Law and Wisdom from Ben Sira to Paul

A Tradition Historical Enquiry
into the Relation of Law, Wisdom, and Ethics

by

Eckhard J. Schnabel

WIPF & STOCK · Eugene, Oregon

Wipf and Stock Publishers
199 W 8th Ave, Suite 3
Eugene, OR 97401

Law and Wisdom from Ben Sira to Paul
By Schnabel, Eckhard J.
Copyright©1985 Mohr Siebeck
ISBN 13: 978-1-61097-349-6
Publication date 3/14/2011
Previously published by J. C. B. Mohr, 1985

Schnabel, Eckhard J.:
Law and wisdom from Ben Sira to Paul: a tradition historical enquiry into the relation of law, wisdom, and ethics / by Eckhard J. Schnabel. –
Tübingen: Mohr, 1985.

To Barbara

Preface

It is a generally acknowledged fact both among Old Testament scholars and New Testament scholars, as well as among experts in the literature of early and later Judaism, that the correlation of law and wisdom is of paramount importance for Jewish and Christian theology and ethics. It is therefore all the more surprising that this correlation has never been the subject of a major monograph. There are only a handful of articles which correlate law and wisdom at least in the title: K. Hruby (1967), A.R. von Sauer (1972), E. Zenger (1973), J. Marböck (1976), G.T. Sheppard (1978). The study of J. Blenkinsopp on wisdom and law in the Old Testament (1983) is rather brief and gives but limited remarks on this correlation.

The present study was written to fill this apparent gap and to make a contribution to the investigation of the theology of early Judaism and early Christianity, focusing on the correlation of law and wisdom in Ben Sira, in other early Jewish documents including Qumran, and in the thinking of Paul the Apostle.

This book is a revised and abridged version of my Ph. D. thesis which was submitted to the University of Aberdeen in August 1983. I am indebted to my supervisor, Professor Robin S. Barbour, for his constant encouragement, and to Professors I. Howard Marshall and William Johnstone who read various parts of the manuscript and made helpful comments. My thanks go also to Professor Matthew Black of St. Andrews who acted as external reader of the original thesis for his suggestions. Naturally the usual caveats against guilt by association apply. I would also like to thank several friends: Dr. Helge Stadelmann for his relevant suggestions in connection with his own work on the Jewish wisdom tradition which finally led me to my dissertation topic, and Dr. Henry Lazenby, Hans Bayer, and Bob Yarbrough for succeeding now and then in challenging me to transcend the spheres of law and wisdom thus making my time at King's College even more memorable. B. Yarbrough helped reading the proofs.

I also would like to record my gratitude to the Arbeitskreis für evangelikale Theologie (AfeT) of the Deutsche Evangelische Allianz for its financial assistance during the final year of research, and for its contribution of a substantial printing grant. Finally, I wish to express my sincere thanks to Professor Martin Hengel of Tübingen for accepting this study for publication in the WUNT series.

My wife was of invaluable help in many ways. She is certainly a true embodiment of the dictum of Ben Sira, the scribe and wise man: קנה אשה ראשית קנין עזר ומבצר ועמוד משען (Sir 36,24). The dedication of this study to her requires therefore no further comment but rather an exclamation mark.

Grossbottwar, January 1984   EJS

Contents

Preface	V
Contents	VII
Abbreviations	XI
Introduction	1
Chapter One: Ben Sira's Identification of Wisdom and Law	**8**
§ 1 Introductory Survey	10
§ 2 Ben Sira's Concept of Wisdom	16
2.1. Wisdom and Creation	16
2.2. Wisdom and Salvation-History	20
2.3. Summary	28
§ 3 Ben Sira's Concept of Law and the Commandments	29
3.1 Terminology	31
3.2. Law and Creation	42
3.3. Law and Salvation-History	44
3.4. Law and the Fear of the Lord	45
3.5. The Function of the Law	46
3.6. Motives of Obedience	55
3.7. Halakhah in Sirach	57
3.8. Old Testament Quotations and Allusions	60
3.9. Summary	62
Excursus I: The Identity and History of the Sopherim	63
§ 4 Ben Sira's Identification of Law and Wisdom	69
4.1. The Exegetical Evidence	69
4.2. The Nature of the Identification	79
4.3. The Rationale behind the Identification	84
4.4. The Consequences of the Identification	87
4.5. Conclusion	89

Chapter Two: Wisdom and Law in the Intertestamental Literature — 93

§ 5 Earlier Jewish Writings from Palestine — 95
   5.1. Baruch — 95
   5.2. The Ethiopic Book of Enoch — 100
   5.3. The Psalms of Solomon — 112

§ 6 Earlier Jewish Writings from Alexandria — 119
   6.1. The Letter of Aristeas — 119
   6.2. The Third Sibylline Oracle — 124
   6.3. The Wisdom of Solomon — 129

§ 7 Later Jewish Writings from the First Century A.D. — 134
   7.1. The Fourth Book of Maccabees — 134
   7.2. The Fourth Book of Ezra — 138
   7.3. The Apocalypse of Baruch — 152

§ 8 Conclusion — 162

Chapter Three: Law and Wisdom in the Dead Sea Scrolls — 166

§ 9 Introduction — 166

§ 10 Law and Commandments: The Rule of Life — 169
   10.1. The Significance and Role of the Law — 169
   10.2. Terminology — 171
   10.3. The Concept of Revelation — 172
   10.4. The Law and the Covenant — 174
   10.5. The Law and the Creator — 178
   10.6. The Study of the Law — 181
   10.7. The Halakhah of the Community — 183
   10.8. The Function of the Law and Motives of Obedience — 187
   Excursus II: Qumran, the Law, and Legalism — 188

§ 11 Wisdom: Universal-Systematic Blueprint for Creation and Salvation — 190
   11.1. The Significance of the Sapiential Tradition — 190
   11.2. Terms and Genres — 195
   11.3. Wisdom, God, and Creation — 199
   11.4. Wisdom, Revelation, and the Covenant — 201
   11.5. Wisdom and Teaching — 203
   11.6. Conduct and Ethics — 204

§ 12 Law and Wisdom	206
12.1. Exegetical Evidence	207
12.2. The Nature of the Identification	221
12.3. Summary	225

Chapter Four: Wisdom and Law in Pauline Christology and Ethics   227

§ 13 Introduction	227
13.1. The Conceptual Heritage of Paul	227
13.2. Paul and the Correlation of Law and Wisdom	232
13.3. Methodological Considerations	234
§ 14 Christ and Wisdom	236
14.1. Wisdom Christology in Recent Research	237
14.2. Exegetical-Conceptual Evidence	240
14.3. Theological-Hermeneutical Evidence	260
§ 15 Christ and the Law	264
15.1. Christ and Torah in Recent Research	264
15.2. Exegetical Evidence	271
15.3. Theological Evaluation	292
15.4. Conclusion: Wisdom and Law in Paul's Christology	298
§ 16 The Christian Way of Life	299
16.1. Foundational Motivations	301
16.2. Binding Norms: The Law Aspect	310
16.3. Guiding Criteria: The Wisdom Aspect	323
16.4. Conclusion: Normativity and Wisdom in Paul's Ethic	338

Chapter Five: Conclusions   343

Select Bibliography	351
Index of Passages	379
Index of Authors	413
Index of Subjects	421

Abbreviations

1. Books of the Bible

Gen, Ex, Lev, Num, Deut, Josh, Judg, Ru, 1,2Sam, 1,2Kgs, 1,2Chr, Ezr, Neh, Esth, Job, Ps, Prov, Qoh, Cant, Is, Jer, Lam, Ez, Dan, Hos, Joel, Am, Obad, Jon, Mic, Nah, Hab, Zeph, Hag, Zech, Mal.

Mt, Mk, Lk, Joh, Acts, Rom, 1,2Cor, Gal, Eph, Phil, Col, 1,2Thess, 1,2Tim, Tit, Phlm, Heb, Jas, 1,2Pet, 1,2,3John, Jude, Rev.

2. Apocrypha and Pseudepigrapha

AntBibl, ApcBar, Aristob, AssMos, Bar, En(eth), En(hebr), EpArist, 4 Ezr, JosAs, Jub, Judt, 1,2,3,4Macc, PsSal, Ps(syr), SapSal, Sib, Sir, TestXIIPatr (TReu,TSim, TLev, etc.).

3. Dead Sea Scrolls (Qumran)

CD, 1QS, 1QSa, 1QSb, 1QM, 1QH, 1QpHab, 1QDireMoshe (22), 4QOrd$^{a\text{-}c}$ (159,513, 514), 4QpIs$^{a\text{-}e}$ (161-165), 4QpNah (169), 4QpPs^a (171), 4QFlor (174), 4QTestim (175), 4QBer (286), 4QDibHam$^{a\text{-}c}$ (504-506), 4QPrFêtes$^{a\text{-}c}$ (507-509), 4QShir$^{a\text{-}b}$ (510-511), 4QMessAr, 11QPs^a, 11QPs^{a}DavComp (27,2-11), 11QMelch, 11QT.

4. Other Ancient Sources

Philo and Josephus: the conventional sigla are used.
Rabbinic writings: the conventional sigla are used.
Other ancient writings: the conventional sigla are used.

5. Periodicals, Series, Reference Works

AA	Archäologischer Anzeiger
AB	Anchor Bible
AGSU	Arbeiten zur Geschichte des Spätjudentums und Urchristentums
ALGHJ	Arbeiten zur Literatur und Geschichte des hellenistischen Judentums
AnBibl	Analecta Biblica
ANRW	Aufstieg und Niedergang der römischen Welt, ed. H. Temporini, W. Haase
APOT	The Apocrypha and Pseudepigrapha of the Old Testament, ed. R.H. Charles
ATD	Altes Testament Deutsch
AThANT	Abhandlungen zur Theologie des Alten und Neuen Testaments
AThD	Acta Theologica Danica
BA	Biblical Archaeologist
BAL	Berichte über die Verhandlungen der Sächsischen Akademie zu Leipzig
BBB	Bonner Biblische Beiträge

BDR	Blass/Debrunner/Rehkopf, Grammatik des neutestamentlichen Greichisch, 15. Auflage, 1979
BETL	Bibliotheca Ephemeridum Theologicarum Lovaniensium
BEvTh	Beiträge zur Evangelischen Theologie
BFCTh	Beiträge zur Förderung Christlicher Theologie
BHH	Biblisch-historisches Handwörterbuch, ed. B. Reicke, L. Rost
BHTh	Beiträge zur Historischen Theologie
Bib	Biblica
BiKi	Bibel und Kirche
BJHIL	Bibliographie zur jüdisch-hellenistischen und interestamentarischen Literatur, ed. G. Delling
BJRL	Bulletin of the John Rylands Library
BJS	Brown Judaic Studies
BK	Biblischer Kommentar
BNTC	Black's New Testament Commentaries
BTB	Biblical Theology Bulletin
BWANT	Beiträge zur Wissenschaft vom Alten und Neuen Testament
BZ	Biblische Zeitschrift
BZAW	Beiträge zur Zeitschrift für die alttestamentliche Wissenschaft
BZNW	Beiträge zur Zeitschrift für die neutestamentliche Wissenschaft
CB	Coniectanea Biblica
CBQ	Catholic Biblical Quarterly
CRAI	Comptes Rendues de l'Académie des Inscriptions et Belles-Lettres
CIJ	Corpus Inscriptionum Judaicarum, ed. J.B. Frey
CThJ	Calvin Theological Journal
DEB	Documents pour l'Étude de la Bible
DJD	Discoveries in the Judaean Desert (of Jordan)
EB	Études Bibliques
EJ	Encyclopedia Judaica
EKK	Evangelisch-Katholischer Kommentar
EQ	Evangelical Quarterly
EThR	Études Theologiques et Religieuses
EvTh	Evangelische Theologie
EWNT	Exegetisches Wörterbuch zum Neuen Testament, ed. H. Balz, G. Schneider
ExpTim	Expository Times
FRLANT	Forschungen zur Religion und Literatur des Alten und Neuen Testaments
FThS	Freiburger Theologische Studien
GCS	Die Griechischen Christlichen Schriftsteller der ersten drei Jahrhunderte
GThA	Göttinger Theologische Arbeiten
HAT	Handbuch zum Alten Testament
HBT	Horizons in Biblical Theology
HLJ	Hastings Law Journal
HNT	Handbuch zum Neuen Testament
HR	History of Religions
HThK	Herders Theologischer Kommentar

Abbreviations

HThR	Harvard Theological Review
HUCA	Hebrew Union College Annual
ICC	International Critical Commentary
Int	Interpretation
IZBG	Internationale Zeitschriftenschau für Bibelwissenschaft und Grenzgebiete
JAAR	Journal of the American Academy of Religion
JBL	Journal of Biblical Literature
JBR	Journal of Bible and Religion
JE	Jewish Encyclopaedia
JES	Journal of Ecumenical Studies
JETS	Journal of the Evangelical Theological Society
JJS	Journal of Jewish Studies
JJSoc	Jewish Journal of Sociology
JNSL	Journal of Northwest Semitic Languages
JQR	Jewish Quarterly Reivew
JR	Journal of Religion
JRE	Journal of Religion and Ethics
JSHRZ	Jüdische Schriften aus hellenistisch-jüdischer Zeit
JSJ	Journal for the Study of Judaism
JSNT	Journal for the Study of the New Testament
JSS	Journal for Semitic Studies
JThS	Journal of Theological Studies
Jud	Judaica
KEK	Kritisch-Exegetischer Kommentar
KuD	Kerygma und Dogma
LCL	Loeb Classical Library
MGWJ	Monatszeitschrift für Geschichte und Wissenschaft des Judentums
MPTh	Monatszeitschrift für Pastoraltheologie
MS	Monograph Series
MVAG	Mitteilungen der Vorderasiatisch-Ägyptischen Gesellschaft
NF	Neue Folge
NIGTC	New International Greek Testament Commentary
NovTest	Novum Testamentum
NRTh	Nouvelle Revue Théologique
NTA	Neutestamentliche Abhandlungen
NTA	New Testament Abstracts
NTD	Neues Testament Deutsch
NTS	New Testament Studies
NTT	Norsk Teologisk Tidsskrift
OBO	Orbis Biblicus et Orientalis
OTS	Oudtestamentische Studien
PAAJR	Proceedings of the American Academy of Jewish Research
POS	Pretoria Oriental Studies
PTMS	Pittsburgh Theological Monograph Series

PVTG	Pseudepigrapha Veteris Testamenti Graece
PW	Paulys Realencyclopädie der classischen Altertumswissenschaft, ed. G. Wissowa, W. Kroll et al.
PWSuppl	Supplementbände
RAC	Reallexikon für Antike und Christentum, ed. T. Klauser
RB	Revue Biblique
RE	Realencyklopädie für protestantische Theologie und Kirche, ed. A. Hauck, 3. Auflage
REJ	Revue des Études Juives
RGG	Religion in Geschichte und Gegenwart, 3. Auflage, ed. K. Galling
RGVV	Religionsgeschichtliche Versuche und Vorarbeiten
RHPR	Revue d'Histoire et de Philosophie Religieuse
RivBibl	Revista Biblica
RQ	Revue de Qumran
RSPT	Revue des Sciences Philosophiques et Théologiques
RSR	Revue des Sciences Religieuses
RThL	Revue Théologique de Louvain
RTP	Revue de Théologie et de Philosophie
SB	Sources Bibliques
SBL	Society of Biblical Literature
SBLDS	SBL Dissertation Series
SBLMS	SBL Monograph Series
SBLSCS	SBL Septuagint and Cognate Studies
SBLTT	SBL Texts and Translations
SBLSBS	SBL Sources for Biblical Study
SBM	Stuttgarter Biblische Monographien
SBS	Stuttgarter Bibelstudien
SBT	Studies in Biblical Theology
SC	Sources Chrétiennes
SEA	Svensk Exegetisk Årsbok
SGJ	Schriften der Gesellschaft des Judentums
SGV	Sammlung gemeinverständlicher Vorträge
SJLA	Studies in Judaism in Late Antiquity
SJT	Scottish Journal of Theology
SMB	Serie Monografica di 'Benedictina'
SNT	Supplements to Novum Testamentum
SNTS	Society for New Testament Studies
SPB	Studia Post-Biblica
SR	Studies in Religion/Sciences Religieuses
SSN	Studia Semitica Neerlandica
StANT	Studien zum Alten und Neuen Testament
STDJ	Studies on the Texts of the Desert of Judah
StJud	Studia Judaica
StNT	Studien zum Neuen Testament
StPh	Studia Theologica
SUNT	Studien zur Umwelt der Neuen Testaments
SVF	Stoicorum veterum fragmenta, ed. J. von Arnim
SVT	Supplements to Vetus Testamentum
SVTP	Studia in Veteris Testamenti Pseudepigrapha

THAT	Theologisches Handwörterbuch zum Alten Testament, ed. E. Jenni, C. Westermann
ThBeitr	Theologische Beiträge
ThLZ	Theologische Literaturzeitung
ThR	Theologische Rundschau
ThSt	Theological Studies
ThViat	Theologia Viatorum
ThWAT	Theologisches Wörterbuch zum Alten Testament, ed. G.J. Botterweck, H. Ringgren
ThWNT	Theologisches Wörterbuch zum Neuen Testament, ed. G. Kittel, G. Friedrich
ThZ	Theologische Zeitschrift
TSAJ	Texte und Studien zum Antiken Judentum
TThZ	Trierer Theologische Zeitschrift
TU	Texte und Untersuchungen zur Geschichte der altchristlichen Literatur
TyndB	Tyndale Bulletin
UTB	Uni-Taschenbücher
VIKJ	Veröffentlichungen aus dem Institut Kirche und Judentum bei der Kirchlichen Hochschule Berlin
VT	Vetus Testamentum
VuF	Verkündigung und Forschung
WHJP	World History of the Jewish People
WMANT	Wissenschaftliche Monographien zum Alten und Neuen Testament
WThJ	Westminster Theological Journal
WuD	Wort und Dienst
WUNT	Wissenschaftliche Untersuchungen zum Neuen Testament
ZASA	Zeitschrift für Ägyptische Sprache und Altertumskunde
ZAW	Zeitschrift für die alttestamentliche Wissenschaft
ZDPV	Zeitschrift des Deutschen Palästina-Vereins
ZEE	Zeitschrift für evangelische Ethik
ZKTh	Zeitschrift für katholische Theologie
ZNW	Zeitschrift für die neutestamentliche Wissenschaft
ZThK	Zeitschrift für Theologie und Kirche

6. Technical and Other Abbreviations

a.c.	articulus citatus
b	Babylonian Talmud
cf.	confer
col.	columna
ET	English Translation
f	fragment
FS	Festschrift (Hommages, Studies in Honour of, etc.)
G	Greet text of Sirach
H	Hebrew text of Sirach
LXX	Septuagint
m	Mishnah tractate
MS(S)	manuscript(s)
MT	Masoretic Text

n	footnote
NT	New Testament
o.c.	opus citatum
OT	Old Testament
p	Palestinian Talmud
t	Tosefta tractate
v(v)	verse(s)
vol.	volume

Introduction

Any attempt to examine the interrelatedness of such complex phenomena as wisdom and law involves the difficult problem of method. Both law and wisdom are rather fluid concepts, each being characterized by a long historical and theological development which in both cases still cannot be described in a final and definitive way[1].

There is a growing recognition of the fact that wisdom and law are closely associated with each other already in the Old Testament, and that they are interrelated in various ways in the history of Israelite society[2]. Scholars have presented the relationship between OT wisdom and law in different ways.

First, it had been a widely accepted view that the wisdom teaching is the practical application of ethical prescriptions as they are contained in the law as 'objective' teaching to the 'subjective' life

---

1 As regards OT wisdom research, no comprehensive history of research has been written. Brief surveys on the history and the present situation of OT wisdom research include W. Baumgartner, "Die israelitische Weisheitsliteratur", *ThR* 5 (1933) 259-261; R.E. Murphy, "Assumptions and Problems in Old Testament Wisdom Research", *CBQ* 29 (1967) 407-418; R.B.Y. Scott, "The Study of the Wisdom Literature", *Int* 24 (1970) 20-45; J.L. Crenshaw, "Prolegomenon", *Studies in Ancient Israelite Wisdom*, 1976, pp.1-21; R.E. Murphy, "Wisdom – Theses and Hypotheses", *Israelite Wisdom*, FS S. Terrien, 1978, pp.35-42; J.A. Emerton, "Wisdom", *Tradition and Interpretation*, ed. G.W. Anderson, 1979, pp.214-237; G.T. Sheppard, *Wisdom as a Hermeneutical Construct*, BZAW 151, 1980, pp.1-12. It was only recently that a really satisfactory introduction to the Israelite wisdom literature has been written: J.L. Crenshaw, *Old Testament Wisdom: An Introduction*, 1982. A good survey of the research on law done since A. Alt and J. Begrich can be found in A. Renker, *Die Tora bei Maleachi: Ein Beitrag zur Bedeutungsgeschichte von tôra im Alten Testament*, FThS 112, 1979, pp.18-58.
2 Cf. J.L. Crenshaw, "Method in Determining Wisdom Influence upon 'Historical' Literature", *JBL* 88 (1969) 132; J.W. Whedbee, *Isaiah and Wisdom*, 1971, pp. 16f.; P.J. Nel, *The Structure and Ethos of the Wisdom Admonitions in Proverbs*, BZAW 158, 1982, pp.94-97; J. Blenkinsopp, *Wisdom and Law in the Old Testament: The Ordering of Life in Israel and Early Judaism*, 1983, passim.

of man³. This view is not prominent in the recent discussion.

Second, other scholars find parallels between wisdom and law as regards their origin, form, and structure. J.P. Audet argues that the wisdom tradition had its roots in a pre-school and pre-urban civilization and was basically "une tradition de *paideia* domestique"; he compares the origins of law and wisdom and concludes that "sagesse et loi relèvent des mêmes dépositaires de l'autorité domestique et servent les mêmes fins par rapport au bien du groupe"⁴. J. Malfroy asserts that the context in which the Torah is partially presented is characterized by sapiential vocabulary and style⁵. E. Gerstenberger seeks to show a close relationship between the so-called apodictic law, i.e. the categorical prohibitives and Ancient Near Eastern wisdom are related regarding the basic intention (the protection from false ways and the turning down of evil), regarding the content of the prohibitives and the warnings (rules for social conduct), and regarding the common pedagogical aims⁶. The life-setting of the prohibitives and the sapiential admonition is in both cases the ethos of the clan since there are analogical or at least similar circumstances of origin⁷. In a similar manner W. Richter attempts to show that legal prohibitions were the exponents of internal group instruction and that the admonitions of the wise men, as preserved in later collections of proverbial material, were basically of the same substance, i.e. direct adaptations of the early family ethic⁸. J.L. Crenshaw states that the clan ethos "saw the virtual union of law and instruction"⁹. This approach

---

3 Cf. G. von Rad, *Wisdom in Israel*, 1972, pp.87f. who rejects this view which describes, for example, the Decalogue as the ethical norm from which the teachers of the proverbs began.
4 J.P. Audet, "Origines comparées de la double tradition de la loi et de la sagesse dans le Proche-Orient ancien", *25th International Congress of Orientalists*, 1960, pp.356f.
5 J. Malfroy, "Sagesse et loi dans le Deutéronome", *VT* 15 (1965) 49-65.
6 E. Gerstenberger, *Wesen und Herkunft des 'apodiktischen' Rechts*, WMANT 20, 1965, pp.49-65.
7 E. Gerstenberger, o.c., pp.116-129. Cf. H.W. Wolff, *Amos' geistige Heimat*, WMANT 18, 1964 who postulates a "Sippenweisheit".
8 W. Richter, *Recht und Ethos: Versuch einer Ortung des weisheitlichen Mahnspruchs*, StANT 15, 1966.
9 J.L. Crenshaw, *Old Testament Wisdom*, p. 56. See also C.M. Carmichael, "Forbidden Mixtures", *VT* 32 (1982) 394f. who refers to the obvious links between wisdom and law, particularly in early legal development before the formalization of court procedure.

has been criticized as constituting an absolutizing of form on behalf of content.

Third, it has been repeatedly recognized that it was the content and the intention of both law and wisdom which were the impetus for the development which, eventually, led to the identification of the two concepts[10].

Fourth, G. Östborn emphasizes the close ties between the wise men and the priests. According to him, "It is not an easy task clearly to distinguish between cultic literature and Wisdom literature"[11]. As תורה means, according to Östborn, "to show the way", the close relationship between law and wisdom is obvious. Both concepts are associated with דרך which is often used in the sense of "practice" or "mode of procedure"[12]. If associated with תורה, דרך acquires the meaning "the will of Yahweh" (cf. Ps 119,33; Gen 18,19; 1Kgs 2,3; 1Sam 12,23; Deut 11,26ff.). On the other hand Prov 4,11 states that the wise man's תורה contained instruction regarding "the way": the wise man instructs his "son" in the "way of wisdom" (דרך חכמה)[13]. The "way" demonstrated by the teacher of wisdom took the form of "commandments". According to Prov 8,20 the "way of righteousness" and the "paths of judgment" are characteristics of wisdom. Thus, Östborn concludes that "the Wise man's instruction can thus be said to have contained 'law', just as the instruction given by the priests did; and this 'law' was described by the Sage in the same terms as were otherwise employed with reference to the 'law' of Yahweh"[14].

Fifth, T.C. Vriezen points out that the problem of the relation between the will of God and the cosmic order arose at the time when Israel developed a Yahwistic cosmology, when the cosmic

---

10 Cf. W. Richter, *Recht*, pp.140-145 emphasizing that both law and wisdom express ethos; also A. de Pury, "Sagesse et révélation", *RTP* 110 (1977) 36 who states that "dans sa substance morale, la Loi n'apporte donc rien que la sagesse humaine n'ait pas reconnu ou n'aurait pas pu reconnaître par ses propres moyens"; similarly P.J. Nel, *Structure*, p.94.

11 G. Östborn, *Tora in the Old Testament: A Semantic Study*, 1945, p.113.

12 Following H.S. Nyberg, *Studien zum Hoseabuche*, 1935, p.81; G. Östborn, *o.c.*, p.35 refers to Gen 6,12; 19,31; 31,35; Is 10,24.26; Jer 12,16; Hos 10,13; Am 4,10; 8,14.

13 Cf. Prov 1,31; 2,8; 3,17; 6,23; 8,32; 11,20; 12,15; 22,6; Job 23,10-11; 24,13. Cf. G. Östborn, *Tora*, pp.117f.

14 G. Östborn, *o.c.*, p.118.

majesty of Yahweh became the focus[15]. Consequently the relation between revelation (Torah) and reason (wisdom) became a problem which led eventually to the conception of the identity of the two realms.

Sixth, recently D.F. Morgan argued that the deuteronomistic material testifies to the responsibility which the scribe felt for the Torah, an important factor in the development of the later equation of wisdom and Torah[16].

Seventh, other scholars maintain that the similarities in the ethos of wisdom and Torah should be traced back to the common institutional origins[17].

Finally, J. Blenkinsopp seems to assume a combination of some of these factors to be responsible for the confluence of wisdom and law. The Israelite wisdom tradition basically "aimed at promoting order and maintaining an ethical consensus in the society based on the accumulated experience of the past"[18]. This aim corresponds with the fundamental role of law which is to order life in society; thus, "law is, in a certain sense, subsumed under wisdom"[19]. That is, wisdom and law correspond with each other as regards their cultural and sociological origins and as regards their goals and intentions. Blenkinsopp goes on to affirm that Deuteronomy is the "watershed" with its scribal character; here the legal and the sapiential traditions flow together[20].

The identification of law and wisdom no doubt opened up in certain canonical psalms (Ps 1; 19; 119) which state that the law of Yahweh makes wise[21]. It is not possible at this point to include

---

15 Cf. T.C. Vriezen, *Outline of Old Testament Theology*, 1958 (= 1970), pp.25ff., supported by P.J. Nel, *Structure*, 1982, pp.96f.
16 Cf. D.F. Morgan, *Wisdom in the Old Testament Traditions*, 1981, p.104.
17 Cf. J. Bright, "The Apodictic Prohibition: Some Observations", *JBL* 92 (1973) 200f., followed by D. Zeller, *Die weisheitlichen Mahnsprüche bei den Synoptikern*, Forschung zur Bibel 17, 1977, p.29.
18 J. Blenkinsopp, *Wisdom and Law*, 1983, p.74.
19 Cf. J. Blenkinsopp, *o.c.*, p.75; cf. also *ibid.*, pp.74-78. He affirms that the law is "a specialization of tribal wisdom" (pp.80f.).
20 Cf. J. Blenkinsopp, *o.c.*, pp.92-101, particularly p.100. It is not clear which period Blenkinsopp considers to be responsible for the confluence of wisdom and law: early Israelite history (pp.74,80f.), or Deuteronomy which he dates into the 8th century (p.100), or "late" theological wisdom (pp.130-132), or Sirach in the 2nd century (pp.140-145).
21 Cf. H.P. Müller, Art. "חכם", *ThWAT* 2 (1977) 939; he sees "eine erste Identi-

a general discussion of the problems of 'wisdom psalms'[22]. Scholars disagree not only with regard to the extent but also with regard to the content of psalms denoted as 'wisdom psalms'. Over fifty (!) psalms have been labelled 'wisdom psalm' or 'didactic psalm'. One of the main causes for this variance is to be seen in the diverging views regarding the original life-setting of these psalms. One is compelled to conclude that "a genre 'wisdom psalm' as such cannot be reconstructed"[23].

However, T.K. Koo showed that Ps 1; 19; 119 have to be regarded as implying a profound theological connection between the Torah as the revelation of God's wisdom and man's fear of the Lord as a manifestation of wisdom[24]. In this context the "fear of the Lord" sometimes means, *per metonymiam*, the law itself (cf. Ps 19,10; 111,10 LXX; 112,1; 119,38.63; 128,1.4; cf. Sir 1,28; 6,37; 9,16; 28,7)[25]. The ethic of wise living consists in submission under the order which wisdom has perceived. This obedience is identified with submission under the Torah. He is wise who obeys the law.

This identification of wisdom and law is implied as well in Deut 4,6; Mal 2,6-7 (?) and in Ezr 7,25 where "wisdom" is a synonym for the "book of the Torah"[26].

In the post-exilic period the entire theological thinking became sapiential[27]. All the different Jewish schools claimed to possess

---

fizierung des (schriftlich fixierten) JHWH-Gebots mit weisheitlichem Ethos" in Jer 8,8-9 (cf. 18,18) where the priests boast to be "wise" because they possess the "Torah of Yahweh". Cf. also E. Gerstenberger, *Wesen*, p.151; D.F. Morgan, *Wisdom* p.131; H. Gese, "Das Gesetz", *Zur biblischen Theologie: Alttestamentliche Vorträge*, BEvTh 78, 1977, pp.70f.; idem, "Wisdom, Son of Man, and the Origins of Christology: The Consistent Development of Biblical Theology", *HBT* 3 (1981) 35.

22 Cf. J. Luyten, "Psalm 73 and Wisdom", *BETL* 51 (1979) 59-81; L.G. Perdue, *Wisdom and Cult: A Critical Analysis of the Views of Cult in the Wisdom Literatures of Israel and the Ancient Near East*, SBLDS 30, 1977, pp.261-343.

23 J. Luyten, *a.c.*, p.63.

24 T.K. Koo, *Wisdom and Torah, with Special Reference to the Wisdom Psalms*, Ph.D. Diss. Edinburgh, 1979, pp.164-196. Cf. J.P.M. van der Ploeg, "Le Psaume 119 et la sagesse", *BETL* 51 (1979) 87; H. Gese, "Wisdom", *HBT* 3 (1981) 35f.

25 Cf. J. Becker, *Gottesfurcht im Alten Testament*, AnBibl 25, 1965, pp.267-276.

26 Cf. H.P. Müller, in *ThWAT* 2 (1977) 939.

27 Cf. G. Fohrer, in *ThWNT* 7 (1964) 482. G. von Rad, *Theologie des Alten Testaments*, 1, p.439 states that wisdom in this period became the "Form schlechthin, in der alles spätere Theologisieren Israels einherging". See also K. Galling, *Die Krise der Aufklärung in Israel*, 1952, p.18 who refers to rabbinic theology as "eine neue Erscheinungsform der Weisheit"; similarly E. Jacob, "Principe canonique et formation de l'Ancien Testament", *SVT* 28 (1978) 117.

wisdom: the sopherim, the hasidim, the Essenes, the Pharisees, and the rabbis. One can correctly speak of a "sapiential milieu"[28]. At the same time, the Torah became more and more the one entity which regulated practical life in every respect. The Torah penetrated every aspect of life — individual, social, and national[29].

What is, then, the relationship between Torah and wisdom? What is the structure of the identification of Torah and wisdom as we find it in Sirach and in other documents of the intertestamental period? R.E. Murphy wrote in 1967 that "future studies will doubtless wrestle with these questions"[30]. It is surprising that the following fifteen years have not seen such a wrestling with these questions. The present study is therefore a modest attempt to help clarify the answer to these issues.

The current renaissance of research in the area of early Jewish thinking has certainly aided our enquiry. The fact that the literature in this area appears to expand by geometric progression has led some scholars to limit themselves to an analysis of general processes and structures while neglecting verifiable individual observations. Other scholars limited their discussion to the minutiae of redaction-critical and historical questions while neglecting theological conceptions and developments. Trying to avoid these pitfalls we will concentrate on a comprehensive exegetical scrutiny of the relevant texts and on a succinct systematic analysis of the conceptual evidence as regards the relatedness of law and wisdom, and of halakhah and ethics, in the various documents. Taking into account the present state of research, a discriminating use of the sources is a matter-of-course.

As regards the subtitle of our study, the stress is on tradition rather than on history. What makes a study distinctively historical is the comparison and correlation of concept — the unfolding of ideas in different documents — and context — the historical setting of the authors and redactors of these documents. The reason for not focusing on the historical aspect of our enquiry is twofold: the

---

28 Cf. M. Küchler, *Frühjüdische Weisheitstraditionen: Zum Fortgang weisheitlichen Denkens im Bereich des frühjüdischen Jahweglaubens*, OBO 26, 1979, pp.1ff., following J.E. Worrell, *Concepts of Wisdom in the Dead Sea Scrolls*, 1968.

29 Cf. M. Avi-Yonah, Z. Baras, "Society and Religion in the Second Temple Period", *WHJP* I/8 (1977) 42.

30 R.E. Murphy, "Assumptions and Problems", *CBQ* 29 (1967) 418.

evidence for the relevant concepts, especially law and wisdom, is often rather scarce, and the exact historical and conceptual context of the different documents, or of the individual subunits, cannot always be established beyond doubt. Further, it is increasingly recognized that the transition between the different Jewish groups is fluid and that these groups are not homogeneous in themselves. It is much more promising, therefore, and indeed of primary interest, to provide a description of the way in which the correlation of law and wisdom, which is at least after Ben Sira a tradition, has been taken up[31].

---

[31] The original thesis contained an extensive chapter on the correlation of law and wisdom in the Mishnaic system. As this section was rather long and somewhat discursive it was omitted. The fact that the completed system of the Mishnah dates several generations after Paul justifies this omission.

Chapter One

Ben Sira's Identification of Wisdom and Law

The book of Sirach was composed by Jeshua b. Eleazar b. Sira, briefly called Ben Sira, between 190 – 175 B.C. in Jerusalem[1]. It was originally written in Hebrew[2] and later translated into Greek[3] by Ben Sira's grandson in Alexandria after 132 B.C.[4] It is generally acknowledged that Ben Sira was a wisdom teacher. Recently it has been definitely confirmed that he was also a priest and a scribe[5].

There is a fundamental unanimity among scholars as to Ben

---

1 Cf. G.H. Box, W.O.E. Oesterley, "The Book of Sirach", *APOT* 1 (1913) 293; F. Vattioni, *Ecclesiastico*, 1968, p.XVIII; L. Rost, *Einleitung in die alttestamentlichen Apokryphen und Pseudepigraphen*, 1971, p.50; G. Maier, *Mensch und freier Wille*, pp.24f.; O. Eissfeldt, *Einleitung in das Alte Testament*, [4]1976, pp.808f.; M. Hengel, *Judentum und Hellenismus*, WUNT 10, [2]1973, pp.241-245; H. Stadelmann, *Ben Sira als Schriftgelehrter*, 1980, pp.1-3; G.W.E. Nickelsburg, *Jewish Literature between the Bible and the Mishnah*, 1981, pp.55,64; J.L. Crenshaw, *Old Testament Wisdom*, 1982, p.158.

2 On the Hebrew text (H) of Ben Sira see R. Smend, *Die Weisheit des Jesus Sirach: Hebräisch und Deutsch*, 1906; F. Vattioni, *Ecclesiastico: Testoebraico con apparato critico e versioni greca, latina e sirica*, 1968; and the studies by A.A. di Lella, *The Hebrew Text of Sirach: A Text-Critical and Historical Study*, 1966, and H.P. Rüger, *Text und Textform im hebräischen Sirach: Untersuchungen zur Textgeschichte und Textkritik der hebräischen Sirachfragmente aus der Kairoer Geniza*, BZAW 112, 1970.

3 We used the edition of J. Ziegler, *Sapientia Iesu Filii Sirach*, Septuaginta Vetus Testamentum Graecum ... Gottingensis, vol. 12/2, [2]1980.

4 Regarding translations of Sirach, we relied mainly on Box/Oesterley, "The Book of Sirach", *APOT* 1 (1913) 268-517; G. Sauer, "Jesus Sirach (Ben Sira)", *JSHRZ* III/5 (1981) 483-644; G. Snaith, *Ecclesiasticus*, Cambridge Bible Commentary, 1974.

5 See H. Stadelmann, *Ben Sira als Schriftgelehrter: Eine Untersuchung zum vormakkabäischen Sofer unter Berücksichtigung seines Verhältnisses zu Priester-, Propheten- und Weisheitslehretum*, WUNT 2/6, 1980, passim.

Sira's historical and theological importance with regard to the correlation of law and wisdom[6]. It is quite surprising, therefore, to observe that Ben Sira's creative and portentous identification is mostly dealt with in one or two sentences[7]. Only a handful of scholars made some more specific remarks on the background and the nature of this identification[8]. We will start our discussion of Ben Sira's identification of law and wisdom with a survey of these

---

6 An exception seems to be H.F. Weiss, *Untersuchungen zur Kosmologie des hellenistischen und palästinensischen Judentums*, TU 97, 1966, p.192 who states that "Ansätze zu dieser *späteren* (i.e. Rabbinic!) Identifizierung von Weisheit und Tora liegen ... auch schon bei Jesus Sirach vor" (italics by EJS). Similarly U. Wilckens, in *ThWNT* 7 (1964) 504.

7 See the typical statement by B.L. Mack, *Logos und Sophia*, 1973, p.23: "Bekanntlich wird im Sirachbuch die Weisheit mit dem Gesetz identifiziert". See also the brief remarks of W.L. Knox, *St. Paul and the Church of the Gentiles*, 1939, p.60; W. Gutbrod, in *ThWNT* 4 (1942) 1042; W.D. Davies, *Paul and Rabbinic Judaism: Some Rabbinic Elements in Pauline Theology*, 1948 (^{2}1955 = 1962), p.169; W.D. Davies, *Torah in the Messianic Age and/or the Age to Come*, JBL MS 7, 1952; E. Janssen, *Das Gottesvolk und seine Geschichte: Geschichtsbild und Selbstverständnis im palästinensischen Schrifttum von Jesus Sirach bis Jehuda ha-Nasi*, 1971, p.32; E. Jacob, "Principe canonique", *SVT* 28 (1975) 117; J.L. Crenshaw, "Prolegomenon", 1976, p.23; E. Jacob, "Wisdom and Religion in Sirach", *Israelite Wisdom*, FS S. Terrien, 1978, p.256; B.T. Viviano, *Study as Worship*, SJLA 26, 1978, p.132; P. Sigal, *Emergence of Contemporary Judaism*, 1/1, 1980, p.228; J.L. Crenshaw, *Old Testament Wisdom*, 1982, p.155. The commentaries on Sirach which have been assigned by J. Marböck, "Sirachliteratur seit 1966", *ThR* 71 (1975) 184 to the "Gattung der haute vulgarisation" do not go into detail either. For example, O. Schilling, *Das Buch Jesus Sirach*, Herders Bibelkommentar, 7/2, 1956, p.107 says with regard to Sir 24,1-22 that "göttliche Herkunft, Einwohnung in Israel, heilsgeschichtlicher Segen, verpflichtender Anspruch, missionarische Kraft sind die Hauptgedanken dieses Hymnus auf die Weisheit", and he limits his observations on 24,23 to the two sentences: "Die Weisheit ist eingegangen in die Offenbarung und das Gesetz des Alten Bundes ... Hier zeigt sich die Hochschätzung des Gesetzes als des vornehmsten Teils der Offenbarung" (p.111).

8 Cf. O. Kaiser, "Die Begründung der Sittlichkeit im Buche Jesus Sirach", *ZThK* 55 (1958) 51-63, especially 53-58; E.G. Bauckmann, "Die Proverbien und die Sprüche des Jesus Sirach", *ZAW* 72 (1960) 33-63, especially pp.47-56; M. Hengel, *Judentum*, pp.252-254,291f.; J. Marböck, *Weisheit im Wandel: Untersuchungen zur Weisheitstheologie bei Ben Sira*, BBB 37, 1971, pp.81-96; G. von Rad, *Wisdom*, pp.244-247; E. Zenger, "Die späte Weisheit und das Gesetz", *Literatur und Religion des Frühjudentums*, ed. J. Maier et al., 1973, pp.43-56, especially 50-55; M. Gilbert, "L'éloge de la Sagesse (Siracide 24)", *RThL* 5 (1974) 326-348, especially 345-348; J. Marböck, "Gesetz und Weisheit: Zum Verständnis des Gesetzes bei Jesus ben Sira", *BZ* 20 (1976) 1-21; P.S. Fiddes, *The Hiddenness of Wisdom in the Old Testament and Later Judaism*, Diss. Oxford, 1976, pp.309-340; G.T. Sheppard, *Wisdom as a Hermeneutical Construct*, BZAW 151, 1980, pp.19-83 passim; P.J. Nel, *Structure and Ethos*, 1982, pp.92-97.

observations. This will help us to establish a methodological framework for our own treatment of the relevant passages and conceptions.

§1 Introductory Survey

O. Kaiser begins his discussion by recognizing the fact that Ben Sira is the first author clearly to correlate law and wisdom teaching[9]. He goes on to say that in order to establish the way in which Ben Sira links reason and revelation or wisdom and law one has to recognize that he identifies morality and wisdom (pp.56f.). For Ben Sira, 'law' designates the Mosaic law, incorporating all divine commandments of the Pentateuch: "Die Befolgung des im Pentateuch geoffenbarten Gotteswillens erschließt den Weg zu der Weisheit, die Gott denen gibt, die ihn lieben" (p. 57, quoting Sir 2, 15-16; 15,1b; 19,20). All proper and wise behaviour is obedience to the law revealed to Moses. Thus, wisdom is the humble submission to the revealed will of God which man has to receive with fear and trust (p.58). Ben Sira, living in a time of religious insecurity, establishes the foundation of morality (wisdom) as submission to the revealed will of God which is embodied in the Torah.

E.G. Bauckmann states that the association of wisdom and law in Sir is possible only when "eine Seite ihre Eigenart vollständig aufgibt"[10]. The instruction of wisdom is not established on the fact that it is the word of God but on the personal advantage of man (eudaemonism). It is not regarded as strict, divine commandment: Ben Sira does not refer to the Exodus event nor to the notion that Israel is God's possession; he uses אל and אלוהים but not יהוה ; he never refers specifically to the God of Israel; the law and the commandments he mentions are not particularly those of Israel; and the 'covenant' of Sir 24,23 is simply synonymous with 'law' (pp.52-54). Bauckmann concludes: "Das alte Ziel der Weisheitslehre (ist) das neue Ziel des Gesetzes geworden ... Das Gesetz

---

9 O. Kaiser, "Begründung der Sittlichkeit", *ZThK* 55 (1958) 53.
10 E.G. Bauckmann, "Proverbien", *ZAW* 72 (1960) 49.

hat in der Weisheitslehre seine ursprüngliche Funktion als Ordnung des Bundesvolkes verloren und ist selbst zur Weisheitslehre geworden" (pp.55,63). It should be noted that a number of Bauckmann's arguments are hardly supported by the textual evidence as will be seen later. The main question which arises from his remarks is about the meaning of 'law' in Sirach.

M. Hengel points out that in Sir 24 (and also in 17,11; 38, 34c. d; 39,1) "Weisheit und Gesetz sind praktisch eins geworden"[11]. He emphasizes the results of this identification: the universalistic tendency of traditional wisdom is being limited as wisdom becomes the exclusive gift of God to Israel, and the possibility of profane wisdom is excluded. Hengel traces the correlation of law and wisdom back to Deut 4,6 and Ps 1; 119 but emphasizes that "es ist doch noch ein entscheidender Schritt bis zur völligen Identifikation bei Ben Sira" (p.291). He points out that this identification influenced the Palestinian Haggadah, the Alexandrian philosophy of religion, the book of Baruch, the development of christology, and Rabbinic theology (pp.307-318). Thus, Hengel focuses on the results and on the originality of Ben Sira's identification of law and wisdom.

J. Marböck, in an excursus on law and wisdom in Sirach[12], begins his discussion by pointing out that Ben Sira never makes the Torah the direct object of a poem or of a large pericope (p.85). Torah appears as a summary of a wisdom hymn (15,1; 24,23), as part of comprehensive sapiential activities (19,20; 39,1-11), or as part of God's wise order of creation (17,11-12). Then Marböck goes on to discuss Ben Sira's concept of law (pp.86-92).

> He points out that for Ben Sira (1) law and commandments are the norm and the motives of ethical behaviour, (2) law and commandments belong to God's order and are related to wisdom with the commandments being simply the concretization of the comprehensive divine satisfaction, and (3) the law finally appears also as the Mosaic revelation as embodied in the Pentateuch.

It is at this point that Marböck deals with the identification of law and wisdom (pp.89-91).

> He states that in 15,1 Ben Sira presents the law as the reliable and certain way to wisdom. In 19,20-30 the religious aspect of wisdom is being emphasized: wisdom does

---

[11] M. Hengel, *Judentum*, ²1973, p.253.
[12] J. Marböck, *Weisheit im Wandel*, 1971, pp.81-96.

not exist apart from God and his law. In 21,11 we have a climax from law to the fear of God and to wisdom. In 24,23 the Torah is presented as universal creation, wisdom thus being understood as comprehensive cosmic law which permeates creation and history.

Finally, Marböck deals with the motive of Ben Sira's identification of law and wisdom (pp.93-96). The identification was "innerisraelisch vorbereitet" but should rather be understood in the context of Stoic philosophy as "weisheitliche Antwort auf den Hellenismus" (p.93). Following J. Fichtner, K. Schubert and M. Hengel he believes that "Ben Sira seine Zusammenschau von torā and hokmā im Horizont hellenistischer Denkkategorien vollzogen hat" (p.94). Thus, Marböck's discussion raises again the question of the importance and position of the identification of law and wisdom in Sir. He is the first scholar to attempt an explanation of this identification (see further infra, § 4.2.1.). And, finally, he is most emphatic in ascribing the motives for this identification to Hellenistic conceptual categories.

G. von Rad attributes the total identifications "Torah is the fear of God, and wisdom is Torah" to Ben Sira's "didactic zeal"[13]. According to von Rad, Torah in Sir simply defines and interprets the term "fear of the Lord". He believes that Ben Sira is "little ... capable of developing the idea of Torah" as this is not a subject of particular interest to him (p.247). It is obvious again that the role of 'law' in Sir is of utmost importance for our own discussion.

E. Zenger, like M. Hengel, refers to Deut 4,6-8 and Ps 1; 19; 119 as the OT background of Ben Sira's identification of law and wisdom[14]. This correlation freed Torah from the danger of becoming an absolute, timeless entity: Torah acquired a sapiential function. At the same time the identification of wisdom (as order of creation) and Torah led to the development of a Torah theology: Torah itself is regarded as order of creation, as comprehensive order for the fellowship of God, creation, and man. Torah retains both the divine and the human aspect: "Sie ist die von Jahwe in Schöpfung und Geschichte Israels gegebene 'Offenbarungsweisheit', die zu 'Lebensweisheit' verhelfen soll" (p.55). Zenger's discussion focuses, like Hengel's, primarily on the results of Ben Sira's identification of law and wisdom.

---

13 G. von Rad, *Wisdom*, 1972, pp.242-245 (quote on p.245).
14 E. Zenger, "Die späte Weisheit und das Gesetz", 1973, p.50.

M. Gilbert discusses the role of wisdom in creation[15] and then turns to the assimilation of wisdom and Torah. He emphasizes that despite the fact that Torah in Sir 24,23 and elsewhere refers to the Pentateuch, Torah does not simply consist of "codes légaux" which every Jew is supposed to put into practice. Gilbert argues that Prov 8,22-31 and Deut 4,6-8 form the background of the identification. He explains Ben Sira's basic thesis with the following words: "L'ordre primordial que recherchent les sages d'Israel trouve sa meilleure formulation dans la Torah" (p.347). Thus, Ben Sira seeks to justify "le patrimoine sacré de la Torah" (p.348).

A recent article by J. Marböck is the only study which is devoted exclusively to the relationship of wisdom and law in Sirach[16]. In the first section Marböck deals with key texts which bear on the relation between law and wisdom. He emphasizes again[17] that in Sir the law is never the direct subject of a pericope (p.3). He goes on to discuss 17,11-14 and 24,23 in their respective contexts (pp.3-9) and then treats the two topics which arise from these texts: (1) law and the order of creation, and (2) law and the election of Israel (pp.9-13). For Ben Sira the 'horizon of creation' is more important than the law; when he refers to the law he uses very general formulations and never concretizes it (p.10). Ben Sira has "eine offene Konzeption der Tora" (p.11). Israel's election is, in an unprecedented manner, formulated in the sense that wisdom found its valid expression, its dwelling, and its fullness in the law which has been entrusted to Israel (p.13). Thus, Ben Sira's concept of wisdom and law is characterized by the attempt to combine and to do justice to both the universalistic and the particularistic dimension: the width and openness of wisdom in creation, and the election of Israel which is manifest in the law which contains God's wisdom. Finally, Marböck attempts a "geistesgeschichtliche Einordnung" of this conception of wisdom and law (pp.13-21). He traces the roots of this conception back to the OT, especially to Deut 4.6. As to the cause for the identification of law and wisdom he refers again to the Stoic popular philosophy (p.20).

P.S. Fiddes discusses in his dissertation the relationship between

---

15 M. Gilbert, "L'éloge de la Sagesse", *RThL* 5 (1974) 341-345.
16 J. Marböck, "Gesetz und Weisheit: Zum Verständnis des Gesetzes bei Jesus ben Sirach", *BZ* 20 (1976) 1-21.
17 Cf. J. Marböck, *Weisheit*, 1971, p.85.

wisdom and the Torah on the background of Deut 30,11-14; Prov 30,1-6; Ps 19[18]. He concludes that Ben Sira's identification is not a totally new concept but that he makes definite an existing tendency (p.309). He emphasizes that the identification of wisdom with the Torah, with the latter understood as a fixed body of material (p.315), has to be interpreted against the background of the flexible concept of the "fear of the Lord" (p.310). He stresses that Ben Sira's identification should not be derived from the fact that both wisdom and the law are (allegedly) a means of providing an intermediary (as hypostasis). The 'cosmic Torah' was developed at a later stage, particularly in Rabbinic theology, and should not be read back into wisdom (pp.317-321).

G.T. Sheppard deals with the deuteronomistic background of Ben Sira's identification of law and wisdom[19] in a brief article. He develops his views further in his dissertation[20] in which he studies Ben Sira's techniques by which he conformed non-wisdom traditions of the Torah to teach wisdom like that of the biblical tradition. He does not discuss the identification of law and wisdom as such. When he refers to it in his analysis of Sir 24,3-29; 16,24-17, 14 he focuses on its background. He traces 24,23 back to Deut 33, 14 and to other statements in Deut (pp.60-69).

D.J. Harrington observes that Ben Sira identifies wisdom and law[21] but points out that it is "not entirely evident" how these two blocks fit together (p.187 n.3).

G.W.E. Nickelsburg labels Ben Sira's identification of wisdom and Torah as "the heart and dynamic of his thought"[22] and then goes on to make a few observations on Sir 24.

P.J. Nel explains the identification of law and wisdom against the background of the development of Yahwistic theology and cos-

---

18 P.S. Fiddes, *The Hiddenness of Wisdom in the Old Testament and Later Judaism*, Diss. Oxford, 1976, pp.277-340 (on Sirach, pp.309-340). His study is marred by the fact that he hardly enters into a discussion of the scholarly, especially German, literature on the subject.

19 G.T. Sheppard, "Wisdom and Torah: The Interpretation of Deuteronomy Underlying Sirach 24,23", *Biblical and Near Eastern Studies*, FS W.S. LaSor, ed. G.A. Tuttle, 1978, pp.166-176.

20 G.T. Sheppard, *Wisdom as a Hermeneutical Construct: A Study in the Sapientializing of the Old Testament*, BZAW 151, 1980, pp.19-83 passim.

21 D.J. Harrington, "The Wisdom of the Scribe According to Ben Sira", *Ideal Figures in Ancient Judaism*, ed. J.J. Collins et al., 1980, pp.181f.

22 G.W.E. Nickelsburg, *Literature*, 1981, p.59.

mology in which the relationship between the revelation of the created order and the revelation of God's will in the law became a problem[23]. The relation between revelation (law) and reason (wisdom) was eventually solved by the conception of the non-contradictoriness and identity of the two realms.

J.A. Davis regards the correlation of law and wisdom as a fundamental relationship for Ben Sira's thought[24]. He asserts against J. Marböck that the universalistic element was introduced for apologetic and for polemical purposes (p.3) and then goes on to give "a brief and selective account of the relationship between wisdom and law in Sirach" (p.10) by commenting rather briefly on Sir 1; 6,37; 15,1; 24; 29,9 and on the study of the law as search for wisdom.

This survey shows that with the exception of J. Marböck and P.S. Fiddes scholars did not attempt to discuss Ben Sira's concept and correlation of wisdom and law in a methodologically satisfying manner. Very often they simply observe one or two results of the identification, make some remarks on his concept of law, or speculate on the motives behind the identification. In order to arrive at a comprehensive and sound understanding of the conception of law and wisdom in Sir we have to deal adequately with (1) Ben Sira's concept of wisdom with special emphasis on its relation with creation, salvation history, and the "fear of the Lord", (2) the function and importance of the law, and (3) the nature of his identification of law and wisdom, the rationale behind the identification, and its consequences. The first area has been sufficiently researched by J. Marböck, O. Rickenbacher, and M. Löhr. The second area will require more exegetical work than has usually been done. It is hoped that this procedure, together with a more comprehensive discussion of all the relevant texts regarding the third area and a discerning reception of the scholarly opinions on the subject, will enable us to arrive at a balanced analysis of Ben Sira's notion of law and wisdom.

---

23 P.J. Nel, *Structure*, 1982, pp.92-97 relying on T.C. Vriezen, *Outline*, 1966, pp.25ff.
24 J.A. Davis, *Wisdom and Spirit: An Investigation of 1 Corinthians 1,18-3,20 against the Background of Jewish Sapiential Tradition in the Hellenistic-Roman Period*, Ph.D. Diss. Nottingham, 1982, pp.3-10. The remarks of J. Blenkinsopp, *Wisdom and Law*, 1983, on the identification of law and wisdom are very limited dealing only with Sir 24 (pp.143f.).

§2 Ben Sira's Concept of Wisdom

In this section we are able to utilize and summarize the analyses and conclusions of J. Marböck (1971), O. Rickenbacher (1973), and M. Löhr (1975)[25]. They discuss generally the same wisdom pericopes: 1,1-10; 4,11-19; 6,18-37; 14,20-15,10; 19,20-24; 20,27-31; 21,11-28; 24; 37,16-26[26]; 38,24-39,14; 51,13-30[27]. The passages 1,1-10, and 24,1-34 can be considered as summaries of the wisdom conception of Ben Sira regarding wisdom's creational and salvation-historical aspects.

It is generally agreed that wisdom in Sirach has a two-fold character: (1) It is a cosmological entity, and (2) it is the salvation-historical possession of Israel[28]. We will proceed along these lines in our discussion of Ben Sira's wisdom conception.

2.1. Wisdom and Creation

2.1.1. The universality of wisdom. The fact that wisdom which is God's wisdom (1,1; 24,3-4; cf. 1,8; 42,18c.20) and creation which is God's creation are very closely related emphasizes the universality of wisdom. Wisdom was imparted by God to "all his works" (1,9c) and to "all flesh" (1,10a)[29]. Wisdom rules over the

---

25 See further P.E. Bonnard, *La Sagesse en personne*, 1966, pp.53-80; J.L. Crenshaw, *Old Testament Wisdom*, 1982, pp.149-173.

26 Discussed only by O. Rickenbacher, *Weisheitsperikopen bei Ben Sira*, OBO 1, 1973, pp.173-175.

27 The wisdom terminology of Ben Sira is listed by J. Marböck, *Weisheit*, pp.13-15.

28 Cf. J. Marböck, *o.c.*, p.62; M. Hengel, *Judentum*, p.284; E. Zenger, "Späte Weisheit", pp.48f.; H.F. Weiss, *Untersuchungen*, p.197. G. von Rad, *Weisheit*, p.242 distinguishes two senses of the term 'wisdom' in Sir: it is the primeval order which confronts man objectively, and it is a human characteristic which one should be anxious to acquire, and calls this usage a "strangely ambivalent phenomenon" (ibid.).

29 On the expression "all flesh" in Sir see O. Rickenbacher, *Weisheitsperikopen*, pp.25-28. The term τὰ ἔργα in 1,9 (and in 16,26; 17,8; 39,16) refers to God's creation; the underlying Hebrew equivalent is מעשה; cf. D. Barthelemy, O. Rickenbacher, *Konkordanz zum Hebräischen Sirach*, 1973, pp.232f. who list 32 passages in which מעשה is translated by ἔργον. See also M. Löhr, *Bildung aus dem Glauben*, 1975, p.26; J. Haspecker, *Gottesfurcht bei Jesus Sirach*, 1967, pp.67,78, 153,332.

entire earth as well as over all peoples and nations (24,6). The activity of wisdom knows no geographical or national barriers as it includes all spaces and all nations. This rule of wisdom is clearly the expression of its divine function: in the activity and rule of wisdom God himself rules and is active[30].

2.1.2. The order of creation. The wisdom of God is manifest in the order of creation (16,24-17,14; 39,14-35; 42,15-43,33). This notion is especially evident in the large pericope 16, 24-17,14[3]. God's wise order of creation is manifest in all realms: in the cosmos (16,24-28), on earth among man (16,29-17,10), and particularly among God's elect people (17,11-14).

> The first part of the pericope 16,24-17,14 indicates that God assigned to his works, when he created them, their "portion" (μέρις) with regard to their being (16,24H; 16,26G)[31]. He "set in order" his works and their spheres of activity forever (16,27). In the second realm such an order can be found as well: God has set a fixed span of life for man (17,2) and assigned to him the tasks of ruling over creation (17,2b.3-4), of discerning between good and evil (17,7), and of praising him (17,8). God's order of life is most distinct in the third realm, i.e. among his people. 17,14 summarizes what had been said in the previous verses: God's commandments are implicit in the order of creation; conduct in human and divine affairs has been disclosed in a fundamental way[32]. – This order is reflected in the very structure of this passage[33]. In all three parts, Ben Sira refers to law and commandments: God's works obey his "word" (ῥῆμα, 16,28); man is filled with the fear of God (17,8); and God's people received at Sinai the "laws of life" (νόμος ζωῆς, 17,11), his "laws" (τά κρίματα, 17,12), and his commandments (17,14). – The concept of order is further conveyed by the fact that in Sirach God's creational activity can be understood as "mathematisches Zählen, Bestimmen und Zuweisen"[34]. This can be seen in terms like "number" (ἀριθμός, 17,2; cf. 1,9), "to assign, to order"(διαστέλλω,16,26), "to order" (κοσμέω, 16,27), and "portion" (μέρις, 16,26).

In the context of the hymn in 39,14c-35 Ben Sira emphasizes the goodness and purposefulness of all works of God in both creation and history (39,16.33). The order inherent in creation is made explicit with the sapiential terms בעתו (39,16.21.33.34), בעת (39,28), לעת (39,30)[35]. God's activity בעתו (cf. also 10,4;

---

30 Cf. J. Marböck, *Weisheit*, p.62 who points out that such sweeping statements of an all-encompassing rule are made in the OT only of God (cf. p.62 n.72 for references).
31 Cf. the translation of G. Sauer, "Jesus Sirach", *JSHRZ* III/5 (1981) 546. O. Rickenbacker, *Weisheitsperikopen*, p.148 follows S and relates the verse to the stars.
32 Cf. O. Rickenbacher, *o.c.*, pp.148f.
33 Cf. J. Marböck, *Weisheit*, p.136.
34 J. Marböck, *o.c.*, p.137.
35 For a discussion of the term עת in its sapiential usage see J. Marböck, *o.c.*, pp.140f.

43,6) indicates the purposefulness and wisdom of his works. The creation is described as being "good", marked by harmony (39,16. 33; cf. Gen 1,31). God's acts and plans know their proper time. In this context צורך "purpose, requirement, benefit" is a key term for Ben Sira expressing the purposefulness of creation (39,16.21. 30.33; 42,33)[36]. Further, Ben Sira uses חלק in the sense of a discernible order and allocation by God (39,25; cf. also 7,15; 15, 9; 16,26G; 40,1; 44,2). He links God's creational activity very closely with God's ordering and organizing assigning: חלק is often used parallel to ברא and is often identical with ברא (31,13.27=34, 13.27G; 38,1). These terms guarantee the purposefulness and order in God's creation and in God's acts in history as well.

The third large hymn on creation in 42,15-43,33[37] focuses on the מעשי אל (42,15-16), the works of creation, and on God's acting and ruling in creation and in history[38]. Ben Sira stresses the fact that God's works in nature are the revelation of his כבוד (42, 16-17.25; 43,1-2.12)[39]. Again he points out the order and purposefulness of creation (42,23-25; 43,6.10). These concepts are here closely linked with God's omniscience and wisdom (42,18-20) which obviously guarantee this order. In this pericope Ben Sira's ultimate purpose in his discussion of the order of creation becomes obvious: his final goal is the praise of God which is to lead to faith in God's wisdom, i.e. in God himself who is active in creation and history (43,28-32; cf. 1,2-3; 18,4-7)[40].

The works of creation are thus regarded as one path to wisdom: "Der Mensch kann die zugängliche Seite der Weisheit erkennen, so wie sie sich ihm durch ihre Werke erschließt"[41]. Ben Sira pre-

---

36 The root צרך is further used in 8,9; 10,26; 12,5; 13,6; 15,12; 35,2.17; 37,8; 38,1.12; 42,21.
37 On this pericope see M. Löhr, *Bildung*, pp.80-94.
38 God's works in creation are the subject of 1,9.16.26.27; 17,8; his acting in history is thus designated in 11,4; 18,4; 33(36),15; 39,16.33. See J. Marböck, *Weisheit*, pp.147f.
39 This does not, however, constitute an argument for the existence of God from the design of creation. Contra J.G. Snaith, *Ecclesiasticus*, 1974, p.210. God's existence was not denied by Ben Sira's contemporaries.
40 Cf. H. Duesberg, I. Fransen, *Scribes*, p.661, followed by J. Marböck, *o.c.*, p.151. J. Haspecker, *Gottesfurcht*, pp.67f., 152f. points out that for Ben Sira the goal of creation is the fear of the Lord.
41 M.S. Segal, *Sepher Ben Sira'* ²1958, ad Sir 1,6 quoted by O. Rickenbacher, *Weisheitsperikopen*, p.24.

sents the secrets of creation as cause of the inquiry into the locus and origin of wisdom (cf. 1,2-3.6)[42]. But the root and the secrets of wisdom are essentially hidden for man and can be made known only by revelation (cf. 4,18; 24,23-29).

2.1.3. The wisdom figure. In the context of Sir 24 which refers to an 'objective' relationship between wisdom and creation it has been claimed repeatedly that this 'wisdom speculation' has a mythological background.

> W.L. Knox was the first to point out an alleged "affinity to a Syrian Astarte with features of Isis"[43]. This view was defended and developed by H. Ringgren[44] and especially H. Conzelmann[45]. M. Hengel agrees with this interpretation stating that the mythological background of the wisdom speculation is particularly obvious as the parallels to the Hellenistic Isis aretalogies are firmly established[46]. J. Marböck and others follow this view[47].

Recently B. Lang voiced his disagreement with this seemingly prevailing view. Formal affinities say nothing about the provenance of the content which, in this case, can be derived from the Israelite tradition[48]. And even the formal affinities, i.e. the genre of the aretalogy, are not unequivocal.

---

42 Cf. J. Marböck, *Weisheit*, p.32.
43 W.L. Knox, "The Divine Wisdom", *JThS* 38 (1937) 235.
44 H. Ringgren, *Word and Wisdom: Studies in Hypostatization of Divine Qualities and Functions in the Ancient Near East*, 1947, pp.144ff. See also U. Wilckens, *Weisheit und Torheit*, 1959, pp.160-170 (pp.165-168 on Sir 24).
45 H. Conzelmann, "Die Mutter der Weisheit", 1964, pp.225-234 (= *Theologie als Schriftauslegung*, 1974, pp.167-176) arguing that Sir 24,3-6 represents "ein praktisch wörtlich aufgenommenes, nur an zwei Stellen leicht retouschiertes Lied auf Isis" (p.228).
46 M. Hengel, *Judentum*, pp.284-287; supported by O. Kaiser, in *VuF* 27 (1982) 84f.
47 J. Marböck, *o.c.*, pp.48-54; B.L. Mack, *Logos*, p.40; E. Schüssler Fiorenza, "Wisdom Mythology and the Christological Hymns of the New Testament", *Aspects of Wisdom*, ed. R.L. Wilken, 1975, pp.26-31; J.C.H. Lebram, "Jerusalem, Wohnsitz der Weisheit", *Studies in Hellenistic Religions*, ed. M.J. Vermaseren, 1979, pp. 114, 119f., 120-128 (assuming further the influence of Athene); B. Vawter, "Prov 8,22", *JBL* 99 (1980) 206; also J. Blenkinsopp, *Wisdom and Law*, pp.143f. who believes that Ben Sira's identification of wisdom and law is dependent upon the Isis aretalogies and was therefore "natural" since Isis (Matt) stood for cosmic order and presided over the administration of law.
48 B. Lang, *Frau Weisheit*, 1975, pp.152-154. Lang concludes: "Nicht die Göttin Isis, sondern Frau Weisheit als erstes und Gott nahestehendes Geschöpf ist Vorbild der Sophia in Sir 24. An Motive anderer biblischer Schöpfungstexte anknüpfend, hat

An aretalogy is a genre of Greek-Hellenistic literature which acclaimed the *aretai*, i.e. the miraculous deeds of a god or of a miracle-working hero. J. Marböck admits that in Sir 24 the main characteristic of an aretalogy is missing, viz. the documentation of divine power in a miracle[49].

Closely related with the question of the background of Sir 24 is the question whether wisdom in Sir 24 is a hypostasis or not. The majority of scholars regard wisdom here as hypostasis[50]. This interpretation is, however, not undisputed[51]. Recently J. Marböck concluded in his extensive discussion of Sir 24 "daß es nicht Ziel des Selbstpreises sein kann, eine klar umrissene Person oder Hypostase zu zeichnen, sondern durch die Darstellung des Wirkens und der Attribute der Weisheit zu zeigen, wo und wie Gottes Nähe, seine Gegenwart und sein Wirken sich erfahren läßt"[52]. Further, Marböck argued that Ben Sira's divine wisdom, the wisdom 'from above', must not be understood as an intermediary being between God and creation nor as a hypostasis. Wisdom is rather a poetic personification expressing God's nearness, God's acts, and God's personal call[53].

Before we discuss Ben Sira's conception of law we have to clarify first the relationship between wisdom and salvation-history in Ben Sira's thought.

2.2. Wisdom and Salvation-History

Jesus Sirach ein eigenständiges Bild von der Sophia entworfen" (P.154). Cf. G. Pfeifer, *Ursprung und Wesen der Hypostasenvorstellungen im Judentum*, 1967, p.31; P.S. Fiddes, *Hiddenness of Wisdom*, 1976, pp.126-132 stating that there is nothing in Sir 24 "which requires, or is illuminated by, the influence of the figure of Isis" (p.132). Recently H. Gese, "Wisdom", *HBT* 3 (1981) 35f. rejected the view that Sir 24 is based on a pagan myth.

49 J. Marböck, *Weisheit*, p.48 n.13. With regard to the aretalogy see P. Weimar, "Formen frühjüdischer Literatur", *Literatur und Religion des Frühjudentums*, ed. J. Maier et al., 1973, pp.128f. with bibliography.

50 Cf. W. Schencke, *Chokmah*, pp.28-32; N. Peters, *Das Buch Jesus Sirach*, 1913, p.7; H. Ringgren, *Word*, p.113; idem, Art. "Hypostasen", *RGG* 3 (1959) 504-506; M. Hengel, *Judentum*, pp.275-282, 287-289; H.H. Schmid, *Wesen und Geschichte der Weisheit: Eine Untersuchung zur altorientalischen und israelitischen Weisheitsliteratur*, BZAW 101, 1966, pp.149-155; G. Pfeifer, *o.c.*, pp.28-31.

51 Cf. the scholars cited by J. Marböck, *o.c.*, p.66 n.84 and p.130 n.3.

52 J. Marböck, *o.c.*, pp.65f.

53 J. Marböck, *Weisheit*, pp.129f., followed by J.D.G. Dunn, *Christology*, 1980, pp. 170,172 (with n.37 on pp.326f.); cf. also J.L. Crenshaw, *Old Testament Wisdom*, 1982, p.72.

2.2.1. The origin of wisdom. Ben Sira wants to make it clear that God possesses all wisdom and is the one source of true wisdom (1,1; 24,3). This is the second path to wisdom: God reveals to man. Revealed wisdom is παρά κυρίου, from Yahweh (1,1)[54]. It "came forth from the mouth of the Most High" (24,3a). This phrase relates wisdom very closely to the Word of God which is, in the OT, repeatedly described as proceeding from the "mouth of God"[55]. Wisdom is also conceived of as a gift of God (1,10.26; 17, 11; 38,6; 43,33; 45,26; 50,23). God is the ultimate source of wisdom.

2.2.2. Wisdom and Israel. For Ben Sira, wisdom is active in history (1,9-10; 24,6-12; 17,6-9; 43,33). In his great wisdom hymn in chap. 24 he concentrates on the locus of wisdom in the cosmos and among man[56]. Wisdom finally finds a dwelling place (κατέπαυσεν) and inheritance (κατακληρονομήθητι) in Israel (24,8): "Die voll entfaltete Weisheit ist nur in Israel zu finden"[57]. It is not coincidental that the terms of the 'theology of the ark' — the place of rest (מנוחה) and the inheritance (נחלה) — appear in this context[58].

> God's wisdom is where God's mercy is (1,27; 35,14)[59]. God's wisdom is where God's love is. The OT repeatedly points out that Israel is the very sphere of God's love (Deut 7,8.13; 10,13; 23,5; 33,3; Ez 16,8; Is 63,9; 43,4; Hos 11,4; 14,4). The focus of this divine love towards Israel is his holy city. God loves Mount Zion (Ps 78,68) and the gates of Zion (Ps 87,2). He has chosen Zion and made it his dwelling place (Ps 132, 13-14). Sir 24,8-12 resumes this tradition of thought. In the OT wis-

---

54 On παρά with genitive see BDR § 237.1.
55 The following passages refer to the דבר יהוה in the sense of the prophetic speech as proceeding from the mouth of God: Is 1,20; 34,16; 40,5; 45,23; 48,3; 55,11; 62,2; Jer 9,11.19; 15,19; 23,16; Ez 3,17; 33,7; Hos 6,5; Mi 4,4; 2Chr 36,12. Other passages state that משפטים (Ps 119,13), תורה (Ps 119,72), עדות (Ps 119,88), חוקים and מצות (Job 23,12) come from the "mouth of God". In Prov 2,6 it is stated that wisdom (חכמה), knowledge (דעת), and understanding (תבונה) come from the "mouth of God". Cf. K. Weiss, Art. "στόμα", ThWNT 7 (1964) 696.
56 On the wisdom concept in Sir 24 see recently J.C.H. Lebram, "Jerusalem, Wohnsitz der Weisheit", *Studies in Hellenistic Religions*, ed. M.J. Vermaseren, 1979, pp.103-128; H. Gese, "Wisdom", *HBT* 3 (1981) 32-25.
57 M. Löhr, *Bildung*, p.43. Cf. J.C.H. Lebram, a.c., pp.112-120 who stresses the relation between wisdom and the Israelite cult and history in Sir 24. See also J.L. Crenshaw, *Old Testament Wisdom*, pp.149-158.
58 Cf. H. Gese, a.c., p.34.
59 Cf. J. Marböck, *Weisheit*, pp.27-30; O. Rickenbacher, *Weisheitsperikopen*, pp.32f.

dom literature, for all practical purposes, Israel does not occur[60]. For Ben Sira, Israel, Jerusalem, and Zion constitute a prominent theme[61].

God's wisdom found a "dwelling place" and a "place of rest" in Israel. The only passage in the OT which can be compared is Prov 14,33: "Wisdom reposes in the heart of the discerning". Ben Sira refers to the concept of "rest" (נוח) several times[62]. He pictures wisdom as seeking rest and a dwelling place (24,7) which she finally finds in Zion (24,8.11). Thus Israel enters into God's rest.

This rest which God has given to wisdom in Israel can be shared by others: "For at length you will find her rest, and she shall be turned for you into gladness" (6,28). As the dwelling place[63] of wisdom, Israel is her "inheritance"[64]: wisdom had been looking for an inheritance (24,7) which she found, on account of God's initiative, in Israel (24,8). In this inheritance of God, wisdom takes root (24,12) and prospers (24,13-17). Wisdom shares her inheritance with all those who seek her (24,18-20). And all this is the Torah, as inheritance of Jacob (24,23).

Thus, the locus of wisdom is Jacob and Israel (24,8), the temple (24,10a), Zion (24,10b), and Jerusalem (24,11). The section 24, 8-12 "clarifies that wisdom is the divine *shekina* on Zion ... i.e. the cult which, as revelation on Sinai, forms the center of the Torah"[65].

The majority of passages referring to Israel is to be found in the *laus patrum*[66]. Wisdom plays an important part in the history of

---

60 See the brief discussion in O. Rickenbacher, *o.c.*, p.159 who cites Prov 1,1; Qoh 1,12 as exceptions having no theological significance.
61 Cf. O. Rickenbacher, *o.c.*, pp.159-162.
62 Cf. O. Rickenbacher, *o.c.*, pp.138f. for references.
63 In 24,7; 28,16; 47,12-13 the concept of "rest" is combined with the notion of "dwelling".
64 In Deut 12,9-10; 25,19 the terms "rest" and "inheritance" are closely related. Cf. G.von Rad, *Theologie*, 1, p.237; idem, *Gesammelte Studien zum Alten Testament*, pp.87-108; J. Marböck, *Weisheit*, p.62.
65 H. Gese, "Wisdom", *HBT* 3 (1981) 34. G. Vermes, *Scripture and Tradition in Judaism*, SPB 4, ²1973, p.31 points out that in 24,10-13 the word "Lebanon" is used in relation to the temple. It is totally inadequate to interpret 24,1-22 as seeing wisdom as city- and country-goddess who secures the welfare of state and people; contra J.C.H. Lebram, "Jerusalem", 1979, pp.115-119,124-127.
66 44,23; 45,5.11.16.17.22.23; 46,1; 47,2.11G.18.23; 50,13.17.20.22; 51,12c.e.f.o(H). Cf. also E. Janssen, *Gottesvolk*, 1971, pp.16-33 on Ben Sira's "geradliniges Geschichtsbild" (p.16).

Israel. In his introduction (44,1-15), Ben Sira describes the leaders, kings, and prophets of Israel as wise men (44,3-4.15). The wisdom of Solomon is naturally emphasized (47,12.14.17). Moses is described as having received the "law of life and insight (ἐπιστήμη)" (45,5; cf. 17,11).

We have seen that wisdom is closely linked with Israel and her history: Jacob, Israel, the inheritance, the people, the holy city, Zion, Jerusalem, the temple — they are all the locus of wisdom[67].

2.2.3. Wisdom and cult. Closely related with the theme of wisdom and Israel is the relationship between Ben Sira's concept of wisdom and Israel's cult[68]. This is not surprising since Ben Sira was a priest[69].

Besides the main cult pericopes 7,29-31; 31,21-32,20; 38,9-11; 45,23-26 Ben Sira comes to speak of Israel's cult in other contexts as well (cf. 7,8-10; 14,11G; 24,10-11.15; 45, 14-16; 46,16; 47,2; 49,1, 50,1-21). We will briefly comment on these passages, following the analyses of H. Stadelmann.

> In 7,8-10 Ben Sira argues against the misconception of the sacrifice as *opus operatum*. It is the ethical disposition of the person who is sacrificing which decides the effectiveness of the sacrifice. 7,29-31 contains a summons to proper behaviour in cultic matters which is, for Ben Sira, not (!) the product of nomism but essentially the manifestation of an attitude of the heart marked by a living piety (love of God and reverence for the priests) and coupled with just social behaviour (vv. 32-35). —In the context of his 'praise of wisdom' Ben Sira describes in 24,10-11.15 how wisdom came to dwell in the holy city performing the priestly service in the temple. The quintessence and climax of wisdom is her service and rule in the temple[70]. Wisdom is spoken of as one spoke of the cult of the ark, indeed as of the *shekhinah*[71]. In v.15 wisdom is compared with the scents of the temple. — In the lengthy tractate on the Israelite cult in 31,21-32,20 Ben Sira first attacks the abuse of the cult by the impious (31,21-31). This is followed by the presentation of ethical behaviour as spiritual sacrifice (32,1-7) and by a description of the exemplary cultic behaviour of the just (32, 8-13). He concludes in 32,14-20 with an admonition to abstain from unjust sacri-

---

67 These concepts occur, besides in 24,8-12, in the prayer in 36,13-17.
68 See the recent contributions by L.G. Perdue, *Wisdom and Cult*, 1977, pp.188-211 and especially H. Stadelmann, *Ben Sira*, 1980, pp.40-176.
69 Cf. H. Stadelmann, *o.c.*, pp.12-26,40-176 passim. Contra P. Sigal, *Emergence*, I/1, p.227.
70 This is supported by the structure of chap. 24: vv.10-11 form the end and climax of the second stanza (vv.7-11) in which Ben Sira describes the search of a permanent dwelling on earth on the part of wisdom. See H. Stadelmann, *Ben Sira*, pp.51-53; J.C.H. Lebram, "Jerusalem", pp.114f.
71 H. Gese, "Wisdom", *HBT* 3 (1981) 35.

fices. One can indeed refer to a "Kultisierung der Sittlichkeit"[72] by Ben Sira with regard to this important pericope. — In the 'praise of the fathers' Ben Sira deals with Aaron the high priest in 17 verses (45,6-22) whereas Moses is portrayed in only 6 verses (44,23b-45,5). Ben Sira's interest is focused on priestly figures like Phinehas (45,23-25), Samuel (46,13-20), and the high priest Simon II (50,1-21), as well as on kings who stood up for the cult, like David (47,1-11), Solomon (47,12-23), Hezekiah (48,17-22), and Josiah (49,1-3)[73].

2.2.4. Wisdom and the fear of the Lord.

The theme of the fear of the Lord is so prominent in Sirach that J. Haspecker could designate this concept as "Grundthema und wichtigstes Bildungsanliegen Sirachs in seiner pädagogischen Schrift"[74], interpreting it as the formal and material climax even of the wisdom pericopes[75]. Even though this last notion is exaggerated[75] it is nevertheless obvious that the concept of the fear of the Lord is an important feature in Ben Sira's wisdom book: "Der Sirazide fragt nicht nach der Gottesfurcht. Diese ist für ihn eine grundlegend vorgegebene religiöse Größe"[77].

In 1,10 Ben Sira mentions the fear of the Lord for the first time: it is demanded in order to acquire wisdom[78]. This notion is expanded in 1,11-20[79] where the fear of the Lord is described as the way to wisdom: the fear of the Lord is the beginning or essence (ἀρχή) of wisdom (v.14), the fullness of wisdom (πλησμονὴ σοφίας, v.16), the crown of wisdom (στέφανος σοφίας, v.18), and

---

72 Cf. H. Stadelmann, o.c., pp.92ff. passim.
73 Cf. the statement of L.G. Perdue, *Wisdom and Cult*, p.191 that "in a perusal of this eulogy, Sirach may be seen most certainly as a loyalist to the priestly institution of the post-exilic cult, and especially to the office of the high priest". Cf. also H. Stadelmann, o.c., pp.46f.
74 J. Haspecker, *Gottesfurcht bei Jesus Sirach*, AnBibl 30, 1967, p.198.
75 Cf. J. Haspecker, o.c., pp.93,98,141,187 regarding Sir 1,1-10; 4,16-19; 6,18-37; 50,27-29.
76 Cf. the review of R. Murphy in *Bib* 49 (1968) 121 and the remarks by G.von Rad, *Wisdom*, p.242 and J. Marböck, *Weisheit*, pp.16,22,117f.,132f.
77 O. Rickenbacher, *Weisheitsperikopen*, p.12. Cf. J. Haspecker, *Gottesfurcht*, p.337 who states in his conclusion: "Es wird von Sirach ein sehr intensives und lebendiges personales Verhältnis zu Gott vom Gottesfürchtigen verlangt bzw. vorausgesetzt". On the relation between wisdom and the fear of the Lord in Sir see also M. Löhr, *Bildung*, pp.25-48.
78 We read "fear" (G miniscules, S) instead of "love" (G), following R. Smend, *Weisheit*, 1906, p.9; J. Haspecker, o.c., pp.51-53; J. Marböck, *Weisheit*, p.21; O. Rickenbacher, o.c., p.10; G.Sauer, in *JSHRZ* III/5 (1981) 507.
79 Cf. M. Löhr, o.c., pp.27-32.

the root of wisdom (ῥίζα σοφίας/חכמה שרש[80], v.20). The fear of the Lord "is wisdom and instruction" (v.27). In 6,36H (= 6,37G)[81] the fear of the Lord is again presented as a condition and prerequisite for wisdom and instruction (see also 15,1-2; 32,14-16; 39,6; 43,33; 50,28-29).

Wisdom and the fear of the Lord are further closely related with each other by the fact that they share the same fruits: glory (cf. 1,11 with 4,13; 24,16-17), joy and gladness (cf. 1,11-12 with 4,12; 6,28), honour (cf. 1,13 with 6,29; 24,16), and length of days (cf. 1,12 with 1,20). Both wisdom and the fear of the Lord keep from sin (1,21; 24,22).

2.2.5. *The fruit of wisdom.* The way in which Ben Sira describes the growth and the fruit of wisdom equally stresses the close relationship between his concept of wisdom and the realm of Israel's faith and history[82].

The first fruit of wisdom which Ben Sira mentions is שלום/εἰρήνη (1,18)[83], an important theological term in the OT. "Peace" is often seen as God's gift to his people[84]. The notion that *shalom* is a result of wisdom can already be found in Prov 3,2.17 (cf. 12,20). "Good health" (Sir 1,18b) and "length of days" (1,20) are further results of wisdom. Ben Sira points out elsewhere that good health is from the Lord (28,3; cf. 38,2.14G). In the OT "length of days" (ארך ימים, רבה ימים, LXX μακροημέρευσις) is God's gift and reward for faithfulness to his commandements (Deut 4,40; 5,33; 6,2; 11,8-9.18-21; 32,47). In 4,12 רצון "good will, favour with God" (as subject) is described as a further fruit of wisdom. This term which is quite common in Sir[85] is used as an equivalent for

---

80 Thus the reconstruction of H (2Q18) by F. Vattioni, *Ecclesiastico*, 1968, p.7.
81 On this verse see J. Haspecker, *o.c.*, pp.60-64,130f.
82 It seems that this theme has never been discussed previously in detail.
83 O. Rickenbacher, *Weisheitsperikopen*, p.13 follows R. Smend, hesitatingly, in taking the fear of the Lord as subject. However, it is at least equally plausible to take wisdom as subject: both vv.18.20 closely relate wisdom and the fear of the Lord with wisdom clearly being the subject in v.20b. Both verses might contain the same imagery of the tree since στέφανος σοφίας in v.18 has been taken to refer to the crown of a tree (cf. L. Alonso-Schökel, quoted by O. Rickenbacher, *o.c.*, p.13; G. Kuhn in *ZAW* 47 (1929) 289 wants to read *nzr* "shoot, sprout" and not *nṣr*).
84 Cf. G.von Rad, Art. "εἰρήνη", *ThWNT* 2 (1935) 401f.
85 Cf. the list in O. Rickenbacher, *o.c.*, pp.31f.; also G. Schrenk in *ThWNT* 2 (1935) 741f.

wisdom (1,27), law and commandments (2,16; 15,15), and forgiveness (35,5). In the OT רצון is most often used for God's favour, grace, and good will (cf. Deut 33,23; Ps 5,13; 30,6.8; Prov 8,35; 12,2; 18,22; Is 60,10). Another result of wisdom is כבוד / δόξα (4,13; 6,31; 24,16-17; 37,26; 51,17; cf. 44,2) which is a characteristic of Yahweh (17,13; 36,19; 42,16-17; 45,3; 49,12)[86].

Further fruits of wisdom with a similar background are blessing (4,13), blessedness (14,20; 25,9-10), rest (6,28), joy (4,12G; 6, 28), protection (6,29), honour (6,29; 24,16), grace (24,16), and wealth (24,17). Finally, wisdom, like the fear of the Lord, keeps from sin (24,22).

In 24,13-17 wisdom unfolds the blessing of her presence in an impressive series of images, focusing on her growth and fruitfulness[87]. Wisdom presents herself as living, growing, prospering, and blossoming in the entire country, from the Lebanon and Hermon to Engedi and Jericho, and out into the plain. "So erweist sie (i.e. wisdom) sich wieder als in Israels Raum wirksame Größe"[88].

Appendix: The 'Laus Patrum' and Ezra

For a long time, commentators and scholars have been startled by the fact that Ben Sira does not mention Ezra in his review of Israel's history[89]. Different explanations have been given which we will review briefly. Some explanations are so forced or hypothetical that they can be dismissed out of hand. R. Smend thinks that it is pure chance that Ben Sira did not mention Ezra[90]. N. Peters believes that the book of Ezra did not yet exist at Ben Sira's time[91]. Other scholars including K.F. Pohlmann[92], P.R. Ackroyd[93], and R. Rivkin[94] attempt to defend the view that Ben Sira did not know the Chronicler's work. Other scholars tried to explain the omission of Ezra by *material differences* between Ezra and Ben Sira. Box/Oesterley think that Ben Sira, as a representative of the circle of wisdom teachers who had a wide outlook, did not esteem the narrow and legalistic attitude of the scribes around Ezra[95]. E. Jansen

---

86 On the concept of כבוד in Sir see O. Rickenbacher, *o.c.*, pp.46-48.
87 On this passage see especially J. Marböck, *Weisheit*, pp.74-76.
88 J. Marböck, *o.c.*, p.74.
89 Cf. J. Marböck, "Der schriftgelehrte Weise", *BETL* 51 (1979) p.303.
90 R. Smend, *Weisheit*, p.474. Similarly E. Rivkin, "Ben Sira and the Non-Existence of the Synagogue", *In the Time of Harvest*, FS A.H. Silver, 1963, pp.349f. who says that maybe Ezra was not yet known to Ben Sira "because Ezra had not yet attained historical reality yet"!
91 N. Peters, *Das Buch Jesus Sirach*, 1913, p.422.
92 K.F. Pohlmann, *Studien zum dritten Esra*, FRLANT 104, 1970.
93 P.R. Ackroyd, "The Maccabean Dating of OT Literature", *VT* 3 (1953) 116.
94 E. Rivkin, *a.c.*, pp.349f.
95 Box/Oesterley, in *APOT* 1 (1913) 506 in the context of Sir 49,13.

thinks that Ben Sira probably did not value the non-pentateuchal writings as much as he did the Pentateuch[96]. P. Sigal believes that Ezra was omitted because he was "signally ineffective" in his mission which, as a result, had to be repeated by Nehemiah who took more stringent steps[97]. R. Smend[98], T. Middendorp[99], and R.A.F. MacKenzie[100] refer to Ezra's rigoristic dissolution of the mixed marriages which was not appreciated by Ben Sira. However, these material explanations are not conclusive and far from adequate[101].

Numerous explanations focused in recent years on *theological differences* between Ezra and Ben Sira. J.C.H. Lebram thinks that Ezra was probably "Leitgestalt der Chasidäer" who wanted to keep Israel 'clean' by erecting a "fence around the Torah" which was not appreciated by Ben Sira who represented the "priesterliche Konzentration auf das Mosegesetz"[102]. M. Hengel[103] and J. Marböck[104] follow Lebram's explanation. U. Kellermann[105] adduced "kontroverstheologische Gründe": Ben Sira did not reckon Ezra to be an example for Israel since he was for him the chief witness of the totally introvert attitude of the theocratic circles which paralysed the power of resistance to the danger of Hellenism. W.T. in der Smitten[106] developed this argument further without adding substantially new insights. P. Höffken sees the decisive theological difference between Ben Sira and Ezra in the differing evaluation of the role and function of the Levites in Ben Sira and in the Chronicler (including Ezra): as Ben Sira has a different understanding of the theocratic Israel, Ezra is, as "Prototyp des Levitismus", intolerable[107]. Finally, R.A.F. MacKenzie believes that Ben Sira had a "real distaste" or distrust for a written law[108]. Without going into a detailed evaluation of these explanations we note that none of them has received the undivided support of the scholarly world.

The best explanation, in our eyes, seems to be that offered by J.G. Snaith[109] and

---

96 E. Janssen, *Gottesvolk*, 1971, p.22.
97 P. Sigal, *Emergence*, I/1, 1980, pp.115f.
98 R. Smend, *Weisheit*, p.474.
99 T. Middendorp, *Die Stellung Jesu Ben Siras zwischen Judentum und Hellenismus*, 1973, p.66.
100 R.A.F. MacKenzie, "Ben Sira as Historian", *Trinification of the World*, FS F.E. Crowe, 1978, pp.323f. His "working hypothesis", that Ben Sira descended from a family whose members were not in the exile but had remained in Palestine and resented Ezra's imposition of a new and stricter version of the law remains a hypothesis.
101 P. Höffken, "Warum schwieg Jesus Sirach über Esra?", *ZAW* 87 (1975) 185-187.
102 J.C.H. Lebram, "Aspekte der alttestamentlichen Kanonbildung", *VT* 18 (1968) 189 (cf. pp.181f. with n.5).
103 M. Hengel, *Judentum*, p.272 n.281 where he states that Ben Sira rejected any "chasidisch-pietistische Ängstlichkeit und Prüderie".
104 J. Marböck, *Weisheit*, p.91 n.167; idem, "Gesetz und Weisheit", *BZ* 20 (1976) 11. In a recent article, J. Marböck, "Der schriftgelehrte Weise", *BETL* 51 (1979) 303 n.37 states that the question of Ezra's omission is not yet solved.
105 U. Kellermann, *Nehemia: Quellen, Überlieferung und Geschichte*, 1967, pp.114f.
106 W.T. in der Smitten, *Esra: Quellen, Überlieferung und Geschichte*, SSN 15, 1973, pp.69-74.
107 P. Höffen, "Warum schwieg Jesus Sirach über Esra?", *ZAW* 87 (1975) 187-200.
108 R.A.F. MacKenzie, "Ben Sira as Historian", 1978, p.324.
109 J.G. Snaith, *Ecclesiasticus*, 1974, p.247 (not discussed by P. Höffken).

defended by H. Stadelmann[110] which is based on *exegetical reasons*: Ben Sira mentions only those post-exilic persons, apart from his contemporary, Simon the high priest, who were involved in the restoration of the city of Jerusalem and of the temple. And Ezra was not one of the "Erbauer und Ausgestalter des äußeren Zentrums der Hierokratie"[111].

2.3. Summary

We have examined Ben Sira's wisdom conception with its twofold character as a cosmological entity and as the salvation-historical possession of Israel. Wisdom links the two areas of creation and history[112]. God's wisdom is manifest in creation. This explains on the one hand the universality of creation and on the other hand the order of creation. Wisdom is universal, i.e. it knows no geographical or national limits. The order of creation can be observed in the cosmos, among mankind, and among God's people. All of God's works are characterized by goodness and purposefulness, by God's own wisdom.

Wisdom is Yahweh's wisdom and enjoys therefore a special relationship with God's people. Israel's God is the only true source of wisdom. Wisdom can be received as God's gift. Universal wisdom came to dwell, in a rather specific manner, in Israel and especially on Zion in the temple. Israel is thus the inheritance of wisdom. Naturally wisdom played an important role in the history of Israel. The temple with its cult is also presented as the locus of wisdom. Right ethical behaviour (wisdom) is presented as spiritual sacrifice. Consequently, wisdom and piety/faith are closely related: the fear of the Lord is the beginning and the end, the root and the crown of wisdom. The fruits of wisdom in one's life are equivalent to God's grace and favour bestowed upon man.

Ben Sira the scribe and priest incorporated the priestly, the prophetic, and the sapiential traditions of Israel and presented wisdom as being active and essential in all realms of reality: in nature and in history, in the world and in the life of God's people.

---

110 H. Stadelmann, *Ben Sira*, 1980, p.163 n.1.
111 H. Stadelmann, *o.c.*, p.163; similarly E. Janssen, *Gottesvolk*, p.27.
112 Cf. J. Marböck, *Weisheit*, p.68.

§3 Ben Sira's Concept of the Law and the Commandments

It is rather surprising that despite the renaissance of Sirach research[113] Ben Sira's understanding of the law has not been dealt with adequately. G. von Rad discusses the role of the law in Sir only very briefly[114]. He is not very consistent: he states with regard to the numerous references to the law in Sir[115] that the Torah "in the form of law established in writing" plays an important role (p.244) and then goes on to say that Ben Sira needs the concept of the law in order to clarify the idea of the fear of the Lord (ibid.) but that he is little capable of developing the idea of Torah (p.247). He concludes, astonishingly, that "the Torah is not a subject of particular interest to Sirach. He knows about it, it has a part to play, but basically for Sirach it is of relevance only in so far as it is to be understood on the basis of... the great complex of wisdom teachings" (ibid.).

J. Haspecker deals with the law only in conjunction with his discussion of the concept of the fear of the Lord[116]. But he points out that the double reference to the events at Sinai in 17,11-14 and 45,1-5 suggests a "detaillierte Theologie des Gesetzes und der Gesetzesmitteilung" (p.332).

J. Marböck devotes seven pages of his monograph to Ben Sira's concept of law[117] which are helpful in indicating the more important aspects but which leave much to be desired concerning even basic questions like the relevant terminology in Sirach[118]. In his article on law and wisdom in Sir[119] Marböck included no separate

---

113 Cf. J. Marböck, in *VT* 24 (1974) 510; idem, in *BZ* 20 (1976) 1; R.A.F. MacKenzie, "Ben Sira as Historian", 1978, p.312; H. Stadelmann, *Ben Sira*, 1980, p.V.
114 Cf. G. von Rad, *Wisdom*, pp.244-247.
115 On p.244 n.8 he lists 25 references to the law.
116 Cf. J. Haspecker, *Gottesfurcht*, pp.328-332 where he states that the term 'law' belongs "einesteils in die Theologie des Buches, zum anderen Teil in die Ethik" (p.328).
117 J. Marböck, *Weisheit*, 1971, pp.86-92.
118 J. Marböck, *o.c.*, p.86 lists for example πρόσταγμα as one of the four expressions for law in Sir. However, this term occurs only four times (6,37; 39,16.18; 43,13) being of theological significance only in 6,37 where πρόσταγμα κυρίου (6,36H has יראת עליון, "fear of the Most High") is parallel to ἐντολαί/ מ.צות. Marböck admits that he does not attempt to provide a comprehensive discussion of Ben Sira's concept of law (p.81).

treatment of law in Sir, despite the subtitle of the article. He points out "daß das Gesetz, sowohl was das Vokabular als auch die unmittelbare Thematik einzelner Perikopen betrifft, hinter dem Thema der Weisheit und der Gottesfurcht beachtlich zurücksteht; auch der Schöpfungsgedanke ist weitaus zentraler. Das Gesetz ist nie selbständiger Inhalt, sondern begegnet...stets eingeordnet in diese größeren Zusammenhänge"[120].

Although this last observation is generally valid, an investigation of the relevant Greek and Hebrew vocabulary in Sir shows that the law is an important concept for Ben Sira even if he did not 'discuss' it in a particular pericope. Moreover, the fact that Ben Sira often includes references to the law in passages which contain traditional wisdom material (cf. 1,5.26; 19,17.20.24; 24,23; 32, 14-18. 22-23)[121] seems to indicate that the great didactic pericopes on wisdom, on the fear of the Lord, on the destiny of man, on creation, and on the wise man all aim at establishing the Torah as the 'vanishing point' of the activity of the sage[122]. For Ben Sira, a priest and scribe, the law and the commandments formed the very basis of his life and thought. It is always precarious to speculate on the reasons and motives of a person who failed to do or to write this or that. Whether Ben Sira had specific reasons for not 'praising' the law in a hymn or not, the frequency and significance of his references to the law given to Israel by God make a more extensive treatment of the concept of law in Sir imperative.

K. Berger maintains that for Ben Sira (whom he classifies under Jewish-Hellenistic wisdom literature alongside SapSal, Pseudo-Phocylides, and Pseudo-Meander!) νόμος is de facto not the OT law but simply a monotheism linked with general and social virtues[123].

---

119 J. Marböck, "Gesetz und Weisheit: Zum Verständnis des Gesetzes bei Jesus Ben Sira", *BZ* 20 (1976) 1-21.
120 J. Marböck, "Gesetz und Weisheit", *BZ* 20 (1976) 2f. He denies that Ben Sira, when he refers to the law, means the Mosaic Torah (pp.3f.10). This notion is rejected, without exegetical proof, however, by D. Zeller, *Mahnsprüche*, 1977, p.39 n.209.
121 See also the references to wisdom (4,11ff.; 6,18ff.; 20,35ff.), to instruction (6,32ff.), and to the fear of the Lord (10,18ff.; 21,1ff.) which serve the same purpose of referring to the Torah.
122 Cf. M. Löhr, *Bildung*, pp.107f.
123 K. Berger, *Die Gesetzesauslegung Jesu: Ihr historischer Hintergrund im Judentum und im Alten Testament*, Teil I, WMANT 40, 1972, pp.38f.

He goes on to say that "dem Minimum an spezifisch atl Restbestand in diesem Nomos-Begriff entspricht ein Maximum an Nähe zu hellenistischem paränetischem Material ... neben der weitgehenden Übernahme griechischer Laster- und Tugendkataloge zeigen sich jüdische Traditionen nur mehr in der Formulierung bestimmter Sozialgebote"[124].

Since Ben Sira is obviously not a Jewish-Hellenistic writer, Berger's view, at least with regard to Sir, has to be modified.

O. Rickenbacher attempts a thematic treatment of the terms תורה and מצוה in Sir including a list of both terms with their Greek renderings[125]. However, he does not discuss the equally important terms משפט and חוק. His systematic discussion of תורה and מצוה is brief and far from satisfactory. According to him, תורה 'must not be simply identified with the Mosaic Torah given at Sinai but has to be understood in the context of the order of creation. Although this is true for some passages, it is clearly wrong for others.

Before we attempt to analyze the relevant references thematically we will first have to discuss the different terms referring to law in Sir. As this has not been done before in an exhaustive manner we will have to go into more details than we did with regard to Ben Sira's concept of wisdom.

3.1. Terminology

On the basis of the Hebrew[126] and Greek[127] concordances for Sirach we will treat all occurrences of חוק, משפט, מצוה, תורה and דבר יהוה, as well as the occurrences of the Greek terms νόμος, ἐντολή, κρίμα, and λόγος κυρίου, taking note of the immediate contexts, especially of parallel terms.

(1) *Torah*. The term תורה occurs 12 times in Sir: 15,1b; 32 (35), 15a.17b.18b.23a; 33(36), 2a.3b; 41,4a.8b; 42,2a; 45,5d; 49, 4c. Except in 32,17b.18b; 41,4a, תורה is always translated by νόμος.

---

124 K. Berger, *o.c.*, p.46 with regard to Sir 32,23.
125 O. Rickenbacher, *Weisheitsperikopen*, pp.85-89.
126 D. Barthelemy, O. Rickenbacher, *Konkordanz zum Hebräischen Sirach*, 1973.
127 E. Hatch, H.A. Redpath, *A Concordance to the Septuagint and the other Greek Versions of the Old Testament (Including the Apocyphical Books)*, 2 vols., 1897 (= 1975).

In 15,1 the phrase תפש תורה = "to take hold of the law" (cf. Jer 2,8) is parallel with ירא יהוה ="to fear the Lord". The result of both is the gaining of wisdom. In Jer 2,8 this phrase clearly refers to the Torah of the priests (!), very probably the Mosaic legislation[128]. - In 32,15H the phrase דרש תורה = "to seek the law" is used and is directly parallel with דרש אל (v.14a.15c) and with חפצי דרש (v.14c). In Esr 7,10 דרש is used in connection with תורת יהוה, signifying the Mosaic legislation embodied in the Pentateuch[129]. 32,15a can be considered as corresponding to the "fear of the Lord" in v.16a. The context of vv. 14-16 makes it probable that תורה in v.15 has a 'theological' (and not only a purely sapiential) meaning as well[130]. - 32,17H is more difficult to understand. H[B] reads ואחר צרכו ימשך תורה which is best translated as "to force the law to suit one's necessity"[131]. If תורה in v.15 is taken to refer to the written law it is plausible to take the same meaning here[132]. - 32,18H uses the phrase שמר תורה which proves that תורה signifies here God's laws and commands (שמר is used with מצוה/ מצות in 15,15; 32,23H[E]; 37,12; 44,20)[133] despite the fact that תורה corresponds e contrario with איש חכם. - A similar phrase[134] is repeated in 32,23H[B], again clearly referring to the Mosaic law: מצוה in v.22a.b is parallel to תורה in v.23. - In 33,2H תורה is parallel to the "fear of the Lord" in v.1a and to the "word of the Lord" (דבר יהוה) in v.3a. Thus it is plausible to take this as a reference to the Mosaic law as well. The fourth parallel term is again תורה in 33,3bH. - In 41,4 we have the expression תורת עליון which corresponds with the חוקים מות, the fixed order of God with regard to death[135]. Thus, תורה here refers to God's order of creation. - In 41,8 the term תורת עליון is repeated, now referring to the Mosaic law[136]. Ben Sira laments about the wicked and worthless men who have "forsaken" (עזב) the law. In the OT עזב is used 60 times for people who forsake God, his covenant, or his commandments[137]. - In 42,1-8 Ben Sira lists things one should not be ashamed of, or bad habits and abuses from which one should abstain. This list is preceded by the reference to the constitutional foundation of the Jewish state,

---

128 Cf. R. Smend, *Weisheit*, p.139; J. Haspecker, *Gottesfurcht*, pp.140f., 329; J. Marböck, *Weisheit*, p.89; idem, "Gesetz", *BZ* 20 (1976) 10.
129 Cf. the later technical usage of דרש, especially in Rabbinic texts.
130 Cf. J.G. Snaith, *Ecclesiasticus*, pp.157f.; Box/Oesterly, *APOT* 1 (1913) 427; J. Haspecker, *o.c.*, pp.225,227,266 n.48. Contra G. Sauer, *JSHRZ* III/5 (1981) 584 who translates with "Weisung".
131 Following Box/Oesterley, *o.c.*, p.427.
132 This view is shared by T. Middendorp, *Stellung*, 1973, p.163.
133 The phrase שמר מצוה/שמר תורה is very prominent in the OT (50x in Deut, 21x in Ps 119). Cf. G. Sauer, in *THAT* 2 (1976) 985.
134 H[B] has נוצר תורה (cf. Ps 105,45; 119,34; Prov 28,7; נצר with מצוה is used in Ps 78,7; 119,115; see also Ps 119,2.22.33.56.69.110.129.145). H[E] has probably שומר תורה: see the reconstruction by E. Vanttioni, *Ecclesiastico*, p.173. Since H[B] has שמר נפשך / נפשר three times (v.22a.c.23a) the reading of H[E] (נוצר נפשר) should be dismissed.
135 On this meaning of חוק see G. Liedke, in *THAT* 1 (1971) 629f. G translates תורת עליון with εὐδοκία ὑψίστου.
136 See also T. Middendorp, *Stellung*, p.163.
137 See H.P. Stähli, in *THAT* 2 (1976) 251.
138 See G. Liedke, in *THAT* 1 (1971) 630-632.

the Torah[139]. - In 45,5 Ben Sira emphasizes that God gave to Moses the commandment (מצוה), the law of life and discernment (תורת חיים ותבונה) in order that he might teach (למד) Jacob his statues (חקים), Israel his testimonies (עדרת) and decrees (משפטים). This comprehensive enumeration of legal terms, together with the context (the description of Moses in the *laus patrum*), prove that 45,5 is another reference to the Mosaic Torah given at Sinai[140]. - 49,4 has the same phrase as 41,8b: עזב תורת עליון. In the context the kings of Judah are accused of having forsaken the "law of the Most High". Considering the OT context of similar or identical accusations, תורה here must refer to the Mosaic law as well[141].

Thus, of the 12 occurrences of תורה in Sirach, 11[142] refer to the Torah, the *lex revelata*, the constitutional and spiritual basis of Israel's life. The identification of תורה with עדות, חקים, מצוה, and משפטים referring to the Mosaic law makes it plausible to take the other occurrences of 'law' as references to the Mosaic Torah as well[143]. We have to reject O. Rickenbacher's statement that with the exception of 24,23 there is no reason, "die Bedeutung auf eine erst am Sinai ergangene Torah einzuengen"[144].

The fact that the 12 occurrences of תורה in Prov do not refer to God's law in most cases is no proof that the same holds true for Ben Sira's wisdom book. In Prov תורה is often constructed with a genitive indicating the source of instruction, which often is the wisdom teacher or the father (cf. Prov 1,8; 3,1; 4,2; 6,20.23; 7,2; 31,26).

In Sir, however, we have four times the phrase תורת עליון (41,4.8; 42,2; 49,4), four times the correlation of law and the fear of the Lord (15,1; 32,15; 33,2.3), and one reference to the Sinaitic revelation of the Mosaic law (45,5). The references to תורה in 32,17b.18b.23a are linked with the איש חכם, but also with the

---

139 Cf. T. Middendorp, *o.c.*, p.163; J.G. Snaith, *Ecclesiasticus*, p.203; G. Sauer, in *JSHRZ* III/5 (1981) 608.
140 Cf. R. Smend, *Weisheit*, p.428, J. Haspecker, *Gottesfurcht*, p.153 n.65; J. Marböck, "Der schriftgelehrte Weise", *BETL* 51 (1979) 302 who acknowledges the fact that 45,5 refers to the Mosaic legislation, i.e. to the Sinaitic Torah, and not to sapiential instruction.
141 Cf. T. Middendorp, *Stellung*, p.163.
142 The exception is 41,1 where the fixed order of creation is referred to.
143 Cf. T. Middendorp, *o.c.*, pp.162-164. See further infra.
144 O. Rickenbacher, *Weisheitsperikopen*, p.88. His alternative view of the meaning of law in Sirach ("die Torah kann von der Schöpfung an begonnen haben", ibid.) is totally speculative. His explanation that even in 24,23 nothing indicates "daß nicht auch die Torah schon von Angang der Welt und der Menschen an da war" (p.89) is simply an *argumentum e silentio*.

fear of the Lord (v.16), with the keeping of the commandments (v.18bH^{Bm,E}.22a), and with trusting the Lord (v.22b).

(2) *Mizvah*. Ben Sira uses the term מצוה 10 times: 6,36b; 10, 19d; 15,15a; 32(35),18b.22b.d; 37,12b; 44,20a; 45,5c.17a. Except in 32,18b.22d; 44,20, מצוה sg. is translated with ἐντολαί pl[145].

In the OT, especially in Deut, מצוה is used as the designation of a corpus of decrees and commandments, even as designation of the law as a whole: as comprehensive term in conjunction with חקים and משפטים (Deut 5,31; 6,1; 7,11), and in the formula כל המצוה (Deut 5,31; 6,25; 8,1; 11,8.22; cf. Josh 22,3.5; 2Kgs 17,19.37; Jer 32,11). In the deuteronomistic and chronistic context מצוה is often used in sequences of terms for law and commandments which synonymously refer to the whole of, or part of, the law[146]. The evidence in Sirach is as follows.

> In 6,36H (=6,37G) מצוה is parallel to the "fear of the Lord". Ben Sira calls upon his readers to "study" or "meditate upon" (הגה) the commandments of God. The term הגה = "murmelnd bedenken"[147] is used in 14,20 in connection with חכמה but is used in Josh 1,8; Ps 1,2 in connection with תורה . The fruit of this study of the law is insight and wisdom. - In 10,19 מצוה and the fear of the Lord are parallel again. Ben Sira states that those people are worthy of contempt who "transgress" (עבר) the commandments. In the OT עבר is often used for the trangression of the Torah[148]. - 15,5 has שמר מצוה = "to keep the commandments", and parallels the phrase "to act according to God's pleasure (רצון)". Here מצוה refers to the whole law as an expression of the way of life God approves[149]. - Following H^{Bm} and H^E we read in 32,18b יקח מצוה (H^B has ישמר לשון)[150] which is parallel to ישמר תורה in v.18d, referring to the Mosaic law. It also corresponds with the fear of the Lord in v.16. - In 32,22b.d we have again the phrase שמר מצוה (H^B; H^{Bm} has pl. מצות), correlating with נצר תורה in v.23a. - In 37,12 the phrase שמר מצוה is repeated again and is linked in synonymous parallelism with the fear of the Lord. - 44,20 related that Abraham has "kept" (שמר) the "commandments of the Most High" (מצות עליון), "entered into a covenant with him", and accepted circumcision as a mark of the covenant. If מצוה does not refer to the Mosaic Torah here[151] it certainly refers to the *lex revelata*. - In 45,5c

---

145 In 44,20 the Greek text has νόμος. Cf. O. Rickenbacher, *Weisheitsperikopen*, pp. 69-71 for further details.
146 Cf. G. Liedke, in *THAT* 2 (1976) 535f.
147 Cf. L. Koehler, W. Baumgartner, *Hebräisches und Aramäisches Lexikon zum Alten Testament*, ³1967, 1, p.228.
148 With פי יהוה (Num 14,41; 22,18; 24,13; 1Sam 15,24), מצוה (Deut 26,13; 2Chr 24,20), and תורה (Is 24,5). Cf. H.P. Stähli, *THAT* 2 (1976) 204.
149 Cf. J.G. Snaith, *Ecclesiasticus*, p.79.
150 R. Smend and Box/Oesterley read יקח תורה.
151 Cf. J.G. Snaith, *o.c.*, p.219.

מצוה clearly refers to the Mosaic Law. - In 45,17 Aaron is described as having received God's מצות (parallel to חק and משפט). These terms certainly refer to God's revealed law as well, probably to the Mosaic law which was the foundation of the Jewish state ruled by the priests[152].

It follows from this discussion that probably[153] all 10 occurrences of מצוה in Sir refer to the revealed law of God which, in the historical context, would be identified with the Mosaic law. Four times מצוה is linked with the fear of the Lord (6,36; 10,19; 32,18; 37,12). Sir usess מצוה always in the singular: "Für Ben Sira geht es nicht um einzelne Gebote, sondern um die Torah überhaupt, um sie als gesamte"[154].

(3) *Mishpaṭ.* The term משפט occurs 20 times in Ben Sira: 13 references are of theological significance: 32(35),16a.c; 35 (32), 12.17.17; 42,2b; 43,13; 45,5-6.10c.17b.d; 48,7b; 50,19[155]. It is most often translated with $\kappa\rho\iota\mu\alpha$, $\kappa\rho\iota\sigma\iota\varsigma$, or related terms.

In the OT, שפט generally designates "ein Handeln, durch das die gestörte Ordnung einer (Rechts-) Gemeinschaft wiederhergestellt wird"[156]. The phrase משפט יהוה refers to Yahweh's sentence or judgment (cf. Job 40,18; Is 3,14; 30,18) and to his order, way, or legal claim (cf. 2Kgs 17,26-27; Is 51,4; 58,2; Hos 6,5), rarely signifying the law. However, the pl. משפטים refers to the "ins Jahwerecht eingegliederten kasuistischen Rechtssätze"[157] (cf. Lev 18,4ff.; 26,15.43; Deut 33,10; Ps 19,10; 89,31; 119,20.39; Is 26,8-9), and, in connection with other terms for law, משפט / משפטים synonymously designate the commandments of Yahweh. The evidence in Sir is as follows.

In 32,16a.c it is stated that those who fear the Lord "know" (בין) his law (משפט sg.). In the context we have parallel terms for law including תורה (vv.17b.18c) and מצוה (vv.18bH^Bm,E.22b.d). Thus, a reference to the Mosaic law is quite possible. - In 35,12.17 Yahweh is called אלהי משפט, "God of judgment", who, as "righteous judge" (שופט צדק) "exercises justice" (יעשה משפט). There is no reference to the Mosaic law intended. - In 42,2b H^Bm and H^M read משפט instead of מצדיק (G has $\kappa\rho\iota\mu\alpha\tau\alpha$). Since this term is preceded by תורה and חוק we have probably another reference to the written law. - The term זיקות משפט in 43,13 re-

---

152 Cf. T. Middendorp, *Stellung*, p.163; H. Stadelmann, *Ben Sira*, p.154 n.1.
153 The evidence in 37,12 is not as clear as in the other passages.
154 O. Rickenbacher, *Weisheitsperikopen*, p.70.
155 The other 7 occurrences are 4,9H^A; 30,20; 32(35),5b; 38,16c; 39,29; 41,16; 47,10.
156 G. Liedke, in *THAT* 2 (1976) 1001.
157 G. Liedke, in *THAT* 2 (1976) 1009.

fers again to God's judgment (cf. 35,12.17; 39,29). - In 45,5 מׁשפטים is the last term for law after תורה, מצוה, חקים and עדות. Thus, this is a clear reference to the Mosaic Torah. - In 45,10c we have again the meaning "judgment", referring to Aaron's legal responsibilities. - In 45,17b.d מׁשפט is again linked with מצות and חוק, designating the Mosaic law. - Although 48,7 refers to the events at Sinai, מׁשפט does not refer to God's law given to Moses but to God's judgment. - In 50, 19 מׁשפטיו does not designate the Mosaic law either.

Thus, מׁשפט refers to the revealed Mosaic law only in 32,16a.c; 42,2; 45,5.17b.d with the last three references being the most definite ones. In 32,16a.c מׁשפט is linked with the fear of the Lord.

(4) *Ḥuq.* The term חק occurs 21 times in Sir: 11,17c.18a; 14, 12c.17; 16,20; 38,22; 39,31b; 41,2a.3a; 42,2; 43,7a.10a.12a; 44, 5a.20c; 45,5e.7a.17b.c.24a;47,11c. G has 10 timess διαϑήκη and 4 times κρίμα.

The primary meaning of חק is "something scratched on, confining line or limit". It is often used of a fixed order (e.g. of the stars) of God (cf. Gen 47,26; Jdg 11,39; Job 28,26; Ps 148,2-6; Jer 31, 36). Its theological significance lies in the fact that it describes God's acts and orders of creation (Job 38,10.33; Prov 8,27.29; Jer 5,22.24; 33,25), man's 'limits' set by God (Job 14,5.13; 23,14; Prov 30,8), the priestly share in the sacrifices (cf. Ex 29,28; Lev 6, 11), and (mostly with the pl.) also God's law when used in conjunction with other terms for law (with מׁשפטים in Deut 4,1.5.8.14. 45; 5,1.31; 6.1.20; 7,11; 11,32; 12,1; 26,16-17; Neh 1,7; 9,13; 10, 30; 1Chr 22,13; 2Chr 7,17; 19,10; 33,8; Ez 5,6-7; with מצות in Deut 6,2; 8,11; 10,13; 11,1; 28,15.45)[158]. The evidence in Sir is as follows.

> In Sir חק often refers to the fixed orders set by God which affect man: the inescapable lot of death (11,17cH; 14,12.17; 38,22; 41,2a.3a); the particular profession of man as 'temperal order' (11,18H); God's final judgment which the godless take to be far away and uncertain (16,20 H); God's rule over creation and his command initiating judgment (39,31); the cosmic order of stars (43,10); and the fixed times which they indicate. חק also denotes the musical order of composition in the writing of psalms (44,5). But חק also refers to orders of theological significance: the 'order' of circumcision which is God's convenant with Israel (44,20), and the established law or 'order' of a covenant into which certain individuals are placed by God (Levi 45,7; Aaron 45,17; Phinehas 45,24; David 47,11). Finally, חק is used in conjunction

---

[158] Cf. G. Liedke, *THAT* 1 (1971) 627-632. On חק as term for the cosmic order see also S. Aalen, *Die Begriffe 'Licht' und 'Finsternis' im Alten Testament, im Spätjudentum und im Rabbinismus*, 1951, pp.158-163.

of, and synonymous with, תורה, מצוה, and משפט, refering to the Mosaic law (45, 5e.17b.c; cf. 42,2)[159].

Thus, חק refers to the Mosaic law in 42,2; 45,5e.17b.c. In the majority of the other references it signifies God's orders in creation and/or in the history of Israel.

(5) *Dabar Yahweh*. Ben Sira refers 8 times to the דבר יהוה: 33, 3aH; 43,5b.10a.26b.29b; 47,22b; 48,3a; 51,30e. In 7 cases (except 43,29b) G has λόγος κυρίου.

In 33,3 דבר יהוה corresponds with תורה, referring to God's revealed law. In the majority of the other occurrences the term designates God's word which is active in creation (43,5.10.26.29; cf. 48,3).

(6) *Nomos*. The term νόμος occurs in G 26 times which is 9 times the translation of תורה. We will discuss here only those passages which are extant in Greek only (14 references). The others, focusing on the Hebrew original, were treated above.

In the prologue (prol.) νόμος clearly refers to the Pentateuch: vv.1-2 read "the law and the prophets and the others which followed them", and vv.8-10 mentions the "law and the prophets and the other books of the fathers". - In 2,16 νόμος corresponds with God's ῥήματα and ὁδοί (v.15a) thus referring to God's revealed law[160]. - 17,11 is the first verse of the third part of Ben Sira's great pericope on God's wise order in creation which is especially evident among God's people (17,11-14). God gave to Israel "knowledge" (ἐπιστήμη) and the "law of life" (νόμος ζωῆς). As νόμος ζωῆς (v.11b) is parallel to διαθήκη αἰῶνος and God's κρίματα (v.12), and since vv.13-14 obviously refer to the events at Sinai, we take the term "law of life" (cf. 45,5 תורת חיים) to refer also to the Mosaic law[161]. - In 19,17 the νόμος ὑψίστου is to regulate the relationship between human beings. It is linked with the fear of the Lord (v.18a), and with God's commandments (ἐντολή, v.19a). In 19,20 the ποίησις νόμου is linked in synonymous parallelism with the fear of the Lord. In 19,24 the transgression of the νόμος is contrasted with the pious (ἔμφοβος). On the basis of the 'theological' context of these verses we are justified in taking νόμος to refer in all three verses to God's revealed law[162]. - In 21,11 the keeping of the law is equated with the perfection of the fear of the Lord. The context of this verse mentions the "assembly of the godless" (v.9) and the "way of the sinners" (v.10). Thus it is quite probable that νόμος refers to the revealed will of God rather than to sapiential instructions[163]. - The phrase νόμος ὑψίστου in 23,23 certainly refers to the Mosaic

---

159 Cf. also H. Stadelmann, *Ben Sira*, p.154 n.1 who does not list all references of חק, however.
160 Cf. R.J. Banks, *Jesus and the Law*, p.54.
161 Cf. M. Löhr, *Bildung*, pp.54-57; J. Marböck, "Der schriftgelehrte Weise", *BETL* 51 (1979) 302.
162 Cf. J. Haspecker, *Gottesfurcht*, pp.52 n.7,156; acknowledged for 18,20 by J. Marböck, *Weisheit*, p.89.
163 Cf. G. Sauer, *JSHRZ* III/5 (1981) 557.

law: the woman who leaves her husband and commits adultery breaks the (written) law. - In 24,23 the Mosaic law is envisaged as well: βίβλος διαθήκης ὑψίστου (v.23) is equated by synonymous parallelism with νόμον ὃν ἐνετείλατο ἡμῖν Μωυσῆς (v. 23b)[164]. - In 34,8 νόμος also refers to the revealed, written law of God[165]. - 32(35), 1 states that "he who keeps the law increases the sacrifices". Here νόμος clearly refers to the Mosaic (cultic) law. It is paralleled by ἐντολαί in v.2. - 39,8 are part of Ben Sira's description of the scribes and his activities (38,34c-39,11): the scribe studies and mediates (διανοοῦν) on God's law (νόμῳ ὑψίστου, 38,34d) and teaches his instruction (παιδεία διδασκαλίας, 39,8a), and glories in the "law of the covenant of the Lord" (ἐν νόμῳ διαθήκης κυρίου, 39,8b). Here again we have references to the Mosaic law [166].

From the 14 references to νόμος which are extant only in Greek, 12 or possibly 13 refer to the Mosaic law: prol. 1.8; 2,16; 17,11; 19,17.20.24; 21,11(?); 23,23; 24,23; 32(35),1; 38,34d; 39,8. In at least four passages νόμος is linked with the fear of the Lord: 2, 16; 19,20.24; 21,11 (cf. 19,11).

(7) *Entolē*. G uses ἐντολή 18 times which is 7 times the translation of מצוה. We will discuss only the 9 references which are extant only in the Greek MSS: 1,26; 23,27; 28,6.7; 29,1.9.11; 32 (35),2.7.

In 1,26 the keeping of the commandments (ἐντολαί) is presented as the basis for acquiring wisdom, and is related to the fear of the Lord (v.27). Similar passages make it quite plausible to see here a reference to the Torah[167]. - 23,27 is the end of the pericope on the adulterous woman (23,22-27) who had been accused in 23,23 of having been disobedient to the Mosaic law. In v.27 we have the 'moral' of the story: nothing is better than the fear of the Lord, and nothing is sweeter than the keeping of the commandments of the Lord (i.e. the Mosaic law). - In 28,6b Ben Sira summons his readers to keep God's ἐντολαί, reminding them that they have to die (and will face judgment). This is immediately followed by a second call to "remember" God's commandments (28,7a) as well as God's covenant. The last expression proves that in both cases Ben Sira refers to the Mosaic law. - In 29,1 the keeping of the commandments is linked with "practising mercy" and "lending to one's neighbour", suggesting again that an implicit reference to Israel's law is meant here. The same is true for 29,9 where the reader is challenged to support the poor "for the sake of the commandment" (cf. Deut 15,7-11), and for 29,11 where the reader is asked to spend his money "according to the commandments of the Most High". - In 32(35), 2.7 ἐντολαί (and νόμος in v.1) is related to the cultic (Mosaic, levitic) law of Israel (cf. Ex 23,15; 34,20; Deut 16,16; 26,1-4).

---

164 Cf. O. Kaiser, "Begründung der Sittlichkeit", *ZThK* 55 (1958) 56; E. Jacob, "Wisdom and Religion in Sirach", 1978, p.255.
165 Cf. J.G. Snaith, *Ecclesiasticus*, pp.165f.; G. Sauer, *o.c.*, p.588.
166 Cf. M. Löhr, *o.c.*, p.102; J. Marböck, *a.c.*, p.302.
167 Cf. J. Haspecker, *Gottesfurcht*, pp.315f. He points out that the pl. is "Eigenform von G" and that H probably had the sg. (cf. 6,36; 10,19; 15,15; 37,12 etc.). See also M. Löhr, *Bildung*, pp.31f.

Thus, all the 9 references to ἐντολή/ἐντολαί which are extant only in G refer to the Mosaic law. In two passages "commandment(s)" is/are linked with the fear of the Lord: 1,26; 23,27.

(8) *Krima*. The term κρίμα is used 19 times in Sir (4 times for חק and 6 times for משפט. It occurs only in 4 passages which are not extant in H.

> In 17,12b κρίματα clearly refers to the decrees of the Mosaic law since it is parallel to the "eternal covenant" which God made with Israel at Sinai (v.12a) and with the "law of life" which God gave to his people (v.11b)[168]. - In 18,14 κρίματα is parallel to παιδεία and refers to the orders of God. - In 19,25 and 21,5 κρίμα refers to a "judgment" of the wise or the poor.

Thus, 17,12 is the only passage, not extant in H, where κρίματα designates the Mosaic law.

(9) *Logos*. Ben Sira uses the term λόγος 73 times[169].

> 54 times it refers to sapiential concepts with regard to 'speech ethics'. In 5 passages it denotes the word of God in creation (39,31; 42,15; 43,5.10.26) or in prophets (48, 3.5; cf. 45,3), and in one passage it refers to a prophetic utterance (48,1). It does not refer to the Torah of Israel.

We are now able to summarize the terminological evidence with regard to Ben Sira's concept of law. Despite the fact that the law is never the subject of a particular pericope or hymn it must be admitted that the sheer number of unambiguous references to the law of Israel indicates how important and basic the revealed law as (written) *lex revelata* was for Ben Sira[170]. We established 53 or possibly 56 references to the Mosaic law. The evidence can be presented as follows:

---

168 Cf. M. Löhr, *Bildung*, p.55.
169 E. Hatch, H.A. Redpath do not list 36(33),3; 47,22.
170 E.G. Bauckmann, "Proverbien und die Sprüche des Jesus Sirach", *ZAW* 72 (1960) 48 says that Torah, for Ben Sira, refers to the "altergebrachten Ordnungen Gottes für Israel". M. Hengel, *Judentum*, p.253 agrees that, for Ben Sira, *torah* signifies "in der Regel die konkrete Tora Moses" and that the same is true for *miẓvah* (p.253 n.216). Similarly, E. Rivkin, "Ben Sira – The Bridge between Aaronide and Pharisaic Revolutions", *Eretz Israel* 12 (1975) 95 n.1 points out that Ben Sira witnesses to a society "operating on the basis of a literal reading of the Pentateuch". P.S. Fiddes, *Hiddenness*, p.315 says that in Sir 'Torah' is "compact", a fixed body of material. It is difficult to understand how R.A.F. MacKenzie, "Ben Sira as Historian", 1978, p.324 could write that "Ben Sira has a real distaste, or perhaps distrust, for a written law".

Ref.	H	G
Prol. 1	–	νόμος
8	–	νόμος
1,26	–	ἐντολαί
2,16	–	νόμος
6,36	מצות (עליון)	ἐντολαι (κυρίου)
10,19	מצוה	ἐντολαί
15,1	תורה	νόμος
15,15	מצוה	ἐντολαί
17,11	–	νόμος ζωῆς
17,12	–	κρίματα
19,17	–	νόμος ὑψίστου
19,20	–	νόμος
19,24	–	νόμος
21,11	–	νόμος
23,23	–	νόμος ὑψίστου
23,27	–	ἐντολαὶ κυρίου
24,23	–	νόμος
28,6	–	ἐντολαί
28,7	–	ἐντολαί
29,1	–	ἐντολαί
29,9	–	ἐντολή
29,11	–	ἐντολαὶ ὑψίστου
32,15	תורה	νόμος
32,16a?	משפט	κρίμα
32,16c?	משפט	–
32,17	תורה	σύγκριμα
32,18b	מצוה	φόβος ?
32,18d	תורה	–
32,22b	מצוה	ἐντολαί
32,22d	מצוה	–

(Continued on page 41)

(Continued from page 40)

Ref.	H	G
32,23	תורה	νόμος
33,2	תורה	νόμος
33,3a	דבר ייי	λόγος
33,3b	תורה	νόμος
34,8	-	νόμος
35,1	-	νόμος
35,2	-	ἐντολαί
35,7	-	ἐντολή
37,12?	מצוה	νόμος
38,34	-	νόμος ὑψίστου
39,8	-	νόμος κυρίου
41,8	תורת עליון	νόμος ὑψίστου
42,2a	תורת עליון	νόμος ὑψίστου
42,2a	חק	διαθήκη
42,2b	משפט	κρίματα
44,20	מצות עליון	νόμος ὑψίστου
45,5c	מצוה	ἐντολαί
45,5d	תורה	νόμος
45,5e	חקים	διαθήκη
45,5f	משפטים	κρίματα
45,17a	מצות	ἐντολαί
45,17b	חוק	διαθήκη
45,17b	משפט	κρίματα
45,17c	חק	μαρτύρια
45,17d	משפט	νόμος
49,4	תורה עליון	νόμος ὑψίστου

We have seen that Ben Sira never uses the different terms for law in a genitive construction with terms like father, mother, or wisdom teacher (unlike Prov. 34(31),8 is the only passage where a term for law (νόμος) is used parallel with wisdom meaning "instruction" rather than law[171].

In some passages 'legal' terms are used for the order of creation with was established by God: תורה in 41,4; דבר יהוה in 43,1.5. 10.26.29 (cf. 48,3), and especially חק is often used: 44,20; 45,7. 17.24; 47,11.

In at least 17 passages terms for law are closely linked or even identified with the fear of the Lord: תורה in 15,1; 32,15; 33,2.3; מצוה in 6,36; 10,19; 32,18; 37,12; תורה in 32,16a.c; νόμος in 2, 16; 19,11.20.24; 21,11; and ἐντολή in 1,26; 23,27.

In 11 passages terms for law are used in a genitive construction with "the Most High" or with "Lord": 19,17; 23,23.27; 29,11; 38,34; 39,8; 41,8; 42,2; 44,20; 49,4 (cf. also 6,36; 32,16).

In 8 passages terms for law are linked with God's covenant with his people: 17,11.12; 24,23; 28,7; 39,8; 42,2G; 44,20; 45,5. In other cases we have a clear reference to Israel's cultic law: 28,6.7; 29,1.9.11; 35,1.2.7.

In 24,23 and 45,5 the law and the commandments of God are linked with Moses and with the events at Sinai, and thus clearly refer to the Pentateuch (cf. also prol. 1.8).

In view of these facts it is interesting to note that in some 20 passages Ben Sira calls upon his readers to "keep the law" (1,26; 15,1.15; 19,20; 21,11; 23,27; 28,6.7; 29,1; 32,22.23; 35,1.2; 37,12; 44,20; cf. 2,16; 6,36), and not to "break" or "transgress" the law (10,19; 19,24; 49,4; cf. 41,8).

3.2. Law and Creation

It appears to be methodologically unwarranted to identify the 'law' with the divine order which includes the whole creation simply because in 17,11-12 'law' is dealt with in the great pericope on creation[172]. The identification of law and wisdom certainly had consequences (!) for the nature of the law as well as for the relationship between law and creation (cf. §4.2.1.). But a *petitio prin-*

---

171 Similarly E.G. Bauckmann, in ZAW 72 (1960) 48.
172 Contra J. Marböck, *Weisheit*, pp.87f. and idem, "Gesetz", *BZ* 20 (1976) 5f. See also P.S. Fiddes, *Hiddenness*, 1976, pp.317-321.

cipii has to be avoided. Therefore we will start by limiting our observations to those passages where legal terms are directly applied to the order of creation.

> In 41,1 תורה refers to the law of death which God imposed upon man. Ben Sira deals with the subject of death particularly in 17,1-2 and 41,1-4. Death is described as man's inescapable lot, a fixed order imposed by God upon creation. The 'fixed' order of death is a divine חק (11,17H; 14,12.17; 38,22; 41,2.3). - In his great hymn on God's creation in 42, 15-43-33[173] Ben Sira uses legal terms to describe the orders which God laid upon "his works". At the end of his observations on the sun (43,2-4) he quite naturally refers to God who created (עשה) it (43,5; cf. Gen 1, 14-16): "For great is the Lord who made it, and his words (דבריו) make his mighty (ones) brilliant". Although v.5b is not totally clear[174] it is obvious that the whole verse refers to the sun (vv.6-8 describe the moon). God created the sun and imposed upon it his order. The sun obeys the דברים ייי. - The moon (43,6-8) was created by God to regulate (חק) feasts and seasons (v.7; cf. Sir 33,7-9; Gen 1,14). The same applies to the order (חק) of the stars (vv.9-10) which was instituted by God's word (דבר אל) as well (v.10). - In 43,26 Ben Sira underlines the fact that "by his words" (בדבריו) God creates (פעל) what he wills.

Thus we see that Ben Sira does use the terms דבר יהוה, תורה, and especially חק as designating the order which God imposed upon creation: "Alles wird durch das Wort Gottes geschaffen, in seiner Unterschiedenheit geordnet und erhalten ... Zwischen dem schaffenden und dem erhaltenden Wort wird nicht differenziert. Demnach ist Gottes Ordnen und Erhalten sein Schaffen, und die Ordnung (חוק), die auf dem Wort beruht bzw. sein Ausdruck ist, ist das Leben"[175]. However, the number of passages where legal terms are directly linked with creation and its comprehensive orders is not as great as some seem to suggest. If in 24,23 the law is identified with the preceding wisdom and, as a result, is placed into the horizon of creation, then this does not prove that this 'law' is not the Sinaitic revelation but some universal, cosmic law which operates in creation and history (cf. § 4.2.1.)[176]. The con-

---

[173] Cf. M. Löhr, *Bildung*, pp.80-94.

[174] G reads instead of ינצח אבירין: κατέσπευσεν πορείαν = "he hastens its course" in reminiscence of Ps 19,6. J.G. Snaith, *Ecclesiasticus*, p.210 follows G. The plural אבירין is difficult. R. Smend, *Weisheit*, ad loc. emends to אבירו and reads "and his word assures victory to his mighty servant" (i.e. the sun). See also Box/ Oesterley, *APOT* 1 (1913) 474. G. Sauer, *JSHRZ* III/5 (1981) 611 translates "und seine Worte lassen aufstrahlen seine Helden".

[175] M. Löhr, *Bildung*, p.95 in his summary of Ben Sira's concept of creation. Cf. also M. Limbeck, *Von der Ohnmacht des Rechts: Untersuchungen zur Gesetzeskritik des Neuen Testaments*, 1972, pp.18-20.

[176] Contra J. Marböck, "Gesetz", *BZ* 20 (1976) 8. On the meaning of law in 24,23

sequences of the identification of wisdom and law, with regard to the law, will be discussed later (cf. 4.4.1).

3.3. Law and Salvation-History

The fact that in at least ten passages we find the phrase "law of Yahweh" or "law of the Most High" shows the close relation between the law and the God of Israel envisaged by Ben Sira.

In 17,11.12; 24,23; 39,8; 42,2G; 44,20; 45,5 terms for law are linked with the covenant (ברית /διαθήκη)[177]. 17,11.12 belong to the lengthy pericope on God's control of the world (16,24-17,14). After having dealt with God's creation of the universe (16,24-28) and of the earth and of man (16,29-17,10), he turns to the chosen people (17,11-14). Israel is not mentioned until v.17 but it is obvious that the "law of life" (v.11), the "eternal law" (v.12a), the "commandments" (v.12b), and the theophany (v.13) refer to the events at Sinai described in Ex 19-20[178]. The content of the law is summed up and formulated in accordance with the deuteronomistic *Hauptgebot:* to "beware of all unrighteousness" (v.14a), and to love one's neighbour (v.14b)[179]. This summing up of the commandments of the law proves again that the law, in 17,11.12, is not simply the concretization of the comprehensive divine order but very specifically the Mosaic law[180]. - In 24,23 the "book of the covenant of God the Most High" is identified with the "law" which Moses gave to Israel as an "inheritance". We will return to this passage later when we discuss Ben Sira's identification of law and wisdom. We want to point out at this stage that the law mentioned in 24,23 is the Mosaic law and has, as a result, a unique relation with the faith and history of Israel. - 39,8 belongs to Ben Sira's description of the scribe's activities. Being proudly conscious of the rich treasures of knowledge and insight entrusted to him, the scribe glories in the "law of the covenant of the Lord" which unfolds and opens up wisdom. The scribe studies the prophets and the sayings of wise men (39,1-2) but he glories most of all in the (Mosaic) law. - In the *laus patrum* the commandments of God are linked with God's covenant with Abraham (44,20) and with Moses and Israel at Sinai

---

see supra, p.38. Cf. also J.C.H. Lebram, "Jerusalem", 1979, p.111 who defends νόμος in chap. 24 as the Sinaitic law.
177 Cf. G.W.E. Nickelsburg, *Literature*, p.61 who refers to Ben Sira's "covenantal theology" as closely linked with the Torah.
178 Cf. J. Haspecker, *Gottesfurcht*, pp.152f.; J.G. Snaith, *Ecclesiasticus*, p.88; J. Marböck, *Weisheit*, p.87.
179 Cf. Mt 22,36-40.
180 Contra O. Rickenbacher, *Weisheitsperikopen*, pp.148f. O. Kaiser, "Begründung der Sittlichkeit", *ZThK* 55 (1958) 51-63 points out in the context of his discussion of Sir 17,11ff. that "obwohl Sirach unmittelbar vorher von der Schöpfung und der Erkennbarkeit Gottes in seiner Kreatur spricht, zieht er doch nicht die weitergehende Konsequenz, das Gesetz mit der Harmonie des Alls, dem ewigen Logos der Natur zu identifizieren, wie es dann später Philo getan hat" (p.56). Cf. Philo VitMos 2,52.

(45,5). - The term חֹק is used in several instances of God's orders for his people. It refers to circumcision (44,20), to the "eternal" levitical priesthood (45,7.17), to the hereditary rights of the priests granted to Phinehas (45,24), and to the Davidic covenant (47,11; cf. 45,25). - The law is also linked with the sacrifices (35,2-4).

Thus, the law is most intimately linked with Israel's faith and history. It is the very law of Israel's God, given through the mediation of Moses at Sinai, the basis and the content of God's covenant with his people.

3.4. Law and the Fear of the Lord

As we have noted already, Ben Sira parallels law and the fear of the Lord in numerous passages[181]. J. Haspecker pointed out that Ben Sira does not simply or directly identify obedience to the law with the fear of the Lord, not even in the "Grundsatzparänese" in 2,15-16[182]. In the routine parallelism of fear of the Lord/law, the sequence of these two phrases is not optional but dependent upon the focus of the particular passage. If the starting point of the context is a fundamental or 'inner' viewpoint we have the sequence: fear of the Lord - law (cf. 6,37; 15,1; 23,27; 37,12; 39, 1). In this case the second part of the parallelism, the law, appears to be a concretization. On the other hand, if we have the sequence: law - fear of the Lord, the thought progresses from the practical to the fundamental, from the outward to the inward, from the concrete to the more comprehensive realm (cf. 1,26-27; 9,15.16; 21,11; 32,14-16; 32,24-33,1)[183]. This implies that Ben Sira considers the fear of the Lord to be the basis of the obedience to the law.

The fear of the Lord is not 'swallowed up' by the keeping of the law. This fact, on the other hand, makes sure that the keeping of the law is not a routine performance or accomplishment but a result of one's personal commitment and confidence in God who makes the obedience to his law possible (cf. 15,13). In 1,26-27 we

---

[181] See generally the discussion in J. Haspecker, *Gottesfurcht*, pp.63,147,153f.,167f., 328-332.
[182] Cf. J. Haspecker, o.c., pp.287-289.
[183] Cf. J. Haspecker, o.c., p.329. On the structure of 32,14-16 and 32,14-33,1 see ibid., pp.222-227,263-268.

have, therefore, the sequence: obedience to the law - fear of the Lord - faithfulness and humility. The wisdom teaching of Ben Sira is in a fundamental way oriented by the sovereign will of God which dominates all areas of life. But Ben Sira is at the same time conscious of the fact that the wisdom which is found and 'inferred' from the law is not some autonomous advice but demands a correlating personal strong commitment to God. Therefore Ben Sira calls those who reject such 'discipline' by and in the law "offenders" (32,17). Those who fear the Lord and who study law and tradition in a comprehensive manner are conscious of the fact that they thereby encounter the living will of God.

Thus we conclude with J. Haspecker: "So spricht sich an markanten Stellen das Bewußtsein, in der Hingabe an das Gesetz die treue und demütige Auslieferung an den persönlichen Willen Gottes zu vollziehen, recht klar aus"[184].

3.5. The Function of the Law

3.5.1. Norm of moral and social behaviour. Many passages in Sirach indicate that, for Ben Sira, the Israelite law was the norm of moral behaviour[185]. In 19,17 which is the last verse in the section on how to handle malicious gossip (19,4-17)[186], and the last verse in the discussion of rebuke (19,14-17), we read: "Reprove your neighbour before you threaten him, and give place to the law of the Most High" (cf. Lev 19,17!). The law has the ability to convict a person of his guilt and the ability to show him how he should behave.

21,11 concludes the section on the control of sin (21,1-11)[187]: "He who keeps the law keeps his (natural) inclination[188] under

---

184 J. Haspecker, *Gottesfurcht*, p.332.
185 Cf. G.von Rad, *Wisdom*, p.244; J. Marböck, *Weisheit*, pp.86ff. who, however, refers only to 19,17; 23,23; 28,6.7; 29,9.11; 41,8.
186 Cf. J.G. Snaith, *Ecclesiasticus*, pp.97f.
187 Cf. J.G. Snaith, *Ecclesiasticus*, pp.105f.; as possibility in O. Rickenbacher, *Weisheitsperikopen*, p.105. Similarly J. Haspecker, *Gottesfurcht*, p.161 who sees a caesura after v.12. Box/Oesterley, *APOT 1 (1913)* 388; O. Rickenbacher, *o.c.*, pp.104f., and others see 21,11 as the beginning of the section on the contrast between the godly man who is wise and the godless man who is a fool (21,11-28).
188 In 21,11a S reads ܚܫܒܬܗ (as in 15,14 with H יצר; cf. 27,6H) which makes it

control, and accomplished wisdom is the fear of the Lord"[189]. As a result of the chiastic structure of the verse the keeping of the law is parallel to the fear of the Lord, and the control of the יצר is parallel to accomplished wisdom. The control of the 'natural', i.e. evil inclination or tendency can be achieved only by obeying the law which contains the norm for godly behaviour.

23,23 belongs to the section on adultery (23,16-27): the adulterous woman "disobeys the law of the Most High". The sin of adultery consists in breaking the divine law which was laid down in Ex 20,14 and Deut 5,18 and which has to be obeyed as it is God's norm.

28,6-7 concludes the section on forgiveness and divine punishment (27,30-28,7): "Remember the end that awaits you and cease from hate; remember corruption and death and abide by the commandments. Remember the commandments and do not be enraged at your neighbour; remember the covenant of the Most High and overlook ignorance"[190]. Loyalty to God's covenant with Israel is, for Ben Sira, identical with the keeping of the commandments (note the synonymous parallelism in v.7). And the law includes the stipulation not to hate one's "neighbour" or "brother" ($\pi\lambda\eta\sigma\iota\sigma\nu$/ אח/רע)[191] but to love him (cf. Lev 19,17-18)[192].

In 29,9.11 Ben Sira admonishes in the context of his discussion of lending and borrowing (29,1-13): "For the commandment's

---

rather likely that H had כבש יצר; cf. Box/Oesterley, o.c., p.388; R. Smend, *Weisheit*, p.192 (reading כובש יצרו, referring to mAb 4,1); O. Rickenbacher, o.c., p.105. G. Maier, *Mensch und freier Wille*, 1971, pp.92f. states that the $\dot{\epsilon}\nu\nu\dot{o}\eta\mu\alpha$ in 21,11 could well be the translation of an original יצר which then cannot be interpreted here (in contrast to 15,14; 27,6) as a 'neutral' inclination, for it implied "eine Aufspaltung von grundlegendem Wollen und Trieb in der Richtung der späteren rabbinischen Lehre". In a similar way also J. Haspecker, o.c., p.145 n.46. With regard to the Talmudic concept of the יצר הרע see bQid 30b: "I created the evil desire, but I also created the Torah, as its antedote: if you occupy yourselves with the Torah, you will not be delivered into his hand".

189 In 21,11b we follow the translation of R. Smend, M.S. Segal, O. Rickenbacher. NEB translates "wisdom is the outcome of the fear of the Lord".

190 Probably referring to sins which were committed unconsciously. Cf. Box/Oesterley, *APOT* 1 (1913) 408.

191 These terms refer in the context of the OT to the companions of the covenant who have a share in the election and in the covenant with their duties and rights. Cf. J. Fichtner, in *ThWNT* 6 (1959) 310-313.

192 On the passages see H. Stadelmann, *Ben Sira*, pp.128-132.

sake help the poor ... invest[193] your treasure according to the commandments of the Most High". Here again the law is taken to be the norm of all moral and social life (cf. Deut 15,7-11).

The references to the law in 32,17.18.22.23 belong to a pericope which deals with the wise man (in contrast to the fool) whose life is determined by the law and characterized by the fear of the Lord (32,14-33,6). Two basic statements, each consisting of four distichs, on the fear of the Lord and the zeal for the law (32, 14-17 and 32,24-33,3) are followed, respectively, by a general sapiential parenesis (32,18-23 and 33,4-6)[194]. 32,17 forms the end of the first basic statement: "The man of violence[195] will reject reproof, and he forces the law to suit his necessity[196]". Ben Sira contrasts the man who seeks God (v.14) and fears the Lord (v.16) and, as a result, knows God's will (משפט, v.16), with the godless man who does not accept criticism or reproof, not even from the law! He is not willing to adjust his life to the norms of the law but, instead, adjusts the law to his own desires. In 32,18 a general parenesis starts with the words, "A wise man will not conceal wisdom[197], but a scoffer will not keep the commandments[198]; a wise man will not accept a bribe, but the presumtuous and the scoffer will not keep the law". The godless do not keep the law but accept bribes - a familiar theme in the OT[199]. The parenesis ends with the admonition: "In all your ways guard yourself, for he who does so keeps the commandment (מצוה). He who keeps

---

193 Cf. Liddell/Scott, *Lexicon*, s.v. τίθημι A.II.7 "deposit, as in a bank". See also the translations of J. Marböck, *Weisheit*, p.86 and G. Sauer, *JSHRZ* III/5 (1981) 5,575.
194 Following H. Stadelmann, *Ben Sira*, pp.262f.; similarly Box/Oesterley, *APOT* 1 (1913) 426-429.
195 Following H^{Bm} (איש חמס) and similarly G (ἄνθρωπος ἁμαρωλός) rather than H^B (איש חכם). Cf. Box/Oesterley, *o.c.*, p.427; J.G. Snaith, *Ecclesiasticus*, p.157; G. Sauer, *JSHRZ* III/5 (1981) 584.
196 The translation follows Box/Oesterley. G reads καὶ κατὰ τὸ θέλημα αὐτοῦ εὑρήσει (248 ἐξευρισκει) σύγκριμα; S reads "and according to his will (= G) makes his way". G. Sauer, ibid., translates "und entsprechend seinem Plan zieht er die Weisung hin". The root צרך certainly means "need, necessity, want, requirement".
197 Reading חכמה with H^{Bm}. Cf. G. Sauer, *o.c.*, p.584.
198 Reading יקח מצוה with H^{Bm} and H^E (instead of H^B ישמר לשון). Cf. H. Middendorp, *Stellung*, p.163.
199 Cf. Ex 23,8; Deut 16,19; 27,25; Ps 15,5; Prov 6,35; 17,23; Is 1,23; Ez 22,12. Of special importance here is Deut 16,19: "Do not accept a bribe, for a bribe blinds the eyes of the wise (!) and twists the words of the righteous".

the law (תורה) guards himself; and he who trusts in the Lord shall not be brought to shame" (32,22-23). The law and the commandments are to be observed as the norm of one's actions (מעשיך) and of one's behaviour and life-style (דרכיך).

The ethical normativeness of the law is also evident in 35,1-7 where proper ethical behaviour is portrayed as spiritual sacrifice[200]. Ben Sira states that one should practise "works of love" (ἀνταποδιδοὺς χάριν, v.2)[201], carry out "charity" (ποιῶν ἐλεημοσύνην, v.2)[202], and avoid wickedness and injustice (v.3), "for all this (shall be done) on grounds of the commandments" (χάριν ἐντολῆς, v.4).

In the section on good and bad counsellors (37,7-15) Ben Sira first lists unreliable counsellors (v.11) before he goes on to commend consultation with a man who always fears the Lord and who, as he knows, keeps the commandments (v.12), i.e. whose advice will be in accordance with the law.

In his description of the fate and the curses of the sinner (41,5-13) Ben Sira accuses them primarily of having "forsaken (מעוזבים) the law (תורה) of the Most High" (v.8). Similarly Ben Sira points out that except David, Hezekiah, and Josiah all the kings of Judah abandoned (עזב) the law of God.

These passages clearly show that Ben Sira regarded the Mosaic law as norm of one's behaviour with regard to all the 'ways' of life. To keep the law and the commandments is to comply with God's will.

---

200 On this passage see H. Stadelmann, *Ben Sira*, pp.93-99.
201 This term presupposes the Hebrew phrase גמילות חסדים. Cf. Box/Oesterley, *APOT* 1 (1913) 437; H. Stadelmann, *o.c.*, p.96 (who refers to 7,33 and 40,17 where חסד is translated in G by χάρις). In later Rabbinic theology the "works of grace" (גמילות חסדים) included visits to the sick, the putting up of strangers, the equipping of poor brides and bridegrooms, the attendance of weddings and funerals, the comforting of mourners, etc. Cf. Strack/Billerbeck, *Kommentar*, 4, pp.559-510; E. Stauffer, Art. "ἀγαπάω", *ThWNT* 1 (1933) 42-44; G. Bertram, Art. "ἔργον", *ThWNT* 2 (1935) 644.
202 Charity (Hebr. צדקה) was also part of the "good works" (מעשים טובים). Cf. Strack/Billerbeck, *o.c.*, pp.536-558; R. Bultmann, Art. "ἐλεημοσύνη", *ThWNT* 2 (1935) 482. Charity differs from the "works of love" in that the former is done with money whereas the latter can be performed both with money and with personal activity. Charity was directed only towards the poor and the living whereas the "works of love" could benefit the rich and the dead as well. Cf. Strack/Billerbeck, *o.c.*, p.536 with reference to tPea 4,19.

3.5.2. Source of wisdom. Numerous passages indicate that for Ben Sira the study and the keeping of the law led to wisdom[203]. Compared with the general function of the law in the OT this is a new aspect.

<small>The following passages are relevant here. 1,26: "If you desire wisdom, keep the commandments, and the Lord will give it to you in abundance". 6,36: "Ponder the fear of the Most High and think upon his commandments continually; then he will give insight to your heart and in everything which you desire he will make you wise"[204]. 15,1b: "He who observes the law will acquire her (i.e. wisdom)". 15,15: "If you desire, you can keep the commandment, and it is insight (wisdom) to do his pleasure". 19,20: "All wisdom (consists in) the fear of the Lord, and all wisdom includes the fulfilling of the law"[205]. 33,2-3: "He is not wise who hates the law, and he is tossed about like a ship in a storm[206]. A man of insight knows the word of the Lord, and for him the law is as reliable as the consultation of the lots[207]".</small>

The sapiential importance of the Torah is mentioned *expressis verbis* in the two references to the Sinaitic revelation of the law of Yahweh. God gave Israel via Moses "knowledge and the law of life" (ἐπιστήμην καὶ νόμον ζωῆς, 17,11) which is the "law of life and insight" (תורת חיים ותבונה/νόμον ζωῆς καὶ ἐπιστήμης, 45, 5). Thus, Ben Sira clearly states that obedience to God's law and commandments leads to wisdom and is in itself the hallmark of true wisdom.

3.5.3. Measure of piety. Since the law contains the revealed will of God, obedience ot the law indicates one's piety. For this reason Ben Sira linked the love for God and especially the fear of the Lord very closely with the keeping of the law. Those who fear the Lord and love him will steep themselves in the law (2,16). He

---

<small>203 See already J. Haspecker, *Gottesfurcht*, pp.330f.
204 On this passage see J. Haspecker, *o.c.*, pp.130f.
205 On 19,20.24 see J. Haspecker, *o.c.*, pp.155-158.
206 33,2b completed with H^{Bm} and H^E (cf. G). See G. Sauer, *JSHRZ* III/5 (1981) 585.
207 33,3a completed with G ὁ νόμος αὐτῷ πιστὸς ὡς ἐρώτημα δήλων. On this phrase see M. Löhr, *Bildung*, p.112 and H. Stadelmann, *Ben Sira*, pp.262-265 who points out that, at Ben Sira's time, the knowledge of the Torah had taken the place of the old oracle (urim and thummim): "Gerade so zuverlässig, wie einst das unzweideutige Losorakel dem Priester Auskunft über Gottes Willen gab, erschließt sich nun dem verständigen Schriftforscher die Torah. Und wie einst eine gewisse Analogie zwischen priesterlichem Weissagen auf Grund des Loses und dem Offenbarungswort der Propheten bestand, so sind auch nun Lehrerkenntnis produzierende Schriftforschung und Prophetie zwar nicht identische, aber vergleichbare Größen" (p.264).</small>

is worthy of honour who fears the Lord and keeps the commandments (10,19; cf. 19,24). Nothing is preferable or better than to fear the Lord and to keep his commandments (23,27). Obedience to the law indicates whether a person really loves the Lord and fears him.

3.5.4. Rule for cult and jurisdiction. Ben Sira did not retain the cultus *qua lege* justifying all cultic activities nomistically[208]. For him, cultic activity is not the product of nomism but essentially the manifestation of the attitude of one's heart which is characterized by a living piety and by a just social conduct. However, the law is important nevertheless: not as substantiation or motivation in the sense of nomism but as regulation of cultic activity. Being priest and scribe it was natural for Ben Sira to accept the Torah as authority also for this important area of Jewish life.

> Thus Ben Sira says in 7,31: "Glorify God and honour the priest and give (δός) them their portion (חלק) as you have been commanded (צוה): food of the trespass-offering (לחם אברים/ἀπαρχήν) and heave-offering (תרומתיו/πλημμελείας), sacrifices of righteousness (זבחי [צדק]) and holy offerings (תרומת קדש/ἀπαρχὴν ἁγίων)"[209]. The reference to the law implies the regulating normativeness of the law in all matters relating to the cult[210]. The list of offerings and contributions in v.31c.d is rather selective[211] which proves that it is not meant as a legal, casuistic directive but indicates *pars pro toto* the specific regulative function of the Torah. For the priestly portion with regard to the trespass-offering one can compare Num 18,9, for the heave-offering Num 18,11, for the sacrifices Deut 18,3, and for the holy offerings Num 18,19[212].

In 35,6-7 Ben Sira concludes his description of proper ethical conduct as "spiritual sacrifices" with the words, " 'Do not appear with empty hands in the presence of the Lord!' For all this (shall be done) on grounds of the commandment". Although the quote in v.6 (cf. Ex 23,15; 34,20; Deut 16,16; 26,1-4) is not meant to be applied literally but is re-interpreted in a spiritualizing way ("he who exhibits the ethical attitudes and conduct mentioned in vv.

---

208 Contra this widely held opinion see the recent convincing discussion of H. Stadelmann, *Ben Sira*, 1980, pp.67,87ff.
209 On the textual evidence see H. Stadelmann, *Ben Sira*, p.56.
210 Cf. J. Haspecker, *Gottesfurcht*, p.304; O. Rickenbacher, *Weisheitsperikopen*, p.145; H. Stadelmann, *o.c.*, p.68.
211 The list in 45,20c-21b is even more selective.
212 Cf. H. Stadelmann, *o.c.*, p.60. On the priestly portions see generally Lev 5,14-26; Num 18,8-19; Deut 12,6-7.

3-5 fulfills the command not to appear empty before God"), it is nevertheless clear that v.6 is not only a skillfully used support for his (spiritualized) interpretation but is beyond that "eine durchaus praktisch gemeinte Aufforderung"[213]. For Ben Sira the cult is indeed regulated by the law.

The Mosaic law is further the authoritative and regulative basis of jurisdiction. This is explicitly mentioned in 42,4 where Ben Sira stresses that one should not be ashamed of the "law of the Most High" and his "statute" (חוק) nor of the "administration of justice" (מצדיק)[214] which passes sentence upon the wicked. In 45,17 Aaron (and with him the priests in general) is described as having received the commandments (מצות) and the authority (ימשילהו) over statute (חוק) and judgment (משפט). The priests have been given the judicial task of applying the Torah to current legal problems[215]. It was exactly this application of the Torah to current legal problems which gave rise to halakhah. We will investigate later whether traces of halakhah can be found in Sirach (§ 3.7.).

3.5.5. Foundation for teaching. Finally, the law is considered to be the basis and the content of teaching. In 38,34c-39,11 Ben Sira describes the ideal of the *sopher/hakham*, the wise scribe[216]. This pericope consists of four stanzas with four distichs each[217]. The first two stanzas (38,34c-39,3 and 39, 4-5) describe the normal professional life of the *sopher* at the time of Ben Sira. The third

---

213 H. Stadelmann, *o.c.*, p.99.
214 The form מצדיק is part.hiph. of צדק which means in hiph. "to give someone justice, to acknowledge that someone is right or innocent, to help someone gain his rights". Cf. Ex 23,7; Deut 25,1; 2Sam 15,4; 1Kgs 8,32; Ps 82,3; Prov 17,15; Is 5,23.
215 Cf. T. Middendorp, *Stellung*, p.163; H. Stadelmann, *Ben Sira*, p.279.
216 Cf. R.H. Pfeiffer, *History of New Testament Times*, pp.368-370; R. Meyer, in *ThWNT* 9 (1973) 23; M. Hengel, *Judentum*, pp.146,238; E. Schürer, *The History of the Jewish People in the Age of Christ*, 2, 1979, pp.323f.; J. Marböck, "Sir. 38,24-39,11: Der schriftgelehrte Weise: Ein Beitrag zu Gestalt und Werk Ben Siras", *BETL* 51 (1979) 293-316; especially H. Stadelmann, *o.c.*, pp.177-309 (here pp.217-246,284-293); D.J. Harrington, "The Wisdom of the Scribe According to Ben Sira", *Ideal Figures in Ancient Judaism*, ed. J.J. Collins et al., SBLSCS 12, 1980, pp.181-188 passim. See also infra, pp.65f.
217 Cf. O. Rickenbacher, *Weisheitsperikopen*, pp.177-179, followed by J. Marböck, *a.c.*, pp.295f. and H. Stadelmann, *o.c.*, p.221. As regards the analysis of 39,1-11 we follow H. Stadelmann, *o.c.*, pp.221-246.

stanza (39,6-8) deals with the special case of a *sopher* inspired by the free will of God. The last stanza (39,9-11) records the praise given to the scribe by other people.

In 38,34c.d Ben Sira resumes the subject of the wise scribe who had already been mentioned in 38,24 and emphasizes that the study of the law and practical devotion to the fear of the Lord, in their synthesis, are the main characteristics of the *sopher/ hakham*. This twofold introductory statement on the fear of the Lord and the zeal for the law is then unfolded in a chiastic manner in 39,1-5. Ben Sira first describes the investigating and exploring activities of the scribe (vv.1-4), and ends with the prayer life of the scribe, corresponding to the fear of the Lord (v.5). The scribe investigates the biblical books, the law and the prophets (v.1)[218]. He also explores the general wisdom traditions (vv.2-3). Here he concentrates on the traditional wisdom motives of the parable (παραβολαί), riddles (ἀπόκρυφα παροιμίαι), and the discourses of wise men (διηγήσει ἀνδρῶν ὀνομαστῶν) who want to pass on experiences and perceptions. Finally, the travel of the scribe is mentioned as the third source for the gathering of insights and experiences (v.4a)[219]. The exploring and investigating activity of the scribe is essentially receptive and reproductive. After the description of the external scope of the exploration activities of the scribe, Ben Sira returns to the subject of the piety of the scribe, joining v.5 chiastically to 38,34c. The wise scribe seeks his Creator with all his heart, he opens his mouth in prayer, and he makes supplication for his sins. In the words of Stadelmann, "der jüdische Schriftgelehrte ist kein autonomer Intellektueller und auch kein theoretischer Ethiker . . . Bei allem Wissen aber bleibt ein Mann der praktischen Gottesfurcht, die ihren persönlichsten Ausdruck im Gebet findet"[220]. - The third stanza 39,6-8 describes the special case of the inspired scribe. Every human being has been created with "insight of understanding" (ἐπιστήμη συνέσεως, 17,7a), i.e. with the critical ability of discerning between good and evil (17,7b). But it is only "if God the Most High so wills" (ἐὰν κύριος ὁ μέγας θελήσῃ, 39,6a) that some scribes are "filled with the spirit of understanding" (πνεύματι συνέσεως ἐπλησθήσεται, 39,6b). This πνεῦμα συνέσεως is not simply a professional characteristic feature of the scribe but only a "gelegentliches *donum superadditum*"[221]. The activity of the inspired scribe which is portrayed in 39,6c-8 resembles that of the scribe described in 39,1-5. However, whereas the 'normal' scribe was engaged in the reproducing investigation of Torah and tradition, in political service and in personal piety, the inspired scribe is involved, on top of that, (1) in the production of wisdom material, i.e. wise sayings (ῥήματα σοφίας), differ-

---

218 On the question whether 39,1-3 contains a reference to the threefold division of the OT canon see J. Marböck, *o.c.*, p.85; J.G. Snaith, *o.c.*, p.191; H. Stadelmann, *o.c.*, p.223f.
219 Cf. V. Tcherikover, *Hellenistic Civilization and the Jews*, ²1961, p.143; M. Hengel, *Judentum*, pp.243f.; J. Marböck, *Weisheit*, pp.161ff.; H. Stadelmann, *Ben Sira*, pp.229f. The priestly *sopher* who knew the Torah, the law of the Jewish hierocracy, was naturally used for such missions as he had also public tasks to fulfill (cf. Sir 38,33; 45,17).
220 H. Stadelmann, *o.c.*, pp.213f. Cf. J. Marböck, "Der schriftgelehrte Weise", *BETL* 51 (1979) 303-306,314f.
221 G. Maier, *Mensch*, p.37, followed by H. Stadelmann, *Ben Sira*, p.234. On wisdom as special and direct gift of God see ibid., pp.235-238.

ent prayers and liturgical hymns (προσευχαί)[222], v.6c.d, (2) in 'speculative' thinking, i.e. in counsel (βουλή), in knowledge (ἐπιστήμη), and in the secrets of God (ἀπόκρυφα), v.7, and (3) in the pedagogical communication of his wisdom (παιδεία διδασκαλίας): he "makes known[223] the knowledge of his teaching and glories in the law of the covenant of the Lord"[224]. - The last stanza 39,9-11 finally describes the praise which is attributed to the wise scribe by many (πολλοί, v.9a), "from generation to generation" (εἰς γενεὰς γενεῶν, v.9d), by the "congregation" (H עדה, v. 10a), and by the "assembly" (ἐκκλησία, v.10b).

Two passages in the *laus patrum* are also relevant here. At the end of the short pericope on Moses (45,1-5), Ben Sira describes Moses as Israel's teacher of the law: "And he (i.e. the Lord) placed in his (i.e. Moses') hand the commandment (מצוה), the law of life and discernment (תורת חיים ותבונה), that he might teach (למד) Jacob his statutes (חקיו) and Israel his testimonies (עדותו) and decrees (משפטיו)" (45,5c-f)[225].

The pericope on Aaron (45,6-22) begins with the statement that "he (i.e. the Lord) exalted a holy one like him[226], that is Aaron of the tribe of Levi" (v.6). The immediate context of 45,5c-f and v. 6a suggests that Ben Sira intended to place Aaron side by side with Moses not only generally with regard to his importance but rather specifically with regard to his function.

> In the words of H. Stadelmann, "gerade als Empfänger des Gesetzes, in dessen Hand die judiziale Aufgabe der Anwendung der Torah auf aktuelle Rechtsprobleme (das Treffen von Rechtsentscheiden) und die didaktische Aufgabe der Gesetzeslehre vereinigt sind, ist Aaron 'gleich ihm'"[227].

The terminology in 45,17 describing Aaron as recipient and teacher of the law is nearly identical with 45,5: "He gave him (i.e.

---

222 On the production of hymns in Sirach see L. Perdue, *Wisdom and Cult*, 1977, pp.204ff., followed by H. Stadelmann, *o.c.*, pp.242-244.
223 Following O. Rickenbacher, *Weisheitsperikopen*, p.185 who prefers S ܢܚܘܐ to G ἐκφαίνειν. Cf. M. Löhr, *Bildung*, p.107; H. Stadelmann, *o.c.*, p.244.
224 Contra O. Rickenbacher, *o.c.*, p.185 who dismisses G with the comment that "Ben Sira von allem Möglichen spricht, nur eben nicht vom Bundesgesetz". This is simply a *petitio principii*. We have seen that Ben Sira often has terms for law parallel to references to the covenant. S has "law of life".
225 The translation follows H. G mentions only the διαθήκη and the κρίματα which should be taught. Cf. H. Stadelmann, *Ben Sira*, p.278; G. Sauer, *JSHRZ* III/5 (1981) 617.
226 Only G (ὅμοιον αὐτῷ) and S have the phrase "like him". It is easy to understand how this phrase which elevates Aaron to the level of Moses could be eliminated from H. Cf. H. Stadelmann, *o.c.*, p.278 n.3.
227 H. Stadelmann, *o.c.*, p.279.

Aaron) his commandments (מצותיו), and invested him with authority over statute (חוק) and decree (משפט), that he might teach (למד) his people statute (חק) and decree (משפט) to the sons of Israel" (v.17).

The law with all its statutes, decrees, and commandments was the basis and the content of the teaching which was one of the tasks of the priests and especially of the priestly scribes/sages like Ben Sira.

3.6. Motives of Obedience

Ben Sira never refers to the motives for obedience to the law explicitly[228]. As the law per se is never the subject of a pericope he never discusses the obedience to God's revealed will. The basis of his obedience, as Ben Sira sees it, can nevertheless be derived from several passages.

3.6.1. Acquiring wisdom. In several passages obedience to the law is not only identified with "being wise" but is motivated by the acquisition of wisdom which results from the keeping of the law[229]. Ben Sira calls upon those who desire wisdom to "keep the commandments" as God will give wisdom "in abundance" to them who keep his law (1,26). If a man continuously studies the law God will give him insight (6,36). He who abides by the law will receive wisdom (15,1). Sinners will not acquire wisdom (15,7). Complete wisdom can be achieved only by obedience to the law of God (19,20). Those who love, know, and keep the law will be wise and entirely reliable and steady, unlike ships in a storm (33,2-3). Ben Sira challenges his readers, indirectly, that they should keep the law as obedience to the law is the way to (complete) wisdom.

3.6.2. The will of God. Sometimes Ben Sira summons his readers to keep the commandments simply because God himself has

---

[228] For a discussion of the motives of obedience in Judaism see A. Nissen, *Gott und der Nächste im Antiken Judentum*, WUNT 15, 1974, pp.167-219.

[229] Cf. H. Stadelmann, *Ben Sira*, pp.299f.

commanded them. The law is the revealed will of God, and godly people should heed the will of God. It is wise and a sign of insight if a man keeps the law because it is God's "pleasure" (רצון). This motivation for obedience becomes evident in 15,15 and 19,19.

3.6.3. Avoiding sin. A few passages stress the importance of keeping the law since it helps to avoid sin: "He who keeps the law keeps his (natural) inclination[230] under control" (21,11; cf. 41, 8). Obedience to the law enables man to combat effectively his natural, evil desires.

3.6.4. Fear. One should further keep the law because a pious person "fears the Lord", which implies the respect for God's will (23,27; 37,12). Thus, the fear of the Lord which includes attention to God's will being embodied in the revealed law is another motive for the keeping of the commandments.

3.6.5. Love. Closely linked with the motivation by fear is the motivation by love[231]. As in the OT[232], the motive of love for God is seen as the basis of obedience in 2,15.16; 7,30. He who loves God keeps his commandments.

3.6.6. Eternal life. If 19,19 was original[233] we would have a clear reference to immortality in Sirach[234]: "The knowledge of the commandments of the Lord is an instruction to life; and they who do the things that are pleasing to him shall reap at the tree of immortality". A similar correlation of obedience to the law and the attainment of "life" (אתה תחוה) is to be found in 15,15b(H).

---

230 See supra p.46f. with n.188.
231 With regard to the correlation of 'love' and 'fear of the Lord' see J. Haspecker, *Gottesfurcht*, pp.280ff. Compare 1,10 with 1,11-20; 2,15a.16a with 2,15b.16b; 7,29.31 with 7,30. For further references in the intertestamental literature see A. Nissen, *Gott und der Nächste*, p.202 n.492.
232 Cf. Deut 5,10; 6,5; 7,9; 10,12; Neh 1,5; Is 56,6; Dan 9,41; etc.
233 19,18.19. is contained in only a few Greek MSS. Most translators print these verses only in the footnotes; cf. Box/Oesterley, *APOT* 1 (1913) 383; J.G. Snaith, *Ecclesiasticus*, p.98.
234 This would contradict the view of J.G. Snaith, *Ecclesiasticus*, pp.56, 148,186,203 who thinks that Ben Sira did not believe in life after death. Cf. also Box/Oesterley, *APOT* 1 (1913) 388.

We might have an analogous situation in 21,10.11 where Ben Sira describes the "way of the sinner" which is smoothly paved but which eventually leads to the "pits of Hades" (βόθρος ᾅδου), whereas the man who keeps the laws controls his evil desires (and thus does not walk on the "way of the sinner" and thus does not end up in Hades?!).

3.7. Halakhah in Sirach

The existence of halakhah, i.e. 'oral' law standing alongside the written law in Sirach has been both emphatically denied[235] and affirmed[236]. Only a short article in Hebrew has been devoted to this question[237]. Other information has to be gleaned from studies on the development of the early halakhah[238]. The conclusion of L.I. Rabinnowitz may serve as a starting point: in general the legal pattern is that of the written law, but indirect signs of the oral law as it was practiced in Ben Sira's time can be detected[239]. Without attempting to establish a final and complete list of all possible references to traces of the contemporary oral law of Ben Sira's time, we will nevertheless try to indicate the material and systematic evidence with regard to the halakhah in Sirach[240].

4,7 refers to the "assembly" (עֵדָה/συναγωγή) and to the "ruler of the city" (שַׁלִּיט עִיר

---

[235] E. Rivkin, "Ben Sira — The Bridge Between the Aaronide and Pharisaic Revolutions", *Eretz Israel* 12 (1975) 101. He makes the further, rather astonishing, statement that "not once in his entire book does Ben Sira even quote a Biblical verse, much less explicate its meaning" (ibid.). That this evaluation is completely wrong will be shown in § 3.8.

[236] Cf. P. Sigal, *Emergence*, I/1, 1980, p.229: "Examples of Ben Sira's halakhah abound". Unfortunately, Sigal does not list a single reference.

[237] L.I. Rabinowitz, "The Halakhah as Reflected in Ben Sira" (hebr.), *Papers of the 4th World Congress of Jewish Studies*, 1967, 1, pp.145-148.

[238] Cf. Z.W. Falk, *Introduction to Jewish Law of the Second Commonwealth*, AGSU 11, 2 vols., 1972/1978; B.S. Jackson, *Essays in Jewish and Comparative Legal History*, SJLA 10, 1975.

[239] L.I. Rabinowitz, "Halakhah", p.145 bases his discussion of the halakhah in Sirach on 9,8-9 which he interprets in the light of the later Rabbinic evidence and terminology. Then he focuses mainly on 9,9-12 ; 7,30-33 citing Mishnaic and Talmudic parallels.

[240] We rely mainly on the study of Z.W. Falk, *Introduction*, 2 vols., who presents the relevant Mishnaic evidence as well.

עִיר ²⁴¹/μεγιστᾶν) with regard to which one should make oneself beloved. This is a reference to the local government in which the townspeople decided on administrative questions and performed executive functions²⁴². - 4,29 and 7,6-7 refer to the town court in which the local authorities dealt with civil and even criminal cases²⁴³. In 4,29 the judge is admonished that he should verify with whom he is to sit (cf. bSanh 23a). As the judges seem to have been elected by the "assembly" of the townspeople, 7,6 warns that one should not submit one's own candidature unless one is qualified²⁴⁴. A judge who perverted justice was liable to be tried before the town court himself (7,6b.7; cf. 1,30). - In 7,19.26 Ben Sira seems to warn his readers against arbitrary divorce²⁴⁵. - Some have interpreted 8,8-9 as referring explicitly to the oral law as part of the authoritative Jewish tradition²⁴⁶. It seems, however, that this verse should be understood in the context of a sapiential chain of tradition rather than in the context of a (later) legal and 'doctrinal' (or exegetical) chain of tradition²⁴⁷. - 11,7 might refer to the examination of witnesses before a court warning the (potential) judges not to jump to conclusions and not to rebuke a person or a party until the examination of witnesses is over²⁴⁸. - Although the OT provided only for a bailee's oath (Ex 22,6-14; Lev 5,1.21), it seems to have been allowed for any plaintiff who brought no evidence to demand that the defendant take an oath in denial of the claim. An oath had indeed become an informal adjuration of the accused by the accuser and could even be administered out of court (cf. mShebu 5,1). Since false oaths increased there was also a marked tendency to refrain from administering oaths. Thus Sir 23,9-11 objects to the habit of taking oaths²⁴⁹. - 23,22-25 points out that an adulteress offends against the law of God, against her husband, and against the child born by adultery. She will be judged before the local "assembly" (cf. 42,11) where her child is declared a bastard²⁵⁰. - Discussing the financial

---

241 Correcting H^A (שלטון עוד) with S. 10,2 has ראש עיר. Cf. G. Sauer, in *JSHRZ* III/5 (1981) 514.
242 Cf. T. Middendorp, *Stellung*, pp.148,160f.; Z.W. Falk, *o.c.*, p.83.
243 Cf. G. Alon, *Jews, Judaism, and the Classical World*, 1977, pp.388f.; Z.W. Falk, *o.c.*, p.90.
244 Reading "judge" in 7,6a following G (κριτής, also S and L) instead of H^A (מושל). Cf. Box/Oesterley, *APOT* 1 (1913) 338; T. Middendorp, *o.c.*, p.150; J.G. Snaith, *Ecclesiasticus*, pp.41f.
245 Cf. Z.W. Falk, *o.c.*, p.308 who discusses the evidence with regard to divorce in the schools of Hillel and Shammai.
246 Cf. L.I. Rabinowitz, *a.c.*, p.145; T. Middendorp, *o.c.*, p.11 n.1.
247 Cf. H. Stadelmann, *Ben Sira*, pp.304-307 who, with regard to 39,1, acknowledges the fact that the "tradition (שמיעה) of the elders" (8,9a) might contain material from the OT, that 6,35-36 refers to a close affiliation with a personal master or mentor, and that 51,23 explicitly mentions a "house of instruction" (בית מדרש). However, if one compares 8,8-9 with 9,14-15 and takes into consideration the (purely sapiential) context of 51,13-21, it becomes less probable that 8,8-9 refers to the oral law. With regard to the בית מדרש in 51,23 see P.W. Skehan, "The Acrostic Poem in Sirach 51,13-20", *HThR* 64 (1971) 397 who reads בית מוסר following G (παιδείας) and S (yulpānā).
248 Cf. Z.W. Falk, *Introduction*, p.125 referring to mAb 1,9 and other texts.
249 Cf. Z.W. Falk, *o.c.*, pp.129f.; B.S. Jackson, *Essays*, p.248. See also TAsh 2,6 ;TGad 6,4; Philo SpecLeg 2,2-5; Decal 84-86.
250 Cf. G. Alon, *Jews*, pp.388f.; Z.W. Falk, *o.c.*, pp.83,293f. discussing the Mishnaic evidence referring to mSanh 11,1; mKer 1,1; mYeb 4,13.

obligations between husband and wife, Z.W. Falk sees in 25,21-22 a reference to the custom that the bridal gift remains under the control of the wife and that the husband might possibly not have been supposed to enjoy the produce of her property[251]. - 25,25-26; 28,15 can be interpreted as referring to a husband divorcing his wife for a just cause[252]. - 26,29; 27,1-2; 42,4 reflect the common custom of the Second Temple period according to which the townspeople agreed on prices, measures, and wages of labourers (cf. tBM 11,23) in order to avoid profiteering[253]. - Some see a reference to the oral law in the "wisdom spoken by the faithful" in 34, 8[254]. - 34,30 is an explicit reference to corpse-cleanness which is, for Ben Sira, a source of "routine homiletic dicta on the moral life"[255]. - 36,25a(H) has been interpreted by B.S. Jackson in the context of the problem of 'breaking the fence' as *actio de pastu pecoris*[256]. - 37,11h-i is to be understood in the context of the labour law: it is inadvisable to consult with the "yearly hireling"[257] since he is personally involved[258]. - 38,32c.33 describes the deciding factor in the performance of public judicial functions: the qualifications of knowledge. Ignorant artisans were not able to join the elders and scribes and sages in the local government, the 'people's council'[259]. - Some see another direct reference to the oral law in 39,2-3 where Ben Sira describes the scribes as preserving the sayings of famous men and investigating parables and proverbs[260]. -42,3a is part of the partnership law: a man who laid out the money is not to be ashamed to require an account from his partner when he returns from his journey[261]. - 42,3b belongs to the laws regulating the inheritance: the heir is warned not to hesitate to stand on his right as to the "distribution of an inheritance and a property". Sometimes it was necessary to resort to distribution by a court (cf. tPea 4,5)[262]. - 42,7 illustrates the contemporary customs regarding loans and bailments[263]. One used to write a bill as evidence (cf. DJD 2, pp.12,114; mShebi 10, 1; tKet 4,13). Ben Sira warns against the practice of letting objects of bail pass from hand to hand without any bill being written.

This evidence indicates that Sirach contains elements of contemporary halakhah in the areas of constitutional and governmental matters (4,7.29; 7,6.7; 23,24; 38,32.33; 42,11), evidence in

---

251 Cf. Z.W. Falk, *o.c.*, pp.298f.
252 Cf. Z.W. Falk, *o.c.*, p.308.
253 See also mKer 1,7. Cf. Z.W. Falk, *o.c.*, p.203 (note the misprints of the Sirach references!).
254 Cf. J.G. Snaith, *Ecclesiasticus*, pp.165f.
255 J. Neusner, *The Idea of Purity in Ancient Judaism*, SJLA 1, 1973, p.37 (referring to 34,25G).
256 B.S. Jackson, *Essays*, p.261.
257 Reading שכיר שנה with H^{Bm} and H^D (H^B has שומר שוא which makes no sense). Cf. Box/Oesterley, *APOT* 1 (1913) 445; G. Sauer, *JSHRZ* III/5 (1981) 594. G should read correspondingly μισθίου ἐπετείου. For the textual evidence see J. Ziegler, *Sapientia Iesu Filii Sirach*, ^{2}1980, pp.107f.,296. Cf. Deut 15,18.
258 Cf. Z.W. Falk, *Introduction*, p.214.
259 Cf. G. Alon, *Jews*, p.400 n.73; Z.W. Falk, *o.c.*, p.83.
260 Cf. J.G. Snaith, *Ecclesiasticus*, p.192.
261 Cf. Z.W. Falk, *o.c.*, p.230.
262 Cf. Z.W. Falk, *o.c.*, p.349. Cf. E.E. Urbach, *Sages*, 1975, p.511 (on 30,4-6).

courts (11,7), property (36,25), contracts (26,36; 37,11; 41,24; 42,3.8; 43,4), bridal gifts (25,21.22), divorce (7,19.26; 25,25.26; 28,15), and inheritance (30,4-6; 42,2)[264].

3.8. Old Testament Quotations and Allusions

It has been claimed recently that Ben Sira quotes the OT "not once in his entire book"[266]. This view is not shared by other scholars, however. Several studies prove that Ben Sira used the OT rather extensively and in different ways[267].

A. Eberharter distinguishes between (1) allusions ("Anspielungen"), i.e. material and formal reminiscences which leave the possibility of an independent formation open, (2) references ("Anlehnungen") where the subject-matter and form indicate clearly a relationship to OT references, and (3) reflexive combinations of several texts of OT passages[267].

G.T. Sheppard recently designed a more sophisticated checklist of the means of referring to specific OT texts and traditions[268]: (1) full citation of a single biblical text, at least several words in length, without alteration in wording, (2) partial citation of a single biblical text with alteration in wording, including additions and omissions, (3) the use of key words or phrases as *Stichwortverbindungen* with specific texts or traditions, (4) allusions to specific texts or traditions, (5) paraphrase of specific texts or traditions, (6) imaginative choice of metaphors that allow for a variety of free associations with biblical imagery[269]. Sheppard further

---

263 Cf. Z.W. Falk, *o.c.*, pp.204,218.
264 Proving wrong both E. Rivkin, "Ben Sira", 1975, p.101 and J. Marböck, "Gesetz", 1976, p.10 who claim that typically Israelite laws do not occur in Sirach.
265 E. Rivkin, *a.c.*, p.101.
266 A. Eberharter, *Der Kanon des Alten Testaments zur Zeit des Ben Sira. Auf Grund der Beziehungen des Sirachbuches zu den Schriften des Alten Testaments dargestellt*, 1911; J.K. Zink, *The Use of the Old Testament in the Apocrypha*, Ph.D. Diss. Duke University, 1963, pp.78-88,192,200f.,205-207; T. Middendorp, *Stellung*, 1973, pp. 35-91.
267 A. Eberharter, *o.c.*, pp.4f.
268 G.T. Sheppard, *Wisdom*, 1980, pp.100-102.
269 G.T. Sheppard, *o.c.*, pp.100-102 uses Sir 24 as a case study and arrives at the following conclusions (the figures indicate the categories described above): (1)

lists eight possible redactional means of interpreting specific OT texts or traditions with alterations of their original contexts[270].

T. Middendorp attempts to prove that the original text of Sirach did not contain so much borrowed material from the OT. Ben Sira himself formulated his views independently, i.e. he was relatively independent with regard to the wording of the biblical text. Oral tradition is responsible for the frequent "Rückbiegung" of the Sirach text to OT passages[271]. Whether Middendorp's procedure is methodologically sound may be left undecided at this point. His decisions, often based on the priority of an assumed *Vorlage* of G[272] or on the 'motives' of the oral tradents with regard to such "Rückbiegungen", appear at times to be forced and speculative.

A. Eberharter found in Sirach 66 allusions and 67 references to the Pentateuch, 21 allusions and 48 references to the 'former' prophets, 69 allusions and 35 references to the 'later' prophets, and 171 allusions and 125 references to the hagiographa: all in all 327 allusions and 275 references to the OT[273].

Other authors claimed as well that Ben Sira quoted from every book of the OT[274]. J.K. Zink found 10 explicit citations of the OT in Sir[275]. T. Middendorp found 70 allusions to the Pentateuch, 46 allusions to the historical books, 51 allusions to the prophetical books, and over 160 allusions to the hagiographa, altogether ca.

Sir 24,23: Deut 33,4; (2) Sir 24,15: Ex 30,23-24; (3) Sir 24,4b; (4) Sir 24,13-14. 16-17.26; (5) Bar 3,30; (6) Sir 24,13-14.16-17.

270 G.T. Sheppard, *o.c.*, pp.103-108.
271 T. Middendorp, *Stellung*, pp.35-49 discussing 60 passages.
272 See his statement that "G geht auf eine eigene.Vorlage zurück ... wahrscheinlich, daß diese Vorlage von G in den meisten Fällen einen besseren Text hatte als den der Genizafragmente. G hilft der Textkritik oft, Memorierfehler zu sichten. G, von früheren Auslegern oft als ungenau, umschreibend, frei oder erklärend bezeichnet, scheint seiner Vorlage getreu zu folgen" (p.49). In the light of the present text-critical situation of Sirach research, such sweeping statements do not seem to be warranted.
273 Cf. A. Eberharter, *Kanon*, pp.6-52 (my own count).
274 Cf. the list of authors mentioned by P.R. Ackroyd, "Criteria for the Maccabean Dating of the Old Testament Literature", *VT* 3 (1953) 115 n.3.
275 Cf. J.K. Zink, *Use of the Old Testament*, pp.78-88,192,200f.: 1,14 (Prov 1,7; 9,10); 2,18 (2Sam 24,14); 15,19 (Ps 33,18); 17,17 (Deut 32,8-9); 17,27 (Ps 6,6); 20,29 (Deut 16,19); 27,26 (Prov 26,27); 34,16 (Ps 33,18); 36,24 (Prov 18,22); 49,7 (Jer 1,10). He found further 207 implicit citations of the OT (my own count).

330 allusions to the OT[276]. H. Stadelmann touches the question of the OT quotations only briefly in his excursus on "Schriftforschung" in Sir[277]. He finds direct quotations from the Torah (i.e. the Pentateuch) in 35,6 (Deut 16,16), 45,23 (Num 25,13); 23,13 (Deut 33,4).

It would be beyond the scope of this study to give a complete and exhaustive analysis of the technical and material evidence of OT quotations and allusions in Sir, as this would provide material for a monograph of its own. It is obvious, however, that Ben Sira not only knew but also used the OT extensively and in diverse ways.

3.9. Summary

Our treatment of the concept and position of the law and the commandments in Sirach proved that although the law is never the subject of a longer pericope, it is nevertheless of fundamental importance to Ben Sira[278]. The numerous explicit references to the (written) law have even prompted some scholars to believe that Ben Sira's main objective was the 'piety of the law'[279] and that he attempted to establish the Torah as the 'vanishing point' of the diverse activities of the sage[280]. Thus, it seems that Ben Sira did not (!) have a "offene Konzeption der Tora"[281] after all. The terms תורה/νόμος and מצוה/ἐντολαί refer, in the vast majority of the passages, specifically to the Mosaic Torah[282].

When Ben Sira describes the order of creation he sometimes uses legal terms. As such passages are relatively rare it is unwarranted to hold the view that Ben Sira understood the law essentially as a comprehensive cosmic law. The realm of creation is not identical with the realm of the law.

---

276 Cf. T. Middendorp, *Stellung*, pp.49-91 (my own count). For a critical evaluation of Middendorp's procedure cf. H. Stadelmann, *Ben Sira*, p.255.
277 H. Stadelmann, *o.c.*, pp.254f.
278 Cf. already J. Haspecker, *Gottesfurcht*, 1967, p.332.
279 Cf. B.L. Mack, *Logos*, p.26.
280 Cf. M. Löhr, *Bildung*, pp.107f.
281 Contra J. Marböck, "Gesetz", *BZ* 20 (1976) 11.
282 See also M. Hengel, *Judentum*, p.253.

For Ben Sira the law is very closely linked with Israel's history and faith. The law is the word of Yahweh and was revealed at Sinai through the mediation of Moses and thus is, as a result, the foundation, the content, and the aim of the covenant.

The law as *lex revelata* was, in the eyes of Ben Sira, the norm or moral and social conduct, the source and the means of attaining wisdom, the measure of one's devotion to God, the rule for the temple cult and for jurisdiction, and last but not least the foundation or 'text book' for teaching.

Ben Sira challenges his readers to obey the law and to keep the commandments as this is the sure road to wisdom and to a godly life.

Finally we established the existence of halakhic material in Sir as well as his conceptual and material dependence on the OT.

Excursus 1: The Identity and History of the Sopherim

1. Term

The term סופר can be explained on the basis of an 'internal' Hebrew etymology. It is probably a denominative formation with the original sense of "he who makes a ספר (list, written document)". Thus, סופר is a person professionally concerned with books[283]. The Talmudic etymology interprets סופרים as scholars who count the letters of the Torah: "Therefore the early (Sages) were called *Sopherim* because they counted all the letters of the Torah"(שהיו סופרים כל אותירת שבתורה), bQid 30a. If this statement is taken to provide an etymological explanation, it has certainly no historical signficance[284].

סופר can refer to a literate person[285], an elementary teacher, a secretary[286], a secretary of state[287], a temple scribe[288], and a (proto-Rabbinic) scribe[289]. A differentiation with regard to the different usage in subsequent historical contexts and with regard to the technical or honorific usage of סופר is therefore essential.

Attempts to identify the *sopherim* often presuppose that they must correspond to some 'party' or movement. It has to be stressed therefore that *sopherim* is not the name for a party but a professional or educational designation[290]. The term *sopher*

---

283 Cf. E. Schürer, *History*, 2, 1979, p.324 n.2.
284 Cf. E.E. Urbach, *Sages*, 1975, p.568.
285 Cf. the term κωμῶν γραμματεῖς used by Josephus in Ant 16,203; Bell 1,24.
286 2Kgs 25,19: ספר שר הצבא; 2Kgs 12,11: ספר המלך .
287 Ezr 7,12.21: ספר דתא אלה שמיא .
288 Cf. the edict of Antiochos III in Ant 12,142: γραμματεῖς τοῦ ἱεροῦ,
289 In the sense of *Schriftgelehrter*. Cf. Sir 38,24-39,11. On the whole see R. Meyer, *Tradition und Neuschöpfung*, 1965, pp.38-42; idem, in *ThWNT* 9 (1973) 22f.; E. Rivkin, *Hidden Revolution*, 1978, pp.158-160,202f.
290 Cf. M. Hengel, *Judentum*, p.144: "Berufs- bzw. Bildungsbezeichnung"; P. Sigal,

was used as a proper title only in the Tannaitic literature referring to the so-called 'early sages'. Some of the *sopherim* were given titles themselves, such as רבי, רבן, אבא or מורה[291].

2. Identity in history

In pre-exilic times the term *sopher* was used to denote secretaries in the administration of the Israelite monarchy, especially the royal secretary (ספר המלך)[292]. The royal secretary was responsible for the king's correspondence and for the keeping of the official state annals. If we follow J. Begrich and particularly T.N.D. Mettinger, this office was modelled on the 'royal secretary' in Egypt[293]. On this international scale the royal secretaries seem to have been closely related to or even identical with the 'wise men', at least in a secondary sense[294]. The LXX translation of סופר with γραμματεύς fits into this general context.

In the time of Ezra, ספרא seems to have been used as the designation of a Persian office: ספר דתא די אלה שמיא (Ezr 7,12.21), a civil servant "dessen Ressort innerhalb der persischen Verwaltung die Belange des jüdischen Gottes bzw. seiner Gemeinde sind"[295]. This term implies that Ezra is responsible to the Persian king and also that he is invested with authority as state official with regard to the priests in Jerusalem[296]. The activity of Ezra the *sopher* (cf. Ezr 8,1.4.9.13; 12,6.36) "stellte die Weichen für jene Konzentration auf die Torah, die im Judentum der Folgezeit immer stärker zu beobachten ist"[297]. Scribism as ideology begins with the view that the Mosaic law given by God was binding and therefore had to be authoritatively interpreted and applied to daily affairs, a view which has to be traced back to Nehemiah's establishment of the Mosaic Torah as the constitution of Judea. Thus, from the 4th century B.C. onwards, the men who could apply the completed (written) Torah

---

Emergence, I/2, 1980, p.3: "denoting a functionary"; cf. also J. Neusner, "The Formation of Rabbinic Judaism", *ANRW* II/19,2 (1979) 38f.
291 Cf. E. Schürer, *o.c.*, pp.325-327.
292 2Kgs 12,10; 18,37; 19,2; 22,3.8-10.12; 2Chr 34,8; Jer 36,10.12.20-21.
293 Cf. J. Begrich, "Sofer und Mazkir", *ZAW* 35 (1940) 10-15; T.N.D. Mettinger, *State Officials*, 1971, pp.25-51. See also E. Schürer, *o.c.*, p.324.
294 C. Kayatz, *Studien zu Proverbien 1-9*, WMANT 22, 1966, p.13; H. Mantel, "The Development of the Oral Law During the Second Temple Period", *WHJP* I/8 (1977) 55; R. Riesner, *Jesus als Lehrer: Eine Untersuchung zum Ursprung der Evangelien-Überlieferung*, WUNT II/7, 1981, pp.154-156; R.T. Beckwith, "The Pre-History and Relationships of the Pharisees, Sadducees and the Essenes", *RQ* 11 (1982) 19f.
295 Cf. H.H. Schaeder, *Esra der Schreiber*, 1930, p.49, followed by A. Guttmann, *Rabbinic Judaism*, 1970, p.4; W. Rudolph, *Esra und Nehemia*, HAT 20, pp.67,72; R. Meyer, in *ThWNT* 9 (1973) 22f.; W.T. in der Smitten, *Esra: Quellen, Überlieferung und Geschichte*, 1973, pp.105-110; H. Mantel, *a.c.*, p.55. But note the objections raised by S. Mowinckel, *Studien zu dem Buche Ezra-Nehemiah*, 3, 1965, pp. 117-124 who sees 'sopher' in Ezr 7,12 as a scholar in the law rather than as title of a Persian office. Cf. also J. Marböck, "Der schriftgelehrte Weise", *BETL* 51 (1979) 298 n.15.
296 Cf. R. Meyer, in *ThWNT* 9 (1973) 22; K. Galling, *Die Bücher der Chronik, Esra, Nehemia*, ATD 12, 1954, p.205.
297 R. Riesner, *o.c.*, p.162. Cf. also J.Z. Lauterbach, *Rabbinic Essays*, 1973, p.165 who regards the *sopherim* as the successors of Ezra.

constituted an important class or profession. The scribes regarded the study, interpretation, and application of the Torah as the centre of piety[298].

In the pre-Maccabean period we encounter *sopherim* at the temple (Ant 12,142). The temple scribes were literate priests who were responsible for copying the Scriptures, especially the Pentateuch, and for transmitting them with meticulous care. They were the custodians of the Holy Scriptures[299]. It is in the context of this period that we hear of hasidic *sopherim* (1Macc 7,12-13)[300]. They were legal experts who interpreted the law and applied it to new situations. These scribes were searching for a law which would establish the legitimacy of Alcimus[301].

At the beginning of the second century the priest and wisdom teacher Ben Sira uses the word סופר for the first time in the 'technical' sense of 'scribe': the scholar who is סופר and חכם at the same time (38,24: σοφία γραμματέως = חכמת סופר). In 38,24-39,11 he pictures the ideal scribe (see supra §6.5.5.). In 38,24-34b Ben Sira discusses the relation between the *sopher/ḥakham* and the lay people who have other professions. His aim is to show that craftsmen always remain craftsmen and that the highest level of wisdom can be attained only by the (priestly[302]) *sopher* who has the necessary leisure to study the Torah[303]. In 38,34c-39,11 Ben Sira describes then the ideal of scribe as such. In his description of the work of the scribe we find a new and extremely important element: whereas the *sopher* of the Persian per-

---

298 Cf. J. Neusner, "Formation of Rabbinic Judaism", *ANRW* II/19,2 (1979) 38f.
299 Cf. R. Meyer, in *ThWNT* 9 (1973) 22f.; E.E. Urbach, *Sages*, p.568. Some see a reference to the *sopherim* at the temple in Jer 8,8; cf. R. Riesner, *Jesus*, p.160. In TLev 8,17 levitical scribes are expressly mentioned.
300 Cf. R. Riesner, *o.c.*, p.168.
301 R. Meyer, *a.c.*, p.23 identifies these scribes with the temple scribes. But there is nothing in the context of 1Macc 7,12-13 which would warrant this identification. P. Sigal, *Emergence*, I/1, pp.199f. calls the scribes of 1Macc 7,12 "scholastics of Torah" and identifies them as the "new class of proto-Rabbis". This view cannot be justified either, since the text relates these scribes to the hasidim who clearly cannot be regarded as being, exclusively, proto-Rabbis.
302 The apologetic interest of Ben Sira aims at emphasizing that lay people have no business with the priestly scribe. This has been clearly recognized by H. Stadelmann, *Ben Sira*, pp.274-293 passim. The view of H.H. Schaeder, *Esra der Schreiber*, p.59 that in Sir 38,24-39,11 Ben Sira praises the ideal figure of the "schriftgelehrten, torakundigen Laien" is totally erroneous. M. Hengel, *Judentum*, p.146 believes that in this passage the *sopher* has already a relatively autonomous (!) significance, emancipating himself from the priesthood and allowing lay people into his rank in order to combat Hellenism. As regards the historical context, this view seems to be correct. But Ben Sira is seemingly not part of this development but rather opposes it! Cf. H. Stadelmann, *o.c.*, p.292. E. Rivkin, "Pharisaism and the Crisis of the Individual in the Greco-Roman World", *JQR* 61 (1970) 33 proves that Ben Sira underwrites Aaronide authority by pointing out that he reminds his readers of the fate of Dathan, Abiram, and Korah who had dared to challenge Aaron's supremacy (Sir 45,17-19). Cf. E. Rivkin, *Hidden Revolution*, pp.191-207 where he describes the *sopherim* at Ben Sira's time as "Pentateuchalists, hierocratic intellectuals, Aaronide supremacists, and lovers and seekers of Wisdom" who share "only a name with the Pharisees-Hakhamim-Soferim, not an essence" (p.197). It should be noted that Rivkin fails to see the apologetic (!) nature of Ben Sira's description of the *sopher*, and the halakhah existed already in that time.

iod focused his interest exclusively on the Torah (cf. Ezra), we find that the *sopher* of the pre-Maccabean period includes topics and traditions of traditional wisdom (Sir 39,2-3). Ben Sira's *sopher* is an intellectual, not a 'scribe' in the old sense, a scholar, not a copyist, a sage, not a secretary. This fusion of traditional scribal (Torah) erudition and wisdom teaching can also be seen in the telling phrases, mentioned already, of the σοφία γραμματέως = סופר חכמת (Sir 38,24)[304]. With Ben Sira, חכם and סופר are essentially identical terms[305].

R. Meyer's statement that "erst die feste Verbindung von 'Weisheit' und 'Gesetz' beziehungsweise von 'Weisen' und 'Schreibern' als deren Trägern ergibt den komplexen Begriff des Schriftgelehrten"[306] has to be modified, however, with reference to the fact that the term *sopher* and the corresponding 'profession' existed before Ben Sira, denoting the priestly scholar who concentrated on the Torah[307]. R.H. Pfeiffer pointed out that Ben Sira, with his fusion of *ḥakham* and *sopher*, "marks the transition from the Bible to the Talmud, from the authority of inspiration (which he still claims ...) to the authority of learning. The two phases of this study, wisdom and Law, remained basic in Judaism after Sirach"[308].

Others maintain similarly that Ben Sira gives the "first description of the emergent proto-rabbi"[309]. It is necessary, however, to differentiate between the different types of *sopherim* after Ben Sira. As concerns Ben Sira himself, with his claim of possessing the "spirit of understanding" (19,6) and thus being inspired like the prophets, M. Hengel has rightly distinguished two potential directions of further development: (1) the development of a new 'prophecy' founded on the inspired interpretation of law and prophets (as among the Essenes and the Zealots), or (2) the institutionalization of exegesis (as in the later Rabbinic system)[310]. E. Rivkin dissociates Ben Sira and his fellow-*sopherim* completely from the Pharisees whom he takes to be identical with the *ḥakhamim/sopherim*[311]. He does not see, however, that Ben Sira has to defend (!) the priestly-Aaronide *sopherim*, that there are indeed similarities between Ben Sira's *sopher* and the later Pharisaic *sopherim*, and that the early halakhah existed already in Ben Sira's day[312]. Further, Rivkin's exclusive identification of (post-

---

303 Cf. H. Stadelmann, *o.c.*, pp.284-293. On the alleged relation between Ben Sira and the 'Instruction of Cheti' (*ANET*, pp.432ff.) and the 'Praise of the Learned Scribe' (*ANET*, pp.431f.) see the critical assessment, with negative conclusions, by O. Rickenbacher, *Weisheitsperikopen*, pp.186-192, followed by H. Stadelmann, *Ben Sira*, pp.287-290 and J. Marböck, "Der schriftgelehrte Weise", *BETL* 51 (1979) 295.

304 Cf. H. Stadelmann, *o.c.*, p.225. This was already observed by R. Meyer, *Tradition*, pp.41f.; idem, in *ThWNT* 9 (1973) 23; also J. Marböck, *a.c.*, pp.302f.,311-314. E. Rivkin, "Scribes, Pharisees, Lawyers, Hypocrites: A Study in Synonymity", *HUCA* 49 (1978) 139 rightly pointed out that the term γραμματεύς did not keep up with this change in meaning of סופר.

305 Cf. our discussion infra, §4.

306 R. Meyer, *o.c.*, p.42; cf. idem, *a.c.*, p.23; also M. Küchler, *Weisheitstraditionen*, 1979, p.40.

307 Cf. H. Stadelmann, *o.c.*, p.227.

308 R.H. Pfeiffer, *History*, 1949, p.369.

309 P. Sigal, *Emergence*, I/2, 1980, p.18.

310 Cf. M. Hengel, *Judentum*, p.248.

311 E. Rivkin, *Hidden Revolution*, pp.197-204.

312 Cf. L. Finkelstein, "Some Examples of Maccabean Halaka", *JBL* 49 (1930) 20-42; L.I. Rabinowitz, "Halakhah", 1967, pp.145-148.

Hasmonean) *sopherim* with the Pharisees=*hakhamim* is not warranted. One can say, at least, that a similar phenomenology is operative in the sage/scribe of Ben Sira and in the later rabbi[313].

As regards the special case of the 'inspired' scribe, a position which Ben Sira obviously claims for himself, later rabbinic theory assumed for all the rabbis, called חכמים, the authority of both revelation (inspiration) and interpretation (exegesis), based on their succession of both priest and prophet[314].

The Hasmonean period witnessed a second concentration on the Torah as a reaction against the attempt to abolish the law by the Hellenizers[315]. This is true for the Sadducees and for the Pharisees, as well as for the Qumran Community[316]. The scribes were no longer recruited from among the priests only but more and more from among the lay people[317]. Their power was not based any more on priestly descent but on their erudition and expertise in the Torah. Each of the above-mentioned 'parties' or movements had its own scribes who also combined wisdom and law[318].

The Pharisaic scribes came from priestly or non-priestly circles and were involved in the working out of halakhah, especially concerning ritual purity[319]. We know only a small number of scribes who belonged to a Pharisaic community[320]. These scribes were, according to the later Rabbinic tradition, in principle committed to non-writing with regard to halakhah. Their allegiance to the law was strengthened by the fact that the priests were by now no longer the (sole) custodians of the law[321].

There were also Sadducean scribes. It would be very strange if the Sadducees who acknowledged the Torah as sole binding authority would include no professional expositors of the Torah. This is all the more probable since the *sopherim* were, as we have seen, originally recruited from the priests, and the Sadducees consisted largely, if not almost exclusively, of priests. Josephus (Ant 18,16) and the NT (cf. expressions as "scribes of the Pharisees", Acts 23,9; Mk 2,16; Lk 5,30) presuppose that there were Sadducean scribes too[322]. The halakhah to which R. Eliezer b. Zadok refers in mSanh 7,2 (the death penalty by burning is to be applied literally) is described in bSanh 52b as a Sadducean legal practice[323].

---

313 Cf. D.J. Harrington, "The Wisdom of the Scribe", 1980, pp.186f.
314 Cf. P. Sigal, *Emergence*, I/2, p.18.
315 Cf. M. Hengel, *o.c.*, p.563.
316 Cf. H. Stadelmann, *Ben Sira*, pp.227f.
317 Cf. J. Jeremias, *Jerusalem in the Time of Jesus*, ⁵1979, pp.233-235.
318 Cf. E. Schürer, *History*, 2, p.329; R. Meyer, in *ThWNT* 9 (1973) 23; P. Sigal, *o.c.*, I/1, p.3; J. Jeremias, *o.c.*, pp.254-256; H. Mantel, "Development", *WHJP* I/8 (1977) 55; R. Riesner, *Jesus*, pp.168-176. J. Jeremias, *o.c.*, p.254 rightly rejects "the completely false idea that the Pharisees were the same as the scribes". Also J. Neusner, "Formation", *ANRW* II/19,2 (1979) 38 who points out that the rabbinic traditions about the Pharisees before 70 A.D. do not mention a stress on, or even the presence of, the ideal of the study of Torah, and that neither Josephus nor the Gospels confuse the scribes with the Pharisees (pp.39-41). Contra E. Rivkin, "Scribes", *HUCA* 49 (1978) 135-142.
319 Cf. J. Jeremias, *Jerusalem*, pp.256-258.
320 Cf. J. Jeremias, *o.c.*, p.254.
321 Cf. E. Rivkin, "Scribes", *HUCA* 49 (1978) 139.
322 Cf. E. Schürer, *History*, 2, p.329; J. Jeremias, *o.c.*, p.231; J. Le Moyne, *Les Sadducéens*, EB, 1972, pp.41f.,352-354.
323 Cf. E. Schürer, *o.c.*, pp.329f. with n.29. On Sadducean halakhah see J. Le Moyne,

The scribes in Qumran focused on the study of the Torah as well (cf. 1QS 6,6-7). The exploration of the Scriptures remained here the task of the priests and Levites (cf. CD 6,4-6; 13,2-3; 14,7-8; 1QS 2,8-9). But the goal was to provide all members of the Community with a thorough knowledge of the Scriptures. This is probably why they were called "pupils of God" (למודי אל, cf. CD 20,4; 1QH 2,39; 8,36; 1QM 10,10). The priestly 'Teacher of Righteousness' was the expounder of Torah *par excellence* (דורש התורה, CD 6,7.10-11)[324].

It seems that there were also 'independent' scribes. We know of scribes who opposed Sadducean teachers and championed Pharisaic ideas but who did not seem to belong to a Pharisaic community. For example, Yohanan b. Zakkai defends Pharisaic opinions against Sadducean views speaking of himself in the third person (mYad 4, 6)[325]. And the halakhot on ritual purity which characterize the Pharisees are not significant in the traditions on Yohanan b. Zakkai[326]. It could well be that a part of the 'proto-rabbis' stood above the 'parties'[327].

After 70 A.D. scribism changed, introducing important differences with regard to the pre-70 scribal ideology: the temple cult was replaced by the study of the Torah, the priest by the rabbi (= scribe), and the centre of piety shifted away entirely from the temple cult and its sacrifices[328]. Thus the scribal ideal was carried to its logical conclusion: "If study of Torah was central and knowledge of Torah important, then the scribe had authority even in respect to the Temple and the cult; indeed, his knowledge was more important than what the priest knew"[329]. The rabbinism of the early Yavneans, especially Yohanan b. Zakkai, is the continuation of pre-70 scribism.

In the Mishnah, סופר is a title applied only to scribes of earlier times who had already an authority for the Tannaim[330]. The scholar/scribes of Tannaitic times are called חכמים. If סופר (or aram. ספרא) is not meant as a title referring to the 'early sages' it is used as the most common designation for the elementary teacher[331], for a copyist or professional writer[332], for a book-binder[333], or for a town-archivist[334]. Thus the term סופר acquired again its original meaning referring to a person

---

o.c., pp.369-379.

324 O. Betz, *Offenbarung und Schriftforschung in der Qumransekte*, WUNT 6, 1960, pp.19-36; R. Riesner, *Jesus*, pp.170f.
325 Cf. J. Jeremias, o.c., pp.255f. On his disputes with the Sadducees see J. Neusner, *A Life of Rabban Yohanan ben Zakkai*, SPB 6, 1962, pp.52-60.
326 Cf. J. Neusner, *Early Rabbinic Judaism*, SJLA 13, 1975, pp.57f.
327 Cf. R. Riesner, *Jesus*, p.174. It is wrong, however, to identify such 'independent' scribes with the 'proto-rabbis' in contradistinction to the Pharisees who were only interested in the transmission of practical instructions for proper behaviour and showed no interest in wisdom traditions (contra R. Riesner, o.c., p.174). The 'proto-rabbis' were to be found in the diverse Pharisaic communitites as well.
328 Cf. J. Neusner, "Formation", *ANRW* II/19,2 (1979) 38.
329 Cf. J. Neusner, a.c., p.38.
330 Cf. mOrl 3,9; mYeb 2,4; 9,3; mSanh 11,3; mKel 13,7; mPar 11,4-6; mToh 4, 7.11; mTeb 4,6; mYad 3,2. Cf. E. Schürer, *History*, 2, p.325 n.9; J. Jeremias, Art. "γραμματεύς", *ThWNT* 1 (1933) 741.
331 Cf. tMeg 3,19; 4,38; pPea 21a; pHag 76c; pMeg 74a; pYeb 13a; bBB 21b. The elementary school is called בית סופרים or הסופר בית : cf. tSot 6,2; pTaan 69a; bKet 105a.
332 Cf. mGit 8,8; 3,1; 7,2; 9,8; mBM 5,11; mShab 12,5; mSanh 4,3; 5,5.
333 Cf. mPes 3,1.
334 Cf. bBB 21b.

professionally concerned with books and documents[335]. R. Eliezer summed up the new situation lamenting that "since the day that the Temple was destroyed, the ḥakhamim began to be like the sopherim and the sopherim became like ḥazzanim" (mSot 9,15).

§4 Ben Sir's Identification of Law and Wisdom

We are now in a position to understand the nature of Ben Sira's identification of law and wisdom, as well as the rationale behind it and its consequences. Before we discuss the character of the identification, we will first have to focus on the material evidence of the identification in Sirach since this has not been done before[336].

4.1. The Exegetical Evidence

4.1.1. The explicit evidence. In seven passages we find a clear and direct identification of wisdom and law. (1) 15,1: "He who fears the Lord[337] will do this, and he who keeps the law will acquire it (i.e. wisdom)". This verse is the formal and material centre of the wisdom pericope 14,20-15,10[338] in which Ben Sira presents piety as the *conditio sine qua non* for obtaining wisdom[339]. Personal faith which includes obedience to the law will lead to wisdom. As in 24,23 the Torah appears here as the summary of a wisdom hymn, and as in 1,26 obedience to the law is

---

335 Cf. J. Jeremias, *a.c.*, p.741; R. Riesner, *o.c.*, p.184; P. Sigal, *Emergence*, I/2, p.3; E. Schürer, *o.c.*, p.324; A. Gutmann, *Rabbinic Judaism*, p.7. Josephus does not use γραμματεύς for the scribe of his time (except Bell 6,291: ἱερογραμματεῖς) but employs rather paraphrases (cf. Ant 17,149f.) or calls them σοφισταί (cf. Ant 17,152; Bell 1,648).

336 J. Marböck, "Gesetz", *BZ* 20 (1976) 1-21 discusses only 17,11-14; 24,23.

337 H starts 15,1 with כי which is omitted by G and S. We follow O. Rickenbacher, *Weisheitsperikopen*, p.77 who interprets the כי as a *ki-affirmationis* which is generally not translated. Cf. P. Joüon, *Grammaire de l'Hébreu biblique*, 1923 (= 1965), §164b.

338 Cf. J. Haspecker, *Gottesfurcht*, pp.140-142; J. Marböck, *Weisheit*, p.107; O. Rickenbacher, *o.c.*, p.77; J.G. Snaith, *Ecclesiasticus*, p.75.

339 Cf. H. Stadelmann, *Ben Sira*, p.301 n.1.

seen as a prerequisite for attaining wisdom[340]. The law is a sure way to wisdom. To keep the law is to be wise.

(2) 17,11: "He gave them knowledge[341], and he gave them as an inheritance the law of life". The chiastic structure of this verse identifies "knowledge" ($\dot{\epsilon}\pi\iota\sigma\tau\acute{\eta}\mu\eta$) and "law of life" ($\nu\acute{o}\mu o\varsigma\ \zeta\omega\tilde{\eta}\varsigma$) which God gave to Israel (cf. 45,5). In the context of the Sinaitic revelation of God we have here another explicit occurrence of the identification of law and wisdom[342].

(3) 19,20: "All wisdom is the fear of the Lord, and all wisdom is the fulfilment of the law"[343]. As in 2,15-16; 6,36; 15,1 Ben Sira closely links the fear of the Lord, wisdom, and the law. Here the fear of the Lord and wisdom are identified, and it is pointed out that the fulfilment of the law consists in this synthesis[344]. The keeping of God's law equals comprehensive wisdom[345].

(4) 21,11: "He who keeps the law keeps his (natural) inclination under control, and accomplished wisdom is the fear of the Lord"[346]. In v.11b wisdom is identified with the fear of the Lord[347]. The chiastic structure of the verse suggests that wisdom is also identified with the control of the 'natural' inclination (יצר) and the fear of the Lord with obedience to the Torah[348]. It has

---

340 Cf. J. Marböck, o.c., pp.85,88. Taken alone, 15,1b hardly implies the identification of law and wisdom. However, the context is decisive here: Torah is the summary of the wisdom hymn.
341 Box/Oesterley, APOT 1 (1913) 376 suggest that G reads בינה instead of ברית and translate "he set before them the covenant". This emendation would fit the context (cf. the "law of life") but is not warranted by the textual evidence and has to remain speculative.
342 Acknowledged by P.J. Nel, Structure, 1982, p.93.
343 The translation follows O. Rickenbacher, Weisheitsperikopen, pp.99f. who omits ἐν in v.20b in accordance with the fact that in over 20 passages H and S stand against G omitting anything which would correspond to ἐν. If this conjecture is correct, J. Marböck's statement that in 19,20 the law appears as part of more comprehensive sapiential activities (Weisheit, p.85) has to be modified.
344 Cf. M. Löhr, Bildung, p.36.
345 Cf. O. Rickenbacher, o.c., p.100, quoting L. Alonso-Schökel, Proverbios y Ecclesiastico, 1968, ad loc.: "El temor del Señor es sintesis de la sabiduria, complir su ley es toda la sabiduria". We acknowledge the fact that this exegesis rests on an emendation. The text as it is (cf. NEB "all wisdom ... includes the fulfilling of the law") supports rather the correlation of wisdom and law.
346 On the context, the translation, and the meaning of the verse see supra, pp.46f.
347 Cf. J. Haspecker, Gottesfurcht, p.161; J.G. Snaith, Ecclesiasticus, p.106.
348 Cf. O. Rickenbacher, Weisheitsperikopen, p.106; J.G. Snaith, Ecclesiasticus, p.106; H. Stadelmann, Ben Sira, p.222.

not been observed yet that besides this structural parallelism we also find a synonymous parallelism with regard to the content: as obedience to the law leads to inner discipline and a godly life, so does accomplished wisdom which corresponds with commitment to God. In other words: obedience to the law is accomplished wisdom — both are strongly linked with the fear of the Lord, and both are the foundation and the means of attaining a godly life which is in accordance with God's commandments.

(5) 24,23: "All this is the book of the covenant of God Most High[349], the law which Moses imposed upon us, as inheritance for the assembly[350] of Jacob"[351]. The ταῦτα πάντα is usually understood as comprehending wisdom, which functions in creation and in history (24,1-22), as the Mosaic law containing God's will (cf. the term "inheritance") for his people[352]. Wisdom and law are clearly identified. The βίβλος διαθήκης in v.23a is to be understood as synonymous with the book of the law in v.23b[353]. Ben

---

349 Retaining G βίβλος διαθήκης θεοῦ ὑψίστου with J. Marböck, *Weisheit*, pp.35, 40,77; J.G. Snaith, *o.c.*, p.124; M. Löhr, *Bildung*, p.46; G. Sauer, *JSHRZ* III/5 (1981) 565; contra O. Rickenbacher, *o.c.*, pp.126f. followed by H. Stadelmann, *o.c.*, p.248 n.1. It is not necessary to see in 24,23 a tristich: cf. J. Marböck, *o.c.*, p.45.

350 Following S instead of G (συναγωγαῖς). Cf. O. Rickenbacher, *o.c.*, p.167 ; J. Marböck, *o.c.*, p.40.

351 We retain the authenticity of 24,23ff. Cf. M. Hengel, *Judentum*, p.289 n.339, contra W.L. Knox, "The Divine Wisdom", *JThS* 18 (1937) 233,236f. U. Wilckens, *Weisheit und Torheit*, 1959, pp.167f. states that this pericope represents in a later redactor's mind "die zentrale Aussage des ganzen Liedes". We do not take into account the variant in the Syriac version, viz. "all this is *in* the book of the covenant of God Most High", following practically all scholars. If "in" were original, G with its predilection for ἐν (cf. supra n.343) would certainly have translated it. On the relationship of 24,23 with 24,1-22 see also G.T. Sheppard, "Wisdom and Torah", 1978, pp.166-168.

352 Contra J.C.H. Lebram, "Jerusalem", 1979, pp.108-112 who relates ταῦτα πάντα to 24,20-22 and rejects the usual interpretation of this phrase as expressing the identification of wisdom and law since, according to him, this phrase contains only a comparison: "das Gesetz gibt dem Menschen soviel, wie die Weisheit, nämlich ewige Sättigung" (p.110). Wisdom is not identified with the law but the law, as book (!), is seen as mediator of sapiential perception (p.108). Lebram's interpretation does not do justice to the conceptual context of Sir 24. He asserts that such an identification would be not impossible for Ben Sira, historically speaking, referring to Ezr 7,25 and Bar 4,1, assuming, obviously, that Sir 24,23 is the only passage in Sirach which could contain the identification of law and wisdom.

353 Cf. J. Marböck, *Weisheit*, p.77, following E. Kutsch, "Gesetz und Gnade: Probleme des alttestamentlichen Bundesbegriffes", *ZAW* 79 (1967) 18-35, part. p.30 who

Sira often relates the covenant to the revealed law (17,11.12; 24, 23; 28,7; 39,8; 42,2G; 33,20; 45,5)³⁵⁴. 24,23b is a quotation from Deut 33,4³⁵⁵.

> J. Marböck thinks that, as a result of this identification of law and wisdom, "der Begriff des Gesetzes bei Ben Sira ebenfalls eine gewisse Erweiterung und Auffüllung erfahren muß"³⁵⁶. First, the dignity of the law is enhanced: since it is linked with wisdom which is active in creation and in Israel's history, the law is 'projected back' to creation. Second, the law assumes the characteristics of a comprehensive cosmic law which permeates creation and history: it is seen as universal creation-wisdom³⁵⁷. Later rabbinic theology developed this concept of the Torah as cosmological principle³⁵⁸. It has to be emphasized, however, that the law does not give up its identity as God's revealed and authoritative law given to Israel through the mediation of Moses.

The law which dominated the life of the pious Jew is the only source of true wisdom: "Die wahre und letzte Stufe der Weisheit liegt . . .für Ben Sira in der durch Moses vermittelten Offenbarung, die das dauernde und eigentliche Erbe des Volkes ist"³⁵⁹. In 24,25-27 Ben Sira uses poetic metaphors to illustrate the great wisdom of law. The Torah overflows with wisdom — comparable with the overflowing and life-giving waters of the rivers of paradise, the Pishon, Tigris, Euphrates, and Gihon (cf. Gen 2,11-14), to which Ben Sira adds the rivers Jordan and Nile³⁶⁰. Water is of paramount importance for life. For Ben Sira water is a sign of blessing, a symbol

---

      pointed out that in deuteronomistic theology ברית and תורה are used as synonyms.
354 Cf. J. Marböck, o.c., p.78 who quotes (only) 17,12 ; 28,7; and 1Macc 1,56.57 where τὰ βίβλια τοῦ νόμου are parallel to βιβλίον διαθήκης. Contra O. Rickenbacher, Weisheitsperikopen, pp.166f. who states that the object of 'covenant' in Sir is never Israel nor Moses but mankind, the patriarchs, and David. Although this observation is generally true he does not take note of the fact that in the 8 passages mentioned above Ben Sira links the 'covenant' with the (Mosaic) law. Thus, the covenant is indeed related to Israel!
355 Cf. J. Marböck, o.c., p.77; J.G. Snaith, Ecclesiasticus, p.124 ; M. Löhr, Bildung, p.46; H. Stadelmann, Ben Sira, p.250; G.T. Sheppard, "Wisdom and Torah", 1978, pp.168-170.
356 J. Marböck, o.c., p.77, followed by H. Stadelmann, o.c., p.250.
357 Cf. J. Marböck, o.c., p.91; also J. Blenkinsopp, Wisdom and Law, p.144.
358 Cf. H.F. Weiss, Untersuchungen, 1966, pp.283-304.
359 Cf. J. Marböck, o.c., p.78.
360 The context of these verses is clearly the Torah (i.e. the Torah pours out wisdom here, not God). W.L. Knox, "The Divine Wisdom", JThS 3 (1937) 232f. thinks that Sir 24,23-27 is an interpolation because the equation of the masculine νόμος with a river can be understood only on Greek background. This emendation must remain speculative, however.

of life and wisdom (cf. 15,3; 21,13)[361]. The reference to the motive of paradise[362] adds to the significance of the refreshing fullness of life in wisdom which becomes accessible in the Torah[363]. In 24,28-29 Ben Sira applies the motif of the inscrutability of wisdom (cf. 1,2-3.6) to the law which contains this wisdom[364]. The Torah contains this blessing of profound wisdom in such an abundance that despite all scribal study it has been impossible and always will remain impossible to exhaust its meaning[365]. Thus, Ben Sira seems to interpret the law as some kind of final entity and revelation of God[366].

(6) 34,8: "Without lies shall the law be completed, and wisdom finds completion in a mouth which is faithful". The chiastic structure of this verse proves that wisdom and law are identified: "without lies" equals the "faithful mouth", and "law" is parallel to "wisdom", both of which are being "completed".

(7) 45,5c.d: "And he placed in his hand the commandment, the law of life and insight". The phrase תורת חיים ותבונה contains a clear identification of law and wisdom (תבונה)[367]. The context is the Sinaitic revelation of the Torah to Israel.

4.1.2. The implicit evidence. Twelve passages presuppose, imply, or result in the identification of law and wisdom. (1) 1,26: "If you desire wisdom, keep the commandments[368], and the Lord will give it to you in abundance". Obedience to the law is the con-

---

361 Cf. O. Rickenbacher, *Weisheitsperikopen*, pp.109f.
362 Cf. J. Marböck, *Weisheit*, p.78 who refers to the significance of the (eschatological) waters/rivers of paradise in Ez 47; Joel 4,18; Zech 14,8; Ps 36,9; 46,5; as well as to the salvational symbolism of water in Is 12,3; 41,18; Jer 31,12.
363 Cf. H. Stadelmann, *Ben Sira*, p.251.
364 Cf. M. Löhr, *Bildung*, p.46; contra Box/Oesterley, *APOT* 1 (1913) 399; J.G. Snaith, *Ecclesiasticus*, p.124; G. Sauer, *JSHRZ* III/5 (1981) 566 who relate vv.28-29 with wisdom instead of with the law. R. Smend, J. Marböck, O. Rickenbacher, M. Löhr, H. Stadelmann and others relate these verses to the law, which is required by the context. Cf. J.C.H. Lebram, "Jerusalem", 1979, p.107 who relates 24,25-29 to the law or to Moses.
365 Cf. H. Stadelmann, *o.c.*, p.251.
366 Cf. J. Marböck, *o.c.*, p.79 and U. Wilckens, *Weisheit*, pp.167f. who notes that 24, 23 is the central statement of the 'hymn' in which wisdom has become the "Offenbarergestalt κατ 'ἐξοχήν" (p.167).
367 Cf. J. Marböck, *Weisheit*, pp.70,90,130.
368 J. Haspecker, *Gottesfurcht*, p.315 emends into the singular. Cf. O. Rickenbacher, *Weisheitsperikopen*, pp.5,14.

dition for acquiring wisdom. It is true that, in one sense, wisdom is more comprehensive than the Torah since it is the personal gift and presence of God[369]. But this verse also implies that being wise equals the keeping of the law[370]. Obedience to the law will make one wise.

(2) 2,15-16: "They who fear the Lord will not be disobedient to his words, and they who love him will keep his ways. They who fear the Lord will seek his favour, and they who love him steep themselves in the law". These verses link the fear of the Lord with obedience to the law[371]. In 1,14.16.18.20 (cf. 19,20; 21,11; 35,14) the fear of the Lord was described as "beginning" and "fullness", as "crown" and "root" of wisdom. One can say that "die Gottesfurcht ist das Tun der Weisheit, sie ist die Weisheit als Lebensvollzug"[372]. Wisdom cannot be attained without the fear of the Lord which, for its part, is closely connected with the keeping of God's commandments. Again we find an implicit correlation of law and wisdom.

(3) 6,36: "Ponder the fear of the Lord, and study his commandment at all times; then he will give insight to your heart, and in everything which you desire he will make you wise"[373]. As in 2, 15-16 the fear of the Lord is linked with the law. The fear of the Lord and the law are described as being the prerequisites for acquiring wisdom. Ben Sira implies again that for him fearing God and studying (for the sake of keeping) the law leads to wisdom and indeed equals wisdom. The context of this verse (6,18-36) reveals the fact that according to Ben Sira sapiential instruction leads to the study of God's commandments thereby closely linking the objects of sapiential teaching with the Torah, and to the close association of the promises connected with wisdom (cf. the fruit of wisdom which consists in rest, joy, and honour, vv. 19.28-31). These promises come as a result of obedience to the law (cf. Deut

---

369 J. Marböck, *o.c.*, p.89 referring to 39,6; 1,10.26.
370 Cf. P.J. Nel, *Structure*, pp.93,96.
371 J. Haspecker, *o.c.*, pp.328-332 emphasizes that the fear of the Lord is not simply identical with obedience to the law but goes beyond it.
372 M. Löhr, *Bildung*, p.31, referring to J. Haspecker, *Gottesfurcht*, pp.83,96.
373 With regard to text-critical matters in this verse see J. Haspecker, *o.c.*, pp.60-64; O. Rickenbacher, *Weisheitsperikopen*, p.64. J. Marböck, *Weisheit*, p.117 sees this verse as a later redactional interpretation. This view cannot be substantiated, however.

28,1-14!)³⁷⁴. The metaphors in 6,30-31 seem to possess a symbolic significance linking discipleship of wisdom with the study of the law³⁷⁵.

(4) 15,15: "If you desire³⁷⁶ you can keep the commandment, and it is based upon insight, to act according to his pleasure". The phrase "to keep the commandment" corresponds with "to act according to (God's) pleasure". Obedience to God's law is equated with "insight" (תבונה³⁷⁷). The wise man will always keep the commandments.

(5) 19,24: "It is better to lack perception and to be godfearing than to overflow with prudence and to transgress the law"³⁷⁸. This verse parallels 19,20³⁷⁹ and belongs to the brief section on the cleverness and prudence of the godless sinner (19,22-25). The passage shows that the scribe, even as wise man, remains committed to God and his word. It states *ex negativo* that the true wise man will fear the Lord and keep the law.

(6) 24,22: "Whoever listens to me will not be put to shame; and those who perform their work(s)³⁸⁰ in me will not sin". This verse concludes the self-praise of wisdom (24,1-22) and is the last verse of the fourth stanza (vv.19-22) which describes wisdom's invitation to man³⁸¹. Wisdom promises to those who heed her advice and act accordingly a godly life without sin. This implies the identity of wisdom and law since obedience to the law is also said to lead to a disciplined life which avoids sin (cf. 21,11). This is confirmed by the fact that the terms "listen" or "obey" (ὑπακο-

---

374 Cf. M. Löhr, *o.c.*, p.35.
375 Cf. J.G. Snaith, *Ecclesiasticus*, p.40.
376 In 15,15-17 Ben Sira explains his conviction that man was created by God as a free being (15,14) with the threefold use of the verb חפץ. Man can keep the law if he wishes. Cf. G. Maier, *Mensch*, pp.91-97; also O. Rickenbacher, *Weisheitsperikopen*, pp.146f.; M. Löhr, *Bildung*, p.51.
377 H^A and H^Bm read תבונה instead of אמונה in H^B (cf. G πίστιν). H^A is to be preferred. Cf. F. Vattioni, *Ecclesiastico*, p.77; G. Sauer, *JSHRZ* III/5 (1981) 542.
378 J. Haspecker, *Gottesfurcht*, pp.68,156f. follows S: "Es gibt den an Verstand Armen, der der Sünde entgeht, und es gibt den an Verstand Überreichen, der sündigt". But he cannot exclude the terminology of G.
379 Cf. supra, p.70.
380 Following the translation of G. Sauer, *o.c.*, p.565. O. Rickenbacher, *o.c.*, pp.112, 125 translates: "die mir gemäß handeln". G has οἱ ἐργαζόμενοι ἐν ἐμοί.
381 See the structural analysis of O. Rickenbacher, *o.c.*, pp.113-118 who follows L. Alonso-Schökel, *Proverbios y Ecclesiastico*, 1968, ad loc. See also H. Stadelmann, *Ben Sira*, pp.51-53,247f.

ύων) and "doing" (ἐργαζόμενοι) are traditional terms connected with the practice of the law[382].

(7) 24,32-33 is part of Ben Sira's testimony about himself (24, 30-34). As scribe he studies first of all the law in order to attain learning and erudition and wisdom; but his knowledge had become so vast and overflowing (v.31) that he came to share his learning and instruction (παιδεία, v.32) and his teaching (διδασκαλία, v.33) with others. His labours, i.e. his study of God's (written) revelation and of tradition, have not been for himself alone but benefited all those who seek wisdom (v.34). The parallelism of παιδεία (which belongs to the realm of wisdom) and διδασκαλία (which is the result and aim of the study of the law) suggests again a close correlation of wisdom and law. This is supported by the context: "Bei der Arbeit am Gesetz ... überkam ihn (i.e. Ben Sira) auf einmal die Weisheit in ihrer Fülle"[383]. The law appears as the vessel of wisdom. The study and practice of the law will result in wise behaviour.

(8) 33,2-3: "He is not wise who hates the law, and he is tossed about like a ship in a storm. A man of insight knows the word of the Lord, and for him the law is as reliable as the consultation of lots"[384]. Ben Sira emphasizes here that obedience to the law is entirely reliable and steady and therefore unlike ships in storms (v.2) or cartwheels and axles which are always moving (v.5)[385]. V. 2a implies *e contrario* that the wise man will love the law which certainly includes the study and practice of the law. In v.3a it is similarly stated that a "man of insight" (איש נבון) knows God's word. To be wise and steadfast corresponds with dedication to the law.

(9) 38,34c.d/39,8 belong to Ben Sira's description of the *sopher/ḥakham* (cf. § 3.5.5. and Excursus I) who studies God's revelation, the law and the prophets, as well as tradition (38,34d-39,3). The wise scholar meditates upon God's law (38,34c.d). He proclaims the "discipline of his instruction" (παιδεία διδασκαλίας) and is proud of the Israelite law (19,8). Both the person and the activity of the scribe imply the identification of law and wisdom[386].

---

382 Cf. O. Rickenbacher, *Weisheitsperikopen*, p.125.
383 M. Löhr, *Bildung*, p.46.
384 On this verse see already supra, p.50.
385 Cf. J.G. Snaith, *Ecclesiasticus*, pp.159f.
386 See generally H. Stadelmann, *Ben Sira*, pp.228f. with his remarks in the context of his discussion of 38,34c-39,8.

(10) 44,4c: "Wise thinkers in their knowledge of Scripture"[387]. Scholars agree that the term חכמי שיח refers to the scribes[388]. The fact that the wise men study and know God's revealed word implies again a close correlation of wisdom and law. This passage corresponds to 38,34c.d and 39,8.

(11) 51,15c.d: "My foot walked in uprightness; from my youth I became acquainted with her (i.e. wisdom)"[389]. In this autobiographical note which belongs to the epilogue of his book (51,13-30), Ben Sira correlates a pious life ("upright walk", אמתה דרכה, v.15c) with the acquaintance with wisdom (v.15d). Since a "walk in uprightness" is the corollary of obedience to the law this verse implies again the identification of law and wisdom. The man who keeps the law and, as a result, lives a righteous life, is being acquainted with wisdom.

(12) 51,30a.b: "Perform your works in righteousness, and he will give you your reward in his time". In his last appeal which concludes his summons to search for and to study wisdom (51,23-30), Ben Sira presents practical righteousness in life as prerequisite for the attainment of wisdom which is God's "reward" (שכרך / μισθός) for the pious. The "righteousness" of one's works implies the keeping of the law. The man who is obedient to the law will be rewarded with wisdom. Again, commitment to the law leads to wisdom. To keep the law and to be wise is, in the end, the same.

4.1.3. Secondary passages. Two passages in the main body of Sir (1,5; 19,19) and several lines in the prologue (1-3.12-14.29. 35-36) also refer to the identification of law and wisdom. These passages represent later editings of, and additions to, the Ben Sira text. (1) 1,5: "The fountain of wisdom is God's word on high, and

---

387 Cf. G. Sauer, *JSHRZ* III/5 (1981) 615 following L. Delekat, "Zum hebräischen Wörterbuch", *VT* 14 (1964) 32f. (on ספרות in Ps 71,15). See also R. Smend, *Weisheit*, p.418 who translates with "Schriftgelehrsamkeit".

388 Cf. N. Peters, Box/Oesterley, M.S. Segal, H. Duesberg, Y. Yadin; cf. J. Marböck, *Weisheit*, p.166.

389 Following generally H^Q; cf. O. Rickenbacher, *Weisheitsperikopen*, pp.197,202f.; G. Sauer, *o.c.*, p.636.

390 Only extant in a few MSS (cf. the evidence in J. Ziegler, *Sapientia*, p.128); missing in S. Generally regarded as secondary, cf. recently G. Sauer, *JSHRZ* III/5 (1981) 507.

her ways are the eternal commandments"[390]. The synonymous parallelism links "God's word" (λόγος θεοῦ) with the "eternal[391] commandments" (ἐντολαί), both referring to the Israelite law. This verse asserts that the law is the basis and source of wisdom (v. 5a) and contains the normative ("eternal") exposition of wise conduct ("ways") and demeanour (v.5b). Here the identification is most explicit and unambiguous, even more explicit than in Sir[392]. Wisdom seems to have been 'swallowed up' by the law: there is no wisdom besides the law as all wisdom arises out of the law. And to keep the commandments is identical with wise conduct.

(2) 19,19: "The knowledge (γνῶσις) of the commandments (ἐντολαί) of the Lord is life-giving instruction (παιδεία ζωῆς), and those who do what pleases him will reap from the tree of immortality"[393]. The "live-giving instruction" means practised wisdom which results in 'true life', life in its fullness. This instruction for wise conduct is identical with the knowledge of the law. He who knows the commandments knows how to behave 'wisely'. Wisdom and law are identical, wise conduct and obedicnce to the law are the same.

(3) Prol. 1-3. The grandson of Ben Sira begins his prologue to the translation of his grandfather's wisdom book by referring to the threefold division of the Scriptures, the law and the prophets and the writings[394], "for which Israel has to be praised with regard to her instruction (παιδεία) and wisdom (σοφία)" (line 3). The content of God's written revelation is designated as "instruction and wisdom". Thus Ben Sira's grandson, writing near the end of the second century, extended the identification of law and wisdom to an identification of the entire written revelation with wisdom. Anybody who seeks wisdom is referred to the Scriptures. The question whether Ben Sira's grandson is personally responsible for the identification law = wisdom cannot be answered.

---

391 On the concept of eternity in Sir see O. Rickenbacher, *Weisheitsperikopen*, pp.22-24. Often God is linked with the concept of עולם or עד: 1,2.4.9; 2,9; 16,27.28; 18,1; 36,22(!); 39,20; 42,23; 51,8. It is plausible that the commandments are called "eternal" because their author, Yahweh, is eternal.
392 This might be a further, internal, reason for regarding 1,5 as secondary!
393 This verse is extant in L and MS 672. Cf. J. Ziegler, *Sapientia*, p.213.
394 See p.53 with n.218.

(4) Prol. 12-14. The author of the prologue describes Ben Sira's motives in writing his book: he wanted to compile material which deals with "instruction and wisdom" (παιδαία καί σοφία, line 12) in order that all those who seek learning (φιλομαθεῖς) and hold on to erudition (line 13) might be in a better position to make progress with regard to the life according to the law (διά τῆς ἐννόμου βιώσεως, line 14). This implies that for Ben Sira's grandson, wise conduct and learning are identical with the "life according to the law". To be more wise is to be more obedient to the law. He who keeps the law in all areas of life is the truly wise man.

(5) Prol. 29.35-36. In lines 27-36 the grandson describes the external circumstances in which he translated Ben Sira's book. The Jews in Egypt endeavoured to increase their education and learning (παιδεῖα) considerably (line 29) and intended to "live according to the law" (ἐννόμως βιοτεύειν, lines 35-36)[395]. This description implies again the close correlation of wisdom (or "learning") and obedience to the law. The desire to gain more wisdom equals the intention to live according to the law. He who keeps the law is wise and will become increasingly wiser.

4.2. The Nature of the Identification

4.2.1. The universalistic dimension. Most scholars who attempted to explain Ben Sira's identification of law and wisdom refer to the fact that wisdom is seen as the ordering principle of the world, as the primeval order, or as the universal cosmic law, and that this universal wisdom is identified with the law which is seen as part of God's order of creation, and as ordering principle for the life of man. Wisdom and law are correlated in their common universalistic orientation[396]. We have already pointed out[397] that we must avoid making the mistake of postulating a priori the cosmic and universalistic perspective of the Israelite law. We must not confuse

---

395 G. Sauer, *JSHRZ* III/5 (1981) 507 translates lines 35-36: "die es sich vorgenommen haben, ihren Lebenswandel im Sinne des Gesetzes zu führen".
396 Cf. J.L. Koole, "Die Bibel des Ben Sira", *OTS* 14 (1965) 377. J. Marböck, *Weisheit*, pp.68f.,89-94; E. Zenger, "Späte Weisheit", 1973, pp.53-55; M. Gilbert, "L'éloge de la Sagesse", *RThL* 5 (1974) 347f.; J. Marböck, "Gesetz", *BZ* 20 (1976) 6-13. Similarly R.J. Banks, *Jesus and the Law*, p.54.
397 Cf. supra, pp.42f. See also P.S. Fiddes, *Hiddenness*, 1976, pp.317-321.

cause and effect. While it is true that legal terms are used to describe the order of creation (§3.2.) it cannot be maintained that the law per se *equals* God's order of creation and is *therefore* identified with wisdom which is manifest in the order of creation. The law in Sir is primarily the Mosaic law. The universalistic dimension of the law is not the cause but the *result* of its identification with wisdom (cf. §4.4.1.).

When תורה is linked with the order of death which God imposed upon man (41,4) and when דבר ייי and חק are related with different aspects of creation (11,17; 14,12.17; 38,22; 41,2.3; 43,5-10), this does not prove that the written Mosaic Torah is equated with a cosmic, universal ordering principle. It only proves that legal terms can be used in more than just one sense.

Thus it seems to be wrong to conclude from the contexts of 17, 11 and 24,23 that Ben Sira acknowledges the "Schöpfungshorizont ausdrücklich als der *vor* dem Gesetz stehende"[398], as the law, for Ben Sira, signifies indeed both with regard to time and space the Mosaic legislation. Ben Sira was a scribe and a priest. This naturally implies that the Mosaic law was a self-evident, given entity for him. For Ben Sira the Torah is the foundation and the starting point for all his other activities besides the study of the law. It is not wisdom which is confined and limited to the Torah, but the Torah is being 'expanded' to encompass wisdom[399]. The predominantly sapiential character of Sir is due to the purpose and the readers of the book.

We conclude, therefore, that Ben Sira did not identify wisdom and law because both realms had a universalistic dimension. This was not the case with regard to the law, the Mosaic Torah, at least not to begin with. The apparent universalistic dimension of the Torah in Sir should be regarded as the result, rather than the cause, of the identification of law and wisdom[400].

---

398 Contra J. Marböck, *a.c.*, p.10.
399 Cf. H. Stadelmann, *Ben Sira*, pp.228f., following J. Marböck, *Weisheit*, pp.86-96.
400 This is implicitly acknowledged by J. Marböck, *o.c.*, p.91 when he says that Israel's Torah "*bekommt* ... auch einen Zug in Richtung eines umfassenden Weltgesetzes, das Schöpfung und Geschichte durchwaltet" (italics by EJS). Cf. the same statement in idem, "Gesetz", *BZ* 20 (1976) 8. In his discussion, however, Marböck does not differentiate between cause and effect and, as a result, fails to see the consequences of this evidence.

4.2.2. The particularistic dimension. The particularistic dimension of both the Torah and wisdom is one of the reasons for Ben Sira's identification of law and wisdom[401]. We have seen that Ben Sira relates the law in numerous passages very closely with Yahweh[402] and his covenant(s) with his people Israel[403], with the revelatory events at Sinai[404], and even with the Israelite cultic law[405] (cf. §3.3.). On the other hand it is obvious that Ben Sira also provided wisdom with a particularistic perspective: wisdom comes from Yahweh[406], found its dwelling place in Israel[407], and is closely linked with the temple cult and the fear of the Lord (cf. §2.2.).

The ταῦτα πάντα of 24,23 focuses wisdom on the realm of the "covenant of God the Most High" and identifies it with "the law which Moses imposed upon" Israel. Wisdom, after having found its valid expression, its dwelling place, in Israel (24,8-12), found its fullness in the (Mosaic) law which Israel is to heed, to practise, and to teach.

The law and wisdom are one in that they are both God's gift to Israel. Both play a significant role in Israel's faith and history. And both are most important for the individual believer, the pious Jew, and also for the scribe, the *sopher/ḥakham*.

4.2.3. The theological dimension. The theological dimension of Ben Sira's identification of law and wisdom is evident when we look at the basis and focus of this correlation: the submission to God's will as regards the life of the nation and the life of the individual believer. This submission to God's will is the objective of both the law and wisdom and is summarized in the fear of the Lord[408].

In several passages the fear of the Lord and the obedience to

---

401 This is rightly seen by J. Marböck, *a.c.*, p.13.
402 Cf. 19,17; 23,23.27; 29,11, 38,34; 39,8; 41,8; 42,2 ;44,20; 49,4.
403 Cf. 17,11.12; 24,23; 28,7; 39,8; 42,2G; 44,20; 45,5.
404 Cf. 24,23; 45,5.
405 Cf. 28,6.7; 29,1.9.11; 35,1.2.7.
406 Cf. 1,19, 24,3 and the passages which describe wisdom as God's gift (see supra, p.21).
407 Cf. 24,8 and the references to Israel in the *laus patrum* (see supra, p.22 n.66).
408 Cf. P.S. Fiddes, *Hiddenness*, p.310 who states that wisdom and law are identified in Sir by means of the flexible concept of the fear of the Lord.

the law are described as prerequisite and source of wisdom (2,15. 16; 6,36; 15,1; 21,11). 19,20 states unequivocally that the keeping of God's law equals comprehensive wisdom which equals the fear of the Lord (cf. 19,24). The fear of the Lord can be correlated with the law (2,15.16; 19,19.20.24; cf. 1,5; 6,36) and with wisdom (1,14.16.18.20; 15,1; 19,20; 21,11). Obedience to the law and practised wisdom are both pleasing to God (2,15.16; 15,15). God rewards those who keep his commandments and those who are wise with "length of days" (cf. Sir 1,20 with Deut 4,40; 5,33; 6,2; 32,47).

Wisdom and law are one since they are both the expression of God's will for life. To keep the commandments is practised wisdom, and to be wise means to obey the law — both are proof of one's fear of the Lord and of one's desire to commit one's life to God in submitting to his will concerning all areas of life. This theological dimension leads directly to the ethical dimension of Ben Sira's identification.

4.2.4. *The ethical dimension.* The majority of passages which express or imply the correlation of wisdom and law refer to the ethical dimension of the identification[409]. Both law and wisdom aim at leading the individual and the nation to a pious and godly life, to inward and outward discipline.

Wisdom and law, both taken up by and in the fear of the Lord, lead to an upright walk in God's ways (2,15.16; 51,15; cf. prol. 12-14.29.35-36)[410]. Piety characterizes the wise man who keeps the commandments (15,1.15). Both wisdom and law aim at determining one's life (17,11; 45,5; cf. 19,19). Both enable man to keep his sinful desires under control and to avoid sin (21,11; 24,22; 51, 15). Obedience to the commandments has practical, 'wise' results: a

---

409 The ethical foundation of the identification is recognized by O. Kaiser, "Begründung", *ZThK* 55 (1958) 51-63, particularly pp.54-58, but not further elaborated.
410 The concept of life (or generally of human existence) as 'walking a (good or bad) path/walk' is an OT motif which is very prominent in the intertestamental literature. Cf. S. Aalen, *Begriffe*, 1951, p.185. Cf. Sir 5,2.9.; 8,15;12,15; 14,21;17,15; 21,10; 39,24; Tob 4,19; Bar 4,2.13; Judt 13,12; SapSal 5,6;Jub 5,13; 12,21 ;20,3; 21,22; 23,21.26; 25,15; 35,13; TJud 13,2; 23,5; 24,3; TIss 3,1-2;4,6; 5,1.8; TDan 5,5; TNaph 4,1; TAsh 5,4; ApcBar 44,3; 4Ezr 3,8; 7,79.129.133. R.T. Herford, *Pirke Aboth*, 1930, p.39 points out that the term הלכה is a technical term for "the rule of right conduct in life".

pious person will not lie but be faithful in his speech (34,8). All those who keep the commandments and act wisely will not be put to shame (24,22; 32,23; 33,2.3; 44,20). A pious, godly life is a wise life (51,30).

Both the law and wisdom are compared with light which gives orientation. According to 45,17 Aaron had received the task of "enlightening" Israel by the law ($\dot{\epsilon}\nu$ $\nu\dot{o}\mu\omega$ $\alpha\dot{v}\tau o\tilde{v}$ $\varphi\omega\tau\dot{\iota}\sigma\alpha\iota$ 'Ισραήλ [411]). And in 24,32 Ben Sira says that he will "bring instruction ($\pi\alpha\iota\delta\epsilon\dot{\iota}\alpha$) to light as dawn ($\dot{\omega}\varsigma$ $\ddot{o}\rho\vartheta\rho o\nu$ $\varphi\omega\tau\iota\tilde{\omega}$) and will make shine forth ($\dot{\epsilon}\kappa\varphi\alpha\nu\tilde{\omega}$) these things afar off". Both the law and wisdom reveal the will of God in the ethical sphere[412].

Wisdom and law are the prerequisite and basis of piety and at the same time the reward and result of piety. Practical and concrete submission to God's will which is laid down in the Torah and definitively outlined in wisdom implies and necessitates obedience to the commandments and wise conduct. Genuine commitment to God which is expressed in the fear of the Lord is the cause as well as the effect of one's obedience to the law and one's wise behaviour. Right ethical behaviour equals wise conduct and results from obedience to God's revealed law.

4.2.5. The didactic dimension. In several passages Ben Sira points out that those who desire wisdom should keep the law. Commitment to God and obedience to his commandments will unfailingly lead to wisdom (1,26; 6,36; 15,1; 51,30; cf. 1,5; 19,19; prol. 12-14.29.35-36). The scribe who is also a (wisdom) teacher studies both the Torah and wisdom material (38,34d-39,3; 44,4; cf. prol. 7-11). He also communicates both the law with the implications of its commandments and wisdom with its instruction and discipline (24,32.33; 39,8; cf. prol. 12-14.31-36).

The *sopher/ḥakham* studies and teaches both the law and the wisdom traditions, and challenges his students to mediate upon and to keep the law of God as this is the (from now on only?) sure and infallible road to wisdom.

---

411 H and S do not have a verb here. R. Smend, *Weisheit*, ad loc., suggests that the term $\vartheta\omega\tau\dot{\iota}\zeta\epsilon\iota\nu$ is based on an original להורות. Cf. Bar 4,2.
412 On the concept of light in this context see S. Aalen, *o.c.*, pp.178-192 (on Sirach, pp.184f.).

4.3. The Rationale Behind the Identification

4.3.1. Theological motives. The correlation of wisdom and law has undoubtedly an OT background which we described earlier[413].

The key passage in this context is Deut 4,6-8 where the Mosaic law is, indirectly, designated as wisdom[414]. Other important references which prepared the complete identification of wisdom and law are Jer 8,8; Mal 2,6-7 (?); Ezr 7,6.10.25, and the so-called wisdom-psalms Ps 1; 19; 119. Ben Sira, the scribe and Torah scholar, knew these passages and resumed this earlier tradition of the correlation of the two realms of law and wisdom[415]. But it has to be emphasized that it is still a decisive step to the complete identification in Sirach[416].

4.3.2. Philosophical motives. It was especially J. Marböck who maintained that it was the Stoic popular philosophy which caused Ben Sira to combine the Torah and cosmic wisdom[417]. In Stoic

---

413 Seen by J. Marböck, *Weisheit*, pp.82-85,93,95; M. Hengel, *Judentum*, p.291; M. Gilbert, "L'éloge", *RThL* 5 (1974) 346f.; J. Marböck, "Gesetz", *BZ* 20 (1976) 19; E. Jacob, "Wisdom", 1978, p.256; P.J. Nel, *Structure*, 1982, pp.92-97. P.S. Fiddes, *Hiddenness*, 1976, p.309 states that Ben Sira just makes explicit an existing tendency.

414 Cf. especially G.T. Sheppard, "Wisdom and Torah", 1978, pp.166-176. He admits that Deut 4 "does not propose the same full identification" as Sir 24,23 (p.168), but that Deut refers to the book (!) of Torah (Deut 30) which comes near to Israel (Deut 4; 30) from beyond the heavens, and is her wisdom (Deut 4,32; ibid., pp. 169f.).

415 This has been stressed recently by H. Gese, "Wisdom", *HBT* 3 (1981) 35-37. It has been pointed out that Ben Sira stands in the deuteronomistic tradition which makes it even more plausible to assume that he knew Deut 4,6-8. Cf. J. Marböck, *Weisheit*, pp.95f.

416 Cf. M. Hengel, *Judentum*, p.291.

417 Cf. J. Marböck, "Gesetz", p.20 idem, *o.c.*, pp.93f. He contradicts himself when he states that he does not want to maintain or prove that Ben Sira is here 'directly' dependent on Stoicism (ibid., p.145). Marböck follows K. Schubert, *Die Religion des nachbiblischen Judentums*, 1955, pp.16f.: "Durch die Weisheits- und Torahauffassung im Buch Jesus Sirach ist die Begegnung des palästinensischen Judentums mit der stoischen Philosophie in der 1. Hälfte des 2. Jahrhunderts v. Chr. erwiesen, denn sie entspricht im wesentlichen der stoischen Konzeption vom Weltgesetz". Besides K. Schubert and J. Marböck see also M. Hengel, *o.c.*, pp.268, 288f.,291. More cautious is J.L. Koole, "Bibel", *OTS* 16 (1965) 377 n.1: "Ob Ben Sira hier unter hellenistischen (sic) Einfluss steht, darf auf sich beruhen" (quoting Cicero, de natura deorum 2,14.37: "Ipse autem homo ortus est ad mundum contemplandum et imitandum"). Similarly also M. Löhr, *Bildung*, pp.32,48,50.

philosophy, νόμος was the cosmic law. Marböck believes that Ben Sira identified the Israelite law with cosmic wisdom which existed from the beginning in order that the Torah should acquire an ancient dignity, authority, and universality which would present it as of equal rank to the Stoic law of the cosmos.

Our results as regards Ben Sira's concept of law show that for him תורה/νόμος is not some kind of cosmic or universal law but very specifically the Mosaic law, God's written revelation. Thus, Marböck's view is deprived of its basis: Ben Sira's law does not in any way resemble the Stoic cosmic law[418].

In addition to the materialistic and monistic aspects, Stoic physics postulate a strict 'legal' dimension which is immanent in the totality of the world. This determining power is called λόγος, νοῦς (soul, reason, necessity, providence), or god (Zeus). For the Stoics the divine is identical with the living totality of the world. Stoic physics is pantheistic[419]. Thus one should note the following facts: (1) the Stoic 'law' belongs to the realm of Stoic physics and ethics, (2) the monistic and pantheistic aspect of the Stoic cosmic law contradicts everything which Ben Sira would stand for, (3) Ben Sira's grandson never translated תורה or מצוה with λόγος or νοῦς which Stoic physics uses predominantly for the postulated cosmic law, (4) Ben Sira clearly conceives of the Torah as written (!) law which contradicts the Stoics' concept of the cosmic law as the living totality of the world.

Thus, we conclude that the law in Sir has nothing in common with the Stoic cosmic law and that Ben Sira was therefore not influenced by Stoic philosophy when he identified wisdom and law.

---

418 Cf. P.J. Nel, *Structure*, 1982, p.97 who states that the identity of law and wisdom "is not necessarily postulated under pressure of external factors"; cf. also W.D. Davies, *Paul and Rabbinic Judaism*, p.169.

419 Cf. Zeno according to Diogenes Laertius 7,88 (= SVF 1,162): "ὁ νόμος ὁ κοινός, ὅσπερ ἐστὶν ὁ ὀρθὸς λόγος διὰ πάντων ἐρχόμενος, ὁ αὐτός ὤν τῷ Διί, καθηγενόνι τούτῳ τῶν ὄντων διοικήσεως ὄντι" ("the universal law, which is true reason permeating everything, is identical with Zeus, the guide of the pervading of all things".) Similarly Cicero, de re publica 3,33: "Est quidem ver lex recta ratio ... diffusa in omnes"; cf. idem, de legibus 1,6.18; 2,8. Cf. also Chrysippos, Περὶ νόμου, SVF 3,314. Cf. M. Hengel, *Judentum*, p.288; J. Marböck, *Weisheit*, p.94. On Stoic physics see M. Pohlenz, *Die Stoa: Geschichte einer geistigen Bewegung*, 1, 1948, pp.64-110; S. Sambursky, *Physics of the Stoics*, 1959; H.J. Störig, *Kleine Weltgeschichte der Philosphie*, 1, 1974, p.195; F.H. Sandbach, *The Stoics*, 1975, pp.69-94; R.B. Todd, "Monism and Immanence: The Foundations of Stoic Physics", *The Stoics*, ed. J.M. Rist, 1978, pp.137-160.

J. Marböck admits that the Torah, with regard to its content, confronts creation and man as it was given by God and as it is the expression of God's personal will, in contrast to the cosmic law of Stoicism[420]. This fact has been pointed out by H.F. Weiss[421]. Marböck does not see that if the *content* of Torah is incompatible with the Stoic 'law' because it is determined by Yahweh, the *extent* of the Torah *cannot* correspond with it either: the extent of the cosmic law of the Stoics is the cosmos = materia = Zeus. In Sir the scope of the Torah is obviously Israel, God's people! M. Hengel endeavours not to present Ben Sira simply as a Hellenizing Jew[422]. Ben Sira could 'rediscover' in Stoicism a strict urge for ethical conduct, the concept of the value of man as God's first creation, the harmony and purposefulness of the world, and other thoughts. But then Hengel quickly points out that this was simply an "orientalische Rückinterpretation" since the Stoa had grown up on Semitic ground and (therefore?!) had many things in common with the thought-world of the OT. Hengel stresses the fact that Ben Sira did not take over Stoic monism with its identification of god and cosmos. And it is obvious of course that it would have been much more natural for Ben Sira to take the concepts of the importance of ethical conduct, the value of man, the purposefulness of creation, etc., from the OT which he said he studied, than from the philosophy of the 'Gentiles'.

It has to be pointed out further that the view of those scholars who emphasize the Hellenistic influences in Sir[423] is, at least, equalised by the observations of other scholars who stress Ben Sira's commitment to the traditional Jewish faith[424]. Even if it is true that Sir contains reminiscences of Greek literature and education[425], it is obvious that these remained within narrow limits[426]. Ben Sira's grand synthesis of wisdom, law, temple, cult, and Zadokite priesthood cannot be understood on a Hellenistic or Stoic background but must be explained by Ben Sira's focus on God's revelation and God's gifts to his people.

---

420 Cf. J. Marböck, *Weisheit*, p.94.
421 Cf. H.F. Weiss, *Untersuchungen*, p.283.
422 Cf. M. Hengel, *Judentum*, p.268.
423 Besides J. Marböck see T. Middendorp, *Stellung*, 1973, passim; M. Hengel, *Judentum*, pp.265-270.
424 Cf. A.A. di Lella, "Conservative and Progressive Theology: Sirach & Wisdom", *CBQ* 28 (1966) 139-154, here 139-146. Cf. also M. Hengel's review of Middendorp's book in *JSJ* 5 (1974) 83-87. A. Momigliano, *Alien Wisdom*, 1975, pp.95f. says that he cannot see "any clear trace" that Ben Sira had read Greek books; he is convinced that Ben Sira "reaffirmed Jewish traditional faith against the temptations of Hellenism" and "repudiated Greek wisdom" (ibid.). Similarly R.J. Banks, *Jesus and the Law*, 1975, p.54 states that "Hellenistic influence is generally absent". See also the recent remarks of G. Sauer, *JSHRZ* III/5 (1981) 490-492 and of O. Kaiser, "Judentum und Hellenismus", *VuF* 27 (1982) 79-86.
425 Cf. T. Middendorp, *o.c.*, pp.7-34.
426 Cf. G. Sauer, *o.c.*, p.491; he points out that "gerade die genauere Betrachtung einiger Einzelzüge, wie etwa die Stellung zum Arzt, zeigen, daß Sir bei allen neuen Gedanken dennoch im Zentrum seines Gottesglaubens verbleibt" (ibid.).

4.3.3. Historical motives. Besides the theological background of Ben Sira's identification of wisdom and law we might also assume that this correlation was at least facilitated, if not prompted, by the historical circumstances[427]. Ben Sira is the first known representative of the *sopherim/ḥakhamim* who carried on the work of Ezra and of the *ḥasidim*. G.F. Moore believes that the identification of wisdom and Torah was a commonplace in Ben Sira's time[428] as a result of this scribal/sapiential background[429]. Although this cannot be proved it is at least very plausible that Ben Sira, as scribe and priest, studied and taught in an environment which had all the theological *Interpretamente* ready which were needed for the correlation and identification of law and wisdom.

4.4. The Consequences of the Identification

4.4.1. Immediate consequences. First of all, Ben Sira's identification had consequences for the wisdom concept. The universalistic tendency of wisdom is limited and the possibility of profane wisdom is excluded. From now on, wisdom is the exclusive gift of Yahweh to Israel[430]. Ben Sira is 'torahfying' and 'historifying' wisdom[431]. The saving history of revelation is joined to wisdom as order of creation: "On the basis of the identity of wisdom and Torah, the tradition concerned with revelation as a history of salvation was carried over into wisdom in most impressive fashion"[432]. As a result, essentially sapiential instructions are now occasionally substantiated by references to law and revelation[433].

---

427 J. Marböck, *Weisheit*, pp.83-85 is the only scholar who discusses this. He points out that Ezra the scribe played an important role in the development of an environment in which both Torah and wisdom material were studied. This was the case in the later temple schools.

428 Cf. G.F. Moore, *Judaism in the First Centuries of the Christian Era*, 1, 1927, p.265.

429 G. von Rad, *Wisdom*, p.245 explained the "total identification" of wisdom and Torah by Ben Sira's "didactic zeal". It seems that with regard to the number and importance of the passages which refer to this correlation (many occupy a key position in a pericope), this explanation is not fully adequate.

430 Cf. M. Hengel, *Judentum*, pp.252-254. J.L. Crenshaw, "Prolegomenon", 1976, p.26 speaks of a "theologization of wisdom". Cf. also M. Küchler, *Weisheitstraditionen*, 1979, p.43.

431 Cf. E. Jacob, "Wisdom", 1978, p.256.

432 H. Gese, "Wisdom", *HBT* 3 (1981) 35.

433 Cf. D. Zeller, *Mahnsprüche*, 1977, p.40, referring to Sir 3,2; 7,15.29.31; 17,14;

On the other hand, the Torah takes on sapiential perspectives: it is freed from the danger of becoming an absolute, timeless, fossilized entity[434]. The sapiential function of Torah is being underlined, i.e. her task of helping Israel (and the nations!) to cope with life and with history. As the Torah is placed into the horizon of the order of creation, i.e. of wisdom, it assumes a universalistic dimension. The Torah is now itself regarded as some kind of order of creation, as "treibende(s) Grundprinzip der Geschichte Israels" and "umfassende Ordnung für die Gemeinschaft von Gott, Kosmos und Menschheit"[435]. At the same time the identification of law and wisdom can deprive the Torah of her ties with specific contingent events of Israel's history: Israel's election was implied (!) in the presentation of the gift of the Torah in the process of creation. In this context it was only consistent "daß das Gesetz seine Rolle als Weg der Bewährung einer *vorgeordneten* Erwählung auf dem Boden der Geschichte verlor und zur Instanz der Heilsermöglichung schlechthin wurde"[436].

4.4.2. Far-reaching consequences. The far-reaching consequences of Ben Sira's identification of wisdom and law will be only summarized here. It will become evident later that Ben Sira's identification influenced Baruch[437], Palestinian aggadah and the Alexandrian philosophy of religion[438], rabbinic theology with its 'Torah theology' which considers the Torah to be a cosmological principle in the manner of wisdom[439], rabbinic halakhah[440], and finally the development of christology and Christian ethics[441].

19,17; 23,23; 28,6-7; 29,1.9.11G; 32,7; 34,15; 35,23-24; 41,4.
434 Cf. E. Zenger, "Späte Weisheit", 1973, p.50, contra H.H. Schmid, *Wesen*, p.195 who stated that wisdom and law are "eins auch in ihrer Erstarrung".
435 E. Zenger, *a.c.*, pp.54f. Cf. also A. Nissen, "Tora und Geschichte im Spätjudentum", *NovTest* 9 (1967) 250-258; M. Küchler, *Weisheitstraditionen*, pp.41f.
436 K. Müller, "Geschichte, Heilsgeschichte und Gesetz", *Literatur und Geschichte des Frühjudentums*, ed. J. Maier, 1973, p.102.
437 Cf. M. Hengel, *Judentum*, pp.307f.
438 Cf. M. Hengel, *Judentum*, p.292.
439 Cf. E. Zenger, "Späte Weisheit", p.53; M. Hengel, *o.c.*, pp.309-318; H.F. Weiss, *Untersuchungen*, pp.283-304.
440 Cf. P. Sigal, *Emergence*, I/1, 1980, p.229 who calls Ben Sira a "forecaster of the rabbinic halakhah". Cf. also H. Stadelmann, *Ben Sira*, p.227.
441 Cf. M. Hengel, *o.c.*, p.292.

4.5. Conclusion

We have examined Ben Sira's significant and portentous identification of law and wisdom. The fact that this identification is referred to in 19 passages altogether[442] and often occurs at key positions in the different pericopes, shows how important this theologoumenon is for Ben Sira[443].

Ben Sira's identification of law and wisdom is characterized by four dimensions: a particularistic, a theological, an ethical, and a didactic dimension. The universalistic dimension of the Torah was recognized as being one of the results of the identification rather than its basis. The particularistic perspective which lies at the foundation of the identification implies that both the law and wisdom are regarded by Ben Sira as possessions of Israel: they were both given by God to his people, they both have an important and lasting function in Israel's faith and history, and they are both of utmost importance for the pious.

The theological foundation of the identification is summarized by the concept of the fear of the Lord which is the goal of both wisdom and law: God's will for the nation and for the individual is embodied in both law and wisdom.

The ethical dimension of the identification is determined by the fact that both law and wisdom are the basis and prerequisite, the content and realm, the reward and the result of practical and personal piety at the same time. Right ethical conduct is prescribed and described in the law and outlined and concretized in wisdom.

The didactic foundation of the identification is personified in the scribe and wisdom teacher who studies and teaches both law and wisdom and who challenges his students to keep the commandments and to be wise.

Theological and historical motives prompted Ben Sira to iden-

---

442 Besides 5 secondary passages, including the prologue.
443 I cannot agree with M. Black when he says that "the correlation of Torah with wisdom is certainly significant but complete identification is doubtful except in some probably secondary traditions attributed to Ben Sira" (private communication). Both the explicit and the implicit exegetical evidence seems to support our conclusions in an overhelming manner. It is impossible to attribute *all* passages which express the identification law = wisdom to secondary traditions. The complete identification of law and wisdom by Ben Sira is also recognized and acknowledged, though not discussed extensively, by the vast majority of scholars.

tify the two realms of law and wisdom. The identification has an indirect background in deuteronomistic theology and in the wisdom-psalms of the OT. And it was facilitated by the traditions which came together in the person of the scribe who combines the theological emphases of the *ḥasidim, ḥakhamin,* and *sopherim*. Concepts of Stoic philosophy were excluded as motives behind Ben Sira's identification.

The consequences of the identification of law and wisdom were immediate and far-reaching: the universalistic tendency of wisdom was limited, profane wisdom was excluded, and the law acquired a universalistic dimension as comprehensive order for the relationship between God, creation, and man. Both law and wisdom possess a double character: both realms have a cosmological and a salvation-historical aspect[444]. The identification, further, influenced the inter-testamental literature as well as the development of rabbinic and Christian thought.

> As regards the term 'identification', we want to make a few observations on what is meant by identity, as a concept of logic, in this context[445]. If identity is defined as a relation of the terms x and y (or law and wisdom) one can say that x and y are the *same* term when *every* assertion which is true of x is also true of y, and the x and y are not the same if there is at least one assertion which is true of the one but false of the other. Similarly, if the identity is defined as a relation of classes x and y (or 'law' consisting of commandments, and 'wisdom' consisting of the sapiential tradition and theology), class x is identical with class y when, and only when, every member of x is a member of y and vice versa. Identity is a relation which is symmetrical (it is always true that if x is the same as y, y is the same as x), transitive (it is always true that if x is the same as y and y the same as z, x is the same as z), and self-relative (the same term which is antecedent in the relation may always be sequent). The Aristotelian formulation of the law of identity is "presence of the same form in the same matter". One can say that identity in its strictest logical sense can subsist only between a term and itself.
>
> However, the assertion of identity does not exclude difference or diversity: the point of identity may lie entirely in the formal, or in the material, aspect of the complex or its formal element may change without affecting the other element. Thus, there appears to be always a certain degree of arbitrariness involved in deciding how far and to what degree the formal, or the material, constituents can be modified without nullifying the relation of the identity. In the context of our discussion of the identification of wisdom and law, the term 'identify' has to be understood not in the sense of 'determine the identity of' but rather in the sense of 'make identical, or one, with', 'to treat as the same'; 'to associate inseparably'.

---

444 This was recognized by H.F. Weiss, *Untersuchungen*, p.197.
445 Cf. A.E. Taylor, Art, "Identity", *Encyclopaedia of Religion and Ethics*, vol. 7, 1940, pp.95-99; G. Schischkoff, *Philosophisches Wörterbuch*, [19]1974, p.287 for the following observations.

Conclusion

When one attempts to apply these definitions and specifications of (Aristotelian) logic to the concepts and areas of Jewish law and wisdom, one has to notice that this is hardly, if at all, possible. The following reasons explain this difficulty: (1) Neither law nor wisdom are clearly and unambiguously defined or definable terms, concepts, or 'classes'; (2) neither the OT writers nor the Jewish authors of later times discussed law or wisdom according to or in terms of this sort of logic; (3) not even the authors of EpArist, SapSal, 4Macc, or AntBibl who were presumably aware of Greek (Aristotelian) logic treated the concept of law or the concept of wisdom or the correlation of the two concepts systematically or cogently in terms of logic; (4) the notion of identity is expressed in Hebrew (and hence often in LXX Greek!) by nominal sentences (without the copula 'is') or by correlation in a *parallelismus membrorum* which makes it difficult to grasp the systematism of the 'logic' involved. It is obvious that if we tried to present Ben Sira's 'identification' of law and wisdom in the terms mentioned above, the 'identification' would disappear: it is certainly not possible to say that *every* assertion which is true of law is also true of wisdom, or that *every* constituent which makes up 'law' is always also a constituent of 'wisdom'. For this reason we use, instead of the term 'identification', also the term 'correlation' in the sense of a mutual relation of law and wisdom implying an intimate or, after Ben Sira, even a necessary connection.

When we say that Ben Sira identified or correlated law and wisdom, we assert an identity in diversity. However, it is difficult to know whether Ben Sira intended a formal or a material identity or a mixture of both possibilities with the stress on one or on the other. It seems that the latter is more probable, i.e. that Ben Sira identified law and wisdom both as regards the formal and the material aspect. The formal aspect is related to the revelation of God in the history of his people, to the fear of the Lord as goal of God's will for his people, and to the person and function of the scribe as Torah scholar and wisdom teacher. The material aspect is linked with the ethical dimension: both the law and wisdom are the basis, the prerequisite, the realm, and the result of practical God-approved piety. The cosmological dimension which treats God's wise orders of creation as identical with God's law is also (more potentially?!) connected with the material aspect. It would seem to be arbitrary to decide whether the formal or the material aspect of the established identity of law and wisdom is primary or more important.

Our investigation of the subsequent reception and use of Ben Sira's identification of law and wisdom concentrates, after having established the respective notions of law and wisdom in the various documents, on those pericopes which express this identification explicitly. Implicit aspects of the identification with respect to the formal and theological evidence are only occasionally referred to.

We omit Philo from our investigation despite the fact that he has been called the heir of the Jewish wisdom tradition since he shares a common context of meaning and outlook, also as regards wisdom, with SapSal[446]. Philo does link *sophia* and *nomos* (cf. Post 18; Decal 1; SpecLeg 3,6; Som 2, 252). But he does not seem to equate wisdom and Torah explicitly (cf. Virt 62-65) even though there is an implicit relationship, as wisdom is related with, and in fact totally subordinate to, the less personal *logos* (cf. Fug 97.108-109; Som 2,242.245) which is identified with the Mosaic law (cf. Migr 130)[447]. It has to be noted that in Philo the relationship between wisdom and law is "modified in relation to the larger concept of the λόγος and redefined by the methodology and presumptions of allegorical exegesis"[448]. Philo is more concerned with *logos* than with *sophia* or the *cosmos*[449]. For this reason we can leave Philo aside.

---

446 Cf. K.G. Sandelin, *Die Auseinandersetzung mit der Weisheit in 1. Korinther 15*, 1976, p.8 referring to W.L. Knox, H.A. Wolfson, E. Brandenburger, and B.L. Mack.
447 Cf. J.D.G. Dunn, *Christology*, 1980, p.171 with further references.
448 J.A. Davis, *Wisdom and Spirit*, 1982, p.55.
449 On Philo's concept of *logos* see H. Kleinknecht, in *ThWNT* 4 (1942) 86-88; H.F. Weiss, *Untersuchungen*, 1966, pp.248-282; G.D. Farandos, *Kosmos und Logos nach Philon von Alexandria*, Elementa 4, 1976, pp.231-275; J.D.G. Dunn, *Christology*, 1980, pp.220-228.

Chapter Two

Wisdom and Law in the Intertestamental Literature

Ben Sira stands, chronologically speaking, at the beginning of the literary productivity of the intertestamental period[1]. The literature[2] of the 250 years between 180 B.C. and A.D. 70 is characterized by an astonishingly vast array of literary forms[3]. Contemporary research rightly tends more and more in the direction of

---

1 Only EpJer, Ps(syr), and Tob are to be dated earlier. On EpJer see L. Rost, *Einleitung*, pp.53f.; O. Eissfeldt, *Einleitung*, pp.805f.; G.W.E. Nickelsburg, *Literature*, pp.35-38. On Ps(syr) see J.H. Charlesworth, *Pseudepigrapha*, 1976, pp.202-209; A.S. van der Woude, "Die fünf syrischen Psalmen", *JSHRZ* IV/1 (1974) 29-74. On Tob see L. Rost, *o.c.*, pp.44-47; O. Eissfeldt, *o.c.*, pp.790-793; G.W.E. Nickelsburg, *o.c.*, pp.30-35.
2 See generally the introductions of A.M. Denis (1970), L. Rost (1971), O. Eissfeldt ([4]1976), J.H. Charlesworth (1976), and G.W.E. Nickelsburg (1981). Cf. also J.H. Charlesworth, "A History of Pseudepigrapha Research: The Re-emerging Importance of the Pseudepigrapha", *ANRW* II/19,1 (1979) 54-88.
3 Cf. P. Weimar, "Formen frühjüdischer Literatur: Eine Skizze", *Literatur und Religion des Frühjudentums*, ed. J. Maier, 1973, pp.123-162. With regard to the tendency towards *anonymity* or *pseudonymity* see J.A. Sint, *Pseudonymität im Altertum*, 1960; K. Aland, "Das Problem der Anonymität und Pseudonymität in der christlichen Literatur der ersten beiden Jahrhunderte", *Studien zur Überlieferung des Neuen Testaments und seines Textes*, 1967, pp.23-34; W. Speyer, *Die literarische Fälschung im heidnischen und christlichen Altertum: Ein Versuch ihrer Deutung*, Handbuch der Altertumswissenschaft I/2, 1971; M. Smith, "Pseudepigraphy in the Israelite Literary Tradition", *Pseudepigrapha*, 1, ed. K. von Fritz, 1972, pp.189-215; M. Hengel, "Anonymität, Pseudepigraphie und 'Literarische Fälschung' in der jüdisch-hellenistischen Literatur", *Pseudepigrapha*, 1, pp.229-308; B.M. Metzger, "Literary Forgeries and Canonical Pseudepigrapha", *JBL* 91 (1972) 3-24; F. Dexinger, *Henochs Zehnwochenapokalypse und offene Probleme der Apokalyptikforschung*, SPB 29, 1977, pp.60-64; I. Gruenwald, "Jewish Apocalyptic Literature", *ANRW* II/19,1 (1979) 97-102; C. Münchow, *Ethik und Eschatologie: Ein Beitrag zum Verständnis der frühjüdischen Apokalyptik*, 1981, pp.123f.; C. Rowland, *The Open Heaven: A Study of Apocalyptic in Judaism and Early Christianity*, 1982, pp.61-70.

treating early Jewish literature as "eigenständige Zeugnisse einer wichtigen Epoche der jüdischen Geschichte"[4]. The apocalyptic tradition stands out as of prime significance[5]. We will deal with 9 writings of this literature, excluding for the time being the Qumran documents, which refer to Ben Sira's identification of law and wisdom. Since no adequate, comprehensive studies have been written on either the concept of law or on the concept of wisdom in early Jewish literature[6], much groundwork has to be done again.

The question of the unity or the compilation of the different writings can be left out of consideration most of the time since the authors and/or compilers obviously did not discover conflicting concepts of law or of wisdom in the traditions, fragments, or units which they incorporated into their books. In order to avoid the levelling of the texts[7], we will describe the different purposes and contexts of the relevant texts. This makes a succinct treatment of introductory questions necessary.

Intensive analysis of individual passages will prove to be neces-

---

4 G. Mayer, "Zur jüdisch-hellenistischen Literatur", *ThR* 45 (1980) 244.
5 On apocalyptic see recently E. Janssen, *Gottesvolk*, 1971, pp.49-100; J. Barr, "Jewish Apocalyptic in Recent Scholarly Study", *BJRL* 58 (1975) 9-35; P.D. Hanson, *The Dawn of Apocalyptic: The Historical and Sociological Roots of Jewish Apocalyptic Eschatology*, 1975; U. Luck, "Das Weltverständnis in der jüdischen Apokalyptik", *ZthK* 73 (1976) 283-305; J. Carmignac, "Qu'est-ce que l'apocalyptique?", *RQ* 37 (1979) 3-33; F. Dexinger, *Offene Probleme*, 1977, pp.3-94; I. Gruenwald, "Jewish Apocalyptic Literature", *ANRW* II/19,1 (1979) 89-118; G.W.E. Nickelsburg, *Literature*, passim; C. Münchow, *Ethik*, 1981, passim; O.H. Steck, "Überlegungen zur Eigenart der spätisraelitischen Apokalyptik", *Die Botschaft und die Boten*, FS H.W. Wolff, 1981, pp.301-315; K. Koch, et al., eds., *Apokalyptik*, Wege der Forschung 365, 1982; C. Rowland, *Open Heaven*, 1982, passim. It should be noted that we have still no unanimous definition of apocalyptic (cf. C. Münchow, *o.c.*, 1981, p.11).
6 With regard to the concept of law see A. Nissen, "Tora und Geschichte im Spätjudentum", *NovTest* 9 (1967) 241-277, here 260-269; M. Limbeck, *Die Ordnung des Heils: Untersuchungen zum Gesetzesverständnis des Frühjudentums*, 1971 (not treating all documents); R.J. Banks, *Jesus and the Law*, 1975, pp.29-32,50-55,67-70. With regard to the concept of wisdom see M. Küchler, *Frühjüdische Weisheitstraditionen*, 1979 (focusing on the exegetes, historians, Phocylides, Achiqar, TestXIIPatr). These studies are all selective with regard to the material discussed and do not go into great exegetical detail either.
7 As was done in the study of D. Rössler, *Gesetz und Geschichte: Untersuchungen zur Theologie der jüdischen Apokalyptik und der pharisäischen Orthodoxie*, WMANT 3, 1960. For a critique of Rössler's method and position see A. Nissen, "Tora", *NovTest* 9 (1967) 241-277; W. Harnisch, *Verhängnis und Verheißung der Geschichte*, FRLANT 29, 1969, pp.11f., 152f. with n.2.

sary in order to show the particular emphasis of the concepts of wisdom and law within the particular material and conceptual contexts.

We divide the Jewish literature of the intertestamental period into earlier writings from Palestine (§5), earlier writings from Alexandria (§6), and later writings which were composed around A.D. 70 (§7).

§5 Earlier Jewish Writings from Palestine

5.1. Baruch

The pseudepigraphal book of Baruch[8], extant only in Greek[9] but at least partially based on a Hebrew original[10], dates back to the second century[11]. The wisdom poem (3,9-4,4) is embedded between a prose section with a prayer (1,15-3,8) and a Zion poem (4,5-5,9). These sections are bound together by the common theme of exile and return, stressing the notion that the law is the quintessence of all wisdom and God's gift to Israel[12].

---

8 See generally J.J. Battistone, *An Examination of the Literary and Theological Background of the Wisdom Passage in Baruch*, Ph.D. Diss. Duke University, 1968, particularly pp.2-100; L. Rost, *Einleitung*, pp.51-53; A.H.J. Gunneweg, "Das Buch Baruch", *JSHRZ* III/2 (1975) 168-170; O. Eissfeldt, *Einleitung*, pp.802-805; G.W.E. Nickelsburg, *Literature*, pp.109-113.

9 Cf. J. Ziegler, "Baruch", *Septuaginta Vetus Testamentum Graecum*, vol.15, 1976, pp.450-467; E. Tov, *The Book of Baruch*, SBLTT, 1975. We used the translation by O.C. Whitehouse, "The Book of Baruch", *APOT* 1 (1913) 582-595, and by A.H.J. Gunneweg, o.c., pp.171-180.

10 Cf. J.K. Zink, *Use of the Old Testament*, 1963, p.148; L. Rost, o.c., p.51; A.H.J. Gunneweg, o.c., p.170; O. Eissfeldt, o.c., p.803; G.T. Sheppard, *Wisdom*, 1980, p.84 with n.1.

11 G.W.E. Nickelsburg, *Literature*, p.113 points out that the attempts to date Bar by comparing Bar 1,15-3,8 with Dan 9 and PsSal 11 "fall short of certainty", and maintains that the style of Greek indicates 116 B.C. as *terminus ante quem*, with 164 B.C. being a probable date of composition or compilation. See also C.A. Moore, "Toward the Dating of the Book of Baruch", *CBQ* 36 (1974) 312-320 who maintains that 1,15-2,19 and 4,5-5,4 were composed some time during the 4th till 2nd centuries B.C.

12 Cf. L. Rost, *Einleitung*, p.53; G.W.E. Nickelsburg, o.c., p.109; M. Küchler, *Weisheitstraditionen*, pp.39f. Cf. also O.H. Steck, *Israel und das gewaltsame Geschick*

5.1.1. The concept of wisdom. The wisdom terminology in Bar includes the terms σοφία (3,12.23), φρόνησις (3,9.14.29), σύνεσις (3,14.23.32), and ἐπιστήμη (3,20.27.36) which are essentially used as equivalents.

The wisdom pericope[13] begins with the call: "Hear, O Israel, the commandments of life; give ear to understand wisdom" (3,9). The reality of the exile is related to Israel's leaving the "fountain of wisdom" (3,12). The following verses deal with the question of the locus of wisdom. First, various classes of people are described who have not found wisdom (3,16-28). Man is not capable of discerning the way to wisdom (3,29-31). Only God found the way to wisdom (3,32-36), and he has given it to Israel, his people (3, 37-38). This wisdom is embodied in the Torah (4,1-4).

Wisdom and creation are closely related[14]. In 3,24-25 the universe is pictured as "house of God" and "place of his possession". In 3,32c-34 God the Creator is described as having "found out" (ἐξ εὗρεν) the way to wisdom with his own "understanding" (σύνεσις)[15]. God's wisdom and power are emphasized in connection with his activity as Creator (3,32-34) and with the idea of his incomparability (3,35). Wisdom seems to be seen as being universal or cosmic: man is not able to find her and God the Creator is described as possessing wisdom and as knowing the way to wisdom[16]. In contrast to Sir, wisdom is not related to the *order* of creation. In 3,38 the universal presence of wisdom is also stressed[17].

The personification of wisdom in 3,9-4,4 is not as clear as in Sir

---

der Propheten, WMANT 23, 1967, pp.128-133 who stresses the unity of 1,15-5,9.

13 For a recent detailed exegesis of this passage, with special regard for the OT evidence and background, see G.T. Sheppard, *Wisdom*, 1980, pp.85-99. Cf. also P.E. Bonnard, *Sagesse en personne*, 1966, pp.81-88.
14 Cf. J.J. Battistone, *Wisdom Passage*, pp.148-177.
15 The same concept of God as the source of wisdom may be seen in 3,12 where Israel is said to have forsaken the "fountain of wisdom" (πηγὴ τῆς σοφίας). Cf. J.J. Battistone, *o.c.*, pp.180f.; G.T. Sheppard, *Wisdom*, pp.94f.
16 Cf. J.J. Battistone, *o.c.*, pp.149-151. The statement that in Bar wisdom is a "cosmic principle by which the universe is regulated" (ibid., p.177) is not warranted by the text, however.
17 Cf. M. Küchler, *Weisheitstraditionen*, p.39. Some commentators regard 3,38 as a later Christian gloss, even though it is well attested in Greek MSS; cf. G.T. Sheppard, *o.c.*, p.97 n.19.

24: "This poem is *about* her rather than *by* her"[18]. Wisdom is portrayed as the object of man's search rather than as a 'person' who searches the universe herself. The term συνεστράφη in 3,38 is the only example of wisdom being the subject of a verb of action.

The relationship between wisdom and salvation-history becomes obvious in 3,37-4,4 where it is stated that wisdom is God's gift to Israel, being embodied in the Torah. The fruit of wisdom which is "peace" (3,13.14), "length of days" (3,14), "life" (3,14; cf. 3,28), and "light of the eyes" (3,14) also stresses the connection between wisdom and the realm of Israel's faith[19].

> The correlation of wisdom and salvation history in Bar cannot be established, in contrast to Sir, on the basis of the origin of wisdom from Yahweh, the God of Israel's faith and history: the term κύριος is frequently used in 1,5-3,8 (41 times), but never in 3,9-5,9 where θεός is used. Further, Bar does not refer to any connection of wisdom with Israel's history (except the statement that the exile is a result of Israel's forsaking of wisdom) or cult, nor does he relate it to the fear of the Lord (which he mentions only in 3,7; 5,4[20]).

With regard to the background of 3,29-31 it has been pointed out that "in the body of Baruch's prose about wisdom Deuteronomy 30 is paraphrased"[21].

5.1.2. *The law and the commandments*. The terms for law used in Bar are νόμος (2,2.28; 4,1.12), ἐντολαί (3,9; 4,13), and πρόσταγα (1,18; 2,10; 4,1).

The law is never depicted as a universal or cosmic order but is closely related with Israel's history. The basis of the law is intimately linked with God's convenant[22] with Israel (1,18-20; 2,10-12.27-35). The law goes back to Moses who was commanded by

---

18 G.W.E. Nickelsburg, *Literature*, p.112. Contra J.J. Battistone, *o.c.*, pp.168-177 who maintains that in Bar, wisdom exists as an independent entity being "something more than a poetic personification of an abstract quality" (p.169). But Battistone admits that in Bar, wisdom "does not assume the personal qualities of the figure in Proverbs or Sirach" (p.177).
19 G.T. Sheppard, *Wisdom*, p.97 states with regard to 3,37-4,1 that the author in a typological application of passages like Deut 33,10; Ps 78,5; 147,19 "assesses Israel's election in terms of wisdom".
20 Contra M. Küchler, *Weisheitstraditionen*, p.39 who says that Bar never mentions the fear of the Lord.
21 Cf. G.T. Sheppard, "Wisdom and Torah", 1978, p.171 (cf. ibid., pp.172f. for a discussion of this relationship). See also his discussion of this pericope in idem, *Wisdom*, pp.90-93,101.
22 Cf. R.J. Banks, *Jesus and the Law*, pp.30f.

God to write the law (2,2-28). The law is Yahweh's law (note the genitive constructions in 1,18; 2,10; 4,1.13). Israel has to suffer because she had forsaken God's commandments (1,17-22; 2,1-7. 20-26.28-30; 3,2-4.8-13; 4,12-13). Bar also stresses the eternal validity of the law (4,1).

The function of the law consists primarily in being the norm of moral and social behaviour. This is apparent in the verses which describe the reasons for Israel's suffering in the exile: she has not obeyed God's commandments but abandoned the norm of her God. In this sense Bar mentions the "ways of God's commandments" (ὁδοῖς ἐντολῶν θεοῦ) which are paralleled by the "paths of discipline" (τρίβους παιδείας) in his (i.e. God's) righteousness" (4,13).

As to the motives of obedience to the law, it is obvious that the avoidance of sin stands in the centre of interest. Obedience to the law results in a pious life which ensures God's favour and salvation. The motive of the will of God is naturally implied.

5.1.3. The identification of law and wisdom. The identification of law with wisdom is "one of the main points of emphasis of the wisdom passage in 3,9-4,4"[23]. It is carried through in the introduction (3,9-14) and conclusion (4,1-4), and is implied in 3,29-31 which paraphrases Deut 30. With regard to this identification Bar is probably dependent on Sir 24[24].

In 3,9 the "commandments of life" (ἐντολαὶ ζωῆς) are parallel to "understanding" (φρόνησις). These terms are identical: Israel is called upon to listen to both. 3,10-13 deals with the problem of the exile: Israel has forsaken the "fountain of wisdom" (v.12) and refused to walk in the "way of God" (v.13). In order to obtain salvation, Israel is to pursue wisdom so that she may receive life and dwell in peace (v.14). The term "fountain of wisdom" in v.12 presents either God or the Torah as source of wisdom[25]. It is likely that the latter meaning is implied since the term "ways of God"

---

23 J.J. Battistone, *Wisdom Passage*, p.112. Cf. M. Küchler, *Weisheitstraditionen*, pp.39f.; G.T. Sheppard, *Wisdom*, p.84.
24 Cf. M. Hengel, *Judentum*, p.307; M. Küchler, *o.c.*, p.39; see also J.J. Battistone, *o.c.*, p.175; G.W.E. Nickelsburg, *Literature*, p.112; J.L. Crenshaw, *Old Testament Wisdom*, pp.187f.
25 Cf. J.J. Battistone, *Wisdom Passage*, pp.180f.

which follows immediately in v.13 seems to be referring to the Torah (cf. 4,13).

In 4,1-4 the phrase αὕτη ἡ βίβλος serves as formula of identification: the wisdom which God has given to Israel *is* the "book of the commandments of God" (βίβλος τῶν προσταγμάτων τοῦ θεοῦ) and the "law" (νόμος) which endures forever (v.1). In the Torah Israel has access to divine wisdom[26]. The Torah secures Israel's safety and salvation (v.2). It contains God's revealed will to Israel. The Torah is a light illuminating her path (v.3): "Das Gesetz (die Weisheit) gibt die rechte Orientierung für das Leben"[27]. The Torah is a source which shows the things which are pleasing to God, and this knowledge constitutes the source of Israel's happiness. Thus, the Torah is the source of the "glory" (δόξα) of Israel (4,4).

The identification of wisdom and law in Bar lacks any universalistic dimension since the law is not conceived of as a cosmological entity. As in Sir the *particularistic dimension* of the identification is obvious: it is only in Israel and in the Mosaic revelation that law and wisdom are one (4,1-4). The theological dimension is more implicit. The *ethical dimension* is again most prominent: both wisdom (3,20-21.23.27.31) and the law (1,18; 2,10; 4,13) lead to and imply an upright "walk" in God's "ways" (3,13; 4,2). Both wisdom and the law result in the reward of "life" (3,9.14). The consequences of forsaking wisdom and law are the same: God's judgment and the exile (cf. 3,9-14 with 1,17-22; 2,1-7.20-26.28-30; 3,2-4.8-13; 4,12-13).

5.1.4. Summary. The wisdom concept in Bar is characterized by the relationship of wisdom with God's creation and with Israel's faith. The law is always the Mosaic law which is mainly presented as norm for Israel's life and conduct. The identification of the Mosaic law with inscrutable wisdom is the primary *Interpretament* of the wisdom pericope. Law and wisdom are one in the Mosaic Torah which God gave to Israel and which contains the instruction necessary to live a life which is pleasing to God.

---

26 Cf. J.J. Battistone, *o.c.*, p.182.
27 S. Aalen, *Begriffe*, p.185 ad loc.

5.2. The Ethiopic Book of Enoch

The pseudepigraphal apocalypse En(eth)[28] is entirely extant only in Ethiopic[29] with Aramaic[30], Syriac[31], and Greek[32] fragments existing as well. Scholars agree that Aramaic (or Hebrew) was the original language of the greater part of the work[33]. En(eth) is a composite writing[34]. It can be divided into introduction (1-5), the Book of the Watchers (6-36: 6-16 angelology, 17-19/20-36 Enoch's journeys)[35], the Similitudes or Parables (37-71:38-44/ 45-57/58-69), the Astronomical Book (72-82), the Dream Visions or *Tiersymbol-Apokalypse* (83-90), the Admonitions of Enoch (91-105, incorporating the Apocalypse of Weeks in 93,1-14; 91,12-17), and an Addendum (106-108).

The dating of En(eth) has been a notorious problem, especially as regards the Similitudes. Most specialists concur that the earliest

---

28 See generally A.M. Denis, *Introduction aux pseudépigraphes grecs*, 1970, pp.15-30; O. Rost, *Einleitung*, pp.101-106; O. Eissfeldt, *Einleitung*, pp.836-843; J.H. Charlesworth, *Pseudepigrapha*, pp.98-103; G.W.E. Nickelsburg, *Literature*, pp. 47-55,90-94,145-151,214-223. See also R.A. Coughenour, *Enoch and Wisdom*, 1972, pp.1-9,188-212; D.W. Suter, *Tradition and Composition in the Parables of Enoch*, 1979, pp.11-14,23-32.

29 The most recent edition is the one by M.A. Knibb, *The Ethiopic Book of Enoch: A New Edition in the Light of the Aramaic Dead Sea Fragments*, 1, 1978, which is, however, not a critical edition but only the edition of one MS.

30 Edited by J.T. Milik, *The Books of Enoch: Aramaic Fragments of Qumrân Cave 4*, 1976.

31 Published by S.P. Brock, "A Fragment of Enoch in Syriac", *NTS* 19 (1968) 626-631.

32 Re-edited by M. Black, *Apocalypsis Henochi Graece*, PVTG 3, 1970.

33 We use the translation of R.H. Charles, "1 Enoch", *APOT* 2 (1913) 188-281 (substituting 'you' for 'thou', etc.) which uses a much more reliable text than the translation of M.A. Knibb, *Ethiopic Book of Enoch*, 2, 1978, pp.55-251. The edition of M. Black, *The Book of Enoch or II Enoch: A New English Edition with Commentary and Textual Notes*, to be published in 1984 (by Brill, Leiden), will contain an up-date of R.H. Charles' translation (private communication from Prof. M. Black). The translation of E. Rau in *JSHRZ* V has not appeared yet. – With regard to the assumption of an Aramaic original see M.A. Denis, *Introduction*, p.27; M.A. Kbibb, *o.c.*, 2, pp.37-46; G.W.E. Nickelsburg, "Enoch 97-104: A Study of the Greek and Ethiopic Texts", *Armenian and Biblical Studies*, ed. M.E. Stone, 1976, p.92.

34 With regard to the composite nature of En(eth) see A.M. Denis, *o.c.*, pp.15-17; L. Rost, *Einleitung*, pp.103-105; O. Eissfeldt, *Einleitung*, pp.837-839; R.A. Coughenour, *Enoch and Wisdom*, p.2; F. Dexinger, *Offene Probleme*, 1977, pp.17f.

35 See recently J.J. Collins, "The Apocalyptic Technique: Setting and Function in the Book of the Watchers", *CBQ* 44 (1982) 91-111.

portions date back at least to the first half of the second century B.C. (ch. 72-82; 6-36; 83-90)[36]. The Book of Noah which has been incorporated in different parts (6-11; 39,1-2; 54,7-55,2; 60; 65,1-69,25; 106-107) and the Apocalypse of Weeks (93,1-14; 91,12-17) are ascribed to roughly the same period[37]. The Admonitions (91-105) are usually dated to the second half of the second century B.C.[38]. The redactional additions in ch. 1-5; 108 are assigned to the first century B.C.[39] The date of the Similitudes has been much disputed. J.T. Milik went so far as to give A.D. 270 as date of composition of the Parables[40]. This is, however, extremely speculative. The majority of scholars date ch. 37-71 to the first century B.C.[41] or to the middle of the first century A.D.[42].

Thus, the Book of Enoch was compiled, essentially, during the second and first century B.C. and was probably written in Palestine (Jerusalem)[43]. There are close similarities with Qumran theology, but also differences[44] which exclude the assumption of

---

36 Cf. A.M. Denis, o.c., pp.26f.; M. Hengel, Judentum, p.320; M.E. Stone, "The Books of Enoch and Judaism in the Third Century B.C.E.", CBQ 40 (1978) 484, 491; G.W.E. Nickelsburg, Literature, pp.47f.,93. J.T. Milik, o.c., pp.7-28,41-47 gives the following dates: ch. 72-78: the oldest part (p.8); ch.6-36: middle of the 3rd century B.C. (p.27); ch. 83-90: 164 B.C. (p.44). Cf. also R.T. Beckwith, "The Earliest Enoch Literature and its Calendar: Marks of their Origin, Date and Motivation", RQ 10 (1981) 365-403, here pp.365-372; idem, "The Pre-History and Relationships of the Pharisees, Sadducees, and Essenes", RQ 11 (1982) 3-6; C. Rowland, Open Heaven, p.266.
37 Cf. L. Rost, Einleitung, pp.103f.
38 Cf. G.W.E. Nickelsburg, Literature, p.149 who states that a date early in the second century is also possible (ibid., pp.149f.). J.T. Milik, Books of Enoch, pp.47-57 gives 100 B.C. as date.
39 Cf. L. Rost, o.c., p.105; R.A. Coughenour, Enoch and Wisdom, p.202.
40 Cf. J.T. Milik, "Problèmes de la littérature hénochique à la lumière des fragments araméens de Qumrân", HThR 64 (1971) 333-378; idem, o.c., pp.89-98.
41 Cf. O. Eissfeldt, Einleitung, p.839; L. Rost, o.c., p.104; M. Hengel, Judentum, p.321 n.444; M.E. Stone, "Books", CBQ 40 (1978) 492; G.W.E. Nickelsburg, o.c., pp.221-223 ("produced around the turn of the era", p.223).
42 Cf. M.A. Knibb, "The Date of the Parables of Enoch: A Critical Review", NTS 25 (1979) 345-359 (probably written after A.D.66-73); C.L. Mearns, "Dating the Similitudes of Enoch", NTS 25 (1979) 360-369 (written in the late 40's A.D.); D.W. Suter, Tradition, 1979, pp.23-32 (probably in the middle of the 1st century A.D.); also C. Rowland, o.c., p.266; B. Lindars, Jesus Son of Man, 1983, p.5.
43 Cf. L. Rost, o.c., p.105. Cf. R.A. Coughenour, o.c., pp.211f. who opts for Galilee as place of redaction.
44 Especially with regard to the dualism of 1QS and the Messianic expectations. Note also the fact that En(eth) was translated into different languages which was not the case with respect to the proper Qumran writings; cf. C. Münchow, Ethik, p.16.

direct Qumranian authorship[45]. A common hasidic background is more probable. The vast variety of traditions which were incorporated into En(eth) form a "véritable encyclopédie"[46]. Recently, however, it has been shown that En(eth) is not a random selection of traditions arbitrarily arranged but rather a definite literary corpus in which the various parts are arranged in accordance with the biographical information of Enoch's life following the biblical chronology as elaborated by aggadic amplifications[47].

5.2.1. Wisdom traditions in En(eth). The compiler(s) of En(eth) incorporated significant elements of the Jewish wisdom tradition[48]. A list of the wisdom elements in En(eth) includes the following facts: (1) Enoch is depicted as a sage[49]; (2) Enoch's inspiration corresponds with the wisdom writers' inspiration[50]; (3) the recipients of Enoch's instruction[51]; (4) wisdom genres[52]; (5) the numerous ethical admonitions[53]; (6) cosmological material[54]; (7)

---

45 Cf. L. Rost, *Einleitung*, p.105; R.A. Coughenour, *Enoch and Wisdom*, pp.205-207. R.T. Beckwith, "The Earliest Enoch Literature", *RQ* 10 (1981) 365-372 refers the earliest strata to the Essene tradition in its very early stage. See also J.T. Milik, "Problèmes de la littérature Hénochique à la lumière des fragments araméens de Qumrân", *HThR* 64 (1971) 333-378 pointing out regarding the archaeological evidence that the scrolls of the Enoch texts were seemingly excluded from general use in Qumran (ibid., pp.335,338).

46 A. Sabatier, "L'apocalypse juive et la philosophie de l'histoire", *REJ* 40 (1900) LXX; cf. A. Nissen, "Tora", *NovTest* 9 (1967) 248.

47 Cf. D. Dimant, "The Biography of Enoch and the Books of Enoch", *VT* 33 (1983) 14-29.

48 See R.A. Coughenour, *Enoch and Wisdom: A Study of the Wisdom Elements in the Book of Enoch*, Ph.D. Diss. Case Western Reserve University, 1972, particularly pp.34-188; also C. Münchow, *Ethik*, 1981, pp.18,24f.,37,41; and D.W. Suter, *Tradition*, 1979, pp.183f.

49 Cf. 1,1;12,3.4;15,1.

50 Visions: 1,1-2; 71; dreams: 13,8; 14,2-4; 83; 85,1-2; 86,1; 90,39-42; translation: 12,1-11; 70,1-3; 71,1.5; reception of instruction: 17-26; 25,13. Cf. R.A. Coughenour, *o.c.*, pp.72-94.

51 The elect and righteous equivalent to the wise: 1,1-9; 102,4-104,13; the wicked equivalent to the foolish: 1,1-9; 98,1-102,3; kings and mighty: 62,1-63,12; all mankind: 99,10. Cf. R.A. Coughenour, *Enoch and Wisdom*, pp.94-100.

52 Parables: 1,2-3; 37,1-5; 38-44; 45-57; 58-69; the woe-formula (34 times): 94,1-100,9; 103,5.8; 'words of blessing': 1,1; 58,2; 81,4; 91,10; the *Lehreröffnungsformel*: 37,2; 79,1; 83,1; 85,1.2; 91,1.3; 94,1; 108,1. Cf. R.A. Coughenour, *o.c.*, pp.56-72, 129-143.

53 Cf. 5,4-9; 10,15; 79,1; 81,1; 82,1; 91-105. Cf. C. Münchow, *Ethik*, p.41 with n.42 who refers with regard to the Admonitions to 91,10;98,1.3; 99,10;100,6; 101,2-8; 104,12.

54 See especially the Astronomical Book in ch. 72-82. Cf. C. Münchow, *o.c.*, pp.24f.

the uses of the word 'wisdom'[55]. The significance of the wisdom tradition for En is based not only on the sheer quantity of incorporated wisdom elements but also on the fact that wisdom material occurs at vital places in the work. R.A. Coughenour refers to the theological, scribal, and eschatological perspective of wisdom in En: "Theological because it deals with cosmological questions of natural and world order, and of revelation; scribal by virtue of its reputed author, the 'scribe of righteousness' and by virtue of his interpretive task; eschatological wisdom because of its striking note of judgement and its emphasis on the eschaton"[56].

5.2.2. The concept of wisdom. Those parts of En which date to the second century B.C. contain only rare allusions to wisdom, whereas the first century sections (91-105; 37-71) include numerous such references[57].

Wisdom clearly has a universalistic dimension. Wisdom is personified[58] and portrayed as participating in creation: "For you have made and you rule all things, and nothing is too hard for you, wisdom departs not from the place of your throne, nor turns away from your presence. And you know and see and hear everything, and there is nothing hidden from you (for you see everything)" (84,3)[59]. Wisdom is an attribute of the "Lord of Spirits" (48,7; 63,2-3). The heavenly angels are also characterized as being wise (61,7.11). As wisdom found no place to dwell on earth among the wicked, a dwelling place has been assigned to her in heaven where she "took her seat in the midst of the angels" (42,1-2).

On the astronomical chapters see now O. Neugebauer, *The 'Astronomical' Chapters of the Ethiopic Book of Enoch (72-82)*, 1981. The study of E. Rau, *Kosmologie, Eschatologie und die Lehrautorität Henochs: Traditions- und formgeschichtliche Untersuchungen zum äthiopischen Henochbuch und zu verwandten Schriften*, Diss. Hamburg, 1970, was unobtainable.

55 Cf. the next section.
56 R.A. Coughenour, *o.c.*, p.182.
57 Cf. A. Theochares, "The Concept of Wisdom in the Ethiopic Book of Enoch" (Greek), *Deltion Biblikon Meleton* 1 (1972), 287-311, here 291-298.
58 Cf. 42,1 ; 84,3; 91,10 ;94,5. U. Wilckens, *Torheit*, pp.160-162 and others describe the wisdom figure in ch. 42 in terms of a 'myth'.
59 Cf. M. Küchler, *Weisheitstraditionen*, p.76. On creation as order of the world, especially with regard to the Book of the Watchers, see also M.T. Wacker, *Weltordnung und Gericht: Studien zu 1 Henoch 22*, Forschung zur Bibel 22, 1982, pp.297-301.

Consequently, Enoch's observations concerning the heavenly bodies and calendric information are called 'wisdom': "I have revealed to you everything, and given you books concerning all these . . . I have given wisdom to you and to your children, (and your children that shall be to you) that they may give it to their children for generations, this wisdom (namely) that passes their thought. And those who understand it shall not sleep, but shall listen with the ear that they may learn this wisdom, and it shall please those who eat thereof better than good food" (82,1-3)[60]. This universalistic perspective is also evident in the numerous passages that focus on empirical observations which are often linked with cosmic phenomena (cf. 2,1-5,3; 41,3-9; 43,4; 52,1-9; 59,1-3; 60,11-23; 72-82).

We can also discover a particularistic dimension in the wisdom concept of En. Wisdom originates with Yahweh (84,3) and is his gift to his people (5,8 with *passivum theologicum*; cf. also 48,1-2; 91,10; 104,12). Wisdom is very specifically related to the righteous (of Israel — even if the terms 'Israel' or 'Jacob' do not occur explicitly[61]).

> In 14,3 the "word of wisdom" is parallel with the "words of righteousness" (v.1). In 32,3 the "garden of righteousness" contains the "tree of wisdom". In 82,2-4 the righteous are identified with those who learn wisdom, and the "way of righteousness" (v.4) is linked with practised wisdom. In 91,10 the relationship between wisdom and righteousness is most explicit: "And the righteous shall arise from sleep, and wisdom shall arise and be given unto them". 92,1 states that those who accept Enoch's "complete doctrine of wisdom" will practise uprightness and peace. In 99, 10 the "words of wisdom" correspond with the "path of righteousness". In the later Similitudes we find this close relationship between righteousness and wisdom as well (cf. 48,1; 49,1-3; 61,1-13[62]; 63,3; cf. 58,5; 71,3)[63].

The particularistic perspective is also evident in the fruit of wisdom: those who accept and receive and practise wisdom will have life (5,8.9; 82,3; cf. 61,7); they do not sin (5,8.9; 82,3.4; 99,10) but have righteousness (32,3; 82,3.4; 99,10); they will have humil-

---

60 O. Neugebauer, *'Astronomical' Chapters*, p.31 designates 80,1 as "concluding speech of Uriel" and points out that 80,2-82,3 represents "an intrusion of non-astronomical material: apocalyptic and again concluding words to Methuselah".
61 Israel and her history are described, under pseudonyms, in the Dream Visions in 89,16-71 (from the Exodus to the destruction of Jerusalem).
62 On 61,1-13 see R.A. Coughenour, *Enoch and Wisdom*, pp.119-124.
63 On the term 'secret' in En(eth) see R.A. Coughenour, *o.c.*, pp.157-159.

ity (5,8), peace (5,9), joy and gladness (5,9) and eternal life (37,4; 58,3).

The ethical dimension, or rather foundation, of wisdom in En becomes obvious when we consider the numerous ethical admonitions (5,4-9; 10,15; 79,1; 81,1; 82,1; 91-105). In many cases onomastica and astral or calendar observations are connected with ethical admonitions (cf. 2-5; 41,3-9; 43-44; 52; 59; 60,11-23; 80,2-8; 81,4; 82,2-4)[64].

In En wisdom has, for the first time, a new dimension: an eschatological one[65]. Wisdom characterizes the chosen and the righteous ones who will inherit the earth (5,7-9; 91,10; cf. 92,1). Eschatological wisdom is also prominent in the Apocalypse of Weeks[66]. With regard to the 6th week we have a reference to those who "godlessly forsake wisdom" (93,8). In 93,10[67] the "elect righteous" from the "eternal plant of righteousness" (i.e. Israel, cf. 93,5)[68] receive, by revelation, perfect ("sevenfold") "wisdom" which consists of physical, apocalyptic, and mystical speculations. In the Similitudes wisdom is also of eschatological importance. 48,1 describes how the inexhaustible "fountain of righteousness" in paradise[69] is surrounded with many "fountains of wisdom" from which "all the thirsty" drink who then, after having been filled with wisdom, dwell with the righteous. The Elect One or the Son of Man is closely associated with wisdom as well[70]: he is "named"

---

64 See particularly C. Münchow, *Ethik*, pp.16-42 passim who emphasizes that the apocalypse of En(eth) with its correlation of eschatology and ethics incorporated sapiential traditions and material alongside prophetic traditions. He concludes that "das apokalyptische Weltbild ... gibt mit seiner theozentrischen Ausrichtung den theologischen Rahmen für die Tradierung ethischer Aussagen ab, in den sich nun aus der prophetischen Tradition stammende Gattungen ... sowie weisheitliches Traditionsgut einordnen lassen" (p.41).

65 This is stressed by A. Theochares, "Concept of Wisdom", 1972, pp.302-311; R.A. Coughenour, *Enoch and Wisdom*, p.182; M. Küchler, *Weisheitstraditionen*, pp.76-79; C. Münchow, *o.c.*, pp.24f.,41.

66 Cf. F. Dexinger, *Offene Probleme*, 1977, pp.183f.

67 On 93,10 see F. Dexinger, *o.c.*, pp.133-135.

68 This is a reference to the specific group within Israel whose spiritual, intellectual, and religious viewpoints are responsible for the Apocalypse of Weeks.

69 Cf. J. Theisohn, *Der auserwählte Richter*, 1975, p.225 n.11.

70 Cf. generally J. Theisohn, *o.c.*, pp.126-139. See also W.D. Davies, *Torah in the Messianic Age*, p.41; R.J. Banks, *Jesus and the Law*, p.69. As regards the Son of Man in Enoch see now J.J. Collins, "The Heavenly Representative: The 'Son of Man' in the Similitudes of Enoch", *Ideal Figures in Ancient Judaism*, ed. J.J. Collins et

in the context of the "fountain of righteousness" and the "fountains of wisdom" (48,1-2), wisdom is poured out on him (49,1), he is powerful in all the "secrets (!) of righteousness" (49,2), and in him dwells "the spirit of wisdom, and the spirit which gives insight, and the spirit of understanding" (49,3), and he utters "all the secrets of wisdom" (51,3).

5.2.3. The concept of law. In En(eth) the law is primarily, but not exclusively, understood as the universal and comprehensive order of the entire creation[71]. Creation is "Offenbarung des Gehorsam heischenden und Gehorsam findenden, herrscherlichen und schöpferischen Willens Gottes"[72]. The communication of the cosmic conformity to the natural laws can be regarded as communication of Torah as well[73].

In the Book of Noah nature is described as being moved by God's angel on the basis of the divine command (60,11-22; 66,1-2; 69,21-25). The importance of this divine command is stressed (69, 15-21.25).

The cosmological parts of En(eth) emphasize that the world is moved by heavenly beings (18,1-5; cf. 75,1). All days and seasons are under the dominion of mighty angels (72,3; 75,1; 80,1; 82,4.7-10). These heavenly spirits thereby fulfill a "law" which had been given to them: the "laws" and "functions" of the stars (33,3-4), the "law" of the sun and moon (73,1), the "law" of the winds (76,14), "the whole law of the stars of heaven" (79,1-2), the "entire law of the stars" (80,7). This law is binding: the stars (= angels)

---

al., 1980, pp.111-133 who points out that the righteousness of the Son of Man entails wisdom and knowledge (p.118).

71 See M. Limbeck, *Ordnung*, 1971, pp.63-71 and C. Münchow, *Ethik*, 1981, pp.25, 39f. for the following analysis. Cf. also S. Aalen, *Begriffe*, p.177. — We are aware of the lexical difficulties regarding the establishing of the concept of law in En(eth). In the Ethiopic version the terms *cheq* (= hebr. חוק) and *ᶜerit* (= Mosaic law) are missing; the terms *shereᶜat* (= τάξις, διαθήκη, ἔθος) and *teᶜezaz* (= ἐπιταγή, ἐντολή, πρόσταγμα) which can be used as synonyms (cf. 80,4ff.) are rather common and can refer to (1) the cosmic order, (2) the orders and commands of God in general, and (3) the law in an absolute sense. For details see C. Münchow, *o.c.*, p.39.

72 M. Limbeck, *o.c.*, p.64.

73 Cf. C. Münchow, *o.c.*, p.40 referring to "die kosmische Aufweitung des Gesetzesbegriffes, die das Gesetz und die Ordnung des Kosmos mit dem apokalyptischen Weltbild verbindet" (ibid.).

which rose too late (i.e. which did not comply with their law) are being punished (18,11-16; 21,1-6; 80,1-6; cf. 41,5-6). But it is not only the stars, time, or the elements of nature which stand under God's command and rule: the divine predestination of man is also referred to (39,8; cf. 81,1-2; 90,41). This predestination, however, does not lead to indecision or inactivity on the part of man. On the contrary, each individual created being attains perfection by complying with its/his law (39,9; cf. as contrast 80,4-6)[74].

Thus, in En(eth) everything and everybody is under God's one law. The fulfilment of this law by nature can become a model and example for man.

> Thus we read in 2,1-2: "Observe everything that takes place in the heaven, how they do not change their orbits (and the luminaries which are in the heaven), how they all rise and set in order each in its season, and transgress not against their appointed order. Behold the earth, and give heed to the things which take place upon it from first to last, how steadfast they are, how none of the things upon earth change, but all the works of God appear to you".

The non-observance of the cosmic order, on the part of man, is sin (75,2; 80,7; 82,1-5). The stars (angels) preserve among themselves faithfulness (41,5-6; 43,1-2). For man, the absolute integration into the course of the world is of salvational significance[75].

Since the different parts of En(eth), insofar as they contain allusions to contemporary events, always seem to side with the *ḥasidim* and then with the Pharisees[76], it is striking that terms like covenant, Israel, or Torah are nearly totally absent[77]. The particularistic dimension of the law is therefore more implicit than explicit.

> In 89,21-38 the Exodus event, described in pseudonyms, is closely bound up with the giving of the law on Sinai[78]. References to the Torah are to be seen in 5,4; 94,6;

---

74 Cf. M. Limbeck, *Ordnung*, p.68; contra D. Rössler, *Gesetz*, pp.58f.
75 M. Limbeck, *Ordnung*, pp.70f. stresses, however, that the main purpose of En(eth) is not (!) to bring man into harmony with the cosmos as the law and the fulfilment of the law have "nicht schon einen Eigenwert". The aim of En(eth) is the glorification and the praise of God (cf. 36,4; 41,7).
76 Cf. A. Nissen, "Tora", *NovTest* 9 (1967) 247; K. Schubert, *Religionsparteien*, p.28 (with regard to the Similjtudes).
77 Cf. A. Jaubert, *La notion d'Alliance dans le judaisme aux abords de l'ère chrétienne*, 1963, pp.261f.; A. Nissen, *a.c.*, p.248 with n.2; M. Limbeck, *o.c.*, p.72.
78 As in Jub 1,48-50; AssMos 3,11ff.; 4Ezra 5,27; 9,29ff.; 14,3ff. Cf. R.J. Banks, *Jesus and the Law*, p.30. It is unwarranted, however, to conclude from this one pericope in En(eth) that election is subordinated to the law (contra R.J. Banks, *o.c.*, p.30).

99,2.14; 108,1[79]. In 5,4 the wicked are described as having transgressed the law of the Lord. 93,6 emphasizes the eternal character of the law, clearly referring to the law given on Sinai which was binding for all time. In 99,2 the wicked are condemned because they "pervert the words of uprightness" and "transgress the eternal law". 99,14 refers to the law as "the measure and eternal heritage of their fathers". 108,1 mentions that "in the last days" some will keep the law.

This evidence shows that "im Bewußtsein jener Kreise, deren Denken sich in 1 Hen zu Wort meldet, spielte die Thora offensichtlich keine derart (!) dominierende Rolle, daß sich der einzelne *ausschließlich* durch sie von Gott in Anspruch genommen verstanden hätte"[80].

The law has an eschatological perspective as well. The Torah is the means and measure of the judgment. This role of the law is implied in 5,4; 99,2.14[81]. The law is eternally valid (93,6; 99,2.14)[82]. With regard to the Son of Man it has to be pointed out that even though he is only associated with wisdom (48,1-2; 49,1-3; 51,3) and with righteousness (39,6; 48,1-2; 49,2; 53,7; 71,14.16)[83], "we cannot doubt that for the author of the Similitudes the righteous are those who have been faithful to the Torah and it is in accordance with the Torah, we can be sure, that the Elect One shall judge (see 38,2; 39,6; 46,2; 53,6)"[84].

The function of the law is, apart from the cosmological significance, primarily an ethical one: the law is the norm and motive of moral and social conduct. The law is linked with lists of compilations of both positive (91,3-19) and negative (94,6-11; 95,1-7; 96,4-8; 99,1-16; 100,7-10) ethical maxims which often recall the basic moral injunctions of the Decalogue and of the prophets, and whose form has much in common with similar lists in the wisdom

---

79 Cf. R.H. Charles, *APOT* 2 (1913) 190,263,270; A. Nissen, *a.c.*, p.248 n.2 ;M. Limbeck, *o.c.*, p.72; R.J. Banks, *o.c.*, p.30.

80 M. Limbeck, *o.c.*, p.72.

81 The judgment on the basis of one's works is referred to, or implied, in 1,9; 13,6; 38,2-6; 41,1; 81,2-4; 98,6; 99,2; 100,7; 103,3; 104,7. But even those who are faithful to the Torah are dependent upon grace and forgiveness (cf. 92,4). Cf. A. Nissen, "Tora", *NovTest* 9 (1967) 265.

82 This does not necessarily imply an unhistorical conception of the nature of the law. Cf. R.J. Banks, *Jesus and the Law*, p.30 who, however, misunderstood A. Nissen who did not (!) maintain that En(eth) or the other apocalypses did promote an unhistorical concept of law.

83 Cf. R.J. Banks, *o.c.*, p.69.

84 W.D. Davies, *Torah in the Messianic Age*, p.42; cf. also J.J. Collins, "Heavenly Representative", 1980, p.119.

literature[85]. The Torah is clearly the standard and measure of the injunctions. Condemned are theft and enrichment (97,8; 102,9), oppression and exploitation of the poor (96,5; 99,12-13), unjust judgment (95,6), deception and fraud (94,6: 96,7), hate (95,2), murder (99,15), lies (95,6; 104,9), false measures (99,12), wrong calculation of the calendar (87,5), alteration and wrong interpretation of the Torah (104,10; 108,6), magic and astrology (7-8; 9,8), blasphemy and hybris (1,9; 68,4; 101,3)[86]. However, there is a "marked freedom from casuistry in any highly developed form"[87].

5.2.4. Wisdom and law. It has been maintained that in En(eth), as an exception with regard to the other apocalypses, the law is not identified with wisdom[88]. Even though the identification is not as explicit as in Sir or Bar it is nevertheless implicit in a number of passages.

In 5,3-4 the phrase "commandments of the Lord", here to be understood as "the creative word which has established the general order of the created world and by which it operates, the substantial word that orders the societal life of mankind shaped by Torah"[89], occurs in a parable setting forth the results of the 'two ways' which also employs empirical observations for ethical purposes: the commandments of the Lord are seen as wisdom[90].

---

85 Cf. R.J. Banks, *o.c.*, p.52, and C. Münchow, *Ethik*, p.40 who states that even though the Torah is not quoted in En(eth) it is obvious that the admonitions in En(eth) can be phrased as 'general' as they are only because they refer to the presupposed and known Torah of Moses, without quoting it *expressis verbis*. It is inconsistent, however, when Münchow asserts that "die ethische Belehrung der Apokalyptik ist also nicht Tradition des Mosegesetzes, sondern verschiedenartige Traditionen (i.e. cosmological and sapiential ones) entfalten das für die Apokalyptik typische Gottesverständnis ... und Geschichtsverständnis, das die Grundlage abgibt, um das Handeln zu motivieren und zum Tun entsprenchend der Tora aufzurufen" (ibid.).
86 Cf. A. Nissen, "Tora", *NovTest* 9 (1967) 262f. G.W.E. Nickelsburg, "The Apocalyptic Message of 1 Enoch 92,105", *CBQ* 39 (1977) 311 points out that misdeeds of the wicked are often social in nature (95,5-6; 96,5; 97,8; 98,13; 99,11-12.15; 100,7-8), but that the sins of the wicked also have theological dimensions (96,7; 98,9.11.14-15; 99,14). Contra R.J. Banks, *Jesus and the Law*, p.53 who states that the single virtues and vices which are listed in En(eth) are all of a social nature only.
87 R.J. Banks, *o.c.*, p.53.
88 Cf. R.J. Banks, *o.c.*, p.69; U. Luck, "Weltverständnis", *ZThK* 73 (1976) 292; M. Küchler, *Weisheitstraditionen*, p.80.
89 R.A. Coughenour, *Enoch and Wisdom*, p.117.
90 Cf. R.A. Coughenour, *o.c.*, pp.116f.,178.

In 5,8-9 wisdom is closely correlated with the abstaining from sin which will be characteristic of the elect and which is connected with the keeping of the commandments of 5,4.

In 42,1-3 wisdom is pictured as the opposite of unrighteousness which implies that wisdom and righteousness are closely related. And righteousness surely implies and presupposes and results in the keeping of the law. This correlation of wisdom and righteousness is confirmed by 48,1.

The Son of Man is characterized both by wisdom and by righteousness (49,1-3).

In 61,1-13 the commandments are also seen as wisdom[91]: the "measures", "cords", and "ropes" are God's instrument of judgment (which is linked with the "righteous law" and the "covenant" of 60,6), and (!) of wisdom.

In 81,1-4 the commandments of the Lord are identified with 'special' wisdom (which is quite different from the Decalogue!)[92].

In 91,10; 92,1; 93,10 (cf. the contrast in 93,8) wisdom is again correlated with righteousness. In 94,1-5 the "paths of righteousness" are linked with wisdom.

99,10 also implies the identification of Torah and wisdom[93]: those who "accept the words of wisdom and understand them" also "observe the paths of the Most High, and walk in the path of his righteousness". 104,12 again links righteousness with wisdom.

Thus, it can be stated that in En(eth) "with Wisdom ... goes the Torah in its fulness"[94]. Wisdom is "given in and found by doing Torah"[95].

The universalistic dimension of the identification of law and wisdom is evident: both realms are one in the divine creative word which established and which rules the cosmos, ordering everything from the stars down to man[96]. The correlation of wisdom and law in this context can be found in 5,3-4; 81,1-4.

---

91 Cf. R.A. Coughenour, *o.c.*, pp.119-124,178.
92 Cf. R.A. Coughenour, *o.c.*, pp.125f.,178.
93 Cf. A. Nissen, "Tora", *NovTest* 9 (1967) 259.
94 W.D. Davies, *Torah in the Messianic Age*, p.43.
95 R.A. Coughenour, *Enoch and Wisdom*, p.182. His statement that "Enoch has taken over Sirah's identification of Torah and wisdom, understainding by it both the Decalogue and the more inclusive Mosaic law" (p.128) is difficult to defend, formulated as it is, since the evidence with regard to the concept of law/Torah is rather scanty.
96 Cf. C. Münchow, *Ethik*, p.25 who understands the conception of Torah, as both

The particularistic dimension is to be seen in the fact that both wisdom and law are characteristics not of all the "wise of mankind" but rather of the chosen righteous ones (implied: from Israel). To be filled with wisdom is equivalent to being righteous (48,1). Wisdom and righteousness, implying the abstinence from sin which is faithfulness to the law (cf. 5,8-9), are correlated in all parts of En(eth): in the early portions (14,1-3; 82,2-4; 91,10; 92,1; 93,10; 94,1-5; 99,10; 104,12; cf. 5,8-9) as well as in the later Similitudes (42,1-3; 48,1; 49,1-3; 61,1-13; 63,3).

The theological dimension consists in the common origin and basis of law and wisdom: Yahweh, the Creator, the Lord of his people. The righteous and the wise share the same fruit and blessing: life (5,8-9), eternal life (37,4; 58,3), and peace and joy (5,9).

The ethical dimension of this correlation is expressed in the close relationship between wisdom and righteousness which implied obedience to the law. Wisdom is identical with the avoidance of sin (5,8-9). Wisdom excludes iniquity (42,1-3). Where righteousness is, wisdom is, and the wise are, where the righteous are (48,1). The chosen righteous possess perfect wisdom (93,10). The wise walk on the paths of righteousness and are closely linked with "light" which signifies a moral or ethical religious quality[97]. For the chosen and the righteous who are wise there will be light (5, 6-9); the good, i.e. the righteous, are the "generation of light"[98] and will shine whereas the sinners will be thrown into darkness (108,11-14); the righteous will be "in the light of the sun" and are characterized by the "light of eternal life" and the "light of uprightness" (58,3-6).

In En(eth) the correlation of wisdom and law (righteousness) is also characterized by an eschatological dimension which is due to the fact that En(eth) is an apocalypse. The lot of the wise and of the righteous is the same: they will have joy and peace and eternal life and will inherit the earth (5,7-9; 91,10), whereas the sinners and the foolish are condemned (98,6-10). In the Similitudes, the

---

ethical and cosmological law in En(eth), as further development of sapiential notions assimilating thoughts of the stoic-platonic popular philosophy.

97 Cf. S. Aalen, *Begriffe*, pp.177-179.

98 Cf. the phrase "children of uprightness" (105,2), "children of righteousness" (93,2), "children of heaven" (101,1).

Elect One is very closely associated with both wisdom and righteousness[99].

5.2.5. Summary. In En(eth) the wisdom tradition has had many influences on the content and on the form of different portions of this composite apocalypse. The wisdom concept is characterized primarily by a cosmic orientation but is also closely related with the righteous ones of God's people. New is the eschatological aspect of wisdom in En(eth): the elect righteous ones who will be redeemed and awarded eternal life are filled with wisdom, and the Son of Man is also closely associated with wisdom.

The law per se occurs rather seldom and signifies first of all the comprehensive order of creation. The law as Mosaic Torah is more implied than clearly referred to. However, it is obviously presupposed as the decisive norm of all social behaviour as well as the measure of the future judgment. The last function of the law shows that it has also an eschatological dimension.

The identification of the law (righteousness) with wisdom is primarily tied up with the ethical standard(s) which the Lord has imposed upon his people. But it also has a universal and even an eschatological dimension.

5.3. The Psalms of Solomon

The collection of PsSal[100] was originally written in Hebrew[101]

---

99 W.D. Davies, *Torah in the Messianic Age*, p.42 states that "the association of the Elect One with wisdom may also be significant because from early times wisdom had been associated with Torah". Pace J.J. Collins, "Heavenly Representative", 1980, p.188 who asserts that the identification of wisdom and law is "not apparent" in the Similitudes: granted that the identification is not stated explicitly, it can still be argued that it is implied, since the Son of Man is related to both wisdom and righteousness, with the latter presupposing fidelity to the law.

100 See generally G.B. Gray, "The Psalms of Solomon", *APOT* 2 (1913) 625-630; J. Viteau, *Les Psaumes de Salomon*, DEB I/4, 1911, pp.1-252; A.M. Denis, *Introduction*, pp.60-69; L. Rost, *Einleitung*, pp.89-91; O. Eissfeldt, *Einleitung*, pp.826-831; J.H. Charlesworth, *Pseudepigrapha*, pp.195-197; S. Holm-Nielsen, "Die Psalmen Salomos", *JSHRZ* IV/2 (1977) 51-59; idem, "Religiöse Poesie des Spätjudentums", *ANRW* II/19,1 (1979) 172-180; G.W.E. Nickelsburg, *Literature*, pp.203-212.

101 Cf. G.B. Gray, *o.c.*, p.627; J. Viteau, *o.c.*, pp.105-125; A.M. Denis, *o.c.*, p.63; S. Holm-Nielsen, *JSHRZ* IV/2 (1977) 51,53f.; J.H. Charlesworth, *o.c.*, p.195.

but is extant today only in Greek[102] and in Syriac[103]. The 18 psalms were probably written by several authors[104] who were related to Pharisaic circles[105]. Their life-setting was the synagogue services[106]. They originated in Palestine, probably in Jerusalem[107], and were composed in the middle decades of the first century B.C.[108]. The theological emphasis is on the righteousness of God[109] and on the relationship between the pious and the godless[110].

5.3.1. The law. In PsSal 7,9 the term ζυγόν "yoke" could be a reference to the law[111]. In 8,32 we have an ambiguous reference to the law in τὰ κρίματα[112]. 10,4 refers to the witness to God's mercy which is to be found "in the law of the eternal covenant" (ἐν νόμῳ διαθήκης αἰωνίου) i.e. in the Torah[113]. 14,2 refers to

---

102 Cf. the edition by A. Rahlfs, *Septuaginta*, 2, pp.471-489.
103 We use the translations of G.B. Gray, *APOT* 2 (1913) 631-652; J. Viteau, *o.c.*, pp.253-375; S. Holm-Nielsen, *JSHRZ* IV/2 (1977) 62-112.
104 Cf. G.B. Gray, *o.c.*, p.628; O. Eissfeldt, *o.c.*, p.830; S. Holm-Nielsen, *o.c.*, pp.51, 58f.; J. Schüpphaus, *Die Psalmen Salomos: Ein Zeugnis Jerusalemer Theologie und Frömmigkeit in der Mitte des vorchristlichen Jahrhunderts*, ALGHJ 7, 1977, p.142 n.28. The assumption of a single author is defended by J. Viteau, *o.c.*, pp.86-92; G. Maier, *Mensch*, p.281; cf. A.M. Denis, *o.c.*, p.64.
105 Cf. G.B. Gray, *o.c.*, p.630; J. Viteau, *o.c.*, p.106; A.M. Denis, *o.c.*, p.64 (with lit. in n.21); L. Rost, *o.c.*, p.90; G. Maier, *o.c.*, p.295; J. Schüpphaus, *o.c.*, pp.127-137,142 n.28,151,158; S. Holm-Nielsen, *o.c.*, p.59; G.W.E. Nickelsburg, *o.c.*, pp. 203,212.
106 Cf. S. Holm-Nielsen, *o.c.*, p.59; J. Schüpphaus, *o.c.*, pp.150f.
107 Cf. J. Viteau, *o.c.*, pp.92-94,105; G. Maier, *o.c.*, p.281; A.M. Denis, *o.c.*, p.64; O. Eissfeldt, *o.c.*, p.831; J. Schüpphaus, *o.c.*, p.142 n.28.
108 Cf. G.B. Gray, *o.c.*, pp.628-630; A.M. Denis, *o.c.*, p.64; L. Rost, *o.c.*, p.90; O. Eissfeldt, *o.c.*, pp.829f.; J.H. Charlesworth, *o.c.*, p.195; J. Schüpphaus, *o.c.*, pp.105-107,115f.,127-137; G.W.E. Nickelsburg, *o.c.*, p.203.
109 Cf. especially H. Braun, "Vom Erbarmen Gottes über den Gerechten: Zur Theologie der Psalmen Salomos", *ZNW* 43 (1950/51) 1-54.
110 Cf. generally J. Schüpphaus, *Psalmen*, 1977. After a history of research (pp.1-20) followed by a detailed analysis of each psalm (pp.21-82), Schüpphaus discusses the two main topics of the righteousness of God and God's help in hostilities (pp.83-116).
111 Cf. mAb 3,5 עוֹל תּוֹרָה; also Acts 15,10; Gal 5,1; cf. J. Viteau, *Psaumes*, pp.290f.; S. Holm-Nielsen, *JSHRZ* IV/2 (1977) 77. J. Schüpphaus, *o.c.*, p.43 n.145 interprets ζυγός as "das Joch strafender Züchtigung in der Geschichte".
112 Translating "decrees" or "Satzungen"; cf. H. Braun, "Erbarmen", *ZNW* 43 (1950/51) 4,33; M. Limbeck, *Ordnung*, p.89 n.63. J. Viteau, *o.c.*, p.301; G.B. Gray, *APOT* 2 (1913) 642; and J. Schüpphaus, *o.c.*, p.50 translate with "judgments".
113 10,4b is generally regarded as a reference to the Torah; cf. recently J. Schüpphaus,

the pious who "walk" (πορευομένοις) in the righteousness of God's "commandments" (πρόσταγμα) and "in the law" (ἐν νόμῳ) which God imposed upon them in order that they might live. In 14,6 the "sinners" are contrasted with those who break the law (παράνομοι). This term is repeated in 17,24 (ἔθνη παράνομα). In 18,12 which is the last verse of the concluding doxology[114] the order of the "lights of heaven" (v.10) is described (vv.10-12b) without using a legal term.

Thus, the material evidence is rather small and does not allow us to draw far-reaching conclusions with regard to the concept of law in PsSal[115]. Several observations may be made, however. The law has always a particularistic dimension[116]: it is the law of Israel and has to be understood in the context of the covenant (10,4)[117].

The main function of the law is its role as norm of moral and social behaviour. In 14,2 the commandments are linked with those "who walk in righteousness" (τοῖς πορευομένοις ἐν δικαιοσύνῃ). The attitude towards the law is the basis of the distinction between "sinners" and "righteous" which characterizes the PsSal[118].

> In the words of J. Viteau, "au point de vue moral, l'homme est juste ou pécheur. Son libre arbitre et sa conscience ont besoin d'une règle venant du dehors, avec laquelle il puisse diriger sa vie. Dieu la lui a donnée, c'est la 'loi'. Celui qui observe la loi est le 'juste'; celui qui la néglige est le 'pécheur' "[119].

---

o.c., p.54.

114 The doxology in 18,10-14 is probably secondary; cf. J. Viteau, o.c., pp.44f.,373-375; G.B. Gray, o.c., pp.651f.; G. Maier, Mensch, p.298; J. Schüpphaus, o.c., p.74.

115 J. Viteau, o.c., p.223 n.1 stresses the significance of the law for the theology of the PsSal by pointing out that 14,2 states that the law gives "life".

116 The concept of the divine cosmic order is referred to in the concluding doxology in 18,10-12 which has, however, no relationship with the preceding statements on the law. Cf. M. Limbeck, Ordnung, p.89.

117 As regards the concept of the covenant in PsSal cf. A. Jaubert, Notion, 1963, pp.253-257.

118 On the godly and the ungodly cf. J. Viteau, Psaumes, pp.51-56; J. Schüpphaus, Psalmen, pp.94-105. Schüpphaus fails to appreciate the role of the νόμος (cf. pp.100 n.229,122). He states that the focus is on man's basic relationship with God and not (!) on the "Orientierung an einer gesetzlichen Norm" (p.122). However, even though "die Erfüllung bestimmter Gebote und Satzungen, der Gehorsam gegenüber einem festumrissenen Gesetz" (ibid.) may not have a decisive role to play, it has to be pointed out that if they were composed in Pharisaic circles (as Schüpphaus rightly stresses, cf. pp.127-137,151,158), the decisive significance of the law is at least implied. Cf. also G. Maier, Mensch, p.319.

119 J. Viteau, o.c., pp.51f.

This is confirmed by the fact that the "sinners" (ἀμαρτωλός)[120] are described as "lawless" (ἄνομος/παράνομος) in 4,9.11.19.23; 12,1.3.4; 14,6; 17,11.18.24. Their behaviour is characterized by ἀνομία (1,8; 2,3.12; 9,2; 15,8.10), παρανομία (4,1.12; 8,9; 17,20), ἀδικία[121] and ἁμαρτία[122]. They are the "unrighteous" (ἄδικος)[123]. Thus, it can be concluded *e negativo* that obedience to the law is the prerequisite for a godly life. The "righteous" (δίκαιος)[124] and "pious"(ὅσιος)[125] is described explicitly as walking in righteousness with regard to God's commandments (14,2). The righteous is linked with the fear of the Lord (φοβούμενος τὸν θεόν/κύριον)[126] and with his love for God[127]. The sinners who transgress the law do not fear the Lord (4,21) but despise him (4,11; 8,11; 17,5).

The eternal character of the law is stressed in 7,9 (cf. 10,4).

In the messianic/eschatological pericope 17,21-46 the law is not given an explicit role[128]. The Messiah[129] is rather connected with righteousness (17,23.32.37; 18,7) and with the fear of the Lord (17,40; 18,7)[130]. One should note, nevertheless, that the Davidic King is described as the enemy of the "lawless nations" (ἔθνη παράνομα). Although the significance of the law may be implied again, no conclusion can be based on the evidence[131]. Finally,

---

120 1,1; 2,1.16.34.35; 3,9.11.12; 4,2.8; 12,6; 13,2.5.6.7.8.11; 14,6; 15,5.8.10.11.12. 13; 16,2.5; 17,5.23.25.36.
121 2,12; 4,24; 9,3.5.
122 1,7; 2,7.16.17; 3,10; 4,3; 8,8.13; 14,6; 15,11; 17,20; cf. 17,8. Other terms are ὑπερηφανία (17,13) and σκάνδαλον (4,23).
123 4,10; 12,5; 15,4; 17,22. Other descriptive terms for the sinners are βέβηλος (2,13; 4,1; 17,45), ὑπερήφανος (2,31), and ἀνθρωπάρεσκος (4,7.8.19).
124 δίκαιος: 2,34.35; 3,3.4.5.6.7.11; 4,8; 9,7; 10,3; 13,6.7.8.9.11; 14,9; 15,6.7; 16,15.
125 ὅσιος: 2,36; 3,8; 4,1.6.8; 8,23.34; 9,3; 10,5.6; 12,4.6; 13,10.12; 14,3.10; 15,7; 17,16.
126 2,33; 3,12; 4,23; 5,18; 6,5; 12,4; 13,12; 15,13.
127 4,25; 6,6; 10,3; 14,1.
128 Cf. J. Viteau, *Psaumes*, p.80; W.D. Davies, *Torah*, 1952, p.43.
129 According to J. Schüpphaus, *Psalmen*, pp.124-126 we have to distinguish a twofold "Messiasbild": the Davidic King who comes primarily as a political and military leader and king, and the Messiah who is God's messenger and the perfect example for the righteous being dedicated primarily to the inner purification, protection, and guidance of the holy people.
130 In the OT the Messiah is also connected with righteousness (cf. Is 9,7; 11,3-5; 16,5; 32,1; Jer 23,5; 33,15; Ps 72,1-2) and with the fear of the Lord (cf. Is 11,2-3).
131 R.J. Banks, *Jesus and the Law*, p.69 n.1 agrees that in PsSal the term 'law' is not emphasized in passages dealing with the messianic period; he says that 'wisdom' and 'righteousness' are used which are elsewhere equated with the law.

obedience to the commandments is said to lead to eternal life (14, 2-3)[132].

5.3.2. Wisdom. Wisdom terminology is used in several passages: 2,33 encourages those who fear the Lord "with insight" (ἐν ἐπιστήμῃ) to praise the Lord because he will show mercy to them in the judgment. 4,9 refers to σοφία. 10,2.3 mentions the divine "chastening" (παιδεία) with which God wants to "cleanse" (καθαρισθῆναι) his people and "make straight the ways (ὀδοί) of the righteous", as God's mercy is upon those who love him in truth. 14,1 deals with God's παιδεία as well. 16,7.8 resumes the sapiential topic of the godless, beguiling woman[133].

> In 16.7 we have a plea for preservation from any wicked sin and from every wicked woman who causes the fool (ἄφρονα) to stumble. V.8 implores the repulse of any delusion by a beautiful, lawless (παρανομούσης) woman or by sinners in general.

The plea in 16,9 focuses on the instruction with regard to proper behaviour and to the maintenance of a pious conduct. 16,10 asks for truthful speech and the renunciation of meaningless anger. 16,13 points out that "chastisement" (παιδεία) can be endured only with God's help. In 17,23 σοφία is linked with the Messiah (cf. also 17,29.35.37; 18,7)[134].

Wisdom concepts are at issue in the division of men into two classes, the δίκαιος and the ἁμαρτωλός, the צדיק and the רשע[135].

In PsSal wisdom is primarily linked with God: he imposes παιδεία on man (10,2.3; 14,1; 16,13). Wisdom (ἐπιστήμη) is linked, on the human level, with fearing (2,33) and loving (10,2.3; 14,1) the Lord.

Wisdom is a moral and ethical concept: it has to do with "cleaning" and with "straightening" man's "ways" (10,2.3; cf. 16,9) and with staying away from sin (16,7.8).

In the eschatological section the Davidic King, as well as the

---

132 In 3,12; 13,10-12; 14,2-3 those who fear the Lord will inherit eternal life.
133 Cf. J. Schüpphaus, *Psalmen*, p.63 with n.281.
134 Cf. J. Viteau, *Psaumes*, p.223 with n.1; G.L. Davenport, "The 'Anointed of the Lord' in Psalms of Solomon 17", *Ideal Figures in Ancient Judaism*, ed. J.J. Collins et al., 1980, pp.72f.
135 Cf. H.L. Jansen, *Die Spätjüdische Psalmendichtung: Ihr Entstehungskreis und ihr 'Sitz im Leben'*, 1937, pp.12f.; J. Schüpphaus, *o.c.*, pp.94f. Schüpphaus asserts that we observe in PsSal, besides the reception of other traditions, "eine umfangreiche Aufnahme weisheitlicher Tradition" (p.117 n.383).

Messiah, is linked with wisdom[136]: the Davidic King destroys the unrighteous rulers, purges Jerusalem from the nations, and expels the sinners from the inheritance "with wisdom and righteousness" (ἐν σοφίᾳ (ἐν) δικαιοσύνῃ(ς), 17,23), destroying their pride (17,22-25). 17,29 repeats that he will rule the nations "in the wisdom of his righteousness" (ἐν σοφίᾳ δικαιοσύνης)[137]. The Messiah will "bless" the people of the Lord with wisdom (σοφία) and gladness (17,35). He is sinless (17,36) and powerful and "wise by prudent counsel" (σοφός ἐν βουλῇ συνέσεως) with strength and righteousness (17,37)[138]. 18,7 mentions again the wisdom (σοφία) of the Messiah[139].

5.3.3. Law and wisdom.
There is no explicit identification formula in the PsSal which correlates wisdom and law. However, the identification is implied in several passages.

4,8c-13 describes the wicked activities of the pious hypocrites: their eyes are fixed on the house of the steadfast "that they may, like the serpent[140], destroy the wisdom (σοφία) of the neighbour[141] with words of lawlessness (ἐν λόγοις παρανόμων)" (v.9). They are motivated by their "lawless desire" (ἐπιθυμία παρανόμου, v.11), by their sheer "lawlessness" (παρανομία, v.12). Thus, lawlessness is obviously regarded as the opposite of wisdom which implies that obedience to the law is seen as equal to being wise.

14,1-2 characterizes the required conduct of the righteous: he loves the Lord in truth and endures his παιδεία (v.1); he walks (πορεύομαι) in the righteousness of his commandments (δικαιοσύνῃ προσταγμάτων), in his law (νόμος) which leads to eternal life (v.2; cf. v.3). This psalm which has numerous sapiential ele-

---

136 Cf. J. Schüpphaus, *Psalmen*, p.93; G.L. Davenport, "The Anointed", 1980, pp.72-74 (who seems to reckon with only one single anointed figure or Messiah in PsSal 17, see his remark on p.83); P.G.R. de Villiers, "Messiah", *Neotestamentica* 12 (1981) 78.
137 17,22-31 deals with the Davidic King; cf. J. Schüpphaus, *o.c.*, pp.70f.
138 17,32-41 focuses on the Messiah; cf. J. Schüpphaus, *o.c.*, pp.71f.
139 For the links between the Messiah and wisdom see Is 9,6; 11,2; Jer 23,5.
140 Probably referring to Gen 3.
141 G has ἀλλήλων, but the reciprocal meaning does not make any sense. We follow the solution of J. Viteau, *Psaumes*, p.274, followed by S. Holm-Nielsen, *JSHRZ* IV/2 (1977) 71 which assumes an original non-reciprocal רעהו which was misunderstood as being reciprocal. The proper translation would have been τοῦ πλησίον. S has "of each one".

ments[142] makes propaganda "in lehrhaft-unterweisender Form für den Weg des sich der göttlichen Zucht unterwerfenden, dem Gesetz gehorsamen Gerechten"[143]. Implicitly, obedience to the law and the keeping of the commandments is equivalent with adopting the divine παιδεία.

In 16,7-8 "fool" (ἄφρονα) is correlated with lawlessness (παρανομία) which implies again *e contrario* the identity of the 'wise' and those who keep the law.

In these three pericopes the implied identification of law and wisdom obviously has an ethical background. The particularistic limitation to pious Jews is self-evident.

In 17,21-46 the identification of wisdom and law assumes an eschatological dimension. It is true that neither the Davidic King nor the Messiah is explicitly linked with the law but rather with righteousness (17,23.26.29.32.37.40; 18,7.8; cf. 17,22.27) and the fear of the Lord (17,40; 18,7.8; cf. 17,34.39). However, both are described as the enemies of lawlessness (17,24). The statement that the Messiah is taught of God (17,34) and that his "word" will be powerful in judgment (17,41) does not suggest that he will bring a new law. This pericope suggests that "he will establish a condition when the life of righteousness in accordance with the Torah will prevail"[144]. And both the Davidic King and the Messiah are characterized by wisdom (17,23.29.35.37; 18,7). In 17.23.29. 37; 18,7 σοφία and δικαιοσύνη are closely correlated. The future redeemer(s) who possesses wisdom will establish a state of lawfulness.

The theological dimension is implied in the fact that both the law and wisdom are linked with the concept of the fear of the Lord (law: 2,33; 3,12; 4,23; 5,18; 6,5; 12,4; 13,12; 15,13; wisdom: 2,33) and love for God (law: 4,25, 6,6; 10,3; 14,1; wisdom: 10,2.3; 14,1).

---

142 J. Schüpphaus, *Psalmen*, p.59 n.252 refers to the life-motif, the motif of retribution, the contrast righteous/sinner, and the pattern of the two ways.
143 J. Schüpphaus, o.c., p.59.
144 W.D. Davies, *Torah*, p.43.
145 See generally M. Hadas, *Aristeas to Philocrates*, 1951, pp.1-90; A.M. Denis, *Introduction*, pp.105-110; L. Rost, *Einleitung*, pp.74-77; N. Meisner, "Aristeasbrief", *JSHRZ* II/1 (1973) 37-44; O. Eissfeldt, *Einleitung*, pp.817-821; J.H. Charlesworth, *Pseudepigrapha*, pp.78-80; G.W.E. Nickelsburg, *Literature*, pp.165-169.

5.3.4. Summary. The concepts of wisdom and of law are not developed in PsSal to any great extent. In both cases, the ethical and also the eschatological perspectives are prominent. The law is the norm of moral and social behaviour, and, implicitly, obedience to the law is the prerequisite and the basis of righteousness, which is an important concept in PsSal. Obedience to the commandments is the foundation of the distinction between the sinners and the pious — the sinners are "lawless" (ἄνομος/παράνομος), and the pious are "righteous" (δίκαιος). 'Wisdom' and 'discipline' have, on the human level, to do with the goal of living a morally pure life.

The identification of law and wisdom has, as we have pointed out, primarily an ethical orientation but implies a particularistic and a theological foundation as well. Finally, the identification has also an eschatological perspective: both the Davidic King and the Messiah are described as enemies of lawlessness, as aiming at establishing righteousness, and as possessing wisdom.

§6 Earlier Jewish Writings from Alexandria

6.1. The Letter of Aristeas

The Letter of Aristeas[145] is a fictional account (διήγησις) by an anonymous Jew in Egypt in the form of a letter allegedly written to his brother Philocrates by Aristeas, a Greek in the court of Ptolemaios II. It is obvious, however, that EpArist was written by a Jewish-Alexandrian author between 130 and 100 B.C.[146]. EpArist is written in an excellent Hellenistic Greek[147]. It represents an

---

146 Cf M. Hadas, *o.c.*, p.54; W. Michaelis, in *RGG* 1 (1957) 569; K. Stendahl, in *BHH* 1 (1962) 127; A.M. Denis, *o.c.*, pp.109f.; L. Rost, *o.c.*, p.75; N. Meisner, *o.c.*, pp.42f.; O. Eissfeldt, *o.c.*, p.818; G.W.E. Nickelsburg, *o.c.*, p.39. M. Hengel, *Judentum*, pp.55f. n.198 assumes a date between 150 and 130 B.C. S. Jellicoe, "Septuagint Origins: The Letter of Aristeas", *The Septuagint and Modern Study*, 1968, pp.47-50 suggests a date before 170 B.C.
147 Cf. A.M. Denis, *o.c.*, p.108; N. Meisner, *o.c.*, p.39. For an edition of the Greek text see P. Wendland, *Aristeae ad Philocratem Epistula*, 1900; M. Hadas, *Aristeas to*

apology for Judaism defending the LXX and the temple in Jerusalem[148]. It shows among other things "die Verbindung von Kulturoffenheit mit allegorischer Interpretation des Gesetzes und fröhlichem Gehorsam dem Gesetz des Mose gegenüber"[149].

6.1.1. The law. EpArist is not directly interested in theological problems[150]. However, the doctrine of God and the conception of the significance of the Jewish law are the two prominent theological features of the 'letter'[151]. EpArist uses mainly νόμος and νομοθεσία as designations of the Mosaic law and its commandments (3,5,10,15,30,127,131,144,168,171,309,313)[152]. On several occasions the law is also called γραφή (155,168)[153] and τὰ λόγια (158,177)[154].

The author emphasises the divine origin of the law repeatedly: the law is "divine" (θεῖος νόμος, 3) and "of divine origin" (διὰ θεοῦ γεγονέναι, 313; cf. 31), and it was "God who has put (ὁ θεὸς δέδωκε) the thoughts into the hearts of the lawgivers" (240, cf. 139).

The law is "free from all blemish" (ἀκέραιον, 31) and is characterized by "sanctity" (σεμνότης, 31,171). The law is the unique

---

Philocrates, 1951, pp.91-227. We use the translations of H.T. Andrews, *APOT* 2 (1913) 94-122; N. Meisner, *JSHRZ* II/1 (1973) 45-87.

148 S. Jellicoe, *a.c.*, p.50 suggests that EpArist is directed against a rival Greek translation of the OT which had been developed at Leontopolis. Cf. also J.H. Charlesworth, *o.c.*, p.78. See generally D.W. Gooding, "Aristeas and Septuagint Origins: A Review of Recent Studies", *VT* 13 (1963) 357-379 (= *Studies in the Septuagint*, ed. S. Jellicoe, 1974, pp.158-180).

149 K. Stendahl, *BHH* 1 (1962) 128. With regard to the Hellenistic influences in EpArist see V. Tcherikover, "The Ideology of the Letter of Aristeas", *HThR* 51 (1958) 63-66 (= *Studies*, ed. S. Jellicoe, 1974, pp.185-188).

150 Cf. H.T. Andrews, *APOT* 2 (1913) 88.

151 With regard to the doctrine of God see H.T. Andrews, *o.c.*, p.88 and particularly P. Dalbert, *Theologie*, pp.94-98.

152 For a full list see the "index verborum" in P. Wendland, *Epistula*, p.202 s.v. νομοθεσία and νόμος.

153 H.T. Andrews, *o.c.*, p.110 observes that this is probably the first instance where the law is spoken of as Scripture; cf. also M. Hadas, *Aristeas*, p.161 (ad 155). In TZeb 3,4 we find the phrase ἐν γραφῇ νόμου Μωυσέως. But the absolute use of ἡ γραφή is (except in EpArist 155,168) never used elsewhere in the pre-Christian period.

154 This is probably the earliest instance of the application of the term τὰ λόγια to the law as a whole. In the NT cf. Acts 7,38; Rom 3,2; Hebr 5,12. Cf. H.T. Andrews, *o.c.*, p.111.

possession of Israel (15) providing spiritual and moral protection.

> The author asserts that "it has fenced us round with impregnable ramparts and walls of iron, that we might not mingle at all with any of the other nations, but remain pure (ἁγνοί) in body and soul" (139).

In 128-171,306 various commandments of the Jewish law regarding food and purity are interpreted (allegorically). While the law is binding for the Jews it is emphasized that the law's intent is "compatible with the finest in Gentile ethics and wisdom"[155] (cf. the speech of Eleazar in 130-171).

The purpose and the benefits of the law are stated in Hellenistic terms: obedience to the law leads to the "good life", the "right way of living" (καλῶς ζῆν, 127), to "virtue and the perfecting of the character" (πρὸς ἁγνὴν ἐπίσκεψιν καὶ τρόπον ἐξαρτισμόν, 144), to "righteousness" and "justice" (πρὸς δικαιοσύνην, 168), and to "righteous relationships between man and man" (πρὸς τὴν τῶν ἀνθρώπων συναναστροφὴν δικαίαν, 169). The law is the embodiment of truth and points to the "right attitude" or the "right outlook" (πρὸς σημείωσιν ὀρθοῦ λόγου, 161). The law finally provides the person who obeys its commandments with a "perpetual memorial" (279). For man the most important virtue is the keeping of the commandments (127). For the Jew the temple and the cult are of great significance (33-34,83-106)[156]. The significance of the Torah is further underlined by the fact that the author of EpArist calls for an exact textual transmission of the Torah (30-32,176-177)[157].

Thus, the Mosaic law is of particularistic and of universal importance and has a theological, religious, and an ethical dimension, with the latter being specifically emphasized[158].

6.1.2. Wisdom. Several scholars suggested that the table-talk

---

[155] G.W.E. Nickelsburg, *Literature*, p.168. Cf. also V. Tcherikover, "Ideology", *HThR* 51 (1958) 73 who points out that the Torah in EpArist is devoid of any specific Jewish features, and that the allegorical interpretation "turns the Torah into a universal doctrine which may be accepted by every enlightened mind, especially by those who had Greek education".

[156] Thus it can be said that "die Trias Gesetz-Kult-Tempel als Offenbarungsform Gottes spielt im Aristeasbrief eine bedeutende Rolle" (P. Dalbert, *Theologie*, p.96). On 'covenant' in EpArist cf. A. Jaubert, *Notion*, pp.322-329.

[157] Cf. M. Hengel, *Judentum*, p.313 n.420.

[158] Cf. P. Dalbert, *o.c.*, pp.98-102; R.J. Banks, *Jesus and the Law*, pp.54f.

section (172–300)[159] is dependent upon Israelite wisdom material[160]. However, a closer review of this claim proves that this is not the case[161]. The influence of the wisdom tradition can be traced in those parts which were written by the author of EpArist himself, "nämlich bei der Erwähnung Gottes am Schluß jeder Antwort"[162]. The author presents these references to God as proof of the fact that Jewish theology surpasses Greek philosophy: the Jewish translators from Jerusalem are far superior to the Greek philosophers, "since they always made God their starting-point" (235, cf. 200).

Wisdom motifs are implied in terms like "right way of living" (127), "quest for virtue" and "perfecting of the character" (144), "right reason" and "power of reason" (161,162), "due reason" (168), "right relationships between man and man" (169). The terms σοφία and σοφός occur in 107,130,137,139,207,260,271. According to 121 the seventy-two scholars from Jerusalem who were to translate the Torah were chosen, among other reasons, because of their παιδεία.

The answer to Ptolemaios' question, "What is the teaching of wisdom (σοφίας διδαχή)", given by one of the Jewish translators, is a statement of the 'golden rule' in its negative form (207)[163]. The answer to the question "What is the fruit of wisdom (σοφίας καρπός)" is, "that a man should be conscious in himself that he has wrought no evil and that he should live his life in truth. Since it is from these, O mighty King, that the greatest joy and steadfastness of soul and, if you rule in piety, good hopes with God come" (260)[164].

---

159 Cf. J.J. Lewis, "The Table-Talk Section in the Letter of Aristeas", *NTS* 13 (1966) 53-56 who compares EpArist with Ps-Phocylides.
160 Cf. J. Fichtner, *Weisheit*, 1933, p.10; O.S. Rankin, *Wisdom Literature*, pp.2-4,10.
161 Cf. N. Meisner, *Untersuchungen zum Aristeasbrief*, Diss. Berlin, 1973, 2, pp.40-76 (not available); idem, *JSHRZ* II/1 (1971) 41. See already H.T. Andrews, *APOT* 2 (1913) 87 who pointed out that the table-talk section may be dependent upon a collection of 'moral sayings' but that it is not possible to determine whether they were Jewish or Greek.
162 N. Meisner, *JSHRZ* II/1 (1973) 41.
163 Cf. Tob 4,15; hebr TNaph 1,6; Ps-Menander 39f.; bShab 31a bar (Hillel). See also Mt 7,12; Lk 6,31; Acts 15,29; Did 1,2. With regard to the 'golden rule' see generally A. Nissen, *Gott und der Nächste*, WUNT 15, 1974, pp.390-399.
164 Following the translation of N. Meisner, *JSHRZ* II/1 (1973) 78.

Thus, wisdom is, like the law, of universal[165] and of particularistic importance having both a theological and, especially, an ethical dimension.

6.1.3. Law and wisdom. Several passages in EpArist prove that the identification of law and wisdom which was taught and presupposed in the Palestinian wisdom and scribal schools had started to exert a significant influence in Alexandria too[166].

In 31 it is emphasized that the law is "of divine origin, is full of wisdom, and free from all blemish".

In 127 it is stated that the "right way of living" which is the aim and the content of wisdom "consists in the keeping of the commandments" (ἐν τῷ τὰ νόμιμα συντηρεῖν εἶναι).

In 139 Moses the "lawgiver" (ὁ νομοθέτης) is called "a wise man" (σοφὸς ὤν), while the context deals with laws of food and purity.

In 144 the author points out that the law(s) of Moses were made for righteousness' sake "to aid the quest for virtue and the perfecting of the character". Since the last phrase is an exact description of the goals of wisdom we have here another clear example of the identification of the Mosaic law and wisdom. We have a similar thought in 161 where the objective of the (ritual and cultic!) law is described as "truth" and "right attitude"[167]. This thought occurs again in 168-169:

> "All our regulations have been drawn up with a view to righteousness, and nothing has been enacted in the Scripture (γραφή) accidentally (εἰκῇ) or just for the story's sake (μυθωδῶς), but its purpose is to enable us throughout our whole life (ζῆν) and in all our actions (πράξεσιν), to practise (δοκῶμεν) righteousness before all men, being mindful of God, the Ruler. Also with regard to meats and the unclean creeping things and wild beasts, every word (λόγος) aims at righteousness and righteous relationships between man and man (τὴν τῶν ἀνθρώπων συναναστροφὴν δικαίαν)".

The identification of law and wisdom has primarily an ethical dimension: the Jewish law which is true wisdom contains every-

---

165 Cf. M. Hengel, *Judentum*, p.307.
166 Cf. O. Eissfeldt, *Einleitung*, p.818 who states that the author of EpArist aims at providing "die himmelhohe Überlegenheit der mit dem Gesetz identischen jüdischen Weisheit über alle griechische Bildung". See also W. Gutbrod, in *ThWNT* 4 (1942) 1042.
167 H.T. Andrews, *APOT* 2 (1913) 109 translates "indication of right reason"; similarly M. Hadas, *Aristeas*, p.163 who has "a token of right reason".

thing which is needed for a morally perfect character and a perfect life. The motivation of the author of EpArist implies also both the universalistic and the particularistic dimension: the law (as well as wisdom, embodied in the law) is the Mosaic law of the Jews which is to be commended to the Gentiles. And the Mosaic law with its wisdom has a universal significance and should be observed by all, whether they are Jews or Gentiles (note here the significance of the allegorical interpretation[168]).

The motives of the author also imply the didactic dimension: the Jewish law should be made the basis of all, even Gentile, instruction which has as its goal the perfecting of one's character. And the theological dimension of the identification is also implied: it was God who gave the law to Israel via the mediation of Moses.

6.1.4. Summary. Even though the evidence with regard to the concepts of law and wisdom of the author of EpArist is not all too extensive, the nature of the law and the character of the identification of wisdom and law in EpArist can be described in a satisfactory manner.

The law is always the Mosaic law which was given by God for the moral refinement and perfection of the Jews and also of man in general. Even the food laws and other ritual and cultic decrees have an ethical significance, which is deduced via the allegorical interpretation. True wisdom consists in the right way of living and in righteous relationships between people.

The law is clearly identified with wisdom: Moses who gave the law was a "wise man", a sage. The law contains wisdom. And the law has the very same goal as wisdom: "to aid the quest for virtue and the perfecting of character" (144). Thus, the ethical dimension of the identification of law and wisdom is most explicit and most prominent. The universalistic, particularistic, theological, and didactic perspective is implicitly present as well.

6.2. The Third Sibylline Oracle

The Jewish Sibylline Oracle[169] of the Egyptian diaspora was to

---

168 See supra, p.121 n.155.
169 See generally J. Geffcken, *Komposition und Entstehungszeit der Oracula Sibyllina*,

support the Jewish mission by imitating and sometimes even adopting the popular prophetic oracle literature of the Hellenistic period[170]. The significance of this fact is two-fold: "Wie man die Griechen ... zu Auswertern jüdischer Gesetze und Lehren machte, so versuchte man andererseits, heidnische Weissagungen und Weisheit als Verkündigung eigentlich jüdischer Gedanken hinzustellen"[171]. The Sibylline oracles in general are marked by a "syncretistic use of pagan mythologies and conversely by powerful polemics against idolatry and immorality"[172]. As a result we find frequent references to the uniqueness, eternity, and omnipotence of the God of the Jews[173]. Sib 3 is the oldest Jewish Sibylline[174]: the corpus of this oracle was written ca. 140 B.C. in Egypt[175]. It is clearly a composite of heterogeneous sources[176]. Christian interpolations are normally seen in Sib 3,62-96.372(!).776[177]. Sib 3,1-92 was originally the end of Sib 2 and was composed in the first century A.D.[178] Sib 3 is written in Greek hexameters[179].

TU 23, 1903; A.M. Denis, *Introduction*, pp.111-122; V. Nikiprowetzky, *La Troisième Sibylle*, Etudes Juives 9, 1970; L. Rost, *Einleitung*, pp.84-86; J.J. Collins, *The Sibylline Oracles of Egyptian Judaism*, SBLDS 13, 1974; O. Eissfeldt, *Einleitung*, pp.834-836; J.H. Charlesworth, *Pseudepigrapha*, pp.184-188; G.E.W. Nickelsburg, *Literature*, pp.162-165.

170 Cf. M. Hengel, *Judentum*, p.380. He also emphasizes the influence of the apocalyptic tradition (p.461). The propagandistic goal is also acknowledged by A.M. Denis, *Introduction*, p.113; O. Eissfeldt, *Einleitung*, p.835; J.J. Collins, *Oracles*, pp.53-55.

171 L. Rost, *Einleitung*, p.86.

172 G.W.E. Nickelsburg, *Literature*, p.162. On the syncretism in the Oracles see V. Nikiprowetzky, *Sibylle*, pp.112-194; J.J. Collins, *o.c.*, pp.97-115.

173 With regard to the theology of Sib 3 see P. Dalbert, *Theologie*, pp.110-123; V. Nikiprowetzky, *o.c.*, pp.71-194. J.J. Collins, *o.c.*, pp.35-55 focuses on the pattern of eschatology in Sib 3.

174 Only Sib 3-5 appear to be Jewish. Sib 4 should be dated to ca. A.D. 80, whereas Sib 5 was presumably written in the first third of the second century A.D. Cf. J.H. Charlesworth, *Pseudepigrapha*, p.185.

175 Cf. J. Geffcken, *Komposition*, pp.1-7; A.M. Denis, *o.c.*, pp.118-120; J.J. Collins, *o.c.*, pp.28-33; O. Eissfeldt, *o.c.*, p.835; J.H. Charlesworth, *o.c.*, pp.184f.; M. Hengel, *o.c.*, pp.139f.,341,461; G.W.E. Nickelsburg, *o.c.*, pp.162,164. V. Nikiprowetzky, *o.c.*, pp.195-204 attempted to show that Sib 3 was written in the first century B.C. But see J.J. Collins, *o.c.*, pp.32ff. Collins suggests that Sib 3,46-62.75-92.350-380 are first century B.C. additions (ibid., pp.57-71).

176 Cf. J.H. Charlesworth, *o.c.*, pp.184f. and others. Contra V. Nikiprowetzky, *o.c.*, pp.206-225 who attempts to show the unity of Sib 3.

177 Cf. A.M. Denis, *o.c.*, p.118; J.H. Charlesworth, *o.c.*, p.185.

178 Cf. A.M. Denis, *o.c.*, p.119; M. Hengel, *o.c.*, p.351 n.527.

179 We use the edition of J. Geffcken, *Die Oracula Sibyllina*, GCS 8, 1902 (= 1970)

6.2.1. Concepts of revelation.
God is one. He is the Creator and sovereign ruler of the universe. He is the first cause of all that exists. He is eternal and omniscient. And he cannot be known or conceived by man: "Il échappe en son essence à toute prise sensible ou intellectuelle de l'homme qui ne saurait ni l'appercevoir, ni entendre son nom"[180].

God reveals himself[181] to man primarily in nature[182] and in judgment[183]. God's revelation in the events of the Exodus and in the theophany at Sinai is referred to only in 3,248-260. In 3,293 the nightly dreams or visions are described as media of the divine revelation. Prophetic utterances are further means of revelation[184]. The ecstatic inspiration of the Sibylline has to be mentioned in this context as well[185].

6.2.2. The Jewish law.
Numerous passages stress the fact that the Jewish law is of divine origin: "God gave the law (νόμος) forth from heaven" (3,256; cf. 3,768). The law is specifically the "law of the immortal God" (3,275.600), the "law of the mighty God" (3,284.686; cf. 3,246), the "law of the Most High" (3,580. 719).

At times νόμος is connected with lists of compilations of (positive) ethical maxims[186] (3,237-262 with νόμος in 256. 259).

The Gentiles are regarded as ἄνομοι who have never listened to the word of God (3,69-70) and who therefore live a lawless life

---

and the translations of H.C.O. Lanchester, "The Sibylline Oracles", *APOT* 2 (1913) 378-406 and V. Nikiprowetzky, *Sibylline*, 1970, pp.291-353 (text with French translation).

180 V. Nikiprowetzky, o.c., p.71.
181 On the knowledge of God in Sib 3 see V. Nikiprowetzky, o.c., pp.74-76.
182 In earthquakes (σεισμός): 3,449.457; cf. 4,128; 5,291; floods (ὕδωρ): 3,440. 461.824; cf. 4,129.143; thunder (βροντή): 5,298-305; pestilence (λοιμός): 3,266. 332.538.603; famine (λιμός): 3,236.317.476.602.754.
183 Cf. 3,154-174.319.333.669-697. In many instances natural catastrophes are also understood to be divine judgment. On the whole see H.C.O. Lanchester, *APOT* 2 (1913) 375; P. Dalbert, *Theologie*, pp.113f.
184 Cf. the terms προφητεύειν: 3,163.298.491.699.811.822; προφῆται: 582.781.
185 Cf. the terms οἰστρομανής: 3,810; μαινομένην: 3,816.818; ἀνάγκη: 3,296. See the oracles in 3,296-302.490-491.162-163. Cf. V. Nikiprowetzky, o.c., pp.74f.; M. Hengel, *Judentum*, p.391.
186 Cf. R.J. Banks, *Jesus and the Law*, p.52.

(ἄνομος βίος) which equals an unclean life (ἄναγνος βίος, 3,496). Lawlessness and uncleanness are linked with unrighteousness (3,496). Those who do not obey the law will fall under God's judgment (3,569-603.686).

In contrast to the lawless Gentiles, the pious Jews possess the law of God "in righteousness" (3,580; cf. 3,768).

The law will be universally valid (and kept!) in the eschatological kingdom (3,573-583.719-720.757)[187]. The nation of the mighty God "shall be to all mortals the guide of life (βίου καθοδηγοί" (3,195)[188]. God's law which is the most righteous of all on earth (3,719-720) is "l'hymne des justes lois (ἔννομος ὕμνος)" (3,246)[189]. Salvation and peace will only rule when men return to the righteousness of the law (3,580-581)[190]. In 3,275-278 obedience to the law is linked with the fear of the Lord.

Thus, it seems that in Sib 3 the Jewish law appears to be of particularistic and universal, of theological and ethical and even of eschatological significance.

6.2.3. Law and wisdom. Scholars acknowledge the fact that Sib 3 has adopted the identification of wisdom and law[191] even though they do not state the textual or theological evidence. In 3,219-220 the Jewish nation is called "a race of most righteous (δικαιοτάτων) men who ever give themselves up to sound counsel and virtuous deeds (οἷσιν ἀεὶ βουλή τ'ἀγαθή καλά τ'ἔργα μέμηλεν)". Since righteousness is linked with obedience to the law (3,558.720.768) and unrighteousness with uncleanness and lawlessness (3,69-70.496), it can be assumed that 3,219-220 implies the close correlation of wisdom ("sound counsel", "virtuous deeds") with the law ("righteousness").

In 3,573-600 the "holy race of God-fearing men" (εὐσεβέων ἀνδρῶν ἱερὸν γένος) is described as "adhering to the counsels (βουλαῖς) and the mind (νόῳ) of the Most High" (574), honouring the temple (in Jerusalem) and bringing the prescribed ritual offerings (575-579), possessing the law of the Most High "in righteous-

---

187 Cf. W. Gutbrod, in *ThWNT* 4 (1942) 1042; P. Dalbert, *Theologie*, p.115.
188 Cf. also En(eth) 105,1.
189 Following the translation of V. Nikiprowetzky, *Sibylle*, p.303.
190 Cf. M. Limbeck, *Ordnung*, p.89 n.63.
191 Cf. W. Gutbrod, *a.c.*, p.1042; V. Nikiprowetzky, *o.c.*, p.74.

ness" (580). To this race alone God has given "discreet counsel" (εὔφρονα βουλήν, 584) and faith (πίστιν) and an "excellent understanding" (ἄριστον νόημα) in their hearts (585). They keep all the commandments of the law (586-596) and do not transgress the "holy law" (ἁγνὸς νόμος) of the immortal God (600). Thus, the pericope 3,573-600 clearly implies the identification of the (cultic, ritual, and moral) Jewish law with wisdom ("counsel", "mind", etc.).

3,669-697 presupposes *e contrario* this identification: God will bring judgment upon the "undisciplined, empty-minded people" (λαὸν ἀπαίδευτον κενεόφρονα, 670) because they did not know the law (686) but had a "witless mind" (ἄφρονι θυμῷ, 687).

Similarly 3,702-731 contrasts the pondering of the law of the Most High God (719) with going "astray from the path of the Eternal" (721) and having "foolish hearts" (ἄφρονι θυμῷ, 722).

3,762-763 summons to "consecrate your minds (φρένας) within your breasts and eschew unlawful service (λατρείας ἀνόμους): serve the living God". It is clear from the context (cf. 3,764-765) that lawful service is understood to consist in obeying the law. Proper thinking is pictured as identical with "lawful service"[192].

6.2.4. Summary.

Despite the composite and syncretistic nature of Sib 3 which influenced even some of the concepts of revelation (note the role of ecstasy), it is obvious that νόμος refers to the Jewish law including not only moral or ethical or universal rules for behaviour but also cultic and ritual decrees.

The identification of law and wisdom which is apparent in several passages has to be understood primarily as possessing an ethical dimension. The ability to give sound counsel and virtuous deeds equals the keeping of the law with its various commandments. The apologetic and 'missionary' purpose of Sib 3 makes it probable that the universalistic dimension is implied as well: the Gentiles should recognize that the Jewish law is the one true source of

---

[192] The identification of the Jewish law with wisdom can also be observed in the later Sib 5. Sib 5,264-265 states that to be clean means to have within one's heart a mind (νοῦς) which conforms to God's laws. 5,360 refers to "God the Father, the wise (σοφός), the everlasting". 5,384 mentions the "wise" (σοφοί) who will be left and not be destroyed by God's judgment. And 5,509 states that God will destroy all the evil and all the "lawless" (ἀνόμους).

wisdom, and in the future they will themselves arrange their thought and deeds in accordance with this law.

6.3. The Wisdom of Solomon

The originally anonymous writing SapSal[193] was composed in Greek[194] and written by an Egyptian Jew, presumably in Alexandria[195] during the first century B.C.[196] It has proven to be impossible to demonstrate a literary dependence of SapSal on En(eth), on writings from Qumran, or on apologetic Hellenistic Judaism[197]. However, the evidence that SapSal had contact with the world of Jewish apocalyptic and apologetic represented by and in these writings is beyond any doubt[198]. The points of contact be-

---

193 See generally L. Rost, *Einleitung*, pp.41-44; O. Eissfeldt, *Einleitung*, pp.812-816; D. Winston, *The Wisdom of Solomon*, 1979, pp.1-69 (with lit. on pp.70-96); D. Georgi, "Weisheit Salomos", *JSHRZ* III/4 (1980) 391-401 (with lit.); G.W.E. Nickelsburg, *Literature*, pp.175-185.
194 Some scholars assume a Hebrew *Vorlage* for SapSal 1-6, but this cannot be proved despite the *parallelismus membrorum* or the reminiscences of Hebrew diction; cf. L. Rost, *o.c.*, p.42; D. Georgi, *o.c.*, p.392 n.4. We use the edition of J. Ziegler, *Sapientia Salomonis*, Septuaginta Vetus Testamentum Graecum, XII/1 ²1980, and the translations of S. Holmes, "The Wisdom of Solomon", *APOT* 1 (1913) 518-568; D. Winston, *The Wisdom of Solomon: A New Translation with Introduction and Commentary*, AB vol. 43, 1979; D. Georgi, *JSHRZ* III/4 (1980) 402-478.
195 This is generally acknowledged; cf. D. Winston, *o.c.*, p.25. But see F. Zimmermann, "The Book of Wisdom: Its Language and Character", *JQR* 57 (1966) 1-27, 101-135 who argues for an Aramaic original and for Syria as place of origin, and D. Georgi, *o.c.*, p.396 who maintains that "die Annahme der Entstehung der Sap in Ägypten ist ... weder nötig noch möglich", arguing for Syria as place of origin. However, his arguments are rather apologetic and defensive and speculative, and do not convince. — The unity of SapSal is disputed. Some scholars deny the integrity of the book; cf. S. Holmes, *o.c.*, pp.521-524. Others emphasize its unity; cf. L. Rost, *o.c.*, p.43; O. Eissfeldt, *o.c.*, p.816; D. Winston, *o.c.*, pp.12-14; D. Georgi, *o.c.*, p.392. Cf. also G. Ziener, *Die theologische Begriffssprache im Buche der Weisheit*, BBB 11, 1956, p.11.
196 Thus L. Rost, *o.c.*, p.43; O. Eissfeldt, *o.c.*, p.815. However, several dates between 220 B.C. and A.D. 50 have been suggested. Recently G.W.E. Nickelsburg, *o.c.*, p.184; D. Winston, *o.c.*, pp.21-24 argued for a date between 37-41 A.D. (the reign of Caligula), whereas D. Georgi, *o.c.*, pp.396f. argued for a date in the last decades of the 2nd century B.C.
197 Cf. the extensive discussion in C. Larcher, *Études sur le Livre de la Sagesse*, EB, 1969, pp.103-151.
198 Cf. D. Georgi, *o.c.*, pp.394f.

tween SapSal and Philo are even closer[199]. The influence of Greek Hellenistic styles and concepts is evident throughout the book[200].

It seems to be impossible to harmonize SapSal with the purpose of establishing a theological conceptual system.

> In the words of D. Georgi, "Sap will ... trotz ihrer Vertrautheit mit dem philosophischen Wissen der Zeit, keine logisch gegliederte philosophische oder theologische Information geben. In ihrer begrifflichen Buntheit geht sie noch weit über das in der popularphilosophischen Diatribe Übliche hinaus"[201].

SapSal has been described as "weisheitliche Glaubenslehre" for the Jews in Alexandria in the first century B.C.[202] It is an "exhortation to pursue wisdom and thereby to live the righteous life that issues in immortality"[203]. In order to achieve this purpose the author uses the popular Hellenistic genre of the *protreptic*, a treatise that made an appeal to follow a meaningful philosophy as a way of life[204].

6.3.1. Wisdom concepts. If one approaches the main doctrines of SapSal one soon becomes aware of the fact that "its subtle blending of heterogeneous conceptions has inevitably entailed a degree of ambiguity in their formulation which makes it difficult to determine which elements are primary and which are secondary"[205]. This is also the case with regard to the concepts of wisdom in SapSal[206].

Wisdom is presented as a person (1; 6-10)[207], as mediator in

---

199 Especially with regard to Philo's *Quaestiones* and the allegorical commentaries. Cf. C. Larcher, *Études*, pp.151-178.
200 Cf. F. Ricken, "Gab es eine hellenistische Vorlage für Weish 13-16?", *Bib* 49 (1968) 54-68; E. des Places, "Le Livre de la Sagesse et les influences grecques", *Bib* 50 (1969) 536-542; C. Larcher, *o.c.*, pp.181-236; J.M. Reese, *Hellenistic Influence on the Book of Wisdom*, AnBibl 41, 1970.
201 D. Georgi, *JSHRZ* III/4 (1980) 393.
202 M. Küchler, *Weisheitstraditionen*, p.20. Cf. D. Winston, *Wisdom*, pp.63f. who also defends the view that the author is "primarily addressing his fellow Jews in an effort to encourage them to take pride in their traditional faith" (p.63).
203 G.W.E. Nickelsburg, *Literature*, p.175.
204 Cf. J.M. Reese, *o.c.*, pp.117-121; G.W.E. Nickelsburg, *o.c.*, p.175.
205 D. Winston, *Wisdom*, p.33; cf. D. Georgi, *JSHRZ* III/4 (1980) 393.
206 Cf. generally P. Dalbert, *Theologie*, pp.78-85; G. Ziener, *Begriffssprache*, pp.109-113; H. Hegermann, *Schöpfungsmittler*, pp.77f.; U. Wilckens, *ThWNT* 7 (1964) 499f.; P.E. Bonnard, *Sagesse*, pp.89-112; C. Larcher, *Études*, pp.362-414; D. Winston, *o.c.*, pp.33-43.
207 Cf. G. Ziener, *o.c.*, p.112; H.F. Weiss, *Untersuchungen*, pp.199-202; C. Larcher, *o.c.*, pp.398-414; J.M. Reese, *Influence*, pp.36-50; B.L. Mack, *Logos und Sophia*,

creation (8,3-4; 9,1-2.9), as dwelling with God (8,3; 9,4.9-10), as a gift of God (7,7; 8,21; 9,4.10.17), as pervading the entire cosmos and at the same time enjoying intimacy with God (7,24; 8,1-3)[208]. Wisdom is also closely related with πνεῦμα (1,6; 7,22; 9,17)[209] and is also linked with λόγος (9,1.2)[210]. Wisdom represents the whole spectrum of natural science (7,17-21) and teaches all human arts and crafts (7,16; 14,2). Wisdom is the source of all moral knowledge (8,7)[211] and of immortality (8,13). Wisdom is sometimes linked with righteousness (1,5.15; 3,1; cf. 5,1.15). Wisdom is synonymous with divine providence (7,27; 14,3). Wisdom is also the source of prophecy (7,27). The attainment of wisdom implies moral prerequisites: man has to long for wisdom (6,12-13; 8,2.18), and wisdom enters only into pious souls (7,27) and into those who are worthy (6,16).

SapSal makes no mention of the fear of the Lord or of the Jewish sacrificial cult.

6.3.2. *The law.* Although the terms νόμος and ἐντολή[212] occur several times it is obvious that the author of SapSal seems to avoid references to the Jewish (!) law[213]. Possible references to the Jewish law are 2,12; 6,4; 9,9; 18,4.

---

pp.63-107; D. Winston, *o.c.*, pp.34-38. H.F. Weiss, *o.c.*, p.200 says with regard to passages like SapSal 8,3-4; 9,4.9 that "mit solcher Terminologie scheint nun allerdings die Grenze dessen erreicht zu sein, was mit dem jüdischen Monotheismus noch vereinbar ist"; but he points out as well (regarding 7,25-26) that "die Weisheit eben nicht eine selbständige oder etwa gleichwertige Größe neben Gott ist" (ibid.). Similarly J.D.G. Dunn, *Christology*, 1980, pp.172f.

208 Note J.D.G. Dunn, *o.c.*, p.173 who points out on the basis of 7,15-16; 8,21-9,6 that the author of SapSal "has not the slightest thought of equating wisdom with some pantheistic ultimate reason ... of wisdom as an independent divine being. From start to finish the wisdom of which he speaks is the wisdom of God and signifies God's wise ordering of creation and of those who fear him" (ibid.).

209 Cf. C. Larcher, *o.c.*, pp.362-376.

210 Cf. H. Hegermann, *o.c.*, pp.77f. who detects in SapSal the beginning of the "Übergang der Sophiaspekulation auf die Logosgestalt" (p.78) which is more fully developed by Philo. He points out that both λόγος and σοφία are called παντοδύναμος (18,15 and 7,23), and that both reside on heavenly thrones (18,15 and 9,10).

211 Cf. G. Ziener, *o.c.*, pp.109f. who states that the main emphasis of SapSal is the moral significance of 'wisdom'. Similarly S. Aalen, *Begriffe*, pp.175f. point out that according to 7,22-30 wisdom is "die moralische Lichtmacht, die im Menschen wirksam ist" (p.176).

212 νόμος: 2,11.12; 6,4.18; 9,5; 14,16; 16,6; 18,4.9; ἐντολή: 9,9; 16,6.

213 Cf. K. Berger, *Gesetzesauslegung*, 1, p.45 who finds a "faktische inhaltiche Redu-

In 2,12 the wicked are said to plan to entrap the just man since he reproaches them for their "sins against the law"(ἁμαρτήματα νόμου)[214]. In 6,4 the author reproaches the kings that their judgment was not straight and that they "did not keep the law (ἐφυλάξετε νόμον) nor live (ἐπορεύθητε) according to God's will (βουλή)"[215]. In 9,9 Solomon says that wisdom knows what is "right" (εὐθές) according to his "commandments" (ἐντολαῖς), i.e. the commandments of God[216]. 18,4 belongs in the context of the Exodus and refers to the Israelites as people "through whom the imperishable light of the law (τὸ ἄφθαρτον νόμου φῶς) was to be given to the world".

It is evident that this kind of evidence makes it impossible to establish the concept of law of the author of SapSal. It is safe to assume, however, that the law is conceived of as a universal entity. The significance of the particularistic Jewish laws is played down. The ethical perspective of the law is emphasized.

6.3.3. *Wisdom and law*. Recently it has been denied that SapSal identifies wisdom and law[218]. Other scholars defend the view that

---

zierung des atl Gesetzes" and a "weitgehende Identifizierung mit Sozialgeboten überhaupt" in SapSal. However, there is insufficient evidence in SapSal with regard to the concept of law to substantiate this opinion. The brief discussion of the concept of law in SapSal by R.J. Banks, *Jesus and the Law*, pp.31f.,54f. is not satisfactory either. It is true that SapSal refers to the Exodus and God's covenant, but these events are nowhere related to the Jewish law. When Banks states (p.55) that νόμος in SapSal embraces knowledge of the elements of the universe (7,17-21), virtues not drawn directly from the law (8,7), and divination of present riddles and future happenings (8,8), it has to be pointed out that in all these instances no relation to the law in general or to the Jewish law in particular can be detected. As regards the concept of covenant in SapSal cf. A. Jaubert, *Notion*, pp.350-373.

214 G. Ziener, *Begriffssprache*, p.93 thinks that 2,12 expresses the normative character of the Jewish law, and that νόμος designates here "die Summe aller Vorschriften, welche das Leben des Israeliten regeln". D. Winston, *Wisdom*, p.119 does not comment on this phrase.

215 C. Larcher, *Études*, p.203 thinks that here νόμος "renvoie aux grandes obligations de la loi naturelle entérinées par les législations de divers peuples". D. Winston, o.c., p.153 agrees that νόμος here means "natural principles of justice", but emphasizes at the same time that "a number of Jewish Hellenistic writers viewed the Torah itself as an expression of natural law". Cf. EpArist 161; 4Macc 1,16f.; 5,25; Philo Op 3,143; VitMos 2,52; Abr 16,60.

216 S. Holmes, *APOT* 1 (1913) 550 comments that "his devotion to Scripture in this place overcomes the writer's philosophical theories".

217 D. Georgi, *JSHRZ* III/4 (1980) 464f. acknowledges that νόμος is here a reference to the Jewish law. Cf. also D. Winston, *Wisdom*, p.311. With regard to the concept of the obligation to spread the teachings of the Torah to the Gentiles see Is 2; 42,1-6; TLev 14,4; ApcBar 48,40; 59,2; 4Ezr 7,20-24; 14,20.

218 Cf. D. Winston, o.c., p.42 who points out, at least, that this identification is nowhere stated explicitly (!). D. Georgi, o.c., p.395 states that "Sap kennt auch nicht

the author knew and used this identification[219]. The correlation of wisdom and law can be seen as being implied in 2,12: the "sins against the law" are linked in synonymous parallelism with "sins against our discipline" (ἁμαρτήματα παιδείας). Thus, νόμος and παιδεία are closely related.

Further evidence of the implicit identification of law and wisdom is to be found in the passages which compare both wisdom and the law with light[220]: 7,26 states that wisdom is an "effulgence of everlasting light" (ἀπαύγασμα φωτὸς ἀιδίου) which came into the world with creation and which organizes the world and checks darkness and evil. 7,27 says that wisdom dwells in the "friends of God" of all generations. And according to 18,4 Israel possesses the "imperishable light of the law" (τὸ ἄφθαρτον νόμου φῶς)[221].

Further, it has been pointed out in a general way that in ch. 6-10 wisdom becomes an entity "die alle Beziehungen zwischen Gott und dem Frommen umfaßt"[222], and that the author of SapSal seems to avoid the term 'law' for apologetic reasons preferring to speak of wisdom "in welcher sich der Offenbarungscharakter (7,25b) und das Normative (6,18) des Gesetzes finden"[223].

> In other words, "Wisdom is conceived by him (i.e. the author) as a direct bearer of revelation, functioning through the workings of the human mind, and supreme arbiter of all values. She is clearly the Archetypal Torah, of which the Mosaic Law is but an image"[224].

Further, ch. 9-18 seem to present implicitly the Jewish law as a means of overcoming the hiddenness of wisdom: the 'men of the Torah' of the OT are filled with the divine spirit of wisdom (9,10-

---

die Gleichsetzung von Weisheit und Gesetz"; cf. also idem, *o.c.*, pp.435 (ad 9,9), 464f. (ad 18,4).
219 Cf. W. Gutbrod, *ThWNT* 4 (1942) 1042; S. Aalen, *Begriffe*, p.176 n.2; G. Ziener, *Begriffssprache*, pp.93,113; P.S. Fiddes, *Hiddenness*, pp.343-350; B.T. Viviano, *Study*, 1978, p.140. Implicitly acknowledged by D. Winston, *o.c.*, p.43 when he says that the author of SapSal "very likely" believed "that the teachings of the Torah were tokens of Divine Wisdom, and that they were in harmony with the laws of the universe and as such implant all the virtues in man".
220 Contra D. Georgi, *o.c.*, pp.464f. (ad 18,4).
221 S. Aalen, *Begriffe*, p.176 n.2 states in this context with regard to 7,27: "Die Weisheit als moralische Macht fällt zusammen mit dem Gesetz als moralischem 'Licht' ". On 18,4 see ibid., pp.187,194.
222 G. Ziener, *Begriffssprache*, p.113.
223 G. Ziener, *o.c.*, p.93.
224 D. Winston, *Wisdom*, p.43.

18; 10,1-21; 11,1-10) and also provide object-lessons (= wisdom) for admiration and copying of the present generation. And the miracles of the Torah are wisdom object-lessons as well (cf. 11,15-16; 12,24-27; 15,18-19; 16,6).

6.3.4. Summary. In contrast to the concept of wisdom which is prominent in SapSal — even if it is not harmonized into a theological conceptual system due to its eclectic character — the concept of the (Jewish) law is not developed at all. This makes any attempt at establishing an implicit or explicit identification of wisdom and law impossible, not to speak of the nature of such an identification.

Nevertheless we have found several passages in which wisdom and law are closely related if not implicitly identified (2,12 and 7, 26-27 compared with 18,4). Further, the miracles of the Torah seem to have been used as wisdom object-lessons. And finally, wisdom appears to be referred to instead of the Torah as entity which 'contains' the will of God.

§7 Later Jewish Writings from the First Century A.D.

7.1. The Fourth Book of Maccabees

The treatise 4Macc[225] was composed in Greek[226] between A.D. 40 and 118[227] in Alexandria or in Antioch in Syria[228]. 4Macc is a

---

225 See generally L. Rost, *Einleitung*, pp.80-82; O. Eissfeldt, *Einleitung*, pp.831-834; J.H. Charlesworth, *Pseudepigrapha*, pp.151-153; U. Breitenstein, *Beobachtungen zu Sprache, Stil und Gedankengut des Vierten Makkabäerbuches*, ²1978; G.W.E. Nickelsburg, *Literature*, pp.223-227.
226 We use the edition of A. Rahlfs, "Machabaeorum IV", *Septuaginta*, 1, pp.1157-1184; and the translation of R.B. Townshend, "The Fourth Book of Maccabees", *APOT* 2 (1913) 666-685.
227 Cf. O. Eissfeldt, *o.c.*, p.832; J.H. Charlesworth, *o.c.*, p.151. M. Hadas, *The Third and Fourth Book of Maccabees*, 1953, pp.95f. (followed by G.W.E. Nickelsburg, *o.c.*, p.226) suggests A.D. 40. Others suggest A.D. 117/118. L. Rost, *o.c.*, p.82 takes A.D. 70 as *terminus ante quem*. Recently U. Breitenstein, *o.c.*, pp.173-175 defended the first third of the second century A.D. as date of composition.
228 Cf. J.H. Charlesworth, *o.c.*, p.151. For Alexandria, cf. L. Rost, *o.c.*, p.82; O. Eiss-

representative of the earlier form of the diatribe[229] and is strongly dependent upon Greek and Hellenistic philosophy[230]. The author obviously had mastered Greek thought and language[231]. The subject of 4Macc is the proof of the proposition that "inspired reason is supreme ruler over the passions" (1,1)[232]. But the author remained a Jew as "Judaism is the true philosophy"[233] for him.

7.1.1. The law. The term νόμος occurs 38 times in 4Macc, always in the singular[234]. According to 4Macc the OT legislation is the φιλόσοφος λόγος pure and simple (5,35; cf. 7,7)[235]. It is the "divine philosophy" (θεῖα φιλοσοφία, 7,9), "divine legislation" (θεῖος νόμος, 6,21; 5,18; 11,27), "inspired reason" (εὐσεβὴς λογισμός, 17,16), the "rule of philosophy" (ὁ τῆς φιλοσοφίας κανών, 7,21).

The law of God which shows whether one faithfully follows this rule is, specifically, a dietary law (5,2.6; 6,15). To break this

---

feldt, *o.c.*, p.832. For Antiochia, cf. M. Hadas, *o.c.*, pp.109-113; G.W.E. Nickelsburg, *o.c.*, p.226.

229 Cf. L. Rost, *Einleitung*, p.81; O. Eissfeldt, *Einleitung*, p.832; J.C.H. Lebram, "Die literarische Form des vierten Makkabäerbuches", *Vigiliae Christianae* 28 (1974) 81-96; U. Breitenstein, *Beobachtungen*, pp.178f.

230 Often scholars emphasize the Stoic character of 4Macc. See I. Heinemann, *PW* 14/1 (1928) 800-805; L. Rost, *o.c.*, p.81; O. Eissfeldt, *o.c.*, p.832; G. Delling, "Perspektiven der Erforschung des hellenistischen Judentums", *HUCA* 45 (1974) 152-154. However, U. Breitenstein, *o.c.*, pp.159-175 proved that 4Macc contains not only Stoic, but also Cynic, Peripatetic, Epicurean, and Pythagorean concepts, and concludes that the author, Pseudo-Iosephos, was an "unselbständiger, ... recht verständnisloser Kopf" (p.179; cf. pp.132f.). He compares Ps-Iosephos with the author of SapSal whose writing he knew: both authors are Diaspora Jews, influenced by Hellenism but faithful to the law; both give to their rhetorical treatise a philosophical imprint; both link their Jewish faith with the Hellenistic spirit; both teach the immortality of the soul; and both affirm eternal retribution (p.19).

231 With regard to the vocabulary, language, style, and rhetoric of 4Macc see U. Breitenstein, *o.c.*, pp.13-130. He concludes that the author is a "Vertreter des sogenannten Asianismus, im ganzen der pompösen Unterart dieser Stilrichtung" (p.179).

232 "αὐτοδέσποτος ἐστὶν τῶν παθῶν ὁ εὐσεβὴς λογισμός".

233 G.W.E. Nickelsburg, *Literture*, p.226. Cf. L. Rost, *o.c.*, p.82; G. Delling, *a.c.*, p.153; P. Dalbert, *Theologie*, p.9; H. Hegermann, "Griechisch-jüdisches Schrifttum", *Literatur und Religion des Frühjudentums*, ed. J. Maier, 1973 states that "inhaltlich vertritt er ein sich dem Hellenismus gegenüber abschließendes, gesetzesstrenges Judentum". U. Breitenstein, *o.c.*, p.133 asserts that "das jüdische Element überdeckt das echt griechische".

234 Cf. U. Breitenstein, *o.c.*, p.171. See generally A. Jaubert, *Notion*, pp.333-338.

235 Cf.G. Delling, *a.c.*, p.153.

dietary law is "to break the law of the fathers" (τὸν πάτριον καταλῦσαι νόμον, 5,33).

In 4Macc νόμος clearly refers to the Mosaic law, especially to its ritual sections (cf. 1,34; 2,5; 4,23; 5,16-38; 9,15)[236]. The obedience to the Torah is the motivation to go into martyrdom (5,16; 9,1-8; 16,17-22). And the obedience to the Torah is not depicted as a Stoic virtue but as sheer obedience to God (cf. 5,16; 9,2; 16, 17.19)[237].

As "divine philosophy" (7,9; cf. 7,21; 17,16), the Jewish law has a universal dimension. But it is also very closely linked with Israel in general and with Moses in particular (cf. 5,16.33; 9,2; 17, 19). The purpose of 4Macc explains why the ethical dimension of the law is stressed (cf. also 2,8; 13,24.26; 15,9; 19,1). For the author of 4Macc the content of εὐσέβεια is "das unbedingte Ausharren im Gehorsam gegen das Gesetz Gottes"[238].

7.1.2. The concept of wisdom. The definition of σοφία as "the knowledge of things, divine and human, and of their causes" (γνῶσις θείων καὶ ἀνθρωπίνων πραγμάτων καὶ τῶν τούτων αἰτιῶν, 1,16) is clearly Stoic[239]. God himself is "all-wise" (πανσοφὸς θεός, 1,12). Wisdom is "manifested" under the (Stoic) forms (ἰδέαι) of self-control and justice (φρόνησις καὶ δικαιοσύνη) as well as courage and temperance (ἀνδρεία καὶ σωφροσύνη) according to 1,18[240].

7.1.3. Law and wisdom. The Palestinian and Alexandrian identification of law and wisdom can be observed in 4Macc[241]. In

---

236 Cf. R.J. Banks, *Jesus and the Law*, p.54.
237 O. Eissfeldt, *Einleitung*, p.832.
238 G. Delling, "Perspektiven", *HUCA* 54 (1974) 153 quoting 5,9.16; 9,2.
239 Cf. Cicero Tusc 4,57; Seneca Ep 89,4. Cf. U. Breitenstein, *Beobachtungen*, p.159. He emphasizes, however, that the martyrs of 4Macc are nevertheless not (!) Stoic 'wise men' (ibid.).
240 Representing the four cardinal virtues of Stoicism. Cf. O. Eissfeldt, *Einleitung*, p.832. U. Breitenstein, *Beobachtungen*, p.160 points out that both the Stoic main maxim of ethical behaviour, the ὁμολογουμένης (τῇ φύσει) ζῆν (cf. M. Pohlenz, *Stoa*, 1, pp.116-118), and the important Stoic value of the καθῆκον, the obligation of the wise man, are never mentioned in 4 Macc.
241 Cf. M. Küchler, *Weisheitstraditionen*, p.58 who states with regard to 1,15-19 that the author achieves "eine Verbindung von griechischer Definition (16) und jüdischem Dogma (17a), welche in einem Dreierschritt die Weisheit mit dem Gesetz zusammenschließt". U. Breitenstein, *o.c.*, p.171 states that "über seine Philo-

1,17 we read: "This (i.e. wisdom) I take to be the culture acquired under the law (ἡ τοῦ νόμου παιδεία), through which we learn with due reverence the things of God". In other words, the Jewish law is the source of, and contains, παιδεία which is identical (αὕτη δὴ τοίνυν ἐστίν, v.17a) with σοφία.

In 5,35 "wisdom-loving reason" (φιλόσοφος λόγος) is closely linked with the venerated priesthood and with the "knowledge of the law" (νομοθεσίας ἐπιστήμη). The last phrase implies that the Mosaic legislation is said to contain ἐπιστήμη and is at the same time compared with the φιλόσοφος λόγος.

The identification of law and wisdom, i.e. of the 'religious' and of the 'philosophical' realms, is the basis of the equation of reason and piety[242]. The author of 4Macc uses the term φιλοσοφία[243] as designation for the Jewish view of world, life, and religion (cf. 5, 11.22; 7,9 θεία φιλοσοφία of Eleazar; 7,21). For the tyrant the priest Eleazar does not seem to be a philosopher since the old man still adheres to the Jewish religion (5,7). Eleazar answers (5,22): "You scoff at our philosophy (φιλοσοφία), as if under it we were living in a manner contrary to reason (οὐ μετὰ εὐλογιστίας[244])". And the author of 4Macc himself addresses Eleazar as "philosopher of the divine life" (φιλόσοφε θείου βίου) and "you who live in harmony with the law" (ὦ σύμφωνε νόμου) at the same time (7,7).

For the author the 'proper' philosophy (= wisdom) consisted undoubtedly in a pious life according to the Jewish law. The term εὐσέβεια occurs 46 times and is thus one of the most important concepts of 4Macc[245]. The Jewish εὐσέβεια is connected with the Greek concept of ἀρετή (cf. 5,24; 9,29). It is διὰ τὴν εὐσέβειαν[246] that the martyrs go into death. Even reason is subject to

---

sophia lässt Ps-Ios gar keinen Zweifel aufkommen: Sie ist allein durch das *Gesetz* bestimmt". G.W.E. Nickelsburg, *Literature*, p.226 emphasizes that "right reason takes its stand on wisdom, which is the Torah".

242 Cf. S. Lauer, "Eusebes Logismos in IV Macc.", *JJS* 6 (1955) 170-171, and especially U. Breitenstein, *o.c.*, pp.168-173. We rely on Breitenstein for the following observations.

243 Except in 1,1-2 where he uses the term, rather presumptuously, for his own activity. He calls his treatise a φιλοσοφώτατον λόγον.

244 In 4Macc εὐλογιστία is equivalent with λογισμός; cf. 13,5.16.

245 Cf. U. Breitenstein, *Beobachtungen*, p.169.

246 Cf. 5,31; 7,16; 9,6.7.29.30; 11,20; 13,12.27; 15,14; 16,14.17; 17,7; 18,3; cf. 6,22 with the expression ὑπὲρ τῆς εὐσεβείας.

piety; εὐσεβής is used as an attribute with λογισμός and with ἐπιστήμη[247] : "ὁ εὐσεβὴς λογισμός bedeutet die Vernunft, die auf Frömmigkeit beruht, Vernunft, welche ein 'frommes' Leben gewährleistet und um der Frömmigkeit willen sogar den Märtyrertod nicht verachtet. Die Vernunft folgt dem Gebot der Frömmigkeit"[248]. And it is obvious that this εὐσέβεια consists solely in obedience to the law: Eleazar emphasizes that "we, having accepted the divine law (θεῖος νόμος) as the law of our country, do not believe (that) any stronger necessity (ἀνάγκη) is laid upon us than that of our obedience to the law (τῆς πρὸς τὸν νόμον ἡμῶν εὐπειθείας, 5,16)". The philo-sophia of 4 Macc is solely determined by the Jewish law[249].

7.1.4. Summary. For the author of 4Macc the Jewish law is primarily the basis and source of true piety (εὐσέβεια) and "divine philosophy" (θεία φιλοσοφία). It is also the source of σοφία and παιδεία. As true reason and (Jewish) piety are one, so are wisdom and the (Jewish) law. It is obvious that the author of 4Macc knew the Palestinian, and also Alexandrian, identification of law and wisdom and could indeed take it so much for granted that he was able to base his entire treatise on the "inspired reason (as) supreme ruler over the passions" (1,1) on this correlation. For him the law is the basis, the source, and the content of wisdom, and the object of true philo-sophia. The law determines εὐσέβεια, i.e. all ethical and religious behaviour, and it determines and amounts to true reason. And obedience to the Torah, as obedience to God, is the highest value in life, even if it leads into martyrdom.

7.2. The Fourth Book of Ezra

The apocalypse of 4Ezra[250] was originally written in Hebrew[251]

---

247 Cf. U. Breitenstein, *o.c.*, pp.145f. for references.
248 U. Breitenstein, *o.c.*, p.170. He quotes 7,1.4; 8,1; 13,16; 16,4 as further examples for the 'piety' of reason. S. Lauer, "Eusebes", *JJS* 6 (1955) 171 defines εὐσεβὴς λογισμός as "reasoning which follows the rules of piety (these rules being known to us from the divine law)" and, at the same time, as "reasoning for the sake of piety" (ibid.).
249 As a result, νόμος can be exchanged for λογισμός; cf. 2,9-10.
250 See generally B. Violet, *Die Esra-Apokalypse (IV Esra)*, GCS 18, 1910, pp.XII-

or Aramaic[252] which was then translated into Greek. Numerous versions which are based on the Greek translation are extant with the Latin version being the most reliable[253]. Today 4Ezr is generally regarded as a unity, with the exception of the later Christian additions in Greek (ch. 1-2; 15-16)[254]. This does not exclude the possibility that the author used different apocalyptic concepts, traditions, and material[255].

The Jewish author of 4Ezr 3-14 places his writing into a fic-

---

LXIV; G.H. Box, *The Ezra-Apocalypse (2Esdras 3-14)*, 1912, pp.I-LXXVII; idem, "IV Ezra", *APOT* 2 (1913) 542-561; B. Violet, *Die Apokalypsen des Esra und des Baruch in deutscher Gestalt*, GCS 32, 1924, pp.XII-LV; W.O.E. Oesterley, *II Esdras: With Introduction and Notes*, 1933, pp.XI-XLCII; L. Rost, *Einleitung*, pp.91-94; J.M. Myers, *I and II Esdras: Introduction, Translation and Commentary*, AB vol. 42, 1974, pp.105-134 (with up-to-date bibliography pp.135-139); O. Eissfeldt, *Einleitung*, pp.846-849; J.H. Charlesworth, *Pseudepigrapha*, pp.111-116; G.W.E. Nickelsburg, *Literature*, pp.287-294; J. Schreiner, "Das 4. Buch Esra", *JSHRZ* V/4 (1981) 291-309 (with lit.); E. Brandenburger, *Die Verborgenheit Gottes im Weltgeschehen: Das literarische und theologische Problem des 4. Esrabuches*, AThANT 68, 1981, pp.9-57 (with a good introduction on pp.9-21 and a critical analysis of the history of research on pp.22-57).

251 Cf. L. Rost, *o.c.*, p.91; O. Eissfeldt, *o.c.*, p.849; J. Schreiner, *o.c.*, p.295; A.F.J. Klijn, "Textual Criticism of IV Ezra: State of Affairs and Possibilities", *SBL 1981 Seminar Papers*, 1981, p.223.

252 Cf. recently J.M. Myers *o.c.*, pp.115-119; A.F.J. Klijn, *a.c.*, p.223.

253 Cf. J.M. Myers, *o.c.*, p.113; J. Schreiner, *o.c.*, p.296. Regarding the present state of, and the possibilities for, textual cticicism of 4Ezr see now A.F.J. Klijn, *a.c.*, pp.217-227. With regard to the history of transmission of the different versions see B. Violet, *Esra-Apokalypse*, pp.XII-XLVI; idem, *Apokalypsen*, pp.XIII-XXXIX; W. Harnisch, *Verhängnis*, pp.15-17; J.M. Myers, *o.c.*, pp.113-115; J. Schreiner, *o.c.*, pp.292-297. With regard to the Latin version we rely on R. Wever, "IV Ezra", *Biblia Sacra Iuxta Vulgatam Versionem*, 2, pp.1931-1974. We use mainly the translations of G.H. Box, *APOT* 2 (1913) 561-624; J.M. Myers, *II Esdras*, pp.140-354 (with commentary); J. Schreiner, *JSHRZ* V/4 (1981) 310-412.

254 Cf. L. Rost, *Einleitung*, p.93; J.H. Charlesworth, *Pseudepigrapha*, p.112; J.M. Myers, *o.c.*, pp.119-121; G. Mayer, "Zur jüdisch-hellenistischen Literatur", *ThR* 45 (1980) 233; J. Schreiner, *o.c.*, p.233; C. Münchow, *Ethik*, pp.76f.; and especially E. Brandenburger, *Verborgenheit*, pp.27-37,91-149 who established the "spannungsvolle Einheit eines literarischen und theologischen Ganzen" (p.149) on the basis of the deciphering of a shift in the entire process of the apocalypse in visio 4 (9,26-10, 59) which included a turning point in the attitude of Ezra (ibid., pp.58-90).

255 With regard to the alleged dependency of 4Ezr on AntBibl see M.R. James, *Biblical Antiquities*, pp.54-58; B. Violet, *Apokalypsen*, pp.XLII-XLIX; also W. Harnisch, *Verhängnis*, p.11 n.1; J.M. Myers, *o.c.*, p.132; O. Eissfeldt, *Einleitung*, p.853. But note J. Schreiner, *o.c.*, p.300 who points out that "Berührungspunkte in Inhalt und Aussage (sind), auch ohne daß eine Abhängigkeit vorliegen muß, zu erwarten, wenn die beiden Schriften aus der gleichen Zeit und dem nämlichen Milieu stammen. Dies aber dürfe der Fall sein".

tional setting identifying himself, anachronistically, with Salathiel, i.e. Ezra the scribe (3,1). It is obvious that the author lived in Palestine[256] and wrote after A.D. 70 during the last decade(s) of the first century[257].

4Ezr is a document of the late phase of apocalyptic thought and can be regarded as "one of the most brilliant and original of the apocryphal compositions"[258]. It can be assumed that the author is a representative of Pharisaic apocalyptic[259]. He presents his case in a generally clearly arranged manner with three basic characteristics: (1) seven so-called visions containing courses of events[260], (2) the frame narrative[261], and (3) the dialogue between Ezra and the angel Uriel[262].

---

256 Cf. W. Mundle, "Das religiöse Problem des 4. Esrabuches", *ZAW* 6 (1929) 223; A. Nissen, "Tora", *NovTest* 9 (1967) 248; cf. W. Harnisch, *o.c.*, p.15; L. Rost, *o.c.*, p.94 (under the rule of Domitian 81-96 A.D.); J.H. Charlesworth, *o.c.*, p.112; J. Schreiner, *o.c.*, p.302. Others suggest Rome: cf. B. Violet, *o.c.*, p.L; O. Eissfeldt, *o.c.*, p.849.
257 Cf. L. Rost, *o.c.*, pp.93f.; J.M. Myers, *o.c.*, pp.129f.; J.H. Charlesworth, *o.c.*, p.112; O. Eissfeldt, *o.c.*, pp.848f.; W. Harnisch, *o.c.*, p.11; G.W. E. Nickelsburg, *Literature*, p.287; J. Schreiner, *o.c.*, pp.301f.; E. Brandenburger, *o.c.*, p.111 ("knapp vor 100 nach Christus"); C. Rowland, *Open Heaven*, 1982, pp.254f.
258 J.H. Charlesworth, *o.c.*, p.111; cf. W. Harnisch, "Die Ironie der Offenbarung: Exegetische Erwägungen zur Zionsvision im 4. Buch Esra", *SBL 1981 Seminar Papers*, ed. K.H. Richards, 1981, p.80 commenting on visio 4.
259 Cf. W. Harnisch, *Verhängnis*, p.327 with n.4 (lit.); also L.L. Grabbe, "Chronography in 4 Ezra and 2 Baruch", *SBL 1981 Seminar Papers*, ed. K.H. Richards, 1981, pp.58-62; A. Lacocque, "The Vision of the Eagle in 4 Esdras", in *o.c.*, 1981, pp. 237-258, here pp.237,244-249. A different viewpoint is defended by E. Brandenburger, *Verborgenheit*, pp.154-161 who agues that the author of 4Ezr belonged to the cirlce of the (apocalyptic-prophetic) wise who exclusively and esoterically received not only the law but also apocalyptic secrets referring to 12,36-38; 14,6-8. 13.38-47. It should be noted that Brandenburger does not argue specifically against the assumption of a Pharisaic-apocalyptic author.
260 Visio 1: 3,1-5,19; visio 2: 5,20-6,34; visio 3: 6,35-9,25; visio 4: 9,26-10,59; visio 5: 11,1-38; visio 6: 13,1-56a; visio 7: 14,1-50. Only visio 5 (eagle vision) and visio 6 (Son of Man vision), and with certain reservations visio 4 (Zion vision), are visions with interpretations in the strict sense of the word. Cf. E. Brandenburger, *o.c.*, pp.14f.
261 As introduction (3,1-3) and end (14,48), and as link between the visions and the dialogue parts. Cf. E. Brandenburger, *o.c.*, pp.15,91-107.
262 This dialogue takes up at least two thirds of the entire material (visio 1-3). It is still discernible in visio 4 where, however, important changes regarding the subject-matter and the persons are introduced. In 10,29-59 the angel is only *angelus interpres*, not engaging in a critical dialogue with Ezra. On visio 4 see now E. Brandenburger, *o.c.*, pp.58-90 and W. Harnisch, "Ironie", *SBL 1981 Seminar Papers*, pp.79-104.

Regarding this dialogue between Ezra and Uriel it has been shown that the author of the apocalypse expresses questions and laments through Ezra which are answered authoritatively by the angel as God's representative[263]. The laments of Ezra set forth a particular current of thought or *Seinsverständnis* and launch a dialogue as defined by the dispute. The author takes issue with that pressing current of thought proclaiming a specific faith and theology which has its centre in the concept of the "life-giving law" (14,30). He does not vacillate in his judgment "sondern vertritt eine mit seinen Mitteln mögliche Lösung hinsichtlich der vorwurfsvoll, ja teilweise anklagend angefochtenen Gerechtigkeit Gottes (Theodizeeproblem). Diese Lösung erscheint in der Regel durch die Engelreden, die belehren und enthüllen, also offenbaren. Dabei ist in der Sache wichtig, daß das zwar nicht immer, aber doch nicht selten als Ablehnung, Zurechtweisung, als deutliche Korrektur geschieht. Der Verfasser äußert sich also antithetisch"[264]. Thus, as regards the dialogic part (visio 1-3), the opinion of the author is nearly exclusively expressed in the revelatory addresses of Uriel. As regards the visions part proper (visio 4-6), the author's opinion is again set forth in the heavenly revelations of Uriel as *angelus interpres*, but also in the speeches of Ezra in the Zion episode (9,38-10,24) and in the people's episode (12,40b-50) where Ezra takes over the role of Uriel[265]. Finally, as regards the testament part (visio 7), the opinion of the author represents the material position of the revelatory angel vis-à-vis the people. The farewell address expresses what the author intended to submit as solution for the problematic state of affairs, legitimized by Ezra as recipient of ancient revelatory heavenly wisdom[266].

The central problem[267] of 4Ezr is the fall of Jerusalem which had to be regarded as result of Israel's sins and of her disobedience to the law (cf. 3,25.34; 4,24; 8,16-17)[268]. Israel possesses the cov-

---

263 Cf. E. Brandenburger, *Adam und Christus*, 1962, pp.27-39,54-58, followed by W. Harnisch, *Verhängnis*, 1969, pp.60-67 and J. Schreiner, *JSHRZ* V/4 (1981) 302f. See now E. Brandenburger, *Verborgenheit*, 1981, pp.15-21,39-50,144-147; 150f., 156f. (correcting a few minor misunderstandings on the part of W. Harnisch, *o.c.*, pp.45-50). Contra H. Gunkel, "Das 4 Buch Esra", *Apokryphen und Pseudepigraphen des Alten Testaments*, ed. E. Kautzsch, 2, 1900, p.340 who argued that the dialogue expresses the inner struggle of the author who therefore talks with 'two voices'. Contra A.L. Thompson, *Responsibility for Evil in the Theodicy of IV Ezra*, SBLDS 29, 1977, who suggests that the author argues on two levels. Also contra A.P. Hayman, "The Problem of Pseudonymity in the Ezra Apocalypse", *JSJ* 6 (1975) 47-56 who maintains that both Ezra and Uriel reveal the author's thoughts. The assertion of G. Mayer that the problem of the dialogue structure has not yet been solved (in *ThR* 45/1980, p.233) has been taken care of by E. Brandenburger, *Verborgenheit*, 1981, passim.
264 E. Brandenburger, *Verborgenheit*, p.44; cf. ibid., pp.148-152.
265 Cf. E. Brandenburger, *o.c.*, pp.150f.; on the Zion episode see ibid., pp.74-84; and on the people's episode see ibid., pp.118-120.
266 Cf. E. Brandenburger, *o.c.*, p.151; on visio 7 see ibid., pp.10,20,132-147.
267 Cf. generally E. Brandengurger, *Adam und Christus*, pp.27-39,54-58; W. Harnisch, *Verhängnis*, pp.19-60; G.W.E. Nickelsburg, *Literature*, pp.293f.; J. Schreiner, *JSHRZ* V/4 (1981) 302f.; C. Münchow, *Ethik*, p.78; E. Brandenburger, *Verborgenheit*, pp.11-14,17-19,42-50,154-161.
268 With regard to the historical review in 3,4-27 see now P.G.R. de Villiers, "Under-

enant and the gift of the Torah but seems to be unable to overcome the evil which characterizes the human race since Adam. Moreover, Israel was punished by sinful Gentiles who themselves live in peace (3,29-36). These different strands of thought were obviously incomprehensible. Why did God not make his promises true which were connected with Israel's election (3,28-36; 5,28-30; 6,53-59)? Why did God make such a difference between Israel and the Gentiles? As mankind as a whole is subject to sin since Adam (3,5-26), did this not doom to failure God's purposes in creation and salvation right from the start? Since Israel could not avoid sin, as nobody can, is it not God himself who has to be blamed (3,8)?! The "Schöpfertreue und Gerechtigkeit des Gottes Israels" were put into question[269].

The *status quaestionis* of the author of 4Ezr includes thus two realms: the inability to comprehend the ways of God, and a certain agitated indignation regarding the predominance of the evil heart in this world. These two components "thematisieren beide die Unsichtbarkeit heilvollen Ergehens, die Abwesenheit göttlicher Heilsmacht, also die Verborgenheit Gottes im Weltgeschehen"[270].

In his consciously theological solution of the problem[271] the author builds on the prophetic-apocalyptic presupposition that he has insight into the heavenly secrets and that he is therefore able to disclose eschatological revelatory wisdom which can avert the crisis. The skepticism and the arguments with God which are expressed in the thoughts and speeches of Ezra in the dialogue part are characterized as folly and wrong attitude in the testament of Ezra (14,27-35). Wise behaviour is, as regards its content, understood as repentance and execution of the judgment doxology. Zion is confronted with its guilt, is called to repentance, and is promised — on the basis of her agreement with and endorsement of God's wisdom which governs the world — the renewed gift of salvation in the eschatological process. The author thus advances a deuteronomistically interpreted doctrine of aeons[272].

---

standing the Way of God: Form, Function, and Message of the Historical Review in 4 Ezra 3,4-27", *SBL 1981 Seminar Papers*, pp.357-378.
269 W. Harnisch, *Verhängnis*, p.58.
270 E. Brandenburger, *Verborgenheit*, p.165. For an analysis and evaluation of these two realms of the central problem see ibid., pp.161-186.
271 Cf. particularly E. Brandenburger, *o.c.*, pp.186-201.
272 Cf. E. Brandenburger, *o.c.*, p.188. On the doctrine of aeons in 4Ezr see ibid.,

In the words of E. Brandenburger, "das Hauptanliegen des 4Esr ist, daß die in den anfänglichen vorwurfsvollen Klagen zu Wort kommende skeptische Infragestellung Gottes in der Wende visio 4 revidiert wird und von da aus erkennender Glaube die Skepsis im Lobpreis des Waltens Gottes (13,53b-58) überholt. Thema des 4Esr ist insofern die Erkenntnis der Herrschaft Gottes (13,58). In der Zeit der Verborgenheit Gottes im Weltgeschehen hat solche Erkenntnis ein konkretes, geschichtliches Ziel: einerseits die Wiedergewinnung oder die Festigung des Vertrauens in das Walten ... Gottes, andererseits damit zugleich das Durchhalten des Gehorsams gegenüber dem weltordnenden Recht Gottes"[273].

7.2.1. The Jewish law. The Mosaic Torah plays an important role in 4Ezr[274]. Even though the author refers to secret revelations with regard to the end of the present aeon (3,14; 14,5.23-26), it is abundantly clear that for him God has revealed himself in the law. In the Torah God revealed himself and his will to Israel in an unambiguous way[275].

In 4Ezr the law has primarily an eschatological-salvational significance[276]. The angel proclaims that eternal life and the glory of the future aeon is open to all who are obedient to the law[277]. The possibility of the fulfilment of the law is asserted[278]. The significance of the law in 4Ezr is especially apparent in 7,17-25, the first

---

pp.128-132,139.,152f.,174-176,190-196; cf. also W. Harnisch, *Verhängnis*, pp.89-321. As to the concept of the Messiah in 4Ezr see P.G.R. de Villiers, "Messiah", *Neotestamentica* 12 (1981) 90-96; E. Brandenburger, *o.c.*, pp.127,130,140.

273 E. Brandenburger, *o.c.*, p.188. On the chronography in 4Ezr see L.L. Grabbe, "Chronography", 1981, pp.49-63 who emphasizes that the end of the Roman Empire and the restoration of Israel, through God's intervention, were expected in the near future.

274 Cf. generally W. Mundle, "Problem", *ZAW* 6 (1929) 227-231; W. Harnisch, *o.c.*, pp.142-178 passim; M. Limbeck, *Ordnung*, pp.97-102; R.J. Banks, *Jesus and the Law*, pp.30f.,51-53; J.R. Mueller, "A Prolegomenon to the Study of the Social Function of 4 Ezra", *SBL 1981 Seminar Papers*, 1981, pp.259-268; C. Münchow, *Ethik*, pp.89-91,94; E. Brandenburger, *o.c.*, p.44. Brandenburger states that the theology of the author "hat ihr Zentrum im Gedanken des 'lebensspendenden Gesetzes' (14,30)" (p.44; cf. ibid., p.204 s.v. "Gesetz"). The focus on the concept of law is particularly apparent in 3,19; 5,27; 7,79.89.94; 8,56; 9,31.37; 14,21-22.

275 Cf. W. Mundle, "Problem", *ZAW* 6 (1929) 227.

276 Cf. W. Harnisch, *Verhängnis*, pp.145-149; M. Limbeck, *Ordnung*, p.97; C. Münchow, *Ethik*, pp.89f.; also W. Mundle, *a.c.*, p.228 and J.R. Mueller, "Prolegomenon", 1981, pp.263-265. Cf. E. Brandenburger, *Verborgenheit*, p.45 who asserts that for the author the law is "Garant und Träger des Lebens" and "Basis und Verheißungsträger des Heils" (p.62).

277 Cf. 7,10-16.21-25.88-90.127-130; 8,39; 9,7-13. Cf. E. Brandenburger, *o.c.*, p.17 with n.21.

278 Cf. W. Harnisch, *o.c.*, p.152; C. Münchow, *o.c.*, p.89.

pericope in which the angel deals with the topic of the law per se[279].

The central question which is dealt with here is the lot of the righteous and the wicked. The angel says: "Let the many who exist perish rather than that the law of God which has been communicated (to them) be slighted (v.20). For God (deus) has surely commanded (mandans mandavit) those coming (into the world) when they came what to do to live (vivere) and what course to take to avoid being punished (puniri, v.21)". The "lex" of v.17 is, without doubt, the Mosaic Torah[280]; this verse is probably formulated with relation to Deut 8,1. However, "nicht das geschichtliche Geschick Israels, sondern die *eschatologische* Zukunft der *Gerechten* und der *Sünder* ist nach der Auffassung des Apokalyptikers in den Bestimmungen des göttlichen Gesetzes festgelegt"[281]. This is also true for v.21: the attitude towards the law in the present aeon is decisive with regard to the fate of the individual in the future aeon. The verbs "haereditare" and "puniri" in v.17 correspond with the verbs "vivere" and "puniri" in v.21[282]. It is important to note that the recipients of the law in vv.17.20-21 are not mankind in general but Israel[283]. The author stresses his conviction that it is not the *status electionis* which guarantees life but the obedience to God's demands in the law. Thus the contrast just-ungodly, referring to groups within (!) Israel, moves into the centre of the theological conception (cf. 7,17-18). This contrast supersedes the traditional distinction between Israel and the Gentiles, without displacing or annihilating this distinction totally.

Hence, the law fulfills a mediating role between the present and the future aeons since the eschatological salvation and condemna-

---

279 On this passage see W. Harnisch, *o.c.*, pp.147-155; M. Limbeck, *o.c.*, p.97; J.M. Myers, *II Esdras*, pp.207,232,252f. W. Harnisch, *o.c.*, pp.147f. points out that here the author is not satisfied with demonstrating the "Verhängnischarakter der Geschichte" and with proclaiming the concept of the eschatological abolition of the present aeon, but that he supplements the fundamental consideration of 7,2-16 with an equally fundamental discussion of the law in 7,17-25 thus dealing with misunderstandings which could arise from 7,2-16.
280 Cf. G.H. Box, *Ezra-Apocalypse*, p.105; D. Rössler, *Gesetz*, p.50; W. Harnisch, *o.c.*, p.148.
281 W. Harnisch, *o.c.*, p.148; cf. A. Nissen, "Tora", *NovTest* 9 (1967) 264 referring to 3,33; 5,29; cf. also E. Brandenburger, *o.c.*, pp.175f. who refers to the inner connection between the law and the eschatological condition which is defended in 7,20-44.
282 Here "life" (vivere) signifies the eschatological existence in the future aeon which is not subject to mortality any more. This term, mostly in verbal form, occurs in 7,48. 60.66-67.82.92.129.131.137-138; 8,3.6.39.41.54; 9,13.15; 14,22.30. Cf. W. Harnisch, *Verhängnis*, p.149.
283 Contra G.H. Box, *Ezra-Apocalypse*, p.105; idem, *APOT* 2 (1913) 581; W. Mundle, "Problem", *ZAW* 6 (1929) 229. Following W. Harnisch, *o.c.*, p.150 who defends Israel as recipient of the law even with regard to 3,32-36; 7,37.45-46 where the author probably thinks of a "zwar faktische, aber unbewußte Gebotsübertretung (bzw. -bewahrung) der Heiden" rather than presupposing a knowledge of the Jewish law among the Gentiles. Cf. also J.M. Myers, *II Esdras*, p.253. In 7,129-131; 9,29-37; 14,28-32 Israel is clearly presented as recipient of the Torah.

tion are decided by the present attitude towards the law[284]. It is implied and even expressly stated that the divine law can be fulfilled. The author rejects the idea that the norms of behaviour which are laid down in the law (cf. 7,21: "quid facientes ... quid observantes) are beyond the ability of those who live in the present aeon[285]. The pericopes in 7,70-74 and 7,127-131 can be compared with 7,17-25[286].

The law in 4Ezr appears as an absolute entity. This is the case even in those passages where reference is made to the "commandments" (pl.)[287]. The commandments are often linked with God's covenant with Israel (4,23; 5,29; 7,24.83; 8,27), as is the law (3, 15-20; 5,27; 9,29-32; 14,3-6)[288]. The gift of the law is "die ausschließliche Weise der Erwählung Israels"[289].

Thus, the author of 4Ezr defends the salvational-eschatological significance and effectiveness of the law for Israel, implying its ethical dimension[290].

The ethical orientation of the law becomes apparent in the comparison of the Torah with light (lux, lumen) in 14,20-21 (cf. 10, 22)[291]. The law is correlated with life (7,129; 9,31; 14,22.30). It

---

[284] W. Harnisch, o.c., p.145 points out in this context that thus is "die These von der radikalen Diskontinuität der beiden Äonen durch die Behauptung der Kontinuität des Gesetzes zumindest eingeschränkt"; cf. also C. Münchow, Ethik, pp.89, 94. The view that man is judged because he despised the law is also apparent in 7,24.37.72.79.81; 8,56; cf. 7 81; cf. W. Mundle, a.c., p.229. A. Nissen, "Tora", Nov-Test 9 (1967) 264 also stresses that in 4Ezr the Torah is the "Mittel und Maßstab des Gerichts", referring to 7,21-25; 14,35; 9,7; 13,23; 8,31-36; 3,34. Cf. E. Brandenburger, Verborgenheit, p.167 n.66 who points out that the constitutive correlation of law and concepts of judgment is evidenced by the phrases commandments/ precept (3,32-33.35-36), sin/sacrifice (3,29-30.34-35), reward/fruit (3,33), the scales of the judge (3,34). The judgment according to works is mentioned in 6,5; 7,35; 14,35. E. Brandenburger, o.c., pp.154,163,170 showed that the author of 4Ezr did not propagate universal salvation.

[285] This does not mean that the author of 4Ezr denies the fact that most people (like Adam!) were defeated by the attack of the enemy: cf. 7,22-44. On the יצר הרע in 4Ezr see W. Harnisch, Verhängnis, pp.165-175; C. Münchow, Ethik, pp.87-90; E. Brandenburger, Verborgenheit, pp.169-176.

[286] See the detailed discussion of these passages in W. Harnisch, o.c., pp.155-164.

[287] Mandata: 3,33.35.36; 7,72; legitima: 7,24; 9,32; 13,42; dispositiones: 4,23; constitutiones: 7,11; cf. 7,45; sponsiones: 5,29; 7,24; diligentiae: 7,37.

[288] Cf. R.J. Banks, Jesus and the Law, pp.30f.

[289] K. Müller, "Geschichte", 1973, p.103 referring to 5,27.

[290] Cf. E. Brandenburger, o.c., pp.190f. and C. Münchow, o.c., pp.91-95 who emphasize the relatedness of the obedience to the law, i.e. ethics, and eschatology.

[291] Cf. S. Aalen, Begriffe, pp.182,185; W. Mundle, "Problem", ZAW 6 (1929) 228;

is always clear that it is Israel who possesses the law and who is distinguished by it (cf. 5,27; 8,12-29)[292]. The righteous will keep God's ways, i.e. observe the law (cf. 7,88-99; 14,31.34). In 7,79 the fear of the Lord is connected with the keeping of the law. The significance of the law is also stressed by the statement of its eternal duration: the Torah was present in the paradise with Adam *in nuce* (7,11)[293] and it "will not cease" (lex non perit) but it "endures (permanet) in its majesty" (9,37)[294].

The law is also understood to be "das der Weltordnung zugrunde liegende Recht Gottes"[295], a concept which is developed in 3,4-27. In the context of the first component of the theological problem of 4Ezr, the inability to comprehend the ways of God, Ezra examines "ob die mit dem Recht verbundene Grundordnung der Entsprechung von Tun und Ergehen sich im Weltgeschehen realisiert, ob also Gott seiner Funktion als Wahrer der Weltordnung gerecht wird"[296], which is negated in visio 1. With regard to the problem of the evil heart of man, Ezra levels severe objections against the law as "die Welt förderlich ordnendes Recht Gottes" as the predominance of the evil heart prevented the enforcement of God's creational power in the maintenance and protection of the law[297]. The continuous interest of the author lies in the vigorous defense of the law as creational reality as well: "Recht und Gericht Gottes gehören zur Grundordnung der Schöpfung, und zwar so sehr, daß sie im Rang vor der Schöpfungswirklichkeit selbst eingeordnet sind"[298].

To sum up, in 4Ezr the law has a salvational eschatological significance based on the ethical character of its commandments. The law is always Israel's Torah. The pious are called upon to keep

---

W. Harnisch, *o.c.*, pp.203f.; J.M. Myers, *II Esdras*, p.323. For the Torah, or the word, as light cf. Ps 19,8; 119,105; Prov 6,23; SapSal 18,4; Sir 4517G; TLev 14,4; 19,1.

292 Cf. W. Harnisch, *o.c.*, pp.28f.; M. Limbeck, *Ordnung*, pp.97f.
293 Cf. W. Harnisch, *Verhängnis*, p.107 with n.6.
294 Cf. ApcBar 77,15. The term "majesty" or "dignity" (honor) designates "the lasting, effective, directive, proven, moral quality of the law" (J.M. Myers, *II Esdras*, p.271 ad loc.).
295 E. Brandenburger, *Verborgenheit*, pp.166,168 n.67.
296 E. Brandenburger, *o.c.*, p.167.
297 E. Brandenburger, *o.c.*, pp.171-173.
298 E. Brandenburger, *o.c.*, p.190.

the law and to walk in its ways in order to secure eschatological salvation which is decided by one's attitude to God's will as embodied in the Torah. The creational significance of the law for Israel is an important concern for the author of 4Ezr as well.

7.2.2. The concept of wisdom. First it has to be noted that the form of the dialogue in 4Ezr with its succession of questions and answers is "in formaler Hinsicht . . . wohl eine Stilform der Weisheitsbelehrung"²⁹⁹.

Moreover, the historical review in 3,4-27 and other pericopes reflect the author's proximity to wisdom thought as well: this is indicated (1) by the importance of cosmology, (2) by the conception of history as consisting of a predestined course of events which is laid down in the structure of the world, and (3) by the stress on understanding God's way with this world³⁰⁰.

Further, it has been observed that 4Ezr aims at extending the sequence Moses-prophets-Ezra by one term: the wise men (cf. 12, 38; 14,13.26.46)³⁰¹. These wise men are not simply pious people whose task it is to communicate the secret knowledge which 'Ezra' possesses (12,38; 14,26.46)³⁰², but they are teachers like Ezra who continue his activities in the teaching of the law and admonishing the people³⁰³.

---

299 G. von Rad, *Theologie*, 2, pp.325f.; cf. also W. Harnisch, *Verhängnis*, p.65 n.2. K. Müller, "Geschichte", 1973, p.102 points out that 4Ezr is strongly influenced by the concepts of theological wisdom. He criticizes M. Limbeck, *Ordnung*, pp. 97-102 for not taking into account this evidence (ibid., p.102 n.47). See recently E. Brandenburger, *Verborgenheit*, p.63 acknowledging the sapiential origin of the pattern of argumentation in visio 1-3.

300 Cf. P.G.R. de Villiers, "Understanding the Way of God: Form, Function, and Message of the Historical Review in 4 Ezra 3,4-27", *SBL 1981 Seminar Papers*, 1981, pp.364-366, relying on G. Reese, *Die Geschichte Israels in der Auffassung des frühen Judentums*, Diss.theol. Heidelberg, 1967, pp.136-144 who described the affinities of the author of 4Ezr with wisdom thought. It seem to be exaggerated, however, when de Villiers states that 4Ezr has to be understood (exclusively?) in the wisdom context (*a.c.*, p.366). In view of the decisive eschatological and salvational significance of the law it is inadequate to refer to the intellectual understanding of God's ways with the world as *conditio sine qua non* for salvation (contra de Villiers, *a.c.*, pp.361-365).

301 O.H. Steck, *Israel*, 1967, p.179; cf. also B. Violet, *Apokalypsen*, pp.170,192, 196,201. See E. Brandenburger, *Verborgenheit*, pp.154-161,197 who argues that the author of 4Ezr belonged to the circles of (apocalyptic-prophetic) wisdom.

302 Cf. 14,45-46 where they are differentiated from the "worthy (!) and unworthy".

303 Cf. O.H. Steck, *o.c.*, pp.179f. He admits that there is no clear textual proof for this

The motif of understanding and comprehension is important in 4Ezr[304] : in the evil times before the end, and in the time of the messianic woes, understanding of God and his ways will be lacking (3,13; 5,1.10; 14,20-21); and the 70 books of Ezra which were revealed to him by God (14,22) mediate the knowledge of God (12,36.47).

In 4Ezr 'wisdom' is often secret knowledge (14,25-26[305]). In 14,40 the terms "intellectus" and "sapientia" belong to the portraiture of divine inspiration (14,37-44) that led to the writing of the 94 books which included the canonical and the apocryphal treatises[306]. The "light of understanding" (lucerna intellectus) in 14,25 refers to the dictation of these books.

In two passages wisdom appears as person. In 5,9b-10 "reason" (sensus) is said to become obscure and "insight" (intellectus) is "confined to its chamber and sought in vain by many"[307]. This pericope belongs to the long list of "signs" which will happen before the last days (5,1-12). In 13,55 "wisdom" (sapientia) is called "mother" (mater)[308].

In 8,52 wisdom is described as a gift to the redeemed in the future aeon[309]. Whether wisdom has a creational dimension as well must remain an assumption[310].

Thus it is obvious that the wisdom concept is not developed but only referred to in passing, especially since it is conditioned by the

---

interpretation but points out that "da aber Umkehr und Gehorsam des Volkes das eigentliche Ziel des 4Ezr ist ... und Esra selbst dahingehend wirkt, ist Entsprechendes auch von den Weisen zu erwarten" (p.180 n.1).
304 Cf. P.G.R. de Villiers, "Understanding", 1981, pp.361-364.
305 For the expression "fountain of wisdom" (sapientiae fons) in 14,47 see Prov 18,4; Sir 24,30; En(sl) 48,1; 49,1; OdSal 6,8ff. Cf. J.M. Myers, *II Esdras*, p.326. Regarding the significance of the term "secret(s)" in 4Ezr 10,38; 12,36.38; 14,5 see E. Brandenburger, *o.c.*, pp.197-201.
306 Cf. G.H. Box, *Ezra-Apocalypse*, pp.318f.; idem, *APOT* 2 (1913) 623; J.M. Myers, *o.c.*, p.329. B.Violet, *Apokalypsen*, p.200 gives σύνεσις, בינה, תבונה, דעה and σοφία/חכמה as equivalents for "intellectus" and "sapientia"; cf. also E. Brandenburger, *o.c.*, p.11 with n.8.
307 Cf. En(eth) 42; 91,10; 94,5; ApcBar 48,36; 70,5. The Greek equivalents for "sensus" and "intellectus" here are σοφία (σύνεσις) and ἐπιστήμη; cf. B. Violet, *Apokalypsen*, p.27. Cf. also M. Küchler, *Weisheitstraditionen*, p.77.
308 Cf. J.M. Myers, *II Esdras*, p.313 who compares 11QPs^{a}18,5ff.
309 Cf. W. Harnisch, *Verhängnis*, pp.94 n.1, 112 n.1, 126 n.4; E. Brandenburger, *Verborgenheit*, p.83.
310 Assumed by E. Brandenburger, *o.c.*, p.63.

content and purpose of 4Ezr. The fact that the author chose the sapiential form of the dialogue does not mean, of course, that 4Ezr is a 'wisdom book'. This choice can easily be explained by material reasons as this form allows the author to accentuate a particular theological conception of scepticism on the background of a totally different way of thinking. But it is equally obvious that the wisdom tradition has left its marks in 4Ezr: wisdom characterizes certain people who are "wise men"; wisdom appears as a person; wisdom plays an important role in the end times; wisdom is an eschatological gift in the future aeon; and wisdom — this is the apocalyptic element — is esoteric knowledge imparted by ecstatic inspiration. The next section shows that wisdom is also linked with the law.

7.2.3. The law and wisdom. There are several passages which correlate law and wisdom in a very intimate way[311]. In 5,9-11 wisdom is identified with righteousness (iustitia) — both are hiding themselves in the last days — whereas in 7,88-99 righteousness is identical with the keeping of the law. Thus, 5,9-11 implies the identity of law and wisdom.

In 7,70-74[312] the *angelus interpres* emphasizes again that man has no excuse in judgment: he has received "reason" (sensus)[313],

---

311 Contra U. Luck, "Weltverständnis", *ZThK* 73 (1976) 292-294 who maintains that in 4Ezr "die Einheit von Gesetz und Weisheit so nicht besteht" as in Sir and in SapSal but that, instead, it is the apocalyptic teacher who now appears as wisdom teacher: "Jetzt vermittelt der Apokalyptiker das, was der Weisheit zukommt: die Frage nach der Gerechtigkeit zu beantworten angesichts der Welterfahrung" (pp. 293f.). The identity of law and wisdom in 4Ezr is recognized by O.H. Steck, *Israel*, p.180; K. Müller, "Geschichte", 1973, pp.102f.; R.J. Banks, *Jesus and the Law*, p.69; M. Küchler, *Weisheitstraditionen*, p.80; cf. A. Nissen, "Tora", *NovTest* 9 (1967) 248 with n.9; J.M. Myers, *II Esdras*, p.243. E. Brandenburger, *Verborgenheit*, p.197 comes close to an acknowledgement of the identity of wisdom and law in 4Ezr when he states regarding apocalyptic theology as expressed in 4Ezr that "der Gesetzesgehorsam soll durch den Einblick in das die Zeiten übergreifende Sinngefüge als weises Verhalten einsichtig gemacht werden". C. Münchow, *Ethik*, does not refer to the correlation of wisdom and law as regards 4Ezr.
312 On this passage see W. Harnisch, *Verhängnis*, pp.155-163.
313 With regard to the term "sensus" (7,62.64.72) B. Violet, *Apokalypsen*, p.84 suggested the Hebrew term יֵצֶר as original; cf. the discussion in W. Harnisch, *o.c.*, pp. 155-161. Harnisch identifies "sensus" in 7,72 (in contrast to 7,64) with the יֵצֶר טוב (p.161). Cf. A.L. Thompson, *Responsibility*, pp.333f. who demonstrated the weakness of Violet's suggestion. J. Schreiner, *JSHRZ* V/4 (1981) ad loc. solves the

"commandments" (mandata), and the law (lex), but men have committed iniquity despite their reason, they have not observed the commandments, and they have broken the law (v.72). As the terms "sensus", "mandata", and "lex" are parallel and contrasted with "committing iniquity" which consists in breaking the law, it is obvious that here law and wisdom are also identified.

8,7-13 compares the individual who is first sheltered in the mother's womb, tenderly nurtured after birth, and then instructed for life by the parents, with Israel who was "conceived in the choice of the Lord, sheltered and nurtured by him into maturity, and then instructed in his law"[314].

In 8,12 "law" (lex) and "wisdom" (intellectus) stand in synonymous parallelism: law and wisdom are seen as one and the same[315]. True wisdom is obedience to the law, and the keeping of the commandments makes one truly wise.

The identity of law and wisdom is further implied in 8,52-58 where the future eschatological salvation (vv.52-54)[316] and condemnation (vv.55-58) are described. The state of the righteous is portrayed with the language of the paradise: there is the "tree of life" (arbor vitae), "abundance" (abundantia), "repose" and "rest" (requies) — and the righteous will have "achieved goodness" (perfecta est bonitas) and "wisdom" (perfecta sapientia, v.52). This is contrasted with those who perish: they have held God's law in contempt and abandoned his way (via, v.56). Hence, obedience to the law secures goodness and wisdom in the future aeon.

In 13,54-55 the angel correlates in synonymous parallelism the exploration of God's law (lex) and the dedication to wisdom (sapientia). This is an explicit identification of law with wisdom[317].

In 14,25 the "lamp of understanding" (lucerna intellectus) refers to the dictation not only (!) of the 70 books containing apo-

---

problem which is created by the attempt to correlate "sensus" with יֵצֶר by translating "Verstand".

314 J.M. Myers, *II Esdras*, p.258. He compares 8,12 with Sir 17,11 and ApcBar 38,2 "where the law and wisdom are associated but where the former appears as basis for the latter" (p.243).

315 Cf. O.H. Steck, *Israel*, p.180; M. Küchler, *Weisheitstraditionen*, p.80.

316 Cf. W. Harnisch, *Verhängnis*, pp.238f.

317 Cf. also O.H. Steck, *o.c.*, p.180; K. Müller, "Geschichte", 1973, pp.102f. E. Brandenburger, *Verborgenheit*, p.85 simply refers to the fact that Ezra's wisdom is mentioned alongside his obedience to the law.

calyptic-esoteric information, but also of the 24 books of the Jewish law which is compared with light (lux) in 14,20-21. Again the identity of law and wisdom is implied.

Finally, the description of 'Ezra' as rabbi or scribe (cf. 8,28-29; 13,54-55; 14,13.19-22.50), as a teacher of the people (cf. 8,29; 12,40-50; etc.), and as a wise man (cf. 14,13.40.50)[318] also implies the identity of law and wisdom which had become 'embodied' in the person of the *sopher/ḥakham*.

The identification of law and wisdom in 4Ezr has three dimensions: an ethical, an eschatological, and a didactic perspective. This indicates the main orientation of the concept of law which is much further developed than the concept of wisdom. Both the law with its commandments and wisdom contain the norms and guidelines for the 'ways' in which man is to please God (cf. 5,9-11/7,88-99; 7,72; 8,12.52-56). Law and wisdom are further significant with regard to the eschatological existence in the future aeon of salvation (cf. 8,52-56). And finally, law and wisdom are one in the person of the scribe (cf. 13,54-55; 14,13.25.37-48).

7.2.4. Summary. The significance of the law is one of the most important concepts in 4Ezr. The Mosaic Torah is understood as *ius talionis*, as impartial norm of the judgment which measures the conduct of man in the present aeon and decides his eschatological fate in the future aeon. The knowledge of the law enables each individual to obtain the qualification which is needed for the reception of salvation[319].

'Wisdom' is the label for esoteric-apocalyptic knowledge. Wisdom appears as a person and is an eschatological gift in the future aeon.

Law and wisdom are clearly identified in a number of passages, both explicitly and implicitly. In accordance with the purpose of 4Ezr as well as with the concept of law, this identification has primarily an ethical and an eschatological dimension: obedience to God's commandments leads to righteousness, which is wisdom, and finally decides the individual's eternal, eschatological state in

---

318 Cf. A. Nissen,"Tora", *NovTest* 9 (1967) 248 n.9; E. Janssen, *Gottesvolk*, 1971, pp.96-100.
319 Cf. W. Harnisch, *Verhängnis*, p.325.

the future aeon. In addition, as in Sirach (and the rabbinic circles to whom 4Ezr might be ascribed!), the person of the scribe/sage incorporates this identification as well.

7.3. The Apocalypse of Baruch

The Apocalypse of Baruch[320] is entirely extant only in a Syriac translation[321] which is a version of the Greek translation[322] of the Hebrew original[323]. ApcBar is generally regarded as a unity[324]. Striking parallels between ApcBar and both AntBibl[325] and 4Ezr[326] have been observed[327]. ApcBar was certainly written be-

---

320 See generally R.H. Charles, "2 Baruch", *APOT* 2 (1913) 470-481; B. Violet, *Die Apokalypsen des Esra und des Baruch*, GCS 32, 1924, pp.LVI-XCVI; P.M. Bogaert, *Apocalypse de Baruch: Introduction*, SC 144 1, 1969, pp.21-459; L. Rost, *Einleitung*, pp.94-97; O. Eissfeldt, *Einleitung*, pp.850-853; J.H. Charlesworth, *Pseudepigrapha*, pp.83-86; A.F.J. Klijn, "Die syrische Baruchapokalypse", *JSHRZ* V/2 (1976) 103-123; G.W.E. Nickelsburg, *Literature*, pp.281-287.
321 Cf. the edition by A.M. Ceriani, *Apocalypsis Baruch Syriace*, Monumenta Sacra et Profana, Bibliotheca Ambrosiana, Mediolani, 1871, V, pp.113-180; S. Dednering, "Apocalypse of Baruch", *The Old Testament in Syriac*, IV/3, 1973, pp.1-50. With regard to the textual evidence see espeically P.M. Bogaert, o.c., pp.33-56.
322 With regard to the Greek Oxyrhynchos fragments of ApcBar see A.M. Denis, *Introduction*, pp.182-186.
323 Cf. R.H. Charles, o.c., pp.472-474; B. Violet, o.c., pp.LXVII-LXXIII; L. Rost, o.c., p.95; O. Eissfeldt, o.c., p.853; A.F.J. Klijn, o.c., p.110; cf. G.W.E. Nickelsburg, o.c., p.287. The attempt by P.M. Bogaert, o.c., pp.353-380 to demonstrate that ApcBar war originally written in Greek (Koine) is, in the light of the arguments adduced for an Hebrew original, and with regard to the close relationship with the (originally Hebrew) 4Ezr not really convincing. We relied on the translations of R.H. Charles, *APOT* 2 (1913) 481-526; P.M. Bogaert, o.c., 1, pp.461-528; A.F.J. Klijn, *JSHRZ* V/2 (1976) 123-191.
324 Contra R.H. Charles, *APOT* 2 (1913) 474-476. Cf. B. Violet, *Apokalypsen*, pp. LXXIIIf.; P.M. Bogaert, *Apocalypse*, 1, pp.80-88; L. Rost, *Einleitung*, p.97; W. Harnisch, *Verhängnis*, pp.13f.; cf. also A.F.J. Klijn, *JSHRZ* V/2 (1976) 111-113; C. Münchow, *Ethik*, p.96.
325 Cf. B. Violet, o.c., pp.LXXVII-LXXXI; P.M. Bogaert, o.c., 1, pp.242-258; A.F.J. Klijn, o.c., p.113.
326 Cf. B. Violet, o.c., pp.LXXXI-XC; O. Eissfeldt, *Einleitung*, p.853; L. Rost, o.c., p.97; A.F.J. Klijn, o.c., p.113; J. Schreiner, *JSHRZ* V/4 (1981) 301; cf. also A. Nissen, "Tora", *NovTest* 9 (1967) 249; C. Müncow, o.c., pp.96f.
327 The exact nature of the relationship especially between ApcBar and 4Ezr is still being disputed since the arguments for the priority of 4Ezr do not seem to be compelling. Cf. W. Harnisch, o.c., p.11 n.1; G.W.E. Nickelsburg, *Literature*, p.287. A.F J. Klijn, o.c., p.133 suggests that the two writings belong to the same apocalyptic tradition, thus avoiding the question of dependency.

tween A.D. 90 and 130[328] in Palestine[329], displaying "viele als rabbinisch bekannte Vorstellungen"[330].

In ApcBar the "spannungsreiche Gedankengang" which we observed in 4Ezr is missing[331]. In the statements of 'Baruch' the view of the author is much more reflected than in the statements of 'Ezra' in 4Ezr. The visionary in ApcBar adopts and takes over God's instructions and directions much more than 'Ezra'. For this reason his statements are only seldom corrected by the mouth of the Lord (cf. 15,1ff.; 17,1ff.; 19,1ff.; 23,2ff.; 48,26ff.). The main question in ApcBar is not the 'why' with regard to Zion's downfall but the 'when' with regard to the time of the final fulfilment of the divine promise[332]. Jerusalem's fall is attributed to the sins of the "two tribes which remained" (1,2-4) and is regarded as the just judgment of God (44,5-6; 67,2-4)[333]. God himself was the initiator of the destruction of Jerusalem (cf. 5,3; 6,4ff.; 7,1-2; 8,1-2). But this judgment is only temporal (1,4; 5,3). The Gentiles will be punished too. The question is only, when[334], and what has to be done in the time which is left.

---

[328] Cf. B. Violet, *o.c.*, pp.XCI-XCIII; P.M. Bogaert, *o.c.*, 1, pp.270-295; W. Harnisch, *o.c.*, p.11; L. Rost, *o.c.*, p.97; O. Eissfeldt, *o.c.*, p.853; J.H. Charlesworth, *Pseudepigrapha*, p.84; A.F.J. Klijn, *o.c.*, pp.113f.; G.W.E. Nickelsburg, *o.c.*, p.287; C. Münchow, *o.c.*, p.97; C. Rowland, *Open Heaven*, p.254.

[329] Cf. B. Violet, *o.c.*, p.XCI who follows F. Rosenthal in ascribing the book to the rabbinic circle in Yabneh under R. Aqiba. Cf. also P.M. Bogaert, *o.c.*, pp.331-334; L. Rost, *o.c.*, p.97; J.H. Charlesworth, *o.c.*, p.84.

[330] A. Nissen, "Tora", *NovTest* 9 (1967) 249 (cf. n.2 for references and topics). Cf. also R.H. Charles, *o.c.*, p.478; B. Violet, *o.c.*, p.XCI; P.M. Bogaert, *o.c.*, p.386; W. Harnisch, *o.c.*, pp.179,327; and A.F.J. Klijn, *o.c.*, p.118 with n.40 who states that if it were true that the rabbis addressed the people as a whole in contrast to the *Apokalyptiker* who spoke to a limited circle of initiated, then ApcBar should not (!) be regarded as belonging to the apocalyptic literature! Cf. with caution L.L. Grabbe, "Chronography", 1981, pp.58-62.

[331] Cf. E. Brandenburger, *Adam*, p.36; W. Harnisch, *o.c.*, p.73; C. Münchow, *o.c.*, p.99.

[332] Cf. C. Münchow, *Ethik*, pp.98-101 who points out that this shift places the emphasis on the realm of the ethos, i.e. on the question of what has to be done after the catastrophe, and on the significance of time, i.e. on the question whether there is enough time left to attain salvation by the fulfilment of the law.

[333] Cf. O.H. Steck, *Israel*, pp.181f.; W. Harnisch, *Verhängnis*, p.73; C. Münchow, *o.c.*, p.98.

[334] On the imminence of the endtime for the author of ApcBar see L.L. Grabbe, "Chronography", 1981, pp.54-58,62f.

7.3.1. The Jewish law.

The Mosaic Torah occupies a central place in the thought of ApcBar[335]. The control of the entire apocalypse can indeed be summarized with the statement in 85,3: "We have nothing now save the Mighty One and his law".

The law[336] is a light given by Moses (17,4) at the time when the covenant was established (17,4-19,1). It enlightens man (38,1-2; 54,5) and separates between life and death (46,3). Darkness, i.e. death, is the result of Adam's sin (18,2). Man has the freedom to choose between light and darkness, i.e. between life and death (54,15.19; 85,7). He who chooses the law receives life (32,1; 38, 1-2; 48,22; 51,3-7; 54,15), the good (44,7), mercy and truth (44, 14), and wisdom and understanding (66,14). The law has to be studied and interpreted (3,6; 46,3) and will remain forever (46,4; 59,2; 77,15-16). The law has to be learnt (32,1; 84,1.9) so that Israel will live in accordance with God's will also in the future (44, 3; 46,5; 82,6).

As regards the numerous statements on the subject of the law we should note that "der Verfasser von sBar das in 4Esr sichtbar werdende theologische Interesse voll und ganz teilt"[337]. The difference between ApcBar and 4Ezr consists in the fact that the apocalyptic *ius talionis* is accentuated in ApcBar in a much more decisive and uncompromising way than in 4Ezr. The reason for this difference is that the author of ApcBar proclaims his own conception through the words of 'Baruch' in a much stronger and clearer way than 'Ezra' in his apocalypse[338].

In 15,1-8 we have the first programmatic statements on the law

---

335 Cf. R.H. Charles, *APOT* 2 (1913) 478; A. Nissen, "Tora", *NovTest* 9 (1967) 249; P.M. Bogaert, *Apocalypse*, 1, pp.386,391; W. Harnisch, *o.c.*, p.179; R.J. Banks, *Jesus and the Law*, p.51. Contra M. Limbeck, *Ordnung*, p.102. With regard to a discussion of the significance and function of the Torah in ApcBar see A. Nissen, *a.c.*, pp.249,264f.; W. Harnisch, *o.c.*, pp.178-222; P.M. Bogaert, *o.c.*, pp.390-392; M. Limbeck, *o.c.*, pp.102-107; R.J. Banks, *o.c.*, pp.30f.,51-53,69; A.F.J. Klijn, *JSHRZ* V/2 (1976) 115f.; C. Münchow, *o.c.*, pp.100,104-106,108-111.

336 For this introductory summary of the significance of the law in ApcBar see A.F.J. Klijn, *o.c.*, pp.115f.

337 W. Harnisch, *Verhängnis*, p.179. We follow him in his presentation of the relationship between the concepts of law and of the two aeons in ApcBar.

338 Contra B. Violet, *Apokalypsen*, p.LXXXIV; R.H. Charles, *APOT* 2 (1913) 478; O. Eissfeldt, *Einleitung*, p.853 and others who maintain that ApcBar was written in marked contrast or even opposition to 4Ezr. Following E. Brandenburger, *Adam*, p.39 with n.1; W. Harnisch, *o.c.*, p.179.

which reflect the intention of the author. He discusses and rejects the objections which the seer had brought forward (cf. 14,1-19) against the traditional form of the doctrine of retribution (cf. 13, 2-12).

> In 15,5-6 we read the decisive words, spoken by God: "Man could indeed not have understood my judgment if he had not received the law and if I had not instructed him in understanding . But now, because he transgressed knowingly, therefore he will be tormented knowingly"[339]. This statement refers back to v.3 where 'Baruch' objected that God's judgment was incomprehensible (cf. 14,8). God points out that 'man', i.e. Israel[340], possessed the law (the Torah) and as a result knew the criteria which will be applied in the final judgment (cf. 84,1). As Israel had received the Torah and had been instructed with regard to its intention, the sinner has no excuse in judgment. In the law God put before each one life and death (cf. 19,1). Man himself can and indeed has to decide his salvation or condemnation in the future aeon. If and when the sinner is tormented he knows (15,6) why since he was always conscious of the dreadful consequences of sinful behaviour (cf. 48,40; 55,2; 85,8-9). With regard to the attainment of the eschatological salvation (15,7-8), resolute devotion to God's law is decisive — the keeping of God's commandments and the willingness to fight evil as long as the present aeon exists[341]. — Thus, it can be said that 15,1-8 is dominated by the conviction "daß zwischen Tun (in diesem Äon) und Ergehen (im künftigen Äon) ein fester Zusammenhang besteht, der auf der einen wie auf der anderen Seite (vgl. 15,5f. mit 15,7f.) durch das *Gesetz* garantiert wird. Denn daß die Sünder auf Grund ihrer Übertretungen dem ewigen Verderben verfallen und daß die Gerechten als Lohn für ihren Gehorsam ewige Herrlichkeit erwerben, ist im Gesetz offenbar"[342].

---

339 We followed the translation of B. Violet and A.F.J. Klijn. With regard to 15,6 see 19,3; 48,40; 55,2; 4Ezr 7,72; Barn 5,4.
340 It can be assumed that 15,5 understands "man" as referring to the members of God's family which is clearly the case in 32,1; 44,3.7; 46,4-5; 77,3.15-16 where Israel is clearly presented as recipient of the Torah. Difficult is 48,10 where it seems that the "inhabitants of the earth" know the law. However, since the dominating thought in ApcBar presupposes and describes Israel (!) as the recipient of the law, and since the general intention of the author aims at demonstrating the liability of the Jews (not of Gentiles) with regard to their knowledge of the law, it seems to be justified to interpret this phrase as being primarily the members of God's people (cf. 15,5-6; 55,2). It is only in 82,6 (EpBar) that the heathen are said to have known, and transgressed, the law. Cf. W. Harnisch, *Verhängnis*, p.182 n.2. Cf. also S. Aalen, *Begriffe*, pp.207-209 who points out that in rabbinic thought mankind is represented by Israel, i.e. that "die Juden als die Menschen κατ'ἐξοχήν aufgefaßt sind" (p.207 n.3). Cf. J. Jervell, *Imago Dei*, FRLANT 76, 1960, pp.32f.; W. Harnisch, *o.c.*, pp.81f.
341 The attainment of righteousness on the ground of works is mentioned or implied in 2,2; 14,7.12; 24,1; 32,1; 51,3.7; 57,2; 63,3; 67,6. Cf. A. Nissen, "Tora", *NovTest* "Tora", *NovTest* 9 (1967) 249; P.M. Bogaert, *Apocalypse*. 1, p.400f.;
9 (1967) 249; P.M. Bogaert, *Apocalypse*, 1, pp.400f.; C. Münchow, *Ethik*, pp.104,
342 W. Harnisch, *o.c.*, p.187. Cf. M. Limbeck, *Ordnung*, pp.104f.; C. Münchow, *o.c.*, pp. 104-106,111.

The legitimacy of divine retribution which will be executed on the sinners at the end of the present aeon on the basis of their attitude and position with regard to the law is demonstrated in 48,38-41.45-47; 54,16-18[343].

The central intention of the author is summarized in 54,21-22 where he states that there exists an indissoluble nexus between historical action and eschatological fate. The *ius talionis* is applied to the teaching of the two aeons, and the execution of the divine retribution is transferred to the otherwordliness of the future aeon.

> 54,22 has been paraphrased in the following manner: "Diejenigen, die sich in diesem Äon beständig an das halten, *was das göttliche Gesetz gebietet*, werden im künftigen Äon von der Nähe Gottes begleitet werden. Die Sünder dagegen (die sich jetzt dem Gottenswillen widersetzen) werden am Ende für immer von der Zukunft (der Nähe Gottes) geschieden, *die das göttliche Gesetz verheißt*"[344].

Faithfulness to the law establishes the qualification for the eschatological glory.

The salvational function of the law in ApcBar is further developed by the comparison of the law with light[345].

> 17,4 mentions Moses who brought the law to Israel and thus "lighted a lamp for the nation of Israel". The parallelism of "law" and "lamp" is carried over to 18,1-2 describing Moses as "he who lighted (the lamp of the law)". Moses "took from the light", i.e. he oriented himself by the light which transmitted (eschatological) life and salvation[346]. The "light of Moses" is contrasted with the "darkness of Adam", i.e. the sphere of death which is represented by Adam[347]. The law is further compared with "light" and a "lamp" in 46,2-3; 59,2, and the law is connected with "light" and "life" in 38,1-2; 45,1-2; 46,2-3; 76,5.

In these passages "light" is not only a symbol for the sphere of life originating in the law but rather a *Chiffre* for the revelatory character of the law. The law is "light" insofar as it uncovers the connection between faithfulness and reward and between sin and punishment, thus making the perception of salvation and judg-

---

343 For a discussion of these passages see W. Harnisch, *Verhängnis*, pp.188-194. The personal responsibility of the individual becomes further obvious in the way ApcBar treats Adam's fall in 54,14-15.19. Cf. W. Harnisch, o.c., pp.194-197; P.M. Bogaert, *Apocalypse*, 1, pp.401f.; C. Münchow, *Ethik*, pp.108-110.
344 W. Harnisch, o.c., p.200. Cf. also A. Nissen, "Tora", *NovTest* 9 (1967) 264f.
345 Cf. S. Aalen, *Begriffe*, pp.186-193; W. Harnisch, o.c., pp.202-206; M. Limbeck, *Ordnung*, p.105 with n.2.
346 In 18,1-2 "light" designates the sphere of life which has its origin in the law. Cf. S. Aalen, o.c., pp.186f.; W. Harnisch, o.c., p.205.
347 Cf. E. Brandenburger, *Adam*, p.37; W. Harnisch, o.c., p.205.

ment possible. In the words of W. Harnisch, "die Wirksamkeit des Gesetzes (als) Licht besteht also darin, daß es die Erkenntnis über den Lebens- und Todesweg schenkt"[348].

The parenetic sections in ch. 31-34; 43-46; 76-77 underline the apocalyptic interest in the law[349]. The seer 'Baruch' admonished his people repeatedly to obey the law in the present aeon since only those who keep the law will escape the eschatological affliction (cf. 31,5-32,1; 44,3-7; 46,5-6; 77,5-7.13-15).

With regard to the law in ApcBar the scribes must be mentioned too. They occupy a "Mittlerposition zwischen der Tora und dem nach den 'Verhaltensmaßregeln der Tora' (59,4) fragenden Volk (44,7; 46,3)"[350]. They transmit the content of the Torah (cf. 84, 9) and interpret its contents (cf. 3,6).

> The pericope 77,13-15 is very significant here. The people lament: " 'For the shepherds of Israel have perished, the lamps which gave (us) light are extinguished, and the fountains have withheld their stream from which we used to drink (v.13). Now we are left in darkness and in the thicket of the wood and in the barrenness[351] of the wilderness' (v.14). And I (i.e. 'Baruch') answered and said to them: 'Shepherds and lamps and fountains come from the law, and though we depart, yet the law abides' (v.15)". The "shepherds and lamps and fountains" are presumably a reference to the prophets, the scribes, and the wise men. When the author says that these men "come from the law" he claims that Israel's relationship with God is exclusively founded on, and rooted in, the law[352]. The pious are to submit to them (46,5) as to God and to the Torah (54,3). In fact, 'Baruch' presents himself as a teacher (of the law)[353].

Thus we see that in ApcBar the law possesses, as in 4Ezr, primarily a salvational eschatological significance based on its ethical dimension. Those who direct their 'ways' aright (cf. 77,6) and

---

348 W. Harnisch, *Verhängnis*, p.205; cf. M. Limbeck, *Ordnung*, p.105 n.2; both follow S. Aalen, *Begriffe*, pp.186-188.
349 Cf. W. Harnisch, *o.c.*, pp.208-215; M. Limbeck, *o.c.*, pp.104f.; C. Münchow, *Ethik*, pp.107f. O.H. Steck, *Israel*, pp.180f. showed that the parenetic sections in ApcBar are rooted in the deuteronomistic theology of history.
350 A. Nissen, "Tora", *NovTest* 9 (1967) 249.
351 Following the translation of A.F.J. Klijn, *JSHRZ* V/2 (1976) 174.
352 Contra D. Rössler, *Gesetz*, p.104. Cf. W. Harnisch, *Verhängnis*, p.213. R.J. Banks, *Jesus and the Law*, p.30 observed rightly that the author of ApcBar subordinated the election to the law; similarly A. Jaubert, *Notion*, p.289 who points out that "il paraît pourtant exact d'affirmer que, dans l'ensemble, la doctrine de l'Alliance s'est muée en une doctrine de Loi". Cf. also C. Münchow, *Ethik*, p.105.
353 After A.D. 70 only the rabbis were the teachers! Cf. also A. Nissen, "Tora", *NovTest* 9 (1967) 249 with n.8. On the *Apokalyptiker* as scribe see E.J. Janssen, *Gottesvolk*, pp.96-100.

keep God's commandments will inherit the future aeon (cf. 44, 15).

7.3.2. The concept of wisdom. As in 4Ezr, the wisdom concept is not developed in ApcBar. In 14,9 God's incomprehensible counsel and wisdom are mentioned (cf. also 21,9-10; 44,6; 54,13; 75, 2). In 28,1 wisdom is related to the understanding of esoteric-apocalyptic knowledge. 38,2 refers to God's wisdom which is "right guidance". The pious who obey God's law have acquired for themselves "treasures of wisdom" and "stores of understanding" (44,14; cf. 38,1; 46,5; 48,24.36; 51,3; 54,5; 59,7). 46,5 links wisdom and understanding with the fear of the Lord[354]. 48,9 is a reference to wisdom as cosmic order when it talks of the "spheres" which God made wise[355]. In 51,3.7 wisdom and understanding are again described, alongside the obedience to the law, as prerequisites for the attainment of eschatological salvation in the future aeon. 54,13 refers to God's "counsel" with which he governs all creatures and links the heavenly "treasures of wisdom" with "fountains of light". Here, "light" can mean three things: the external light which organizes the world and which comes from a heavenly source; the rational world order which is the object of knowledge and which is the content of man's wisdom; and the wisdom in which the pious will participate in the future aeon[356]. According to 59,7 God showed to Moses the "root of wisdom", the "riches of understanding", and the "fountain of knowledge". Finally, 46,4 makes reference to the 'wise man' or sage in Israel.

Thus, wisdom in ApcBar has a cosmic (21,9-10; 44,6; 54,13) and a particularistic (46,5; 59,7) perspective. Wisdom can signify apocalyptic knowledge (28,1) but is not linked with the messiah or his kingdom.

7.3.3. The law and wisdom. In ApcBar the identification of law and wisdom can be observed in many passages[357]. 15,5 parallels

---

354 Cf. the translation of A.F.J. Klijn, *JSHRZ* V/2 (1976) 150.
355 Cf. S. Aalen, *o.c.*, pp.176f.
356 Cf. S. Aalen, *o.c.*, pp.175f.
357 Neither W. Harnisch, nor M. Limbeck, nor C. Münchow mention or discuss the identification of law with wisdom. R.J. Banks, *Jesus and the Law*, p.109 refers to it (quoting 77,16), also M. Küchler, *Weisheitstraditionen*, pp.67,80.

the acceptance of the law with instruction "in understanding"; to have the law is equivalent with "knowing" (v.6).

38,1-2.4 is an important pericope. God is said always to "enlighten" those who are "led by understanding" (v.1). The term "light" is usually connected with the "lamp of the law" (cf. 17,4; 18,1-2; 46,2-3; 59,2). In v.2 the identification is explicit: "Your law is life and your wisdom is the right way"[358]. Law is correlated with wisdom by synonymous parallelism. Law and wisdom have one and the same goal: true life, which consists in walking in the right way. And law and wisdom have the same origin: in the Lord. In v.4 law and wisdom are again synonymously parallel: "My soul has always walked in your law, and from my earliest days I did not depart from your wisdom". To keep the law is to heed God's wisdom. The connection between v.2 and v.4 is rather interesting: the "right way of wisdom" (v.4) corresponds with "walking in God's law" (v.4). Thus 38,1-2.4 identifies law and wisdom in a very intricate but clear manner on the basis of the ethical perspective of the two realms.

44,14 describes the pious who will inherit the future aeon (vv. 12-13): they have acquired "treasures of wisdom" and "stores of understanding", they practised mercy and preserved the "truth of the law". The latter expression probably refers to the keeping of the commandments which confirms the 'validity' of the law. As obedience to the law secures one's participation in the eschatological salvation of the future aeon, the "treasures of wisdom" might very well refer to the good works[359] which are the result of this obedience. Thus, to keep the commandments equals the storing-up of "treasures of wisdom" which guarantee salvation. Such a statement can be made only when obedience to the law is regarded as true wisdom.

46,4 personalizes the identification: the "wise man" and the "son of the law"[360] are one in the rabbinic scribe. 46,5 also im-

---

358 The view that the law is life can be found also in 32,1; 45,2.
359 P.M. Bogaert, *Apocalypse*, 2, p.81 compares 44,14 with 4Ezr 6,5 ("treasures of faith"); 7,77 ("treasure of good works").
360 We have no corresponding expression in Greek nor in Hebrew for Syriac ܟܢܐ ܕܒܪ. R.H. Charles, *APOT* 2 (1913) 504 suggests בר מצוה = "one bound to observe the law", which is rejected by P.M. Bogaert, *Apocalypse*, 2, p.83 since בר מצוה is a rabbinic technical term which does not suit the context. Bogaert suggests that the Syriac might be the translation of the Greek terms νομοδιδάσκαλος or νομικός (ibid.).

plies the close correlation of law and wisdom: 'Baruch' admonishes the people to "obey the law" and to obey those who are "wise and understanding".

In 48,24 the identification is again very explicit: "The law which is among us will aid us, the surpassing wisdom which is in us will help us". As the help which is mentioned in this verse refers to staying away from sin and keeping God's commandments (v.22) as prerequisite for entering into the promised eschatological salvation (v.23), it is evident that the identification of law and wisdom is based again on the ethical dimension of the two entities.

In the same chapter the connection between 48,33.36.38.40.47 implies the identification too: in the last days, which is the time of affliction (v.31), not many wise or intelligent will be found (v.33) since the "multitude of intelligence" and the "multitude of wisdom" have hidden themselves (v.36); people pollute themselves and do not remember God's law (vv.38.40) but transgress it (v.47).

In 51,3.4 we have a description of the righteous and the wicked: the righteous are "justified by God's law", have "understanding in their life", and plant in their heart the "root of wisdom"[361] (v.3). The wicked reject God's law and refuse to accept his wisdom and understanding (v.4). The ethical dimension of the identification is here joined by an eschatological dimension.

52,7 deals again with the righteous: they are saved by their works. This notion is explained by the statement that the law has been their hope, understanding their expectation, and wisdom their confidence. Law, understanding, and wisdom are clearly one, referring to the right ethical conduct which guarantees eschatological salvation.

Considering the fact that the "root of wisdom", the "treasures/riches of understanding", and the "fountain of knowledge" are elsewhere closely linked with the law (cf. 44,14; 48,33-47; 51,3-4), it is possible to see the identification also implied in 59,4.7 where Moses is shown the "principles of the law" (v.4) as well as "the root of wisdom, and the riches of understanding, and the fountain of knowledge" (v.5).

The same is true for 61,4-6 where the righteous under David and Solomon are described: in their time "wisdom" and the "riches

---

361 On the "root of wisdom" see 49,7; 4Ezr 3,22; 8,52-53; Sir 1,6.20; SapSal 3,15.

of understanding" were heard and magnified in the assembly (the Torah?!), and "the righteousness of the precepts of the Mighty One was accomplished in truth" (v.6), i.e. people obeyed the law faithfully and thus achieved righteousness.

Similarly, Hezekiah is synonymously called "wise" and "righteous" in 63,5, and King Josiah "exalted the righteous and honoured all those who were wise in understanding", being himself "firm in the law", according to 66,2.5.

Finally, wisdom and law are identified in 77,16[362]: "Therefore, if you consider the law and keep your eye on wisdom, a lamp will not be wanting, the shepherd will not give way, and the fountain will never dry up"[363].

It is obvious that the author of ApcBar knew and presupposed the identity of law and wisdom. Since the concept of wisdom is hardly developed, and since the concept of law is mainly focused on the ethical and eschatological (and also didactic) function of the Torah, the nature of this identification cannot be explained in as many facets as we found in Sirach. The particularistic dimension of the identification of law and wisdom is taken for granted and often clearly implied. The theological dimension is equally obvious: it is God the Almighty who possesses wisdom and who gave the law to Israel.

The ethical dimension is the decisive one: obedience to the law, walking in God's ways, is true wisdom and leads to "treasures of wisdom" which is righteousness. This achieved righteousness is the basis of the eschatological dimension: obedience to the law, i.e. the storing up of the "treasures of wisdom", leads to the righteousness which guarantees eschatological salvation in the future aeon. The didactic dimension is to be seen in the person of the rabbi who, after A.D. 70, combines the sage and the teacher of the law.

7.3.4. Summary. The law plays a central role in ApcBar. Practical obedience to the law in the present aeon means to walk in God's ways which leads to righteousness which in turn secures eschatological salvation in the future aeon. The identity of law and

---

362 Seen by R.J. Banks, *Jesus and the Law*, p.109.
363 The translation follows A.F.J. Klijn, *JHRZ* V/2 (1976) 174.

wisdom is presupposed from the beginning, and is often made explicit. It has no special function but is taken for granted. To keep the law is to be wise, and to obey the commandments is to store up "treasures of wisdom". Wise lawfulness, or lawful wisdom, guarantees eschatological salvation in the future aeon.

§8 Conclusion

Our analysis of nine extra-biblical writings has shown that the identification of law and wisdom which had been carried through most explicitly by Ben Sira was known, presupposed, implied, and stated explicitly by the respective authors, compilers, and circles in which these writings originated. Law is clearly identified with wisdom in Baruch[364], Enoch[365], the Letter of Aristeas[366], the Jewish Third Sibylline Oracle[367], the Fourth Book of Maccabees[368], the Fourth Book of Ezra[369], and the Apocalypse of Baruch[370]. The same identification is very probably implied in the Psalms of Solomon[371], and in the Wisdom of Solomon[372].

The identification of law and wisdom is to be found in all circles: among hasidic groups (Enoch), in the Pharisaic fellowships (Bar(?), PsSal, 4Ezr, ApcBar), and in the Alexandrian diaspora (EpArist, Sib 3, SapSal, 4Macc). The identification is upheld in the wisdom tradition (SapSal), in apologetic-philosophical treatises (EpArist, 4Macc), in hymnic compositions (PsSal), in parenetic

---

[364] Bar 3,9-14; 4,1-4.
[365] En(eth) 5,8-9; 42,1-3; 48,1; 49,1-3; 61,1-13; 91,10; 92,1; 93,10; 94,1-5; 98,6-10; 99,10; 104,12.
[366] EpArist 31,127,139,144,161,168-169.
[367] Sib 3,219-220.573-600.669-697.
[368] 4Macc 1,17; 5,35; cf. also the concept of εὐσέβεια.
[369] 4Ezr 5,9-11/7,88-99; 7,70-74; 8,7-13.12.52-58; 14,25.
[370] ApcBar 15,5; 38,1-2.4; 44,14; 46,4-5; 48,24.33-47; 51,3-4.7; 59,4.7; 61,4-6; 63,5; 66,2.5; 77,16.
[371] PsSal 4,8-13; 14,1-2; 16,7-8.
[372] SapSal 2,12; 7,26-27; 18,4. See also TLev 13; TNaph 2,9; 8,7-10; arTLev 88-90; AntBibl 20,2-3; 21,2; 23,7; 32,7; Jub 2,2; 4,17; Aristob (PrEv 13,12,8-13; 8,10,4; 13,12,1-2.4).

books (Enoch), as well as in the apocalyptic tradition[373] (Enoch, Sib 3, 4Ezr, ApcBar). The identification is expressed both in Hebrew/Aramaic (Bar, Enoch, PsSal, 4Ezr, ApcBar) and in Greek (EpArist, Sib 3, SapSal, 4Macc).

It is not possible to establish the exact historical development of Ben Sira's identification of law and wisdom in the literature which was produced in the later centuries. At times, the life-setting of the particular writing is not totally clear. In most cases neither the concept of the Torah nor the concept of wisdom are much developed. Often the identification of law and wisdom is simply stated and referred to while the relevant pericopes do not allow a more careful analysis of the character of the identification. However, trends can be indicated.

The main emphasis with regard to the identification of law and wisdom is definitely the ethical dimension of the correlation. This is the case in all the writings studied, with the exception of SapSal. Law and wisdom contain and indicate the norms of moral conduct. Bar stresses that the law and wisdom lead to an upright 'walk'. Enoch emphasizes the close relationship between righteousness, implying obedience to the law, and wisdom. In PsSal obedience to the law is regarded as being equivalent with the adoption of, and submission under, the divine $\pi\alpha\iota\delta\epsilon\iota\alpha$. The author of EpArist wants to demonstrate that the Jewish law is true wisdom, making a morally perfect life and character possible. In Sib 3 the ability to give sound counsel and to perform virtuous deeds equals the keeping of the law. The author of 4Macc is convinced that true philosophy (wisdom) consists in a pious life according to the Jewish law: the Torah is the basis and source of true piety and of divine philosophy. For the author of 4Ezra the law and wisdom contain the norms which are decisive if man wants to walk in God's 'ways' in order to please him and to obtain salvation. Similarly the author of ApcBar is convinced that obedience to the Torah is, and leads to, true wisdom which amounts to righteousness and secures salvation.

The ethical orientation is evident in the fact that both law[374]

---

373 Stressed as a "fundamentaler Glaubenssatz" of apocalypticism by M. Küchler, *Weisheitstraditionen*, p.66.
374 SapSal 18,4; 4Ezr 14,20-21; 10,22; ApcBar 17,1; 38,1-2; 54,5; 18,1-2; 46,2-3;

and wisdom[375] are described as "light". Sometimes the law[376] and wisdom[377] are compared with a 'way' and a 'path'.

The particularistic dimension of the identification of law and wisdom, i.e. the emphasis on the Jewish law and the Jewish realm with regard to wisdom, is taken for granted in most writings rather than elucidated specifically. The Exodus event, the covenant, the theophany at Mt. Sinai, and the person of Moses are mentioned occasionally.

The theological dimension is taken for granted as well. The concept of the fear of the Lord is not prominent in most of the writings discussed[378]. But it is always obvious that the law originated with God and that God possesses wisdom and gives wisdom.

The universalistic dimension of the identification is more in the background. Both wisdom[379] and the law[380] are related to creation and described as being universal. Often the eternal validity of the law is stressed[381]. Apologetic-philosophical treatises like EpArist and 4Macc are naturally more inclined to stress the universal perspective of Jewish law and wisdom.

The didactic dimension tends to be equally in the background. It is present in 4Ezr and ApcBar which know the person of the scribe, the wise teacher of the law.

The eschatological dimension of the identification of law and wisdom goes beyond Ben Sira's conception. It has been discovered in Enoch, 4Ezr, and ApcBar. The Coming One is linked with the

---

59,2. Cf. also TLev 4,3; 18,3; 14,3-4; 19,1; TReu 3,8; AntBibl 9,8; 11,1; 12,2; 15,6; 19,6; 23,10; 33,3.

375 Bar 3,14; SapSal 7,26; cf. En(eth) 5,6-9; 58,3-6; 108,11-14; AntBibl 23,7; 51,4; TLev 18,3.

376 Cf. Bar 3,13; 4,13; En(eth) 99,10; PsSal 14,2; ApcBar 38,4. Cf. also AntBibl 12,4; 21,9; 30,1-2.

377 Cf. Bar 4,13; En(eth) 94,1-5; 99,10; ApcBar 38,2. Cf. also TLev 13,1.

378 Cf. ApcBar 46,5. PsSal is an exception: the righteous are linked with the fear of the Lord in 2,33; 3,12; 4,23; 5,18; 6,5; 12,4; 13,12; 15,13. Cf. also TLev 13,1.7; TJud 16,2; TGad 3,2; TJos 11,1.

379 Cf. Bar 3,24-25.32-34; En(eth) 42,1; 84,3; 91,10; 94,5; SapSal 8,1-4; 7,17-21.24; 9,1-2.9. Cf. also TNaph 2,8-9; 3,2-5.

380 En(eth) 2,1-2; 33,3-4; 60,11-22; 66,1-2; 73,1; 75,1; 76,14; 79,1-2; 80,7. Cf. also TLev 13; TNaph 2,1-3,3; 8,7-10; Jub 1,4.10.26.29; 2,2; 5,13; 7,20; 16,3; 21,5; 23,16; 24,11; 30,21.

381 Cf. Bar 4,1; En(eth) 93,6; 99,2.14; PsSal 7,9; 4Ezr 7,11; 9,37; ApcBar 77,15. Cf. also Jub 2,33; 6,14; 13,26; 15,25; 16,30; AntBibl 11,1-2.5; 9,8.

law[382] and with wisdom[383]. Both obedience to the law and wisdom will characterize the new aeon. Wise, faithful obedience to the law is decisive for obtaining righteousness and for inheriting the eschatological salvation[384].

---

[382] The Son of Man: En(eth) 39,6; 48,1-2; 49,2; 53,7; 71,14.16; the Davidic King: PsSal 17,24. Cf. also TJud 24,1.3.6 (the Messiah) and TLev 18,2.3-5.9.11 (the 'saviour priest').

[383] The Son of Man: En(eth) 48,1-2; 49,1-3; 51,3; the Messiah and the Davidic King: PsSal 17,23.29.35.37; 18,7. Cf. also TLev 18,3.5.7.9 (the 'saviour priest').

[384] Especially stressed in 4Ezr and ApcBar.

Chapter Three

Law and Wisdom in the Dead Sea Scrolls

§9 Introduction

The non-biblical manuscripts from Qumran which were discovered in 11 caves at the northwestern edge of the Dead Sea, situated in the immediate proximity of the communal settlement of Hirbet Qumran, form the textual basis of this section. Academic research[1] seems to have settled the most important fundamental questions of the origin of these texts to such a degree that they do not have to be discussed here again[2]. There exists a wide agreement that the manuscripts of these caves stem from the library of the Essenes, known from ancient sources[3], who had settled in

---

1 For useful surveys see J.A. Sanders, "The Dead Sea Scrolls — A Quarter Century of Study", *BA* 36 (1973) 110-148; J. Licht, "The Qumran Sect and its Scrolls", *WHJP* I/8 (1977) 125-152; G. Vermes, *The Dead Sea Scrolls: Qumran in Perspective*, 1977; A. Dupont-Sommer, "Trente années de recherches sur les manuscrits de la Mer Morte (1947-1977)", *CRAI* 1978, pp.659-677; E. Schürer, *History*, 2, 1979, pp.555-606; H. Bietenhard, "Die Handschriftenfunde vom Toten Meer (Hirbet Qumran) und die Essenerfrage. Die Funde in der WüsteJuda", *ANRW* II/19,1 (1979) 704-778; G.W.E. Nickelsburg, *Literature*, pp.122-160. Cf. also the bibliographies of C. Burchard, *Bibliographie zu den Handschriften vom Toten Meer*, 1, BZAW 76, 1957; 2, BZAW 89, 1965; B. Jongeling, *A Classified Bibliography of the Finds in the Desert of Judah 1958-1969*, STDJ 7, 1971, and the regular up-date in *RQ* by J. Carmignac et al. The lament of O. Betz, *Offenbarung und Schriftforschung in der Qumransekte*, WUNT 6, 1960, p.1, of 13 years ago, that it is hardly possible anymore to keep track of all monographs and articles which have appeared on Qumran, is even more appropriate today.
2 See the statement to the same effect of H. Lichtenberger, *Studien zum Menschenbild in den Texten der Qumrangemeinde*, SUNT 15, 1980, p.13.
3 Josephus Ant 13,171; 18,13-21; Vit 10-11; Bell 2,121-123.128-142.147-149.163; Philo Quod omnis 75-76; Pliny NatHist 5,73. Cf. A. Adam, C. Burchard, *Antike Berichte über die Essener*, ²1972.

Qumran⁴. More specifically, the manuscripts are the product of the literary production and, as regards probably the majority of them, of the copying activity of the group which lived in the settlement. As measure for genuine Qumranian concepts figure mainly 1QM, 1QH, 1QS, CD, and the pesharim⁵. With regard to other texts which do not fit exactly into the spectrum of these main writings, it is often difficult, in the individual case, to prove or to deny Qumranian origin. It is justified⁶, however, to draw upon such texts which are usually relatively short — such as 4Q175, 179, 184, 185, 186; 4QDibHam, 4QShir, 11QPsᵃ 19,1-18; 22,1-15; 27,2-11 — in order to present in a clearer outline the evidence of the typically Qumranian writings⁷.

Recent research assumes that the chief Qumran texts have obtained their present form through an evolutionary process which

---

4 Cf. O. Betz, *Offenbarung*, p.2; K. Schubert, *Religionsparteien*, p.50; E.F. Roop, *A Form-Critical Study of the Society Rule*, 1972, pp.336-361; M. Hengel, *Judentum*, p.395 n.626; G. Vermes, *Qumran*, pp.125-130; J. Licht, "Qumran Sect", *WHJP* I/8 (1977) 146; J.H. Charlesworth, "The Origin and Subsequent History of the Authors of the Dead Sea Scrolls: Four Transitional Phases Among the Qumran Essenes", *RQ* 10 (1980) 216; K.E. Grözinger, *Qumran*, 1981, pp.3f.; G. Vermes, "The Essenes and History", *JJS* 32 (1981) 19-21; G.W.E. Nickelsburg, *Literature*, p.122.

5 Cf. M. Hengel, *o.c.*, p.394; H. Lichtenberger, *o.c.*, p.14. It has been shown recently, on linguistic and literary grounds, that the Temple Scroll (11QT) which dates into the Hasmonean period was not composed by a Qumranian author. Cf. B.A. Levine, "Preliminary Reflections on the Temple Scroll", in J. Neusner, *A History of the Mishnaic Law of Holy Things*, SJLA 30, vol. 6, 1980, pp.XVIII-XX; L.H. Schiffman, "The Temple Scroll in Literary and Philological Perspective", *Approaches to Ancient Judaism*, 2, BJS 9, ed. W.S. Green, 1980, pp.143-159. Schiffman assumes that 11QT was "composed by a group that was ideologically aligned between Qumran sectarianism and the Pharisaic tradition, tending toward Pharisaism" (p.154). Pace H. Lichtenberger, *o.c.*, p.14 who includes 11QT in the genuine Qumran corpus.

6 Cf. H. Lichtenberger, *o.c.*, p.45.

7 With respect to the major Qumran texts we use the edition of E. Lohse, *Die Texte aus Qumran: Hebräisch und Deutsch*, ²1971, and the translation of G. Vermes, *The Dead Sea Scrolls in English*, ²1975 (= 1982), being the most accessible. With regard to the other Qumran texts we used the editions and translations in the respective volumes of the *Discoveries in the Judaean Desert (of Jordan)*: D. Barthelemy, J.T. Milik, *Qumran Cave 1*, *DJD* 1, 1955; M. Baillet, J.T. Milik, R. de Vaux, *Les 'Petites Grottes' de Qumrân. Exploration de la falaise. Les grottes 2Q, 3Q, 5Q, 6Q, 7Q à 10Q. Le rouleau de cuivre*, *DJD* 3, 1962; J.A. Sanders, *The Psalms Scroll of Qumrân Cave 11 (11QPsᵃ)*, *DJD* 4, 1965; J.M. Allegro, *Qumrân Cave 4: I (4Q158-4Q186)*, *DJD* 5, 1968; M. Baillet, *Qumrân Grotte 4: III (4Q482-4Q520)*, *DJD* 7, 1982.

seems to mirror somehow the historical development of the Qumran Essenes[8]. References from contemporary history, archaeological evidence, and palaeographical data reveal that the Qumran Community proper has a history of over 200 years, beginning in the second half of the second century B.C. and ending with the First Jewish War.

> R.T. Beckwith assumes on the basis of the date of the Book of Dreams in En(eth) 89-90 that the proto-Essene movement which preceded the emergence of the Essene party proper must have commenced in or around 251 B.C. He maintains that these 'proto-Essenes' seem to have been originally "associates" (*haberim*) in the existing (proto-) Pharisaic societies. He characterizes the Essenes as a reforming (not 'conservative') movement exhibiting several major similarities with the Sadducees[9].

J.H. Charlesworth concludes from the evidence of the history of the group in Hirbet Qumran that "Essene theology was not a monolithic closed system but developed during the 200 years of the existence of the Qumran Essenes"[10].

However, M. Hengel points out that despite the tradition history of some of the texts they can still be regarded as being characteristic of the basic Essene teaching since the strict discipline and consistency of the Community render the co-existence of different, consciously contradicting 'theologies' very improbable[11]. Even though, e.g., 1QS and CD might have gone through a literary evolution and consist of different units, hymns, catechetic instructions, liturgic formulae, and judicial stipulations, this does not prove that different *Lehrtopoi* were adopted at different historical stages. He concludes that "die angeblichen theologischen Differ-

---

8 See the studies of J. Becker, *Das Heil Gottes: Heils- und Sündenbegriffe in den Qumrantexten und im Neuen Testament*, SUNT 3, 1964; A.M. Denis, *Les thèmes de connaissance dans le Document de Damas*, Studia Hellenistica 15, 1967; P. von der Osten-Sacken, *Gott und Belial: Traditionsgeschichtliche Untersuchungen zum Dualismus in den Texten aus Qumran*, SUNT 6, 1969, P. Garnet, *Salvation and Atonement in the Qumran Scrolls*, WUNT II/13, 1977; H. Lichtenberger, *Studien*, SUNT 15, 1980.

9 Cf. R.T. Beckwith, "The Significance of the Calendar for Interpreting Essene Chronology and Eschatology", *RQ* 9 (1980) 167-202; idem, "The Pre-History and Relationships of the Pharisees, Sadducees and Essenes: A Tentative Reconstruction", *RQ* 11 (1982) 3-46, here 3-6, 32-38.

10 J.H. Charlesworth, "The Origin and Subsequent History of the Authors of the Dead Sea Scrolls", *RQ* 10 (1980) 233.

11 M. Hengel, *Judentum*, p.406 n.674 arguing contra J. Becker, *Heil Gottes*, 1964, pp. 39-59.

enzen sind überwiegend durch die verschiedene Form der einzelnen literarischen Einheiten bedingt"[12].

§10 Law and Commandments: The Rule of Life

No comprehensive study on the concept of law in Qumran has yet been written. The major contributions for our brief and synthetic presentation of the Qumranian concept of law come from F. Nötscher, H. Braun, O. Betz, M. Limbeck, J.A. Huntjens, and H. Lichtenberger[13]. The concept and content of Essene halakhah has been discussed by J.M. Baumgarten and L.H. Schiffman[14].

10.1. The Significance and Role of the Law

The supreme goal of the Community is expressed in the opening lines of 1QS where the members of the Community are exhorted to "seek God (דרש אל) with a whole heart and soul, and do what is good and right before him as he commanded (צוה) by the hand of Moses and all his servants the Prophets" (1,1-3). The Community is referred to as "house of the law" (בית התורה, CD 20, 10.13) and "community of the law" (יחד בתורה, 1QS 5,2). Its members are people who "observe the Torah" (עושי התורה 1QpHab 8,1; 12,5).

People who join the Community "return to the law of Moses" (שוב אל תורת משה, CD 15,9.12; 16,1-2.4.5; cf. 1QS 5,9). In the

---

12 M. Hengel, ibid.; cf. also E.P. Sanders, *Paul and Palestinian Judaism*, 1977, p.238 n.1.

13 F. Nötscher, *Zur theologischen Terminologie der Qumrantexte*, BBB 10, 1956, pp. 43f.,63-71; H. Braun, *Spätjüdisch-häretischer und frühchristlicher Radikalismus*, 1, BHTh 24, 1957, passim; O. Betz, *Offenbarung und Schriftforschung in der Qumransekte*, 1960, passim; M. Limbeck, *Ordnung*, 1971, pp.119-189; J.A. Huntjens, "Contrasting Notions of Covenant and Law in the Texts from Qumran", RQ 8 (1974) 361-380 passim; H. Lichtenberger, *Studien*, 1980, pp.200-212.

14 J.M. Baumgarten, *Studies in Qumran Law*, SJLA 24, 1977; L.H. Schiffman, *The Halakhah at Qumran*, SJLA 16, 1975.

oath of entrance (1QS 5,7-11; CD 15,5-15; 1QH 14,17-18; cf. Josephus Bell 2,139-142) the novice pledges himself to practise the whole law with all its implications, even unto death (cf. CD 16,8-9). Thus, 'conversion' was identical with the study of, and perfect obedience to, the law of Moses as revealed to and interpreted by the "sons of Zadok" (cf. 1QS 5,8-9)[15]. The entrance into the Community is dependent upon the total and unlimited fulfilment of the Torah.

The keeping of the law guarantees God's blessing, and disobedience results in curse. This is apparent in the formulae of blessing and curse[16]. Thus, 4QBer[a] (286) 10 2,12[17] states that the wicked are cursed because they are eager to "alter (להמיר) the commandments of the Torah". The law is the decisive factor in one's relationship to God.

The leaders of the Community are to be characterized by perfection in all which is revealed in the law (1QS 8,1-2). The Teacher of Righteousness is the "interpreter of the law" (דורש התורה, CD 6,7; 7,18) *par excellence* (cf. also 1QS 14 f9,6-8; 1QpHab 5,10-12; 7,4-5; 4QpPs[a] 2b,2).

The basic importance of the law for the Community is further evident in passages like CD 7,16-19; 1QH 4,10; 5,11; 6,10; 1Qp Hab 7,10-12; 8,1; 12,4-5; 4QpPs[a] 1,2-3; 4QDibHam[a] f1 2,13.

Thus, the basis of the Community has been described as displaying a "devotion extrême à la Torah, norme de vie absolute et idéal de perfection"[18]. The law is certainly a fundamental

---

15 Cf. H. Gabrion, "L'interpretation de l'Ecriture dans la littérature de Qumran", *ANRW* II/19,1 (1979) 819; similarly P. Garnet, "Qumran Light on Pauline Soteriology", *Pauline Studies*, FS F.F. Bruce, ed. D.A. Hagner et al., 1980, pp.20-22.
16 Cf. H. Lichtenberger, *Studien*, pp.99-116, 201.
17 Preliminary edition by J.T. Milik in *JJS* 23 (1972) 130-137.
18 H. Gabrion, "Interpretation", *ANRW* II/19,1 (1979) 818. Scholars were never cautious with regard to their evaluation of the role and observance of the law in Qumran (in marked contrast to other aspects of Qumranian theology!) which was labelled 'strict', 'legalistic', etc.; cf. M. Delcor, "Contributions à l'étude de la législation des sectaires de Damas et de Qumrân", *RB* 61 (1954) 533-553; *RB* 62 (1955) 60-75; H. Braun *Qumran und das Neue Testament*, 2, 1966, pp.229-235; cf. also the quotations in M. Limbeck, *Ordnung*, p.22 with nn.37-39. The study of H. Braun, *Radikalismus*, 1, 1957 was very influential; he concluded that the different Qumran writings have one point in common; the "Radikalisierung" or "Verschärfung" of the Torah. For a criticism of H. Braun see O. Betz, *Offenbarung*, p.18 n.4; M. Limbeck, *o.c.*, pp.24-28.

factor for and in the Community, determining man in the totality of his life's references and relationships[19].

10.2. Terminology[20]

The term תורה occurs frequently in the Qumran texts[21] and obviously refers to the Mosaic law (Pentateuch) if not to the OT as a whole[22]. Another frequent term for law is חוק [23] referring both to the Torah[24] and to the order of creation set up by God[25]. The term מצוה is usually *terminus technicus* for the commandments of the Torah[26]. The term משפט[27] is not used to describe the law

---

19 Cf. H. Lichtenberger, *Studien*, p.201. He points out that the totality of this claim corresponds with the deuteronomistic concept of law. The question whether we have to speak of 'legalism' with regard to the Qumranian concept of law will be discussed in Excursus II.

20 Cf. K.G. Kuhn et al., *Konkordanz zu den Qumrantexten*, 1960; idem, "Nachträge zur 'Konkordanz zu den Qumrantexten' ", *RQ* 4 (1963) 163-234; and the indices of Hebrew words in *DJD* 3, 1962; *DJD* 4, 1965, *DJD* 5, 1968; *DJD* 7, 1982.

21 תורה occurs 30x in CD, 13x in 1QS, 5x in 1QpHab, and in 1QH 4,10; 5,11; 6,10; 1QSa 1,11; 1Q22 1,4; 2,9; 1Q27 5,2; 4QpIs^a D2; 4QpIs^c 12.14; 4QpPs^a 1,3; 2,3. 15.23; 4,8; 4QFlor 1,7.11; 4QDibHam^a f1-2 2,13; f4,8; 4Q487 f2,5; 4Q513 f4,5; 11QPs^a 18,12; 24,8.

22 Notice the role of the Psalms (11QPs^a) and of the Prophets (pesharim) for the community. M. Limbeck, *Ordnung*, pp.177f. with n.233 maintains that תורה in the 'Teacher psalms' (1QH 4,10; 5,11; 6,10) does not signify the Mosaic law but "(von Gott kommende) Weisung". This is, however, not the case, cf. S. Holm-Nielsen, *Hodayot: Psalms from Qumran*, AThD 2, 1960, pp.286f. with n.23: since 1QH makes a far greater use of the Prophets and the Psalms than of the Pentateuch, תורה probably refers there to the OT as a whole.

23 חוק occurs 19x in 1QS, 13x in CD, 9x in 1QH, and in 1QSa 1,5.7; 2,21; 1QSb 3, 24; 1QpHab 2,15; 8,10.17; 1QM 10,10.12; 13,12; 1Q16 12,1; 1Q34 f3 2,2; 1Q38 12,1; 1Q51 2; 4QTestim 29; 4QpIs^c f4-7 2,5; 4QpHos f7-9,2; 4Q487 f21,3; 4QM^a f1-3,3; 4Q502 f1-2; 4QDibHam^a f6,3; f3 2,14; 4QPr Fêtes^b 2,3; 4QShir^b f48-51 2, 4; f63-64 2,3; 4Q512 f82,2; 4Q515 f2,1.

24 Especially in 1QS, CD, and 1QH. This is extremely important for the Qumranian concept of law since חוק, in the OT, is not used as term for the law as a whole. In this context here חוק/חקים is a substitute for מצוה/מצות. Cf. M. Limbeck, *o.c.*, pp.47f., 179,181.

25 On חוק as law of time see 1QS 9,14.23; 10,26; as order of all created things see 1QH 7,34; as cosmic order see 1QS 10,1.6.8.11; 1QH 1,10; 1QM 10,12-13; cf. 1QpHab 7,13. Cf. M. Limbeck, *o.c.*, p.48.

26 מצוה occurs 14x in CD, and in 1QS 8,17; 1QSb 1,1; 1QpHab 5,5; 1QH 16,13.17; 17,7; f2,8; 1Q22 2,1.11; 1Q25 1,4; 4QpHos^a 2,4; 4QpHos^b f23,1; 4Q184 1,15;

as a whole[28]. On several occasions the term refers particularly to the law of the Community derived through the medium of exegesis[29].

With regard to the content of the law, two terms are to be noted. נגלות/נגלה[30] designate the "revealed things", i.e. God's clear, revealed precepts in the Torah which are known to everyone and which need no interpretation[31]. The root גלה stands for the process of revelation[32]. On the other hand, the terms נסתר / נסתרות[33] refer to the "hidden things", i.e. those precepts of the law (especially with regard to the calendar, the sabbath, the festivals) for which only the Community has the correct interpretation[34]. These "hidden things" are known to the Community as the result of (progressive) revelation (גלה) or interpretation (מדרש, פרוש)[35].

10.3. The Concept of Revelation

10.3.1. Terms and concepts. The concept of revelation in the Qumran Community has been studied by O. Betz[36]. The process

---

4Q501 f1,7; 4QDibHam[b] f121,2; 6Q16 3,2 Cf. generally M. Limbeck, *o.c.*, pp.40, 181.

27 משפט occurs 53x in 1QS, 48x in 1QH, 38x in CD, 10x in 1QpHab, 8x in 1QSa. The occurrence in other texts cannot be listed here.

28 Cf. M. Limbeck, *o.c.*, p.41 n.42a who states that משפט in CD means "Norm für das persönliche Verhalten wie für die Rechtsprechung" (cf. CD 5,9).

29 Cf. CD 7,1-3; 12,19-20; 14,17-19; 15,10-13; 20,27-32; 1QS 8,17-18.24-25; 9,14-15. Cf. L.H. Schiffman, *Halakhah*, pp.42-49.

30 Cf. 1QS 1,9; 5,9.12; 8,1.15; 9,13.19; 1QH 14,16; CD 5,5; 15,13; 4QPrFêtes[b] f2,4.

31 Cf. O. Betz, *Offenbarung*, p.7; L.H. Schiffman, *Halakhah*, pp.22-32; H. Gabrion, "Interpretation", *ANRW* II/19,1 (1979) 820.

32 גלה occurs 17x in 1QH, 8x in CD, 8x in 1QS, and in 1QM 10,11; 1Q26 1,4; 1Q27 f1 1,5.6; 2,1; 4QpIs[c] f1-2,3; 4QpNah f3 2,5; 3,4; 4Q177 f5-6,9; 4Q485 f3,2; 4QPrFêtes[b] f2,4.

33 Cf. 1QS 5,11; 8,11; 9,17; 11,6; 1QH 11,19; f55,1; CD 3,14; 4Q512 5,15; 4QPrFêtes[b] f2,4; 4QPrFêtes[c] f212,1; 5Q13 1,2.

34 Cf. L.H. Schiffman, *o.c.*, pp.22-32; H. Gabrion, *a.c.*, pp.820f.; J.M. Baumgartner, "The Unwritten Law in the Pre-Rabbinic Period", *JSJ* 3 (1972) 24 (= *Studies in Qumran Law*, 1977, p.30).

35 Cf. §10.3., 10.6., and 10.7.

36 Cf. O. Betz, *o.c.*, especially pp.3-154. See also F. Nötscher, *Terminologie*, 1956, pp.68-71.

of revelation is described with the term גלה[37]. It is interesting to note that the law is never called 'revelation' in the sense that God has 'revealed' (גלה) the law. Rather, it is said that God has "commanded" (צוה) the law (cf. 1QS 1,2-3; 5,8; 8,15; 1Q22 1,4). In many passages the law is linked with God as its source and origin without necessarily using the terms גלה or צוה[38].

The law requires further revelation in order to be understood: as Moses was mediator of the divine will (1QS, 1,2), so the prophets also revealed the law. On Sinai God spoke to Moses face to face proclaiming to him the "words of the Torah" (דבר התורה, 1Q22 1,1-4). And the prophets "have revealed (גלו) by his Holy Spirit" (1QS 8,16).

The Community continues this revelation of that which is meant by the Mosaic Torah and by the prophets (cf. 1QS 1,9; 5,9; 8,1; 9,13)[39]. The oath of entrance contains the basic stipulation for the novice to "return" (לשוב) to the entire Mosaic law "in accordance with all that has been revealed of it (הנגלה ממנה) to sons of Zadok, the keepers of the covenant and seekers of his will" (1QS 5,8-9). This progressive revelation of the law is necessary in order that the "hidden things" (נסתרות) come to light. Thus we find in many texts an "articulated emphasis on revelation as a continuing process involving a constant search for new illumination"[40].

In legal texts this revelation is tied more to an exposition of the Mosaic Torah and of the prophets, whereas in the Hymns it appears more in the form of direct inspiration[41]. The realm of di-

---

37 See supra, n.32.
38 God is depicted as the source of the law in 1QS 1,3.7.12.14; 2,15; 3,5.6.9; 4,3; 8, 15-21; 1QSb 1,1-3; CD 2,18.21; 3,2.6; 5,21; 9,7.8; 19,32; 1QH 15,11-12.19; 16,13. 17; 1QpHab 1,11; 2,15; 5,5; 8,16-17; 1Q22 1,4; 2,1-2.11; 4Q501 7; 4QDibHam[a] f1 2,13; f2 5,14; 4QDibHam[b] f121,2; 4Q166 2,4; 4Q185 2,3-4; 11QpIs[b] 2,7; 11Q-Melch 12; 11QT 54,5-14; 11QPs[a] 18,14; 24,9. In these passages the genitive is often used to denote God as the source of the law.
39 Cf. H. Braun, *Radikalismus*, 1, p.18.
40 J.M. Baumgarten, *Studies*, pp.29f. He concludes that "the Qumran exegetes, while ... recognizing the authority of the Pentateuch, thought of it as only one of the relevations received by Moses, the others being embodied in their arcane writings" (p.35).
41 Cf. M. Hengel, *Judentum*, p.403. Hengel points out that this different emphasis is not necessarily a contradiction: it can be explained by the differing literary forms of the statements as well as by the fact that divine illumination is also needed for

vine revelation can be defined with the term אמת[42], a central concept for Qumranian theology: "Was Gott tut, mitteilt und fordert, ist אמת"[43].

Moses and the prophets have already been mentioned as mediators of revelation. Other persons in this category include Zadok-Hilkiah (CD 5,5), Ezra (CD 1,6-12), and the Teacher of Righteousness (CD 1,11-12; 7,14-19)[44].

10.3.2. Symbols and images. The reception of revelation[45] is compared with the opening of man who is understood to be 'closed', especially in the Hymns. In this context גלה is used in its literal sense "to open": God "opens" the ears (1QH 1,21; 6,4; 18,4.20), the eyes (1QH 18,19), and the heart (1QH 12,34; 18, 24) of man. As his 'closed' organs are opened, man receives revelation.

Different images are used to describe the quality of the revelation. It is described as light (cf. 1QH 4,5.23.27; 1QS 2,3; 3,19-20; 11,3.5), as water (cf. CD 3,16-17; 6,2-11; 1QH 2,18-19; 4,5-6), as life-giving and nourishing power (cf. 1QH 7,21-22; 5,23).

God's Spirit has an important part to play in the process of revelation[46]. The revealing activity of the Spirit is not emphasized as such. The texts focus more on the purification which prepares man for the reception of revelation and on the knowledge which is given by the Spirit as power of revelation. Both the teacher and the student of the Torah are inspired by the Spirit. The revelation which is a product of the interpretation of the Scriptures and the revelation given by God's Spirit are one.

10.4. The Law and the Covenant

---

the knowledge of the secrets of God's revelation in the Scriptures (cf. 1QH 12,11-13). On the concept of revelation in 1QH see S. Holm-Nielsen, *Hodayot*, 1960, pp. 282-290; H.W. Kuhn, *Enderwartung und gegenwärtiges Heil: Untersuchungen zu den Gemeindeliedern von Qumran*, SUNT 4, 1966, pp.22-24, 139-175.

42 אמת occurs 133x in K.G. Kuhn's *Konkordanz*, and "Nachtrag".
43 M. Hengel, *Judentum*, p.402 n.652. Cf. also O. Betz, *Offenbarung*, pp.53-59; J. Becker, *Heil*, pp.155-160.
44 Cf. O. Betz, *o.c.*, pp.11f.
45 Cf. O. Betz, *o.c.*, pp.110-154.
46 Cf. O. Betz, *o.c.*, pp.135-142 for references.

10.4.1. Terms. As the covenant between God and his people is the key to the understanding of the OT, so covenant theology forms the foundation of the basic beliefs of the Qumran Community[47]. The term ברית is frequently used in the Qumran texts[48]. Often reference is made to Moses in connection with the covenant and/or the law[49].

10.4.2. Sinai, Israel, and the Community. There is no question that the Community believed in the mediation of the law by Moses (cf. 1QS 1,2-3). The Sinaitic covenant as such enters the picture especially through the reference in the history of the Community to the ברית ראשנים, the covenant God made with the forefathers (cf. CD 1,4; 3,10; 4,9; 6,2; 8,16-18)[50]. God established his eternal covenant with those Israelites who kept the commandments and who, therefore, constitute the remnant (cf. CD 3,12-13). From this group to which God revealed his will (CD 3,13-16) arose, after an initial stage (CD 3,16-17), the Community (CD 3,18-20; cf. 1,4-11). It is obvious that the Qumran group saw itself to be in continuity with Israel and with God's acts for his people.

---

47 Cf. A. Jaubert, *Notion*, pp.116-249; J. Becker, *Heil*, pp.60-65; A.S. Kapelrud, "Der Bund in den Qumran-Schriften", *Bibel und Qumran*, ed. S. Wagner, 1968, pp.137-149; J.A. Huntjens, "Contrasting Notions of Covenant and Law in the Texts from Qumran", *RQ* 8 (1974) 361-380; G. Vermes, *Dead Sea Scrolls*, ²1975, pp.25-29, 35-38; idem, *Qumran*, 1977, pp.165-175; R.J. Banks, *Jesus and the Law*, pp.33-35; E.P. Sanders, *Paul*, pp.240-271; H. Lichtenberger, *Studien*, pp.200-207. It should be noted that M. Limbeck, *Ordnung*, pp.119-189 in his discussion of the concept of law in Qumran refers to the covenant only in passing (cf. p.129); this explains the one-sidedness of his presentation. In a short article, N. Ilg, "Überlegungen zum Verständnis von ברית in den Qumrântexten", *BETL* 46 (1978) 257-263 deals with the concept of covenant with regard to the general priestly consciousness during the initial stage of the history of the Community.

48 ברית occurs 42x in CD, 32x in 1QS, 27x in 1QH, 13x in 1QM, 7x in 1QSb, and in 20 further references listed by K.G. Kuhn. Add now 4Q183 f1 2,3; 4Q185 3,3; 4Q176 16,5; 4Q179 f1 1,4; 4Q491 f8-10 1,7; 4Q497 1,5; 4Q501 1,2.7; 4Q503 4,3; 4QDibHamᵃ f1-2 2,9; 3,9.18; 4,6; 5,8.9; 6,8; f2 7,9; 4QPrFêtesᵇ f4,2; 4QPrFêtesᶜ f18,2; f97-98 1,8; f188,2; 4QShirᵇ f63-64 2,5; 3,5; 4Q512 12,12; 5Q13 28,3; 6Q16 3,1; 11QPsᵃ 21,17.

49 Moses is mentioned 11x in CD, and in 1QS 1,3; 5,8; 8,15.22; 1QM 10,6; 1QH 17,12; 1Q22 1,1.11; 2,5.11; 4,3; 1Q62 2(?); 4Q158 f7-8,3; 4Q159 f1 2,17; 5,4.7; 4QFlor f1-3 2,3; 4QTestim 1; 4QOrdᵃ 2,17(?); 4QDibHamᵃ f1-2 2,9; 3,12; 5, 14; f3 2,16; f4,8; f6,12; 4QDibHamᵇ f122,1; 4QPrFêtesᶜ 2,4; 4QOrdᵇ 4,5; 6QD 3,4.

50 Cf. H. Lichtenberger, *Studien*, pp.203f.; also A. Jaubert, *Notion*, pp. 120-139.

But there is also a discontinuity with the total history of Israel which is characterized by apostasy — apart from the remnant who kept the commandments[51] when Israel went astray and was consequently punished. The Qumran group believed that the broken covenant has been established anew in the existence of the Community to which the members of their fellowship belong as a result of their repentance. This "new covenant" or "covenant of God" is oriented by the law which, according to their conviction, is only kept in the Community. As a result, the Community is separated, and has to be kept separated, from the rest of the Jews.

10.4.3. The faithful remnant. Israel is thus split into two: there is the remnant who kept the divine commandments, and there is Israel who went astray (cf. CD 3,12-15; 4,1). This leads to the conclusion that the concept of election has been narrowed down to the separated Community which is the only guarantor of salvation. Here the Community is identical with the "convenant of grace" (ברית חסד, 1QS 1,8).

The separation of the Community from Israel has to be seen against the background of its aim to achieve a perfect adjustment to God's character (cf. CD 2,20-3,12)[52]. God hates the spirit of dark-

---

[51] See also those passages which show that the Qumran group regarded itself to be in the same situation as the Jews who returned from the Exile (CD 20,11-12; cf. 6,5). Cf. H. Gabrion, "Interpretation", *ANRW* II/19,1 (1979) 816; also K. Schubert, *Qumran-Essener*, pp.73-76.

[52] Cf. M. Limbeck, *Ordnung*, pp.120-123; he refers to CD 5,16; 8,3.13.18-19; 1QS 5, 12; 1QM 3,6; 4QFlor 1,5-6; 4QTestim 23-24. H. Braun, *Radikalismus*, 1, p.15 states that "in der Sekte bildet die radikale Torabeobachtung den Hauptgrund für die Konstituierung einer eigenen Gemeinde". This is right if the Community's observance of the law is seen as integral part of the Qumranian aim of the 'imitation of God' who hates evil and loves the good. Cf. F.J. Helfmeyer, " 'Gott nachfolgen' in den Qumrantexten", *RQ* 7 (1969) 81-104; M. Limbeck, *o.c.*, p.122; H. Lichtenberger, *Studien*, p.201; G. Klinzing, *Umdeutung des Kultus in der Qumrangemeinde*, 1971, p.153. H. Lichtenberger, *o.c.*, p.206 concludes with regard to the pesharim that the obedience to the Torah effects the separation between those who "despise the Torah" (1QpHab 1,11) and the Community which follows the Torah and its interpretation by the Teacher. The members of the Community are those who "observe the Torah" (1QpHab 8,1; 12,5). Cf. also P.R. Davies, "The Ideology of the Temple in the Damascus Document", *JJS* 33 (1982) 287-301 who emphasizes that the temple, in CD, is not an issue in its own right but that the temple represents only one aspect of the Community's existence "which was based on the conviction that only it fulfilled, because only it possessed, the divine law in its fulness

ness and all those who live in this spirit (1QS 3,26-4,1). He hates all sinners (CD 1,21; 1QS 2,15; 1QH 11,8; 1QM 3,6.9) and turns away his face from all who sin (CD 1,3-4; 2,8)[53]. Therefore the Community hates the sinners too and separates itself from them.

> The deviation from the other branches of Judaism was surely affected by the particular Qumran doctrines, especially with regard to the calendar[54]. But such doctrines were derived from the Torah and, in the eyes of the Community, the non-acknowledgement of these 'commandments' which were hidden in the Torah was equivalent to the contempt of the law, i.e. of the divine will[55].

The basic attitude of the member of the Community and the tenor of his entire life is summed up in 1QS 9,24: "Nothing shall please him save God's will".

10.4.4. Covenant and the Community. Entrance into the Community is equivalent with the "return to the law" (שוב אל תורה) and with submission to the divine commandments (cf. 1QS 3,9-11; 5,8-9; CD 15,5-11). Sometimes reference is made to the "new covenant" (ברית החדשה, cf. CD 6,19; 8,21; 20,12; 1QpHab 2,3-4)[56]. The members of the Community regard themselves as the true heirs to God's eternal covenant with Israel. To enter the Community and to enter the covenant are the same[57]. The temple symbolism in Qumran makes it clear that the Community ascribed to itself present salvation[58]. With respect to the novice the covenant

---

and in its detail (*prws*)" (p.298). Contra J.H. Huntjens, "Notions", *RQ* 8 (1974) 364 who concludes that the question of the calendar per se was "the single most decisive issue that led to the secession of the 'sect' from Jerusalem to Qumran".

53 M. Limbeck, *o.c.*, p.121 states with regard to CD 2,21; 3,8 that sin, for the Community, is "die Eigenwilligkeit des Menschen, der seine Geschöpflichkeit nicht anerkennen will". Cf. also H. Lichtenberger, *o.c.*, p.208. On the question of dualism see especially P. von der Osten-Sacken, *Gott und Belial,* 1969, passim, and H. Lichtenberger, *o.c.*, pp. 51-53; 190-200, 233f.

54 On the calendar see infra, § 10.7.3.

55 It seems that this separation of the Community from Israel gives us the best explanation for the Qumran esoteric. Cf. M. Limbeck, *Ordnung*, p.123 with n.20. H. Braun, *Radikalismus*, 1, pp.18-24 provides a different explanation.

56 On the term "new covenant" cf. E.P. Sanders, *Paul*, pp.240-242; cf. generally A. Jaubert, *Notion*, pp.209-249.

57 Cf. J.A. Huntjens, "Notion", *RQ* 8 (1974) 367 with reference to 1QS 1,8.16.24; 2,10-13.18; 5,9.20; 6,15.19; 8,16; 1QSa 1,2; 1QSb 5,21; CD 1,20; 2,20; 3,10; 6,11; 9,3; 15,5.

58 Cf. H.W. Kuhn, *Enderwartung*, p.167 referring to the implicit "Grundverständnis der göttlichen Heilsgegenwart". Regarding the temple symbolism and the statements on atonement and salvation cf. recently H. Lichtenberger, "Atonement and

refers to the "Bundesverpflichtung, die im Einhalten des Gesetzes besteht. Insofern herrscht die Tendenz vor, den Bund als Zusage Gottes durch die Verpflichtung zu ersetzen, die der Eintretende in der Gesetzesobservanz auf sich nimmt"[59].

Thus we find rather diverse theological statements in the Scrolls with regard to law and covenant[60]. The covenant is seen as divine promise to the pious, but also as obligation of man to keep the law. With respect to the latter the Qumran group has been called "a covenant community tied to the law"[61].

10.5. The Law and the Creator

10.5.1. Terms. It was especially M. Limbeck who developed the Qumranian concept of law against the background of the order of creation[62]. He shows[63] that חוק and משפט refer not only to law and the commandments but also to the cosmic order[64], to the law of time[65], and to the order of all created things[66]. Another important term is תכון which is used[67] as designation for the order established by God[68] and for the order given to the Community[69].

Sacrifice in the Qumran Community", *Approaches to Ancient Judaism*, 2, BJS 9, ed. W.S. Green, 1980, pp.159-171.

59 H. Lichtenberger, *Studien*, p.206. Similarly M. Limbeck, *Ordnung*, p.129 who states that the Qumranian unconditional assent to God's law has to be seen as an attempt "auf die von Gott im Bund angebotene Gemeinschaft vorbehaltslos einzugehen".

60 Cf. J.A. Huntjens, "Notions", *RQ* 8 (1974) 361-380; R.J. Banks, *Jesus and the Law*, p.33; H. Lichtenberger, *o.c.*, p.207. On law and covenant in 1QH see J. Becker, *Heil*, pp.60-65.

61 J.A. Huntjens, *a.c.*, p.368.

62 M. Limbeck, *o.c.*, pp.119-174. His study has been received favourably; cf. the reviews of O. Plöger in *ThLZ* 97 (1972) 830-834; H. Cazelles in *VT* 23 (1973) 382f.; J. Murphy-O'Connor in *RB* 81 (1974) 300f.; and the remark of H. Lichtenberger, *o.c.*, p.218 n.116.

63 M. Limbeck, *o.c.*, p.48.

64 חוק in 1QS 10,1.6.8.11; 1QH 1,10; cf. 1QM 10,12.13; חקק in 1QpHab 7,13; 1QS 10,1; 1QH 1,24; משפט in 1QS 10,7.9; 11,10.

65 חוק in 1QS 9,14.23; 10,26.

66 חוק in 1QH 7,34; משפט in 1QS 3,16.17; 4,18; 1QH 1,9.16; 14,20; CD 12,15.

67 Cf. M. Limbeck, *o.c.*, pp.49,131-133,176-179. He attempts to prove that כון/מכון are key terms of the preaching of the Teacher himself (p.133), and that the strong emphasis in Qumran thought and life on the order of creation has to be traced back to the Teacher (p.179).

68 Cf. 1QS 8,4; 9,12.18; 10,5.7.9; 1QH 12,5.8.9; 1QpHab 7,13; 1Q27 f1,6.

Further, מחשבה is used for God's plan of creation[70]. Other terms in this context are נתיבות and משא[71].

> In 1QS 3,15-17 it is said that "from the God of knowledge comes all that is and shall be (כול הווה ונהייה). Before ever they existed he established (הכין) their whole design (מחשבתם), and when, as ordained for them, they come into being, it is in accord with his glorious design (כמחשבת) that they accomplish their task without change. The laws of all things (משפטי כול) are in his hand and he provides them with all their needs". - 1QM 10,12-13 explains that God is the creator of the earth "and of the laws (חוקים) dividing it into desert and grassland". - 1QH 1,9-13 asserts that God created all the spirits and established a law (משפט) for all their works and made the winds "according to their laws" (לחוקיהם). Cf. also 1QH 12,5-11; 1Q34bis 2,2-3; 4Q180 1-5[72].

10.5.2. The order of creation and the Community.

God's order of creation is of crucial and practical importance with regard to the "appointed times" like morning and evening (i.e. the coming and going of the sun), the sabbaths, the first days of the quarters as days of transition, the sabbath years, and the jubilees. As these times and days were appointed by God as specific signs of his grace, the Community endeavoured in a most scrupulous way to observe them as such. In the words of M. Limbeck, "nach qumranischem Verständnis war die Zeit und Welt, in der der Mensch lebt, ihrer Struktur nach von Gott bestimmt. Deshalb war es in ihren Augen die primäre Aufgabe des Menschen, diese Strukturen in seinem Leben zu achten. Die der Welt von Gott gegebene Ordnung wurde so — um Gottes willen — zum Maß und Gesetz des menschlichen Lebens"[73]. The order of the times and seasons was seen as expression and realization of God's salvational purposes aiming at establishing Israel's fellowship with God. The observance of this order of the times implied the acceptance of God's offer.

It seems that the Essenes regarded the "ordnende, schöpferische Bestimmung Gottes, durch die allein alles Grund und Bestand erhält" as identical with the "ordnende(n) Wille(n) Gottes dem eigenen Volk gegenüber"[74]. The use of the term חוק implies a

---

69 Cf. 1QS 5,3.7; 6,4.8.9.10.22; 7,21; 8,19; 9,2.7.21.
70 Cf. 1QS 3,15-16; 4,4; 11,11.19; 1QH 1,13; 18,22; f17,3; f20,4.
71 Cf. 1QH 1,12-16.
72 4Q180 has been designated as "The Ages of Creation" by J.M. Allegro in *DJD* 5 (1968) 77-79.
73 M. Limbeck, *Ordnung*, p.167.
74 M. Limbeck, *o.c.*, p.181.

concept of law according to which the cosmic order and Israel's law constitute but one reality. The Community understood itself as part of the work of creation which was essentially determined by the will of God. The divine orders and stipulations inherent in creation and given to Israel were experienced as a unity. Thus it was natural for the Community to organize its life in a basic and scrupulous conformity and harmony with the laws of both the Torah and creation[75]. At the same time the strictly observed order of the Community is determined by the divine Spirit[76].

Despite the emphasis upon the order of creation it has to be pointed out that "die Ordnungen der Gemeinde dienen ... letztlich in allem der besseren Einhaltung des Gesetzes und damit der Sicherung der reinen Heilsgemeinde... Die Ordnungen der Gemeinde sind abgeleitet, sie entfalten kein Eigenleben gegenüber dem Gesetz, dessen Einhaltung sie dienen"[77]. This is true with respect to the liturgic process of blessing and cursing, the judicial regulations regarding penalties, and the regulations for and the mode of the admittance of novices.

10.5.3. The origin of concepts. Even if Limbeck's assumption that the strong emphasis on the creational aspect of the concept of law in Qumran has to be traced back to the Teacher[78] must remain speculative, it nevertheless provides a good explanation for the observed concentration on the order of creation. The Teacher was in all probability a priest who worked and lived in Jerusalem. The very fact that he is called מורה, combined with the evidence regarding his exegetical functions in the Community, make it plausible to assume that he was a scribe as well[79]. Further, the Community had strong links with the wisdom tradition and its

---

75 Cf. M. Limbeck, *o.c.*, p.182. Cf. also H. Lichtenberger, *Studien*, p.207 who states that in CD 2,21; 3,8 two normally separate concepts are united: God as giver of the commandments, and God as creator of man.
76 Cf. M. Limbeck, *o.c.*, pp.183-189.
77 H. Lichtenberger, *o.c.*, p.217.
78 Cf. M. Limbeck, *o.c.*, pp.131-133,179-182.
79 With regard to the person of the Teacher of Righteousness see G. Jeremias, *Der Lehrer der Gerechtigkeit*, 1963, pp.140-166; G. Vermes, *Qumran*, pp.142-146,152f. Cf. also W.H. Brownlee, "The Background of Biblical Interpretation at Qumran", *BETL* 46 (1978) 183-193 who demonstrated that the scribal and interpretive traditions of the sopherim are to be found in the Qumran texts (pp.188-193).

theology as will be seen later. And these three aspects — the priestly background, the exegetical/scribal functions, and the sapiential orientation — would place the Teacher into the immediate proximity of the priest, scribe, and wisdom teacher Ben Sira and his school in Jerusalem[80]. Fragments of copies from Ben Sira's wisdom book have been discovered in the caves of the desert Community[81], and there are also other links between Sirach and Qumran[82].

10.6. The Study of the Law

10.6.1. Foundations. The acknowledged obligation of perfect obedience to the Mosaic Torah and the prophets was based on an extraordinary devotion to the study of the Scriptures[83]. The members of the Community are described as people who separated themselves "from the habitation of ungodly men" and went into the wilderness "to prepare the way of him" (1QS 8,12-14). This "way of the Lord" is equated with the study of the law (1QS 8,15).

The importance of Torah study for the Community is seen most clearly in 1QS 6,6-8 where it is stated that "in a place in which

---

80 Cf. J.E. Worrell, *Concepts of Wisdom in the Dead Sea Scrolls*, 1968, pp.167f. who makes the hypothetical assumption that the Teacher was "perhaps a sage-teacher with a school much like that seen in Sirach" (p.168).

81 2Q18 f1 (Sir 6,14-15); f2 (Sir 6,20-31), edited by M. Baillet, *DJD* 3 (1962) 75-77; 11QPs^a 21,11-22,1 (Sir 51,13-20b.30b), edited by J.A. Sanders, *DJD* 4 (1965) 79-85; cf. also J. Rabinowitz, "The Qumran Original of Ben Sira's Concluding Acrostic on Wisdom", *HUCA* 42 (1971) 173-184).

82 Cf. J. Carmignac, "Les rapports entre l'Ecclésiastique et Qumrân", *RQ* 3 (1961) 209-218; M.R. Lehmann, "Ben Sira and the Qumran Literature", *RQ* 3 (1961) 103-116; D. Lührmann, "Ein Weisheitspsalm aus Qumran", *ZAW* 80 (1968) 87-98. The attempt of H. Germann, "Jesus ben Siras Dankgebet und die Hodajoth", *ThZ* 19 (1963) 81-87 to identify (!) Ben Sira and the Teacher has to be rejected.

83 See generally M. Delcor, "Contribution à l'étude de la legislation des sectaires", *RB* 62 (1955) 66-69; F.F. Bruce, *Biblical Exegesis in the Qumran Texts*, 1959; O. Betz, *Offenbarung*, pp.15-72; H. Braun, *Qumran und das Neue Testament*, 2, pp.301-325; E. Slomovic, "Toward an Understanding of the Exegesis in the Dead Sea Scrolls", *RQ* 7 (1969) 3-16; D. Patte, *Early Jewish Hermeneutic*, 1975, pp.299ff.; W.H. Brownlee, "The Background of Biblical Interpretation at Qumran", *BETL* 46 (1978) 183-193; G. Vermes, "The Qumran Interpretation in its Historical Setting", *SJLA* 8 (1975) 37-49; H. Gabrion, "Interpretation", *ANRW* II/19,1 (1979), 779-848.

there are ten, there shall not be absent a man expounding (דורש) the law day and night, always alternating each with his neighbor. And the assembly shall be assidous to read the Bible (ספר) as a community one-third of each night of the year, and to expound (דרש) the law and recite benedictions as a community"[84]. The phrase in 1QS 6,7 shows that the study of the Scriptures was the activity of all members of the Community at least four hours a day. Taking into account 1QS 6,3-4 and 5,21-22 it is obvious that the priests were entrusted with the study of the law in a special way.

Further, the Teacher of Righteousness was looked upon as *the* interpreter of the law (cf. CD 6,7-11; 1QpHab 2,8). In 1QS 8,11-12 we read of the איש הדורש, the expounder of the law.

The Qumranian interpretation of the law is further distinguished by its claim to inspiration and infallibility[85]. The correct interpetations of the *niglot* and *nistarot* is believed to be known only by the Community and derived by divinely inspired biblical exegesis[86].

10.6.2. Exegetical techniques. An exact observance of the law necessitated the exegesis of the Mosaic Torah[87], leading to the halakhah of the Community. But the Qumranians interpreted the books of the prophets as well[88].

<small>These interpretations are called 'pesharim' since each section of an interpretation which follows a biblical quotation is introduced by formulae using the word פשר,</small>

---

84 Following the translation and analysis of L.H. Schiffman, *Halakhah*, 1975, pp.32f.
85 Cf. G. Vermes, *Dead Sea Scrolls*, ²1975, p.37; H. Gabrion, "Interpretation", *ANRW* II/19,1 (1979) 821f.
86 Cf. L.H. Schiffman, *o.c.*, pp.75f.
87 It is important to note that it is exegesis, not (esoteric) revelation, which is at the basis of the Qumran legislation. Cf. H. Gabrion, *a.c.*, pp.822f. who states that "pour tout ce qui touche à la juridiction, la Torah est l'unique charte de la Communauté" (p.823). This seems to be the case despite those remarkable features of the newly published 11QT which suggest that the Essenes (?) regarded the Temple Scroll as quintessential Torah, the true word of God. Cf. J. Milgrom, "The Temple Scroll", *BA* 41 (1978) 109,119.
88 Cf. 1QpHab, 1QpMic (14), 1QpZeph (15), 1QpPs (16), 3QpIs (4), 4QpIs^{a-c} (161-165), 4QpHos^{a-b} (166-167), 4QpMic (168), 4QpNah (169), 4QpZeph (170), 4QpPs^{a-b} (171,173). For a convenient, recent edition of these (fragmentary) commentaries, with translation and notes, see M.P. Horgan, *Pesharim: Qumran Interpretations of Biblical Books*, CBQ MS 8, 1979.

"interpretation"[89]. They have been called "companions to the biblical text"[90] which unravel section by section the mysteries which were believed to be contained in the text. The pesharim established references between these mysteries and the time of the Community as (eschatological) end-time and interpreted them in terms of the history, life, and beliefs of the Community.

Two general methods of exegesis were *perush* (פרוש), a technique which made it possible to derive (new) relevant laws from biblical verses without the use of proof-text[91], and *midrash* (מדרש), the derivation of a law through biblical exegesis, aggadic and especially halakhic exegesis[92]. This leads us to a brief discussion of the Essene halakhah.

10.7. The Halakhah of the Community

10.7.1. Halakhah and oral law. The exegetical techniques of פורש and מדרש which were applied both to the נגלות and the נסתרות form the basis of the Qumranian legislation[93]. It is important to note that the Qumran Community did not hold to an oral law concept[94]. This concept is entirely absent from Qumran. The *nistar* is not the equivalent of the later rabbinic oral law as it is derived (only) through divinely-inspired exegesis; the *perush* is also integrally connected with the text, based upon the specific Qumranian interpretation. Similarly, *mizvah* as term for the sec-

---

89 On the word and genre of the 'pesher' see O. Betz, *Offenbarung*, pp.77-80; F.F. Bruce, *Exegesis*, pp.7-10; I. Rabinowitz, "Pêsher/Pittârôn: Its Biblical Meaning and its Significance in the Qumran Literature", *RQ* 8 (1973) 219-232; G. Dautzenberg, *Urchristliche Prophetie: Ihre Erforschung, ihre Voraussetzungen im Judentum und ihre Struktur im ersten Korintherbrief*, BWANT 104, 1975, pp.43-64; D. Patte, *Hermeneutic*, pp.299ff.; M.P. Horgan, *o.c.*, pp.230-237; G. Brooke, "Qumran Pesher: Towards the Redefinition of a Genre", *RQ* 10 (1981) 483-503; H. Lichtenberger, *Studien*, pp.154-156.
90 M.P. Horgan, *o.c.*, p.259.
91 Playing the same role as the rabbinic concept of the 'oral law'. Cf. L.H. Schiffman, *Halakhah*, 1975, pp.36-41; H. Garbrion, "Interpretation", *ANRW* II/19,1 (1979) 823f. with n.212.
92 Cf. L.H. Schiffman, *o.c.*, pp.57-60; H. Gabrion, *a.c.*, pp.823f.
93 Cf. L.H. Schiffman, *o.c.*, pp.22-76 with regard to the halakhic terminology in Qumran.
94 The later rabbinic 'oral law' concept means that there are laws which are not linked to any Scriptural derivation but were given orally on Sinai and passed down from Moses through the generations.

tarian legal traditions shows no evidence of oral transmission or of a claim to authority based on oral tradition[95]. The Scriptures are the sole source and basis of halakhah in Qumran[96].

The halakhah is the fruit of progressive revelation and is linked with further exegesis[97]. The Community had no scruples about writing down their halakhic rulings: written transmission was the norm at Qumran[98]. The Community made an unrestricted use of extra-biblical writings, including halakhic texts which were recorded for the edification of the initiates and for their fortification against apostasy[99].

1QSa 1,1-6 seems to imply that such writings were recited at public gatherings and studied as part of the curriculum[100]. This substitution of the reading of the Torah (cf. Deut 31,10) by the reading of the "laws of the covenant" seems to be an "indication of the almost canonical status to which they were elevated"[101].

> The peculiar method of rephrasing the biblical laws while inserting the elaborations of the Qumranian tradition in 4QOrd[102] serves to "erase the distinction between biblical and non-biblical rules and to lend to all sectarian ordinances the aura of Mosaic authorship"[103]. This is supported by 11QT which systematically changes, in the quotations from the Pentateuch, the 3rd person to the 1st person and uses, as in other canonical books, square brackets for the tetragrammaton; even the non-biblical

---

95 L.H. Schiffman, *Halakhah*, pp.20,32,40,48. Cf. J.M. Baumgarten, "The Unwritten Law in the Pre-Rabbinic Period", *Studies in Qumran Law*, 1977, pp.13-18; H. Gabrion, "Interpretation", *ANRW* II/19,1 (1979) 822.
96 Contra J.A. Huntjens, "Notions", *RQ* 8 (1974) 366 who says with regard to CD 9-16 that the Qumran halakhah is not developed by exegesis but "stated as already well-established and absolute legal maxims". Also contra D. Flusser, "The Jewish Religion in the Second Temple Period", *WHJP* I/8 (1977) 11 who states that the Essenes developed the oral law in a peculiarly sectarian manner, but that we have no special information about the theoretical attitude of the Essenes to the oral law.
97 Cf. S.T. Kimbrough, "The Ethic of the Qumran Community", *RQ* 6 (1969) 497 who calls attention to the openness within the Community which permitted real discussion of the halakhah with a real possibility of change (cf. 1QS 6,9-13) and concludes that "the moral life had a certain contextuality which required the discussion of Halakah" (ibid.).
98 Cf. J.M. Baumgarten, *a.c.*, pp.15-18,29f.; L.H. Schiffman, *o.c.*, pp.60-76.
99 Cf. J.M. Baumgarten, *Studies*, p.35.
100 Here the "laws of the covenant" (cf. 1QSa 1,5; CD 10,6; 20,29) refer to the laws of the Qumran Community.
101 J.M. Baumgarten, *Studies*, pp.15f.
102 4QOrd^{a-c} (159,513,514) in *DJD* 5 (1968) 6-9 (J.M. Allegro) and *DJD* 7 (1982) 287-298 (M. Baillet).
103 J.M. Baumgarten, *o.c.*, p.17.

sections are formulated as direct revelation of God (in the 1st person!) to Moses[104]. Thus 11QT presents itself as part and content of the Torah[105].

The recording of halakhah and the position of halakhah in Qumran as such are related to the unique concept of revelation held by the Community. However, the authority of Qumranian halakhah is not expressly derived from the notion that it is the product of revelation. Its authority is based on the fact that it is derived exclusively from exegesis and thus directly linked with the authority of the Scriptures. On the other hand, the exegesis of the Community is indeed linked with (progressive) revelation.

10.7.2. Halakhic characteristics. Scholars have tried to establish a relationship between the Pharisaic/rabbinic and the Essene halakhah, especially with regard to CD[106]. Some scholars hold the view that there is a "detailed agreement between Qumranian halakhah and the Pharisaic"[107]. As both the Qumran Community and the Pharisees may be traced back to the hasidim[108], it is not at all surprising to find similar concepts and halakhot[109]. Recent studies

---

104 Cf. J. Maier, *Die Tempelrolle vom Toten Meer*, UTB 829, 1978, p.11; J. Milgrom, "The Temple Scroll", *BA* 41 (1978) 109.
105 As regards the provenance of 11QT see supra, p.167 n.5.
106 The pioneer work here was written by L. Ginzberg, "Eine unbekannte jüdische Sekte", *MGWJ* 55-58 (1911-1914). Until 1958 only a few studies appeared, basically extending Ginzberg's analyses. Cf. J.M. Baumgartner, *Studies*, p.3.
107 E.P. Sanders, *Paul*, p.239, relying mainly on C. Rabin, *Qumran Studies*, 1957.
108 With regard to the Essenes and the initial stages of the Community see M. Hengel, *Judentum*, pp.417,457,566; G. Vermes, *Qumran*, pp.148,150,152f.; J.H. Charlesworth, "Origin and Subsequent History", *RQ* 10 (1980) 218-222; R.T. Beckwith, "Pre-History and Relationships", *RQ* 11 (1982) 3-46. On the hasidim as the common root of Essenes and Pharisees cf. M. Hengel, *o.c.*, pp.321,462f.,566f.
109 Cf. J.H. Charlesworth, *a.c.*, pp.223f. who believes that 'phase two' of the history of the Community saw an influx of Pharisees which explains the similarity of theological perspectives. He builds his case on the studies of J.T. Milik, *Ten Years of Discovery*, SBT 26, 1959, pp.87-93 and J. Murphy - O'Connor, "La genèse littéraire de la Règle de la Communauté", *RB* 76 (1969) 528-549; idem, "The Essenes in Palestine", *BA* 40 (1977) 100-124. Recently J.T. Milik published a Pharisaic type of phylactery from Qumran; cf. *DJD* 6 (1977) 47. See also J. Neusner, "'By the Testimony of Two Witnesses' in the Damascus Document IX, 17-22 and in Pharisaic-Rabbinic Law", *RQ* 8 (1973) 197-217; L.H. Schiffman, *Halakhah*, p.135; N.L. Rabinowitch, "Damascus Document IX,17-22 and Rabbinic Parallels", *RQ* 9 (1977) 113-116; B.S. Jackson, "Damascus Document IX,16-23 and Parallels", *RQ* 9 (1978) 445-450.

demonstrate that the halakhah of CD and other texts reflects the Zadokite priesthood as well[110].

> The halakhic evidence of the Temple Scroll shows that the regulations of the group or author responsible for this text differ from rabbinic law[111], suggesting a separate halakhic tradition[112].

10.7.3. Halakhic material. Sources of Qumranian halakhah are mainly CD, 1QS, 1QM, 4QOrd^{a-c}[113], 4Q502[114], 4Q512[115]. Important subjects in Qumranian halakhah are the calendar[116], the sabbath[117], jurisprudence[118], and questions of purity[119].

---

110 Cf. H. Mantel, "The Dichotomy of Judaism During the Second Temple", *HUCA* 44 (1973) 86; L. Rosso-Ubigli, "Il Documento di Damasco e la halakah Settaria", *RQ* 9 (1978) 357-399; and J.M. Baumgarten, "The Pharisaic-Sadducean Controversies about Purity and the Qumran Texts", *JJS* 31 (1980) 157-170 who bases his discussion of Qumran halakhah on 11QT establishing points of agreement between Qumranian and Sadducean (Boethusian!) halakhah.
111 Cf. the stipulations that the Passover sacrifice can be eaten in (!) the temple (11QT 17,8-9; but see bZer 56b), that a dead fetus makes an entire household unclean (11QT 50,10-12; but see bHul 1a), that marriage to one's niece is prohibited (11QT 66,16-17; but see b Yeb 62b). See also 11QT 3,5-6; 19,5; 23,4; 43,4; 46,1-3.
112 Cf. M.R. Lehmann, "The Temple Scroll as a Source of Sectarian Halakhah", *RQ* 9 (1978) 579-587.
113 *DJD* 5 (1968) 6-9 (J.M. Allegro), *DJD* 7 (1982) 287-298 (M. Baillet).
114 *DJD* 7 (1982) 81-105 (M. Baillet), called "Rituel de Mariage".
115 *DJD* 7 (1982) 262-286 (M. Baillet), called "Rituel de Purification".
116 Cf. A. Jaubert, "Le calendrier des Jubilés et les jours liturgiques de la semaine", *VT* 7 (1957) 35-61; J.M. Baumgarten, "The Beginning of the Day in the Calendar of Jubilees", *JBL* 77 (1958) 355-360; A. Jaubert, "Jésus et le calendrier de Qumrân", *NTS* 7 (1960/61) 1-30; K.G. Kuhn, "Zum essenischen Kalender", *ZNW* 52 (1961) 65-73; J.M. Baumgarten, "The Calendar of the Books of Jubilees and the Bible", *Studies*, pp.101-114; A. Strobel, "Zur Funktionsfähigkeit des essenischen Kalenders", *RQ* 3 (1962) 395-412; J.M. Baumgarten, "The Counting of the Sabbath in Ancient Sources", *VT* 16 (1966) 277-286; M. Limbeck, *Ordnung*, pp. 134-175; J.M. Baumgarten, "4QHalakah^a 5, the Law of Hadash, and the Pentecontad Calendar", *JJS* 27 (1967) 36-46; H. Burgmann, "Die Interkalation in den Jahrwochen des Sonnenkalenders", *RQ* 10 (1979) 67-82; R.T. Beckwith, "The Significance of the Calendar for Interpreting Essene Chronology and Eschatology", *RQ* 10 (1980) 167-202; idem, "The Earlier Enoch Literature and its Calendar: Marks of their Origin, Date and Motivation", *RQ* 10 (1981) 365-404.
117 Cf. the extensive study of L.H. Schiffman, *Halakhah*, pp.77-133; cf. also P. Sigal, *Emergence*, I/1, 1980, pp.297-302; T.Zahavy, "The Sabbath Code of Damascus Document X,14-XI,18: Form Analytical and Redaction Critical Observations", *RQ* 10 (1981) 589-692.
118 Cf. J.M. Baumgarten, "On the Testimony of Women in 1QSa", *JBL* 76 (1957) 266-269; G. Vermes, "Sectarian Matrimonial Halakhah in the Damascus Role", *JJS* 25 (1974) 197-202; J.M. Baumgarten, "The Duodecimal Courts of Qumran, Revela-

10.8. The Function of the Law and Motives of Obedience

10.8.1. The function of the law. To sum up, the law and the commandments including the halakhic stipulations have been, and are, progressively revealed by God to the Community representing the true covenant of God. As such the law is the rule of the life of the Community in general and of its members in particular. The law is the "way of perfection" (תמים דרך, 1QS 8,18.21)[120] of the Community. It is the norm for cultic and juristic matters[121], and the norm of moral behaviour[122]. The law is the foundation for teaching (cf. 1Q22 2,9; 1QpHab 2,8-9). One passage presents the law as the source of wisdom (4QDibHam^a f1 2,13-15). The fear of the Lord as related to the law is not a prominent concept in Qumran; it seems to occur only in 1QSb 1,1-2 (cf. 11QT 54,5.14).

Finally, the law seems to possess an eschatological-apocalyptic function as well. The priestly messiah, the "messiah of Aaron", is the "interpreter of the law" (דורש התורה, 4QFlor 1,11; cf. CD 7,18)[123], the final teacher "who shall teach righteousness at the end of days" (CD 6,11) and who brings the proper interpretation of the prophets (1QpHab 2,9-10)[124].

---

tion, and the Sanhedrin", *JBL* 95 (1976) 59-78; L.H. Schiffman, "The Qumran Law of Testimony", *RQ* 8 (1975) 603-612.

119 Cf. J.M. Baumgarten, "The Essene Avoidance of Oil and the Laws of Purity", *RQ* 6 (1967) 183-193; idem, "The Exclusion of Netinim and Proselytes in 4QFlorilegium", *RQ* 8 (1972) 87-96; idem, "Controversies about Purity", *JJS* 31 (1980) 157-170.

120 Cf. also 1QS 1,13; 3,1-4.8-12; 9,19; 1QSb 1,1-2; 5,22; CD 1,20-21; 2,15-16; 7,4-5; 1QH 6,20; 4Q184 14-17; 4QShir^b f2 1,6; 11QPs^a 17,2-3. The members are described as "those who have chosen the way" (1QS 9,17-18) and as the "perfect of way" (תמימי דרך, 1QS 4,22; cf. 1QH 4,21.24; CD 20,6-7).

121 Cf. 1QS 5-9; 1QSb 3,22-24; CD 3,5-16; 5,6-7; 6,14-21; 9-16; 1Q22 1,2-9; 4Q166 2,16; 4QOrd^b f3,5; 4Q512 f1 12,4; cf. 11QT 51,5-9; 56,3-4.21; 57,13-14; 59,3-9.

122 Cf. 1QS 1,26; 3,1; 6,6-7; 1QSb 1,1-2; CD 6,14-21; 7,2.6-8; 4Q184 14-17; 4QpIs^b 2,1-10; 4QDibHam^a f2,13-14; 11QPs^a DavComp (27,2-11).

123 See G. Vermes, *Qumran,* 1977, pp.185,195f. He points out that CD 7,18-20 discovers in Num 24,17 the announcement of the coming of both the "Interpreter of the law" (= the Star) and the "Prince of the whole Congregation" (= the Sceptre), while the quotation of Num 24,17 in 4QTestim 12 is usually understood as referring to the kingly messiah only (p.196). Cf. also O. Betz, *Offenbarung,* pp.34f.; G. Jeremias, *Lehrer,* pp.289-292; R. Riesner, *Jesus als Lehrer,* p.308.

124 According to 11QT 56,20-21; 57,12-14 (cf. 58,18; 59,13-21) the future king of Israel has to consult the priests' interpretation of the Torah before he makes his decisions.

10.8.2. The motives of obedience. With regard to motives of obedience, the claim of the will of God[125] and the attainment of eternal life as reward[126] are prominent. Other passages imply as motives the effort to avoid sin[127], to become or to stay pure[128], and fear and love[129].

Excursus II: Qumran, the Law, and Legalism

In 1966 H. Braun wrote that most scholars rightly regarded the attitude of the Qumran Community as "ernsteste, besonders strenge Gesetzlichkeit"[130]. He speaks of rigorism, narrow observances, and dry legalism. It is undisputable, of course, that we find a rigorous obedience to the Torah in Qumran[131]. However, it is questionable whether this rigorism with regard to the obedience to the Torah can be equated with legalism. The statements of J.A. Huntjens demonstrate, unintentionally, the importance of a clear presentation which distinguishes between legal rigorism and legalism. He states with regard to CD and 1QS that the legalistic notion of the Qumranian covenant concept is especially evident in the term "new covenant" which, according to him, is almost exclusively identified with the issue of the interpretation of the Torah and with the question of the sabbath and the festivals[132]. He believes that the question of the calendar was "the single most decisive issue" which led to the secession of the Qumran group from Jerusalem to the desert (p.364). He then attempts to support his thesis that such a rigid and legalistic notion of covenant is persistent in the Qumran texts by trying to prove that Qumran halakhah is not developed by exegesis but "states as already well-established and absolute legal maxims" (p.366). He concludes that the Community had a "very rigid and severely legalistic understanding of the law as an absolute maxim to be followed and obeyed" (p.368), that the legalism of the Community "and the whole issue of the law and the covenant is reduced to the question of the calendar" (p.369), and that the main exegetical aim in Qumran was "to seek biblical support for the sect's dating of the Sabbath and the festivals and for refining the regulations for the correct observance of the Sabbath" (ibid.). However, if we take into account the fact that (1) Huntjens overemphasizes the significance of the calendric issue, (2) he has a totally erroneous conception of the origin and function of Qumranian halakhah, and (3) he has a one-sided view of the objectives of Qumranian exegesis, not much of his "rigid and severe legalism" remains. Huntjens realizes this himself and therefore establishes a "highly spiritualized notion of covenant law as faith in the eschatological purpose of God revealed through

---

125 Cf. 1QSb 1,1-2; CD 2,14-21; 3,2-6.11-12.15; 4QpPs^a 1,2-5; 4QDibHam^a fl 2,13-14.
126 Cf. CD 3,15-16.20; 7,5-6; 19,1-2; 1Q22 2,1-5; 1Q34^{bis} 2,6-7.
127 Cf. CD 2,15-18; 4QDibHam^a fl 2,13-14; cf. 11QT 59,9-10.
128 Cf. CD 7,5-6.
129 For fear cf. 1QS 4,3; 1Q22 2,9-10; for love cf. CD 19,2; 1QH 16,13.17.
130 H. Braun, *Qumran und das Neue Testament*, 2, pp.229f. Cf. his earlier studies "Beobachtungen zur Tora-Verschärfung im häretischen Judentum", *ThLZ* 79 (1954) 347-352; idem *Spätjüdisch-häretischer und frühchristlicher Radikalismus*, 1, 1957, passim.
131 Cf. M. Hengel, *Judentum*, p.404; J.A. Huntjens, "Notions", *RQ* 8 (1974) 362-369.
132 J.A. Huntjens, "Notions", *RQ* 8 (1974) 362f.

scripture" (p.378) discussing mainly passages from 1QpHab and 1QH[133]. He concludes that particularly 1QH has the tendency to internalize and spiritualize the law as being centered in the heart. The law, he says, is still a law which has to be obeyed; but here obedience is a response to, and acceptance of, the revealed law or covenant purpose of God, corresponding to an act of faith. Huntjens explains the fact that these two notions of law (and covenant) occur in the Qumran texts side by side with the reference to the priestly-apocalyptic nature of the sect (p.379). We doubt, however, whether these two differing notions of law are so much different with regard to the Qumran texts. It is important to note that the necessity of obedience to the law is implied in the 'internalized' notion of law as well (as Huntjens admits). We suggest that the difference between these notions of law should be explained on the basis of the different literary genres — *hodayot* or hymns have necessarily a more 'internalised' or 'spiritual' thrust than the *serekh* or manual — rather than by resorting to the assumption of a neat confluence of priestly and of apocalyptic traditions which did not 'merge' in the Community but found their different expressions in different documents. Even though CD, 1QS, and 1QH have to be ascribed to different periods and authors, they nevertheless reflect together (!) the theological perspectives and the practical piety of the Community. Further, it has to be pointed out in principle that the law is *not* the centre of *all* thinking in Qumran. The central salvational property of the Community is not the law but the Community itself and the affiliation with and membership in it[134]. As regards the Community's function as a means of salvation, four vehicles of salvation were considered to be available: (1) the teaching and knowledge of the Community, especially of the law, (2) the holy atmosphere of the Community, (3) the exclusiveness of the Community, and (4) the discipline of the Community[135]. The obedience to the law and the regulations and orders of the Community serve, in the final analysis, the securing and the protection of the pure fellowship which possesses God's salvation[136]. For the member of the Community, righteousness does not (!) come by works of law even though human righteousness is works of law for him[137]. It is clear at the same time, however, that even for the members of the Community there is no salvation without obedience to God in and through his law. The classification as צדיק is based on the election by God's predestining grace and involves, at the same time, the obedience to the law: "doing the law is the condition of remaining elect"[138]. Obedience to the commandments is required as a condition for remaining in the covenant. Further, the final objective of the pious life was not mere obedience to the law and the commandments per se but rather the glory and the praise of God[139]. Therefore, love for God[140] and love for the

---

133 J.A. Huntjens, "Notions", *RQ* 8 (1974) 370-378. He also refers to 1QM 13,2-4; 10,8-11; 11,7-8; 1QS 3,13-4,25; 1Q34bis 2,3-4; 1Q27 3-8. He points out, and rightly so, that this side has received insufficient attention (p.378). R.J. Banks, *Jesus and the Law*, p.58 asserts that the law obviously did not fill the thought and worship of the Community to the exclusion of everything else.
134 Cf. G. Klinzing, *Umdeutung des Kultus*, 1971, p.153.
135 Cf. P. Garnet, "Qumran Light on Pauline Soteriology", 1980, p.20.
136 Cf. H. Lichtenberger, *Studien*, p.217.
137 Cf. J. Becker, *Heil*, p.125; E.P. Sanders, *Paul*, pp.305-312.
138 E.P. Sanders, *o.c.*, p.312.
139 Cf. M. Limbeck, *Ordnung*, pp.170-173 referring to 1QS 10,8-9; 1QH 1,27-31; 4, 27-40; 10,9-12.
140 Cf. CD 20,21; 1QH 14,26; 15,9-10; 16,7.13.

brethren[141] occupies a central position in the Community. Finally, it has been pointed out that "the stress laid upon ethical obligations entails the preservation of many Old Testament prophetic and wisdom emphases"[142].

Thus, we conclude that the Qumranian notion of law is not legalistic in the proper sense of the term[143] but is rather inseparably linked with the notions of election and grace. The character of this linkage is still a paradox which is expressed by U. Wilckens in the following manner: "Für die Qumrangemeinde bedeutet die Rechtfertigungserfahrung sola gratia selbstverständlich eine erneute, unbedingte Verpflichtung zu radikaler Gesetzeserfüllung; das sola fide geht hier zusammen mit den Gesetzeswerken"[144].

§11 Wisdom: Universal-Systematic Blueprint for Creation and Salvation

Several scholars have discussed the influence and effects of the sapiential tradition on the Qumran Community and its texts. The most comprehensive study written so far is the unpublished dissertation of J.E. Worrell[145]. With regard to other relevant studies in this area the names of F. Nötscher, A.M. Denis, C. Romaniuk, W.L. Lipscomb, and M. Küchler have to be mentioned[146].

11.1. The Significance of the Sapiential Tradition

11.1.1. Qumran as wisdom community. J.E. Worrell has de-

---

141 Cf. CD 6,21; 1QS 1,9; 2,24; 4,4-5; 5,25.
142 R.J. Banks, *Jesus and the Law*, p.58. Similarly P. Garnet, *a.c.*, pp.20-22 who states, however, that the phrase "justification by works of the law" is still valid for Qumran: "In spite of the emphasis on the covenant community, obedience was essential if either community or the individual were to find acceptance with God" (p. 22).
143 Cf. R.J. Banks, *o.c.*, pp.57f.
144 U. Wilckens, *Römer*, 1, EKK VI/1, 1978, p.248.
145 J.E. Worrell, *Concepts of Wisdom in the Dead Sea Scrolls*, Ph.D Diss. Claremont Graduate School, 1968.
146 Cf. F. Nötscher, *Terminologie*, pp.38-48,50-63,71-76; A.M. Denis, *Les thèmes de connaissance dans le Document de Damas*, 1967; C. Romaniuk, "Le thème de la sagesse dans les documents de Qumran", *RQ* 9 (1978) 429-435; W.L. Lipscomb, "Wisdom at Qumran", *Israelite Wisdom*, 1978, pp.277-285; M. Küchler, *Weisheitstraditionen*, 1979, pp.88-133.

scribed the Qumran Community as "wisdom community"[147]. This claim can be substantiated on the basis of the sapiential phraseology which is diffused throughout the Qumran texts (§ 11.2.1), the occurrence of literary genres which are characteristic of the wisdom tradition, and the sapiential propensities of documents like 1QS and CD whose function was the regulation of the life of the Community (§ 11.2.2.), the frequency and content of the pericopes related to the wisdom tradition and of sapiential concepts (§ 11.1.2.), the claim of the Community to possess wisdom (§ 11.5.), the emphasis on teaching (§ 11.6.) and right ethical conduct (§ 11.7.), as well as on the basis of the inevitable relationship with the contemporary sapiential milieu[148].

The possible self-understanding of the Qumran group as wisdom community is especially evident in the use of the term עצה, "counsel/council"[149]. The משכיל, clearly a term of the wisdom tradition, appears to have been one of the most prestigious personages of the Community: he was probably identical with the *mebaqqer* or "guardian", the teacher of the Community[150]. The people who wanted to join the Community are characterized as possessing דעת (cf. 1QS 1,11-13).

M. Küchler concludes from this evidence that "die Mönchsgemeinde von Qumran war für die damalige Zeit eine demonstrative Verwirklichung ... einer apokalyptisch-weisheitlichen Gruppe, welche in der Bemühung um die 'Einsicht des Lebens' und das 'Wissen der Ewigkeit' verharrte (vgl. 1QS 2,3) und so 'Zeuge(n) der Wahrheit' (1QS 8,6) sein wollte"[151].

---

147 J.E. Worrell, *o.c.*, pp.120-154 passim, followed by M. Küchler, *o.c.*, pp.90f.
148 Cf. M. Hengel, "Qumran und der Hellenismus", *BETL* 46 (1978) 333-372. Cf. also H. Lichtenberger, *Studien*, p.127 who states, following Hengel, that Jewish wisdom and Hellenism prepared the way for an individualization which characterizes the conditions for life in the Community. J.E. Worrell, *Concepts*, pp.123-129 discusses the testimonies of Josephus and Philo on the sapiential background of the Community: Josephus mentions Judah the Essene who revealed mysteries and secrets (Bell 1,87ff.) and refers to the Essene knowledge of prophetic apothegms (Bell 2, 159); and Philo adduces the Essenes as cardinal example for the most excellent *sophia* in Israel (Quod omnis 72-91). This evidence is, as Worrell admits (p.128), not conclusive as such, however.
149 Cf. J.E. Worrell, *o.c.*, pp.129-150; idem, "עצה: 'Counsel' or 'Council' at Qumrân", *VT* 20 (1970) 65-74.
150 Cf. G. Vermes, *Dead Sea Scrolls*, pp.22-25; idem, *Qumran*, p.91; J.E. Worrell, *o.c.*, pp.150-154; W.L. Lipscomb, "Wisdom at Qumran", 1978, p.277.
151 M. Küchler, *Weisheitstraditionen*, p.91.

W.L. Lipscomb acknowledges the fact that numerous passages in the Qumran texts employ wisdom terminology and reflect a concern for knowledge and teaching[152]. He disagrees, however, with the claim that such elements are really sapiential. He states that they are neither sapiential on the grounds of gaining consistent personal experience of the divine world order, nor are they sapiential on the basis of form: "The object of wisdom at Qumran was the revealed mysteries of God's predestined plan of salvation, knowledge of sectarian doctrine" (p.278). He believes that the employed sapiential terminology "provides only the external garb which clothes the central concern of the sect about God's predestined plan and the imminent eschaton" (ibid.). With regard to the ethical dualism which others attributed to the wisdom tradition[153] he says that in the sapiential tradition the dichotomy righteous/wicked is gleaned from humanity's own experience of the divine world order, whereas in Qumran the ethical dualism is divinely predestined truth revealed by God only to the true Israel. He finally claims that there are not true wisdom texts among the scrolls of undisputed Essene authorship (ibid.). The following arguments answer Limpscomb's objections.

(1) Methodological difficulties in establishing the influence of the wisdom tradition in a given text exist not only with regard to Qumran alone but also with regard to the OT literature, i.e. such difficulties cannot be used as an argument. (2) It is true that the form of a text and/or the endeavour to gain consistent personal experience of the divine world order are characteristic for wisdom. However, Qumran stands not at the beginning of the wisdom tradition where the *gaining* of such an experience was foundational, but at the end of the Jewish wisdom tradition where it was possible to *use* such experiences which had been made by others. The Qumranian worldview (cf. §10.5.2., 11.3.) is an unambiguous example for this. (3) Lipscomb neglects to take into account the crucial fact that wisdom had been identified with the law before the Qumran texts were written. As a result, wisdom and doctrine were not mutually exclusive. (4) The diversity of wisdom terms, the frequency of their occurrence, the significance of clear wisdom emphases, the structure of much of the life of the Community, and the explicit world-view prove that the employed sapiential terminology is not just "external garb". (5) With regard to the dualism of the Community many questions are still open[154] so that we should be cautious not to draw any inferences based on its supposed origin. (6) Limpscomb's conviction that there exist no true Qumranian wisdom texts is based, in his case, on a *petitio principii*: all sapiential elements are "superimposed upon the esoteric sectarian doctrine of an apocalyptic community" (p.278). Moreover, it seems to be clear that there are some links between the wisdom tradition and the origins and concepts of apocalyptic[155]. (7) Finally, it is not possible any longer (i.e. after the publication of *DJD* 7,

---

152 Cf. W.L. Lipscomb, "Wisdom at Qumran", 1978, pp.277f.
153 Cf. J.E. Worrell, *Concepts*, pp.280-357; J.G. Gammie, "Spatial and Ethical Dualism in Jewish Wisdom and Apocalyptic Literature", *JBL* 93 (1974) 356-385.
154 Cf. H. Lichtenberger, *Studien*, pp.190-200. Cf. also G. von Rad, *Theologie*, 2, pp. 214-221; idem, *Wisdom*, pp.263-283.
155 With respect to the relationship between wisdom and apocalyptic, Lipscomb is ambiguous. He states on the one hand that wisdom was one of the factors which contributed to the origin and development of apocalyptic thought ("Wisdom at Qumran", p.282 n.7), but on the other hand he says that P.von der Osten-Sacken and K. Koch presented "cogent challenges" to G.von Rad's thesis that the origins of apocalyptic thought may be seen in the wisdom literature (ibid.). See G. von

1982) to maintain that there exist no wisdom compositions of Qumranian origin: 4Q486[156], 4Q487[157], 4Q489[158] are possibly sapiential compositions, and 4QShir, representing 'Hymns of the Sage'[159], is clearly of Qumranian origin. And with regard to texts where the Essene authorship is disputed (e.g. 4Q185[160]) it has to be pointed out that they were used and copied in Qumran and therefore must surely reflect the self-understanding of the Community in *some* way.

It is true that it would be exaggerated to label the central concern of the Community as sapiential. Therefore the objection to the classification of the Qumran group as 'wisdom community' might be warranted after all. But it is obvious that the Community belonged to the contemporary sapiential milieu just as the other Jewish groups did and that it was strongly based upon, and molded by, wisdom perspectives.

The significance of wisdom for a proper understanding of the Qumran Community is further underscored by the fact that the "gift of knowledge" which is nearly exclusively described with perfecta in 1QH is linked with the entrance into the Community. The reception of revelatory knowledge coincides with the "einmalige Faktum" of the entrance into the group[161].

Thus, J.E. Worrell arrives at the conclusion that "Qumran's

Rad, *Theologie*, 2, pp.214-221; idem, *Wisdom*, pp.263-283, and his critics P.von der Osten-Sacken, *Die Apokalpytik in ihrem Verhältnis zu Prophetie und Weisheit*, Theologische Existenz heute 157, 1969; K. Koch, *Ratlos vor der Apokalyptik*, 1970, pp.43-45; also F. Dexinger, *Offene Probleme*, 1977, pp.39-43. Recently I. Gruenwald, "Jewish Apocalyptic Literature", *ANRW* II/19,1 (1979) 92f. suggested that apocalyptic should not be explained by either/or theories as it is to be viewed within a framework which is by and large independent of Scripture. Gruenwald states that *if* apocalyptic is to be viewed mainly in relation to Scripture, it should be linked with "para-prophecy" which contains many wisdom elements. C. Münchow, *Ethik*, 1981, pp.12,113-117 demonstrated that the apocalyptic movement, whole continuing the prophetic tradition, incorporated numerous sapiential elements and concepts; cf. also H. Gese, "Wisdom", *HBT* 3 (1981) 37f.; C. Rowland, *Open Heaven*, 1982, pp.203-208.

156 4Q486: *DJD* 7 (1982) 4-5 (M. Baillet) going back, at least, to the first part of the 1st century B.C.
157 4Q487: *DJD* 7 (1982) 5-10 (M. Baillet) consisting of 53 fragments which are mostly too small to give any meaning. On calligraphic grounds the fragments date around 70 B.C.
158 4Q489: *DJD* 7 (1982) 73-74 (M. Baillet) consisting of 15 hymnic or sapiential fragments. The script dates back to Herodian times (turn of era).
159 4QShir^a(510): *DJD* 7 (1982) 215-219 (M. Baillet) dating into the last quarter of the 1st century B.C. These hymns are clearly of Essene character (p.215). 4QShir^b (511): *DJD* 7 (1982) 219-262 (M. Baillet) with 224 fragments date to Herodian times resembling the Teacher hymns.
160 Cf. H. Lichtenberger, "Eine weisheitliche Mahnrede in den Qumranfunden (4Q-185)", *BETL* 46 (1978) 151-162.
161 Cf. H.W. Kuhn, *Enderwartung*, pp.155-161, referring to 1QH 1,21; 7,26-27; 11,3-4. 9-10.15-17.27-28; 10,13-14.28-29; 14,13.

terminological and structural implementations provide a prime historical example of sapiential items gathered into a superimposed system and perspective . . . The Community of Qumran was a 'wisdom community' in the sense that their categories for self-understanding came through the 'sapiential milieu'. Their terms of self-designation appropriated wisdom concepts for specific ends"[162].

11.1.2. The Qumranian world-view. The pericope 1QS 3,15-4, 26 shows a striking accumulation of abstract terms, and it is obvious that the anthropological terminology of this and of other Qumran texts is closely linked with that of late wisdom. We find an effort to employ a systematic, even 'philosophical', conceptuality which is unprecedented in the Hebrew language before that time[163]. In 1QS 3,15-4,26 we have an attempt to interpret "all that is and shall be" (הווה ונהייה, 3,15), i.e. being and process, creation and history, on the basis of a theological approach in a systematic form.

> In the words of M. Hengel, "bei den Essenern wird — m.E. zum ersten Mal in der jüdischen Geistesgeschichte — ansatzweise ein *'System' universaler Weisheit* vorgelegt, das Gott, Himmel und Erde, Menschheit und Geschichte umfaßt und in dem alle Phänomene von Natur — oder besser Schöpfung — und Geschichte ihren bestimmten Ort zugewiesen erhalten"[164].

This systematic blueprint of the Community is, of course, totally theocentric: God's free counsel and revelation is the basic and constant point of departure. "Er beruht im vollen Sinn des Wortes auf 'apokalyptischer Weisheit', die dem Nicht-Erwählten verborgen bleibt"[165].

11.1.3. Origin of concepts. Some scholars point out parallels between the Essene and the gnostic concept of knowledge[166]. But this view has been rejected on good grounds[167]. The Qumran dual-

---

162 J.E. Worrell, *Concepts*, pp.390-393.
163 Cf. M. Hengel, *Judentum*, p.396.
164 M. Hengel, "Qumran und der Hellenismus", *BETL* 46 (1978) 352.
165 M. Hengel, *a.c.*, p.353; cf. also C. Rowland, *Open Heaven*, pp.115-120.
166 Cf. K.G. Kuhn, "Die in Palästina gefundenen hebräischen Texte und das Neue Testament", *ZThK* 47 (1950) 203f.; C. Colpe, in *RGG* 2 (1958) 1651.
167 Cf. H.W. Kuhn, *Enderwartung*, p.142 (with regard to the hymns of the Community in 1QH), referring to the theological wisdom of the Palestinian sources, the con-

ism has been traced back to Iranian origins, but this derivation has not been unanimously accepted either[168].

The Qumranian 'system of universal wisdom' has its source in the OT tradition, especially late wisdom, and has parallels in ancient oriental wisdom[169]. There are many common points between wisdom in Qumran and wisdom in the OT: (1) the practical character of wisdom, (2) the concept of wisdom as the principle of a morally correct life, (3) the reference to God as the one who possesses true wisdom in a unique way, (4) the thought that man's wisdom is but the participation in God's wisdom, (5) the relationship between sin and folly, (6) the conviction that wisdom not only assures the honesty of moral life but also guarantees eternal life, (7) the notion that wisdom is the highest value[170]. The differences between biblical and Qumranian wisdom[171] can be explained on the basis of the exclusive self-understanding of the Community with its apocalyptic-eschatological emphases.

11.2. Terms and Genres

11.2.1. Wisdom terms. Scholars have long recognized the fact that the Qumran texts use sapiential vocabulary with a remarkable frequency[172]. Especially terms of cognition are numerous: ידע[173],

---

cepts of 'knowledge' and 'insight' in the apocalyptic literature as prerequisites for understanding the 'revelational knowledge' in 1QH (pp.142-154). Cf. also J.E. Worrell, *Concepts,* p.203; B. Reicke, "Traces of Gnosticism in the Dead Sea Scrolls?", *NTS* 1 (1954/55) 137-141; idem, "Da‘at and Gnosis in Intertestamental Literature", 1969, pp.246-250.

168 Cf. the discussion in H. Lichtenberger, *Studien,* pp.196-200. Cf. B. Otzen, "Old Testament Wisdom Literature and Dualistic Thinking in Late Judaism", *SVT* 28 (1975) 146-157; J.G. Gammie, "Spatial and Ethical Dualism", *JBL* 93 (1974) 356-385; J.E. Worrell, *o.C.,* pp.280-357; W.L. Lipscomb, "Wisdom at Qumran", p.278.

169 Cf. M. Hengel, *Judentum,* p.396; idem, "Qumran", *BETL* 46 (1978) 353.

170 Cf. C. Romaniuk, "Le thème de la sagesse", *RQ* 9 (1978) 433f.

171 In the biblical tradition wisdom is available to everyone, whereas in Qumran it is only for the members of the Community. Wisdom as direct object of praise, not uncommon in the biblical tradition, is rare in Qumran, as is the poetic personification of wisdom. Also, in Qumran we have not found the phrase that the fear of the Lord is the beginning of wisdom, which is so frequent in Prov and Sir.

172 Cf. F. Nötscher, *Terminologie,* pp.38-79; H.W. Kuhn, *Enderwartung,* pp.139-141; S. Wagner, "ידע in den Lobliedern von Qumran", *Bibel und Qumran,* FS H. Bardtke, 1968, pp.232-252; J.E. Worrell, *Concepts,* pp.181-236; B. Reicke, "Da‘at und

משכיל[181], דעת[174], דעה[175], בין[176], בינה[177], חכם[178], חכמה[179], שכל[180], ערמה[182], מחשבה[183], תושיה[184]. Attempts to differentiate the mean-

---

Gnosis", 1969, pp.246-249; C. Romaniuk, a.c., pp. 429-435; M. Küchler, *Weisheitstraditionen*, pp.88-91.

173 ידע occurs 73x in 1QH, 20x in CD, and in 1QpHab 7,2.4; 1QS 4,25.26; 5,11.19; 6,25; 8,18; 10,16; 1QM 10,16; 11,15; 13,3; 18,10; 1QSa 1,10.10.28; 1Q18 1,2; 1Q22 1,11; 1Q27 f1 1,3.4.8; 2,11; 1Q34 f3 2,3.7; 1Q36 1,4; 21,1; 2Q22 1 2,1; 3Q14 11,1; 4QFlor 5,3; 4Q180 f2-4 2,10; 4Q181 2,5; 4Q491 f11 1,23; 4Q160 1,5; f3-4 2,5; 4Q177 f1-4,12; 4Q185 f1-2 2,7.15; 3,13; 4Q502 f28,2; 4Q503 4,7; f51-55,9.13.14; f72,2; 4QDibHam[a] f1-2 2,10; f4,5.14; f8 recto 10; 4QDibHam[c] f131-132,10; 4QPrFêtes[b] f1,1; f2,4.5; 4QShir[b] f2 1,2; 2,6.9; f42,7; f48-51 2,7; 11QPs[a] 18,2.2.3.4.4.12.13; 19,2; 21,13; 26,12. Total: 161 occurrences.

174 דעת occurs 17x in 1QS, 17x in 1QH, and in 1QpHab 11,1; 1QM 17,8; 1QSb 4,27; 5,25; CD 2,3.4; 10,10; 1Q36 12,2; 4Q502 f10,3; 4Q503 4,4; 4QShir[b] f2 1,6; f18 2,8; f19,3; f28-29,3; f43,2; f63-64 2,4; f71,4; f93,1; f96,4; f124,3; f131,2; 4QS1 39 f1 1,18; 40 f24,2; 4QpPs[a] f1-2 1,19; 4QDibHam[a] 8 recto 5; 6Q18 5,3; 11QPs[a] 19,14; 26,11. Total: 62 occurrences.

175 דעה occurs in 1QS 3,15; 7,4; 9,18; 11,6.15.18; 1QH 1,26; 11,8.28; 12,10; 14,25; f4,15; f8,9; CD 15,15; 20,5; 1Q27 f1 1,7; 4QDibHam[a] f4,4; 4QDibHam[c] f131-132, 9; 4QShir[a] f1,2; 4QShir[b] f1,8; f143,2. Total: 21 occurrences.

176 בין occurs 16x in 1QH, 12x in CD, 5x in 1QS, and in 1QSa 1,5.28; 1Q27 f1 1,3; 1Q34 f3 2,3.4; 2Q27 1,4; 4Q160 f3-4 2,6; 4Q186 f2 1,1.1; 4QpNah f3-4 2,5; 3,1.4; 4QDibHam[a] f1-2 2,17; f6,3.4; 4Q485 f1,6; 4Q487 f17,2; 4QPrFêtes[c] f4,4; f12 1,13; f97-98 1,2.4, 5Q13,1.9. Total: 55 occurrences.

177 בינה occurs 17x in 1QH, and in 1QS 4,3; 11,1; 1QM 10,10.16; CD 5,16.17; 1Q29 13,2; 1Q40 1,3; 4Q158 f1-2,8; 4Q502 f2,4; 4Q503 f51-55,13; f216,3; 4QDibHam[a] f5 2,8; f8 recto 5; 4QPrFêtes[c] f122,9; 4QShir[a] f1,6; 4QShir[b] f18 2,6.8; f48-51 2,1; f186,1. Total: 37 occurrences.

178 חכם occurs in CD 6,3; 1QSa 1,28; 2,16; 1QH 1,35; 3,14; 11QPs[a] 27,2.

179 חכמה occurs 8x in 1QH, and in 1QS 4,3.18.22.24; CD 2,3; 4Q487 f2,8; 4QPrFêtes[c] f16,7; f55,2; 11QPs[a] 18,3; 26,14. Total: 18 occurrences. The relatively rare occurrence of חכמה/חכם is to be explained by (1) the effort to avoid the official Pharisaic use of the term on the basis of Qumran's purist reaction (cf. J.E. Worrell, *Concepts*, pp.154,183-186), and (2) the emergence of the noetic-reflective perception and the resulting greater differentiation of the revealed 'knowledge' to which the old term חכמה could no longer do justice (cf. M. Hengel, *Judentum*, p.402 n.651; also M. Küchler, *Weisheitstraditionen*, p.89).

180 שכל occurs, as verb and noun, 29x in 1QH, 15x in 1QS, and in CD 13,7.11; 1QSa 1,7.17; 1QM 10,10; 4QS1 39 f1 1,21; 4Q184 1,13; 4Q185 f1-2 1,13; 4Q502 f2,4; 11QPs[a] 18,5; 19,3. Total: 55 occurrences.

181 משכיל occurs in 1QS 3,13; 9,12.21; 1QSb 1,1; 3,22; 5,20; CD 12,21; 13,22; 1QH f8,10; 4QShir[a] f1-4; 4QShir[b] f2 1,2. Total: 11 occurrences.

182 ערמה occurs in 1QS 4,6.11; 10,25; 11,6; 1QH 1,35; 2,9; CD 2,4; 1QpHab 7,14; 4Q491 f11 1,10; 4Q502 f16,3. Total: 10 occurrences.

183 מחשבה occurs 13x in 1QH, 10x in 1QM, 8x in 1QS, and in 1QpHab 3,5; CD 2,6; 1Q29 13,4; 4QFlor 1,8.9; 4QM[a] 12; 4QDibHam[a] f4,4; f6,2; f24,3; 4Q491 f8-10 1,12; f14-15,8.8; 4Q498 f3 1,3; 4Q502 f6,2; 4Q503 f51-55,13; 4QPrFêtes[c] f23 1,2; 4QShir[b] f22,4; f23,4; f26,2; f42,7; f63-64 2,3; f100,2. Total: 53 occurrences.

184 תושיה occurs in 1QS 10,24; 11,6; CD 2,3.

ing of these terms[185] should not be carried too far since they are, in the Qumran context, nearly synonymous[186]. They demarcate the sphere in which "alles Wichtige an Wissen und Erkenntnis vor sich geht" und characterize the Community as the place "an dem entscheidendes Wissen von Gott geschenkt, von den Mönchen aufgenommen und gehütet und miteinander im 'Weisheitsrat' (1QS 10,24) erwogen wird"[187]. The above-mentioned group of terms possesses the greatest weight in Essene theology[188].

> The frequent occurrences of wisdom terms in 1QH is particularly remarkable. The roots חכם, בין, שכל, ידע and their derivates occur 171 times in 1QH, fragments included, in most cases referring to the "gegenwärtige Sein des Qumranfrommen in der Gemeinde"[189]. Thus we find the "Hymnik als locus der Erkenntnis-Reflexion"[190] which is rather typical for the concept of wisdom as gift in the apocalyptic tradition. The use of ידע in 1QS shows a "definite predilection for practical implications"[191].

Other important wisdom terms are עצה[192], סוד[193], and למד[194].

---

185 Cf. F. Nötscher, *Terminologie*, pp.44-63; J.E. Worrell, *o.c.*, pp.187-212; C. Romaniuk, "Le thème de la sagesse", *RQ* 9 (1978) 429-433.
186 Cf. C. Romaniuk, "Thème", *RQ* 9 (1978) 433; M. Küchler, *Weisheitstraditionen*, p.90; already observed by H. Braun, *Radikalismus*, 1, p.22 n.4. See for example the combination of sapiential terms in 1QH 11,27-28.
187 M. Küchler, *o.c.*, p.90.
188 Cf. M. Hengel, *Judentum*, p.401.
189 H.W. Kuhn, *Enderwartung*, p.140; he mentions 100 occurrences in the 'Community hymns' and 20 occurrences in the 'Teacher hymns' (including the references of גלה), obviously not including the fragments.
190 M. Küchler, *o.c.*, p.90.
191 B. Reicke, "Daʿat and Gnosis", 1969, pp.247f.
192 עצה occurs 40x in 1QS, 10x in 1QH, 5x in 1QpHab, and in 1QSa 1,3.26.27; 2, 2.9.11; 1QSb 3,28; 4,24.26; 5,25; CD 5,17; 12,8; 13,17; 20,24; 1QM 3,4; 13,11; 1Q14 10,6; 1Q38 8,1; 4QFlor 1,17.17; 4QpIs^d 1,2; 4Q502 f305,1; 4QpNah 2,5.6. 9; 3,7.8; 4QpPs^a 2,19; 4Q491 f11 1,11; 4QShir^b f23,1; f48-51 2,1; 4Q515 f1,2.2; f23,1; 5Q18 1,2. Total: 80 occurrences.
193 סוד occurs 29x in 1QH, 10x in 1QS, and in CD 14,10; 19,35; 1QM 13,9; 1Q38 8,1; 1Q46 1,1; 4Q180 1,10; 4Q486 f1,5; 4Q491 f10 2,17; 4Q502 f19,1; f23,4; f24,4; f116,2; f177,1; 4QDibHam^a f4,21; 4QShir^b f10,11; f26,3; f28-29,3; f44-47 1,2; f52-59 3,5; f63 3,2; f63-64 2,1; 4Q512 3,13. Total: 61 occurrences. On עצה and/or סוד cf. J.E. Worrell, *Concepts*, pp.129-150; idem, "עצה: 'Counsel' or 'Council' at Qumrân", *VT* 20 (1970) 65-74; O. Betz, *Offenbarung*, pp.50-53.
194 למד occurs in 1QS 3,13; 9,13; 1QSa 1,7; 1QH 2,17; 1QM 6,12.13; 10,2.10; 14,6; 4Q169 f3-4 2,8; 4Q491 f8-10 1,4; 4Q495 f1,2. Total: 12 occurrences. On למד and other terms for teaching (השכיל, הבין, הודיע) see J.E. Worrell, *o.c.*, pp. 156-160.

Wisdom metaphors include the water imagery[195] and, further, terms like "light"[196] and "way"[197].

11.2.2. Wisdom genres. The Community Rule 1QS has been described as "a teacher's manual authorized by the Rabbim and intended to provide material from which the Instructor could draw in his didactic work and material which might serve to remind him of the kind of behaviour the Rabbim expected of him"[198]. If this is a correct evaluation of 1QS[199], it is obvious that 1QS has to be regarded as belonging to the wisdom tradition. It seems that CD 13-16 is the fragment of a 'Community Rule' too[200].

Another wisdom genre is the sapiential poem, represented by 4Q184[201] and 4Q185[202]. The texts 4Q486, 4Q487, 4Q489, and 4QShir are probably wisdom poems with a hymnic character.

---

195 Terms like "fountain", "spring": מעין occurs in 1QS 3,19; 10,12; 11,7; 1QH 1,5; 5,26; 6,17; 8,6.12; 12,13; 1Q35 2,1; 1Q36 12,2; מקור occurs 17x in 1QH, and in 1QS 3,19; 10,12; 11,3.5.6.; 1QM 7,6; 1QSb 1,3.6; 3,19; 1Q16 8,2; 4QDibHam^a f1-2 5,2; 4QShir^b f44-47 1,1; f52-59 3,2; f63 3,1; 4QOrd^c f1 1,4. Total: 32 occurrences.

196 אור occurs as noun 16x in 1QS, 10x in 1QH, 10x in 1QM and in CD 5,18; 13,12; 1Q14 22,2; 1Q27 f1 1,6; 4QFlor f1-2 1,9; 4QpIs^d 1,6; 4QSl 40 f24,4; 4Q177 f1-4, 8; f10-11,7; f12-13 1,7.11; 4Q185 f1-2 1,13; 4Q186 f1 2,7; 3,6; 4Q487 f37,2; 4Q491 f8-10 1,14; 4Q497 f9,2; 4Q503 3,9.10; 4,1.2.5; 8,8.9.10; 11,2; f10,1; f13, 1.2; f18,3; f24-25,7; f21-22,1; f14,1; f15-16,6; f19,2; f51-55,6.8.14; f56-58 2,2; f65,3; f215,7; 4QShir^a f1,7; f6,1; 4QShir^b f2 1,4; 4Q512 f191,1; f227,3; 4Q517 f16,2; 8Q5 1,3; 11QPs^a 26,11; 27,2.2. Total: 87 occurrences.

197 דרך occurs 43x in 1QS, 23x in 1QH, 22x in CD, and in 1QM 3,10; 14,7; 1QSa 1,2.17.28; 1QSb 5,22; 1Q17 1,4; 1Q19 1,3; 1Q22 2,8; 1Q30 2,2; 2Q22 2,3; 4QFlor f1-2 1,14; 4QpIs^b 1,5; 4QpIs^c 1,3; 4Q158 f1-2,10; 4Q176 f18,2; 4QSl 39 f1 1,22; 40 f24,7; 4Q183 f1 2,5; 4Q184 f1,8.9.9.14.16.17; 4Q185 f1-2 2,1; 4Q486 f1,3; 4Q491 f8-10 1,5; 4Q497 f6,2; 4Q499 f5,2; 4Q502 f119,1; 4QDibHam^a f1-2 5,20. 20; f4,13; f8 recto 13; f17 2,4; 4QDibHam^b f121,1; 4QPrFêtes^c f296,1; 4QShir^a f1,9; 4QShir^b f2 1,6; f10,8; f63 3,3; 4Q517 f17,2; 11QPs^a 21,13; 22,10; 27,3. Total: 134 occurrences.

198 E.F. Roop, *Form Critical Study*, 1972, p.335 (conclusion).

199 Roop's study is approvingly quoted by H. Lichtenberger, *Studien*, pp.35f.

200 Cf. H. Lichtenberger, *o.c.*, p.37.

201 Classified as a "short sapiential poem" by R.D. Moore, "Personification of the Seduction of Evil: 'The Wiles of the Wicked Woman' ", *RQ* 10 (1981) 505. Cf. also G. Vermes, *Dead Sea Scrolls*, p.255.

202 Cf. H. Lichtenberger, "Mahnrede", *BETL* 46 (1978) 151-162; G. Vermes, *o.c.*, p.257.

Several texts have been classified as "wisdom texts with a didactic nature"[203]: 1 Q26, 4QOrNab, 11QPs^aDavComp.

The astronomical-astrological fragments of 4Q180, 4Q186, 4Q247, 4Q260, 4Q317, 4Q384-390 can be attributed to wisdom genres as well[204].

No proverbial texts have been found in Qumran which is rather surprising when we consider the large influence of the wisdom tradition on the Community. The fact that Qumran seems to have had no room "für die Lebensweisheit der Sprüche und überhaupt für eine geschliffenere Formulierung der Lebensregulative in Sentenzen und Bildworten, welche aus sich selbst sprechen und kontextunabhängig sind"[205], can be explained (1) by the great importance of the manuals 1QS and CD for the Community, and (2) by the urgent reference of all individual actions to the great decisions of the near future.

11.3. Wisdom, God, and Creation

11.3.1. Theocentric wisdom. In the Qumran texts, terms and concepts of knowledge are often linked with a reference to God[206]. God is the אל הדעות, the "God of knowledge" (1QS 3, 15; 1QH 1,26; 12,10; f4,15). God is the מקור דעת, the "source of knowledge" (1QS 10,12; 11,3; cf. 1QH 2,18; 5,26; 8,6; 12,29). He possesses knowledge, and he passes on knowledge. God is omniscient[207]. The systematic 'blueprint' of the Essenes is totally theocentric: the point of departure is God's free counsel and revelation[208].

---

203 Cf. M. Küchler, *Weisheitstraditionen*, p.106.
204 Cf. M. Küchler, *o.c.*, p.108.
205 M. Küchler, *o.c.*, p.96.
206 Cf. 1QS 3,15; 4,3.4.18.22; 10,12; 11,3.18.19; CD 2,3-4; 1QpHab 7,14; 1QH 1,7. 8.14.19.21.26; 2,18; 4,13; 5,26; 7,27; 8,6; 9,17.23.31; 10,14; 11,8.9.12.16.27.28; 12,10.11.13.29; 13,8.13; 14,8.12.27; 15,12; 4Q185 1,14; 2,11; 4QShir^a 1,2; 4Q-Shir^b f1,7-8; f2 1,6.7; 2,7-9; f18 2,8; f29,3; f49,1; f63-64 2,4; f63 3,1-4; f96,4.
207 Cf. CD 2,6-8; 1QM 18,10; 1QH 1,7; 7,13; 9,12.17-30.
208 Cf. M. Hengel, "Qumran", *BETL* 46 (1978) 353. Cf. also F. Nötscher, *Terminologie*, pp.40f.; J.E. Worrell, *Concepts*, p.204; M. Hengel, *Judentum*, p.402. A.M. Denis, *Les thèmes de connaissance*, p.78 demonstrates that in CD knowledge is derived from God himself.

11.3.2. The order of creation. In several passages a special functional recognition with regard to creation is given to God's wisdom and knowledge.

In 1QS 3,15-18 we read that "from the God of knowledge (אל הדעות) comes all that is and shall be (הויה ונהייה). Before ever they existed he established (הכין) their whole design (מחשבתם), and when, as ordained for them, they come into being, it is in accord with his glorious design (כמחשבת כבודו) that they accomplish their task without change. The laws of all things (משפטי כול) are in his hand and he provides them with all their needs". - In 1QH 1,7.14[209] it is stated in a similar manner that "by your wisdom (בחכמתכה) all things, exist from eternity, and before creating (ברא) them you knew their works for ever and ever ... You have fashioned (כון) all their inhabitants according to your wisdom (בחכמתכה)". In the 'Hymn to the Creator' we read: "Separating light from deep darkness, by the knowledge of his mind (בדעת לבו) he established (מכין) the dawn ... Blessed be he who makes (עשה) the earth by his power, establishing (מכין) the world in his wisdom (בחוכמתו). By his understanding (בתבונתו) he stretched out the heavens" (11QPs^a 26,4-8).

The order of the world created by God's wisdom is expressed in 1QH 1,7-15; 12,5-11 with phrases like "the law (משפט) of the spirits'" "the laws (חוקים) of the mighty winds", "the paths (נתיבות) of the stars", "the laws (חוקות) of the great light of heaven", "the statute (תכון) and signs of every dominion", "the certain law (תכון נאמונה)", "the precept which is and shall be for ever and ever without end (תעודת הויה והיאה תהיה)". It has been observed already that חוק and משפט are often used as designations of the order of creation set up by God[210]. The universality of wisdom is not a prominent concept; it is implied in 1QS 3,15; 1QH 9,17[211].

11.3.3. Sapiential personifications. J.A. Sanders pointed out that 11QPs^a 18 (= Ps (syr) 2) has close connections with wisdom speculation, probably even implying the personification of wisdom[212]. The Qumranian origin of this pericope is disputed[213].

---

209 See also 1QH 12,5-11; 13,8-10.13.
210 Cf. supra, p.171 with n.23 and §10.5.1-2.
221 Cf. M. Küchler, *Weisheitstraditionen*, p.94 who points out that "eine universale Präsenz der 'Weisheit' bei den Menschen wie in Sir 1,10; Bar 3,38 ist undenkbar".
212 J.A. Sanders, "Two Non-Canonical Psalms in 11QPs^a", *ZAW* 76 (1964) 57-75; idem, *DJD* 4 (1965) 69; cf. also J.C.H. Lebram, "Die Theologie der späten Chokma", *ZAW* 77 (1965) 202-211, here 202f.
213 J.A. Sanders, *DJD* 4 (1965) 69 states that "there is nothing of necessity Qumrânian in the psalm". Similarly D. Lührmann, "Ein Weisheitspsalm aus Qumran (11-

Sanders asserts that the personification of wisdom is not found in any other Qumran text[214]. The absence of the personification or hypostatization of wisdom has been observed by others as well[215].

This absence can be explained by pointing out (1) that the feminine hypostasis of God probably appeared as too mythological for the Community, (2) that such a personification was superfluous as the Community itself claimed a rather close and intimate fellowship with God, and (3) that therfore a personification or hypostasis did not fit into the strict outlines of Essene theology[216].

11.4. Wisdom, Revelation, and the Covenant

11.4.1. Revealed wisdom. For the Qumran Community the present aeon is characterized by a fundamental lack of wisdom. The wicked of Israel who are the sons of darkness walk in the spirit of falsehood, which is the spirit of folly (1QS 4,24), performing deeds of folly (1QH 4,8; 13,4). It is only the Community which possesses wisdom, revealed by God. This distinctive wisdom which separates the Community from the rest of Israel is expressed and contained in the "mysteries" (רזים) of God. And in the context of the Community the רזים correspond to the divine גלה[217].

Thus it can be said that "wisdom and revelation become specialized correlatives in the Scrolls, with inspiration as much possession by wisdom as possession of wisdom"[218]. And it is in or by his wisdom that God reveals his secret counsel to the Community (cf.

QPs^a XVIII)", *ZAW* 80 (1968) 88 concluding from a form-critical analysis that it is different from the Essene psalms in 1QH (pp.90f.). W.L. Lipscomb, "Wisdom", p.279 agrees that Lührmann's arguments to the effect that the Essenes *could* not have written the psalms are unconvincing.

214 J.A. Sanders, *DJD* 4 (1965) 69.
215 J.A. Worrell, *Concepts*, pp.230-236; M. Hengel, *Judentum*, pp.296f.; M. Küchler, *o.c.*, p.94.
216 Cf. J.E. Worrell, *o.c.*, pp.231f., following H. Ringgren, *The Faith of Qumran*, 1963, pp.81-93; M. Hengel, *o.c.*, p.397 n.633.
217 Cf. F. Nötscher, *Terminologie*, p.72; J.E. Worrell, *o.c.*, p.178; M. Küchler, *Weisheitstraditionen*, pp.92f.
218 J.E. Worrell, *o.c.*, p.177, referring to those passages where sapiential terms are linked with רזים, and to the parallels between רז and סוד. Cf. also W.L. Lipscomb, "Wisdom", 1978, p.277; C. Rowland, *Open Heaven*, pp.115-120.

1QS 2,3; 4,2; CD 2,12-13; 1QH 1,21; 9,31; 11,9-10.27-28). Here, as with regard to creation, God is the מקור דעת, the "source of knowledge".

> M. Hengel states in this context that "das Wissen über die tieferen Zusammenhänge in Schöpfung und Geschichte ... stammen aus ihm (i.e. Gott) allein, und nur der ist weise, dem Gott durch seinen Geist die Geheimnisse seines Willens geoffenbart hat"[219].

The communication of this divinely revealed knowledge is achieved through teaching (cf. § 11.5.). We pointed out earlier that God's counsel and revelation is the point of departure of the Qumranian theocentric and systematic blueprint of the created world, known only to the Community.

The Teacher of Righteousness plays an important role in the revelatory communication of divine wisdom. He assumes the central role as revealer[220]. The essential connection of the Community with the secrets of God consists in the Teacher's enlightenment concerning the Qumranian possession and communication of wisdom and salvation.

11.4.2. Wisdom and the covenant. It has been pointed out already that for the individual the reception of the gift of knowledge coincides with the entrance into the Community[221]. In other words, "the gift of knowledge is the means of effecting the election"[222]. It is in this context that 1QS 4,2-14 underscores the wisdom of the צדיק which enables him to grasp God's wonders and which is granted only to the elect[223]. The content of revelatory and revealed knowledge deals with the present salvation given by God to the Community (cf. 1QH 7,26-33; 11,3-14). The children of God's truth "jubilate in eternal knowledge" (1QM 17,8). There are "wise men" (חכמים, 1QSa 1,28; 2,16; 1Q22 2,8-9) and "men of knowledge" (אנשי דעות, CD 20,4) in the Community. The

---

219 M. Hengel, *Judentum*, p.402 referring to 1QS 11,3-7; idem, "Qumran", BETL 46 (1978) 357.
220 F. Nötscher, *Terminologie*, p.51; G. Jeremias, *Lehrer*, pp.141,150-166; J.E. Worrell, *Concepts*, pp.163-169,379-385; M. Küchler, *Weisheitstraditionen*, pp.92f.
221 Especially in the 'Community hymns' in 1QH; cf. H.W. Kuhn, *Enderwartung*, pp. 155-163.
222 E.P. Sanders, *Paul*, p.260, quoting 1QH 14,25-26.
223 Cf. B. Sharvit, "The Virtue of Wisdom in the Image of the Righteous Man in the Manual of Discipline" (hebr), Beth Mikra 59 (1974) 526-530.

"spirit of knowledge" (רוח דעת) has been given to, and is active in, the Community[224]. There are also passages which describe the gift of knowledge as eschatological endowment (cf. 1QS 4,22; 1QH 3,22-23; 11,12; 1Q27 fl 1,7; 4QMessAr 1,3-10; 4QpIs^a f8-10,11-24)[225]. The unpublished text 4QAhA attributes great wisdom to the priestly messiah[226].

11.5. Wisdom and Teaching

11.5.1. The importance of teaching. Teaching is an essential wisdom category. That this is true for Qumran[227] becomes obvious when we consider the terms used to describe the process of teaching: למד (pi), הבין, הודיע, and השכיל. These terms refer (1) to God's revelation of wisdom to the Community[228], and (2) to the teaching within the Community[229]. In the different texts we find numerous wisdom forms and elements which serve a didactic function[230]. The manual form of CD and of 1QS[231] underscore the importance of sapiential teaching for Qumran.

11.5.2. The Teacher of Righteousness. The מורה הצדק received his wisdom from God (cf. 1QpHab 7,4) and passed it on to the Community (1QH 2,9-10; 1QpHab 2,1-3; CD 1,1-12). Some scholars assume that the Teacher might have been a sage/teacher in Jerusalem[232]. His wisdom was, however, not the common wis-

---

224 Cf. 1QSb 5,25; 1QH 14,25; 4QShir^a f1,6; 4QShir^b f18 2,6; 4QSl 37-40; 11QPs^a 19,14.
225 Cf. H.W. Kuhn, *Enderwartung*, pp.166-175 concluding that passages like 1QS 4,22; 1Q27 fl 1,7; 1QH 11,12; 7,27 show "daß man der gegenwärtigen Offenbarungserkenntnis den Sinn eines eschatologischen Geschehens im strengen Sinn geben konnte" (p.168). Cf. also P.G.R. de Villiers, "The Messiah and Messiahs in Jewish Apocalyptic", *Neotestamentica* 12 (1981) 88.
226 Cf. J. Starcky, "Les quatres étapes du messianisme à Qumrân", *RB* 70 (1963) 492; cf. R. Riesner, *Jesus als Lehrer*, p.308.
227 Cf. J.E. Worrell, *Concepts*, pp.156-160; W.L. Lipscomb, "Wisdom", 1978, p.277.
228 למד: 1QH 2,17; 11QPs^a 24,8; הודיע: 11QPs^a 19,2-3; 1QH 4,27-28; 7,27; 10,5. 14; הבין: 11QPs^a 24,8; 1QH 11,22.28; 12,33; השכיל: 1QH 7,26; 9,16; 10,4. 6-7; etc.
229 Cf. 1QS 3,13; 4,22; 9,13-14; CD 1,11-12.
230 Cf. J.E. Worrell, *o.c.*, pp.160-163.
231 Cf. E.F. Roop, *Form Critical Study*, 1972, pp.310-335 (conclusion).
232 Cf. J.E. Worrell, *o.c.*, pp.167f.

dom of the 'old' sage but a unique prophetic-apocalyptic wisdom[233].

11.5.3. The maskil. It has been pointed out already (§ 11.1.1.) that the משכיל seems to have been one of the most important persons in the Community, probably being identical with the מבקר and the דורש התורה, the "guardian" and the "interpreter of the law"[234]. The *maskil* was the teaching functionary in the Community, communicating its doctrines to the members[235].

> He is to "teach the saints to live according to the Book of the Community Rule, that they may seek God with a whole heart and soul, and do what is good and right before him as he commanded by the hand of Moses and all his servants the Prophets" (1QS 1,1-3). According to 1QS 3,13-14 the *maskil* is to "instruct (להבין) all the sons of light and shall teach (ללמד) them the nature of all the children of men according to the kind of spirit which they possess". Cf. further 1QS 9,12-20.

11.6. Conduct and Ethics

11.6.1. Wisdom and ethics. Wisdom and ethics are linked in passages which deal with the examination of the novices and the members of the Community.

> In 1QS 5,20-21 we read that "when a man enters the covenant to walk according to all these precepts that he may join the holy congregation, they shall examine his spirit in community with respect to his understanding (שכלו) and his practice of the law (מעשיו בתורה)". In CD 13,11 it is similarly stated that the novice shall be examined "with regard to his deeds (מעשיו), understanding (שיכלו), strength, ability, and possession". When the novice has completed his year of probation "the congregation shall deliberate his case with regard to his understanding (שכלו) and his observance of the law (מעשיו התורה)" (1QS 6,18).

Each member of the Community "shall strengthen his loins that he may perform his tasks (עבודת מעשו) among his brethren in accordance with his understanding (שכלו) and the perfection of his way (תום דרכו)" (1QSa 1,17-18). Thus the rank of each member in the hierarchy of the Community depended on this examination of his spirit (רוח) with regard to his understanding (שכל) and

---

233 Cf. J.E. Worrell, *o.c.*, pp.379f.
234 Cf. G. Vermes, *Dead Sea Scrolls*, pp.19-25; J.E. Worrell, *o.c.*, pp.150-154.
235 Cf. W.L. Lipscomb, "Wisdom", 1978, p.277.

his "works of the law" (מעשי בתורה) which seem to be envisaged as objectively discernible qualities[236].

As to the Qumranian parenesis it has been observed that the Essene exhortations have two general characteristics: the emphasis on separation leading to purity, and the emphasis on knowledge and understanding[237]. The cosmic-ethical dualism is rooted in the wisdom tradition as well[238].

11.6.2. Ethics and law. The study of the law, together with all divine knowledge given to the Community, aims at man's conduct[239]. This can be seen in the intensity and significance of terms like עשה, מעשים, עלילות, and הלך used with regard to man[240]. Right conduct (cf. 1QS 1,2: "to do what is good and right before him") is explained materially by the law and the prophets (cf. 1QS 1,3). The conduct which is pleasing to God can be achieved by absolute obedience to the divine commandments in the Community — exclusively in contrast to, and in separation from, the wicked (cf. the polemic in 1QS 5,11-12)[241]. God can be sought only in the Torah. The relationship between Torah and ethics in the Community is a vital, but also a complex relationship[242]. The Community requires absolute obedience to, and reverence of, the law and the prophets. But with regard to the morality of its ethic we observe "an environmental conditioning of behaviour by law and obligation"[243].

We discussed already the crucial significance and inspired status of Qumran halakhah (§ 10.7.). Halakhic discussions made an adjustment of the rules of the Community possible. For the Community, the Torah discloses also the "hidden things", i.e. the doctrines peculiar to the Community which are derived by (inspired)

---

236 Cf. J.E. Worrell, *Concepts*, pp.227-230; H. Lichtenberger, *Studien*, p.216.
237 Cf. E.P. Sanders, *Paul*, pp.312f.
238 Cf. B. Otzen, "Old Testament Wisdom Literature and Dualistic Thinking in Late Judaism", *SVT* 28 (1975) 146-157.
239 Cf. S.T. Kimbrough, "The Ethic of the Qumran Community", *RQ* 6 (1969) 483-498. He characterizes Qumran's faith as "religion of deed rather than of creed" (p.495).
240 Cf. H. Braun, *Radikalismus*, 1, p.24.
241 Cf. H. Lichtenberger, *Studien*, pp.201f.
242 Cf. S.T. Kimbrough, "Ethic", *RQ* 6 (1969) 493f.
243 S.T. Kimbrough, *a.c.*, p.495. He characterizes the Qumran ethic as "ethic of limited flexibility" (pp.483,498).

exegesis. As a result, Qumran ethics comprises holiness, purity, worship (at the proper times!), sacred meals, social policies (with regard to marriage, private property, etc.), virtues, love and hate, and justice. For the Community the high complexity of their ethic did not bury its ultimate goal: to achieve symmetry between the righteousness of God and man's activity[244]. The orientation by the law, i.e. the Scriptures and the halakhah, gave to man a "sicheres Bezugssystem in seinem Verhältnis zu Gott und zu seinem Nächsten"[245]. The underlying presuppositon implies that man is indeed able to keep the law and to decide in liberty regarding his behaviour. The radical emphasis on the necessity to keep all (!) divine commandments reveals "eine mechanisierende Gleichmachung zwischen Wichtigem und Unwichtigem, also ein Verzicht auf Einheitlichkeit"[246].

The keeping of the law (including the halakhah) is often described as "perfection of way" (תמים דרך). This notion is expressed in 1QS 8,10.18.21; 9,2.5.9[247]. This phrase is a characteristic description of the life in the Community[248].

It has to be pointed out, however, that man, in Qumran theology, is always dependent upon God with regard to the forgiveness of sins and salvation. Nevertheless, atonement is still linked with conduct: it is only possible in the submission of the individual and of the entire Community to the divine will as it is embodied in the law[249].

§12 Law and Wisdom

The correlation of law and wisdom in Qumran has not been studied in depth by any scholar. M. Hengel believes that the re-

---

244 Cf. S.T. Kimbrough, a.c., p.497.
245 H. Lichtenberger, o.c., p.204.
246 H. Braun, *Radikalismus*, 1, pp.28f.
247 See also the phrase תמימי דרך in 1QS 4,22; 1QM 14,7; 1QH 1,36; 1QSa 1,28; 4QMa f8-9,5; 4QSl 39 f1 1,22; 4QShira 1,9; 4QShirb f10,8; f63 3,3. Compare the phrases הלך תמים בדרכיו in 1QS 4,22; ישרי דרך in 1QH 2,10; and תמים בכול דרכיו in 11QPsaDavComp 3.
248 Cf. G. Klinzing, *Umdeutung des Kultus*, 1971, pp.98f. who states with regard to the background of the cultic meaning of תמים that "auch das, was an die Stelle des Opfers tritt, wird mit kultischen Maßstäben gemessen" (p.98).
249 Cf. H. Lichtenberger, *Studien*, pp.210-212.

Exegetical Evidence 207

latedness of Essene theology to history prevented the identification of God's knowledge or 'plan for the world' with the Torah, thus differing from Ben Sira and later Pharisaic-rabbinic thought[250]. Other scholars seem to be inclined to recognize a Qumranian relationship between law and wisdom but limit themselves to very brief remarks[251]. The only exception is J.A. Davis whose comments, however, are still rather provisional[252]. We will first analyze individual texts before we arrive at a synthesis of the nature of the correlation of law and wisdom in the Qumran writings.

12.1. The Exegetical Evidence

12.1.1. Explicit evidence. There are 11 passages which refer rather explicitly to the close correlation and identification of law and wisdom. (1) 1QS 3,1: "His soul detests the wise teaching (יסורי דעת) of just laws (משפטי צדק)". The term יסור is not prominent in the OT[253] but is used in the Qumran texts[254] with the meaning "instruction", "direction", "reprimand". The phrase משפטי צדק is used elsewhere[255] and means here, especially in conjunction with the verb חזק, the commandments of the law (including the specific Qumran halakhah)[256]. 1QS 2,26-3,1 can also be translated: "his soul rejected the instruction of knowledge; he has not held on to the just precepts"[257]. According to this division of the text we have a chiasm where "instruction" corresponds

---

250 M. Hengel, *Judentum*, p.421.
251 Cf. F. Nötscher, *Terminologie*, p.63; J.E. Worrell, *Concepts*, p.229; B. Sharvit, "The Virtue of Wisdom" (hebr), *Beth Mikra* 59 (1974) 526-530; E.P. Sanders, *Paul*, p.271; C. Romaniuk, "Thème", *RQ* 9 (1978) 431 n.2; H. Gabrion, "Interpretation", *ANRW* II/19,1 (1979) 830.
252 Cf. J.A. Davis, *Wisdom and Spirit*, 1982, pp.26-33.
253 Cf. only Job 40,2 with the (disputed) meaning of "the one who reprimands", "grumbler"; cf. L. Koehler, W. Baumgartner, *Lexikon*, 2, p.399. The noun occurs in Sir 40,29 and the verb in Sir 4,19; 6,33; 7,23; 10,1.25; 30,13 and is translated in most places with παιδεύειν.
254 Cf. 1QH 17,22; CD 7,5.8; 19,4; 1Q34 f3 2,7.
255 Cf. 1QS 4,4; 9,17; CD 20,30.31; 1QH 1,23.26; f5,1; 1QSb 2,26.
256 Cf. the translations of G. Vermes and E. Lohse.
257 Following E. Lohse, *Texte*, p.9.

with "precepts". Reference is made here to those who refuse to enter the Community. This pericope states then (1) that the "instruction of knowledge", i.e. wisdom, is the result of the law, or (2) that wisdom is equivalent to the law.

(2) 1QS 3,15-17: "From the God of knowledge (אל הדעות) comes all that is and shall be. Before ever they existed he established their whole design (מחשבה), and when as ordained for them, they come into being, it is in accord with his glorious design (מחשבה) that they accomplish their task without change. The laws of all things (משפטי כול) are in his hand and he provides them with all their needs". This pericope[258] is closely linked with 1QH 1,1-19 (cf. also 1QH 13,7-13; 15,12-26)[259] embodying the determination of all being and all processes in creation and establishing the framework for the following dualistic and predestinational statements. Everything happens according to a plan which God the Creator has established even before creation. The phenomena of the world move not in accordance with an autonomous static world order but according to a plan which was set up in an exact manner before creation. As all works of creation are determined, so is man in his ways and in the sequence of the generations. The term משפטים is used as a designation for the precepts or laws which determine the affairs of the world[260]. Hence we encounter the creational aspect of the correlation of wisdom and law here: God's wisdom is apparent in the design (מחשבה) of creation and in the laws (משפטים) of nature.

(3) 1QS 9,17: "He (i.e. the *maskil*) shall conceal the teaching of the law (עצת התורה) from men of falsehood (אנשי העול), but shall impart true knowledge (דעת אמת) and righteous judgment (משפט צדק) to those who have chosen the way (דרך)". The *maskil* is required to conceal the "counsel" or teaching of the law — obviously implying the Qumranian halakhah — from the wicked, not giving them a share in the interpretation of the Torah by the Community and thus in the way of salvation[261]. This pericope cor-

---

258 Cf. P.von der Oster-Sacken, *Gott und Belial*, pp.123-131; H. Lichtenberger, *Studien*, pp.187-189.
259 P.von der Osten-Sacken, *o.c.*, p.131 assumes "daß der Abschnitt (i.e. 1QS 3,15-17) aus dem Gut der Loblieder schöpft".
260 Cf. 1QH 1,9.16 and similar formulations in 1QS 10,16.
261 Cf. H. Lichtenberger, *o.c.*, p.213.

relates wisdom and law in two ways: (1) the Torah is the basis of "counsel"[262], and (2) the teaching and counsel of the Torah is equivalent to the "knowledge of truth"[263].

(4) CD 6,2-5: "But God remembered the covenant with the forefathers, and he raised from Aaron men of discernment (נבונים) and from Israel men of wisdom (חכמים), and he caused them to hear. And they dug the well: the well which the princes dug, which the nobles of the people delved with the stave (Num 21,18). The well is the law (התורה), and those who dug it were the converts of Israel who went out of the Land of Judah to sojourn in the land of Damascus". This passage relates Num 21,18 to the history and self-understanding of the Community. Wise men from the priests (Aaron) and from the laity (Israel) are said to have listened to God and "dug the well" (cf. also CD 3,16-17), i.e. strove after a specific and exemplary approach to the law[264]. Without discussing the precise interpretation of this 'well-midrash' in CD 6,2-11[265], it is still obvious that נבונים and חכמים are said to be engaged in the exposition of the proper, i.e. Essene, interpretation of the Torah. These terms seem to be designations for priestly scribes and lay scribes who study the Torah. This corresponds with the picture of the ideal scribe presented by Ben Sira and by the Pharisaic and later the rabbinic circles[266].

(5) 1QM 10,9-11: "Who is like your people Israel which you have chosen for yourself from all the peoples of the lands; the people of the saints of the covenant (ברית), instructed in the laws (מלומדי חוק) and learned in wisdom (משכילי בינה) ... who have heard the voice of majesty and have seen the angels of holi-

---

262 Cf. O. Betz, *Offenbarung*, p.50 who states with regard to the phrase עצת התורה that "die Tora gleicht nach dieser Wendung einer Person, die den Frommen berät, wie es etwa die Weisheit tut". He observes further that the phrase עצת אל in 1QS 1,8.10.13; 3,6; 1QH 6,11.13; etc., is identical with the עצת התורה (p.51).
263 Interpreting דעת אמת as a genitive construction, as G. Vermes and T.H. Gaster ad loc. Pace E. Lohse, *Texte*, p.35.
264 J. Murphy-O'Connor, "A Literary Analysis of Damascus Document VI,2-VIII, 3", *RB* 78 (1971) 230 interprets the phrase "to dig the well", especially with regard to CD 6,8-11, as meaning "unless read in the perspective of a special teaching the Law does not release its life-giving force".
265 Cf. O. Betz, *Offenbarung*, pp.23-35; J. Murphy-O'Connor, "Literary Analysis", *RB* 78 (1971) 210-232, here 228-232.
266 Cf. J.A. Davis, *Wisdom and Spirit*, pp.26f. stating that CD 6,2-11 describes the Torah, as interpreted by the sect, as source of wisdom.

ness, whose ear has been unstopped (מגולי ארון) and who have heard profound things (עמוקות)?". This pericope [267] describes Israel as the object of divine election. On the background of the general context of 1QM, Israel has to be understood here as limited to the Community which is engaged in the eschatological battle[268]. The theme of election is linked with the instruction of Israel in the divine law[269]. The remarkable accumulation of wisdom terminology in 10,10-11 in this context of election and instruction in the law can be compared with Deut 4,6-14. The phrase מלומדי חוק refers to the law[270] which possibly includes here the Community's peculiar halakhah. The קול נכבד, i.e. the "voice of majesty" or "glorious voice" has to be linked very probably with the Sinai events as well, referring to "la voix élevée majestueuse, imposante, qui a résonné sur la montagne du Sinai"[271]. Although angels had no function in the communication of Sinaitic law in the OT tradition, they were indeed related to the Sinaitic events in the extra-biblical tradition and in the NT[272]. This pericope clearly correlates learning (מלומדי) in the law and knowledge (משכילי) in wisdom in synonymous parallelism.

(6) 1QH 1,1(?)-20. This creation hymn is similar to the creation hymn in 1QM 10,8-16, both with regard to the overall framework of the works of creation mentioned and with regard to individual terms which are used[273]. But the hymn in 1QH 1 has strong deter-

---

267 1QM 10,8-16 has been classified as a creation hymn. Cf. P.von der Osten-Sacken, *Gott und Belial*, p.59 with n.1; P.R. Davies, *The War Scroll from Qumran*, Biblica et Orientalia 32, 1977, p.95; H. Lichtenberger, *Studien*, pp.185f.
268 Cf. H. Lichtenberger, *o.c.*, pp.185f.
269 The concept of law is of basic importance for 1QM. Cf. Y. Yadin, *The Scroll of the War of the Sons of Light Against the Sons of Darkness*, 1962, pp.4f. who points out that with regard to the eschatological war expected by the Community the exact fulfilment of the Mosaic law was an essential condition. He states that "the fact that the angels fight on their side obliges the Sons of Light to conduct themselves in accordance with all the Biblical laws of purity ... This basic conception passes through the scroll like a purple thread. It determines its content, structure, and sequence" (p.5).
270 Cf. the connection with the law in Deut 4,14; Ps 119,12; Ezr 7,10. Cf. Y. Yadin, *Scroll*, p.306.
271 B. Jongeling, *Le Rouleau de la Guerre*, STDJ 2, 1959, p.137; Y. Yadin, *o.c.*, p.306 (as possibility). Cf. Ex 20,18-19; Deut 4,12; 5,22-23; cf. Hebr 12,19.
272 Cf. Deut 33,2 LXX; PesiqR 21 (103b-104a); ShemR 29 (88d); BemR 11 (164b); Pesiq 108a; Josephus Ant 15,136; also Acts 7,38.53; Gal 3,19; Hebr 22,2. Cf. H.L. Strack, P. Billerbeck, *Kommentar*, 3, pp.554-556.
273 Cf. Y. Yadin, *o.c.*, p.306; H. Lichtenberger, *Studien*, pp.167f. For a recent analysis

ministic overtones referring to the predestination of all created beings (1,7-15) and of man (1,19). The pericope underscores the conviction that God's wisdom finds expression in his creation with its order of time and nature[274]. God's wisdom is referred to with the terms עצה (1,5), חכמה (1,7.14.19), ידע (1,7), and דעת (1, 19). The prescience (1,7.19) and omniscience (1,8) of God the Creator are described. This wisdom of God is expressed in the order of creation which is described with the terms משפט (1,9.16), חוקים (1,10), נתיבות (1,12), משא (1,12), חפצים (1,13), and קצים (1,16). Thus we have here again the close correlation of God's wisdom and the laws of creation. The same is true for 1QH 12,5-11.

(7) 1QH 4,9-11: "And they, teachers of lies and seers of falsehood, have schemed against me a devilish scheme, to exchange your law (תורתכה) engraved[275] on my heart, for the smooth things (חלקות)[276] (which they speak) to your people. And they withhold from the thirsty the drink of knowledge (משקה דעת) and assuage their thirst with vinegar[277]". This pericope belongs to the 'Teacher hymns'[278]. The term תורה and משקה דעת are synonymous: the enemies of the Community, or of the Teacher, took away the Torah, i.e. the proper understanding of the law, and they withheld the "drink of knowledge". Instead of the Torah they present "smooth things", i.e. their own particular halakhah, and instead of the "drink of knowledge" they offer some intoxicating drink. Thus the Torah is equivalent with the "drink of knowledge"[279].

---

of the structure and the poetic techniques of several hymns of 1QH see B.P. Kittel, *The Hymns of Qumran: Translation and Commentary*, SBLDS 50, 1981. The passages which are relevant for our discussion are not treated.

274 Cf. S. Holm-Nielsen, *Hodayot*, p.19; M. Mansoor, *The Thanksgiving Hymns*, 1961, p.34.
275 Cf. Deut 6,7.
276 This term, especially in the phrase דורשי חלקות, is taken by many scholars to refer to the Pharisees.
277 Cf. Ps 69,22 where the usual translation is "vinegar". According to S. Holm-Nielsen, *Hodayot*, p.82 it refers more probably to an intoxicating drink.
278 Cf. J. Becker, *Heil*, pp.54f.; H.W. Kuhn, *Enderwartung*, pp.23f. But see recently D. Domkowski Hopkins, "The Qumran Community and 1QHodayot: A Reassessment", *RQ* 10 (1981) 323-364 passim.
279 Cf. S. Holm-Nielsen, *o.c.*, p.82 who says that דעת refers here, based upon the law,

The term משקה "drink" is a metaphor for studying which is well known in the later rabbinic literature[280]. According to mAb 1,4 R. Yose b. Joezer said: "Drink with thirst their (i.e. the sages') words" (שותה בצמאה את דבריהם). The same metaphor occurs in BemR 14,11: "We are your disciples and we drink from your waters". See also bBQ 62a with the phrase אין מים אלא תורה. We discussed already CD 6,4 with the interpretation of הבאר היא התורה.

(8) 1QDireMoshe 2,8-9: "When I have established the covenant and commanded the way (צוות את הדרך) in which you shall walk, appoint wise men (הבו לכם חכמים) whose work it shall be to expound (לבאר) to you and your children all these words of the law (כול דברי התורה)"[281]. In this farewell discourse Moses admonishes Israel to keep the law and the commandments and to appoint special teachers of the law. The pericope 2, 8-9 is based on Deut 1,13[282] where Moses tells the people of Israel to "choose some wise, understanding and respected men (אנשים חכמים ונבנים וידעים)" from each tribe as overseers, officials, and commanders (cf. Deut 1,15). In our pericope here the חכמים are described as people who expound (לבאר)[283] the Torah, i.e. as scribes.

(9) 4QMessAr 1,3-11. This Aramaic text[284] seems to be the horoscope of the final "prince of the congregation" or the royal messiah[285]. His education can be compared with the schedule out-

---

"to truth by virtue of God's revelation in contrast to the lies of man". Cf. also F. Nötscher, *Terminologie*, p.62.

280 Cf. M.R. Lehmann, "Talmudic Material Relating to the Dead Sea Scrolls", *RQ* 1 (1959) 392; M. Mansoor, *Thanksgiving Hymns*, p.124.
281 The lacunae have been restored with J.T. Milik, *DJD* 1 (1955) 93; cf. also G. Vermes, *Dead Sea Scrolls*, p.226; T.H. Gaster, *Dead Sea Scriptures*, 1976, p.374.
282 The preceding sentence in 2,7-8 is clearly a rearrangement of Deut 1,12. Cf. J.T. Milik, o.c., p.94.
283 באר pi means "to explain", "to expound". It is used with regard to the law in Deut 1,5.
284 First edited by J. Starcky, "Un texte messianique araméen de la grotte 4 de Qumrân", *Mémorial du cinquantenaire de l'École des langues orientales anciennes de l'Institut Catholique de Paris*, 1964 pp.51-66; cf. also J. Carmignac, "Les Horoscopes de Qumrân", *RQ* 5 (1965) 206-217; J.A. Fitzmyer, "The Aramaic 'Elect of God' Text from Qumran Cave IV", *CBQ* 27 (1965) 348-372. 4QMessAr has to be dated on paleographical grounds to the end of the 1st century B.C.; cf. J. Starcky, a.c., p.54 with n.1; M. Hengel, *Judentum*, p.434. J.A. Fitzmyer, a.c., pp.370-372 contests the view that this is a messianic text and suggests that it belongs to literature concerned with the birth of Noah.
285 Cf. J. Starcky, "Texte messianique", p.51 with n.2; J. Carmignac, "Horoscopes", *RQ* 5 (1965) 217; M. Hengel, *Judentum*, p.434; G. Vermes, *Dead Sea Scrolls*, p. 268.

lined in 1QSa 1,6-18[286]. The text stresses the unusual knowledge of the messiah: he "knows (ידע) one thing from another" (1,3); he acquires wisdom (יערם) and learns understanding (ידע), so that even professional seers will come to him on their knees[287] (1, 6); he possesses counsel (מלכה) and prudence (וערמומה) and knows (יד) the secrets (רזים) of all the peoples (1,7-8). It is further said that "he knows the three books (מנדע תלתת ספריא)" (1,5).

> The phrase תלתת ספריא has always been a puzzle for the scholars. J. Starcky understands the phrase to be an allusion to the mystery involved in the manifestation of the 'elect of God' suggesting that these books were of eschatological, perhaps even astrological, character[288]. J. Carmignac suggests that these "three books" are the "Book of Study" (ספר ההגו) of CD 10,6; 13,2 (cf. 1QSa 1,7), together with the "Manual of Discipline" (1QS) and the "Zadokite Document" (CD)[289]. J.A. Fitzmyer takes the phrase to be a general reference to apocalyptic books such as the "books of the living" of En(eth) 47,3, the "heavenly tablets" of En(eth) 81,1-2; Jub 30,22, or the "book of man's deeds" of Ps 56,9; Dan 7,10; En(eth) 90,17, without being specific, real books[290]. T.H. Gaster rejects these suggestions presuming that the number "three" need not be taken literally but refers to the usual standard two or three textbooks[291]. According to his reading of the text these are books which have to be mastered by the average man in order to be educated but with which the "wondrous child" will be able to dispense[292]. G. Vermes suggests that the "three books" refer to the three sections of the Hebrew canon[293].

It cannot be decided whether the "three books" are indeed a reference to the Hebrew Scriptures[294]. However, when we consider the significance of the commandments of the law and of specific halakhic rules for the Community, it can be assumed that the "three books" refer by all means to the authoritative writings of the Community, whether to the Hebrew Scriptures, to written

---

286 Cf. G. Vermes, *o.c.*, p.268.
287 Cf. the translation of T.H. Gaster, *Dead Sea Scriptures*, p.449.
288 Cf. J. Starcky, *a.c.*, pp.56f.
289 Cf. J. Carmignac, *a.c.*, p.212.
290 Cf. J.A. Fitzmyer, "Aramaic 'Elect of God' Text", *CBQ* 27 (1965) 362f.
291 Cf. T.H. Gaster, *o.c.*, pp.475f. who points out with regard to the solution of J. Carmignac that it cannot be proved that these documents existed together at the time 4QMessAr was composed and asks whether the "wondrous child" was a Qumranite "who had to be reared in what were, after all, manuals for a sect 'preparing the way' for his advent".
292 Cf. T.H. Gaster, *o.c.*, p.476 (his translation on p.449).
293 G. Vermes, *Dead Sea Scrolls*, p.268.
294 This interpretation is rejected by J. Starcky, "Texte messianique", p.57; J.A. Fitzmyer, *CBQ* 27 (1965) 362; T.H. Gaster, *Dead Sea Scriptures*, p.476.

halakhic regulations, or both. A ספר was a valuable and honoured means of communication and tradition and surely reserved for the essential properties of the Community. And the "three books" are presented as the source of the child's extraordinary knowledge and wisdom[295]. Thus, the law or the laws are again identified with wisdom.

(10) 11QPs^a 18,10-13: "From the gates of the righteous (פתחי צדיקים)is heard her (i.e. wisdom's) voice (קול), and from the assembly of the pious (קהל חסידים) her song (זמרה). When they eat with satiety she is cited (נשמרה), and when they drink in community together, their meditation (שיחתם) is on the Law of the Most High (בתורת עליון); their words (אמריהמה) on making known (להודיע) his might. How far from the wicked is her word (אמרה), from all haughty men to know her"[296].

> It is disputed whether 11QPs^a 18 is a Qumranian composition. Some scholars opted for an Essene origin of the psalm[297], other scholars pointed out that there is nothing in the psalm which is exclusively Qumranian[298]. The arguments against the possibility of Qumranian origin are not totally convincing[299]. J.A. Sanders points out that "it is inevitable that one should think of Qumran in dealing with the psalm"[300]: particularly 18,11-12 reflects the common meals of the Community, the life of sacramental eating and drinking accompanied by meditation and discussion of the law, and the task of the covenanted people (cf. 1QS 6,4-8). The term תמימים is attested in many passages as designation for the members of the Community[301]. Nevertheless, the archaizing language and the theology of the psalm as well as considerations with regard to the inclusion of the psalm in the Psalm Scroll make it plausible to reckon with a proto-Qumranian or hasidic origin[302]. Thus we will treat 11QPs^a 18 not

---

295 Cf. J.A. Fitzmyer, *a.c.*: p.362; contra the reading and interpretation of T.H. Gaster, *o.c.*, pp.449,476.
296 11QPs^a 18,1-16 = Ps(syr) 2,1-39. Cf. *DJD* 4 (1965) 64-70 (J.A. Sanders).
297 M. Delcor, "Cinq nouveau psaumes esséniens", *RQ* 1 (1958) 85; M. Philonenko, "L'origine essénien des cinq psaumes syriaques de David", *Semitica* 9 (1958) 35-48; J.E. Worrell, *Concepts*, pp.271-275. See implicitly T.H. Gaster, *Dead Sea Scriptures*, pp.125-127,219f. who includes it in "Poems from a Qumran Hymnal" (pp. 217-227). He understands 11QPs^a 18 as an "invitation to grace after meals", known in rabbinic literature as *birkhat zimmun* (cf. pBer 7,2; mAb 3,3-4).
298 Cf. J.A. Sanders, *DJD* 4 (1965) 69; D. Lührmann, "Weisheitspsalm", *ZAW* 80 (1968) 87-98; A.S. van der Woude, "Die fünf syrischen Psalmen", *JSHRZ* IV/1 (1974) 35; W.L. Lipscomb, "Wisdom", pp.278f.
299 Cf. W.L. Lipscomb, *a.c.*, p.279.
300 Cf. J.A. Sanders, *o.c.*, pp.69f.,75.
301 Cf. supra, p.187 with n.120.
302 Cf. J.A. Sanders, *o.c.*, p.70; H. Bardtke, "Literaturbericht", *ThR* 35 (1970) 221-226; M. Hengel, *Judentum*, p.323; W.L. Limpscomb, *a.c.*, pp.278f. Pace A.S. van der Woude, *o.c.*, p.35 who classifies the psalm as late wisdom and dissociates it from proto-Essenic circles.

as a primary witness for the theology of the Community[303]. However, the probable hasidic origin of the psalm plus the fact that it was incorporated in 11QPs[a] and handed down in the Community allows us to assume that 11QPs[a] 18 at least reflects the theology of the Qumran group.

The group which is designated as צדיקים, תמימים, טובים, חסידים (18,1.10.11.13) possesses wisdom (חוכמה) with regard to the task of proclaiming God's might (18,3-4.12-14). The good and pious ones "cite" wisdom (נאמרה), i.e. speak of her (18,11) while they eat and drink. If 11QPs[a] 18 is indeed a *birkhat zimmun*[304], the identification of law and wisdom is very clear: the call to join in the 'grace after meals' was then coupled with an invitation to participate in the "talk about the Torah" as "words of the Torah" (דברי תורה) had to accompany the meal. The "citing" of wisdom which is probably a reference to the "voice" and "song" of wisdom (18,10.11)[305] corresponds then with the "words of the Torah"[306]. Even if we have to regard 11QPs[a] 18 simply as a wisdom hymn[307], wisdom is identified with the law: the righteous proclaim wisdom (18,10-11) and talk about wisdom (18,11-12), and they mediate on the law (18,12)[308].

(11) 11QPs[a] 24,8: "Grant me understanding (הבינני), O Lord, in your Law (בתורתכה), and teach me (למד) your ordinances (משפטיכה)"[309]. The psalm in 11QPs[a] 24 is probably of hasidic origin[310] but has not such a close relationship to Qumran theology or phraseology as 11QPs[a] 18[311]. Hence we will not use it with regard to any conclusions as to Qumranian theology. We note, however, that the identification of law and wisdom is very obvious

---

303 Cf. H. Lichtenberger, *Studien*, p.43.
304 Cf. T.H. Gaster, *o.c.*, pp.126f. See also J.A. Sanders, *o.c.*, p.68 who classifies the psalm, on form-critical grounds, as a *berakhah* or "call to worship", but then decides to call it more generally a "sapiential hymn".
305 Cf. J.A. Sanders, *DJD* 4 (1965) 67.
306 Cf. T.H. Gaster, *Dead Sea Scriptures*, p.126 who states that the "voice of wisdom" is a common rabbinic synonym for the Torah.
307 Cf. J.A. Sanders, *o.c.*, p.68; D. Lührmann, "Weisheitspsalm", *ZAW* 80 (1968) 87-98; M. Hengel, *Judentum*, p.323.
308 Cf. M. Hengel, *o.c.*, p.323 who takes 11QPs[a] 18 to be a sapiential psalm stating that "der Psalm zeigt auch deutlich, daß auch die 'Frommen' eigene 'Weisheitsschulen' besaßen, in deren Mittelpunkt 'ihre Meditation über der Tora' (שיחתם בתורת עליון) stand".
309 11QPs[a] 24,3-17 = Ps(syr) 3,1-38. Cf. *DJD* 4 (1965) 70-75 (J.A. Sanders).
310 Cf. M. Hengel, *o.c.*, p.325.
311 Cf. J.A. Sanders, *o.c.*, p.75.

in this psalm: the study of the law and of its commandments leads, with the help of God, to wisdom and understanding.

12.1.2. Implicit evidence. There are 12 passages which imply the same identification of law (including Qumran halakhah) and wisdom. For reasons of space we will not engage here in detailed exegetical analyses but will simply present the conclusions which we have to draw from the individual pericopes.

(1) 1QS 1,11-13. This pericope asserts that all those who enter the Community shall bring all their knowledge (דעת), powers (כוח), and possessions (הון) into the Community "that they may purify their knowledge (לברר דעתם) in the truth of God's precepts (חוקים)[312]" and order their powers and possessions according to God's "counsel" and "way of perfection", i.e. according to Qumranian halakhah[313]. This instruction implies that (1) the reliable commandments of God correspond with God's "counsel" (עצה) and "way of perfection" (תם דרכים), i.e. with God's law including the particular stipulations and interpretations of the Community, and (2) that this law, if studied properly (in the Community!), leads to a purer and better knowledge. In other words, the proper understanding of the law results in pure, i.e. proper wisdom.

(2) 1QS 2,2-3. The priests are to bless all men who "walk perfectly" in all the ways of God (ההולכים תמים בכול דרכיו), i.e. who obey all the commandments of God[314]. The main part of the blessing says: "May he lighten your heart with life-giving wisdom (שכל חיים) and grant you eternal knowledge (דעת עולמים)" (2, 3). Thus, people who obey the law are blessed with ever-increasing wisdom and knowledge. To be wise implies the keeping of the law[315]. And obedience to the law is the prerequisite and the guarantee of wisdom.

(3) 1QS 4,2-6. This pericope describes the character of the Sons of Light whose heart is enlightened (להאיר) and who walk on the

---

312 On the term חוק see supra, p.171.
313 Cf. J. Becker, *Heil*, p.165.
314 In the context of the Qumranian reverence of the law and in the corresponding obedience to the commandments, this is the meaning of this phrase. Cf. also H. Lichtenberger, *Studien*, p.205.
315 Cf. F. Nötscher, *Terminologie*, p.64.

"paths" (דרכים) of true righteousness and who fear (פחד) the laws (משפטים) of God (4,2). In 4,3-6 different gifts of the Spirit are mentioned, among them understanding (שכל), intelligence (בינה), mighty wisdom (חכמת גבורה)[316]. Again, obedience to the law is closely related with the gift of wisdom.

(4) 1QH 1,34-36. This admonition links the wise men (חכמים) with the just men (צדיקים) and with the perfect of way (תמימי דרך)[317]. For the Community the concepts of צדקה and תום are intricately linked with the keeping of the Mosaic law and their halakhah. Hence wisdom is again linked with obedience to the law.

(5) 1QH 12,32. Here again דעת is linked with צדקה[318]. Knowledge is equivalent to righteousness which is God's gift but also, for the Community, dependent on the keeping of the law[319].

(6) 1QpHab 2,8-10. The context applies Hab 1,5 to the history of the Qumran Community dealing in 2,7 with the "final generation" in which "the priest" (הכוהן) will play an important role (2,8): God has put "understanding" into his heart (נתן אל בינה[320], 2,8) to interpret (לפשור) all the prophets through whom God predicted the future of his people and of the Community (2, 9-10). If the restoration of the lacuna in 2,8 is correct, we have another implicit identification of the Torah (here with the focus on the prophets) with wisdom: the priestly messiah who is elsewhere called "interpreter of the law"[321] has been given special wisdom to understand and to interpret the prophets. That is, a proper and relevant understanding of the prophets — an important

---

316 Cf. P. von der Osten-Sacken, *Gott und Belial,* p.153 with n.1 who compares these sapiential gifts of the Spirit with 1QH 12,11-13; 4,31-32.
317 Cf. S. Holm-Nielsen, *Hodayot,* p.27; H.W. Kuhn, *Enderwartung,* p.160.
318 1QH 12,32 uses צידרוק which occurs only here and in 1QH f2,16. According to M. Jastrow, *Dictionary,* s.v., this term means "justification" in the rabbinic literature. There seems to be no great difference in meaning with regard to צדק. Cf. S. Holm-Nielsen, *o.c.,* p.207.
319 Cf. J. Becker, *Heil,* p.167 who speaks with regard to the soteriological statements in 1QH of "solia gratia innerhalb des Gesetzesgehorsams".
320 Restored following E. Lohse, *Texte,* p.228; G. Vermes, *Dead Sea Scrolls,* p.236; M.P. Horgan, *Pesharim,* pp.13,25. Cf. also I. Rabinowitz, "The Second and Third Columns of the Habbakuk Interpretation Scroll", *JBL* 69 (1950) 33f., who suggests בלבו חכמה which is possible in terms of the context; with the usual full writing of חוכמה the word would be too long, however. Cf. M.P. Horgan, *Pesharim,* p.26.
321 See supra, § 10.8.1.

part of the Torah for the Community — is dependent upon wisdom given by God.

(7) 4QSl 39 f1. The first part of the 'Angelic Liturgy'[322] presents a series of blessings pronounced by each of the seven archangels conceived of as the angelic counterpart of the priestly benediction in Num. 6,24-27[323]. In f1 1,17-18 (blessing no. 4) the blessing is pronounced on those who "walk uprightly" (הולכי ישר), who "lay the foundations of truth", who exalt "true knowledge" (דעת אמתו). Here again the life in obedience to the commandments of the law is regarded as equivalent to true wisdom. In vv. 21-22 (blessing no. 6) the "mighty in wisdom" (גבורי שכל) are identified similarly with the "perfect of way" (תמימי דרך). In vv.24-25 (blessing no. 7) the "holy founders of knowledge" (קדושים ממיסדי דעת) are linked with those "who exalt his statutes" (מרומי משפטיו).

(8) 4Q184 f1,14-17. In the so-called 'Wiles of the Wicked Woman'[324], an allegorical wisdom poem on apostasy[325] or on the character of evil[326], several synonymous and parallel terms are used to designate God's faithful people as object of the seduction: "a righteous man (איש צדיק) . . . a perfect man (איש עצום) . . . the upright (ישרים) . . . the righteous elect (בחירי צדק) . . . the firmly established (סמוכי יצר) . . . those who walk uprightly (הולכי ישר)" (vv.14-15)[327]. It is further said of them that they keep the commandments (נצר מצוה) and that they walk in the "ways of righteousness" (דרכי צדק, v.16) and in the "paths of uprightness" (דרכי שוחה, v.17), and are faithful to the statute

---

322 See the *editio princeps* by J. Strugnell, "The Angelic Liturgy at Qumran, 4Q Serek Sîrîot Haššabat", *SVT* 7 (1960) 318-345; cf. also G. Vermes, *Dead Sea Scrolls*, pp.210-213; T.H. Gaster, *Dead Sea Scriptures*, pp.283-295. The text 4QSl has to be dated to ca. 60 B.C.; cf. J. Strugnell, *a.c.*, p.319.
323 Cf. T.H. Gaster, *o.c.*, pp.285f.
324 Cf. the edition by J.M. Allegro, *DJD* 5 (1968) 82-85, and the notes of J. Strugnell, "Notes en marge", *RQ* 7 (1970) 263-268; also G.Vermes, *Dead Sea Scrolls*, pp.255-257; T.H. Gaster, *Dead Sea Scriptures*, pp.493-503; and the study of R.D. Moore, "Personification of the Seduction of Evil: 'The Wiles of the Wicked Woman'", *RQ* 10 (1981) 505-519.
325 Cf. T.H. Gaster, *o.c.*, p.495.
326 Emphasized by R.D. Moore, *a.c.*, p.506 and passim.
327 Following the translation of J.M. Allegro, *o.c.*, p.83 and J. Strugnell, *a.c.*, p.268 (correcting the text of Allegro with Strugnell, *a.c.*, pp.265f.). Cf. similarly the recent translation of R.D. Moore, *a.c.*, pp.507f.

(חוק, v.15). The righteous are those who are morally perfect, obeying faithfully the commandments and precepts of the Torah, including the specific Qumran halakhah (חוק). The opposite of this righteousness by keeping the Torah is foolishness and wantonness[328]. The reference to foolishness plus the context of this wisdom poem imply that true wisdom is thought to be equivalent to moral perfection which is taken to be the direct result of one's faithful obedience to Torah.

(9) 4Q185 f1-2 1,13-2,1. The text 4Q185[329] has been identified as sapiential *Mahnrede*[330] "mit der zentralen Referenzgröße der Weisheit und/oder des Gesetzes"[331].

> The *Mahnrede* summons Israel, and indeed all peoples[332], not to close their minds to the divine will but to obey it and hence receive salvation and life. The question of how the divine will shows itself leads directly into the problem of the text: the suffixes of the 3rd person fem.sg. may refer to wisdom or to the law[333]. It seems to be obvious that the identification of law and wisdom is carried through here as well[334].

In f1-2 1,13-2,1 man is summoned to "draw wisdom (וחכמו)[335] from the mighty wisdom of God (מן גבורת אלהים)[336]" (1,14) and to "do his good pleasure" (עשו רצונו)[335] (2,1), remembering the miracles which he wrought in Egypt (1,15). In the context of the Exodus event, God's "pleasure" or "will" (1,15 immediately preceding 2,1) may very well refer to the Sinaitic legislation, in which case wisdom would clearly be identified with the law. The pericope f1-2 2,2-11 confirms this: reference is made to the

---

328 See the להביל and פחז in 1,15.
329 Cf. the edition by J.M. Allegro, *DJD* 5 (1968) 85-87, and the notes of J. Strugnell, a.c., pp.269-273; see also G. Vermes, o.c., pp.257-259; T.H. Gaster, o.c., pp.430-432; H. Lichtenberger, "Eine weisheitliche Mahnrede in den Qumranfunden (4Q-185)", *BETL* 46 (1978) 151-162; M. Küchler, *Weisheitsperikopen*, pp.103-105. We use the translations of J. Strugnell, a.c., pp.272f. and H. Lichtenberger, a.c., passim.
330 Cf. H. Lichtenberger, "Mahnrede", *BETL* 46 (1978) 151,161; similarly J. Strugnell, "Notes", *RQ* 7 (1970) 269.
331 M. Küchler, *Weisheitstraditionen*, p.103 n.22a. 4Q185 is pre-Qumranian, but was used and probably copied in Qumran; cf. H. Lichtenberger, a.c., pp.161f.
332 Cf. H. Lichtenberger, a.c., p.153.
333 Cf. J. Strugnell, a.c., p.269; H. Lichtenberger, a.c., p.152; M. Küchler, o.c., p.103.
334 Cf. H. Lichtenberger, a.c., p.152.
335 Cf. the reconstruction by J. Strugnell, a.c., p.270.
336 Interpreting גבורה in its intellectual sense as elsewhere in the Qumran texts; cf. J. Strugnell, a.c., p.270.

"words of Yahweh" (דברי יהוה, 2,3) and the "path (נתיבה)[337] he appointed for Isaac" (2,4) which are identified with "his wisdom" (חכמתו)[338] in 2,11. The two macarisms in f1-2 2,8-13 and 2,13-15 refer to wisdom and/or the law[339]: it has been demonstrated with regard to 2,12 that "die Gaben die für das Tun des von Gott gebotenen Weges gegeben werden, sind eben die, die in weisheitlichen Texten die Gaben der Weisheit sind"[340]. These gifts are "length of days" (ארך ימים)[341], "fatness of bone" (דשן עצם), i.e. luxuriant strength[342], "joy of heart" (שמחת לבב)[343], "riches" (עשר) and "honour" (בבור)[344].

(10) 4QDibHam[a] f1-2 2,12-15. In the prayers of 4QDibHam[345], Israel is described as having been elected by God (f1-2 3,9; 4,3. 5)[346]. In 2,12-15 God's miracles are mentioned which he did in the "eyes of the nations". God is 'reminded' that his name has been "called over Israel" (נקרא שמכה עלינו). These statements might establish the Exodus event and the Sinaitic covenant as the context of our pericope. God is implored to lead Israel to total repentance and to "implant" his law (לטעת תורתכה) in their hearts (2,13) so that they might never depart from it to any degree (2, 14). This implantation of God's law in the human heart is then described as "healing" (רפא) from foolishness (שגעון), blindness (עורון), and aberration of heart (תמהון לבב). This plea implies clearly the identity of wise conduct and obedience to Torah, of wisdom and law.

(11) 4QShir[b] f1,7-8. This pericope belongs to the collection of

---

337 Cf. J. Strugnell, a.c., p.271 contra J.M. Allegro, *DJD* 5 (1968) 85 who reads חתימה.
338 Thus the reconstruction of J. Strugnell, a.c., p.271.
339 Cf. J. Strugnell, a.c., pp.269,273; M. Küchler, o.c., p.105.
340 H. Lichtenberger, "Mahnrede", *BETL* 46 (1978) 152.
341 Cf. Prov 3,16; Sir 1,20; Bar 3,14.
342 Cf. Prov 15,30; cf. Sir 1,18.
343 Cf. Qoh 5,19; Sir 4, 12G; 6,28.
344 Restored tentatively with H. Lichtenberger, a.c., p.162 with n.70. With regard to honour as gift cf. Prov 3,16; 8,18; Sir 4,13; 6,31; 24,16-17; 37,26; 51,17; with regard to riches cf. Prov 3,16; 8,18; Sir 24,17.
345 Cf. the *editio princeps* by M. Baillet, "Un recueil liturgique de Qumrân, grotte 4: 'Les Paroles des Luminaires'", *RB* 68 (1961) 195-250; idem, *DJD* 7 (1982) 137-175. Cf. also G. Vermes, *Dead Sea Scrolls*, pp.202-205; T.H. Gaster, *Dead Sea Scriptures*, pp.269-281. Scholars agree that 4QDibHam is a pre-Qumranian, hasidic writing; cf. K.G. Kuhn, "Nachträge", *RQ* 4 (1963) 168f.; G. Vermes, o.c., p.202; H. Lichtenberger, *Studien*, p.93 n.1; M. Baillet, o.c., p.137.
346 Cf. H. Lichtenberger, o.c., pp.185f.

hymns labelled 4QShir[347] which were written by a *maskil*. Reference is made to the "glory of God of knowledge" (כבוד אלוהי דעות) which is shining in "his words" (באמרין). Whether these "words" of God refer to his word of creation or to the words of legislation, it has to be noted that God's wisdom is present in his word. In f2,5-7 the remnant of God is mentioned, the true Israel, who "keeps the way of God (שומרי דרך אלוהים) and the path of his holiness (מסלת קודשו)", obviously referring to the keeping of the commandments. The writer continues that "for the saints of his people true insight (הנבונה)[348] consists in the knowledge of God (בדעת אלוהים)". This could be interpreted in such a way that the keeping of the ways of God amounts to true insight and is possible only on the basis of the knowledge of God.

(12) 11QPs^{a}DavComp (27,2-11). The only prose section of the Psalms Scroll[349] contains a midrashic supplement on the poetic activities of David who is credited with 4,050 compositions. David is called חכם and סופר (v.2) and described as being "discerning" (נבון) and "perfect in all his ways" (תמים בכול דרכיו, v.3), and possessing a "discerning and enlightened spirit" (רוח נבונה ואורה, v.4). Finally, he is credited with the divine gift of prophecy (בנבואה) as source of his compositions (v.11).

> Thus, "at Qumran, David was thought of not only as a musical composer and author of the Psalter under prophetic inspiration, but also as *hakham*, capable of the kind of thinking elsewhere attributed to the great Wisdom teacher Ben Sira"[350].

Hence, the Scriptures (here with the focus on the Psalter) are said to be both divinely inspired and closely related to scribal wisdom.

---

347 See the *editio princeps* by M. Baillet, *DJD* 7 (1982) 215-262. This collection of hymns is clearly of Qumranian origin; cf. M. Baillet, o.c., pp.215,220. We follow the (French) translation of Baillet.
348 Translating the definite article in הנבונה as "*true* wisdom".
349 11QPs^{a}DavComp (27,2-11). See the *editio princeps* by J.A. Sanders, *DJD* 4 (1965) 91-93; cf. also G. Vermes, *Dead Sea Scrolls*, pp.264f. This pericope dates probably to the beginning of the 1st century A.D.; cf. J.A. Sanders, *The Dead Sea Psalms Scroll*, 1967, pp.134f.
350 J.A. Sanders, *DJD* 4 (1965) 92.

12.2. The Nature of the Identification

12.2.1. The creational dimension. Several passages equate wisdom which is manifest in the order of creation with the laws established by God (1QS 3,15-17; 1QH 1,1-20; 12,5-11; and possibly 4QShir^b f1,7-8). The terms used for, and in connection with, the sapiential order of creation include מחשבה, דעת, דעות, חוכמה, עצה (cf. §11.3.2.). The laws of nature are referred to as חוקים, נתיבות, משפטים (cf. § 10.5.1.).

It is significant to note that תורה is never used for the order of creation[351]. As the Pentateuch and the entire Hebrew canon were esteemed in an exceptional manner, the Community refrained from transferring the characteristic designation תורה to the realm of creation. Instead, it used חוק and משפט which designated elsewhere the Scriptures including its own particular halakhah.

For the Qumran group, the laws of creation were basically one with the laws of the Community which were, in their opinion, directly and unquestionably based on the written law. And the laws of the order of creation were an expression and embodiment of God's great wisdom.

12.2.2. The particularistic dimension. We have seen earlier that both the law and wisdom were closely and at times even exclusively related to the Qumran Community. The law is interpreted, understood, and kept properly, above all, in the Community, especially with regard to matters which the later rabbis called halakhah (cf. § 10.4, 10.7.). The Community was convinced that it was the only group which lived in harmony with the God-given lawful order of creation (cf. § 10.5.2.). The Community was further convinced of the fact that God's wisdom which was embodied in the order of creation had been revealed especially and exclusively to them (§ 11.4.1.), and that the spirit of wisdom determined the life in the Community (cf. § 11.4.2.).

This particularistic dimension can be observed in the immediate context of the identification of law and wisdom as well. In texts which belong either to the pre-Qumranian or to the early Qumranian periods (1QM 10,9-11; 1Q22 2,8-9; 4Q185 f1-2 1,13-2,1.2-

---

351 At this point we want to point out again that the Qumran Community does not use the personification of wisdom (cf. § 11.3.3.).

11), the identification is expressed in the wider context of Israel and the covenant with the fathers. The texts which were written in the main and the later periods of the Community use the identification in the narrower context of the Community which possesses and obeys both the law and the divine wisdom in an exclusive manner (1QH 4,9-11; 1QS 1,11-13; 9,17; CD 6,2-5; cf. 4QShir^b f2,5-7)[352]. One pre-Qumranian text which was used in the Community also refers to the (implicit) identification (4QDibHam^a f1-2 2,12-15).

Only the pre-Qumranian *Mahnrede* 4Q185 f1-2 1,13-2,1 can be interpreted as implying the universal aspect of the identification of law and wisdom.

12.2.3. The ethical dimension. It has been pointed out earlier that Qumran ethics is based upon the Torah and the particular halakhah of the Community, and has strong links with the wisdom tradition (cf. § 11.6., 11.1.1-2.). The most important context of the identification of law and wisdom in the Qumran texts is the ethical context.

In several passages the identification is linked with the concept of צדקה (1QS 3,1; 4,2-6; 9,17; 1QH 1,34-36; 12,32; cf. 11QPs^a 18,10-13; 4Q184 f1,14-17) which is the basic requirement of Qumran ethics[353].

In other texts the identification is related to the concept of תמים/תום (1QS 1,11-13; 2,2-3; 1QH 1,34-36; 4QS1 39 f1 1,21-22; cf. 11QPs^a 27,2-11).

Many texts refer to the identification of law and wisdom in connection with the "the way" (דרך) or the upright or proper "walk" (הלך) (1QS 1,11-13; 2,2-3; 4,2-6; 9,17; 1QH 1,34-36; 1Q22 2,8-9; 4QS1 39 f1 1,17-18.21-22; 4QShir^b f2,5-7; cf. 4Q185 f1-2, 2,2-11; 11QPs^a 27,2-11).

Some passages place the identification in the context of the human heart (1QS 2,2-3; 4,2-6; 1QH 4,9-11; 4QDibHam^a f1-2 2, 12-15).

---

352 J.A. Davis, *Wisdom and Spirit*, 1982, pp.26-28,33 asserts that the concept of wisdom in Qumran is not identical with the law per se but understood to be "co-essential with the sectarian interpretation of the law" (p.33). However, this is no proof that the correlation of law and wisdom was redefined in Qumran since the law always (!) existed (only) as interpreted law.

353 Cf. S.T. Kimbrough, "Ethic", *RQ* 6 (1969) 485.

The members of the Community considered a righteous, proper conduct to be possible (only) on the basis of the written revelation, i.e. the Scriptures and their own particular regulations which had to be faithfully obeyed, and in accordance with the God-given wisdom which had to be appropriated in the Community. Law and wisdom were one in everyday life.

12.2.4. The didactic dimension. The identification of wisdom and law in the Community is embodied in the offices and figures of the Teacher of Righteousness, the *maskil*, and the priestly messiah, as well as in the function of the wise men/scribes.

The Teacher is described as having received particular wisdom and knowledge from God which he passed on to the Community (cf. § 11.5.2.), and at the same time he is the interpreter of the law *par excellence* (cf. § 10.1.).

The *maskil* — the designation and the implied function belong to the sapiential tradition — who seems to have occupied the office of the "interpreter of the law" in the Community, is the teaching functionary (cf. § 11.5.3.). The *maskil* is directly linked with the correlation of law and wisdom (cf. 1QS 9,17).

The priestly messiah who will give the true interpretation of the prophets is also directly connected with both wisdom and the law (cf. 1QpHab 2,8-10).

Two passages relate the חכמים to the study of the law (cf. CD 6,2-5; 1Q22 2,8-9). A pre-Qumranian text refers to David as חכם and סופר (11QPs[a] 27,2-11). It seems that, for the Community, wisdom was both the prerequisite for, and the result of, the study of the law, while the law could be studied, interpreted, and taught properly only by wise people.

12.2.5. The eschatological dimension. Both wisdom and the law have eschatological dimensions in Qumran thought. The priestly messiah comes as interpreter of the law (cf. CD 7,18; 4QFlor 1,11) who teaches righteousness at the end of days (CD 6,11; 1QpHab 2, 9-10). The royal messiah is associated with the "three books" (4QMessAr 1,5) which might be a reference to the sum of authoritative writings of the Community including the Scriptures. Wisdom and knowledge are described as eschatological gifts (cf. § 11. 4.2.) and are associated with the royal messiah (1QpHab 2,8-10).

In each of these two texts the law is implicitly identified with wisdom.

12.2.6. The theological dimension. The reason why this aspect of the correlation of wisdom and law is mentioned last is that the concept of the fear of the Lord as submission under God's will is basically absent from the Qumran writings and is never mentioned in conjunction with the identification of law and wisdom. However, it is self-evident that the identification cannot be separated from the theological dimension: wisdom and knowledge are unique possessions of God and were given by him to the Teacher and his Community, and the law was divinely revealed to Moses and the forefathers, as well as interpreted properly and taught adequately (only) in the Community. We observed earlier that the "walk" in the perfect "way" is always dependent upon God (cf. § 11.6.2.). God is the ultimate source of both law and wisdom, of halakhah and of proper behaviour.

12.3. Summary

We have established the crucial role of the law for the Qumran Community. The orientation by the law is a fundamental datum of Qumran theology. The law has been revealed to Israel but is understood and interpreted properly only in the Community. Progressive revelation guarantees the knowledge of the "hidden things". The members of the Community strive to live in perfect accordance with God's written law and in complete harmony with the divine orders of creation.

We have also seen that the Qumran world-view, life-style, and vocabulary have strong connections with the sapiential tradition. The Community indeed claims distinctive and exclusive wisdom and knowledge for its members who are the "sons of light" who know God's secrets.

We have further seen that the Community knew the identification of law and wisdom and used it in a similar manner as other intertestamental writers and groups used it. The ethical dimension of the correlation is in the foreground. Particularistic, didactic, and eschatological perspectives are present, and the theological aspect is clearly implied. The creational (rather than universalistic!) dimension is an important characteristic of Qumran theology[354].

It should be noted that the identification of law and wisdom is to be observed in the hasidic pre-Qumranian texts (4Q185, 11QPs^a 18; 24; 4QDibHam^a), in the early Qumran writings (1QM, 1QH), in the major texts (1QS, CD 1QpHab, 4QShir^b), and in late Qumran writings (4QS1, 11QPs^a DavComp).

We conclude with a quote from M. Hengel in which he correlates wisdom, knowledge, scribal erudition, right conduct, salvation, and revelation with regard to the Qumran Community: "Nur der Weise und Gelehrte, der über die beherrschende und durchdringende Kraft des Denkens verfügt, kann wirklich fromm, wirklich gut sein. Die Erkenntnis erhält dabei den Charakter des Heilswissens, das dem irrenden Menschen durch Gottes Offenbarung erschlossen werden muß"[355].

---

[354] Cf. H. Lichtenberger, *Studien*, p.238 who emphasizes the outstanding role of creation aspects for Qumran anthropology.

[355] M. Hengel, "Qumran und der Hellenismus", *BETL* 46 (1978) 357. See also H. Gabrion, "Interprétation", *ANRW* II/19,1 (1979) 830 who states that "la connaissance n'a d'importance à Qumran que dans la mesure où elle permet à ceux qui la possèdent de conformer leur vie à l'exigence authentique de la Loi".

Chapter Four

Wisdom and Law in Pauline Christology and Ethics

Our final chapter deals with the theology of the former Pharisee and later apostle Paul, focusing on the questions whether the correlation of wisdom and law which played such a crucial role in the intertestamental period was taken up by Paul and, if the answer is yes, in which way it affected the content of his theology.

§13   Introduction

Before we attempt to understand Paul's conception of σοφία and νόμος, both in the realm of his convictions regarding the person and mission of Jesus Christ, and in the realm of Christian conduct, we first have to establish the basis of our discussion, especially since we are looking for the manner in which these two conceptions are correlated. We will first of all deal with the question whether the background of Paul's origin makes it plausible to assume Paul's familiarity with the correlation of law and wisdom. Second, we will seek to find an explicit exegetical expression of Paul's awareness of this correlation. Finally, methodological considerations will have to clarify our approach to the Pauline corpus as a whole.

13.1. The Conceptual Heritage of Paul

13.1.1. Geographical origins. Paul was born in Tarsus, the capital of the Roman province of Cilicia in Asia Minor (Acts 21, 39;

22,3)[1]. It is disputed whether Paul also grew up in Tarsus, or whether he was brought to Jerusalem at a very early age and subsequently spent his childhood and youth there. The latter view was suggested by W.C. van Unnik[2] who argued, on the basis of a fixed literary unit which Luke used in Acts 22,3 (cf. Acts 7,20-22), that Paul was born (γεγεννημένος) in Tarsus, brought up (ἀνατεθραμμένος) in Jerusalem (by his mother)[3], and educated (πεπαιδευμένος) in Jerusalem (by father and teacher). This interpretation of Acts 22,3 explains the language employed by Luke best and has been widely accepted with convincing reasons[4]. Gal 1,22 cannot be used as argument against this interpretation since Paul was indeed unknown to the Aramaic-speaking Christians in Jerusalem[5]. Thus it is justified to reckon with Paul's upbringing in Jerusalem from a very early age onwards. This implies that the Palestinian influence on Paul, as regards his formative years as a young man, is very significant[6].

---

1 On the historical reliability of Luke see I.H. Marshall, *Luke: Historian and Theologian*, 1970, pp.21-76; M. Hengel, *Zur urchristlichen Geschichtsschreibung*, 1979, pp.36-39,54-61; also C. Burchard, *Der dreizehnte Zeuge: Traditions- und kompositionsgeschichtliche Untersuchungen zu Lukas' Darstellung der Frühzeit des Paulus*, FRLANT 103, 1970, pp.28,169-173 and J. Roloff, *Die Apostelgeschichte*, NTD 5, 1981, pp.2-12 (with whose view that Luke, the author of Acts, did not know Paul personally we cannot agree, however).
2 Cf. W.C. van Unnik, "Tarsus or Jerusalem: The City of Paul's Youth" (1952), *Sparsa Collecta*, SNT 29, 1973, pp.259-322.
3 On the meaning of ἀνατρέφειν cf. W.C. van Unnik, a.c., pp.282-292,295f. who shows that this term was used for the context of the parental home.
4 Cf. E. Haenchen, *Apostelgeschichte*, KEK 3, [13]1961, p.554 n.1; G. Ogg, *The Chronology of the Life of Paul*, 1968, p.6; C. Burchard, o.c., pp.32,34f.; H. Conzelmann, *Apostelgeschichte*, HNT 7, [2]1972, p.134; I.H. Marshall *Acts of the Apostles*, TNTC, 1980, pp.353f.; S. Kim, *Origin*, pp.33-38; also M. Hengel, "Die Ursprünge der christlichen Mission", *NTS* 18 (1971/72) 23f.
5 Cf. M. Hengel, *Geschichtsschreibung*, pp.71f.
6 Cf. C. Burchard, *Zeuge*, pp.34f. n.42 who links the Palestinian-Jewish stamp of Paul's theological training with his upbringing in Jerusalem; cf. also S. Kim, *Origin*, pp.38f. who asserts that the fact that Paul was brought up in Jerusalem weakens the view which sees Tarsus with its Hellenistic context as an important factor for Paul's career. It is clear, of course, that Palentinian Judaism was not free from Hellenistic elements, and it is beyond doubt that Paul was well acquainted with the Jewish-Hellenistic (Alexandrian) tradition. It is simply a matter of emphasis when we point out that Paul's formative (!) years were spent in Jerusalem rather than in Tarsus. Cf. M. Hengel, o.c., p.71 and W.G. Kümmel, *Theologie*, [4]1980, p.124 who points out that it is difficult, in specific contexts, to decide on which religion-historical presuppositions Paul bases his arguments.

13.1.2. Sociological origins. Paul's family traced its roots to the tribe of Benjamin (cf. Phil 3,6; Rom 11,1)[7]. Although it lived, for some time, in Tarsus in the Diaspora it was native to Palestine and had always preserved close Palestinian family connections[8]. Paul's self-designation as "Hebrew" in Phil 3,5 and 2Cor 11,22 could well imply a linguistic and cultural distinction, referring in a Palestinian context to Jews whose mother tongue was Aramaic, and in a Diaspora context to Jews who were born in Palestine or who were at least closely linked with Palestine[9]. Paul's upbringing and education are responsible for his basic Palestinian 'outlook', and Aramaic was presumably his mother tongue[10]. Paul was certainly bilingual speaking Grek as well. It seems that Paul belonged to the Greek speaking synagogue in Jerusalem (cf. Acts 6,9; 9,29)[11]. The fact that Paul was born a Roman citizen (Acts 22,27-28) means that he belonged to the social élite[12]. It is not clear whether Paul was a member of the Sanhedrin in Jerusalem[13].

13.1.3. Theological origins. Paul was the son of a Pharisee (cf. Acts 23,6)[14] who made sure that he received a strictly 'orthodox'

---

[7] I.e. to those people who had not lost their tribal identity during the exile; cf. Neh 11,7-9.31-35. Cf. F.F. Bruce, *Paul*, p.41. On the Benjaminite families in the post-exilic period cf. J. Jeremias, *Jerusalem*, pp.227f.

[8] This seems to be the sense of the statements in 2Cor 11,22; cf. W. Gutbrod, in *ThWNT* 3 (1938) 393; M. Hengel, *o.c.*, pp.70f. Cf. Acts 23,16.

[9] Cf. recently M. Hengel, "Zwischen Jesus und Paulus: Die 'Hellenisten', die 'Sieben' und Stephanus", *ZThK* 72 (1975) 151-206, here 169-171; F.F. Bruce, *o.c.*, pp.42f.; S. Kim, *o.c.*, pp.34f. (lit.).

[10] Cf. Acts 26,14. Cf. W.C. van Unnik, "Tarsus", p.304; F.F. Bruce, *o.c.*, p.43.

[11] Cf. F.F. Bruce, *Acts*, p.133; W.C. van Unnik, "Tarsus", p.299; M. Hengel, "Ursprünge", *NTS* 18 (1971/72) 23; idem, *Geschichtsschreibung*, p.72; S. Kim, *Origin*, pp.37f.; J. Roloff, *Apostelgeschichte*, pp.113-157.

[12] Cf. F.F. Bruce, *o.c.*, pp.37f. On Paul's rights as Roman citizen cf. C. Burchard, *Zeuge*, pp.37-39. Cf. also R.F. Hock, "Paul's Tentmaking and the Problem of his Social Class", *JBL* 97 (1978) 555-564 who confirms Paul's aristocratic origin. We cannot, however, follow Hock's presentation and evaluation of Paul's work ethic. On Paul's attitude to work see now W. Schrage, *Die Ethik des Neuen Testaments*, 1982, pp.221f.

[13] This is asserted, on the basis of Acts 26,10, by H. Conzelmann, *Apostelgeschichte*, p.138; C. Burchard, *o.c.*, p.46; I.H. Marshall, *Luke*, p.393; J. Roloff, *o.c.*, p.352; cf. G. Schneider, *Apostelgeschichte*, HThK 5/2, 1982, p.373 n.45. But see A. Oepke, "Probleme der vorchristlichen Zeit des Paulus" (1933), *Das Paulusbild in der neueren Forschung*, ed. K.H. Rengstorf, 1964, pp.410-446, here 418,422f.

[14] Emphasized by C. Burchard, *o.c.*, p.39; M. Hengel, *o.c.*, p.71.

education. Later Paul was a Pharisee himself (Phil 3,5; Acts 23,6; 26,5). He studied under the leading Pharisaic Torah scholar Gamaliel the Elder (Acts 22,3) who was a member of the Sanhedrin (Acts 5,34)[15] and a leading Torah scholar in the first half of the 1st century. Paul was a zealous Pharisee striving to keep the entire law as well as the ancestral traditions, and he was well versed in the application of scribal distinctions, methods, and categories[16]. It is difficult to decide whether Paul was an ordained Torah scholar (i.e. a rabbi in the official later terminology), a γραμματεύς [17] or not[18]. Scholars who take Acts 26,10 literally, assuming that Paul was an official member of the Sanhedrin, often regard Paul as an ordained rabbi[19].

If Paul indeed grew up and was educated in Jerusalem in a Pharisaic and scribal setting, his knowledge of Greek thought and literature[20] and his familiarity with the LXX has to be traced back to the following sources: (1) the school of Gamaliel in which rudiments of Greek learning could well have been passed on[21], (2) the period between Paul's return from Damascus after his conversion and the beginning of his ministry in Antioch which is linked with Tarsus (cf. Acts 9,30; 11,25), and (3) the time of Paul's

---

15 There is no reason to doubt the accuracy of Luke's information here; cf. I.H. Marshall, *o.c.*, p.354; M. Hengel, *o.c.*, p.71; also J. Roloff, *o.c.*, pp.100f; contra E. Haenchen, *Apostelgeschichte*, p.554.
16 The latter fact is stressed and developed by B. Gerhardsson, "1 Kor 13: Zur Frage von Paulus' rabbinischem Hintergrund", *Donum Gentilicium*, FS D. Daube, ed. E. Bammel et al., 1978, pp.185-209; H. Hübner, "Gal 3,10 und die Herkunft des Paulus", *KuD* 19 (1973) 222-231; also S. Belkin, "The Problem of Paul's Background", *JBL* 54 (1935) 41-60; J. Jeremias, "Paulus als Hillelit", *Neotestamentica et Semitica*, FS M. Black, ed. E.E. Ellis et al., 1969, pp.88f.
17 Cf. J. Jeremias, "War Paulus Witwer?", *ZNW* 25 (1926) 310; idem, *Jerusalem*, p.255 n.34. On the ordination (סמיכה) of the later rabbis see H.D. Mantel, *Studies*, pp.214-216.
18 Cf. A. Oepke, "Probleme", pp.410-446 who characterizes Paul as a Pharisee who persecuted the Christians privately while having an "offiziöse Protektion" (p.426), i.e. not officially as an ordained rabbi. Cf. also C. Burchard, *Zeuge*, pp.33 with n.36,46; also J. Blank, *Paulus und Jesus*, StANT 18, 1968, pp.218-221.
19 Differently C. Burchard, *o.c.*, p.46 who maintains that Paul was a Pharisaic member of the Sanhedrin.
20 Cf. K.H. Schelkle, *Paulus: Leben-Briefe-Theologie*, 1981, pp.42-45 (lit.).
21 Note that Simon b. Gamaliel I is reported to have had students who studied "the wisdom of the Greeks" (bSot 49b). Cf. F.F. Bruce, *Paul*, p.126; S. Kim, *Origin*, pp.37f. Note further that Paul probably belonged to a Greek-speaking synagogue in Jerusalem.

missionary career which started in the regions of Syria and Cilicia which confronted him with the Hellenistic world and in the context of which he identified, as far as possible, with the Gentiles (cf. 1Cor 9,19-23)[22].

13.1.4. Summary. Paul's training as Pharisee and Torah scholar surely brought him in contact, apart from the Torah, with the corpus of Pharisaic traditions which included writings like PsSal, Tob, and Judt, and conceptions and motifs which eventually flowed into ApcBar, 4Ezr, AntBibl, and the Mishnah[23]. It can be further assumed that Paul was equally familiar with the hasidic writings such as En, Jub, and TestXIIPatr. Paul's knowledge and reception of the apocalyptic tradition is easily recognized[24]. The assumption that Paul, through his training under Gamaliel, must have come into contact with the corpus of the extra-biblical Jewish literature, including the wisdom literature[25], is substantiated by the fact that Paul exhibits similarties of thought and expression with these writings[26]. It seems safe to assume that Paul knew Sir[27].

---

22 Cf. W.C. van Unnik, "Tarsus", p.305; F.F. Bruce, *o.c.*, p.127; also S. Kim, *o.c.*, pp.37f. who quotes E.E. Ellis, *Paul's Use of the Old Testament*, 1957, pp.12ff. stating that Paul's occasional deviations from the LXX in favour of the Hebrew text show that he knew the latter. Scholars who assert that Paul grew up in Tarsus emphasize consequently the correspondingly early influences of Hellenism on Paul's thought; cf. G. Turbessi, "L'Apôtre Paul, 'homme de Dieu' ", *Paul de Tarse*, ed. L. de Lorenzi, 1979, pp.101-162, here 106-120.

23 The Pharisaic origin of these writings is basically acknowledged.

24 Cf. recently H. Paulsen, *Überlieferung und Auslegung von Römer 8*, WMANT 43, 1974, pp.111-119; and J. Baumgarten, *Paulus und die Apokalyptik: Die Auslegung apokalyptischer Überlieferungen in den echten Paulusbriefen*, WMANT 44, 1975, pp.55-243.

25 Cf. J.A. Fischer, "Pauline Literary Forms and Thought Patterns", *CBQ* 39 (1977) 208-223 who bases his observations on the hypothesis that Paul stands in the mainstream of the Jewish wisdom tradition.

26 Paul 'alludes' to Sir 26x, to Bar 3x, to En 7x, to Jub 3x, to 3Ezr 1x, to 1Macc 1x, to 2Macc 5x, to 3Macc 4x, to AssMos 2x, to Tob 2x, to TestXIIPatr 13x, to PsSal 7x, and uses thoughts which are later also expressed in 4Macc (11x), 4Ezr (10x), and ApcBar (13x). These figures are based on the appendix "loci citati vel allegati" in Nestle-Aland, *Novum Testamentum Graece*, 1979, pp.769-775. It has to be pointed out with H. Conzelmann, "Paulus und die Weisheit" (1965), *Theologie als Schriftauslegung*, BEvTh 65, 1974, p.179 that it is not possible to prove a direct literary dependence of Paul upon certain extra-canonical wisdom writings but that there exists "weithin ein enger Motiv-Zusammenhang".

27 Note the 26 'allusions' which are to be found throughout the Pauline corpus (in Rom, 1Cor, Eph, Phil, Col, 1Thess; 1Tim, 2Tim).

The assumption that Paul also knew the Jewish-Hellenistic (wisdom) tradition[28] is substantiated by 'allusions' to SapSal[29].

As Paul obviously was well familiar with the various Jewish traditions and writings, particularly the Pharisaic and apocalyptic ones, it is difficult to avoid the conclusion that Paul was aware of the correlation and identification of law and wisdom[30]. This is confirmed by the explicit exegetical occurrence of this correlation in Rom 2,17-24.

13.2. Paul's Familiarity with the Correlation of Law and Wisdom

In Rom 2,17-24 Paul deals with the deplorable dichotomy between the (legitimate) claim and the actual existence of the Jews. The pericope 2,17-24 is a typically Pauline anacoluthon[31] consisting of two parts[32]. The first section (vv.17-20) consists of five short parallel phrases in vv.17-18 connected with καί, followed by five parallel units in vv.19-20, and describes the privileges and claims of the Jew. The privilege of being a Jew depends on the gift

---

28 Cf. E. Brandenburger, *Fleisch und Geist: Paulus und die dualistische Weisheit*, WMANT 29, 1968, pp.223-229 concluding that essential elements of Paul's theology presuppose the dualistic wisdom of Hellenistic Judaism as historical conceptual background.

29 Altogether 40 'allusions'. Cf. K. Romaniuk, "Le Livre de la Sagesse dans le Noveau Testament", *NTS* 14 (1967/68) 498-514 (on Paul, pp.503ff).

30 D. Georgi, *The Records of Jesus in the Light of Ancient Accounts of Revered Men*, Protocol of the 4th Colloquy of the Center for Hermeneutical Studies, 1975, pp.6f. maintains that Paul was "thoroughly influenced by the various branches of the Jewish wisdom-movement" which is evident in his precise use of specific terms and patterns. When he states that "Paul is our first literary evidence for an encounter between wisdom-schools and Pharisaism, scribal training and Pharisaic piety" (p.7), Georgi implies that the wisdom tradition and the Pharisaic tradition had existed side by side for nearly 150 years without having penetrated each other. It seems to be impossible to speak of 'the' wisdom movement and 'the' wisdom schools after (!) Ben Sira had identified law and wisdom which also 'merged' the institutions of law and wisdom. Also contra H. Conzelmann, "Paulus und die Weisheit", p.179 who assumes (rightly) a close relationship between Paul and the Jewish wisdom tradition and then maintains that Paul had a 'wisdom school' in Ephesus "wo man 'Weisheit' methodisch betreibt bzw. Theologie als Weisheitsschulung treibt" (ibid.).

31 Cf. BDR §468.2; also G. Bornkamm, "Paulinische Anakoluthe im Römerbrief", *Das Ende des Gesetzes*, 1, [5]1966, pp.76-78 who states that "die Diskrepanz von Anspruch und Leistung spiegelt sich in der Inkongruenz der ganzen Satzkonstruktion" (p.78).

32 See especially U. Wilckens, *Römer*, EKK 6/1, 1978, pp.146f. E. Käsemann, *Römer*, HNT 8a, [4]1980, p.65 calls this pericope a "rhetorisches Meisterstück".

of the Torah on which the Jew rightly relies (v.17b). The Torah contains the will (θέλημα/רצון) of God and makes possible the discernment (δοκιμάζειν) of the essentials (τὰ διαφέροντα) of human life (v.18)[33]. As divine revelation, the Torah is the "embodiment" (μόρφωσις), i.e. the true, fixed, and binding form ('Gestalt') of knowledge (γνῶσις) and truth (ἀλήθεια), v.20. Here νόμος designates the actual 'book' (or scroll!) of the Torah[34]. The Torah contains God's (!) knowledge[35] and truth[36]. The participial phrase in v.20c ἔχοντα τὴν μόρφωσιν τῆς γνώσεως καὶ τῆς ἀληθείας ἐν τῷ νόμῳ which functions as summary of the statements in vv.17-20[37] obviously presupposes the identity of law and wisdom: God's wisdom which is truth pure and simple has assumed a recognizable form in the Torah[38]. Paul says, in other words, that for the Jew God's wisdom and God's law are one and the same. The knowledge of God's will which is laid down in the Torah enables the Jew to discern what is essential in life (v.18b) – which is the fundamental aim of sapiential concerns. Thus, if the Jew adopts and follows God's wisdom, i.e. receives instruction (κατηχεῖν) by the law (v.18c), law and wisdom are one also on the human level (and not only on the theo-logical level).

Paul's awareness of the fundamental identity of law and wisdom as expressed in 2,18.20c[39] can be further substantiated by the four substantives in vv.19-20b which characterize the Jew who

---

33 Cf. U. Wilckens, *Römer*, 1, p.148; H. Schlier, *Römerbrief*, p.83; E. Käsemann, *Römer*, p.65.
34 Cf. J. Behm, Art. "μόρφωσις", *ThWNT* 4 (1942) 762 who translates μόρφωσις here as "leibhafte Darstellung", "Verkörperung". Cf. W. Bauer, *Wörterbuch*, col. 1045 s.v. referring to Josephus Bell 2,292; Ant 12,256; followed by E. Käsemann, *o.c.*, p.66; U. Wilckens, *o.c.*, p.149.
35 Emphasized by R. Bultmann, *ThWNT* 1 (1933) 705; H. Schlier, *o.c.*, p.85; E. Käsemann, *o.c.*, p.66; U. Wilckens, *o.c.*, p.149. Despite the missing genitive (subjective), γνῶσις designates here, as דעת in the OT, the knowledge of the demanding will of God as present ἐν τῷ νόμῳ.
36 Cf. E. Käsemann, *o.c.*, p.66 referring to ApcBar 44,14: "truth of the law".
37 Cf. U. Wilckens, *o.c.*, p.147; E. Käsemann, *o.c.*, p.65; H. Schlier, *o.c.*, p.85.
38 The presence of the identity of law and wisdom in Rom 2,20c is implicitly acknowledged by U. Wilckens, *o.c.*, p.149 when he writes that "es ist darum nicht seine eigene *Weisheit*, deren er sich rühmt, sondern allein diejenige *Gottes*, wie sie *in der Tora zu Wort gekommen* ist".
39 Cf. also M.J. Suggs, " 'The Word is Near You': Rom 10,6-10 within the Purpose of the Letter", *Christian History and Interpretation*, FS J. Knox, ed. W.R. Farmer et al., 1967, p.304 (note the misprint 3,20).

claims to be the Torah teacher of the non-Jewish world. The pagan, as he does not possess the law, is blind (τυφλός), in darkness (ἐν σκότει), foolish (ἄφρων), immature (νήπιος). The Jew, as he possesses the law, claims the authority to be the guide (ὁδηγός), light (φῶς), educator (παιδευτός), teacher (διδάσκαλος). All these predicates refer to the communication of the Torah[40]. The motif of blindness/darkness and enlightenment (v.19)[41] is dependent on the correlation of law and wisdom[42]: both the Torah[43] and wisdom[44] are regarded as light. The motif of instruction (v.20a.b) presupposes this correlation as well: the functions of the educator and teacher are tasks of the wisdom teacher[45] and are here clearly related to the Jewish Torah teachers[46].

Hence, Rom 2,17-20 is a clear proof that Paul was familiar with, and prepared to apply, the correlation of law and wisdom. This passage is the only explicit (!) occurence of this correlation in the Pauline corpus.

13.3. Methodological Considerations

Having established Paul's familiarity with the correlation of law and wisdom we are now ready to inquire to what extent, and in what degree, this correlation affected Paul's theological concep-

---

40 Cf. O. Michel, *Römer*, p.129; E. Käsemann, *Römer*, p.66; U. Wilckens, *Römer*, 1, p.148.
41 For the rich Jewish background and the relevant material see H. Schlier, *Römerbrief*, p.129; U. Wilckens, *o.c.*, pp.148f.
42 Cf. H. Conzelmann, Art. "φῶς", *ThWNT* 9 (1973) 317,337; also U. Wilckens, *o.c.*, p.148 n.381 who relates ὁδηγός to the Jewish (rabbinic) conception of the law as the "way" or "halakhah": wisdom/Torah, possessed by the Jew, is the guide of the gentiles. Wilckens refers for this concept to Prov 2,12-15; 3,17; 4,11-12; 6,22-23; 8,20.22(LXX).34; Sir 6,26-27; SapSal 9,11; 10,10.17; Sib 3,194-195; En(eth) 105,1; Josephus Ap 2,41; Philo Abr 19.
43 Cf. Ps 19,9; 119,101.130; Sir 45,17; TLev 4,3; 18,3; 14,3-4; 19,1; TReu 3,8; SapSal 18,4; AntBibl 9,8; 11,1; etc.; 4Ezr 14,20-21; 10,22; ApcBar 17,4; 38,1-2; etc.
44 Cf. Qoh 2,13; 8,1; Sir 24,32; Bar 3,14; SapSal 7,20; TLev 18,3; AntBibl 23,7; 51,4.
45 Mentioned by U. Wilckens, *o.c.*, p.149 n.384.
46 Cf. O. Michel, *Römer*, p.129 who sees in v.20a.b a reference to the Jewish scribe who teaches the proselyte; cf. also H. Schlier, *Römerbrief*, p.85; C.E.B. Cranfield, *Romans*, 1, 1975, p.167; U. Wilckens, *Römer*, 1, p.149.

tions[47]. The first area of investigation is Pauline christology[48]. We do not intend to provide a survey of the contribution of recent research into Paul's christology[49]. We will delineate relevant perspectives of wisdom christology and of Christ's relationship with the law according to Paul in order to ascertain whether the correlation of law and wisdom exercises any function. The second area of our investigation deals with soteriological anthropology, i.e. with the Christian ethic in the context of Paul's theology. Here we attempt to answer the question whether Pauline ethics is determined by the fundamental identity of law and wisdom.

It is obvious that the scope of this projected procedure is so extensive that a historical exegesis of individual passages can be pursued only at strategic points of the discussion. We are conscious of the fact that this implies the danger of superficiality, especially with regard to pericopes like the Christ-hymns in Phil and Col, or Paul's awareness and conviction of pre-existence christol-

---

47 We base our investigation of Pauline theology on Gal, 1Thess, 1/2Cor, Rom, Phil, and Col. Regarding Col, the close relationship with the theology of the undisputed Pauline letters is generally recognized today; cf. E. Lohse, *Kolosser*, KEK 9/2, pp. 249-257; W.G. Kümmel, *Einleitung in das Neue Testament*, [18]1973, pp.298-305; E. Schweizer, *Kolosser*, EKK, 1976, pp.20f. The differences have been spelled out most recently by J. Gnilka, *Kolosserbrief*, HThK 10/1, 1980, pp.4-19. Recently E. Schweizer, o.c., pp.26f.; W.H. Ollrog, *Paulus und seine Mitarbeiter*, WMANT 50, 1979, pp.219-233,236-242; J. Gnilka, o.c., p.22 asserted that Timothy might have written Col. Many scholars defend Pauline authorship of Col; cf. W.G. Kümmel, o.c., pp.299-303 (lit. p.299 n.12; add J.A.T. Robinson, *Redating the New Testament*, 1976, p.62). — As regards Eph, only of secondary importance for our investigation, W.G. Kümmel, o.c., pp.315-320 gives a good summary of the arguments contra Pauline authorship. Recent major defenses of Pauline authorship of Eph include M. Barth, *Ephesians*, 1974, pp.3-50; A. van Roon, *The Authenticity of Ephesians*, 1974; J.A.T. Robinson, o.c., pp.63f. — The relative chronology of the Pauline Epistles has been discussed most recently by H.H. Schade, *Apokalyptische Christologie bei Paulus*, GThA 18, 1981, pp.173-190 who assumes as sequence: 1Thess, 1Cor, 2Cor, Gal, Rom, Phil. Many British scholars regard Gal as the earliest of Paul's extant letters (cf. F.F. Bruce, *Galatians*, 1982, p.55 n.56 lit.). The same chronological order — Gal, 1Thess, 1Cor, 2Cor, Rom — is also followed by H. Hübner, *Das Gesetz bei Paulus*, FRLANT 119, [3]1982 (cf. the remark on p.131).

48 As regards Paul's knowledge of Jesus see D.M. Stanley, "Pauline Allusions to the Sayings of Jesus", *CBQ* 23 (1961) 26-39; J. Blank, *Paulus und Jesus*, 1968; H.W. Kuhn, "Der irdische Jesus bei Paulus", *ZThK* 67 (1970) 295-320.

49 Cf. particularly J.D.G. Dunn, *Christology in the Making*, 1980 (with a comprehensive list of the relevant literature on pp.356-403); S. Kim, *Origin*, 1981, pp.100-268; H.H. Schade, *Apokalyptische Christologie*, 1981.

ogy[50]. In the discussion of secondary literature we will discuss the major and the more recent positions and contributions.

§14 Christ and Wisdom

In recent years, scholars focused more than before on traits in Paul's theology which make it rather probably that Paul took up significant theologoumena of Jewish wisdom theology in his presentation of christology. Scholars focus more and more on the influence, reception, and significance of the Jewish wisdom tradition in and for both the person and the teaching of Jesus and the Gospel traditions[51]. The discussion of a Pauline wisdom christol-

---

50 Cf. R. Hasenstab, *Modelle paulinischer Ethik: Beiträge zu einem Autonomiemodell aus paulinischem Geist*, 1977, p.149 who points out that, as a result of a "hermeneutische Grauzone" which exists between historical-critical exegesis and systematic theology, exegetical and systematic interests cannot be brought to congruence.

51 Cf. R. Bultmann, *The History of the Synoptic Tradition*, (^{2}1931), 1968, pp.69-108 ("Logia: Jesus as the Teacher of Wisdom"); T.Y. Mullins, "Jewish Wisdom Literature in the New Testament", *JBL* 68 (1949) 335-339; A. Feuillet, "Jésus et la Sagesse divine dans les évangiles synoptiques", *RB* 62 (1956) 161-196; idem, *Le Christ Sagesse de Dieu d'après les Épîtres Pauliniennes*, 1966, pp.386-388; W.A. Beardslee, "The Wisdom Tradition and the Synoptic Gospels", *JAAR* 35 (1967) 231-240; F. Christ, *Jesus Sophia: Die Sophia-Christologie bei den Synoptikern*, 1970; M.J. Suggs, *Wisdom, Christology and Law in Matthew's Gospel*, 1970; J.M. Robinson, "Logoi sophon: On the Gattung of Q", *The Future of our Religious Past*, FS R. Bultmann, 1971, pp.84-130; S. Schulz, *Q: Die Spruchquelle der Evangelisten*, 1972, pp.336-345; N. Perrin, "Wisdom and Apocalyptic in the Message of Jesus", *SBL Proceedings*, 2, 1972, pp.543-570; S. Aalen, "The Conceptions of Wisdom and Jesus' Christological Self-Consciousness" (Swedish), *SEA* 37/38 (1972/73) 35-46; R.G. Hamerton-Kelly, *Pre-existence, Wisdom, and the Son of Man*, SNTS MS 21, 1973, pp.22-102 passim; M.D. Johnson, "Reflections on a Wisdom Approach to Matthew's Christology", *CBQ* 36 (1974) 44-64; U. Luck, "Weisheit und Christologie in Mt 11,25-30", *WuD* 13 (1975) 35-51; J.M. Robinson, "Jesus as Sophos and Sophia: Wisdom Tradition and the Gospels", *Aspects of Wisdom*, ed. R.L. Wilken, 1975, pp.1-16; M. Hengel, *The Son of God*, 1976, p.74; R.A. Edwards, *A Theology of Q: Eschatology, Prophecy and Wisdom*, 1976, pp.58-79; D. Zeller, *Die weisheitlichen Mahnsprüche bei den Synoptikern*, 1977; idem, "Weisheitliche Überlieferung in der Predigt Jesu", *Religiöse Grunderfahrungen: Quellen und Gestalten*, ed. W. Strolz, 1977, pp.94-111; W. Grundmann, "Weisheit im Horizont des Reiches Gottes: Eine Studie zur Verkündigung Jesu nach der Spruchüberlieferung Q", *Die Kirche des Anfangs*, FS H. Schürmann, ed. R. Sch-

ogy is becoming increasingly lively as it is obvious that Paul must have been aware of the early traditions which linked Jesus and wisdom.

In this paragraph we will scrutinize these efforts at clarifying the sapiential elements and features of Paul's christology. After a brief survey of the main contributions and propositions, we will give a succinct exegetical and conceptual analysis of the relevant passages indicating the tradition-historical origins before we present the theological and hermeneutical evidence of wisdom christology in a more systematic manner.

14.1. Wisdom Christology in Recent Research

It seems that H. Windisch was the first scholar who attempted to demonstrate that Pauline christology has been decisively influenced by the Jewish wisdom tradition and that Paul clearly identified the pre-existent Christ with the Jewish divine wisdom[52].

In the subsequent discussion, some scholars attempted to clarify the process by which Paul came to describe Christ in terms of wisdom. W.D. Davies starts from the Jewish identification of Torah and wisdom and points out that, as Paul regarded Jesus as the 'new Torah', he ascribed to him the attributes of wisdom as well, thus asserting Christ's pre-existence and activity in creation[53].
S. Kim maintains that Paul described Christ in terms of wisdom as

---

nackenburg, 1977, pp.175-199; H.J. de Jonge, "Sonship, Wisdom, Infancy: Luke 2,41-51a", *NTS* 24 (1978) 317-354; F.W. Burnett, *The Testament of Jesus-Sophia: A Redaction-Critical Study of the Eschatological Discourse in Matthew*, 1979; P.E. Bonnard, "De la Sagesse personnifiée dans l'Ancien Testament à la Sagesse en personne dans le Nouveau", *BETL* 51 (1979) 136-139; M. Hengel, "Jesus als messianischer Lehrer der Weisheit und die Anfänge der Christologie", *Sagesse et Religion*, Colloque de Strasbourg Octobre 1976, 1979, pp.148-188; R. Riesner, *Jesus als Lehrer*, WUNT 2/7, 1981, pp.330-344; H. Gese, "Wisdom", *HBT* 3 (1981) 40-45.

52 H. Windisch, "Die göttliche Weisheit der Juden und die paulinische Christologie", *Neutestamentliche Studien*, FS G. Heinrici, ed. A. Deissmann, 1914, pp.220-234. The critique of Windisch's position by B. Botte, "La Sagesse et les origines de la christologie", *RSPT* 21 (1935) 385-417 is unfounded. The criticism of R. Scroggs, "Paul: ΣΟΦΟΣ and ΠΝΕΥΜΑΤΙΚΟΣ", *NTS* 14 (1967/68) 33 with n.1 stating that Paul's key christological motifs cannot be derived from wisdom concepts and that the issue of 'wisdom' is treated by Paul in any important way only in reaction to the situation in Corinth, is not valid. See our discussion below.

53 W.D. Davies, *Paul and Rabbinic Judaism*, 1948, ²1955, pp.147-176.

a result of the Damascus christophany where he became convinced that Jesus is the "image of God" and the Son of God[54]. H. Conzelmann suggests that Paul's reworking of wisdom theology and wisdom traditions should be linked with a school of Paul, located probably in Ephesus, in which 'wisdom' was methodically taught and discussed[55].

The second main focus in the discussion of Paul's wisdom christology is the conception of the pre-existence of Christ. Many scholars including E. Schweizer, R.G. Hamerton-Kelly, M. Hengel, H. Merklein, S. Kim and others assert that (Hellenistic) Jewish wisdom theology determined the context of the conceptual genesis of pre-existence christology[56]. The interpretation of the relevant pericopes and concepts by these scholars has been challenged most recently by J.D.G. Dunn, even though he acknowledges the fact that Paul undoubtedly attributed the role of wisdom to Christ[57].

The significance of wisdom theology for Paul's thinking has been further underlined with regard to the christological formula of the Son's sending into the world[58] and of Christ's mediation at

---

54 S. Kim, *Origin*, 1981, pp.114-131,161,257-260.
55 H. Conzelmann, "Paulus und die Weisheit", *NTS* 12 (1965/66) 231-244 (= *Schriftauslegung*, 1974, pp.177-190); also idem, "Die Schule des Paulus", *Theologia Crucis-Signum Crucis*, FS E. Dinkler, ed. C. Andresen et al., 1979, pp.85-96; followed by B.A. Pearson, "Hellenistic-Jewish Wisdom Speculation and Paul", *Aspects of Wisdom*, ed. R.L. Wilken, 1975, pp.43-66, here pp.43-45.
56 E. Schweizer, "Zur Herkunft der Präexistenzvorstellung bei Paulus", *EvTh* 19 (1959) 65-70 (= *Neotestamentica*, 1963 pp.105-109); idem, "Aufnahme und Korrektur jüdischer Sophiatheologie im Neuen Testament" (1962), *Neotestamentica*, pp.110-121; R.G. Hamerton-Kelly, *Pre-existence, Wisdom, and the Son of Man: A Study of the Idea of Pre-existence of the New Testament*, SNTS MS 21, 1973, p.192 and passim; M. Hengel, *The Son of God: The Origin of Christology and the History of Jewish-Hellenistic Religion*, 1976, pp.48-51,66-76; H. Merklein, "Zur Entstehung der urchristlichen Aussage vom präexistenten Sohn Gottes", *Zur Geschichte des Urchristentums*, ed. G. Dautzenberg et al., 1979, pp.33-62, followed by R. Riesner, "Präexistenz und Jungfrauengeburt", *ThBeitr* 12 (1981) 185f.; S. Kim, *o.c.*, pp.114-131,257-260 passim.
57 J.D.G. Dunn, *Christology*, 1980, pp.162-212 (on Christ and wisdom in Paul, cf. pp.176-196). Dunn thinks that it is at least questionable whether Paul thereby "intended to assert the pre-existence of Christ, or to affirm that Jesus was a divine being personally active in creation" (p.194), and that the relevant passages should not be understood as "ontological affirmations about Christ's eternal being" (p. 195).
58 E. Schweizer, "Zum religionsgeschichtlichen Hintergrund der 'Sendungsformel' Gal 4,4f; Rom 8,3f; John 3,16f; 1John 4,9" (1968), *Beiträge*, 1970, pp.83-95; M. Hengel, *Son*, pp.66-76.

creation[59]. The more general concept of the finality of Christ regarding God's purpose for man and for creation is also traced back to wisdom theology[60].

It was particularly A. van Roon who argued that Paul did not know or use wisdom christology[61]. U. Wilckens maintained in his dissertation that 'wisdom' as christological designation has to be attributed to the Corinthians and should hence be understood on the background and in the context of the gnostic conception of the redeemer figure, concluding that Paul's purely soteriological-theological understanding of wisdom excludes any essential relationship between Paul and wisdom christology[62]. Wilckens' view was sharply criticized[63], and recently Wilckens corrected his earlier opinion asserting that if we have to reckon with a wisdom christology at all, it is Paul's, that we cannot assume that the Corinthian opponents were gnostics, and that Paul's position is not always polemical but often positively argumentative[64].

The list of scholars who reckon now with Jewish wisdom theology as significant and directly influential matrix for Pauline conceptions of Christ is rather extensive[65]. Without entering into a de-

---

59 E. Schweizer, "Kolosser 1,15-20" (1969), *Beiträge*, pp.113-144.
60 A. Feuillet, *Christ Sagesse*, EB, 1966 stating that Paul's central idea is "le Christ par qui nous sommes sauvés et en qui nous vivons ... c'est cette même Sagesse de Dieu par laquelle et en laquelle aux origines tout fut créé" (p.275); J.D.G. Dunn, *Christology*, pp.176-196 passim; S. Kim, *Origin*, pp.114-131, 257-260.
61 A. van Roon, "The Relation between Christ and the Wisdom of God according to Paul", *NovTest* 16 (1974) 207-239. J.D.G. Dunn, o.c., p.325 n.19 remarks that van Roon only plays down or ignores the most obvious parallels in the wisdom literature.
62 U. Wilckens, *Weisheit und Torheit: Eine exegetisch-religionsgeschichtliche Untersuchung zu 1.Kor. 1 und 2*, BHTh 26, 1959, pp.5-96,205-224 (cf. pp.97-213 for the religion-historical material), also idem, in *ThWNT* 7 (1964) 518-525.
63 Cf. M.H. Scharlemann in *CBQ* 21 (1959) 190; K. Koester in *Gnomon* 33 (1961) 590-595; C. Colpe in *MPTh* 52 (1963) 489-494; K. Niederwimmer, "Erkennen und Lieben: Gedanken zum Verhältnis von Gnosis und Agape im ersten Korintherbrief", *KuD* 11 (1965) 80-82 with n.11; K. Prümm, "Zur neutestamentlichen Gnosis-Problematik: Gnostischer Hintergrund und Lehreinschlag in den beiden Eingangskapiteln von 1Kor?", *ZKTh* 87 (1965) 399-442; 88 (1966) 1-50; R. Scroggs, "Paul", *NTS* 14 (1967/68) 33-55; R. Baumann, *Mitte und Norm des Christlichen*, NTA NF 5, 1968, pp.72-78,116ff.
64 U. Wilckens, "Zu 1Kor 2,1-16", *Theologia Crucis-Signum Crucis*, FS E. Dinkler, ed. C. Andresen et al., pp.501-537 (= "Das Kreuz Christi als die Tiefe der Weisheit Gottes: Zur 1. Kor 2,1-16", *Paolo a una chiesa divisa*, ed. L. de Lorenzi, 1980, pp.43-81).
65 Cf. E.B. Allo, "Sagesse et pneuma dans la première épître aux Corinthiens", *RB*

tailed analysis of the various convictions and assumptions regarding Paul's wisdom christology which both complement and contradict each other at different points, suffice it to say that it is safe to count upon the fact that Paul's theology implies a wisdom christology[66] which bears, in one way or another, on the christological conceptions of pre-existence, mediation at creation and redemption, the sending of the Son, and the "image of God". Before we can describe the systematic evidence we first must analyze the relevant passages.

14.2. Exegetical-Conceptual Evidence

14.2.1. Gal 4.4. The phrase ἐξαπέστειλεν ὁ θεὸς τὸν υἱὸν αὐτοῦ marks the beginning of a christological-soteriological formula[67].

---

43 (1934) 321-417; M.M. Bourke, "The Eucharist and Wisdom in First Corinthians", *Studiorum Paulinorum Congressus I*, 1963, pp.367-381; P.E. Bonnard, *La Sagesse en personne annoncée et venue: Jésus Christ*, 1966, 133-140; U. Luck, "Weisheit und Leiden", *ThLZ* 92 (1967) 253-258; F. Hahn, "Methodenprobleme einer Christologie des Neuen Testaments", *VuF* 15 (1970) 16; E. Schüssler Fiorenza, "Wisdom Mythology and the Christological Hymns of the New Testament", *Aspects of Wisdom*, ed. R.L. Wilken, 1975, pp.17-41; B.A. Pearson, "Hellenistic-Jewish Wisdom Speculation and Paul", *o.c.*, pp.43-66; K.G. Sandelin, *Die Auseinandersetzung mit der Weisheit in 1. Korinther 15*, 1976; R.S. Barbour, "Creation, Wisdom and Christ", *Creation, Christ and Culture*, FS T.F. Torrance, ed. R.W.A. McKinney, 1976, pp.22-42; idem, "Wisdom and the Cross in 1 Corinthians 1 and 2", *Theologia Crucis*, 1979, pp.57-71; F.F. Bruce, *Paul*, pp.123f.; P.E. Bonnard, "Sagesse", *BETL* 51 (1979) 139-145; W.G. Kümmel, *Die Theologie des Neuen Testaments*, [4]1980, pp.107, 145; J.N. Aletti, *Colossiens 1,15-20: Genre et exégèse du texte. Fonction de la thématique sapientielle*, AnBibl 91, 1981, particularly pp. 141-182; G. Gese, "Wisdom, Son of Man, and the Origins of Christology", *HBT* 3 (1981) 23-57. See also E. Brandenburger, *Fleisch und Geist: Paulus und die dualistische Weisheit*, WMANT 29, 1968, passim.

66 Using the term 'wisdom christology', we do not imply that there existed independent 'christologies' of different Christian communities. Cf. M. Hengel, *Son*, 1976, p.57. — Earlier studies on NT christology did not include a discussion of wisdom christology; cf. O. Cullmann, *The Christology of the New Testament*, 1959; F. Hahn, *Christologische Hoheitstitel: Ihre Geschichte im frühen Christentum*, FRLANT 83, 1963 (= [4]1974); also J.C. Beker, *Paul the Apostle: The Triumph of God in Life and Thought*, 1980.

67 Many scholars assume a pre-Pauline origin; cf. E. Schweizer, "Hintergrund", *Beiträge*, p.94; idem, *ThWNT* 8 (1969) 376; L. Goppelt, *Theologie*, 2, 1976, pp.400-404; F. Mussner, *Galaterbrief*, p.272; H.D. Betz, *Galatians*, p.206, and others. But see S. Kim, *Origin*, pp.112-114 who argues for Pauline origin. On the christological-eschatological meaning of Gal 4,4 in its context cf. P. von der Osten-Sacken, "Das

Even though the language of this phrase does not seem to convey necessarily the concept of the Son's pre-existence[68] the concept is nevertheless in all probability implied[69]: the sending of God's Son into earthly existence (note the following (!) aor. γενόμενον ἐκ γυναικός)[70] presupposes the Son's being prior to his existence as man, especially in view of the fact that Paul clearly regarded Jesus as divine[71]. This is confirmed by the close parallel in SapSal 9,10 where wisdom is described as dwelling with God even before creation and as being sent by God from heaven and from the throne of his glory: the verb ἐξαποστέλλειν which Paul uses only in Gal 4,4.6[72] occurs also in SapSal 9,10 (with regard to wisdom) and the link between the sending of the Son and the sending of the Spirit in Gal 4,4.6 is parallel to the sending of both wisdom and the spirit in SapSal 9,10.17[73].

If SapSal 9,10 or the Jewish wisdom theology in general[74] provide indeed the conceptual (not necessarily linguistic) background

---

paulinische Verständnis des Gesetzes im Spannungsfeld von Eschatologie und Geschichte", EvTh 37 (1977) 549-587, here 551-560.

68 Cf. H.D. Betz, *o.c.*, pp.206f.; J.D.G. Dunn, *Christology*, pp.38-44,46 taking it as a possibility which, however, he does not take to be likely; also F.F. Bruce, *Galatians*, p.195.

69 Cf. E. Schweizer, "Herkunft", *Neotestamentica*, pp.108f.; idem, *ThWNT* 8 (1969) 376f., 385,388; H. Schlier, *Galaterbrief*, p.196; G. Hamerton-Kelly, *Pre-existence*, p.112; M. Hengel, *Son*, pp.10f.; L. Goppelt, *o.c.*, pp.400f.; P. Stuhlmacher, "Zur paulinischen Christologie" (1974), *Aufsätze*, 1981, p.213; F. Mussner, *o.c.*, p. 272; F. Froitzheim, *Christologie und Eschatologie bei Paulus*, 1979, pp.50-54; W.G. Kümmel, *Theologie*, p.151; R. Riesner, "Präexistenz", *ThBeitr* 12 (1981) 181; S. Kim, *Origin*, p.81; F.F. Bruce, *o.c.*, p.195.

70 This phrase refers to Christ's birth "out of" a human mother; cf. H.D. Betz, *o.c.*, p.207 with n.49. It is difficult to grasp the logic of Dunn's interpretation of this phrase when he states that "γενόμενον (born) refers to Jesus as one who had been born, not necessarily to his birth as such ... the reference is simply to Jesus' ordinary humanness, not to his birth" (*o.c.*, p.40). Surely, ordinary humanness not only implies, but is dependent upon birth!

71 See Paul's use of the κύριος title for Jesus Christ, and his presentation of soteriology in general; see also Phil 2,6.

72 Correcting S. Kim, *Origin*, p.118 who states that Paul uses it only in Gal 4,4.

73 Cf. E. Schweizer, "Herkunft", p.108; idem, "Hintergrund", p.92; idem, *ThWNT* 8 (1969) 377; G. Hamerton-Kelly, *Pre-existence*, p.111; L. Goppelt, *Theologie*, 2, p.400. Note J.D.G. Dunn, *Christology*, pp.39f. who attempts to establish Jesus' way of speaking about himself as the more plausible background of Gal 4,4 (referring to Mk 9,37; 12,6; Mt 15,24; Lk 4,18).

74 Cf. F. Mussner, *Galaterbrief*, pp.272f.; S. Kim, *o.c.*, pp.118f.; H. Merklein, "Entstehung", p.34 and passim; also H.D. Betz, *Galatians*, p.206 n.41; F.F. Bruce, *Galatians*, p.195.

for the statement in Gal 4,4, it would be implied that the Son is to be identified with wisdom.

> This is acknowledged by Dunn[75] who then proceeds, however, to point out (1) that this would not be a natural inference for Paul's readers since *sophia* is feminine and was never called God's 'Son' before, and (2) that Paul's references to Christ's identity with wisdom are often linked with cosmic contexts (1Cor 8,6; Col 1,15-17). It should be noted, however, that 1Cor 1,24.30 where Paul explicitly identifies Christ with God's wisdom belongs to a definitely soteriological context (as Gal 4,4!). The fact that 1Cor was written after Gal does not prove that the equation was made for the first time by Paul in 1Cor 1,24.30. And, further, the argument of the feminine character of 'wisdom' carries no decisive weight since Paul describes Christ in terms of (still fem.) wisdom in many other passages. This suggests that the correlation of wisdom and Christ does by no means necessitate the total formal identification of these two 'entities', especially since *sophia* is not a genuine hypostasis or distinctive heavenly being, but rather a conception or way of theologizing.

It is obvious, however, that Gal 4,4 is not an explicit (!) statement of wisdom christology. At the most it presupposes conceptions — the divine sending of the pre-existent mediator of salvation — which would be significant in wisdom christology.

14.2.2. 1Cor 1,24.30. The statements that Christ is θεοῦ σοφία (1,24) and σοφία ἀπό θεοῦ (1,30) express clearly and explicitly a link between Christ and wisdom[76]. In order to understand this link, several general observations have to be made.

> The discussion about the nature of the opposition in Corinth is still going on. It is widely recognized today that one should not look for a Gnostic background of Paul's opponents[77]. Most scholars interpret 1Cor today rather on the background of Jewish wisdom theology[78]. The subject of the divisions in the Corinthian church is usually related to the treatise on wisdom and folly in 1Cor 1-4, but this relation has not yet

---

75 Cf. J.D.G. Dunn, *o.c.*, p.39.
76 On 1Cor 1,30 see most recently U. Schnelle, *Gerechtigkeit und Christusgegenwart: Vorpaulinische und paulinische Tauftheologie*, GThA 24, 1983, pp.44-46 who relates this verse to traditional baptismal terminology without discussing the relevance of wisdom theology/christology here.
77 Cf. H.R. Balz, *Methodische Probleme der neutestamentlichen Christologie*, WMANT 25, 1967, pp.157f.; R. Baumann, *Mitte und Norm*, pp.280f.; K.D. Sandelin, *Auseinandersetzung*, pp.91-105,149-153; M. Hengel, *Son*, pp.76 n.133; U. Wilckens, "Kreuz Christi", pp.68-81; R. McL. Wilson, "Nag Hammadi and the New Testament", *NTS* 28 (1982) 297 ("on the line of development which led from Wisdom speculation into Gnosticism"); G. Sellin, "Das 'Geheimnis' der Weisheit und das Rätsel der 'Christuspartei' (zu 1Kor 1-4)", *ZNW* 73 (1982) 71,97.
78 Cf. most recently J.A. Davis, *Wisdom and Spirit: An Investigation of 1 Corinthians 1,18-3,20 against the Background of Jewish Sapiential Tradition in the Hellenistic-Roman Period*, Ph.D.Diss. Nottingham, 1981, particularly pp.59-151.

been satisfactorily clarified[79]. - Paul's terminology in 1Cor both in general and as regards the use of σοφία is also still disputed. It is not clear whether or to what extent Paul took up the terminology of the opponents, or was influenced by their terminology, or altered the meaning of their relevant key terms[80]. As regards the term and concept of σοφία, the issue between the Corinthians and Paul is also still debated: 'wisdom' has been explained (1) on the basis of the Greek philosophical tradition, (2) as esoteric truth revealed in the utterances of the pneumatics, or (3) as related to Jewish wisdom theology[81]. It is clear, however, that 'wisdom' in 1Cor 1-3 is not understood as a (pre-existent) divine hypostasis[82].

It depends on one's understanding of these complex issues how the statements on Christ as linked with wisdom are related to the progress of thought in 1Cor 1-3[83]. The majority of scholars today acknowledge the fact that in 1,24.30 Jesus Christ is credited with the functions of salvation which the Jewish wisdom tradition ascribed to wisdom[84].

J.A. Davis asserts that Paul's concern in 1Cor 1-3 is shaped by his attempt to depreciate the value of a claim to the Corinthians' Torah-centristic wisdom by giving a new locus to God's wisdom in 1,24.30: in Christ a new wisdom has come into being, providing life, holiness, and redemption, and replacing the Torah as the definite locus of

---

79 Cf. E. Best, "The Power and the Wisdom of God: 1 Corinthians 1,18-25", *Paolo a una chiesa divisa*, ed. L. de Lorenzi, 1980, p.10. For the most recent discussion of this problem see G. Sellin, "Geheimnis", *ZNW* 73 (1982) 69-96 who maintains that there was probably only the rivalry between Paul's and Apollos' 'party', with the 'Christ party' expressing the self-understanding of Apollos. As to the often attempted reconstruction of the Corinthians' theology, future research should take into account the four relevant criteria established by U. Wilckens, "Kreuz Christi", 1980, pp.60f.
80 Cf. J.M. Reese, "Paul Proclaims the Wisdom of the Cross", *BTB* 9 (1979) 149.
81 Cf. E. Best, *a.c.*, pp.19-22. Regarding the term σοφία λόγου (1,17) see now R.A. Horsley, "Wisdom of Word and Words of Wisdom in Corinth", *CBQ* 39 (1977) 224-239; E. Best, *a.c.*, pp.13-16; U. Wilckens, *a.c.*, pp.59-67.
82 Cf. H. Conzelmann, "Paulus und die Weisheit", p.183; H. Lietzmann, *Korinther*, p.10; H. Conzelmann, *Erster Korintherbrief*, p.10; E. Best, *a.c.*, p.35; J.D.G. Dunn, *Christology*, p.80; H. Weder, *Das Kreuz Jesu bei Paulus*, FRLANT 125, 1981, p.155 n.124. Contra R.G. Hamerton-Kelly, *Pre-existence*, pp.112f.
83 For a good analysis of the context of 1Cor 1-2 cf. F. Froitzheim, *Christologie*, pp. 66-77; U. Wilckens, *a.c.*, pp.43-46; G. Sellin, *a.c.*, pp. 72f. Unfortunately J.A. Davis, *Wisdom*, 1982, does not discuss these issues but simply presupposes a Corinthian "Torah-centristic wisdom".
84 Cf. W.D. Davies, *Paul*, pp.154f.; M. Hengel, *Son*, p.74; P. Stuhlmacher, "Achtzehn Thesen zur paulinischen Kreuzestheologie" (1976), *Aufsätze*, pp.202f.; R.S. Barbour, "Wisdom and the Cross", 1979, p.68 (with caution); P.E. Bonnard, "Sagesse", *BETL* 51 (1979) 140; J.D.G. Dunn, *o.c.*, pp.167,177f.; S. Kim, *Origin*, p.117; E. Best, *a.c.*, p.35 (limiting wisdom here to that "which meets the real need of the Greek who seeks wisdom ... Christ is the meaning of existence and the meaning of God").

divine wisdom[85]. It is correct that Paul presents Christ as the new and definite locus of wisdom. But it is without exegetical foundation when Davis states that, as a result of Paul's effort to attack the Corinthians' 'Torah-centristic wisdom', the Torah is replaced: (1) Paul does not polemize against the Torah in the context of 1Cor 1,3, and (2) a Torah-centricity of wisdom at Corinth cannot be established from the text. The latter cannot be proved with the titles in 1Cor 1,20, and M. Hengel cannot be adduced as support either[86].

Thus, according to Paul the crucified Christ is the wisdom of God[87], "the embodiment of God's plan of salvation and the measure and fullest expression of God's continuing wisdom and power"[88].

In the next large pericope on wisdom in 1Cor 2,6-16 Paul wants to establish why the λόγος τοῦ σταυροῦ is the true λόγος σοφίας, i.e. why and how the content of wisdom is God's plan of salvation with its climax of "die im Kreuz Christi eröffnete Heilswirklichkeit"[89]. As Paul makes no further explicit use of Christ's identification with wisdom in this passage[90], there is no need to discuss it here[91].

14.2.3. 1Cor 8,6. It is recognized that this verse contains pre-Pauline and pre-Christian elements[92], but at the same time it has been pointed out that Paul's contribution as regards the actual formulation should not be underestimated since there is no real

---

85 J.A. Davis, *Wisdom*, pp.67f.,74.
86 Contra J.A. Davis, *o.c.*, stating that Hengel believes that 1Cor 1,24.30 is most naturally understood against a Torah-centristic background. However, M. Hengel, *Son*, p.74 simply states that Paul's appeal to the Corinthians (!) in 1Cor 1,30 "in essentials embraces all the functions of salvation which the pious Jews ascribed to Wisdom-Torah", without identifying the Corinthians with these "pious Jews".
87 The stress is on θεοῦ; cf. U. Wilckens, "Kreuz Christi", p.99; H. Weder, *Kreuz Christi*, p.155 n.124.
88 J.D.G. Dunn, *Christology*, p.179.
89 U. Wilckens, *a.c.*, p.59; cf. G. Sellin, "Geheimnis", *ZNW* 73 (1982) 82f.
90 Cf. R.S. Barbour, "Wisdom and the Cross", p.67.
91 Cf. J.A. Davis, *o.c.*, pp.79-151 who understands 1Cor 2,6-17 to contain Paul's teaching on wisdom: "Paul sets forth something of the character of the new sophia which has been brought into being as a result of God's action" (p.151), pointing out its christological essence.
92 Cf. K. Wengst, *Christologische Formeln und Lieder des Urchristentums*, StNT 7, 1972, pp.136-141; R. Kerst, "1Kor 8,6: Ein vorpaulinisches Taufbekenntnis?" *ZNW* 66 (1975) 130-139; R.A. Horsley, "The Background of the Confessional Formula in 1Kor 8,6", *ZNW* 69 (1978) 130-135; J. Murphy-O'Connor, "1Cor VIII, 6: Cosmology or Soteriology?", *RB* 85 (1978) 253-267; J.D.G. Dunn, *Christology*, p.179. Regarding Stoic parallels cf. E. Norden, *Agnostos Theos*, 1913, pp.240-250, 347f.; H. Conzelmann, *Korinther*, p.171f.; R. Kerst, *a.c.*, pp.131f. As regards the unity of 1Cor 8-10 cf. now M. Bouttier, "1Co 9-10 considéré du point de vue de son unité", *Freedom and Love*, ed. L. de Lorenzi, 1981, pp.205-225.

parallel to Paul's affirmation here⁹³. Paul's statement extends the Jewish monotheistic confession εἷς θεός to the double confession εἷς θεός-εἷς κύριος⁹⁴. Paul stresses the essential unity of creation (ἐξ οὗ τὰ πάντα ... δι᾽ οὗ τὰ πάντα, v.6b.d) and salvation (ἡμεῖς δι᾽ αὐτοῦ, v.6d) since those Corinthian Christians who have knowledge should be aware of their responsibility when they deal with created things⁹⁵. The phrase εἷς κύριος Ἰησοῦς Χριστὸς δι᾽ οὗ τὰ πάντα καὶ ἡμεῖς δι᾽ αὐτοῦ expresses the conviction that Jesus Christ as Lord is the mediator of both creation and salvation (as the new creation!)⁹⁶.

> Dunn's attempt to make the assumption plausible that Paul does not comment on the act of creation in the past "but rather about creation as believers see it now" (p.181) does not convince: (1) It is rather unlikely that Paul's readers in the 1st century would have differentiated between the past act of creation and the present interpretation of creation without being interested in the former; (2) Christ's mediation at creation (v.6d) is formally parallel to God's activity in creation (v.6b) and should therefore also be understood in the absolute sense (note the κύριος title in v.6c!); (3) Paul refers by no means to the believers' view of salvation but rather to their responsibility to God the Creator (ἡμεῖς εἰς αὐτόν, v.6b) and to their salvation through Christ (ἡμεῖς δι᾽ αὐτόν, v.6d); (4) the presence of pre-Pauline elements from Jewish monotheism and Stoic cosmology confirms that Paul does indeed comment on the past action of creation.

It appears to be beyond doubt that Paul consciously describes Christ in wisdom language: Christ, as is divine wisdom in the Jewish sapiential theology, is the creative and salvational power and action of God⁹⁷. The description of Christ as mediator of creation

---

93 Cf. A. Feuillet, *Christ Sagesse*, pp.69-81 (Paul adapted an older confession); W. Thüsing, *Per Christum in Deum*, NTA NF 1, 1965, pp.225-232 (formulated by Paul and used in proclamation); H. Langkammer, "Literarische und theologische Einzelstücke in 1 Kor 8,6", *NTS* 17 (1971) 193-197 (composed ad hoc from older individual elements); cf. also R.S. Barbour, "Creation", p.30 with n.5; J.D.G. Dunn, *o.c.*, pp.179,181.
94 Regarding the monotheistic formula cf. C.H. Giblin, "Three Monotheistic Texts in Paul", *CBQ* 37 (1975) 527-247, here 529-537; J. Murphy-O'Connor, "Freedom of the Ghetto", *Freedom and Love*, 1981, pp.25-27.
95 Cf. J.D.G. Dunn, *o.c.*, pp.180,329 (arguing contra J. Murphy-O. Connor, *a.c.*, who asserts an exclusively soteriological meaning). Note also the views of F. Hahn and R. Pesch in the discussion of Murphy-O'Connor's paper (*o.c.*, pp.42f.).
96 This is generally recognized; cf. H. Lietzmann, *Korinther*, p.37; A. Feuillet, *o.c.*, p.78; H. Langkammer, *a.c.*, pp.196f.; R.G. Hamerton-Kelly, *Pre-existence*, p.130; R.S. Barbour, *a.c.*, pp.30f.; idem, "Wisdom", p.69; C. Senft, *1 Corinthiens*, 1979, p.111.
97 Most scholars agree that Paul describes Christ in terms of the Jewish wisdom theology; cf. E. Schweizer, "Herkunft", p.106; A. Feuillet, *Christ Sagesse*, pp.78-82; H.

which seems to be the natural consequence from his identification with wisdom implies or presupposes a pre-existence christology[98].

14.2.4. 1Cor 10,4. This verse belongs to Paul's aggadic midrash on Ex 13,21 (cloud); 14,21-22 (sea); 16,4.14-18 (manna); 17,6; Num 20,7-14 (spring)[99] which Paul uses in order to substantiate his warning to see the danger of presumption in view of apparent privileges[100]. The phrase ἡ πέτρα δὲ ἦν ὁ Χριστός[101] is explained by virtually all commentators in the light of the Jewish Hellenistic wisdom tradition in whose Exodus exegesis σοφία played a significant role[102]. In SapSal 10,17-18; 11,4 σοφία is described as having guided and protected the Israelites in the wilderness who drank from the "flinty rock" (πέτρα ἀκρότομος). Philo (All 2,86; Det 115-8) explicitly equates this rock (ἀκρότομος πέτρα) with σοφία (and λόγος).

> In the Palestinain Jewish exegesis, the "rock" became a peripatetic or wandering rock which followed the Israelites and which is then linked with the *shekhinah* of Yahweh (cf. tSuk 3,11ff.; TO ad Num 21,19-20; cf. AntBibl 10,7; 11,5). This is the background for the πνευματική ἀκολουθοῦσα πέτρα of 1Cor 10,4.

The fact that the interpretations of Philo and Paul differ as re-

---

Conzelmann, *Korintherbrief*, p.172 with n.49; P. Stuhlmacher, "Christologie", *Aufsätze*, p.213; R.S. Barbour, "Wisdom", p.68; F. Froitzheim, *Christologie*, pp.165, 167,182f.; H. Gese, "Wisdom", *HBT* 3 (1981) 46; J.M. Reese, "Christ as Wisdom Incarnate", *BTB* 11 (1982) 45f.; also H.F. Weiss, "Schöpfung in Christus: Zur Frage der christologischen Begründung der Schöpfungstheologie", *Zeichen der Zeit* 31 (1977) 434f. Pace G. Sellin, "Geheimnis", *ZNW* 73 (1982) 96.

98 Cf. E. Schweizer, *a.c.*, p.106; H. Conzelmann, *o.c.*, p.172; P. Stuhlmacher, *a.c.*, p.213; E. Froitzheim, *o.c.*, pp.50,54; H.D. Betz, *Galatians*, p.206 n. 47; S. Kim, *Origin*, p.119; J.M. Reese, *a.c.*, p.46.

99 Cf. H. Conzelmann, *o.c.*, p.194; R.G. Hamerton-Kelly, *Pre-existence*, p.131; F. Hahn, "Teilhabe am Heil und Gefahr des Abfalls: Eine Auslegung von 1Kor 10,1-22", *Freedom and Love*, 1981, pp.149-171, here 154-158.

100 Recently R.L. Jeske, "The Rock was Christ: The Ecclesiology of 1Corinthians 10", *Kirche*, FS G. Bornkamm, ed. D. Lührmann et al., 1980, pp.245-255 attempted to demonstrate that the scopus of 1Cor 10 is the ecclesiology of the Corinthians which Paul comments upon and adjusts.

101 Those who take 1Cor 10 to belong to the Corinthians' exegesis and theology regard 10,4b as Pauline; cf. U. Luz, *Das Geschichtsverständnis des Paulus*, 1968, pp.118f.; R.L. Jeske, *a.c.*, p.246. M. Hengel, *Son*, p.73 attributes the exegesis of 10,1-4 to non-Pauline Greek speaking Jewish Christians since it is not typically Pauline.

102 Cf. H. Lietzmann, *Korinther*, p.45; H. Conzelmann, *Korintherbrief*, p.196; U. Luz, *o.c.*, pp.11–119; M. Hengel, *o.c.*, pp.72f.; R.L. Jeske, *a.c.*, p.246; W.F. Orr, J.A. Walther, *I Corinthians*, 1976, p.245.

gards the details of the allegorical application proves that there is a common tradition which linked the rock with wisdom. It is obvious, therefore, that in 1Cor 10 Paul interprets Christ in terms of[103] the Jewish divine wisdom which was regarded as mediator of (creation and) God's salvation in the history of Israel[104]. This means that Christ's pre-existence is implied here as well[105]: Christ as mediator of God's saving revelation accompanied Israel in the desert.

14.2.5. Rom 10,6-7. This passage contains Paul's second quotation contrasting Moses with the righteousness by faith. The quotation is based on Deut 30,12-14 which is modified in various ways[106] with the main goal of eliminating all references to the

---

103 A.T. Hanson, *Jesus in the Old Testament*, 1965, pp.16-23 attempts to refute the view that 10,3-4 is a typological exegesis, arguing for a relation of identity.

104 Most scholars agree that Paul, here, attributes to Christ functions of Jewish divine wisdom thus describing Christ in terms of wisdom; Cf. E. Schweizer, "Herkunft", p.106; W.D. Davies, *Paul*, p.153; A. Feuillet, *Christ Sagesse*, pp. 103-109; K. Romaniuk, "Livre", NTS 14 (1967/68) 510f.; H. Conzelmann, *Korintherbrief*, p.196; R.G. Hamerton-Kelly, *Pre-existence*, pp.131f.; M. Hengel, *Son*, pp.15,72f.; F. Froitzheim, *Christologie*, p.54 n.136; C. Senft, *1 Corinthiens*, p.129; R.L. Jeske, "Rock", p.248; S. Kim, *Origin*, pp.116f. Contra J.D.G. Dunn, *Christology*, p.184 who maintains that despite Paul's possible awareness of Philo's identification of the rock with wisdom, Paul wanted to say that as the rock was wisdom in the Alexandrian allegory, so the rock was Christ in the Christian typology. However, since Paul obviously identified Christ with divine wisdom in other contexts (explicitly acknowledged by Dunn) it is difficult to see how Paul could say "the rock was Christ" without implying Christ's correlation with wisdom at the same time if he was indeed aware of the Alexandrian Exodus exegesis, which is likely.

105 Cf. E. Schweizer, *a.c.*, p.106; O. Cullmann, Art. "πέτρα", ThWNT 6 (1959) 97; A. Feuillet, *o.c.*, p.106; C.K.Barrett,*1 Corinthians*, p.223; H. Conzelmann, *o.c.*, p.196; A.T. Hanson, *Studies in Paul's Technique and Theology*, 1974, p.149; R.G. Hamerton-Kelly, *o.c.*, pp.131f.; M. Hengel, *o.c.*, p.72; C. Senft, *o.c.*, p.129; R.L. Jeske, *a.c.*, p.248; S. Kim, *Origin*, pp.116f.; F. Hahn, "Teilhabe", 1981, p.156 n.24 (also pp.190,201 in the discussion). Contra J.D.G. Dunn, *o.c.*, pp.183f. who suggests that one should understand this passage not as an allegory of past realities but rather as a typological allegory of present spiritual realities. However, the (durative) imperfecta in the context (note ἐγενήθησαν in v.6 and συνέβαινεν in v.11!) serve to describe the events in their progress and duration (BDR § 327.1), which confirms that 10,1-4 is indeed an allegory of past events. The imperfect in v.4b which is used instead of the pure exegetical praesens (cf. 1QS 8,7; CD 20,3; Acts 4,11 which are not discussed by Dunn, *o.c.*, p.330 n.78) is therefore not symbolical (Dunn gives no example of an imperfect being used as interpretative key in an allegory). The real presence of Christ in the wilderness is the systematic presupposition of the whole exegesis; cf. H. Conzelmann, *o.c.*, p.196.

106 Cf. O. Michel, *Römerbrief*, pp.324,328; E. Käsemann, *Römer*, p.278; U. Wil-

Torah. Where Deut 30 speaks about the law, Paul speaks about Christ: Christ has not to be sought in heaven or hades[107] but is "near" in the proclamation of the kerygma. Scholars have noted that Paul does not use the christological interpretative elements of 10,6-7 with the pattern of humiliation and exaltation elsewhere (except in Phil 2,6-11)[108], as he normally prefers to speak of the cross and the resurrection. This fact has prompted several scholars to assume that Paul took over the quotation from Deut 30, together with its interpretation, from the early Christian tradition and that this tradition is rooted in the broad Jewish tradition-historical context of sapiential concepts transferred to the Torah[109]. The parallel with Bar 3,29-30 is striking where Deut 30,12-13 is interpreted in terms of wisdom[110] and has therefore often been used as substantiation of the assumption that Paul implies here the identification of Christ with divine wisdom: Paul replaced wisdom with Christ as the object or person searched for[111].

Dunn argues that the identification Christ-wisdom depends on the hypothesis that Paul assumed that his readers would recognize the Baruch allusion to wisdom and would thus see the implied identification (p.185). He states that in this case the envisaged interpretative equation becomes "a little complex" (ibid.): Christ=the 'commandment' (Deut 30,11)=wisdom (Baruch's interpretation). Dunn prefers the alternative: as different schools of Judaism interpreted Deut 30,11-14 differently, apply-

---

ckens, *Römer*, 2, 1980, pp.224f. C.E.B. Cranfield, *Romans*, 2, 1979, p.524 rightly points out that we have here not an arbitrary typology but "true interpretation in depth". Concerning Paul's use of the *pesher* method cf. U. Wilckens, o.c., p.225 with n.1005.

107 The pre-existence and incarnation of Christ do not seem to be implied here; cf. E. Schweizer, "Hintergrund", p.94; E. Käsemann, *Römer*, p.278; J.D.G. Dunn, *Christology*, pp.184-187; differently C.K. Barrett, *Romans*, p.199; C.E.B. Cranfield, *Romans*, 2, p.525. Cf. R.G. Hamerton-Kelly, *Pre-existence*, who does not discuss this passage.
108 Cf. E. Käsemann, o.c., pp.278f.; U. Wilckens, *Römer*, 2, p.226.
109 Cf. recently M.J. Suggs, " 'The Word is Near You': Rom 10,6-10 within the Purpose of the Letter", 1967, pp.304-312; E. Käsemann, o.c., pp.278f.; U. Wilckens, o.c., p.226. Not seen by M. Black, "The Christological Use of the Old Testament in the New Testament", *NTS* 18 (1971/72) 9 who assumes a Jewish midrash on the Torah as (exclusive) background. As regards the possibility of a link between Christ and Torah in this pericope see infra, p.292 n.319.
110 Cf. E. Schweizer, "Herkunft", p.107; A. Feuillet, *Christ Sagesse*, pp.325f.; U. Luz, *Geschichtsverständnis*, p.92; E. Käsemann, o.c., pp.279f.; J.D.G. Dunn, o.c., p.185f; G.T. Sheppard, *Wisdom*, pp.90-93,101.
111 Cf. H. Windisch, "Weisheit", p.223; B.A. Pearson, "Wisdom Speculation", p.62 n.20; M. Black, a.c., p.9; E. Käsemann, o.c., p.280; S. Kim, *Origin*, pp.117,130 (answering the objection of W.D. Davies, *Paul*, p.154).

ing it to wisdom (Bar 3,29-30) or to the Torah (Targum Neofiti), so Paul applied it to Christ. Now, it should be noted that Philo refers to Deut 30,11-14 seven times[112] interpreting it in terms of τὸ ἀγαθόν (Post 84-88; Mut 236-239; Som 2,180; Praem 80-81), ἡ ἀρετή (Quod omnis 68), and the moral admonitions of the law which can be fulfilled (SpecLeg 1,301; Virt 183-184; also Praem 80-81). It should be noted that Praem 80-81, which combines the scopus of "the good" and of the observable commandments, highlights in the same context σοφία, and that both "the good" and "virtue" are linked by Philo with wisdom (cf. Her 98 and All 1,103; Virt 8; VitMos 76). This means that the Jewish tradition which interpreted Deut 30,12-13 in terms of wisdom is predominant. There are no early examples for the application of this passage to the Torah.

As Rom 10,6-7 can well be understood in terms of wisdom christology, Paul says here in effect that Christ as wisdom is, although not present on earth, still not hidden or inaccessible but "near" (10,8 using Deut 30,14) in the proclamation of the kerygma which speaks of the righteousness by faith.

14.2.6. Rom 11,33-36. There is a broad consensus in scholarship concerning the literary analysis and tradition-historical background of this Pauline hymn[113]. As it is not necessary for our purposes to enter into a detailed exegesis, suffice it to say that the three questions in vv.34-35 relate in reverse order to the three parallel terms in v.33a which depend on βάθος[114]. The scopus is not the essentially inscrutable God[115] or his characteristics but the fundamentally incomprehensible fact that God acts *sub contrario*, bringing discredit upon the wisdom of the world and making righteous the ungodly[116]. The πλοῦτος (θεοῦ) is the eschatological abundance of salvation which is rooted in God's glory (9,23; cf. Phil 4,19; Col 1,27) and given in Jesus Christ[117]. It corresponds

---

112 Not four times, as asserted by H. Chadwick, "St. Paul and Philo of Alexandria", *BJRL* 48 (1965/66) 295 quoted by J.D.G. Dunn, *Christology*, p.331 n.83.
113 Cf. O. Michel, *Römerbrief*, pp.354 n.3 (lit),361f.; E. Käsemann, *Römer*, p.308; U. Wilckens, *Römer*, 2, p.269. G. Bornkamm, "Der Lobpreis Gottes: Röm 11,33-36" (1951), *Das Ende des Gesetzes*, p.71 emphasized the sapiential background; cf. also R. Deichgräber, *Gotteshymnus und Christushymnus in der frühen Christenheit*, SUNT 5, 1967, p.63.
114 Cf. U. Wilckens, *ThWNT* 7 (1964) 518f.; R. Deichgräber, *Gotteshymnus*, p.62; E. Käsemann, *Römer*, p.309; U. Wilckens, *Römer*, 2, p.269.
115 The inscrutability of God is an important subject of Jewish wisdom theology (cf. Job 28,28; Prov 30,1-6; Sir 24,28-29; 42,15-25; Bar 3, 29-32; SapSal 9,10-18), of OT prophecy (Is 40,12-26; 55,8-11), and in apocalyptic (4Ezr 3,11; 5,36-40; 6,1-6; 8,20-23; ApcBar 14,8-11). Cf. U. Wilckens, *o.c.*, p.270.
116 Cf. E. Käsemann, *o.c.*, p.309 referring to 1Cor 1,19; U. Wilckens, *o.c.*, p.269.
117 Cf. H. Schlier, *Römerbrief*, p.345.

with the depths of God's gifts of salvation in 1Cor 2,9.12. The σοφία (θεοῦ), here, is not so much the wisdom of the Creator and of creation as in 1Cor 1,21 but the wisdom in the context of Christ (cf. 1Cor 1,24.30!), the wisdom which is in *Christus solus*, the paradoxical 'logic' of God's mercy in the *iustificatio impiorum* (cf. v.32)[118]. God's σοφία is incomprehensible since nobody has been his "counsellor (σύμβουλος, v.34b) — nobody except God's own wisdom which is his "counsellor" regarding all his works (SapSal 8.4.9; cf. 9,9)[119]. It is this wisdom which is in Christ. The γνῶσις θεοῦ is God's own knowledge with which he has chosen his people (8,29; 11,2; cf. 1Cor 8,3; Gal 4,9)[120]. God's "knowledge" is incomprehensible since nobody has "known" (ἔγνω) his "mind" (νοῦς, v.34a)[121] — nobody except God's own wisdom which knows God's secrets and plans (cf. Prov 8,22-31; Sir 1,1-8; 24,1-5; SapSal 6,22; 7,15-21.26-30; 8,4.9; 9,9-13.16-17)[122]. And it is again this knowledge or wisdom[123] which is in Christ. Finally, the cosmological formula ἐξ αὐτοῦ καὶ δι' αὐτοῦ καὶ εἰς αὐτὸν τὰ πάντα (v.36) emphasizes both the salvation-historical and the creational significance of Christ[124].

Thus, it seems to be possible to find traces of Paul's wisdom christology in this pericope[125]: God's inscrutable riches, wisdom, and knowledge are closely linked with Jesus Christ who not only knew and knows God's works and plan[126] in contrast to man, but

---

118 Cf. H. Schlier, ibid., E. Käsemann, *o.c.*, p.309; U. Wilckens, *o.c.*, p.269.
119 Cf. U. Wilckens, *o.c.*, p.271.
120 Cf. H. Schlier, *o.c.*, pp.345f.; E. Käsemann, *o.c.*, p.309; U. Wilckens, *o.c.*, p.269.
121 In 1Cor 2,16 Paul answers the same question as in Rom 11,34a positively. On the difference between the meaning see U. Wilckens, *Römer*, 2, p.271 n.1203.
122 Cf. U. Wilckens, *o.c.*, p.271 with n.1204.
123 For Paul, σοφία and γνῶσις are not essentially different; cf. C.K. Barrett, "Christianity at Corinth", *BJRL* 46 (1963/64) 275f.; H. Schlier, "Die Erkenntnis Gottes nach den Briefen des Apostels Paulus", *Gott und Welt*, FS K. Rahner, ed. J.B. Metz et al., 1964, p.525 n.28; R. Baumann, *Mitte*, p.118; J.D.G. Dunn, *Jesus and the Spirit*, ²1978, p.415 n.107; cf. also E. Lohse, *Kolosser*, p.130 referring to Qoh 1, 16-18; 2,26; 7,12; 9,10LXX; Sir 21,13; 1QS 4,3.22; 1QH 1,18-19; CD 2,3 where the two concepts occur side by side.
124 Cf. U. Wilckens, *o.c.*, p.272.
125 Recognized apparently only by P.E. Bonnard, *Sagesse*, pp.136f.; idem, "Sagesse", *BETL* 51 (1979) 142.
126 E. Käsemann, *Römer*, p.310 is right in pointing out that Paul, in Rom 11,36, does not argue christologically in any explicit way but that he leaves the τὰ πάντα

embodied, i.e. revealed and effectively realized, God's wisdom in bringing salvation to man.

14.2.7. Phil 2,6-11. The Christ hymn in Phil 2,6-11 is one of the most difficult and therefore one of the most discussed pericopes of the Pauline corpus[127]. The two questions of structure and of the religion-historical background are of crucial significance for the understanding of the hymn[128]. Most scholars assert that the hymn implies or expresses the thought of Christ's pre-existence[129], although others have argued against it[130]. It has been stressed recently that the focal point or *Aussageakzent* of the hymn (in the

---

undefined ("schwebend"), and that Paul refers, as in 1,18ff.; 5,12ff.; 8,19ff. to the universal salvation whose centre is christology.

127 Cf. R.P. Martin, *Carmen Christi: Philippians 2,5-11 in Recent Interpretation and in the Setting of Early Christian Worship,* SNTS MS 4, 1967 for a review of research until 1963. Add now the major contributions by J. Gnilka, *Philipperbrief,* HThK X/3, 1968, pp.111-147; H.W. Bartsch, *Die konkrete Wahrheit und die Lüge der Spekulation: Untersuchungen über den vorpaulinischen Hymnus und seine gnostische Mythisierung,* 1974; O. Hofius, *Der Christushymnus Philipper 2,6-11: Untersuchungen zu Gestalt und Aussage eines urchristlichen Psalms,* WUNT 17, 1976; J.D.G. Dunn, *Christology,* pp.114-121; H.H. Schade, *Christologie,* 1981, pp.64-69; T. Nagata, *Philippians 2,5-11: A Case Study in the Contextual Shaping of Early Christology,* Ph.D. Diss. Princeton Theological Seminary, 1981, B. Mengel, *Studien zum Philipperbrief: Untersuchungen zum situativen Kontext,* WUNT 2/8, 1982, pp. 245-250.

128 Since E. Lohmeyer's analysis, the vast majority of scholars take the hymn to be pre-Pauline; cf. H. Weder, *Kreuz Jesu,* 1981, p.209 n.333 (lit.). Some scholars still assert that Paul might well have written it himself, using traditional formulations; cf. R. Deichgräber, *Gotteshymnus,* p.120 n.2 (lit.); also W.G. Kümmel, *Theologie,* pp.135f.; S. Kim, *Origin,* pp.147-149; cf. R.P. Martin, *Carmen Christi,* pp.42-62.

129 Cf. D. Georgi, "Der vorpaulinische Hymnus Phil 2,6-11", 1964, pp.276-278; J. Gnilka, *o.c.,* pp.144-147; P.G. Hamerton-Kelly, *Pre-existence,* pp.156-168; R.P. Martin, *o.c.,* pp.99-133; L. Goppelt, *Theologie,* 2, pp.401f.; O. Hofius, *o.c.,* pp.14f., 56f.; M. Hengel, `Son,` pp.71f.; P. Stuhlmacher, "Christologie", *Aufsätze,* p.213; G. Barth, *Philipper,* 1979, p.45; F. Froitzheim, *Christologie,* pp.50,54 n.136; H. Merklein, "Entstehung", p.34; W.G. Kümmel, *o.c.,* p.136; S. Kim, *o.c.,* p.265; H.H. Schade, *o.c.,* pp.68f.; R. Riesner, "Präexistenz", *ThBeitr* 12 (1981) 182; H. Weder, *o.c.,* pp.210f.; M. Hengel, *Atonement,* 1981, p.74; T. Nagata, *o.c.,* pp.172f., 209,293,296; B. Mengel, *o.c.,* p.247.

130 Cf. A. Feuillet, *Christ Sagesse,* pp.348f.; C.H. Talbert, "The Problem of Pre-existence in Phil 2,6-11", *JBL* 86 (1967) 141-153; H.W. Bartsch, *o.c.,* pp.77f.; J. Murphy-O'Connor, "Christological Anthropology in Phil 2,6-11", *RB* 83 (1976) 25-50 passim; G. Howard, "Phil 2,6-11 and the Human Christ", *CBQ* 40 (1978) 368-387; J.D.G. Dunn, *o.c.,* pp.114-121.

present form and context) is Christ's death on the cross (2,8c!), i.e. Paul's *theologia crucis*[131].

As to the traditional background, it has been maintained that concepts of the Heracles myth, the anthropos myth, the heavenly Son of Man, the Suffering Servant, the OT Righteous One, the gnostic *Urmensch* redeemer myth, or concepts of Jewish wisdom or of the two Adams are crucial[132]. If the Adam-Christ typology, i.e. Adam christology, provided the exclusive background for the hymn[133], the latter would be irrelevant for our inquiry. However, numerous scholars maintain that Jewish wisdom theology is at least part of the interpretative context of the hymn[134].

Without being able at this point to enter into a detailed discussion of the relevant words and concepts in Phil 2,6-11, we want to suggest that concepts of Adam and wisdom christology together provide the best background for the hymn. Several reasons make

---

[131] Cf. O. Hofius, *o.c.*, pp.12-17,56-67. See also H. Weder, *o.c.*, pp.209-217 stating that the historical identity of Jesus of Nazareth is expressed in the horizon of the 'mythological' identity of Christ (as the pre-existent heavenly redeemer). Cf. also B. Mengel, *o.c.*, 1982, pp.245-250.

[132] See the critical discussions of R.P. Martin, *Carmen Christi*, pp.120-133, 154-164; J. Gnilka, *Philipperbrief*, pp.138-144; J.T. Sanders, *Christological Hymns*, pp.58-72; K. Wengst, *Formeln*, pp.149-155; G. Barth, *Philipper*, pp.45-47; T. Nagata, *Case Study*, pp.30-66,302-335.

[133] Some scholars assert that Adam christology provides the most probable background; O. Cullmann, *Christology*, p.181; A. Feuillet, *Christ Sagesse*, pp.343-345; H. Bartsch, *Wahrheit*, pp.32,37; J.D.G. Dunn, *Christology*, pp.114-119 (p.310 n.64 lit.); S. Kim, *Origin*, p.265.

[134] Cf. E. Schweizer, *Erniedrigung und Erhöhung bei Jesus und seinen Nachfolgern*, AThANT 28, ^{2}1962, pp.98-102; D. Georgi, "Hymnus", pp.266-291; J.T. Sanders, *o.c.*, pp.72f., 86 n.1,135f.; H. Bartsch, *o.c.*, pp.32,77; H.M. Schenke, "Die Tendenz der Weisheit zur Gnosis", *Gnosis*, FS H. Jonas, ed. B. Aland, 1978, pp.351-372, here 365-372 (comparing Phil 2,6-11 with the sapiential Nag Hammadi text Silvanus of Codex VII, particularly Silv 110,13-111,20; 112,8-113,23); J. Murphy-O'Connor, "Anthropology", *RB* 83 (1976) 25-50, here 31-49; E. Schüssler Fiorenza, "Wisdom Mythology", p.26; R.S. Barbour, "Wisdom", p.68; W.G. Kümmel, *Theologie*, p.136; H.H. Schade, *Christologie*, p.239 n.292 (mentioning the gnostic myth as alternative); cf. also G. Barth, *o.c.*, pp.46f. who assumes a gnostic background but does not exclude the wisdom speculation. J.D.G. Dunn, *o.c.*, p.312 n.87 admits "broad similarities" with the wisdom theology and wisdom tradition but "prefers to concentrate on the direct influence from the Adam motif" (ibid.), without providing arguments which would explain why he does not refer to the wisdom tradition as well and more specifically. H. Weder, *o.c.*, p.211 n.343 emphasizes that the religion-historical background is not a unity and mentions the possibility of a (Hellenistic-Jewish) sapiential background. T. Nagata, *o.c.*, p.305 rejects a sapiential background of the hymn.

this suggestion plausible: (1) The Adam-Christ typology has to be explained as the application of sapiential (!), apocalyptic, and rabbinic-exegetical traditions to the resurrected Christ[135], i.e. Adam christology already includes wisdom elements; (2) the concerns of both Adam christology (stressing the humanity of Christ and developing anthropology and soteriology) and wisdom christology (stressing the divinity of Christ and developing the concept of Christ as mediator of creation, revelation, and salvation)[136] can be found in the hymn; (3) there are also other passages where elements derived from Adam christology and wisdom christology are found together[137].

Granted that the points of contact with the Adam motif are crucial for an understanding of the hymn, it seems to be possible to assume also that elements of wisdom christology stand directly behind some of the hymn's concepts, especially if the hymn expresses the pre-existent Christ's descent from heaven, his humiliation, and his incarnation[138].

Christ's pre-existence[139] is indicated (1) by the phrase ὅς ἐν μορφῇ θεοῦ ὑπάρχων (v.6a) with μορφή θεοῦ describing the specific form ('Gestalt') of Christ as to his divine status before his self-humiliation; (2) by the phrase οὐχ ἁρπαγμὸν ἡγήσατο τὸ εἶναι ἴσα θεῷ (v.6b) which describes the attitude of the heavenly Christ who did not regard his position of honour — being ἴσα θεῷ (as *res rapta*) — as booty (ἁρπαγμός), i.e. as something to be (selfishly) exploited and kept; and (3) by the phrase ἑαυτὸν ἐκένωσεν which

---

135 Cf. H.H. Schade, *Christologie*, pp.83f. See H.W. Bartsch,*Wahrheit*, p.77 who refers to the early (Jewish) Christian tradition "die bei der weisheitlichen Interpretation von Gen 1,26f.; 5,1-3,5 (sic!) einsetzt" as background of the pre-Pauline hymn which interpreted Christ as second Adam. In his survey of research on the background of Adam christology, S. Kim, *Origin*, pp.162-193 concludes that the origin of Paul's Adam-Christ typology has not been clarified (p.193, quoting E. Käsemann, *Römer*, p.136). Regarding recent discussions of Paul's Adam christology see J.D.G. Dunn, *Christology*, pp.98-128 (focusing on the question of pre-existence) and S. Kim, *o.c.*, pp.162-193,260-266; also H.H. Schade, *o.c.*, pp.69-87.
136 Cf. S. Kim, *o.c.*, p.266 in his summary of his treatment of wisdom christology (pp. 258-260) and Adam christology.
137 Cf. S. Kim, *o.c.*, p.267 referring to 2Cor 3,18-4,6; Rom 8,29-30; Col 1,15-20.
138 Cf. M. Hengel, *Son*, pp.71f. referring explicitly to Sir 24.
139 Cf. the references supra n.129. The basic problem of Dunn's interpretation of Phil 2 is his exclusive (and admirably consistent!) reference to Adam christology as interpretative key to the hymn.

denotes Christ's voluntary renunciation of his divine, heavenly status and position, i.e. the incarnation (as self-humiliation).

The following considerations substantiate the case for pre-existence in Phil 2,6-11. As regards the first argument, we point out that it is not possible to equate the μορφή θεοῦ with the εἰκών τοῦ θεοῦ and link it with Adam created in the image of God and sharing in the δόξα of God (contra Dunn, p.115) since (1) μορφή cannot be exchanged for εἰκων, not even in Hellenistic usage[140], and (2) the LXX uses neither μορφή nor δόξα for Adam in Gen. Dunn does not explain the change from the μορφή θεοῦ to the μορφή δούλου satisfactorily: it cannot be established that according to Jewish or early Christian thought Adam lost God's "image" (admitted by Dunn, p. 311 n.70), and to say that Adam "lost his share in God's glory and became a slave" (Dunn, p.115) is without exegetical basis. Adam was created in the "image of God" but did not (!) share in the "form of God", and this is the fundamental difference between Adam and Christ! Jesus Christ changed his "form" or status from θεός to δοῦλος whereas Adam who was man (אדם) and remained man, suffered ('only') a reduction of the divine "image" which had then various consequences.

As regards the second argument, it should be noted that even when ἴσα θεῷ is translated with "equivalent to, of the same value" and distinguished from ἐν μορφῇ θεοῦ[141], it is still possible to understand the term ἁρπαγμός in the sense of *res rapta* rather in the sense of *res rapienda*: Christ, even though he shares the "form of God", is not totally 'identical' with God (the Father) but rather "of the same value" (i.e. divine), sharing the same status[142]. This leads directly into trinitarian considerations which Paul of course does not elucidate explicitly. If one understands ἁρπαγμός in the sense of *res rapienda*, the concept of Christ's pre-existence is still present: "der Satz sagt, daß Christus zwar (präexistent) in der Wirklichkeit Gottes war, sich aber nicht als Gott neben Gott etablierte"[143]. It is unconvincing to link the "equality with God" with Adam's (and hence Christ's) temptation (contra Dunn, pp.115f.) since (1) there is no obvious reference to Gen 3,5 in the context; (2) the thing to be 'grasped' is something positive in Phil 2,6 (equality with God), whereas in Dunn's interpretation it is something negative (as temptation); and (3) Adam's temptation was not equality with God in an ontic sense but rather the attainment of a *Seinsweise* (היה כאלהים) which makes the knowledge of good and evil (ידע טוב ורע), i.e. autonomous mastery of life, possible (Gen 3,5.22): "Es geht um eine göttliche, eine auf das höchste gesteigerte Befähigung zur Bewältigung des Daseins"[144].

Finally, as to the third argument, Dunn's translation of ἐκένωσεν as "he made himself powerless"[145] is not tenable: κενοῦν means "to make empty, to destroy" and has nothing to do with 'power' but refers to the (voluntary) loss or renunciation of something. It is true that "Christ faced the same archetypal choice that confronted

---

140 Cf. D.H. Wallace, "A Note on Morphē", *ThZ* 22 (1966) 22f.; C. Spicq, "Note sur ΜΟΡΦΗ dans les papyrus et quelques inscriptions", *RB* 80 (1973) 44, 570f.; W. Pöhlmann, in *EWNT* 2 (1981) 1091.
141 T. Holtz, in *EWNT* 2 (1981) 494.
142 Cf. W. Trilling, in *EWNT* 1 (1980) 375 with further evidence.
143 T. Holtz, in EWNT 2 (1981) 494.
144 C. Westermann, *Genesis*, Bk I/1, 1974, p.337.
145 J.D.G. Dunn, *Christology*, p.117 following M.D. Hooker, "Philippians 2, 6-11", *Jesus und Paulus*, FS W.G. Kümmel, ed. E.E. Ellis et al., ²1978, p.161.

Adam" (Dunn, p.117). However, if Jesus was only and simply human (seemingly presupposed by Dunn, when he argues against Christ's pre-existence) he could not have possibly faced the same (!) choice as Adam since he would not have been sinless and so he would have had nothing to loose in the first place.

Thus, we conclude that Phil 2,6-11 contains not only the anthropological[146] but also the ontological aspect of christology in the context of wisdom christology.

14.2.8. Col 1,15-20. The vast majority of scholars regards this pericope as a pre-Pauline hymn which was incorporated into Col attaching interpretative phrases[147]. Questions of structure and original form of the hymn[148] are not really relevant for our inquiry and can therefore be left aside[149]. Many scholars agree that the hymn consists of two strophes: the first (vv. 15-18a) deribes Christ's role in creation (protology), and the second (vv. 18b-20) his role in redemption (soteriology)[150]. The view that

---

146 Cf. D. Georgi, "Hymnus", 1964, pp.266-291 passim; J.T. Sanders, *Hymns,* p.86 n.1; H.W. Bartsch, *Wahrheit,* pp.32,77; J. Murphy-O'Connor, "Anthropology", *RB* 83 (1976) 31-49; H.M. Schenke, "Tendenz", 1978, p.372.

147 For surveys of research see H.J. Gabathuler, *Jesus Christus, Haupt der Kirche – Haupt der Welt: Der Christushymnus Kolosser 1,15-20 in der theologischen Forschung der letzten 130 Jahre,* AThANT 45, 1965; E. Schweizer, "Kolosser 1,15-20" (1969), *Beiträge,* pp.113-144; idem, "Zur neueren Forschung am Kolosserbrief (seit 1970)", *Theologische Berichte,* ed. J. Pfammatter et al., 1976, pp.163-191; P. Benoit, "L'hymne christologique de Col 1,15-20: Jugement critique sur l'état des recherches", *Christianity, Judaism and other Greco-Roman Cults,* FS M. Smith, 1, 1975, pp.226-263. As regards the *theologiegeschichtliche* significance of the hymn cf. now J. Gnilka, *Kolosserbrief,* 1980, pp.77f. Some argue still for a Pauline authorship of the hymn; cf. W.G. Kümmel, *Einleitung,* pp. 301f.; N. Kehl, *Der Christushymnus im Kolosserbrief: Eine motivgeschichtliche Untersuchung zu Kol 1,12-20,* SBM 1, 1967, pp.163f.; S. Kim, *Origin,* pp.144-147 (p.144 n.3 lit.). Recently J.C.O'Neill, "The Source of Christology in Colossians", *NTS* 26 (1980) 87f. argued, unconvincingly, that Col 1,15-20 is not a hymn as it uses "language of public declaration" (p.89).

148 On the structure of the hymn cf. J. Gabathuler, *o.c.,* pp.125-131; A. Feuillet, *Christ Sagesse,* pp.246-269; K. Wengst, *Formeln,* pp.170-175; E. Schweizer, *Kolosser,* pp.50-52; J. Gnilka, *o.c.,* pp.52-59; J.N. Aletti, *Colossiens 1,15,20,* 1981, pp.1-47. Cf. C. Burger, *Schöpfung und Versöhnung: Studien zum liturgischen Gut im Kolosser- und Epheserbrief,* WMANT 46, 1975, pp.3-79 who separates consistently the analysis of the original from the adapted hymn.

149 Similarly J.D.G. Dunn, *Christology,* p.188.

150 Cf. J.N. Aletti, *o.c.,* p.21 listing E. Käsemann, J. Jervell, K.G. Eckart, H. Hegermann, H.M. Schenke, E. Bammel, R. Deichgräber, E. Norden, J. Lähnemann, E. Zeilinger, C. Burger, H. Conzelmann (and agrees, cf. p.45); add J.D.G. Dunn,

wisdom language and wisdom theology provide the best, though not exclusive, background of the hymn is nearly unanimously accepted[151]. The following remarks follow the recent significant monographs of Dunn and Aletti[152].

The statement that Christ is the εἰκὼν τοῦ θεοῦ τοῦ ἀοράτου (v. 15a; cf. 2Cor 4,4) has to be traced back to Jewish wisdom theology which described wisdom as "image of God" (SapSal 7,26; Philo All 1,43)[153] and manifestation of the invisible God[154]. The second title of Christ, πρωτότοκος πάσης κτίσεως (v.15b)[155] is also dependent upon the wisdom tradition which described wisdom as first creation or "firstborn" (cf. Prov 8,22-25; Sir 1,4; 24, 9; SapSal 9,9; Philo Quaest in Gn 4,97; Virt 62; Ebr 30-31)[156].

---

o.c., p.188. Many scholars see 1,17-18a or 1,16f-18a as *Zwischenstrophe* thus assuming three parts; cf. J.N. Aletti, o.c., pp.23f.; add now J. Gnilka, o.c., p.58.

151 Cf. W.D. Davies, *Paul*, pp.150-152; H.J. Gabathuler, o.c., p.133; A. Feuillet, o.c., pp.163-273; N. Kehl, o.c., pp.61-76,104-108; E. Lohse, *Kolosser*, pp.85-90; E. Schweizer, o.c., pp.56-63,72; C. Burger, o.c., pp.42,49f.; P. Stuhlmacher, "Christologie", *Aufsätze*, p.213; R.S. Barbour, "Wisdom", p.68; J.D.G. Dunn, o.c., pp. 188-194; S. Kim, o.c., pp.258f.; H. Gese, "Wisdom", *HBT* 3 (1981) 47-50; J.M. Reese, "Christ as Wisdom Incarnate", *BTB* 11 (1982) 4-6; W. Schenk, "Christus, das Geheimnis der Welt, als dogmatisches und ethisches Grundprinzip des Kolosserbriefes", *EvTh* 43 (1983) 141,143. Several scholars restrict the wisdom parallels to the first part of the hymn. Cf. also J.T. Sanders, *Hymns*, pp.75-87 who concludes that the formal matrix of the hymn, i.e. the thanksgiving form, belongs to the psalmography of the wisdom school.

152 J.D.G. Dunn, *Christology*, pp.188-194 focuses on the question whether the hymn expresses Christ's pre-existence, and comes to a negative answer.

153 On Philo's εἰκών-conception cf. H. Hegermann, *Schöpfungsmittler*, pp.96-99; E. Schweizer, *Kolosser*, p.57. Cf. generally A. Feuillet, *Christ Sagesse*, pp.166-175; N. Kehl, *Christushymnus*, p.61; R. Deichgräber, *Gotteshymnus*, p.153; E. Lohse, *Kolosser*, pp.86f.; C. Burger, *Schöpfung*, p.42; F. Zeilinger, *Der Erstgeborene der Schöpfung*, 1974, pp.108f.; E. Schweizer, *Kolosser*, pp.56-58; M. Hengel, *Son*, p. 75; J. Gnilka, *Kolosserbrief*, pp.60f.; V.A.R. Raj, *The Cosmic Christ of Colossians*, Th.D. Diss. St.Louis, 1981, pp.94f.; J.D.G. Dunn, o.c., pp.165,188; J.N. Aletti, *Colossiens 1,15-20*, pp.82-87. For a general discussion of εἰκών-christology cf. S. Kim, *Origin*, pp.137-268.

154 Cf. J.D.G. Dunn, o.c., p.188 who emphasizes that wisdom as the "immanence of God" — "that which man may know of God and of God's will" — provides the background.

155 According to J.D.G. Dunn, o.c., p.189 this contested phrase describes Christ's precedence in rank rather than priority in time (p.333 n.108 with lit.). E. Schweizer, o.c., pp.58f. understands the phrases in a comparative manner in the sense of "früher als . . . vor aller . . ."; cf. also J.N. Aletti, o.c., p.70; J. Gnilka, o.c., pp.62f; this comparative understanding implies anteriority, i.e. pre-existence.

156 Cf. H. Hegermann, o.c., p.99; E. Schweizer, o.c., p.58f. with n.133; A. Feuillet, o.c., pp.185-202; E. Lohse, o.c., pp.87f.; R. Deichgräber, o.c., p.153; C. Burger,

The phrase ἐν αὐτῷ ἐκτίσθη τὰ πάντα (v. 16a) has been traced back to wisdom terminology as well: Christ as wisdom is God's creative power in a cosmological context[157]; v.17 belongs to the same wisdom context (cf. Prov 8,27-30; Sir 1,4; 24,9; 43,26; Philo Her 189,199; Fug 112; Quaest in Gn 2,118; Aristob PrEv 7,14, 1)[158].

> H. Gese states with regard to the first strophe of the hymn that it expresses "the fundamental recognition of Christ's essence in his relation to the being of creation", and that the sapiential christology of the hymn affirms the "identity of Sophia and Christ under the aspect of sin"[159].

The first phrase of the second strophe — Christ is ἀρχή, πρωτότοκος ἐκ τῶν νεκρῶν (v.18b) — reminds us again of wisdom language (cf. Prov 8,22-23; Philo All 1,43)[160]: as the exalted one, Christ is the "beginning", i.e. the effective presence of divinity "die als Schöpferkraft ein weiteres Werden aus sich heraussetzt"[161], and the "firstborn" from the dead, i.e. the author of the eschatological new creation. As regards the term πλήρωμα (v.19)[162], a sapiential background has been suggested as well (cf. Prov 8,12-14; Bar 3, 38; Sir 24,4-11)[163]: Christ is the cosmic presence of God whose action and manifestation have been focused in Christ's life, death, and resurrection[164], in Christ's pre-existence, earthly life, and post-existence[165].

---

o.c., pp.44f.; J.D.G. Dunn, o.c., pp.165,189; S. Kim, o.c., p.259; J.N. Aletti, o.c., pp.63-70; differently N. Kehl, o.c., pp.85-88; P. Beasley-Murray, "Colossians 1,15-20: An Early Christian Hymn Celebrating the Lordship of Christ", *Pauline Studies*, FS F.F. Bruce, ed. D.A. Hagner et al., 1980, p.171 (reference to birthright).

157 Cf. N. Kehl, *Christushymnus*, p.106; A. Feuillet, "La création de l'univers 'dans le Christ' d'après l'Epître aux Colossiens (1,16a)", *NTS* 12 (1965/66) 1-9; J. Gnilka, *Kolosserbrief*, pp.64f; J.D.G. Dunn, *Christology*, p.190; also E. Lohse, *Kolosserbrief*, pp.89f.

158 Cf. N. Kehl, o.c., p.105; A. Feuillet, *Christ Sagesse*, pp.202-217; F. Zeilinger, *Erstgeborene*, p.201; J. Gnilka, o.c., pp.66f.; J.D.G. Dunn, o.c., pp.165f.191.

159 H. Gese, "Wisdom", *HBT* 3 (1981) 48,50.

160 Cf. E. Lohse, o.c., p.97; A. Feuillet, o.c., p.218; J.D.G. Dunn, o.c., p.191; S. Kim, *Origin*, p.259.

161 E. Schweizer, *Kolosser*, p.63.

162 On this term cf. A. Feuillet, o.c., pp.229-238,275-319; N. Kehl, o.c., pp.110-125; C. Burger, *Schöpfung*, pp.47-49; J.N. Aletti, *Colossiens 1,15-20*, pp.77-81 (p.77 n.106 lit.); J. Gnilka, o.c., pp.72f.

163 Cf. A. Feuillet, o.c., pp.236-238; H. Langkammer, "Die Einwohnung der 'absoluten Seinsfülle' in Christus", *BZ* 12 (1968) 258-263, followed by J.N. Aletti, o.c., p.80 with n.124; also C. Burger, o.c., p.49; J.D.G. Dunn, o.c., pp.192f.

164 Cf. J.D.G. Dunn, o.c., p.193.

165 The presence of pre-existence christology in the Colossian hymn is nearly unani-

Dunn's case against pre-existence christology in this hymn evacuates the clear statements in 1,15b.16a.f.17a of their obvious meaning[166]. As regards for example the phrase ἐν αὐτῷ ἐκτίσθη τὰ πάντα (v.16a), it is not only attractive (Dunn, p. 190) but unavoidable to interpret it in terms of Christ's pre-existence. The differentiation between wisdom by which all things were created and Christ who later "became" this wisdom (Dunn, pp.190,334 n.121) is rather artificial and is thwarted by the fact that the scopus of Col 1,15-20 is Christ and not wisdom (the latter is but the conceptual background of some terms): Paul's readers understood the hymn not in terms of wisdom — which later supposedly "became" (when? how?) Christ Jesus — but in terms of Christ! This means that the ἐν αὐτῷ describes (only) what happened in connection with Christ and not what happened in connection with wisdom (as now embodied in Christ). It is difficult to see how Paul could stress here "the continuity between God's creative power and Christ" (p.190) without implying that Christ himself was active in, or present at, creation. The aor.pass. ἐκτίσθη clearly refers to an event in the past[167].

To sum up, the author of the hymn attributed the sapiential functions of creational and salvational mediation to Jesus Christ thus portraying the pre-existent, incarnate, and exalted Christ in the light of the Jewish divine wisdom[168].

Aletti's attempt to avoid the conclusion that Christ was identified with wisdom is rather artificial: (1) He never offers a methodological discussion of the term 'identification' which can be understood in various ways; (2) his treatment of the wisdom figure in the Jewish tradition (pp.152-165) remains ambiguous as he understands personified wisdom as "réalité énigmatique" with a polymorphic character; (3) he emphasizes that wisdom expresses essentially God's relation with his creation and neglects the role of 'wisdom' in God's dealings with his people; (4) he therefore has to argue in a rather awkward manner when he notes that 1Cor 1,30 expresses only a 'functional' identification of Christ and 'wisdom' since Christ is not simply God's

---

mously acknowledged; cf. recently L. Goppelt, *Theologie*, 2, pp.403f.; F. Froitzheim, *Theologie*, p.50; H. Merklein, "Entstehung", 1979, p.34; W.G. Kümmel, *Theologie*, p.151; J. Gnilka, *Kolosserbrief*, pp.61,63-66,77; J.N. Aletti, *Colossiens 1,15-20*, pp.141-147.

166 Cf. I.H. Marshall in his review, *Trinity Journal* 2 (1981) 244f.

167 The perf. ἔκτισται (v.16e) cannot be used to gloss over the aor. ἐκτίσθη (v.16a); contra J.D.G. Dunn, *Christology*, p.334 n.120. The change from aor. to perf. has to be understood as progression "vom Schöpfungsakt zum Schöpfungszustand" (J. Gnilka, *o.c.*, p.65).

168 Cf. J.D.G. Dunn, *o.c.*, pp.187-196 passim; S. Kim, *Origin*, p.259; J.N. Aletti, *o.c.*, pp.148-180. Contra W. Schenk, "Christus", *EvTh* 43 (1983) 138-155 passim who rejects the view that Col 1,15-20 implies or expresses Christ's pre-existence or mediation at creation (pp.142f.) and concludes that "dieser pseudepigraphe Paulus präsentiert sich als 'Entdecker' jenes zentralen Weltgeheimnisses, daß dieser Jesus — von seiner Taufe und seinem Sühnetod her — die Weltseele ist, die die Welt zusammenhält (v.17 συνέστηκεν). Die Welt ist ein οἶκος . . . Pazifizierung und 'Versöhnung' gibt es, weil am Kreuz die vermeintlichen Hausbesitzer als Hausbesetzer entlarvt und entmachtet sind".

relation to man or to creation but the Son "sans que cette relation au Père implique nécessairement une relation aux hommes" (p.163); (5) he seems to presuppose that wisdom has to be conceived of as a real hypostasis if the identification with Christ should make any sense as otherwise Christ would be identified with a chimera (p. 157), which is not the case, however.

14.2.9. Col 2,3.

The statement that in Christ there are πάντες οἱ θησαυροὶ τῆς σοφίας καὶ γνώσεως ἀπόκρυφοι explicates once again wisdom christology[169]. Even though this is not always recognized[170], scholars always pointed out the sapiential background of the concepts which are used in this verse.

In Prov 2,3-6LXX we have the concepts θησαυροί, σοφία, γνῶσις, and also σύνεσις and ἐπίγνωσις (cf. Col 2,2!). Sir 1,5 refers to θησαυροὶ σοφίας. Bar 3,15 mentions the θησαυροί of σοφία which dwell exclusively with God. SapSal 7,14 describes σοφία as θησαυρός which includes God's friendship. Is 45,3LXX speaks of the θησαυροί . . . ἀπόκρυφοι which communicate the knowledge (γνῶσις) of God. And En(eth) 46,3 refers to the Son of Man who reveals all hidden treasures (note that the Son of Man in En is also associated with wisdom)[171].

The statement in 2,3 does not state primarily that Christ is the subject of all human knowledge[172] — this is but the consequence of Paul's assertion — but that Christ, as God's wisdom, is "the sole repository of what men may know of God's character"[173]. Again, functions of wisdom are transferred to Christ[174]: he is the most clear and most definite embodiment of God, the

---

169 Cf. H. Windisch, "Weisheit", p.225; W.D. Davies, *Paul*, p.173 with n.6; A. Feuillet, *Christ Sagesse*, p.172; R.P. Martin, *Colossians*, pp.69f.; F.F. Bruce, *Colossians*, p. 224; M. Hengel, *Son*, p.72; P.E. Bonnard, "Sagesse", *BETL* 51 (1979) 142; J. Gnilka, *Kolosserbrief*, p.111.

170 Surprisingly, neither J.D.G. Dunn, *Christology*, nor S. Kim, *Origin*, make anything of this verse.

171 Cf. generally A. Feuillet, *Christ Sagesse*, pp.53f., 236,258; F. Zeilinger, *Erstgeborene*, p.111 n.134; E. Schweizer, *Kolosser*, p.94 with n.286; J. Gnilka, *Kolosserbrief*, p.111; even A. van Roon, "Relation", *NovTest* 16 (1974) 237f. (admitting that Paul relates Christ to wisdom but rejecting the term 'wisdom christology' nevertheless).

172 Thus E. Schweizer, *o.c.*, p.94, referring to K. Barth, *Kirchliche Dogmatik*, II/1, p. 285; similarly E. Lohse, *Kolosser*, p.129.

173 R.P. Martin, *Colossians*, p.70 quoting C.F.D. Moule who stated that "Christ has become to Christians all that the Wisdom of God was, according to the Wisdom literature, and more still" (p.69).

174 Cf. M. Hengel, *Son*, p.72.

revelation of God's μυστήριον (v.2) which is the gospel or God's plan of salvation which Christ embodies[175].

14.3. Theological-Hermeneutical Evaluation

14.3.1. Cosmological aspects. Jewish wisdom theology, and particularly its speculation regarding divine wisdom, focused on wisdom's function in creation (cf. § 2.1.). When Paul identified Christ as wisdom, Christ of necessity assumed creational and cosmological significance[176]. The "Lord Jesus Christ" is the mediator of creation. The cosmos is "through him" (1Cor 8,6; Rom 11,36; Col 1,16). He is the "firstborn of all creation (Col 1,15): "in him" all things were created (Col 1,16), and "in him" all things hold together (Col 1,17), and "to him" are all things (Col 1,16). Christ is the agent, the sustainer, and the goal of creation[177]. Like wisdom, Christ was active in creation. Like wisdom, Christ is the order of creation. And, unlike wisdom but as a result of God's own wisdom, Christ is the goal of creation.

14.3.2. Soteriological aspects. The second focus of wisdom theology, especially after the exile, was wisdom's significance for and in God's history with his people (cf. § 2.2., 5.1.1.). Divine wisdom was intimately linked with Israel and Zion, with the cult, and with the Torah. The soteriological significance of Christ is naturally not dependent upon his identification with wisdom but on the events of the cross and the resurrection[178].

---

175 Cf. J.D.G. Dunn, *Christology,* pp.235f.; S. Kim, *Origin,* p.78 n.1.
176 Cf. also P. Stuhlmacher,"Christologie", *Aufsätze,* 1981, p.213.
177 Cf. S. Kim, *Origin,* p.259. Cf. our discussion in § 14.2. Most scholars agree that Christ as wisdom implies that he was active in creation. In order to avoid the conclusion that Christ's mediatorship in creation implied or presupposes his pre-existence, J.D.G. Dunn, *Christology,* p.195 argues that all Paul wanted to say when he identified Christ with wisdom was that "the same divine wisdom which was active in creation we believe to have been active in Jesus". It escapes me how Dunn can write in the next sentence that "divine wisdom is not to be recognized as *wholly identified* with Jesus" (italics his) and yet not infer that Christ, as wisdom of God, was active in creation too. One could also say that God acted 'in and through' the OT prophets who performed miracles and proclaimed God's word, as did Jesus!
178 On Paul's understanding of the cross cf. H. Weder, *Kreuz Jesu,* pp.121-252.

However, several aspects of Paul's soteriology are very closely linked with wisdom theology. (1) The christological perspective of the designation of Christ as "Son" (of God) is, among other traditions which are more directly revelant (e.g. messianology), also related to wisdom theology: Christ as God's wisdom is God's Son in terms of a most intimate relationship with God[179]. (2) God's "sending of the Son" for the salvation of the world is to be understood against a sapiential background as well (cf. Gal 4,4; Phil 2,6-11). (3) Christ as wisdom is the embodiment and realization of God's plan of salvation: the crucified Christ is God's wisdom (1 Cor 1,24.30) and the mediator of our salvation (1Cor 8,6; cf. Rom 11,36). (4) As divine wisdom, Christ was present in God's mightiest act of his history with his people, i.e. in the Exodus (1Cor 10, 4). (5) Christ as wisdom of God is familiar with God's works and plans, and embodied and realized this wisdom of God in and by the eschatological *iustificatio impiorum* (Rom 11,33-35). (6) As divine wisdom, Christ is not only the "firstborn" of creation (Col 1,15) but also the "beginning" and the "firstborn" of the eschatological new creation (Col 1,18). (7) As revelatory manifestation of God's "secret", Christ embodies God's plan of salvation and consequently represents the divine "treasures of wisdom" (Col 2, 3). (8) Even though the exalted Christ is not present on earth he is, as God's wisdom, still present in the proclamation of the Gospel (Rom 10,6-7)[180].

---

179 Cf. M. Hengel, *Son*, pp.41-56,66-76; S. Kim, *o.c.*, pp.117-119,259; H. Gese, "Wisdom", *HBT* 3 (1981) 45f. For an extensive treatment of the term and related concepts of "Son of God" cf. recently J.D.G. Dunn, *Christology*, 1980, pp.12-64.
180 K.G. Sandelin, *Auseinandersetzung*, 1976, concludes after examining 1Cor 15,22-28.44b-49.57 that Christ is given characteristics of the Alexandrian wisdom figure: (1) he is described as "life-giving spirit" (pp.24-28); (2) he is presented as *Heilsraum* (cf. the expression "in Christ") and sphere of eternal life (pp.49-60); (3) he is described as ruler who is subject to God and fights against enemies (pp.60-90). Sandelin denies, however, that Paul regarded Christ as 'incarnated *sophia*', especially since the Alexandrian *sophia* which calls upon man to attain salvation by fulfilling the law belongs to those powers which Christ overcomes (1Cor 15,24-26). Regarding Sandelin's study, which has been well received – cf. the reviews of J.F. Collange in *RHPR* 57 (1977) 547f.; J. Cahill in *CBQ* 40 (1978) 446-448; E.E. Ellis in *JBL* 98 (1979) 305f. – it has to be pointed out that Sandelin (1) seems to regard a concept as sapiential if it just occurs somewhere in the wisdom literature or in the Philonic corpus, (2) never defines what 'wisdom' is, and (3) does not delineate his methodological presuppositions.

14.3.3. Ontological aspects.

In our exegetical discussion of the relevant Pauline pericopes we could not avoid the conclusion that certain statements on Christ as the wisdom of God should be understood not merely in a functional manner but rather in ontological respects[181]. (1) As "image" of God and "firstborn" of (the old and the new) creation (Col 1,15) — concepts which sapiential theology links with the (poetic) wisdom figure — Christ not only 'functions' as God's wisdom but is God's wisdom[182]. (2) Christ's mediatorship in creation (1Cor 8,6; Rom 11,36; Col 1,15-18) is to be linked with pre-existence christology[183]. Other interpretations of these passages evacuate the relevant words and concepts of their obvious and most natural meaning. (3) The christological title "firstborn of all creation" (Col 1,15) seems to express the anteriority of Christ prior to creation. (4) The concept of "sending" (the Son) (Gal 4,4, cf. Phil 2,6-11) also implies the pre-existence of Christ, as we have seen. (5) Christ's presence in salvation history as divine wisdom (1Cor 10,4) also expresses Paul's understanding of the person of Christ as pre-existent saviour.

Thus, wisdom christology implies or pre-supposes pre-existence christology[184]: Christ, as God's wisdom, existed before creation.

---

181 Pace J.D.G. Dunn, *Christology*, p.195 who states that "to understand the Wisdom passages as ontological affirmations about 'Christ's eternal being' is most probably to misunderstand them" asserting that they have to be understood rather as saying that "Christ represents what God is" (ibid.). Even though it might be true that Paul was not aiming (!) at winning men to "belief in a pre-existent being" (ibid.), it is still clear, in our eyes, that the ontological identity of Christ is expressed in these passages.

182 We are not convinced that such an identification is "an illegitimate transfer of twentieth-century presuppositions to the first century", as J.D.G. Dunn, *o.c.*, p.195 argues. It seems, rather, that the rejection of such an identification is an unnecessary transfer of modern distinctions and cautions to the time of Paul.

183 Thus the vast majority of scholars; cf. the discussion in §14.2. for literature. F. Froitzheim, *Christologie*, 1979, pp.54f. n.136 argues against the exclusive derivation of the pre-existence conception of Paul from sapiential motifs. Although it is true that Paul's pre-existence statements are not specifically connected with a particular christological title, it is wrong to limit the possibility of sapiential influence to those passages in which Christ is presented in a non-soteriological context as mediator of creation with the argument that *sophia* is a- or trans-historical (ibid.). We noted above that (1) wisdom is closely linked with Israel's history and (specific!) cult, especially in the later stages, and (2) that creation and history cannot be neatly separated in a biblical context.

184 Cf. P. Stuhlmacher, "Christologie", *Aufsätze*, p.213 who points out that "diese Dimension des präexistenten Seins und Wirkens Jesu wurde urchristlich gewonnen

He was God's mediator in creation and, after being sent by the Father into the world, also mediator in salvation (as new creation) — already in God's dealings with Israel, but then primarily and fundamentally in revealing the riches of God's wisdom at the cross which nullified the wisdom of the world, justifying the unjust. It was inevitable that such christological reflections led to trinitarian questions[185].

14.3.4. Revelatory aspects. The pre-existent Christ was not only the mediator of creation and salvation but also of revelation. As "image of the invisible God" (Col 1,15) Christ has solved the old problem of the hiddenness and inaccessibility of God. Christ, as God's wisdom, is the full and perfect and visible manifestation and revelation of God[186]. The true character of divine wisdom is to be read off not from creation but from the cross (1Cor 1,18-25)[187]. The same thought is expressed in Rom 10,6-7; 11,33-36; Col 2,3.

14.3.5. Summary. For Paul[188], Christ was the wisdom of God. As mediator of creation, salvation, and revelation, the "Lord Jesus Christ" manifested the finality of God's own purposes. As mediator of creation, Christ as divine wisdom was the agent and is the sustainer (order!) and the goal of creation. As mediator of salvation, Christ as divine wisdom is the "Son" sent by the Father into the world embodying and realizing his plan of salvation in history and is still present in the preaching of the Gospel. Christ's mediatorship in creation, his sending into the world, and his presence in Israel's salvational history all imply that Christ, as God's wisdom,

---

    durch eine weisheitlich-messianische Aufweitung der ... christologischen Ursprungstraditionen". Cf. also recently J.M. Reese, "Christ as Wisdom Incarnate", *BTB* 11 (1982) 45f.

185 Cf. M. Hengel, *Son*, p.70. It is not necessary to assume that a pre-existence christology presupposes the hypostatization of wisdom with Christ then being identified with the hypostasis or figure of wisdom.
186 Cf. S. Kim, *Origin*, p.259; V.A.R. Raj, *Cosmic Christ*, 1981, pp.123-125.
187 Cf. J.D.G. Dunn, *Christology*, p.195.
188 It is irrelevant for our study whether Paul developed a full wisdom christology himself for the first time, as S. Kim, *Origin*, p.258 thinks, or whether it goes back to the early Palestinian Christian community and/or to Jesus' own teaching, as M. Hengel, *Son*, p.74 asserts.

is not only 'post-existent' with God as the exalted one but that he was pre-existent with God before creation. Finally, Christ as divine wisdom has epistemological significance as mediator of revelation. Christ is the fullest and most perfect visible manifestation of God.

§15 Christ and the Law

In the preceding paragraph we established the fact that Paul's christology involved the correlation of Christ and wisdom. Before we can discuss the question whether the traditional identification of wisdom and law with which Paul was familiar had any influence upon the formulation of his christological convictions we must first establish the relationship between Christ and the Torah as envisaged by Paul. We will proceed as we did in our discussion of wisdom christology: a brief introduction into recent research regarding Paul's theology of the law is followed by a concise treatment of relevant passages which relate Christ and the Torah and a systematic analysis of the theological evidence. As regards the handling of the primary and secondary sources[189] in this paragraph, the methodological considerations of § 13.3. apply here as well.

15.1. Christ and the Torah in Recent Research

It was particularly W.D. Davies who asserted that, for Paul, Jesus Christ was a 'new Torah'[190]. He is aware of the fact that Paul never refers to Christ as 'new Torah' explicitly but states that

---

[189] As regards the literature on the concept of law in Paul cf. H. Schlier, *Galater*, pp. 176f. n.2; G. Friedrich, in *ThWNT* 10/2 (1979) 1190-1195; H. Hübner, *Das Gesetz bei Paulus*, FRLANT 119, ³1982, pp.189-198; idem, Art. "νόμος", *EWNT* 2 (1981) 1158-1161. For a good survey of the older literature cf. O. Kuss, "Nomos bei Paulus", *MüThz* 17 (1966) 173-227; for the more recent contributions cf. A. van Dülmen, *Die Theologie des Gesetzes bei Paulus*, SBM 5, 1968, pp.231-257.

[190] W.D. Davies, *Paulus*, pp.110-176, attempting to demonstrate that both the word of Jesus (pp.110-146) and the person of Jesus (pp.147-176) formed a 'new Torah' for Paul.

this identification is "clearly implied" in 2Cor 3,4-18[191]. As proof for his thesis that Paul interpreted Christ in terms of the old Torah, Davies adduces simply his conviction that this connection explains best Paul's wisdom christology[192].

In her book on Paul's theology of the law, A.van Dülmen discusses all passages in Gal and Rom where νόμος occurs and concludes in her theological section that Paul's theology of the law is christologically defined: there is a continuity between the Torah and Christ in the sense that Christ is (1) the end of the law as way of salvation, and at the same time (2) the pneumatic fulfilment and reinvigoration of the law as expression of God's will, so that Christ, in a certain sense, assumes the place of the Torah as, for Paul, the life "in Christ" replaces the life "under the law"[193].

In the 1970's no monograph except Hübner's appeared on Paul's theology of the law[194]. But numerous articles discussed Paul's conception of the relationship between the Torah and Christian ethics[195], the Spirit[196], the Gospel[197], and Christ[198], or focused on the question of the end and/or the fulfilment of the

---

191 Cf. W.D. Davies, o.c., p.149. On 2Cor 3,4-18 see infra, § 15.2.6.
192 Cf. W.D. Davies, o.c., p.150 and passim. This procedure is far from satisfactory and does not convince. The lack of definite evidence for the view that Paul saw Christ as new Torah was pointed out already in the reviews of J. Jeremias in ThLZ 74 (1949) 148 and W.G. Kümmel in Judaica 7 (1951) 302.
193 A. van Dülmen, Theologie, p.168, particularly pp.185-230. Note C. Haufe in ThLZ 96 (1971) 348f. who points out several inconsistencies in van Dülmen's argumentation.
194 Unfortunately, the dissertation of B.C. Wintle, The Law of Moses and the Law of Christ: An Exegetical Study of Pauline Teaching on the Authority of the Law over the Christian Believer, Ph.D.Diss. Manchester University, 1977, was not published. Cf. infra, pp.267.
195 Cf. A Feuillet, "Loi ancienne et morale chrétienne d'après l'Épitre aux Romains", NRTh 92 (1970) 785-805; M. Barth, "Die Stellung des Paulus zu Gesetz und Ordnung", EvTh 23 (1973) 496-526; J. W. Drane, "Tradition, Law and Ethics in Pauline Theology", NovTest 16 (1974) 167-178.
196 Cf. E. Lohse, "ὁ νόμος τοῦ πνεύματος τῆς ζωῆς: Exegetische Anmerkungen zu Röm 8,2", Neues Testament und christliche Existenz, FS H. Braun, ed. H.D. Betz et al., 1973, pp.279-287; H.D. Betz, "Geist, Freiheit und Gesetz", ZThK 71 (1974) 78-93; J. Blank, "Gesetz und Geist", The Law of the Spirit in Rom 7 and 8, ed. L. de Lorenzi, 1976, pp.73-100.
197 Cf. F. Mussner, Galaterbrief, ³1977 pp.277-290; P. von der Osten-Sacken, "Das paulinische Verständnis des Gesetzes im Spanungsfeld von Eschatologie und Geschichte", EvTh 37 (1977) 549-587.
198 Cf. H. Schürmann, " 'Das Gesetz des Christus' (Gal 6,2): Jesu Verhalten und Wort

law[199], or discussed Paul's attitude towards the law in a more general way[200].

As regards the relation between the Torah and Christ and Christian ethics, H. Schürmann asserts that Paul took Jesus' exemplary conduct and word to be the *Mitte* of all claims on the life of the Christian, calling it "the law of Christ" (Gal 6,2): as to its content it is contrasted with the Mosaic law which is revised and is concentrated upon the commandment of love, and as to its form it has the highest possible authority, replacing the Mosaic law[201].

As regards the validity of the Torah in Paul's theology, F. Hahn takes phrases like νόμος πίστεως (Rom 3,27), ὁ νόμος τοῦ πνεύματος (Rom 8,2) or νόμος τοῦ Χριστοῦ (Gal 6,2) as references to the OT Torah[202] which goes back to God himself and always remains the δικαίωμα of God, which incorporates the 'dialectic antithetic of the "law of sin (and) of death" and the "law of life", and which is newly qualified as a result of the eschatological renovation or reinstatement of the Torah in the sending of the Son of God, thus

---

als letztgültige sittliche Norm nach Paulus", *Neues Testament und Kirche*, FS R. Schnackenburg, ed. J. Gnilka, 1974, pp.282-300; J.A. Sanders, "Torah and Christ", *Int* 29 (1975) 372-390; E.M. Young, " 'Fulfill the Law of Christ': An Examination of Gal 6,2", *SBT* 7 (1977) 31-42.

199 P. Stuhlmacher, " 'Das Ende des Gesetzes': Über Ursprung und Ansatz der paulinischen Theologie", *ZThK* 67 (1970) 14-39; (= *Aufsätze*, 1981, pp.166-192); E.P. Sanders, "On the Question of Fulfilling the Law in Paul and Rabbinic Judaism", *Donum Gentilicium*, FS D. Daube, ed. E. Bammel et al., 1978, pp.103-126.

200 Cf. F.F. Bruce, "Paul and the Law of Moses", *BJRL* 57 (1974/75) 259-279; J. Blank, "Erwägungen zum Schriftverständnis des Paulus", *Rechtfertigung*, FS E. Käsemann, ed. J. Friedrich et al., 1976, pp.37-56; F. Hahn, "Das Gesetzesverständnis im Römer- und Galaterbrief", *ZNW* 67 (1976) 29-63; E.P. Sanders, *Paul*, pp.474-511; J.A. Sanders, "Torah and Paul", *God's Christ and His People*, FS N. Dahl, ed. J. Jervell, 1977, pp.132-140; W.W. Wuellner, "Toposforschung und Torahinterpretation bei Jesus und Paulus", *NTS* 24 (1978) 463-483; P. von der Osten-Sacken, "Paulus und das Gesetz", *VIKJ* 8 (1978) 59-66; H. Schlier, *Grundzüge einer paulinischen Theologie*, 1978, pp.77-97; C.E.B. Cranfield, *Romans*, 2, 1979, pp.845-862; F. Festorazzi, "Coherence and Value of the Old Testament in Paul's Thought", *Paul de Tarse*, ed. L. de Lorenzi, 1979, pp.165-173.

201 H. Schürmann, " 'Das Gesetz des Christus' (Gal 6,2): Jesu Verhalten und Wort als letztgültige sittliche Norm nach Paulus", *Neues Testament und Kirche*, FS R. Schnackenburg, ed. J. Gnilka, 1974, pp.289-294.

202 H. Hahn, "Gesetzesverständnis", *ZNW* 67 (1976) 37f.,47f.,57, following G. Friedrich, "Das Gesetz des Glaubens", *ThZ* 10 (1954) 401-417 (= *Auf das Wort kommt es an*, 1978, pp.107-122) and E. Lohse, "Exegetische Bemerkungen", 1973, pp. 279-287.

preserving the continuity of the OT law as revelation of God's will and at the same time abolishing its character as νόμος τῶν ἔργων[203]. Thus, according to Hahn, the assumption of an *abrogatio legis* or of a *nova lex* in Paul is wrong. One has to speak, rather, of an *interpretatio Christiana* of the OT.

P. von der Osten-Sacken asserts in a similar manner that the time of the law, for Paul, has come to an end only on the christological level with those who believe in Christ still being determined by the law which is in operation as eschatological factor of judgment as a result of Christ's death and resurrection. Thus, on the anthropological-soteriological level, the sinner is condemned by the law which is still valid and the believer fulfills the law by faith which works through love[204].

B.C. Wintle argues that Israel's election and the giving of the law have to be understood in their salvation-historical context as subordinate to God's purpose of creating a new humanity in Christ: the law was given to make man aware of his bondage to sin leading inevitably to God's judgment[205]. Christ brought the life which the law promised but could not give. He has superseded the law since he is, as "image of God", the final revelation of God. The believer, by faith in Christ, is redeemed from the condemnation of the law (pp.131-163). As he is "in Christ", he is no longer "under the law", and by the Spirit (pp.202-237) he fulfills the requirements of the law, in love. The term "law of Christ" is a general way of emphasizing that the believer stands under the will of God which is his saving purpose to create in Christ a new humanity. The life of the Christian is to be determined by moral conformity to Christ (pp. 261-298).

P. Stuhlmacher distinguishes four lines of thought in Paul's 'dialectic' theology of the law. (1) The church lives in the time and realization of the new covenant obligation of Jer 31,31ff. as a result of Christ's death and resurrection. (2) In and with Christ the time of freedom from the Mosaic law has begun. (3) The church

---

203 Cf. F. Hahn, "Gesetzesverständnis", *ZNW* 67 (1976) 60-63.
204 P. von der Osten-Sacken, "Das paulinische Verständnis des Gesetzes im Spannungsfeld von Eschatologie und Geschichte", *EvTh* 36 (1977) 549-587, here 567-569; also idem, "Das Evangelium als Einheit von Verheissung und Gesetz: Grundzüge paulinischer Theologie", *ThViat* 14 (1977/78), 87-108, here 90-99.
205 B.C. Wintle, *Law of Moses and Law of Christ*, 1977, pp.39-130.

has to prove this freedom to be good in the power of the Holy Spirit under the "Torah of Christ" (Gal 6,2). (4) This "Torah of Christ" is, as eschatological counterpart to the Sinai Torah, identical with the Zion Torah which is established by Jesus and which has as its centre the commandment of love and the fundamental claims of the decalogue thus reaching the goal of the spiritual intention of the Sinai Torah[206].

H. Schlier believes that the law is an offer of Christ for those who believe in him: the "law of Christ" is the Mosaic law which has been 'freed' on the basis of its fulfilment by Christ and consequently can be heard and fulfilled again as original will of God. Paul fights for the restitution of the Torah, God's instruction for life[207].

H. Hübner has written the most significant monograph on Paul's theology of the law, focusing on the development of his thinking from Gal to Rom[208]. He sees in Gal an essentially negative attitude towards the law differentiating, on the basis of Gal 3, between (1) the intention of God, (2) the immanent intention of the law, and (3) the intention of the law-giver (angels/demons). In Gal, Paul advocates a conscious abrogation of essential parts of the Torah (pp.16-43). As regards Rom, Hübner agrees basically with F. Hahn and finds a positive role of the law with "love" constituting the fulfilment of the Torah and essentially abrogating the cultic commandments of the Torah (pp.44-80). Hübner interprets νόμος in Rom 3,27; 8,2 as reference to the OT Torah (pp.118-129) without, however, linking the "law of faith" of Rom 8,2 with the "law of Christ" in Gal 6,2.

C.E.B. Cranfield emphasizes in his commentary that, for Paul, the law is not abrogated by Christ[209].

In 1980 several articles discussed the terms "law of the Spirit", "law of Christ", "law of faith", attempting to evaluate their significance in the light of the fact that Christ is "the end of the law" for Paul[210]. Recently C.T. Rhyne investigated the background,

---

206 P. Stuhlmacher, "Gesetz", *Aufsätze*, 1981, pp.156-159. The eschatological Zion Torah is described *o.c.*, pp.142-146,148-150.
207 H. Schlier, *Grundzüge*, 1978, pp.77-97, here 93-95.
208 H. Hübner, *Gesetz*, 1978 (³1982!). We use the third edition. Cf. also idem, Art. "νόμος", *EWNT* 2 (1981) 1158-1172, here 1167-1170.
209 C.E.B. Cranfield, *Romans*, 2, 1979, pp.852-861.
210 Cf. P.W. Meyer, "Romans 10,4 and the End of the Law", *The Divine Helmsman*,

meaning, and context of the phrase νόμον ἱστάνομεν in Rom 3,31 emphasizing that Paul used the conception of faith establishing the law to explain the latter's validity for the believer and the church[211].

From other recent contributions to our subject[212], we want to point out finally the article by U. Wilckens on the development of Paul's conception of the law[213] in which he discusses not only the statements on law in Gal and Rom (as Hübner) but also those in 1/2Cor and in Phil 3. He sees the position of Rom to be a revision of the "Kampfposition" of Phil and Gal which has to be explained by the occasion of the letter. In Gal we see a tremendous concentration on the commandments of the Torah to the commandment of love, resulting in the fact that the cultic and ritual injunctions are abrogated. At the same time it is obvious that the Torah as such and as a whole is not (!) abrogated but receives from Christ a positive-binding significance for the Christian. The "law of Christ" (Gal 6,2) is the Torah in its determinedness by Christ which is fulfilled by the Christian in the Spirit and in love (pp.164-176). In Rom, Paul still advocates the negative function of the law (of Phil 3 and Gal 3,19-20) regarding the sinner and regarding its total lack

---

FS L.H. Silbermann, ed. J.L. Crenshaw, 1980, pp.59-78; L.E. Keck, "The Law and 'The Law of Sin and Death' (Rom 8,1-4): Reflections on the Spirit and Ethics in Paul", *o.c.*, pp.41-57; A. Feuillet, "Loi de Dieu, loi du Christ et loi de l'Esprit d'après les épîtres pauliniennes: Les raports de ces trois lois avec la Loi Mosaique", *NovTest* 22 (1980) 29-65; W.S. Campbell, "Christ as the End of the Law in Rom 10,4", *Studia Biblica 1978*, 3, ed. E.A. Livingstone, 1980 pp.73-81; H. Räisänen, "Das 'Gesetz des Glaubens' (Rom 3,27) und das 'Gesetz des Geistes'(Rom 8,21)", *NTS* 26 (1980) 101-117.

211 C.T. Rhyne, *Faith Establishes the Law*, SBLDS 55, 1981.

212 Cf. H. Räisänen, "Paul's Theological Difficulties with the Law", *Studia Biblica 1978*, 3, 1980, pp.301-320; U. Luz, in R. Smend, U. Luz, *Gesetz*, 1981, pp.89-112; G. Dautzenberg, "Paulus und das Alte Testament", *BiKi* 37 (1982) 21-27; A. Maillot, "Essai sur les citations vétérotestamentaires contenues dans Romans 9 à 11, ou comment se servir de la Torah pour montrer que le 'Christ est la fin de la Torah' ", *EThR* 57 (1982) 55-73; W.D. Davies, "Paul and the Law: Reflections on Pitfalls in Interpretation", *Paul and Paulinism*, FS C.K. Barrett, ed. M.D. Hooker et al., 1982, pp.4-16 (shortened version of his article, with the same title, in *HLJ* 29/1978, pp. 1459-1504) emphasizing the complexity of Paul's view of the Torah on his Jewish background and asserting that Paul reassessed the law in the light of Jesus' messiahship; H. Räisänen, *Paul and the Law*, WUNT 29, 1983.

213 U. Wilckens, "Zur Entwicklung des paulinischen Gesetzesverständnisses", *NTS* 28 (1982) 154-190; cf. also idem, "Statements on the Development of Paul's View of the Law", *Paul and Paulinism*, 1982, pp.17-26.

of salvational power, but at the same time he seeks to establish the law (Rom 3,31) by pointing out its positive significance in the life of the Christian (Rom 8,2) as "law of the Spirit" and "law of life" (pp.184f.).

This survey leads to two important observations. First, the question of the development of Paul's theology of the law is still debated. Rather than assuming decisive changes in the content of Paul's conceptions[214], we side with those who explain the differences in Paul's statements on the significance and validity of the law on the basis of (1) different lines of thought which can be correlated, (2) the different perspectives of Paul depending on the occasion of the letters, or (3) developments in presentation[215].

---

214 Cf. especially the study of H. Hübner, *Gesetz*; also J.W. Drane, *Paul, Libertine or Legalist? A Study in the Theology of the Major Pauline Epistles*, 1975, pp.34f., 62,68,135 etc. As regards Drane's study, the critique of W. Bieder in *ThZ* 32 (1976) 109f. is totally ill-conceived when he assumes Drane's "theologiegeschichtliche Bindung" to Anglicanism leading him to a presentation of Paul, as regards Rom, as a "Kirchenvater der anglikanischen Kirche ... die die goldene Mitte zwischen 'Protestantismus' und 'Katholizismus' darstellt" (p.110), since Drane is not an Anglican in the first place! On the development of Paul's thinking in general see now also P. Benoit, "Genèse et évolution de la pensée paulinienne", *Paul de Tarse*, 1979, pp.75-100.

215 Cf. e.g. F. Hahn, "Gesetzesverständnis", *ZNW* 67 (1976) 30,57-60; E.P. Sanders, *Paul*, p.433 n.9; P. Stuhlmacher, "Gesetz", *Aufsätze*, pp.156f.; similarly W.D. Davies, "Paul and the Law", 1982, pp.8-10; obviously also P. von der Osten-Sacken, "Verständnis", *EvTh* 37 (1977) 549-587; U. Luz, in R. Smend, U. Luz, *Gesetz*, p.153 n.170 (arguing contra Hübner). Cf. also B.H. Brinsmead, *Galatians — A Dialogical Response to Opponents*, SBLDS 65, 1982, pp.115-127 who shows that it was the specific law tradition of the opponents with its tendency towards exclusivism and calendrical observance which called forth the "unusually negative treatment from Paul" (p.127). U. Wilckens, "Entwicklung", *NTS* 28 (1982) 180 calls the position of Paul in Rom a 'revision' or 'correction' of earlier statements, but then goes on to explain the position in Rom on the basis of the particular occasion of the letter (pp.180f.) which seems to indicate that he would maintain the basic reconcilability of Paul's statements on the law. The rather polemic article of H. Räisänen, "Difficulties", *Studia Biblica 1978*, 3, 1980, pp.301-320 in which he asserts that Paul the theologian had vast problems with the law which Paul the man was unable to digest is totally unconvincing; e.g. the fact that Cranfield and Käsemann differ diametrically in their understanding of the relation of law and Gospel in Paul (p.307) is surely no proof for the view that Paul had difficulties with the law! I regret that it was too late for me to discuss Räisänen's most recent book, *Paul and the Law*, WUNT 29, 1983, as fully as I would have wished. His conclusion that Paul's speech about the law was deliberately "loose" and "vague" and that his understanding of the nature and role of the law is "strangely ambiguous", problematic, and full of difficulties and inconsistencies (cf. particularly pp.199-202,264-269) is exegetically unwarranted (cf. §15.2. for a discussion of some relevant

Second, the central issues in Paul's theology of the law are linked with the question of the hermeneutical significance of the statement that Christ is the "end of the law" and the related question of the meaning of the phrases "law of Christ", "law of faith", and "law of the Spirit". We are therefore justified when we focus subsequently on these statements and phrases as they are not only crucial for our inquiry into the christological significance of the traditional correlation of law and wisdom but also for a proper understanding of Paul's theology of the law and hence also of his parenesis.

15.2. Exegetical Evidence

15.2.1. Gal 3,19-25. The related questions of the purpose of the Mosaic law and of the Christian's liberation from the law are treated in Gal 3,19-25[216]. As concerns Paul's discussion of the permanent validity of the promise in 3,15-18, one might conclude from 3,17 that Paul denies the divine authority of the law. Hence Paul inserts a rather concise digression[217] on the Jewish law to prevent such a wrong conclusion.

The two double statements in v.19b-e are chiastically explained in vv.20-25: v.20 elucidates the two final phrases in v.19d.e referring to the origin of the law, and vv.21-25 dwell on the function of the law (cf. v.19b.c), first warding off a wrong conclusion (v.21) and then presenting Paul's own view (vv.22-25)[218]. As regards the assumed origin of the Jewish law, some scholars assert that Paul

---

passages) and theologically both unfounded and implausible. He does not discuss the correlation of different lines of thought in Paul which other scholars hold logical and coherent. His conclusions are in fact preconceived ideas which are read back into the texts. Räisänen is seemingly not interested even in an attempt to arrive at a coherent picture of Paul's position as regards the law. Coherence and consistency of Paul's theological position(s) is much more likely than ambiguity and secondary rationalizations.

216 For a detailed exegesis cf. H.D. Betz, *Galatians*, pp.161-180; also U. Wilckens, "Entwicklung", *NTS* 28 (1982) 171-173. As regards the theology of Paul's opponents in Galatia cf. now B.H. Brinsmead, *Galatians*, 1982.
217 Cf. H.D. Betz, *o.c.*, p.163.
218 Cf. G. Ebeling, *Die Wahrheit des Evangeliums*, 1981, pp.257f.; see H.D. Betz, *o.c.*, pp.163-171 for a detailed analysis of v.19.

emphasizes in v.19 the absenteeship of God in the communication of the law and demonizes the law as "law of angels"[219].

Without detailed analysis of vv.19d.e.20 suffice it to say that (1) the ἄγγελοι are not regarded as evil, neither therefore the Torah[220]; (2) the divine origin of the law is not denied[221]; (3) even though the disputed meaning of μεσίτης[222] implies a depreciatory aspect[223] which results in the Torah being described as inferior, this does not mean that Paul wants to disparage the law, but that (4) Paul, arguing against people who magnified the law unduly over against the Gospel (promise), depicts here the law as *nuda lex* in a narrow sense, i.e. not the law "in the fullness and wholeness of its true character, but the law as seen apart from Christ"[224];

---

219 Cf. especially H. Hübner, *Gesetz*, pp.28f.,78; similarly H. Schlier, *Galater*, pp.157f.
220 Cf. H. Schlier, *o.c.*, p.158; H.D. Betz, *Galatians*, p.169; C.E.B. Cranfield, *Romans*, 2, p.858; F.F. Bruce, *Galatians*, p.177; H. Räisänen, *Paul*, pp.131f.; see also T. Callan, "Pauline Midrash: The Exegetical Background of Gal 3,19b", *JBL* 99 (1980) 550-554. Contra H. Hübner, *o.c.*, p.28. Hübner's interpretation of Gal 3,19-20 regarding the role and nature of the angels in the promulgation of the law has been repeatedly criticized; cf. D.R. de Lacey, in *JStNT* 4 (1978) 71; U. Luz, in *ThZ* 35 (1979) 122; J. Plevnik, in *Bib* 61 (1980) 296. H. Räisänen, *o.c.*, pp.131f.
221 Cf. T. Callan, *a.c.*, p.554; A. van Dülmen, *Theologie*, pp.44f.; R. Bring, *Christus und das Gesetz*, pp.73-78,95; C.H. Giblin, "Three Monotheistic Texts in Paul", *CBQ* 37 (1975) 541; H. Schlier, *o.c.*, p.158; F. Mussner, *Galaterbrief*, p.247 with n.17; B.C. Wintle, *Law*, p.78 n.14; C.E.B. Cranfield, *o.c.*, p.858; F.F. Bruce, *o.c.*, pp.175,177,180. Contra H.D. Lührmann, *Galater*, p.62; H. Hübner,*o.c.*, pp.29f.; also U. Wilckens, "Entwicklung", *NTS* 28 (1982) 172.
222 Most scholars interpret the mediator as referring to Moses; cf. H. Hübner, *o.c.*, p.29; H.D. Betz, *o.c.*, p.170; C.E.B. Cranfield, *o.c.*, p.858; R. Callan, *a.c.*, pp.555-564; B.H. Brinsmead, *Galatians*, pp.116f., 284 n.10 (referring to AssMos 1,14; 3,12; Philo VitMos 3,19 and, with caution, Heb 8,6; 9,15; 12,24). Others see in the mediator the angel of the presence; cf. A. Vanhoye, "Un médiateur des anges en Ga 3, 19-20", *Bib* 59 (1978) 403-411, followed by F.F. Bruce, *o.c.*, p.179; H. Räisänen, *o.c.*, p.130.
223 This is unanimously acknowledged. H.D. Betz, *o.c.*, pp.171f. explains, for example, that Paul describes here the mediator as the representative of a plurality in contrast to God's oneness, that this plurality need not to be identified with the angels, and that "Paul argues that anything that stands in contrast to the oneness of God is inferior. Since the concept of mediator presupposes by definition a plurality of parties, it is inferior and, consequently, renders the Torah inferior". Cf. similarly U. Wilckens, *a.c.*, p.172; B.H. Brinsmead, *o.c.*, pp.116-118, 284 n.11.
224 C.E.B. Cranfield, *Romans*, 2, p.859, quoting J. Calvin, *Institutes of the Christian Religion*, 2.7.2.; cf. also F.F. Bruce, *Galatians*, p.179; F. Hahn, "Gesetzesverständnis", *ZNW* 67 (1976) 59; also B.C. Wintle, *Law*, p.78 who emphasizes that Paul's main concern is not to demonstrate the inferiority of the law per se "but only that the giving of the law did not alter the conditions of God's promise to Abraham".

(5) the characterization of the law as stipulated by angels via a mediator has to be understood in the context of the Galatians' concerns regarding circumcision and the observation of certain days, months, times, and years (cf. Gal 4,10)[225].

As regards the function of the Jewish law, Paul states that the law was "added" in order to condemn the transgressions as such[226] until the coming of Christ (v.19b.c) enclosing everything under sin (v.22a) and keeping everybody in custody until Christ (vv.23-24), and that with Christ's coming we are no longer "under the law" (v.25).

Scholars have interpreted these statements as signifying the abrogation of the Torah with Christ being the *terminus ad quem* of the Torah[227]. This view has been disputed, however[228]. It suffices here to point out that Paul (1) does not refer to a new Torah which is to be given in the messianic age and thus to be connected with Christ[229], (2) wants to avoid the total separation of the Torah (of Moses) and the promise (to Abraham) in v.21a: the law is not directly opposed to the promise, for the law was not given by God to create (!) life in and for the sinners (v.21) but only to condemn sinners as sinners (vv.23-24)[230], (3) describes the function of the law in its salvation-historical significance and necessity[231] as "prison warden" (v.23) and "slave attendant" (v.24), (4) argues here and in Gal as a whole that faith in Jesus

---

225 Cf. M. Limbeck, *Von der Ohnmacht des Rechts: Untersuchungen zur Gesetzeskritik des Neuen Testaments*, 1972, pp.93f. n.28 who points out that the Jewish tradition attributed such regulations to the angels who gave them to Moses, referring to 1QS 10,1-8; Jub 1,27.29; 2,1.25-26.29.30; 6,20.22; 15,25-28. He concludes that "wenn die Galater diese Vorshriften ernst nehmen, folgen sie eigentlich dem Geheiß der Engel — und damit war für Paulus die Möglichkeit gegeben, die Beobachtung dieser Anordnungen mit dem früheren Götzendienst der Galater zu identifizieren" (p.94 n.28).

226 Thus taking χάριν in the causal sense; cf. F. Mussner, *Galaterbrief*, p.245 with n.5; U. Wilckens, "Entwicklung", *NTS* 28 (1982) 171. Pace H.D. Betz, *Galatians*, pp. 164-167; H. Hübner, *Gesetz*, p.27.

227 Cf. F. Mussner, o.c., p.246; H. Hübner, o.c., p.34; B.C. Wintle, o.c., pp.105-107; also F.F. Bruce, *Galatians*, pp.176,182f., H. Räisänen, *Paul*, pp.43f.

228 Cf. H.D. Betz, o.c., p.178f.; C.E.B. Cranfield, o.c., pp.857-859.

229 Cf. H.D. Betz, o.c., p.168.

230 Cf. U. Wilckens, "Entwicklung", *NTS* 28 (1982) 172; also B.C. Wintle, *Law*, p.78.

231 Cf. H.D. Betz, *Galatians*, pp.165,178 who emphasizes that Paul was convinced of the necessity of the Torah "even if this necessity consists of the negative role which this Torah plays".

Christ is the sole constitutive basis for salvation (and not the Torah)[232], (5) sees, consequently, the Torah not as abrogated, evil entity but as outstripped in its specific structure which characterizes its position *ante Christum crucifixum*[233], and, finally, (6) leaves several questions concerning his theology of the law unanswered at this point in this pericope[234].

Thus, we conclude that Paul, in Gal 3,19-25, does not deny the divine origin of the Torah, nor does he advocate the abrogation of the Torah. Rather, his statements, which have to be understood against the polemic background of Gal, describe the law *post Christum* as seen *sine Christo*. It is this law which is inferior to the promise, which is temporary, and which was unable to produce life and righteousness.

15.2.2. Gal 5,14. The statement that ὁ πᾶς νόμος is "fulfilled" (πεπλήρωται) in the one commandment of love resumes Paul's treatment of the subject of the law (3,19-25). It is generally agreed that ὁ πᾶς νόμος does not refer to the sum-total of the individual precepts of the Torah but to the law as a whole[235] as God's demand. The gnomic pass.perf. of πληροῦν is crucial for a proper understanding of Paul's thought here[236]: to "fulfill" the law means to "do" the law in the sense of ποιεῖν, πράσσειν, φυλάσσειν, i.e. to 'perform' the law and to meet its requirements[237].

H.D. Betz wants to distinguish between the 'doing' of the Torah (Gal 5,3) and the

---

232 In this context Paul can speak of his death both to the law (Gal 2,19) and to the cosmos (Gal 6,14). Cf. H.D. Betz, *o.c.*, p.179.

233 Cf. F. Hahn, "Gesetzesverständnis", *ZNW* 67 (1976) 62; C.E.B. Cranfield, *Romans*, 2, p.859; similarly E. Jüngel, *Paulus und Jesus*, ⁵1979, pp.59f.

234 Cf. H.D. Betz, *o.c.*; pp.175f.; G. Ebeling, *Warheit*, pp.268f.

235 Cf. BDR §275.3; also H.D. Betz, *Galatians*, p.275; F. Mussner, *Galaterbrief*, p.370; F.F. Bruce, *Galatians*, p.241; H. Hübner, "Das ganze und das eine Gesetz", *KuD* 21 (1975) 239-256; idem, *Gesetz*, pp.37f.; U. Wilckens, "Entwicklung", *NTS* 28 (1982) 174. Cf. also B.H. Brinsmead, *Galatians*, p.119 who asserts that the issue in Paul is the law as a whole, the law in principle.

236 Acknowledged by H. Hübner, *o.c.*, p.76 in his discussion of the parallel passage Rom 13,8-10 but not consistently applied in his treatment of Gal 5,14 where he simply presupposes the meaning "to do" (p.37).

237 Cf. C.K. Barrett, *Romans*, p.251; U. Wilckens, *Römer*, 3, 1982, pp.68,71 with n.393; H. Schlier, *Galater*, p.244; F. Mussner, *o.c.*, p.370 (who rightly points out that one should see no alternative between πληροῦν in the sense of 'fulfilling the law' and 'doing' it, and πληροῦν in the sense of summary and centre of purpose); also U. Wilckens, *a.c.*, p.175.

'fulfilling' of the Torah (Gal 5,14)[238]. However, he does not specify what πληροῦν should mean in contrast to ποιεῖν. The notion of H. Hübner that πᾶς νόμος in Gal 5, 14 is a critical-ironic phrase which contrasts the quantitative fulfilment of the 'totality' of the law by the Christian with the Jewish quantitative fulfilment of all commandments of the Torah, i.e. that the whole Mosaic law is not (!) identical with the 'whole' law of the Christian (i.e. the commandment of love), thus differing drastically from Paul's later view in Rom 13,9[239], has to be rejected. Paul wants to say in Gal 5 that only the Christian who is justified by faith is able to fulfill the law, as it is 'summarized' in the law of love, "in Christ", and in the power of the Spirit (5,5-6)[240].

Paul states that the Christian who has received the Spirit, who is "in Christ", and whose faith is working through love (5,5-6), fulfills the Torah as a whole in the law of love (cf. Lev 19,18) as the latter is the basic principle or common denominator of the Torah[241].

The commandment of love is interpreted as basic principle of the Torah in connection with the rabbinic practice of the כלל[242]. The *kelal* is a technical term in the context of legal discussions designating (1) a general term or principle in contrast to the specific, or (2) a general rule in relation with the individual laws which are summed up in this rule[243]. As the *kelal* is not a מצוה, and as λόγος in Gal 5,14 need not mean "commandment", it is wrong to speak of a material reduction of the Torah to a single commandment[244]. - The commandment of love is interpreted as common denominator of the Torah in connection with the term ἀνακεφαλαιοῦσθαι in Rom 13,9: the law of love is of dominating significance in the total framework of the Torah[245]. This term does not mean completion or reduction of a multiplicity to a unity, but concentrated reference of the various individual commandments to one point of reference[246].

Thus, Paul does not imply the total abrogation of the Torah

---

238 H.D. Betz, *o.c.*, p.275.
239 H. Hübner, *o.c.*, pp.38,76-78.
240 Cf. U. Wilckens, *Römer*, 2, p.69 n.383; idem, *a.c.*, p.189 n.64. The view of Hübner that Gal 5,14 has nothing to do with Rom 13,8-10 has been criticized repeatedly; cf. U. Luz, *ThZ* 35 (1979) 123; J. Plevnik, *Bib* 61 (1980) 296. Gal 5,14 and Rom 13,8-10 are usually related with each other; cf. H.D. Betz, *o.c.*, p.275 n.31.
241 On the law of love in Judaism cf. K. Berger, *Gesetzesauslegung*, 1, pp.99-136; A. Nissen, *Gott und der Nächste*, 1974, pp.224-244,389-416.
242 Cf. F.F. Bruce, *Galatians*, p.241, quoting H.J. Schoeps, *Paul*, p.208.
243 Cf. A. Nissen, *o.c.*, p.400.
244 Contra H. Hübner, *Gesetz*, pp.38f.,76f., H. Räisänen, *Paul*, pp.26f.
245 Cf. U. Wilckens, *Römer*, 2, pp.68f.
246 Cf. H. Schlier, in *ThWNT* 3 (1938) 681; S. Lyonnet, "La charité plénitude de la loi (Rm 13,8-10)", *Dimensions de la vie chrétienne*, ed. L. de Lorenzi, 1979, p.156; W. Schrage, *Ethik*, p.197; also H. Merklein, in *EWNT* 1 (1980) 197 who defines this term in Rom 13,9 (with reference to Gal 5,14!) as summary of the law as a whole.

nor its partial reduction to the commandment of love[247] but asserts that the requirement of the entire law is "fulfilled" (perfect!) by the Christian when he meets the obligation of love[248]. The law fulfilled in love[249] is not means of salvation, but has to be seen as "the ethical channel through which the new life in Christ flows"[250]. Freedom from the Torah is to be realized in the fulfilment of the Torah.

For the Christian, living in the Spirit, the condemning law is a past entity which does not apply anymore, whereas the law per se and as a whole still applies and is totally fulfilled where Christians comply with the one commandment of love. The Torah receives its controlling centre — the one law of love — on the basis of the

---

247 Contra H. Halter, *Taufe und Ethos: Paulinische Kriterien für das Proprium christlicher Moral*, FThS 106, 1977, pp.119-121 who asserts a reduction or concentration of the Torah to the love of one's neighbour: the Torah has ceased to be the ultimate criterion for God's will but has become a "Fundgrube" of the will of God whose superior criterion is now "die Zuwendung Gottes zum Menschen durch und in Jesus Christus" (p.121). There is an unresolved ambiguity in Halter's position: on the one hand he rejects the notion that the claims of the law have become irrelevant for the Christian (p.120), and on the other hand he asserts that for the Christian the law stands under the 'crisis' of the superior motivating criterion of God's love expressed in Christ (p.121).
248 Cf. O. Merk, *Handeln aus Glauben: Die Motivierungen der paulinischen Ethik*, 1968, pp.9f.,70,74 who asserts that "in der inneren Bezogenheit von Gottes Liebeshandeln und dem Liebesdienst der Gemeinde ist die Stellung des Gesetzes für den Christen fixiert. Die Totalität des Gesetzes ... wird zusammengefaßt in der Totalität der Selbstpreisgabe ..., und so ist mit dem Hinweis auf das Gesetz als Begründung für sein Tun dem Christen die Möglichkeit genommen, seinen Liebesdienst im Sinne eines κατὰ σάρκα ... zu tun" (p.70). Cf. also H. Ridderbos, *Paul*, pp.155, 282; W.G. Kümmel, *Theologie*, pp.164f.,202; A. van Dülmen, *Theologie*, pp.60f.; W. Schrage, *Ethik*, p.198; U. Wilckens, "Entwicklung", *NTS* 28 (1982) 174f.
249 T.J. Deidun, *New Covenant Morality in Paul*, AnBibl 89, 1981, pp.150-187 is ambiguous concerning the role of the law for the Christian as regards Gal 5,14: on the one hand he states that God's demands expressed in the law are not laid aside but are 'fulfilled' in God's love which has been given to the Christian (pp.153f.) and that Christian love does not constitute an ethical norm which replaces the context of God's demand (p.168), and on the other hand he asserts that, for Paul, the law is "a privileged (but not the only one) means of supporting and illustrating ethical claims to which he believes — on grounds which have nothing to do with the Law as such — the Christian is liable" (pp.159f.).
250 C.K. Barrett, *Romans*, p.251 discussing Rom 13,10 and referring to Gal 5,14; cf. also S. Lyonnet, "Charité", 1979, pp.158-163. H.D. Betz, *Galatians*, p.275 is surely right when he asserts that "the commandment to love functions in Paul's theology in a different way compared with the commandments to do the Torah in Jewish theology".

central point of view of faith in the crucified and exalted Lord Jesus Christ. From this follows that not all commandments of the Torah retain their validity. But the Torah as such and as a whole is not abrogated[251].

15.2.3. Gal 6,2.

Paul's statement "bear one another's burdens, and by doing so you will fulfill the law of Christ" (ἀναπληρώσετε τὸν νόμον τοῦ Χριστοῦ) has puzzled many scholars, as it seems to advocate what Paul rejected earlier, viz. that the Christians are to keep the law. The key term is νόμος τοῦ Χριστοῦ which is mostly interpreted in terms of a polemic intention of Paul's part who is said to use νόμος here homonymously for Jesus' ethical teaching or Jesus' way from the *kenosis* to the cross[252], or the commandment of love[253], or the Christian imperative in its totality[254].

Taking into consideration the wider context of this statement

---

[251] Cf. U. Wilckens, "Entwicklung", *NTS* 28 (1982) 173-175. He states that the cultic (4,10) and ritual (2,14) commandments of the Torah are therefore to be regarded as abrogated (p.175). We prefer not to speak of abrogation which carries the sense of repealing or doing away with the law: Christ has fully met the requirements of the Torah as way to salvation and is therefore the only way to salvation. The Torah in its cultic and ritual aspects as way to salvation has been fully realized by Christ and was hence replaced by faith in Christ.

[252] Cf. E. Bammel, "Νόμος Χριστοῦ", *TU* 88 (1964) 120-128; A. van Dülmen, *Theologie*, pp.66f.; F. Mussner, *Galaterbrief*, p.399; D. Lührmann, *Galater*, pp.96f.; F.F. Bruce, *Galatians*, p.261; H. Schürmann, "Gesetz", 1974, pp.289-294; E.M. Young, "Law of Chfist", *SBT* 7 (1977) 31-42; also B.H. Brinsmead, *Galatians*, 1982, pp.173-178 who regards the "law of Christ" as heading of Gal 5-6 which develop the dominical saying recorded in 5,14. For a critique of the view that the "law of Christ" refers to an early codification of the teaching of Christ cf. B.C. Wintle, *Law*, 1977, pp.299-321.

[253] Cf. W. Schrage, *Einzelgebote*, pp.99f.250; D.A. Stoike, *'The Law of Christ': A Study of Paul's Use of the Expression in Galatians 6,2*, Th.D.Diss. School of Theology at Claremont, 1971, passim; H. Schürmann, *Orientierungen am Neuen Testament*, 1978, pp.33-37,96; J.F. Collange, *De Jésus à Paul: L'éthique du Nouveau Testament*, 1980, pp.60f.; U. Schnelle, *Gerechtigkeit*, 1983, pp.63f.

[254] Cf. F. Mussner, *o.c.*, p.285; G. Strecker, "Autonome Sittlichkeit und das Proprium der christlichen Ethik bei Paulus", *ThLZ* 104 (1979) 872; B.C. Wintle, *o.c.*, pp. 224f. with n.75 (recognizing only a formal similarity with the Torah – the aspect of obligation in Christ's body; he does not even discuss the possibility of a material correspondence with the Torah, as qualified by Christ); H. Schürmann, *o.c.*, p.37 ("wie es entgegentritt in der Lehrtradition der Kirche"); A. Feuillet, "Loi de Dieu", *NovTest* 22 (1980) 43-57 (asserting that the "law of Christ is "l'impératif moral qui découle de l'indicatif baptismal", p.61), H. Räisänen, *Paul*, pp.77-82 ("the way of life characteristic of the church of Christ", p.82).

which has to be linked with Gal 5,6.14, we understand νόμος τοῦ Χριστοῦ as reference to the Torah as defined and qualified by Christ[255]: (1) in 5,14 νόμος clearly refers to the Torah; (2) the term ἀγάπη relates 5,14 to 5,6; (3) the declaration ἐν Χριστῷ Ἰησοῦ is the crucial heading of 5,13ff. which explicates the thesis of 5,6; (4) in 5,6 ἐν Χριστῷ Ἰησοῦ is parallel to (ἐν) πνεύματι in 5,5 which is again explicated in 5,13ff.; (5) thus, the love of the brother is founded in the love of Christ (2,20) and results from the gift of the Spirit (5,16.22ff.); (6) consequently the law can and should be fulfilled[256] by the righteous ἐκ πίστεως Χριστοῦ who is ἐν Χριστῷ and guided ἐν πνεύματι: this happens when he practices ἀγάπη which consists in bearing one another's burdens[257]. As "law of Christ", the Torah is *a posteriori* the measure and standard of the Christian life[258].

It is not impossible to derive the actual term νόμος τοῦ Χριστοῦ from the Galatian opponents who might have linked Christ with the messianic Torah[259] and thus combined obedience to Christ

---

255 Cf. E. Jüngel, *Paulus und Jesus*, ⁵1979, p.61; A. van Dülmen, *Theologie*, pp.66-68; U. Wilckens, *Römer*, 1, p.245; H. Schlier, *Grundzüge*, p.94; H.D. Betz, *Galatians*, pp.166,179,229f.; and especially U. Wilckens, "Entwicklung", *NTS* 28 (1982) 175f. Similarly also F. Hahn, "Gesetzesverständnis", *ZNW* 67 (1976) 57. It is interesting to note that H. Hübner, *Gesetz*, does not deal with this phrase: he treats Gal 6,2 only with regard to the term τὰ βαρή (pp.82f.,86f.); when he quotes E. Jüngel he accepts his view only with regard to Rom 8,2 (p.129). U. Schnelle, *Gerechtigkeit*, p.195 n.274 discards Hahn's view without giving arguments.

256 The reading of the future tense ἀναπληρώσετε in (P⁴⁶) B G and in most ancient versions is to be preferred to the aor.imp. ἀναπληρώσατε (א A C D^gr K) on the basis of attestation and transcriptual probability; cf. B.M. Metzger, *Textual Commentary*, p.598; also F. Mussner, *Galaterbrief*, p.398 n.23; H.D. Betz, *o.c.*, p.299; F.F. Bruce, *Galatians*, p.261.

257 Cf. U. Wilckens,*a.c.*, pp.175f.; H.D. Betz, *o.c.*, p.300; also B.H. Brinsmead, *Galatians*, pp.177-180 who is, however, not totally clear as to his interpretation of "law" here: he does not explain whether "law" refers only to Jesus' ethical teaching, taken up by the opponents and by Paul, or whether it includes the Torah, as under the Lordship of Christ (p.180) as well.

258 Cf. E. Jüngel, *o.c.*, p.61 n.1 stating that "statt *in lege (sub lege)* lebt der Christ *cum lege*"; O. Merk, *Handeln*, pp.76f. asserting that the "law of Christ" is the law which Christ has fulfilled for us and which is therefore the "law of the Spirit of life in Christ Jesus" (Rom 8,2) which demands in the Spirit and can be fulfilled (only) in the Spirit.

259 Cf. H.D. Betz, *Galatians*, pp.300f.; U. Wilckens, "Entwicklung", *NTS* 28 (1982) 176, following W.D. Davies, *Paul*, pp.69-74,142-145,174-176; idem, *Torah*, pp.91f.; H.J. Schoeps, *Paul*, pp.172f., also B.H. Brinsmead, *Galatians*, pp.175-177. Wilckens admits that the Jewish notion of a messianic Torah does very probably not go back

with obedience to the Jewish Torah. This thinking is refuted by Paul since Gal 5,13, asserting that (1) freedom from the law is the obligation to fulfill the law in terms of the law of love, that (2) the law of love is to be made specific on the basis of the love of the crucified Christ in terms of the treatment of Christians who have sinned.

15.2.4. 1Cor 7,19. When Paul states, in the context of a discussion of Christian freedom (7,17-24), that "circumcision is nothing and uncircumcision is nothing, but the keeping (τήρησις) of God's commandments (ἐντολῶν)", he implies that even for Gentile Christians the keeping of the commandments of the Torah has a positive significance[260]. The ἐντολαὶ θεοῦ should be interpreted in terms of the commandments of the Jewish law[261] rather than in terms of Christian 'rules' of the new life[262], as Paul's statement obviously carries a rather polemic tone. As a result of God's κλῆσις (7,17.20), the Torah is modified in a rather essential respect, i.e. insofar as the Torah establishes the salvation-historically relevant difference between Jews and Gentiles. But at the same time the commandments of the Torah, as commandments of God, are not only declared as binding but pronounced as 'fulfillable' only and specifically ἐν Χριστῷ[263].

Obviously Paul describes the situation and life of the Christian: the material parallels in Gal 5,6; 6,15 explain the τήρησις in terms of the πίστις which expresses itself through ἀγάπη (5,6) and in terms of the καινὴ κτίσις (6,15)[264]. The fact that Paul refers to

---

to the 1st century A.D. By way of contrast cf. M. Hengel, "Zwischen Jesus und Paulus", *ZThK* 72 (1975) 191f. who claims that Gal 6,2 shows the original tradition-historical origin of Paul in the Christian Jewish-Hellenistic circle around Stephen.

260 This is seen clearly by U. Wilckens, *a.c.*, p.158; also H. Riesenfeld, Art. "τήρησις", *ThWNT* 8 (1969) 146.
261 Cf. U. Wilckens, *a.c.*, p.159; H. Räisänen, *Paul*, p.68; also H. Riesenfeld, ibid.; O. Merk, *Handeln*, p.110; obviously also W. Schrage, *Ethik*, p.197.
262 Cf. C. Senft, *1 Corinthiens*, p.97; W.F. Orr, J.A. Walter, *I Corinthians*, p.216; also C.K. Barrett, *First Corinthians*, p.169 explaining it as "the will of God as disclosed in his Son"; and seemingly W. Schrage, *o.c.*, p.178. Also T.J. Deidun, *Morality*, 1981, p.160 who does not want to exclude the possibility, however, that the "commandments of God" might "coincide (at least in part) with the impositions of the Law".
263 Cf. U. Wilckens, "Entwicklung", *NTS* 28 (1982) 159.
264 Cf. G. Schrenk, in *ThWNT* 2 (1935) 549; H. Riesenfeld, in *ThWNT* 8 (1969) 146;

the fulfilment of the commandments of the Torah as ethical reality of the Christian existence as a matter-of-course is no real contradiction to his more 'dialectic' statements on the law in Gal and Rom. This fact can be explained (1) on the basis of the central importance of conversion as radical moral turn from evil to true righteousness (cf. 1Cor 6,9-11), and (2) with the reference to the fact that the doctrine of justification of Gal and Rom supplies the substantiating context of this ethical turn[265].

15.2.5. 1Cor 9,19-23. In this pericope[266] Paul explains his ἐλευθερία (9,1) as apostle which enables him to relinquish the right to maintenance (vv.7ff.) and to become a δοῦλος for all people in the context of his missionary enterprise in order to lead many to Christ (v.19). This missionary principle is then illustrated by his behaviour towards Jews and Gentiles (vv.20-21) and by his behaviour towards weak Christians (v.22a). In both cases Paul wants to emphasize his personal adaption to different people in different situations. To the Jews, Paul becomes a Jew, i.e. "to those under the law (ὑπὸ νόμον) as one under the law (ὑπὸ νόμον)" (v.20a) even though, as a Christian, he is "not under the law" (v. 20b). In the same manner he becomes to the lawless (ἄνομοι) one who is lawless (ἄνομος, v.21a) even though as a Christian he is "not lawless", i.e. not outside of the law of God[267] but within the law of Christ (μὴ ὢν ἄνομος θεοῦ ἀλλ' ἔννομος Χριστοῦ, v.21b). Paul refers here to the Jewish Torah in its function as criterion of the salvation-historical differentiation between the Jews who have the law and the Gentiles who do not have the law[268].

C.K. Barrett, *First Corinthians*, p.169; U. Wilckens, *a.c.*, p.158 (referring also to Rom 2,13; 8,4; 13,8-10; Gal 5,17).

265 Cf. U. Wilckens, *a.c.*, p.159.

266 Cf. G. Bornkamm, "Das missionarische Verhalten des Paulus nach 1Kor 9, 19-23 und in der Apostelgeschichte", (1966), *Geschichte und Glaube*, 2, Gesammelte Aufsätze 4, 1971, pp.149-161, here 149-153; C.H. Dodd, "'Ἔννομος Χριστοῦ'"(1953), *More New Testament Studies*, 1968, pp.134-148; G. Galitis, "Das Wesen der Freiheit: Eine Untersuchung zu 1 Kor 9 und seinem Kontext", *Freedom and Love*, 1981, pp.127-141, here 136f.; and especially U. Wilckens, *a.c.*, pp.159f. whom we follow in our analysis.

267 Clearly referring to the Mosaic Torah. Contra A. Feuillet, "Loi de Dieu", *NovTest* 22 (1980) 41f. who assumes that "law of God" means "toute loi divine positive".

268 Cf. Rom 2,12.14. Cf. H. Lietzmann, *Korinther*, p.43; C.K. Barrett, *First Corinthians*, p.212; U. Wilckens, *Römer*, 1, p.132; M. Limbeck, in *EWNT* 1 (1980) 254.

With regard to Paul's rhethorically polished statement in an adversative *parallelismus membrorum*, three observations are of paramount significance. First, νόμος stands always for the Torah, otherwise the elaborate parallelism becomes rather imprecise[269].

Second, in this way the incongruence of μὴ ὤν αὐτὸς ὑπὸ νόμον (v.20b) over against μὴ ὤν ἄνομος θεοῦ ἀλλ' ἔννομος Χριστοῦ (v.21b) takes on a specific meaning: the genitive θεοῦ is not meant to distinguish the law of God from the Torah as law of Moses, but rather emphasizes that Paul who is not under the dominion (ὑπό!) of the Torah has yet by no means left the realm of the Torah as *God's* Torah but is, as a Christian, rather 'within' the Torah, viz. the Torah as controlled (and thus qualified) by Christ[270].

Third, as a result the other incongruence becomes understandable[271]: the Jews are "under the law" (ὑπὸ νόμον), i.e. controlled by the law as slave-holder and in need of liberation, and the (Gentile!) Christian is "in the law" (ἔννομος), i.e. in the realm of the law as controlled by Christ[272].

Consequently, the phrase ἔννομος Χριστοῦ (which has to be linked with Gal 5,14; 6,2; Rom 3,31; 8,2-4)[273] characterizes the

---

269 Cf. C.K. Barrett, *o.c.*, pp.212-214; A. van Dülmen, *Theologie*, p.123 with n.162; U. Wilckens, "Entwicklung", *NTS* 28 (1982) 160. Contra H. Conzelmann, *Korintherbrief*, p.190; C.H. Dodd, " Ἔννομος Χριστοῦ", passim; C. Senft, *1 Corinthiens*, p.124; H. Balz, in *EWNT* 1 (1980) 1113f. and others who interpret νόμος in v.21b as "uneigentlich gebraucht" (H. Conzelmann, *Korintherbrief*, p.190) in terms of "the divine imperative to which he is subject" (T.J. Deidun, *Morality*, p.210 n.177).

270 Cf. U. Wilckens, "Entwicklung", *NTS* 28 (1982) 160; also H. Ridderbos, *Paul*, pp. 284f. Contra H. Lietzmann, *Korinther*, p.43; C.H. Dodd, " Ἔννομος Χριστοῦ", pp. 96-110; B.C. Wintle, *Law*, p.263; A Feuillet, "Loi de Dieu", *NovTest* 22 (1980) 42-57 who see νόμος in v.21b as reference to a 'new law' in terms of Jesus' ethical teaching or example, or as general Christian morals. We cannot follow U. Schnelle, *Gerechtigkeit*, 1983, pp.51f. who believes that Paul makes no basic statements on the significance of the law in 1Cor 9,20-22 but simply describes the paradoxical nature of the apostle's missionary existence, taking the law only as an example. The exegesis of H. Räisänen, *Paul*, p.81 is unsatisfactory: he states that v.21 simply asserts "that Paul is *bound* by God's will which, again, has something to do with Christ".

271 Note the remark of C.K. Barrett, *First Corinthians*, p.212 that v.21 is "one of the most difficult sentences in the epistle".

272 Cf. U. Wilckens, *a.c.*, p.160 asserting that the Torah itself as God's law is not removed and that Christ is not the antipode of the Torah but its Lord; cf. also H. Schlier, *Grundzüge*, p.94. The term ἔννομος Χριστοῦ is *gen. separationis*, cf. BDR § 182.4.

273 Cf. C.K. Barrett, *o.c.*, p.213; U. Wilckens, *a.c.*, p.160.

Christian existence "in Christ" as life in the realm of the Torah as controlled (and fulfilled) by Christ.

15.2.6. 2Cor 3,4-18. Paul's description of his apostolic ministry and the midrashic treatise on the letter and the spirit and on the old and the new covenant (cf. Ex 34,28-35; Jer 38,31-34; Ez 36-37) has been often discussed[274]. The scopus of this pericope is doubtless the elaboration of the fundamental difference between the proclamation of the law in the synagogue and the apostolic proclamation of Christ. I.e. it describes the *de facto* (not *de jure*!) difference between the ministry of Moses whose preaching was not believed as it was addressed to dead hearts — to people who (mis-)used the law in a legalistic manner — and the ministry of Paul whose preaching led to the salvation of the Corinthians (context!)[275].

The following observations can be made. First, in vv.4-6 Paul describes his apostolic ministry in terms of the καινή διαθήκη which is qualified not by the "letter" but by the "spirit". Without entering into a detailed analysis[276], we observe that γράμμα has to be understood in terms of the Jews' legalistic (mis-) use and interpretation of the Torah, which becomes manifest only in the con-

---

[274] Besides the commentaries cf. M. Rissi, *Studien zum zweiten Korintherbrief*, AThANT 56, 1969, pp.22-41; J.D.G. Dunn, "2 Corinthians 3,17 – 'The Lord is the Spirit' ", *JThS* 21 (1970) 309-320; J.F. Collange, *Enigmes de la deuxième épître de Paul aux Corinthiens*, SNTS MS 18, 1972, pp.56-125; C.J.A. Hickling, "The Sequence of Thought in 2 Corinthians Chapter Three", *NTS* 21 (1974) 380-395; B.C. Wintle, *Law*, 1977, pp.115-121; R.S. Rayburn, *The Contrast Between the Old and New Covenants in the New Testament*, Ph.D.Diss. Aberdeen University, 1978, pp.302-396; A.T. Hanson, "The Midrash in 2 Corinthians 3" *JSNT* 9 (1980) 2-28; J.A. Fitzmyer, "Glory Reflected on the Face of Christ (2Cor 3,7-4,6) and a Palestinian Jewish Motif", *ThSt* 42 (1981) 630-644; E. Richard, "Polemics, Old Testament, and Theology: A Study of 2Cor 3,1-4,6", *RB* 88 (1981) 340-467; P. von der Osten-Sacken, "Geist im Buchstaben: Vom Glanz des Mose und des Paulus", *EvTh* (1981) 230-235; T.E. Provence, " 'Who is Sufficient for these Things?': An Exegesis of 2Corinthians 2,15-3,18", *NovTest* 24 (1982) 54-81; U. Wilckens, "Entwicklung", *NTS* 28 (1982) 159-161; U. Schnelle, *Gerechtigkeit*, 1983,pp.50f.

[275] Cf. particularly R.S. Rayburn, *o.c.*, pp.302-328 and passim who emphasizes that Paul does not contrast the Old/New Testaments or the law/the Gospel.

[276] On vv.4-6 cf. J.F. Collange, *o.c.*, pp.56-66; H. Baum, *Mut*, 1977, pp.123-140; R.S. Rayburn, *o.c.*, pp.329-351; E. Richard, *a.c.*, pp.349-351; T.E. Provence, *a.c.*, pp. 62-68.

text of the reality of the πνεῦμα, rather than as simple equivalent of the Torah as such[277].

> We agree with H. Hübner when he writes that γράμμα "nicht das Gesetz schlechthin als in sich todbringend artikuliert . . . sondern insofern es nur auf Stein bzw. mit Buchstaben geschrieben ist und darauf harrt, auf 'Tafeln, die fleischerne Herzen sind' (= 'Brief Christi', 3,3) geschrieben zu werden. Das Gesetz ist also auf Geist hin angelegt. Es ist aber γράμμα, insofern ihm der Jude falsch begegnet"[278].

It is wrong to assume that Paul implies here the abrogation of the old law and the old dispensation as having been abolished by the new covenant[279]. Moses is not (!) employed as representing the ministry of the OT or the ministry of the 'law' (as opposed to the Gospel)[280].

Second, in vv.7-11 Paul compares the "glory" of the old and the new covenants, using three times the *qal va-homer (a minori ad majus)*[281]. Even though Paul points out that the δόξα of the ministry (!) of Moses "is being done away" (καταργουμένη, v.7; cf. v.11) it is important to note that δόξα is still ascribed to the ministry of Moses and that this δόξα is not regarded as done away yet[282]. The contrast between Moses and Paul is not a contrast between "no glory" and "glory", nor even between the functions of the two "glories", but between a greater and a lesser glory[283].

---

277 Cf. C.K. Barrett, Second Corinthians, 1973, pp.112f.; R. Bultmann, Zweiter Korintherbrief, 1976, p.80; M. Rissi, Studien, pp.132-134; J.F. Collange, Enigmes, pp. 64f.; R.S. Rayburn, Contrast, pp.329-351; T.E. Provence, "Exegesis", NovTest 24 (1982) 65-68 (misrepresenting the position of R. Bultmann on p.64 with n.29!); also C.E.B. Cranfield, Romans, 1, pp.339f.; 2, p.854; U. Wilckens, "Entwicklung", NTS 28 (1982) 162.
278 H. Hübner, Art. "γράμμα", EWNT 1 (1980) 623.
279 Contra J.D.G. Dunn, "2 Corinthians 3,17", JThS 21 (1970) 310f.; A. Feuillet, "Loi de Dieu", NovTest 22 (1980) 63; T.J. Deidun, Morality, pp.203,206f., and others.
280 Emphasized by R.S. Rayburn, o.c., p.351 pointing out that even the ministry which provokes γράμμα is treated positively by Paul (p.348).
281 On vv.7-11 cf. J.F. Collange, o.c., pp.67-84; R.S. Rayburn, o.c., pp.352-355; T.E. Provence, a.c., pp.68-73.
282 Emphasized by P. von der Osten-Sacken, "Geist", EvTh 41 (1981) 231 pointing to the four praesenta in vv.7.11.13.14. The participle καταργουμένην in v.7 is a present participle; cf. J.F. Collange, Enigmes, p.76; R.Bultmann, Zweiter Korintherbrief, p.83 who sees it as substitute for the verbal adjective "vergänglich"; differently e.g. C.K. Barrett, Second Corinthians, p.116. The term καταργεῖν expresses the transitoriness of the Mosaic order of salvation; cf. H. Hübner, EWNT 2 (1981) 661.
283 Cf. E. Richard, "Polemics", RB 88 (1981) 73; also P. von der Osten-Sacken, a.c.,

Third, in vv.12-18 Paul contrasts the "veiling" of the old covenant and the openness in the new covenant[284]. Paul elaborates on the abiding and open character of the new covenant which is contrasted with the old covenant under which the people hardened their minds, not seeing the goal (τέλος, v.13b) of the glory of the fading old covenant. This goal was to lead the people to faith rather than to works[285]. The old and the new ministries differ regarding the activity, or lack of activity, of the Spirit in the heart of man: "The Old Covenant was the ministry of the law without the empowering work of the Spirit; the New Covenant is the ministry of the law with the Spirit's empowerment to accomplish the law's demands"[286].

To sum up, Paul does not attack the law as past entity. He refers to the Torah in terms of γράμμα in the context of the πνεῦμα, i.e. in terms of its legalistic misunderstanding by the Jews. Since the Spirit was not active, transforming man's heart, the old covenant is inferior to the new covenant which will also abide forever. In the old covenant, man in unbelief received the law as external

---

p.231; U. Wilckens, "Entwicklung", *NTS* 28 (1982) 161. R.S. Rayburn, *Contrast*, pp.352-355 argues that 3,7-11 carries on the distinction in 3,3 of no salvation/salvation, disbelief/faith, heart of stone/heart transformed by the Spirit.

284 On vv.12-18 cf. W.C. van Unnik, " 'With Unveiled Face': An Exegesis of 2 Corinthians 3,12-18", *NovTest* 6 (1963) 153-169 (= *Sparsa Collecta*, 1, 1973, pp.194-210); J.F. Collange, *o.c.*, pp.85-125; R.S. Rayburn, *o.c.*, pp.355-396; E. Richard, *a.c.*, pp.354-359; T.E. Provence, "Exegesis", *NovTest* 24 (1982) 73-81.

285 For this interpretation of τέλος cf. M. Rissi, *Studien*, p.31; T.E. Provence, *a.c.*, pp. 75-77. Note R.S. Rayburn, *o.c.*, pp.374-376 who interprets the term as Christ: for Paul the glory on the face of Moses was the glory of Christ (pp.372f.). On Rom 10, 4 cf. §.15.2.9.

286 T.E. Provence, *a.c.*, p.77 referring to Ez 36,26; cf. also P.E. Hughes, *Second Corinthians*, pp.94,97,100, quoting R. Bultmann, *Theology*, 1, pp.262f.; also C.E.B. Cranfield, *Romans*, 1, pp.855-857; M. Rissi, *Studien*, p41. Cf. also R.S. Rayburn, *Contrast*, pp.384-396 passim who compares the relationship of the old/new covenant with the relationship between flesh/Spirit, between the 'old'/'new' man, between death/life (pp.395f.): the new covenant belongs to the 'new' man made new in Christ (pp.386f.), whereas the old covenant is the broken relationship between God and Israel, between God and the 'old' man with his heart of stone rejecting the Gospel of Christ in unbelief (pp.390-392, rejecting the identification of the old covenant with the Sinaitic law, pp.389f.). It is not possible at this point to discuss the validity of Rayburn's interpretation of the old and new covenant in 2Cor3. We simply note here that his conclusions as regards the status of the OT law for Paul are in accordance with our own argumentation. On the fruit of the Spirit or the transformation of the Christian (vv.17-18) cf. A. Feuillet, *Christ Sagesse*,

letter which then condemned him; in the new covenant the law is written internally on the believer's heart who through faith in Christ is enabled to fulfill the law[287].

15.2.7. Rom 3,27-31. After having argued that both Jews and Gentiles have sinned and that therefore justification based on works of the Torah is impossible (1,18-3,20), Paul explains the revelation of the righteousness of God[288] (3,21-31). He defends and elucidates his conviction that righteousness is by faith on the basis and as a result of the atoning act of God's righteousness in Christ's death (3,21-26). In 3,27-31 Paul resumes the discussion with the Jewish partner from 3,1-8[289]. Since the law is not the locus of the justification of the sinner but of sin, and since justification is on the basis and as the result of Christ's death on the cross, by faith, and apart from the law (3,21-26), Paul asks, "Where then is boasting?" (v.27), continuing the subject of 2,17-29. He points out that God has excluded boasting once and for all (aor. pass. ἐξεκλείσθη, v.27) since both Jews and Gentiles are justified on the basis of πίστις (vv.29-30) without ἔργα νόμου (v.28).

Taking this scopus for granted, v.27b presents a problem. The phrase νόμος ἔργων can easily be explained in connection with 2,

---

pp.113-161; J.F. Collange, *Enigmes*, pp.106-125; J.A. Fitzmyer, "Glory", *ThSt* 42 (1981) 630-644.

287 Cf. P.E. Hughes, *Second Corinthians*, pp.94-100; T.E. Provence, "Exegesis", *NovTest* 24 (1982) 77 stating that "the law is common to both covenants"; similarly U. Wilckens, "Entwicklung", *NTS* 28 (1982) 162f. who states that the Torah as γραφή (not as γράμμα!) possesses the highest authority in the Christian church insofar as it testifies to Christ, thus belonging closely together with the Gospel (p.162), and who compares the relation of the old and the new covenant in 2Cor 3 with the relation of the ὑπὸ νόμον and ἔννομος Χριστοῦ in 1Cor 9,20-21(p.163); see also idem, "Statements", 1982, p.20 asserting that 2Cor 3,4-18 "is a consideration, with a polemical purpose, of the opposition between gospel and Law in the light of salvation history". Contra H. Räisänen, *Paul*, pp.44-46,243-245.

288 On the phrase and concept of the δικαιοσύνη θεοῦ cf. P. Stuhlmacher, *Gerechtigkeit Gottes bei Paulus*, FRLANT 87, ²1966; K. Kertelge, '*Rechtfertigung' bei Paulus: Studien zur Struktur und zum Bedeutungsgehalt der paulinischen Rechtfertigungslehre*, NTA NF 3, ²1971; J.A. Ziesler, *The Meaning of Righteousness in Paul*, 1972; U. Wilckens, *Römer*, 1, 1978, pp.202-233 (with lit.); K. Kertelge, Art. "δικαιοσύνη", *EWNT* 1 (1980) 784-796 (lit.); P. Stuhlmacher, "Die Gerechtigkeitsanschauung des Apostels Paulus", *Aufsätze*, 1981, pp.87-116.

289 Following the analysis of U. Wilckens, *Römer*, 1, pp.93,161-163,171f.,183f., 244. Most recent commentators treat 3,27-31 as a unit; cf. E. Käsemann, *Römer*, pp. 95-99; C.E.B. Cranfield, *Romans*, 1, pp.218-224; U. Wilckens, o.c., pp.244-257.

13 and 3,20.28: it means "die Tora, sofern sie Werke der Gerechtigkeit fordert und allein an ihnen die Rechtfertigung bemißt"[290].

The crux of the verse is the phrase νόμος πίστεως concerning which several significant observations are in order. The paradoxical formulation νόμος πίστεως is not be to understood rhetorically in the sense of (salvational) order, norm, or principle[291] but literally as Torah[292]: (1) this interpretation guarantees a continuous progression of thought in the context of Rom 3; (2) it is not possible to interpret the two νόμοι of 3,27 as two different orders of salvation which both come from God and which succeed one another chronologically, since νόμος ἔργων is not God's old order of salvation but expression of a human attitude towards God's Torah which is wrong in a fundamental way[293]; (3) in 8,2 we find a sim-

---

290 U. Wilckens, *o.c.*, p.245; also H. Hübner, "Pauli theologiae proprium", *NTS* 26 (1980) 465; idem, *Gesetz*, pp.95f.,118; P. von der Osten-Sacken, *Römer 8 als Beispiel paulinischer Soteriologie*, FRLANT 112, 1975, p.245; C.E.B. Cranfield, *o.c.*, p.220 n.3.

291 Contra H. Lietzmann, *Römer*, p.52; R. Bultmann, *Theology*, 1, p.281; A. van Dülmen, *Theologie*, p.87; E. Käsemann, *Römer*, p.96; O. Michel, *Römerbrief*, p.155; H. Schlier, *Römerbrief*, p.116; also C.K. Barrett, *Romans*, p.83 who rejects the meaning 'principle' but then advocates the sense of "religious system"; further F.F. Bruce, "Paul and the Law of Moses", *BJRL* 57 (1974/75) 259; G.E. Ladd, *Theology of the New Testament*, ²1975, p.504; J. Blank, "Gesetz und Geist", *The Law of the Spirit in Rom 7 and 8*, 1976, p.97 (advocating the meaning "order" or "dimension" in the sense of πίστις!); H. Räisänen, "Das 'Gesetz des Glaubens' (Rom 3,27)", *NTS* 26 (1980) 112 (assuming the meaning "die Heilsordnung, die auf Glauben fundiert ist"); also idem, *Paul*, pp.50-52. As regards Räisänen's critique of the position of G. Friedrich, P. von der Osten-Sacken, and F. Hahn we point out that in his interpretation of the aor.pass. ἐξεκλείσθη, Räisänen overaccentuates God's activity by ascribing to God what is 'expected' of faith, and that it is a wrong antithesis if he contrasts God and man antithetically as subjects in the "law of faith" as faith is, according to Paul, in the final analysis gift of God (cf. also H. Hübner, *Gesetz*, pp.136f.). Räisänen uses Cranfield's (deliberately ambiguous) interpretation of the *passivum divinum* without discussing the fact that Cranfield still interprets νόμος πίστεως in terms of the OT law!

292 Already H. Cremer, *Biblisch-theologisches Wörterbuch*, ⁴1885, s.v. νόμος; then especially G. Friedrich, "Das Gesetz des Glaubens: Röm 3,27", *ThZ* 10 (1954) 401-417 (= *Auf das Wort kommt es an*, 1978, pp.107-122); E. Lohse, "ὁ νόμος τοῦ πνεύματος τῆς ζωῆς", *Neues Testament und christliche Existenz*, FS H. Braun, ed. H.D. Betz et al., 1973, pp.281f.; F. Hahn, "Gesetzesverständnis", *ZNW* 67 (1976) 38,41,47-49; P. von der Osten-Sacken, *Römer 8*, pp.245f.; idem, "Das paulinische Verständnis des Gesetzes", *EvTh* 37 (1977) 568; H. Hübner, "Proprium", *NTS* 26 (1980) 465f.; idem, *Gesetz*, pp.95,118-120; C.E.B. Cranfield, *Romans*, 1, p.220; U. Wilckens, *Römer*, 1, p.245.

293 Cf. H. Hübner, *o.c.*, pp.119f. who then attempts to reconcile his interpretation with that of E. Käsemann, *o.c.*, p.96.

ilar antithesis with νόμος as generic term of the Christian's state of and life in salvation[294].

Further, νόμος πίστεως is not a reference to the Jewish law in its function as a witness[295], nor a term for the proper Christian behaviour with regard to God's will as it is expressed in the Torah[296], since (1) the *media* in the two contrary phrases are not the demands of the law (works/faith) but the character of the Torah as law of *God*, and since (2) with that interpretation faith, functionally, becomes works again[297]. The phrase νόμος πίστεως signifies, rather, "die im Glauben zu ihrer ursprünglichen Bestimmung gekommene Torah"[298].

> Hübner is correct when he asserts that 3,27 expresses the contrast of "ein je verschiedenes Verhalten zur Torah, gründend in einer *toto caelo* verschiedenen Sicht der Torah: Mißbrauch des Gesetzes aus dem Mißverständnis, es zum Hinstellen eigenproduzierter Gerechtigkeit benutzen zu müssen, oder rechte Verwendung des Gesetzes, die nur aus Glauben möglich ist"[299].

When and where God reveals his righteousness in Christ and therefore "by faith" (v.22), the Torah has been excluded as law which demands works and which therefore condemns the sinner (vv.21.28) and appears as law which is related to faith (v.21) and is thus not abrogated — it is God's law — but established (ἱστάνομεν, v.31). Now the law fulfills again its original intended purpose, "Gerechte dem Leben zuzusprechen"[300] — not by itself but rather διὰ πίστεως.

---

294 Cf. § 15.2.8.
295 Thus G. Friedrich, "Gesetz", *ThZ* 10 (1954) 401-417; E. Lohse, "νόμος", 1973, pp.279-287. Rejected by H. Hübner, *Gesetz*, p.119; U. Wilckens, *Römer*, 1, p. 246; U. Luz, in R. Smend, U. Luz, *Gesetz*, p.105.
296 Thus P. von der Osten-Sacken, *Römer 8*, p.245; similarly C.E.B. Cranfield, *Romans*, 1, p.220.
297 H. Hübner, *o.c.*, pp.122f. and U. Wilckens, *o.c.*, p.245 with n.766. The latter seems to take place in the case of P. von der Osten-Sacken, *o.c.*, p.232 when he states that salvation (!) consists "nach wie vor in der Erfüllung des Gesetzes". It should be also noticed (ad Wilckens) that the absolutely gracious nature of justification does not totally nullify faith as an act of man.
298 U. Wilckens, *o.c.*, p.247 pointing out that the *media* in the two contrary phrases is the character of the Torah as law of *God* with the νόμος ἔργων linked with man's (attempted) justification and the νόμος πίστεως with faith (p.245).
299 H. Hübner, *o.c.*, p.119; cf. also O. Merk, *Handeln*, p.10. It is not impossible to bring the views of Wilckens and Stuhlmacher to congruence, provided Stuhlmacher could see a more direct material (!) relationship between the Mosaic Torah and the eschatological Zion Torah.
300 U. Wilckens, *Römer*, 1, p.249. Also H. Hübner, *Gesetz*, p.124 who paraphrases

Stuhlmacher interprets the "Torah of Christ" and the "Torah of faith" in terms of the eschatological 'Zion Torah'[301] which, according to him, is not simply identical with the Mosaic Torah "sondern bringt deren geistliche Intention dadurch zum Ziel, daß sie der Mosetora eschatologisch entspricht"[302]. Following H. Gese[303], Stuhlmacher sees the 'Zion Torah' only as eschatological perfection of the Sinaitic Torah's "geschichtliche Vorläufigkeit" [304]. It should be noted, however, that Jer 31,33 refers explicitly to תורתי "my torah", i.e. the same law of God which is given in a new way and in a new context: man will receive a new heart and a new spirit leading to a new obedience to the (same) Torah. Similarly Ez 36,27 speaks in the same eschatological context of חקי and משפטי (also 37,24), obviously referring to God's eternally valid commandments: the heart and the spirit of man will be new but nothing indicates that God's commands will be new also. Note further that the commentaries by H. Wildberger and H.W. Wolff[305] do not treat the passages which Gese adduces as describing the new eschatological 'Zion Torah' as being distinct from the Sinaitic Torah. It is obvious that these texts are not interested in the character of the Torah as such[306]. Finally, Gese's attempt to describe the relationship between the Sinai Torah and the 'Zion Torah' is neither clear nor convincing. Reading Gese's book one cannot avoid the suspicion that the texts are not always allowed to speak for themselves but are 'coordinated' in a pre-conceived system which leads often to rather apodictic conclusions[307]. For this reason his views regarding an eschatological 'Zion Torah' should not be used as basis for interpreting Paul's theology of the law.

15.2.8. Rom 8,1-4. In 8,1-4 Paul substitutes the exclamation of thanksgiving in 7,25a by developing christologically 7,6. The 'thesis' of v.1 is defended in v.2 in the light of the larger subject of the liberation from the law. The phrase νόμος τῆς ἁμαρτίας καὶ τοῦ θανάτου (v.2) is a summary of 7,13-23, referring stringently to the Mosaic Torah which is, as "law of sin", not sin itself (cf. 7,7!) but revealing and effectuating sin as sin (7,13) and which is, as "law of death", not death-effecting in itself (7,13) but adjudging

---

v.31 as "wir stellen das Gesetz hin, indem wir kategorisch seine jüdische Fehlinterpretation ablehnen. Wir stellen die ureigene Intention des Gesetzes hin, indem wir energisch die Intention Gottes mit dem Gesetz vertreten". Cf. also E. Jüngel, *Paulus und Jesus*, p.61.

301 P. Stuhlmacher, "Das Gesetz als Thema biblischer Theologie" (1978), *Aufsätze*, 1981, pp.158-161; also idem, "Gerechtigkeitsanschauung", *o.c.*, pp.112f.
302 P. Stuhlmacher, "Gesetz", p.159.
303 Cf. H. Gese, "Das Gesetz", *Zur biblischen Theologie*, 1977, pp.74-77.
304 Cf. P. Stuhlmacher, *a.c.*, p.143.
305 Cf. H. Wildberger, *Jesaja*, BK X/1, 1972, pp.75-90 (on Is 2,1-5); idem, X/2, 1978, pp.959-969 (on Is 25,6-8); H.W. Wolff, *Dodekapropheton 4: Micha*, BK XIV/4, 1982, pp.82-99 (on Mi 4,1-8).
306 Cf. R. Smend, in R. Smend, U. Luz, *Gesetz*, 1981, p.43 asserting that the subject of these passages is the assurance of salvation.
307 Cf. the review of S. Wagner, in *ThLZ* 106 (1981) 876-878. See also H. Räisänen, *Paul*, pp.239f.

its death penalty to the sinner and keeping him in custody in his "body of death" (7,24)[308].

If, then, man is set free (ἠλευθέρωσεν) "in Jesus Christ" from the Torah which has this double effect, how can the power of the Spirit which liberates man and gives him life be called νόμος? Many scholars solve this problem by understanding νόμος τοῦ πνεύματος τῆς ζωῆς rhetorically as (salvational) order or rule[309]. This interpretation has been challenged recently in a convincing way[310]: (1) the term νόμος τοῦ πνεύματος refers very likely back to 7,14 where the Torah is characterized as πνευματικός; (2) the phrase νόμος τῆς ἁμαρτίας καὶ τοῦ θανάτου in the same verse is used in a stringent manner in the immediate previous context of Rom 7 and refers clearly to the Mosaic Torah; (3) in the immediate following context in 8,3-4 Paul uses νόμος again stringently as reference to the Mosaic Torah; (4) in classical and Hellenistic Greek νόμος is not used as designation for the world order per se (rather as term for the power which creates and maintains the world order and thus is identified with Zeus) nor (νόμος c.gen.) for differing, even antithetical 'orders' or 'norms'[311].

Thus, we conclude that the statement in 8,2 describes the can-

---

308 Following the excellent analysis of U. Wilckens, Römer, 2, 1980, pp.121f. A different structural analysis was recently put forward by P. Lamarche, C. le Du, Épître aux Romains V-VIII: Structure littéraire et sens, 1980, pp.61-63.
309 Cf. G. Friedrich, "Gesetz", p.407; C.K. Barrett, Romans, p.155; J. Blank, "Gesetz", 1976, pp.97,106f. (discussion); H. Schlier, Römerbrief, pp.238f.; O. Michel, Römerbrief, p.249; A. van Dülmen, Theologie, pp.119f.; B.C. Wintle, Law, p.135; E. Käsemann, Römer, p.205; C.E.B. Cranfield, Romans, 1, pp.375f. (changing his earlier view, cf. n.4); H. Räisänen, "Gesetz", NTS 26 (1980) 113-116; A. Feuillet, "Loi de Dieu", NovTest 22 (1980) 57-61; L.E. Keck, "The Law and 'The Law of Sin and Death' (Rom 8,1-4)", 1980, pp.46-49; T.J. Deidun, Morality, pp.193-203, 255f., H. Räisänen, Paul, pp.50,52.
310 Cf. E. Jüngel, Paulus und Jesus, p.61; C.E.B. Cranfield, "St.Paul and the Law", SJTh 17 (1964) 61f.; E. Lohse, "νόμος", 1973, pp.279-287; P. von der Osten-Sacken, Römer 8, pp.226-234; E. Lohse, "Zur Analyse und Interpretation von Röm 8,1-17", The Law of the Spirit, 1976, p.139; F. Hahn, "Gesetzesverständnis", ZNW 67 (1976) 47f.; P. von der Osten-Sacken, "Verständnis", EvTh 37 (1977) 568; H. Hübner, Gesetz, pp.124-127,188; idem, "Proprium", NTS 26 (1980) 466; U. Wilckens, Römer, 1, 1978, p.245; 2, 1980, pp.122f.; H. Hübner, Art. "νόμος", EWNT 2 (1981) 1170; U. Wilckens, "Entwicklung", NTS 28 (1982) 185; idem, "Statements", 1982, p.24.
311 For the last point cf. U. Wilckens, Römer, 2, p.122 with n.491. H. Räisänen, Paul, pp.50f. n.34 has misunderstood Wilckens who does not claim that νόμος does not mean 'rule' or 'order' in classical Greek.

cellation of all condemnation (v.1) as change in the law from its condemning function to a function which cancels this condemnation.

> In the words of Wilckens, Paul asserts a *"Wende im Gesetz selbst von seiner verurteilenden zu seiner diese Verurteilung aufhebenden Funktion. Die überlegene Kraft der Gnade über die universale Verurteilungskraft des Gesetzes (5,20f) ist als göttliche Kraft der Negation zugleich die Kraft, die im Gesetz selbst als dem Gesetz Gottes die dem Gesetz als göttlichem Verurteilungsspruch überlegene Wirkung zum Zuge bringt. In der Entgegensetzung von νόμος und νόμος in 8,2 spiegelt sich die Entgegensetzung von Gott in Kreuz und Auferweckung Christi"*[312].

The genitives τοῦ πνεύματος and τῆς ἁμαρτίας describe the powers which control the νόμος, and the genitives τῆς ζωῆς and τοῦ θανάτου describe the effect of the law under the respective controlling power. The phrase ἐν Χριστῷ Ἰησοῦ is "die hermeneutische Ortsbestimmung der ganzen Aussage und also ... ihre entscheidende Mitte"[313]. As a result of the believer's being ἐν Χριστῷ and having received and being controlled by the πνεῦμα, he has ζωή (as καινὴ κτίσις, cf. Gal 6,15; 2Cor 5,17!) and is enabled to fulfill the demands of the law (8,4; cf. 2,13; 13,8.10!): the Spirit is not only the power of the justification of the sinner who was condemned to death by the Torah, but now, "in Christ", also the power in which the Torah, controlled by the Spirit, is being fulfilled[314].

15.2.9. Rom 10,4.
This verse belongs to the context of 10,1-21 in which Paul treats Israel as having rejected the righteousness of God which can be obtained by all who believe. In v.4 he explains why (γάρ) the Jews have wrong knowledge or understanding (ἐπίγνωσις, v.2). Paul states that Christ is the τέλος of the νόμος for righteousness which is for everyone who believes (v.4). Schol-

---

312 U. Wilckens, *o.c.*, p.123; similarly H. Hübner, *o.c.*, pp.125f.
313 U. Wilckens, *Römer*, 2, p.123; cf. idem, "Entwicklung", *NTS* (1982) 185.
314 Cf. F. Hahn, "Gesetzesverständnis", *ZNW* 67 (1976) 47; E. Lohse, "Analyse", 1976, p.139; H. Hübner, *Gesetz*, p.127f.; U. Wilckens, *o.c.*, pp.128f. (rejecting pronouncedly the notion of an *abrogatio legis* for the Christian); idem, *a.c.*, p.185; cf. also H. Schlier, *Grundzüge*, p.92; C.E.B. Cranfield, *Romans*, 1, p.384; W.G. Kümmel, *Theologie*, pp.201f.; O. Merk, *Handeln*, p.10; W. Schrage, *Ethik*, 1982, p.197 (stating that the Torah becomes a posteriori as "law of Christ" binding for the Christian). J. Blank, *Paulus und Jesus*, pp.294f. is ambiguous. H. Räisänen, *Paul*, pp.51f. is not able to refute successfully the exegesis of Hahn, Hübner, von der Osten-Sacken, and Wilckens.

ars agree that νόμος is a reference to the Mosaic Torah (note the context, particularly 9,31).

The *crux interpretum* is the precise meaning of τέλος which can be understood in terms of fulfilment, or goal, or end. We follow Wilckens who combines the understanding in terms of goal and in terms of end[315]. Christ is (1) the goal of the law insofar as he ended its function of condemning the sinner — the person who believes in Christ is in accordance with God's righteousness which brought the law to its end in Christ's atoning death (cf. the context vv.3-4)[316]. Or Christ is the end of the advertisement of the sarkic abuse of the law as "law of works" and as way to righteousness[317]. And Christ is (2) the goal of the law (cf. the context 9,31) insofar as be brings righteousness to the believer thus doing what the law could not do (8,3), fulfilling what the Jews expected from the law. Christ is the goal of the law which the Jews have "pursued" (9,31): the pursued righteousness which was originally the goal of the Torah, and this righteousness was wrought by Christ for the believer[318]. Christ who was the goal of the Torah has not

---

315 H. Räisänen, *Paul*, p.53 with n.48 has misunderstood the position of U. Wilckens. Räisänen admits that Paul could have written that Christ is the goal of the law (p.56).
316 Cf. U. Wilckens, *Römer*, 2, p.222, following A. von Dülmen, *Theologie*, pp.126f., 217f.
317 Cf. C.F.D. Moule, "Obligation in the Ethic of Paul", *Christian History and Interpretation*, FS J. Knox, ed. W.R. Farmer et al., 1967, pp.402f.; J. Munck, *Christ and Israel*, 1967, p.83; A van Dülmen, *o.c.*, pp.126f.; G.E. Ladd, *Theology*, pp.502f.; O. Merk, *Handeln*, p.10; W.G. Kümmel, *Theologie*, p.162; P. Stuhlmacher, "Achtzehn Thesen", *Aufsätze*, pp.194f.; M. Hengel, *Son*, p.74 (asserting a "christologically motivated abrogation of the law, its abolition as way of salvation"); F. Hahn, "Gesetzesverständnis", *ZNW* 67 (1976) 50; W.D. Davies, "Paul and the Law", *HLJ* 29 (1978) 1476; idem, "Paul and the Law", 1982, p.9; H. Schlier, *Grundzüge*, pp.92f.; B.C. Wintle, *Law*, p.127; U. Luz, in R. Smend, U. Luz, *Gesetz*, 1981, p.93; H. Hübner, *Gesetz*, p.129; idem, Art. "νόμος", *EWNT* 2 (1981) 1170. This interpretation does not imply an abrogation of the Torah per se; contra T. Deidun, *Morality*, 1981, p.152 n.7 who interprets τέλος νόμου as "the termination of the Law's rôle in God's plan of salvation". This is rightly emphasized by C.E.B. Cranfield, *Romans*, 2, p.519 who does not see, however, that νόμος can still mean "end" when νόμος is qualified: not νόμος per se is terminated but its abuse as νόμος ἔργων.
318 Cf. U. Wilckens, *o.c.*, p.223; also C.E.B. Cranfield, *o.c.*, p.519; R. Bring, *Christus und das Gesetz*, pp.35-72; B.C. Wintle, *o.c.*, p.127; P.W. Meyer, "Romans 10,4 and the End of the Law", *The Divine Helmsman*, FS L.H. Silberman, ed. J.L. Crenshaw, 1980, pp.59-78; similarly W.S. Campbell, "Christ as the End of the Law in Romans 10,4", *Studia Biblica 1978*, 3, pp.76f.

abrogated the Torah as such. Christ has (only) terminated and hence abrogated — for those who believe "in him"! — the sarkic abuse of the Torah as way to salvation as well as the condemning function of the Torah[319].

15.3. Theological Evaluation

15.3.1. Soteriological aspects. As a result of Christ's death, resurrection, and exaltation, brought home to Paul in a rather dramatic manner on the road to Damacus, Paul's treatment of the role, validity, and significance of the Jewish Torah focused on the new soteriological status of the Torah[320].

Thus, already in his earliest letters to the Christians in Galatia and Corinth, Paul emphasizes that the Torah, after the Christ event, has no soteriological functions left. With Jesus' mission it had become clear that the Torah could not impart life (Gal 3,21) but functioned as prison warden and slave attendant (Gal 3,23-24). With Jesus' death on the cross, the sole constitutive basis of justification and salvation is faith in Jesus Christ rather than the control and rule of the Torah (Gal 3,25). God's call in Christ effected a fundamental modification of the Torah's salvation-historical and soteriological differentiation between Jews and Gentiles on the basis of circumcision (1Cor 7,19): circumcision as obedience to the Torah is not necessary any more since now God's call is not dependent on, and restricted to, circumcision but is to be heard and received in and through Jesus Christ. It does not matter any more whether a person is a Jew or a Gentile: believers in Christ are not under the dominion ($\dot{v}\pi\acute{o}$!) of the Torah (1Cor 9, 20). Among the Jews the Torah had degenerated to $\gamma\rho\acute{a}\mu\mu a$, being understood in a purely legalistic manner as way to salvation (2Cor

---

[319] It is unlikely that in 10,6-7 Paul implicitly intends to link Christ and the Torah, as Paul's concern in the context is the contrast between Christ and the Torah, and as Paul obviously eliminates all references to the Torah (cf. U. Wilckens, *Römer*, 2, pp.225f.). The traditional Jewish interpretation of Deut 30,12-14 makes it plausible to assume that Paul describes Christ in 10,6-7 in terms of wisdom. Cf. supra, §14.2.5.

[320] The decisive role of Paul's Damascus experience in this respect is stressed by P. Stuhlmacher, "Gesetz", *Aufsätze*, pp.155f. and S. Kim, *Origin*, pp.128f.

3,6). As a result, the glory of the old covenant was lesser than the glory of the new covenant (2Cor 3,7-11). Before Christ, the preaching of the Torah was lacking the accompanying activity of God's Spirit. 'After' Christ, i.e. in the context of the new covenant, preaching is linked with the power of the Spirit (2Cor 3,12-18).

In his letter to the Romans, Paul elaborates on these convictions. Sinful mankind cannot possibly be justified by God as a result of "works of the law" (Rom 1,18-3,20) but rather on the basis and as a result of the realization of God's righteousness in Christ's atoning death, apart from the law (3,21-26). As both Jews and Gentiles are justified on the basis of faith rather than on the basis of obedience to the law (3,28-30), all boasting is excluded (3,27). Thus, man's improper use of the law as way to righteousness is rejected. The condemning function of the Torah as γράμμα ἀπόκτεινον and as master has become obsolete as a result of the Christ event (7,1-6). Without Christ, the Torah reveals and judges sin as sin and thus leads to death (7,13-23; 8,2). The power of the Spirit, through Jesus Christ, liberated the believer from the Torah as controlled by sin. Thus, Christ is the end of the Torah as concerns its condemnatory function in the context of its sarkic abuse (10,4). The Torah has no soteriological functions at all. Christ is the exclusive σωτήρ, and salvation is only by faith in him, on the basis of God's free grace.

15.3.2. Salvation-historical aspects. In polemical contexts Paul can make harsh and depreciatory statements on the Torah seen as *ante Christum crucifixum*: the law was "added", via a mediator, in order to condemn the transgressions as such, thus functioning as prison warden and slave attendant (Gal 3,19-25). The *nuda lex*, i.e. the law without Christ, dominates and rules over man who is ὑπό (1Cor 9,20; Gal 3,23; cf. Rom 6,14.15; Gal 4,5.21;5,18) and who misunderstands the Torah legalistically as γράμμα (2Cor 3,4-18) requiring ἔργα (Rom 3,28), not taking into consideration the fact that, as such, it is ruled by the power of sin and that it leads therefore to death (Rom 7,13-23; 8,2). In this respect, Christ is the end (τέλος) of the Torah for the believer (Rom 10,4).

Christ is the end of the Torah as condemning power in that he is, at the same time, the goal (τέλος) of the Torah (Rom 10,4) insofar as he brought that righteousness which the Torah could not bring (Rom 8,3; 9,31). As the sinless Son of God, Christ met the requirements of the Torah and took upon himself the Torah's judgment of sin and sinner in his atoning and vicarious death on the cross as curse of the law "for us" (Gal 3,13)[321]. Therefore, salvation is not by obedience to the Torah but by faith in Christ.

In this soteriological and salvation-historical framework the Torah is affected in a fundamental way. It is excluded as way to righteousness and life, but it is still included as the holy and good will of God (Rom 7,12) which never lacked δόξα entirely (2Cor 3, 7-11). Man is not ruled by the Torah any more — rather, the Torah is ruled by Christ and qualified by the Spirit[322] and by faith which the Spirit gives. Thus, Paul speaks of the "Torah of Christ" (Gal 6,2; 1Cor 9,21), i.e. of the Torah which is fulfilled by Christ and in Christ and which has thus come under the rule of Christ[323]. Paul speaks of the "Torah of faith" (Rom 3,27), i.e. the Torah which is related to faith thus establishing (Rom 3,31) God's original intention which consisted in giving life to the righteous. And Paul speaks of the "Torah of the Spirit" (Rom 8,2), i.e. the Torah which is controlled by the Spirit leading to life as he also controls the life of the believer, enabling him to fulfill the law (Rom 8,4).

The Torah as qualified by Christ, as controlled by the Spirit, and as linked with faith, is fully relevant for the Christian (1Cor 7, 19) and fully realizable by the Christian who is "in Christ" and who has received the Spirit when he complies with the one commandment of love (Gal 5,14; 6,2; Rom 13,8-10), living by the power of the Spirit (2Cor 3,4-18). In this sense the Torah, as "Gesetz ohne Gesetzlichkeit"[324], is still standard for the Christian's life.

It has been pointed out already in the course of our exegetical discussion that it is wrong to imply an abrogation of the Torah as

---

321 Cf. P. Stuhlmacher, "Achtzehn Thesen", *Aufsätze,* pp.195f.; M. Hengel, *Atonement,* 1981, particularly pp.33-65; on Gal 3,13 in the context of Paul's message of the cross cf. H. Weder, *Kreuz Jesu,* 1981, pp.186-193.

322 On the relationship between the Spirit and Christ in Paul cf. J.D.G. Dunn, *Jesus and the Spirit,* ²1978, pp.318-326, here 322-324 discussing 1Cor 15,45; Rom 8,9-11; 1Cor 6,17; 12,4-6, passages in which Paul expresses this relationship in terms of equation: Christ *is* the Spirit.

323 Cf. U. Wilckens, "Was heißt bei Paulus: 'Aus Werken des Gesetzes wird kein Mensch gerecht'?" (1969), *Rechtfertigung als Freiheit: Paulusstudien,* 1974, pp.77-109, here p.109.

324 K. Niederwimmer, Art. "ἐλεύθερος", *EWNT* 1 (1980) 1056.

such on the part of Paul[325]. We can speak more accurately of a *abrogatio servitudinis sub lege*[326]. The Christian is now *cum lege*[327], himself controlled (and loved!) by Christ and empowered by the Spirit, in faith.

This new location of the Torah "in Christ Jesus" has important hermeneutical consequences. The Torah which is still valid for the Christian is not a reduced Torah — reduced to the commandment of love — nor a new Torah — containing the ethical teaching of Jesus — but the Torah as revelation of God's will as realized in the history of salvation which culminated in the cross and resurrection of Christ. Even though one has to note that the Torah as a whole is still valid for the Christian (Gal 5,14), it is obvious that the ritual and ceremonial parts of the Torah have to be seen in a totally new light, viz. as realized in Christ[328]. They are not abrogated but rather fulfilled by and in Christ, and hence also by the believer who is "in Christ".

15.3.3. Revelatory aspects. There is no doubt that Paul regarded the Torah as revelation of God: the Torah is νόμος (τοῦ) θεοῦ (1 Cor 9,21; Rom 7,22.25; 8,7) and its commandments are ἐντολαί θεοῦ (1Cor 7,19). The statement that the Torah is νόμος ἅγιος (Rom 7,12; cf. 1,2) implies that it belongs to God and originated with God[329]. The Torah is good (ἀγαθός) because it is God's will (Rom 7,12; 12,1)[330]. The declaration that the Torah is spiritual

---

325 Cf. also A. van Dülmen, *Theologie*, pp.204-230; M. Limbeck, *Ohnmacht*, pp. 98f.; R.S. Rayburn, *Contrast*, pp.219-233. Contra H. Räisänen, *Paul*, pp.42-93.
326 Cf. U. Wilckens, *Römer*, 2, 1980, p.71.
327 Cf. E. Jüngel, *Paulus und Jesus*, p.61 n.1.
328 It is obvious that Paul does not differentiate between the ritual and ceremonial, and the ethical parts of the Torah. It is equally obvious, however, that Christ's death as atoning sacrifice made a fundamental difference in Paul's attitude towards the former which has come to its τέλος in Christ (Rom 10,4). Cf. R. Bultmann, *Theology*, 1, p.261 who states "that the identity of meaning in the cultic, ritual and the ethical demands exists only for the man who has not yet come to faith, and that in faith itself an unconsciously working principle of criticism is provided". T. Holtz, "Zur Frage der inhaltlichen Weisungen bei Paulus", *ThLZ* 106 (1981) 393 refers to this complex of thought as a central problem of Paul's theology of the law which has not yet been solved.
329 Cf. U. Wilckens, *Römer*, 2, p.83; C.E.B. Cranfield, *Romans*, 1, p.343; H. Schlier, *Römerbrief*, p.226.
330 Cf. U. Wilckens, *o.c.*, p.83; H. Schlier, *o.c.*, p.226.

($πνευματικός$, Rom 7,14) also asserts its divine origin[331]. Even in Gal the divine origin of the Torah is not denied[332]: the passives $προσετέθη$ and $εδόθη$ in Paul's digression regarding the Torah in Gal 3, 19.21 indicate the divine origin of the Torah[333].

There is no statement in the Pauline corpus to the effect that Christ was of revelatory significance with regard to the mediation of the Jewish (messianic) Torah. As the phrase $νόμος τοῦ Χριστοῦ$ (Gal 6,2; 1Cor 9,21) refers unequivocally and exclusively to the Mosaic Torah, as qualified by Christ, it is further wrong to assume, on the basis of this phrase at least, that Paul regarded Jesus Christ as the bringer of a new Torah. There are no other statements by Paul which imply or express the notion that Christ was a new Torah or brought a new Torah[334]. Jesus Christ possessed for Paul no explicit[335] revelatory significance linked with Torah.

15.3.4. Ontological aspects. As Paul did not describe Christ as identical with, or as the bringer of, a new messianic Torah, it is obvious that Paul did not state any ontological relationship between the Torah and Christ[336]. If, for the writers of the Synoptic

---

331 Cf. E. Käsemann, *Römer*, p.191; C.E.B. Cranfield, *o.c.*, p.355; U. Wilckens, *o.c.*, p. 86; also H. Schlier, *o.c.*, p.229.
332 Cf. F.F. Bruce, *Galatians*, pp.175,177,180.
333 Cf. H. Schlier, *o.c.*, p.247 n.17.
334 Pace W.D. Davies, *Paul*, pp.147-176 who admits that Paul never calls Jesus a 'new Torah' explicitly; he believes nevertheless that 2Cor 3,4-18 implies this conviction (but see supra, § 15.2.6.); cf. also idem, *Torah*, 1952, pp.85-94. Many scholars found Davies' view that Paul regarded Christ as messianic new Torah problematic; cf. W.G. Kümmel, *Judaica*, 7 (1951) 302; A. Feuillet, *Christ Sagesse*, pp.191-193; M.E. Thrall, "The Origin of Pauline Christology", *Apostolic History and the Gospel*, FS F.F. Bruce, ed. W.W. Gasque et al., 1970, pp.310f.; M. Hengel, *Son*, p.68 n. 123. The picture might be different in the case of the Synoptic Gospels and of Stephen who, according to Hengel, saw Jesus as the new law-giver or the bringer of a new Torah who developed the true and original will of God for the commencing Kingdom of God; cf. M. Hengel, "Zwischen Jesus und Paulus", *ZThK* 72 (1975) 191f.,195f.; idem, *o.c.*, pp.67-71; idem, "Jesus und die Torah", *ThBeitr* 9 (1978) 171. In the same vein cf. H. Merklein, "Entstehung", 1979, p.56 who assumes that the Synoptic Jesus-Sophia-Logia presuppose the identification of Jesus with the law.
335 As Paul regarded Jesus as pre-existent Son of God he would not exclude an implicit relationship between Christ and the giving of the Torah. However, Paul did not think through consistently such trinitarian questions here.
336 Pace W.D. Davies, "Paul and the Law", *HLJ* 29 (1978) 1482f.; idem "Paul and the Law", 1982, p.12 asserting that Paul personalized the concept of Torah by identifying it with Christ.

Gospels as well as for Stephen, the true will of God was embodied in the teaching of the messiah Jesus and no longer in the Mosaic Torah[337], the same cannot be said for Paul. When Paul asserts that Christ is the "end" of the law (Rom 10,4), it is true that this conviction "challenges the claim of the law in principle"[338] — but only as "fundamental expression of the unique soteriological function of the crucified and exalted Jesus as the all-embracing final eschatological revelation of God"[339]. That is, for Paul, Christ 'terminated' and hence 'replaced' the Torah only (!) in the soteriological realm (cf. §15.3.1.), not as revelation of God's will and claim — as such, Paul in fact "establishes" the Torah (Rom 3,31). As regards the ontological realm, Paul does not relate Christ and the Torah.

15.3.5. Summary. For Paul, the Torah has lost all soteriological significance with the death and resurrection of Christ. Polemical statements against Judaizing opponents who denied the exclusive (!) soteriological role of Christ wanting to retain obedience to the Torah as crucial for salvation can lead Paul to negative affirmations regarding the Torah (in Gal especially). Paul, however, never doubts the divine origin of the law nor, therefore, its continuous validity as revelation of God's will. The Torah has come to its end, solely, as regards its condemning function and as regards its sarkic abuse as way to righteousness. Christ has taken upon himself the condemnation of the sin of the world and has brought righteousness to those who are linked with him. Therefore, Christ is the τέλος of the Torah. As such, the Torah is defined and qualified by Christ as νόμος τοῦ Χριστοῦ. Consequently, *post Christum crucifixum,* the law becomes the measure and standard of the Christian life, fulfillable in the realm of the Spirit who transforms the believer who is a new creation "in Christ", and in the realm of faith. Christ is the hermeneutical location and the crucial centre of the Torah. Yet, Christ has no revelatory or ontological relationship with the Torah. The Torah is and remains the νόμος τοῦ θεοῦ.

---

337 As maintained by M. Hengel, *o.c.*, p.73 n.2.
338 M. Hengel, *o.c.*, p.74.
339 M. Hengel, ibid.

15.4. Conclusion: Wisdom and Law in Paul's Christology

The main result from our treatment of Paul's wisdom christology and his theology of the law in the light of his christology can be succinctly formulated in the following manner: Paul, even though he was familiar with the already traditional correlation and identification of law and wisdom, did not make use of it in the formulation and presentation of his christology.

In the delineation of his christology, Paul did take up significant elements of the Jewish wisdom speculation, i.e. of the poetic personification of wisdom, and related these elements to Christ. As a result one can justly speak of a Pauline wisdom christology. Cosmological, soteriological, revelatory, and ontological aspects of the wisdom figure are transferred by Paul to Christ, or rather employed in the description of Christ as the pre-existent Son sent by God, as the mediator and sustainer of creation, as the image of God and the embodiment and realization of God's wisdom, i.e. the full and perfect manifestation of God.

But Paul never correlates Christ and the law. The fact that Christ is τέλος νόμου does not mean that he is the full and perfect 'embodiment' of the law. It means that he is the (only!) one who has fully fulfilled the Torah and has thus subjected the law to himself as νόμος τοῦ Χριστοῦ which appears to the believer — who is ἔννομος Χριστοῦ — as νόμος πνεύματος and νόμος πίστεως, but which is still νόμος τοῦ θεοῦ. Whereas Christ is described in terms of wisdom, Christ is not described in terms of Torah[340]. Rather, the Torah is described and defined in terms of Christ.

In the realm of christology, Paul abandoned the functional identity of law and wisdom. Paul could use the characteristics of divine wisdom, but he could not use essential functions of Torah in the context of the 'old' covenant which linked Torah with wisdom: the fundamental function of Torah which linked it with wisdom was its soteriological role as way of and to righteousness. It was in all probability at this very point that Paul had to give up the identity of law and wisdom: the cosmological, ontological, and theological functions of wisdom could well be used for the de-

---

340 We noted above that Paul eliminates all references to the Torah when he uses Deut 30,12-14 to describe the presence of Christ in Rom 10,6b-8.

scription of the person and work of Christ, but the transfer of the theological (actual) functions of Torah to Christ would have led to serious misunderstandings.

The function of the Torah in the salvation of man was shattered by Christ's death and resurrection. We have therefore spoken of a christologically motivated abrogation of the Torah in the soteriological realm which obviously excludes the transfer of the soteriological functions of the Torah to Christ. Paul does not want his readers to get the impression that Christ, as embodiment of God's will, brought a new Torah which man has to fulfill. Paul's central concern was that his readers understood the exclusive soteriological significance of Christ who fulfilled the Torah in his death and resurrection for us. A new law would not solve man's predicament as God's eternal claims would still apply. The only possible solution for man's 'problem' was God sending his Son to fulfill the Torah and to die on the cross for him.

Consequently, Paul abandoned the functional identity of Torah and wisdom on the christological level for soteriological reasons. Christ who is God's wisdom is not God's (new) Torah but brought the realization of God's Torah by fulfilling it himself, and fulfilling it for us, thus defining and qualifying the Torah in the light of the climax of God's history of salvation: the Torah comes under the rule of Christ and thus under the 'rule' of those who are, by faith, in Christ and controlled by the Spirit.

§ 16 The Christian Way of Life

In our final section we investigate the question what import the law and Jewish wisdom have for the Christian ethic as presented and substantiated by Paul. The issue of the place of the law in Pauline ethic leads to the important questions of the relationship of Gospel and law and of indicative and imperative, and of the existence of binding norms for individual, specific behaviour. Much has been written on these matters both by Protestant and Catholic scholars. We will occasionally touch upon the first two areas (in § 16.1.), but we will dwell more on the question of normativity in Pauline ethics (§ 16.2.).

The issue of the place of wisdom in Paul's ethic seems never to have been dealt with systematically even though scholars are aware of the formal and material links between Paul's parenesis and the Jewish wisdom tradition. We will focus particularly on the theological and ethical functions of wisdom theology in Paul's ethic (§ 16.3.). This procedure will help us to determine whether Paul's ethic implies or is even based upon the traditional correlation of law and wisdom. The fact that Paul did not employ this correlation on the christological level does not preclude the possibility that he uses it on the ethical level. This possibility cannot be ruled out as the traditional correlation of law and wisdom had its main focus in the ethical realm.

We will discuss Paul's parenesis as a whole[341] without taking into account the different chronological and contextual settings of his letters, mainly because no developments in Paul's thinking as to both the motivations and the norms of Christian behaviour have been traced[342].

We are aware of the fact that one cannot speak of Paul's 'ethics' since this term implies some sort of scientific treatise, delineating a moral 'system', something which is obviously not extant in the Pauline corpus[343]. The term 'parenesis' as well as the term 'ethos' are equally not unproblematic[344]. However, as these terms have

---

341 Cf. generally W. Schrage, *Die konkreten Einzelgebote in der paulinischen Paränese: Ein Beitrag zur neutestamentlichen Ethik*, 1961, pp.13-48; V.P. Furnish, *Theology and Ethics in Paul*, 1968, pp.242-279; F. Laub, *Eschatologische Verkündigung und Lebensgestaltung nach Paulus*, 1973, pp.1-24; and R. Hasenstab, *Modelle paulinischer Ethik: Beiträge zu einem Autonomie-Modell aus paulinischem Geist*, 1977, pp.29-138 for useful surveys of the main interpretations of Paul's ethic.

342 Cf. W. Schrage, o.c., pp.187-271 passim; O. Merk, *Handeln aus Glauben: Die Motivierungen der paulinischen Ethik*, 1968, pp.245f. (arguing contra L. Nieder, *Die Motive der religiös-sittlichen Paränese in den paulinischen Gemeindebriefen*, 1956, pp.141ff.); W. Schrage, *Ethik*, 1982, p.155.

343 Cf. V.P. Furnish, o.c., pp.208-212 who therefore prefers to speak of Pauline 'ethic', taking into account the fact that the dynamic of indicative and imperative in Paul's thought presupposes theological convictions which, although formulated not self-consciously, underlie his concrete, specific exhortations.

344 Cf. A. Grabner-Haider, *Paraklese und Eschatologie bei Paulus: Mensch und Welt im Anspruch der Zukunft Gottes*, NTA NF 4, 1968, p.4 who suggests that the term parenesis should be avoided since the terms παραινεῖν and παραίνησις occur only in Lk 3,18(D) and Acts 27,9.22 (and in SapSal 8,9; 2Macc 7,25.26; 3Macc 5,17; 7,12 in LXX), referring to H. Schlier, J. Schniewind, W. Joest, E. Schlink, and O.

become very much established in the discussion of the relevant material, especially, as regards the last two terms, on the continent, we will still use them.

We distinguish motivations which are related to the foundation of Christian behaviour (§ 16.1.), binding norms for Christian behaviour (§ 16.2.), and guiding criteria relevant for the practical and specific application of these forms in the Christian life (§ 16.3.).

16.1. Foundational Motivations

16.1.1. Introduction. It was particularly O. Merk who researched the theological basis, the technique, and the content of the motivations in Paul's ethic[345]. The classification of the various motives varies widely[346]. As pointed out above, we want to distinguish between foundational motivations which touch on the basis of the Christian life, and binding norms and guiding criteria which are relevant for the practical working out of the Christian life. The various motivations which will be discussed below are, essentially, the unfolding of God's salvational action[347]. This theological or theocentric foundation of the Christian life is obvious in many parenetic contexts in Paul's letters[348].

Not only the classification but also the nomenclature of the foundation and motivation of Paul's parenesis varies. Some scholars, for example, subsume nearly every aspect of Paul's thinking

---

Michel. He prefers the term 'paraklesis' as a more appropriate term for the early Christian mission and preaching practice. The term 'ethos', widely used in German literature, seems to have a different meaning in the Anglo-Saxon realm, but is still used (cf. J. Nel, B. Gerhardsson).

345 Cf. O. Merk, *Handeln*, pp.43-229 (exegesis), 231-248 (systematizing conclusions); cf. also K. Romaniuk, "Les motifs parénétiques dans les écrits pauliniens", *NovTest* 10 (1968) 190-207; P. Grech, "Christological Motives in Pauline Ethics", *Paul de Tarse*, 1979, pp.541-558.

346 P. Grech, *a.c.*, e.g. distinguishes between 'classified' motives (pp.542-548) which include the appeal to common sense, social reasons, scriptural authority, and theological, salvation-historical, eschatological, and ecclesiological motives, and the proper christological motives (pp.548-555).

347 Cf. O. Merk, *o.c.*, pp.4-41,235-248; V.P. Furnish, *Theology*, pp.213f.; H. Ridderbos, *Paul*, pp.258-265; H. Halter, *Taufe*, p.457f.

348 Cf. O. Merk, *o.c.*, pp.235-237 mentioning Gal 5,13-6,10; 1Thess 4,6-8; 5,1-10; 1Cor 6,1-20; 8,1-11,1; 12-13; 2Cor 8-9; Rom 12-13; 15,7; Phil 2,6-18; Col 3,1-4.

under the category 'eschatology', including christological aspects³⁴⁹. Realizing the interrelatedness of these areas, depending on the respective definitions, we prefer to hold these areas apart since eschatology, even in the broad sense of the term, is but a partial function of Paul's theological conception of the ethos, evidenced by the multiplicity of his parenetic motivations³⁵⁰. A similar situation prevails regarding the term salvation-history. We discuss, however briefly, therefore, the christological (including soteriological), the salvation-historical, the pneumatological, the ecclesiological, and the eschatological motivation of Paul's parenesis.

16.1.2. Christological motivation. Recent studies have confirmed that the proprium of the Pauline ethos consists "in der Christusbezogenheit der ethischen Weisungen, in denen das Christusereignis pneumatologisch, ekklesiologisch und anthropologisch reflektiert ist"³⁵¹. This foundational christological motivation comprises the past of Christ's death and resurrection, the present of Christ's salvation and lordship, and the future of Christ's return.

> According to 2Cor 5,14-15 Christ died for all so that those for whom he died shall no longer live for themselves but for the one who died for them and was raised from the dead. Rom 14,9 asserts that Christ died and was raised in order that he might be Lord of the dead and of the living.

Paul obviously ascribes to Christ's salvational death and resurrection power and authority.

> In the words of W. Schrage, "mit dem Tod Jesu Christi sind das neue Leben und der Gehorsam der Christen mitgesetzt, und zwar nicht nur als ethische Verpflichtung,

---

349 Cf. H. Halter, *Taufe*, p.339 who defines eschatology as "das pln Verständnis des Heilshandelns Gottes durch Christus und der dadurch geschaffenen Situation; similarly W. Schrage, *Einzelgebote*, pp.15f.,20-26; A. Grabner-Haider, *Paraklese*, pp. 33-44,58-112 and others.
350 Cf. C. Münchow, *Ethik*, 1981, p.150.
351 G. Strecker, "Autonome Sittlichkeit und das Proprium der christlichen Ethik bei Paulus", *ThLZ* 104 (1979) 871 summarizing the results of the studies of H. Halter and R. Hasenstab. See further O. Merk, *Handeln*, pp.15-41,237f.; V.P. Furnish, *Theology*, pp.216-226; G. Eichholz, *Theologie*, pp.265-268; H.D. Wendland, *Ethik des Neuen Testaments*, ²1975, pp.49-88; H. Ridderbos, *Paul*, pp.206-214; F. Festorazzi, "Originalità della morale cristiana secondo San Paolo", *Dimensions de la vie chrétienne*, 1979, pp.548-555; J.F. Collange, *Éthique*, pp.55-61; W. Schrage, *Ethik*, 1982, pp.155-230 and passim.

sondern als Realität . . . Das befreiende Herrsein Jesu ist Ausgangs- und Zielpunkt christlichen Lebens und christlicher Ethik"³⁵².

That the lordship of Christ is based on, and rooted in, what Jesus Christ did for man becomes apparent when one considers the relationship between justification and sanctification in Rom 6, 12-23³⁵³. In view of God's action in Christ, the believer must be obedient (Rom 1,5), as faith and obedience are closely related by Paul (cf. Rom 1,8 with 16,19 and Phil 2,12 with 2,17; cf. Rom 15, 18; 2Cor 10,5-6)³⁵⁴. Obedience as proof and test of faith is the thankful recognition of the fact that God has accepted the ἀσεβής as justified in Christ, that God wants to keep and preserve him, that God has 'monopolized' him, and that God's gift of δικαιοσύνη is to realize itself constantly as indwelling power making the justified one into an instrument of righteousness (Rom 6, 13.19)³⁵⁵. The believer who is ἐν Χριστῷ is at the same time ἐν κυρίῳ — an important expression in the context of Paul's ethos³⁵⁶.

Thus, the work and the lordship of Jesus Christ are of basic importance for the Christian ethic according to Paul³⁵⁷.

16.1.3. Salvation-historical motivation. Paul sees the locus of the Christian ethos to be the time between Christ's resurrection

---

352 W. Schrage, *Ethik*, p.161. Cf. also G. Eichholz, *Theologie*, p.272 who asserts in this context: "daß wir Jesus Christus gehören, entnimmt uns uns selbst, unserer Verfügungsgewalt, und macht uns frei zum Dienst für Christus und für den Nächsten". Also H. Halter, *Taufe*, p.326 who concludes that "als der in Christus neu von Gott herkommende und auf Gott hingehende neue Mensch ist der getaufte Glaubende zu einer dieser Heilsbewegung entsprechenden, fruchtbringenden neuen Existenz ermächtigt und gefordert".

353 Cf. U. Wilckens, *Römer*, 2, 1980, pp.5-42 passim (pp.5f. lit., add O. Merk, 'Handeln, pp.28-41). For the question of the relation of indicative and imperative which is relevant here cf. § 16.2.1.

354 Cf. O. Merk, *o.c.*, p.13; C.E.B. Cranfield, *Romans*, 1, pp.66f.; U. Wilckens, *Römer*, 1, pp.66f.

355 Cf. O. Merk, *Handeln*, p.13 referring to E. Käsemann, "Gottesgerechtigkeit bei Paulus", *Exegetische Versuche und Besinnungen*, 2, 1964, p.187.

356 Cf. W. Schrage, *Ethik*, p.162 referring to 1Cor 7,39; 11,11; Phil 4,4; 1Thess 4,1; he asserts that "wer 'in Christus' ist, der ist eben damit eo ipso dem Herrn im Gehorsam unterstellt: 'Leben wir, so leben wir dem Herrn' (Röm 14,9f)".

357 Cf. also 1Thess 5,10; 1Cor 1,13; 3,23; 5,7; 6,12-20; 7,21-24.32-35; 8,11-13; 10,14-22; 11,3-5.11; 2Cor 5,13-15; 8,8-9; Rom 12,1-2; 14,7-9; Phil 2,6-11; Col 3,17-18. Cf. O. Merk, *o.c.*, pp.45-229 passim, 237-239; P. Grech, "Motives", 1979, pp.549-552.

and his return. The Christian ethos is related to, and relevant for, the time 'between the ages', taking into account the tension between the 'already' and the 'not yet'. Accordingly, the Christian ethic has been termed interim ethics, church ethics, or *ethica viatorum*[358]. The 'interim' is both the time of salvation (cf. 2Cor 6,2) and the time of *Bewährung* which is a "Zeit des Gefordertseins, der In-Dienst-Nahme durch Gott"[359]. The believer who has been justified by the revelation of God's righteousness in Jesus Christ responds by obedient behaviour which corresponds to this righteousness and holds out, in the present time of salvation, the dialectic between the salvation which has already happened and is his, and the salvation which will happen and will fully become his (cf. Phil 2,12-13). This dialectic is the ground for the dialectic of the indicative and the imperative: the old aeon has been overturned by Christ but the new aeon has not begun in universal fulness and perfection. And this togetherness of the present evil aeon and the beginning of the new aeon, the new creation, corresponds with the situation of the believer 'between the times'[360].

As a result of this tension between the 'already' and the 'not yet', Paul exhorts believers not to live after the pattern of this aeon (Rom 12,2), implying that this is at least a possibility. He warns them of specific acts of the sinful nature (Gal 5,19-21) and tells them to examine everything and to hold on (only) to the good (1Thess 5,21), knowing that many things are not useful for the believer (1Cor 10,23). And Paul is very much aware of the fact that Satan is still a real threat for the Christians and consequently admonishes them to beware of him (Rom 16,20; 1Cor 7,5; 2Cor

---

358 Cf. O. Merk, *o.c.*, pp.14f.,37; H.D. Wendland, *Ethik*, p.51; H. Ridderbos, *Paul*, p. 257; O. Cullmann, "Les conséquences éthiques entre le 'déjà' et le 'pas encore' ", *Paul de Tarse*, 1979, pp.559-574; W. Schrage, *o.c.*, pp.158f.; see also H. Halter, *Taufe*, pp.14-17,27 who describes the present consensus among Catholic moral theologians as regards "dans Situiert-Sein des christlichen Ethos in der Heilsgeschichte" (p.17). Cf. also J. Ellul, *The Ethics of Freedom*, 1976, p.11. The term 'interim ethics' goes back to A. Schweitzer but is used here in a different, more positive sense.

359 Cf. O. Merk, *o.c.*, p.14.

360 Cf. O. Merk, *o.c.*, p.37; H. Ridderbos, *Paul*, p.257; O. Cullmann, "Conséquences", 1979, pp.559-574 passim; W. Schrage, *Ethik*, p.158. T.J. Deidun, *Morality*, 1981, pp.51-84 claims that the inward activity of the Spirit as fulfilment of the promises concerning the new covenant is the ground of the imperative.

2,11) and of the manifold temptations (1Cor 10,13; Gal 6,1; 1Thess 3,5). which are sure to present themselves.

6.1.4. Pneumatological motivation.

The pneumatological motive of Paul's ethic can be regarded as the concretization of the christological foundation[361]. The Christian life can be defined as a "walk" in the Spirit (Gal 5,25; cf. Rom 8,4), producing the "fruit" of the Spirit (Gal 5,22). The gift of the Spirit is the fundamental power and principle of the new life[362]. The Spirit determines the entire life of the believer and of the church (1Cor 12,11). The Spirit is "Inbegriff des neuen Lebens bis in die Einzelheiten und Alltäglichkeiten hinein"[363] (cf. Rom 5,5; 8,9.14.26-27; 12,4ff.; 15,16; 1Cor 12,3-11; Gal 3,3; 5,22-25).

The renewal of the believer by the Spirit includes, above all, the realm of moral decisions and moral conduct[364]. The believer is 'developed' by the Spirit externally via the apostolic exhortation (1Thess 4,1-8; 1Cor 7,40), the brotherly admonition (Gal 6,1), the example of others (1Thess 1,6-7), the offices and charismata of the church (1Cor 12-14; Rom 12,4-8), and the worship service (1Cor 14; Col 3,16), and internally via perception (1Cor 2,10-16; Col 1,9-10), faith (2Cor 4,13), hope (Rom 5,5; 8,16-17; 15,13), prayer (Gal 4,6; Rom 8,15.26-27), and love (Rom 5,5; 15,30; Gal 5,22)[365]. The Spirit enables the believer to fulfill the will of God (Rom 8,4; cf. Gal 5,13-14.16.25)[366].

---

361 Cf. H.D. Wendland, *Ethik*, p.53 referring to Rom 8,1ff. and Gal 5,13ff. Cf. also W. Schrage, *o.c.,*. p.167 who, however, should not quote Rom 12,1 in this context translating λογικὴ λατρεία as "geistlicher Gottesdienst": the meaning "geistig" or "intelligent", "understanding" worship is clearly to be preferred; cf. C.E.B. Cranfield, *Romans*, 2, pp.604f.; H.W. Bartsch, Art. "λογικός", *EWNT* 2 (1981) 877; U. Wilckens, *Römer*, 3, 1982, pp.4-6.
362 Cf. H. Ridderbos, *Paul*, pp.214-223; W. Schrage, *Einzelgebote*, pp.20,71f.; O. Merk, *Handeln*, pp.18f.,39f.; G. Eichholz, *Theologie*, pp.273f.; H. Halter, *Taufe*, pp.409-427 (pp.683f. lit.!); W. Schrage, *Ethik*, pp.167ff.
363 W. Schrage, *Einzelgebote*, p.71.
364 Cf. H. Halter, *o.c.*, pp.412f. who defines the Spirit and his activity as "wirkmächtiges Anwesen Gottes unter den Menschen ... die subjektive Dimension des objektiven Wirkens Gottes".
365 Cf. H. Halter, *o.c.*, p.420 whose biblical references, however, are not all relevant in this context.
366 Cf. H. Halter, *Taufe*, pp.423f. who states that "als im Geiste zu einer neuen Existenz Ermächtigte sind die Christen zu einer dieser Ermächtigung entsprechenden

16.1.5. Ecclesiological motivation.
It has been indicated that the ethic according to Paul can be defined as 'church ethic'. The ecclesiological motives of Paul's parenesis have been pointed out repeatedly[367]. Paul makes *individualethische* statements[368] only very seldom and relates even them, essentially, to the Christian community[369]. The church is particularly the locus of discovering and discerning the will of God.

Consequently, Paul's exhortations as regards discernment and perception are in the plural (Rom 12,2; Phil 1,9-10; 4,8; Col 1,9-10). He admonishes the believers τὸ αὐτό and τὸ ἓν φρονεῖν (Rom 12,16; 15,5; 2Cor 13,11; Phil 2,2; 4,2)[370]. The reference to the conduct of other believers or churches can become a decisive argument (1Cor 11,16). In the dispute between the 'weak' and the 'strong', the reference to the believers' responsibility to each other is a crucial part of Paul's response[371].

The λόγος σοφίας (1Cor 12,8) seems to be a charism which refers to decisions in the ethical realm[372]. The conceptions of the οἰκοδομή[373] of the church and the κοινωνία[374] in the church are relevant here also. It is a matter-of-course for Paul, however, that the τὸ αὐτὸ φρονεῖν is not *eo ipso* legitimated but has to conform

---

Existenz gefordert — das Treiben des Geistes ist ein ermöglichendes und forderndes" (p.424).

367 Cf. W. Schrage, *Einzelgebote*, pp.174-181; O. Merk, *Handeln*, pp.19,237-239; H.D. Wendland, *Ethik*, pp.64-69; H. Halter, *o.c.*, pp.427-452; H. Schürmann, *Orientierungen*, pp.64-88; F. Festorazzi, "Originalità", 1979, pp.249-253; P. Grech, "Motives", 1979, pp.547f.; J.F. Collange, *Éthique*, pp.220-231; T.J. Deidun, *Morality*, pp.215-217,222f.; W. Schrage, *Ethik*, pp.213f.

368 Cf. the statements on ἀρετή (Phil 4,8) , on the σῶμα of the individual Christian (Rom 12,1; 1Cor 6,13), on personal suffering (Rom 8,18; 2Cor 4,17; etc.); and on ἐγκράτεια (Gal 5,23; cf. 1Cor 7,9; 9,25). Cf. W. Schrage, *Ethik*, pp.209-213.

369 Cf. H.D. Wendland, *o.c.*, p.65; W. Schrage, *o.c.*, 213 concluding that "am sittlichen Verhalten des Christen als einzelnem Individuum hat Paulus kein sonderlich großes Interesse" (ibid.). It is obvious, of course, that Paul regards the church not as transcendent, theoretical reality but as the fellowship of individual believers in Christ!

370 Cf. W. Schrage, *Einzelgebote*, pp.174-176.

371 Cf. J. Murphy-O'Connor, "Freedom", 1979, pp.21-32, here p.32.

372 W. Schrage, *Einzelgebote*, pp.180f.

373 Cf. O. Michel, Art."οἰκοδομέω", *ThWNT* 5 (1954) 139-151; O. Merk, *Handeln*, pp. 237f.; J. Pfammatter, Art. "οἰκοδομή", *EWNT* 2 (1981) 1211-1218.

374 Cf. J. M. McDermott, "The Biblical Doctrine of ΚΟΙΝΩΝΙΑ", *BZ* 19 (1975) 64-77, 219-233; G. Panikulam, *Koinōnia in the New Testament: A Dynamic Expression in the Christian Life*, AnBibl 85, 1979; J. Hainz, Art. "κοινωνία", *EWNT* 2 (1981) 749-755.

to a superior norm since the majority does not automatically possess the truth (cf. Rom 15,5; Gal 2,6.14)[375].

Most scholars refer to a sacramental foundation of the Christian ethos which we want to include in the ecclesiological basis. The main focus here is on the function of baptism as inauguration of the new existence in Christ and as motive for Christian behaviour[376]. Catholic and most Protestant scholars seem to agree that baptism is both a cognitive and a causative event[377] — despite the fact that Paul does not present a proper 'doctrine' of baptism nor treats baptism thematically, and that the question of infant baptism, generally presupposed by these scholars, cannot be answered positively on the basis of the NT documents[378]. It can be said with certainty, however, that Paul does correlate baptism (as causative act? or as testimony?!), justification, and sanctification (Rom 6)[379].

16.1.6. Eschatological motivation. The final foundational motivation of Paul's ethic is the eschatological motive. We take 'eschatological' here not in the broad sense of the term[380] referring to the presence of salvation but rather in the strict sense as comprising the hope (or the future) of salvation. For Paul, the hope regarding the future carries weight for the present behaviour of the believer[381].

---

375 Cf. W. Schrage, *o.c.*, p.177. Pace the Catholic scholars H. Halter, *Taufe*, p.439 (who refers to an "Interaktionsprozess ekklesialer 'Normfindung'", pp.451f.); H. Schürmann, *Orientierungen*, pp.64-88 (who concludes that "die apostolische Kirche schrieb sich selbst die letztlich entscheidende sittliche Erkenntnisfähigkeit und eine hohe Weisungsvollmacht zu wenn es darum ging, den Willen Gottes zu erkenen. Der nachapostoloschen Kirche kommt diesselbe doch wohl ebenfalls zu", p.86); T.J. Deidun, *Morality*, pp.222-225 (who affirms the obligation of clerical celibacy in this context!).

376 Cf. Schrage, *o.c.*, pp.49,187; O. Merk, *o.c.*, pp.19-28,34,41; H. Halter, *o.c.*, pp.289-303; H. Schürmann, *o.c.*, pp.94f.

377 Cf. H. Halter, *o.c.*, p.291 (pp.684f. n.18 lit.); for the Protestant side cf. recently U. Schnelle, *Gerechtigketi*, 1983, passim.

378 Note the explicit remark to this effect by H. Halter, *Taufe*, pp.30,292!

379 Cf. O. Merk, *Handeln*, pp.19-41; W. Schrage, *Ethik*, pp.164f.; also U. Wilckens, *Römer*, 2, pp.5-62 passim and U. Schnelle, *Gerechtigkeit*, pp.33-161 passim.

380 Cf. supra p.302 with n.349.

381 Cf. W. Schrage, *Einzelgebote*, pp.20f.; K. Romaniuk, "Motifs", *NovTest* 10 (1968) 192f.,197; O. Merk, *o.c.*, pp.238,240-243; H. Schürmann, *Orientierungen*, pp. 93f.; F. Festorazzi, "Originalità", pp.248f.; P. Grech, "Motivations", pp.546f.;

Several scholars have pointed out that the view is wrong which explains Paul's use of parenesis by his diminishing *Naherwartung* — the element of the proximity of the parousia is of secondary importance for Paul's ethical motivations[382]. This is corroborated, for example, by the fact that the orientation of the admonitions by the end is characteristic for Paul already in 1Thess (cf. 4,6; 5,9-10; also 3,12-13; 5, 23).

In the context of the relatedness of christology, eschatology, and ethics, Paul's references to the future have (1) a critical function for the present stressing the 'not yet', and (2) a constructive function for the present pointing the believer to the future and determining his understanding of the present in which his actions take place[383].

The concept of the judgment according to works (Rom 2,5-11. 16; 1Cor 3,13; 2Cor 5,9-10; cf. Gal 6,8; Phil 1,10; Col 3,25; 1Thess 4,3-6) serves the elaboration of Christian behaviour in the 'interim', i.e. it serves "der Verklammerung der Rechtfertigung als *articulus fidei constituens* mit der darauf beruhenden Ethik als *articulus fidei consequens*"[384].

The concept of reward (Rom 2,7; 1Cor 3,8.14; 4,5; 9,24-25; 15,58; Gal 6,7-10; Phil 3,14) also plays an important role as regards encouragement and exhortation in Paul's parenesis. Other significant notions in this eschatological context are the nearness

---

J.F. Collange, *Éthique*, pp.64-68; H.H. Schade, *Christologie*, 1981, pp.135-156 passim; C. Münchow, *Ethik*, 1981, pp.150-168 passim; W. Schrage, *Ethik*, p.275.

382 For details see W. Schrage, "Zur formalethischen Bedeutung der paulinischen Paränese", ZEE 4 (1960) 207-233, here 209-218; H. Ridderbos, *Paul*, p.275; P. Grech, a.c., p.547; A. Vögtle, "Paraklese und Eschatologie nach Röm 13,11-14", *Dimensions de la vie chrétienne*, 1979, pp.179-194, here 189-194; H.H. Schade, o.c., p.143; W. Schrage, *Einzelgebote*, pp.16,173f.
383 Cf. C. Münchow, *Ethik*, p.167.
384 C. Münchow, o.c., p.161 emphasizing further that the concept of judgment according to works does not imply or establish the validity of the *Tun-Ergehen-Zusammenhang* but rather challenges the Christian to protect the new creation in the present somatic existence as he lives not in the time of perfection but in the time of ethics (p.167). Cf. also W. Schrage, *Ethik*, p.175 who asserts that Paul does not call upon the Christian, here, to seek salvation on the basis of his own strength, and continues: "Aber die Christen werden danach gefragt werden, ob sie das *sola gratia* auch wirklich *sola*, ganz und total haben gelten lassen, was sie mit Gottes Gaben angefangen haben, ob sie auch wirklich vom Eschaton her und in der Kraft des Geistes gelebt und den Heilsweg in Christus nicht verlassen haben" (ibid.). — On the concept of judgment in Paul see particularly L. Mattern, *Das Verständnis des Gerichtes bei Paulus*, AThANT 47, 1966; E. Synofzik, *Die Gerichts- und Vergeltungsaussagen bei Paulus*, GThA 8, 1977; U. Wilckens, *Römer*, 1, 1978, pp.127-131,142-146.

of the "day" (Rom 13,11-14[385]; 1Thess 5,1-11[386]) or the "day of Christ" (1Cor 1,8; Phil 1,6; 2,16), and the expectation of the σωτήρ Jesus Christ (Phil 3,20). All of these aspects of Paul's (futuristic) eschatology emphatically refer the believer to ethical responsibility.

16.1.7. Summary. One specific characteristic in Paul's ethic, compared with the contemporary Jewish and Hellenistic ethos, is first of all the motivation, i.e. the correlation of the ethos with the christological and eschatological foundation[387]. This correlation is then also significant for the material elaboration of the ethos which, however, we cannot discuss at this point.

As regards the technique of motivation, several concluding remarks may be made[388]. (1) Paul sees a plurality of motivations, and the implied heterogeneity of the motivations makes it impossible to reduce the latter to a single motive[389]. (2) The variety and the very use of the motivations show that Paul makes it a point to gain the understanding of the churches and to render the exhorta-

---

385 See recently A. Vögtle, "Paraklese und Eschatologie nach Röm 13,11-14", 1979, pp. 179-194 passim.
386 Cf. W. Harnisch, *Eschatologische Existenz: Ein exegetischer Beitrag zum Sachanliegen von 1 Thessalonicher 4,13-5,11*, FRLANT 110, 1973, pp.52-158; F. Laub, *Eschatologische Verkündigung*, 1973, pp.157-164; H.H. Schade, *Christologie*, 1981, p.137-140.
387 Emphasized by C. Münchow, *Ethik*, p.163.
388 Cf. O. Merk, *Handeln*, pp.232-235 who includes motives — under the headings 'individual motivations' and 'rare motivations' (pp.240-245) — which are discussed in § 16.3.
389 Thus one should refrain from describing Paul's ethic as 'ethics of freedom', 'ethics of love', 'telos ethics', etc. The plurality of motivations stems from Paul's "Zug zur Konkretisierung"(W. Schrage, *Einzelgebote*, p.61) which is to be distinguished from casuism or legalism; cf. W. Schrage, *o.c.*, pp.59-71 passim; H. Ridderbos, *Paul*, pp.272-278; W. Schrage, *Ethik*, pp.178-181. Cf. also E. Schweizer, "Ethischer Pluralismus im Neuen Testament", *EvTh* 35 (1975) 397-401 with W. Schrage, "Korreferat", *EvTh* 35 (1975) 402-407 who prefers to speak of plurality instead of pluralism. — One should note the difference to Stoic ethics where practical consequences of moral teachings are drawn only rarely; cf. W. Schrage, *Einzelgebote*, pp.59f. with n.3; for a comparison of Stoic ethics and NT ethics cf. recently T. Herr, *Naturrecht aus der kritischen Sicht des Neuen Testaments*, 1976, pp.128-133; pace R. Hodgson, *Die Quellen der paulinischen Ethik*, Diss. theol. Heidelberg, 1976, pp.109-141 who admits that we find no quotation of, or allusion to, specific Stoic dicta but arrives nevertheless on the basis of formal and material correspondences at the "Annahme einer quellenmäßigen Abhängigkeit" (p.138).

tions intelligible and comprehensible[390]. (3) This implies that the motivations are not all equally significant in a given pericope: in a particular context often only one or two substantiations are dominant with other motives being additional. (4) There is no pericope in which the motivations are opposed to each other[391].

Paul motivates the Christian ethos by unfolding God's action in and through the Lord Jesus Christ: "Durch die Motivierungen des von ihm geforderten Tuns soll dem Christen bewußt werden, daß er in Gottes Handeln hineingestellt ist"[392].

16.2. Binding Norms: The Law Aspect

16.2.1. Introduction. The concreteness and multiplicity of Paul's motivations and exhortations cannot be used as an argument to prove that Paul's ethic is not only situationally oriented but also situationally conditioned (and therefore only historically valid): (1) many exhortations occur in pericopes which are not (!) dependent upon a specific situation and occasion (cf. Rom 12-13; Gal 5-6; 1Thess 4)[393], and (2) Paul expects from all (!) Christians a behaviour which is the result and the realization of God's action in and through Christ which is, however, not uniform behaviour.

This leads us to the question whether Paul was committed to norms in the elaboration of the Christian ethos. Attempting to

---

[390] One should not play understanding and conviction off against obedience since these concepts are not mutually exclusive, and since Paul is definitely looking for obedience as well. Contra J. Becker, "Das Problem der Schriftgemäßheit der Ethik", *Handbuch der christlichen Ethik*, 1, ed. A. Hertz et al., 1978, p.257 who states that "nicht Gehorsam, sondern Überzeugung wird gesucht".

[391] Stated by O. Merk, *Handeln*, p.234 as result of his extensive and thorough exegesis of Paul's parenetic texts.

[392] O. Merk, *o.c.*, p.240.

[393] Stressed recently by W. Schrage, *Ethik*, pp.180f.; also idem, "Deutung", *ZEE* 4 (1960) 225-233; H. Ridderbos, *Paul*, pp.276f. Contra e.g. H. Schürmann, *Orientierungen*, 1978, p.110 who states that "je konkreter die Wertungen und Weisungen materialiter werden, desto mehr muß ihre universale Verbindlichkeit hinterfragt werden ... Die universale und zeitlose Allgemeinverbindlichkeit muß immer dann ernstlich überprüft werden, wenn Paulus operative Handlungsnormen für geschichtlich veränderte Situationen und Umstände oder Anweisungen und Mahnungen für konkrete Einzelfälle gibt". It is the classical Kantian proposition when Schürmann suggests that moral-theological hermeneutics and moral reason determine Christian conduct in the final analysis (ibid.).

answer this question, one should clearly distinguish between the question of normativity in and for Paul and the question of normativity of Paul (for today). It seems that the negative answer given by many scholars to the second question also decides the answer to the first question[394]. Such scholars protest against a biblical ethos which claims to be more than a noncommittal paradigmatic commentary on the 'commandment' of love. They attempt to justify their position pneumatologically, ecclesiologically, rationalistically, or by reference to 'love'. They claim that the decisive norm(s) or criteria of Christian conduct, for Paul (and hence for us), is the life in the Spirit[395], the context of the church[396], the function of renewed reason[397], and the fundamental requirement of love[398].

It has to be pointed out, however, that when Paul writes about the perception of the will of God for living, he refers to the Spirit very seldom and rather reluctantly and never as implying a contrast to or autonomy from any *verbum extermum*[399].

---

394 A recent example is G. Strecker, "Autonome Sittlichkeit und das Proprium der christlichen Ethik bei Paulus", *ThLZ* 104 (1979) 871 who asserts that the Christian ethos is accidental and "nicht wirklich normschöpferisch, weil es im Gegebenen die aktuelle Forderung Gottes entdeckt". Cf. also J.T. Sanders, *Ethics*, 1975, p.64 who thinks that situation ethics is unavoidable (as regards Paul's ethos!).

395 Cf. R. Schnackenburg, *Moral Teaching*, p.277; K. Niederwimmer, *Begriff der Freiheit*, 1966, pp.168-220; K.H. Schelkle, *Theologie*, 3, p.55; H.D. Wendland, *Ethik*, pp.53f., 87; G. Therrien, *Le discernement dans les écrits Pauliniens*, EB, 1973, pp. 268-271,284-286,304f.; H. Halter, *Taufe*, pp.424-427,475; B.C. Wintle, *Law*, pp. 202-237,321; J.D.G. Dunn, *Jesus and the Spirit*, pp.222f.; B. Gerhardsson, *Ethos*, 1981, p.71; E. Lohse, "Kirche im Alltag: Erwägungen zur theologischen Begründung der Ethik im Neuen Testament", *Kirche*, FS G. Bornkamm, ed. D. Lührmann et al., 1980, pp.409f.; T.J. Deidun, *Morality*, 1981, pp.51-84,169.

396 Held mainly by Catholic scholars; cf. recently H. Halter, *o.c.*, pp.439, 451f.,475; H. Schürmann, *Orientierungen*, pp.37,86f.; T.J. Deidun, *o.c.*, pp.222-225.

397 Cf. V.P. Furnish, *Theology*, p.230; H. Halter, *o.c.*, p.475; R. Hasenstab, *Modelle*, pp.190-193,203; H. Schürmann, *o.c.*, p.110; J. Becker, "Schriftgemäßheit", pp. 259f.; E. Lohse, *a.c.*, pp.409f.; F. Hahn, "Christologische Begründung", *ZNW* 72 (1981) 94; also C. Münchow, *Ethik*, pp.163f.

398 Cf. K. Niederwimmer, *o.c.*, pp.211f.; V.P. Furnish, *o.c.*, pp.233-237,241; H.D. Wendland, *Ethik*, pp.59-63,86f., J.T. Sanders, *Ethics*, pp.50-60,64f.; E. Lohse, "Kirche im Alltag", 1980, pp.401-406,412,414; C. Münchow, *Ethik*, pp.164f.;J.C. Brunt, "Love, Freedom, and Moral Responsibility", *SBL 1981 Seminar Papers*, ed. K.H. Richards, 1981, p.27; cf. also J.F. Collange, *Éthique*, pp.145-161; T.J. Deidun, *o.c.*, pp.85-103,149f.169,222.

399 Cf. W. Schrage, *Einzelgebote*, pp.75,87,173; idem, *Ethik*, p.181f.; H. Ridderbos, *Paul*, pp.282f.; also V.P. Furnish, *o.c.*, pp.231-233; T.J. Deidun, *o.c.*, p.219.

The same can be said with regard to the church, reason, and love — concepts which are important for Paul as concerns the practical and specific implementation of the ethos. We will deal with these and with other similar concepts in §16.3. treating them as guiding criteria of the Christian ethos according to Paul.

The presence of binding obligation in the Christian life can be established, apart from Paul's conception of the law and its validity for the believer (cf. supra, §15 passim), by referring to such concepts in Paul's parenesis as ἀνάγκη (Rom 13,5; Col 3,18), ὀφείλειν (Rom 13,7.8; 15,1.27; 1Cor 11,10; 7,3; 2Cor 12,14), δεῖ (1Thess 4,1-2; 2Thess 3,7), or κανών (Gal 6,16)[400].

Further, it must be emphasized that it is not possible to derive specific norms for Christian conduct from the indicative-imperative relation since for Paul the Christian existence and divine norms never become simply identical: norms and commandments always remain an apposite entity for the Christian[401]. Heteronomy, not autonomy, is the locus of the Christian ethos according to Paul.

Schrage wants to avoid the term 'norm' for Paul since the concept of norm(s) could be understood in a static way and could easily provoke the legalistic misunderstanding of a deontological ethic which would ignore the results of behaviour. He prefers the term 'criteria' which, according to him, holds together the more dynamic-historical freedom and the "Verbindlichkeit" of Paul's (and of the NT's) ethos[402]. We prefer to hold these two aspects separate, to start with, discussing first the binding norms and the resulting "Verbindlichkeit"[403] of ethics according to Paul (§ 16.2.) and then dealing with the more dynamic, historical, or 'free' as-

---

400 Cf. W. Schrage, *Einzelgebote*, pp.96-98.
401 Cf. W. Schrage, *o.c.*, pp.82f. It is not clear what W. Schrage, *Ethik*, p.160 means when he writes in the context of his discussion of the indicative-imperative relation, with regard to the studies of G. Stählin and H. Schlier on the verb *parakalein*, that "der Anspruch(impliziert) einen Zuspruch und der Zuspruch einen Anspruch" showing that ethics does not belong into the category of law. In the OT the "Zuspruch" was primary as well: note the opening clauses of the decalogue in Ex 20!
402 W. Schrage, *o.c.*, pp.18,189 following C. Link, "Überlegungen zum Problem der Norm in der theologischen Ethik", *Schöpferische Nachfolge*, FS H.E. Tödt, 1978, pp.95-113.
403 The term "verbindlich" is usually translated with "binding" or "obligatory", concepts which clearly presuppose or imply norms!

pect of Christian behaviour which we related to the wisdom aspect (§ 16.3.). This methodological procedure will help us to avoid confusing fundamental norms of behaviour and secondary, though equally important, criteria for the realization of these norms in Christian conduct.

16.2.2. The Word of God (Torah). We have seen in § 15 that, as a result of God's action in and through Christ, the Torah is nullified as *conditio salutis* but is still valid as revelation of the will of God. The law as 'order of relation' has come to its end in Christ but remains valid as material norm and standard of life. We pointed out that the new locus of the law "in Christ" had certain consequences for the law: the ritual and ceremonial commandments are not to be fulfilled literally anymore as they are already fulfilled "in Christ", whereas the ethical norms and commandments are affirmed as valid for Christian behaviour — realizing of course that Paul does not reflect upon this differentiation in a systematic or theoretical manner. For Paul, the Christian is not exempt from keeping the commandments (cf. 1Cor 7,19).

Consequently we have to reckon with the fact that Paul regards the OT, as qualified by Christ, as authoritative standard for the Christian ethos[404].

This evidence can be further substantiated on the basis of parenetic contexts as follows[405]. (1) The more or less faithful takeover and usage of individual OT verses, especially of the parenetic proverbial material, is rather revealing, particularly as this happens in a totally natural and mater-of-course manner[406]. (2) The oc-

---

[404] This is acknowledged by R. Bultmann, *Theology*, 1, p.341; W. Schrage, *Einzelgebote*, pp.228-238; O. Merk, *Handeln*, p.10; K.H. Schelkle, *Theologie*, 3, p.47; T. Herr, *Naturrecht*, 1976, pp.221f.227; H. Ridderbos, *Paul*, pp.278-288 (on the so-called "tertius usus legis"); R.S. Rayburn, *Contrast*, pp.215-219; O. Cullmann, "Conséquences", 1979, pp.195-198; E. Reinmut, *Geist und Gesetz: Studien zu Voraussetzungen und Inhalt der paulinischen Paränese*, Diss. Halle, 1981 (unobtainable, but cf. the report in *ThLZ* 107/1982, cols.633f.); T. Holtz, "Frage", *ThLZ* 106 (1981) 394f.; W. Schrage, *Ethik*, 1982, pp.195-198. Contra e.g. P. Stuhlmacher, "Gesetz", *Aufsätze*, pp.159-161; P. Grech, "Motives", pp.544f.; B. Gerhardsson, *Ethos*, pp.64-66,81.

[405] Cf. W. Schrage, *o.c.*, pp.196f.; T. Holtz, *a.c.*, pp.394f.

[406] Cf. W. Schrage, *Einzelgebote*, p.223 with n.205 listing Rom 12,16 (Prov 3,7); 12, 17 (Prov 3,4); 12,19 (Deut 32,35); 12,20 (Prov 25,21-22); 1Cor 5,13 (Deut 17,7); 6,16 (Gen 2,24); 15,32 (Is 22,13); 13,5 (Zech 8,17); 2Cor 8,15 (Ex 16,18); 8,21

casional introductory formula γέγραπται γάρ (Rom 12,19; 14,11), καθὼς γέγραπται (Rom 15,3; 2Cor 8,15; 9,9), and φησίν (1Cor 6,6) prove that Paul does not quote or use the OT unconsciously without reflection. (3) The substantiating γάρ in Rom 12,19; 14, 11 establishes the authoritative character of the OT quotations. (4) The fact that in 1Cor 5,13; 2Cor 8,15; 9,9 the OT quotes conclude a train of thought shows likewise that Paul regards the OT as authoritative. (5) The inalienable validity of the Torah as norm of life can be ascertained by an *Umkehrschluß* from Rom 4,15 (cf. 5,13-14) where παράβασις is simply and only the transgression (!) of the order of the Torah[407].

> It is misleading when W. Schrage speaks of a dialectical reception of OT ethic by Paul, stating that the OT becomes binding for the Christian (only) a posteriori[408]. The OT receives its authority not only from its relation to Christ but from its stipulation by God and from faith in the revealed identity of God[409]. The OT is normative a priori as God's revelation; a posteriori is only the new, proper relation to it. The theological locus of the law has changed with regard to salvation[410] but has remained unchanged as regards revelation and authority. Some commandments are fulfilled "in Christ" and have therefore no more binding force for the Christian. Other, particularly the ethical, commandments retain their normativity as being God's eternal will. The examples which Schrage adduces to show that Paul takes up the OT selectively and critically even as regards ethical orders (celibacy and the prohibition of divorce) do not prove his point[411].

It has to be emphasized in this context that for Paul (as for the people in the OT, in early Judaism, and in the early church!) the law existed only as interpreted law but was, however, still and pre-

---

(Prov 3,4); 9,7 (Prov 22,8); 9,9-10 (Ps 112,9; Is 55,10); Phil 2,15 (Deut 32,5); Col 2,2 (Is 29,13).
407 Emphasized by T. Holtz, "Frage", *ThLZ* 106 (1981) 395.
408 Cf. W. Schrage, *Einzelgebote*, pp.236-238; idem, *Ethik*, pp.197f.
409 Cf. T. Holtz, ibid.
410 Cf. supra, § 15.3.2. Note also the relevant statement of T. Herr, *Naturecht*, p.227: "Der theologische Ort des Gesetzes ergibt sich erst als Funktion der Offenbarung: das Gesetz ist der Gnade nachgeordnet".
411 Cf. W. Schrage, *o.c.*, p.197. As concerns celibacy, Gen 2,18 is a general statement and not meant as establishing the necessity (!) of marriage for everybody, whereas Paul does not argue against marriage per se in 1Cor 7,26. As concerns the prohibition of divorce, 1Cor 7,10 is not totally absolute (cf. 7,11.15!) and should be regarded moreover as reinstitution of God's original will or order of creation (with the allowance of divorce, and of polygamy, in the OT being what Lutheran scholars call "Notordnung"). Schrage gives no criteria which Paul would have used in 'selecting' ethical material from the OT. Schrage would have a more consistent position if he had a proper understanding of Rom 3,27; 8,2; Gal 6,2 (pace W. Schrage, *Ethik*, pp.197f.).

cisely *the* law: for Paul, Jesus' interpretation was at the same time the fulfilment of the law. However, "gleichwohl bleibt seine Forderung des Gesetzes — des Gesetzes, das auf Gottes ursprünglichen Willen hin durch Jesus erschlossen wurde"[412].

Thus, the Torah is for Paul not an arbitrary, accidental, basically removable, historically contingent and approved order which could be easily superseded by another, nationally and historically equally contingent and approved order. For Paul the Word of God is the unshakable and always valid order of life[413]. Even the Gentile Christian church in Corinth was to submit to the order of the *nomos*!

16.2.3. The words of Jesus. The exegetical evidence leaves no doubt that dominical sayings possessed in Paul's eyes an absolute authoritative and matter-of-course validity[414]. Direct references[415] to dominical sayings are relatively rare (1Cor 7,10; 9,14; cf. also 1Cor 11,23; 1Thess 4,15). But the way in which Paul employs them shows that he regarded the words and commandments of Jesus as normative and binding tribunal, possessing a conclusive and irrefutable authority. Schrage is correct when he declares that "das Gewicht dieser Tatsache wird durch die geringe Zahl der zitierten Herrenworte kaum beeinträchtigt"[416]. Possible reasons for the rarity of references to dominical sayings are (1) the literary genre of the letter which is suited only in a limited way to take up such sayings[417], and (2) the factuality of the numerical limitedness of dominical sayings as such and also with respect to the specific variety of topics Paul deals with and with respect to his different cultural and socio-economic milieu in the diaspora[418]. It is worth

---

412 T. Holtz, "Frage", *ThLZ* 106 (1981) 394.
413 Cf. T. Holtz, *a.c.*, pp.394f.
414 Cf. W. Schrage, *o.c.*, pp.200-202; also idem, *Einzelgebote*, pp.241-249; H.D. Wendland, *Ethik*, p.35; K.H. Schelkle, *Theolgie*, 3, pp.51f.; T.J. Deidun, *Morality*, p.175.
415 As concerns material reminiscences and indirect correspondences between words of Jesus in the Synoptic Gospels and Paul's parenesis cf. the list in W. Schrage, *o.c.*, p.243 n.250; also idem, *Ethik*, p.201.
416 W. Schrage, *Ethik*, p.200.
417 Cf. T.J. Deidun, *Morality*, p.175 who points out that possibly Paul used dominical sayings to a much larger extent in his preaching; similarly K.H. Schelkle, *Theologie*, 3, p.51 who refers to the dominical saying in Paul's address in Acts 20,35.
418 Thus W. Schrage, *o.c.*, p.201.

pointing out that with the exception of 1Cor 11,23-26 all dominical sayings which Paul adduces are related to Christian behaviour[419].

It was (and in some, mainly Catholic, circles still is) held that the earthly life of Jesus is a clear and definite criterion for behaviour in Paul's parenesis[420]. It is obvious, however, that the life (!) of Jesus is never used by Paul as articulated, external ethical criterion[421]. On the other hand, it would be wrong to deny any relevance of the life of Jesus for the Christians' behaviour in the context of Paul's ethos[422]. Even though some passages which are adduced do not refer to the 'earthly' Jesus but to the obedience of the pre-existent Jesus Christ (as 2Cor 8,9; Phil 2,6-11), the concept of Jesus being an example for the believers cannot be totally excluded[423], and even though the passages which refer explicitly to the *mimesis* of Christ (1Cor 11,1; 1Thess 1,6; also Rom 15,3.7) convey Paul's *theologia crucis* and conception of ἀγάπη, they still indicate a "bestimmte Grundrichtung christlichen Lebens"[424].

It is nevertheless obvious that Paul has hardly drawn upon the historical life and work of Jesus for the concrete orientation of Christian conduct. Jesus' message and words are adduced in a more unambiguous way as decisive norm for the Christian ethos.

16.2.4. The dicta of the apostle. Besides God's revealed Word in the Torah and in the words of Jesus, Paul regards his apostolic instructions or commandments as normative. The following facts are relevant here[425]. First, Paul as apostle of Jesus Christ is con-

---

419 Cf. W. Schrage, o.c., p.202.
420 Cf. V.P. Furnish, *Theology*, pp.218-223; K.H. Schelkle, o.c., pp.50-55; H. Halter, *Taufe*, pp.331-339 (pp.659f. n.44 lit.); P. Grech, "Motives", pp.552-558; A. Feuillet, "Loi de Dieu", *NovTest* 22 (1980) 43; J.F. Collange, *Éthique*, pp.197-203.
421 Cf. T.J. Deidun, o.c., pp.221f.
422 Pace O. Merk, *Handeln*, p.238 who explains Paul's occasional challenges to take Jesus as one's example simply as "Hinweis auf die Wirklichkeit des Todes Christi in ihrer Auswirkung auf die Gegenwart".
423 Cf. T. Nagata, *Philippians 2,5-11*, 1981, pp.333-350 who points out that for Paul the Christ-hymn provided "a prototype which defined the way of Christian life" (p.349), as the alternative between a purely soteriological and an ethical interpretation is misleading.
424 Admitted by W. Schrage, *Ethik*, p.199; cf. also B.C. Wintle, *Law*, 1977, pp.274-283.
425 For the following see especially W. Schrage, *Einzelgebote*, pp.102-140; also J.H.

scious of the fact that he speaks in the name of Christ (cf. 1Cor 1,10; Rom 14,14; 1Thess 4,1) and of God (cf. 2Cor 2,17;1Thess 2,13), i.e. that God and Christ are the true authors and originators of the apostolic message and parenesis. For this reason the apostolic message and parenesis are binding and obligatory.

Second, apart from verbs like παρακαλεῖν, ἐρωτᾶν, νουθετεῖν we find authoritative verbs in Paul's parenesis such as θέλειν (Rom 16,19; 1Cor 7,7.32; 10,20; 2Cor 12,20), παραγγέλλειν (1Cor 7, 10; 11,17; 1Thess 4,11; cf. 2Thess 3,4.6.10.12), ἐπιτάσσειν (Phlm 8) and διατάσσεσθαι (1Cor 7,17; 11,34; 16,1). The apostolic exhortations obviously claim validity and demand obedient fulfilment.

Third, even though Paul seeks understanding rather than blind obedience, he reckons quite naturally with the fact that his demands will be obeyed (cf. 2Cor 2,9; 2Thess 3,4)[426].

Fourth, the fact that all Christians in a given church irrespective of sex or social status are equally held responsible and liable to the apostolic exhortations, that all Christians in all churches are subject to basically the very same apostolic claims, and that many apostolic injunctions are constructed with the imp.praes., establishes not only the unchangeability of the will of God but also the fundamental significance of the office of the apostle through which God made known his will[427].

Fifth, the unsystematic and often paradigmatic character of the individual apostolic instructions by no means invalidates the normativeness of the individual commandments: Paul's ethic in his various letters is characterized by a material agreement in the fundamental outlines and motives and by the basic reference of

---

Schütz, *Paul and the Anatomy of Apostolic Authority*, 1975; B. Holmberg, *Paul and Power: The Structure of Authority in the Primitive Church as Reflected in the Pauline Epistles*, CB NT Series 11, 1978.

426 Cf. W. Schrage, *Einzelgebote*, pp.109-115.
427 Cf. W. Schrage, *o.c.*, pp.117-122. On the office of the apostle see K.H. Rengstorf, Art. "ἀπόστολος", *ThWNT* 1 (1933) 406-446; T. Holtz, "Zum Selbstverständnis des Apostels Paulus", *ThLZ* 91 (1966) 324-330; K. Kertelge, "Das Apostelamt des Paulus, sein Ursprung und seine Bedeutung", *BZ* 14 (1970) 161-181; F. Hahn, "Der Apostolat im Urchristentum: Seine Eigenart und seine Voraussetzungen", *KuD* 20 (1974) 54-77; J.A. Kirk, "Apostleship since Rengstorf: Towards a Synthesis", *NTS* 21 (1974/75) 249-264; F. Agnew, "On the Origin of the Term Apostolos", *CBQ* 38 (1976) 49-53; J.A. Bühner, Art. "ἀπόστολος", *EWNT* 1 (1980) 342-351.

individual and specific decisions to the theological contexts and to facts of principle⁴²⁸.

Sixth, the emphasis which Paul places on teaching (διδαχή, διδάσκειν) and on communicability (παράδοσις), also as regards parenetic material (cf. 1Thess 4,1-2; Rom 16,17; 1Cor 4,17: ὁδοί), proves that for Paul there exist universal norms and commandments which remain the same despite changing times and situations, and which are to be followed by the believers in all churches thus accentuating a continuum which is valid πανταχοῦ (1Cor 4,17) despite all dynamic and actuality⁴²⁹.

Seventh, the fact that Paul calls for the *mimesis* of the apostle as concerns his conduct (1Cor 4,16-17; 11,1; Phil 4,9; 3,17) is relevant for the question of normativity also⁴³⁰.

Thus, we conclude that the apostolic exhortations and commands imply not only a historical *prae* but also a material criterion which is and remains the normative rule and standard for Christian behaviour.

16.2.5. The orders of creation.

Finally the OT belief in creation plays a significant role as norm in Paul's ethic even though it is not the basic or most important one⁴³¹. It should be noted at the outset that for Paul creation theology is creation christology⁴³². Thus, Paul has no 'creation ethic' as such, advocating independent norms of creation. But God's salvational action in and through Christ makes the world (κόσμος) recognizable again as God's creation (κτίσις). With and in Christ, the true will of the Creator is and can be fulfilled, especially since Christ is the manifestation of

---

428 Cf. W. Schrage, *Einzelgebote*, pp.122-129.
429 Cf. W. Schrage, *o.c.*, pp.129-140 who concludes "daß es für die Gemeinde eine vorgegebene paränetische Paradosis gibt, die als kritische Norm allem Wandel der Christen vorgeordnet und gegenüber bleibt. Damit bestätigt sich auch hier die bleibende Verbindlichkeit der apostolischen Gebote" (p.140). He writes succinctly that "wer das Gebot der Stunde sucht, darf das des Apostels nicht verlieren" (p. 174).
430 Cf. W. Schrage, *o.c.*, p.106; J.H. Schütz, *Paul*, pp.226-232; W. Schrage, *Ethik*, p.182. On Paul as an example cf. also B.C. Wintle, *Law*, pp.261-274.
431 Emphasized by G. Strecker, "Sittlichkeit", *ThLZ* 104 (1979) 871. For the following cf. W. Schrage, *Einzelgebote*, pp.210-228; idem, *Ethik*, pp.192-195.
432 Cf. T. Herr, *Naturrecht*, pp.137-270 passim, particularly pp.184-199. He states that "das Neue an der urchristlichen Schöpfungsbetrachtung ist die Deutung von der Mitte des Christusereignisses her" (p.189) as "Christus ist, naturrechtlich gesprochen, das Seinsprinzip aller Dinge" (p.199). Cf. also W. Schrage, *Ethik*, p.192.

the wisdom of God and the mediator of creation (cf. 1Cor 8,6). Consequently, as the earth belongs to the Lord in its totality (1Cor 10,26), everything is clean and pure (Rom 14,20). The believer's relationship with the world is neither exclusively positive nor negative, it is rather dialectical: "Christen sind nach Paulus gleich weit entfernt von Weltverachtung wie von Weltvergötterung, von Weltflucht wie von Weltsucht"[433].

The reason for the normative validity of the order of creation has to be sought not only in the work of Jesus Christ who made the κόσμος recognizable again as God's κτίσις but also in the reference of the Torah to creation[434]. As we have seen, in Judaism the Torah was regarded as cosmic and creational principle — as a result of its correlation with wisdom. Despite the fact that we do not know exactly in what matter Paul shared this view, it is evident that he knew of the reality of a νόμος ἄγραφος or νόμος φύσεως among the pagans (Rom 2,14-15)[435].

Consequently, Paul seems to reckon with the ontological (theoretical?) possibility of moral behaviour among the pagans despite their sin and im-morality. That is, Paul assumes the existence of a norm of proper behaviour to which the pagans are tied despite all factual (!) transgression[436]. This is confirmed in Paul's parenesis by passages like 1Thess 4,12; 1Cor 10,32; Col 4,5 and by the multiple reception of formal and material elements of Hellenistic and Jewish ethic. Thus there exists a partial (!) ethical consensus as regards the content and the criteria of moral behaviour for both Christians and non-Christians.

---

433 W. Schrage, *o.c.*, p.193; cf. idem, *Einzelgebote*, p.211 referring to the "kritische Mitte zwischen Verweltlichung und Entweltlichung".
434 T. Holtz, "Frage", *ThLZ* 106 (1981) 395 argues that the Torah's reference to creation provides the reason for the inalienable validity of the Torah. However, the Torah is first of all revelation and only secondarily order of the world. This means that the validity of the Torah is to be derived from the identity of God (as Holtz states, ibid.) and hence from the fact of revelation, and not from the fact that it is the norm of life and of the world.
435 Cf. W. Schrage, "Zur Ethik der neutestamentlichen Haustafeln", *NTS* 21 (1975) 21; T. Herr, *Naturrecht*, pp.155-164; U. Wilckens, *Römer*, 1, pp.133-135; W. Schrage, *Ethik*, p.191. We explain this conception not with a reception of Hellenistic philosophical and ethical conceptuality (pace Wilckens) but on the background of the Jewish correlation of law and wisdom.
436 Cf. W. Schrage, *Einzelgebote*, p.192 going on to discuss Rom 1-2; 7; 13,3 (pp.193-196).

It is therefore correct when C. Münchow states, commenting on Paul's understanding of history: "Es geht um das Heil unter den Bedingungen dieser Welt und nicht um eine Welt des Glaubens, die sich neben der Realität der Welt etabliert"[437]. And T. Herr asserts that "der in Christus sich auch für den Kosmos auftuende neue Hoffnungshorizont erlaubt auch ein erlöstes Sich-Einlassen mit der Welt und ihren Werten, wozu nicht zuletzt das Naturrecht gehört"[438].

As the normative, divinely revealed Torah found expression in the orders of the world and in the orders of intact life — resulting from the fact that the Torah is identical with (divine, cosmic, and ethical) wisdom — these orders are also, essentially, normative.

Standards for Christian conduct referred to by Paul include (1) nature ($\varphi \acute{v} \sigma \iota \varsigma$) which can refer to God's original order of creation (Rom 1,26) or to historical orders such as custom and approved tradition (1Cor 11,14); (2) orders of creation such as marriage (1 Cor 7)[439], state (Rom 13,1-7)[440], and work (1Thess 5,14; cf. 2 Thess 3,6-7.11)[441]; (3) the respect of convention (Rom 13,13; 1 Cor 7,35; 13,5; 14,40; 1Thess 4,12).

Even though these orders belong to this world which perishes, Paul is absolutely certain, on the basis of his belief in creation, that the world, until the final transformation of all earthly reality, will not be left to chaos. God the Creator has not given up his creation, and therefore "this world" remains God's creation as man, even as sinner, remains God's creature: *simul peccator et creatus*[442]. This means for the believer that, as regards sin, he is separated from the world and yet remains, as creature, within the divine orders and the conventions which God has given and established for the preservation of man.

Consequently, the Pauline ethic implies this twofold criterion for Christian behaviour as regards the present world and its orders:

---

437 C. Münchow, *Ethik*, p.152.
438 T. Herr, *o.c.*, p.210 asserting also that "in Christus ist das Humanum wieder aufgerichtet und neu umschrieben, die Ebenbildlichkeit wieder hergestellt worden" (p.209). It should be noted, however, that this "Ebenbildlichkeit" has its locus "in Christ" and not in the "Humanum"!
439 Cf. the discussion in W. Schrage, *Ethik*, pp.194f.,216-220.
440 Cf. recently U. Wilckens, "Der Gehorsam gegen die Behörden des Staates im Tun des Guten: Zu Römer 13,1-7", *Dimensions de la vie chrétienne*, 1979, pp.85-130; idem, *Römer*, 3, 1982, pp.28-66 (pp.28f. lit.); W. Schrage, o.c., pp.226-230; R. Heiligenthal, "Strategien konformer Ethik im Neuen Testament am Beispiel von Röm 13,1-7", *NTS* 29 (1983) 55-61.
441 Cf. W. Schrage, *o.c.*, pp.220-222.
442 Cf. W. Schrage, *o.c.*, p.195.

the Christian cannot and may not anticipate the new order arbitrarily and independently as long as God lets the old order exist, and at the same time he cannot and may not give up either the waiting for the new order which is beginnning nor his commission to penetrate the orders of the world with *agape*[443]. This second criterion leads us to the question of the freedom of Christian ethics.

16.2.6. Summary. The Christian ethic according to Paul is based on, or rather derived from, specific and binding norms. The law, i.e. God's revelation in the OT as fulfilled and qualified by and in Christ has a constitutive significance for the Christian ethos. The message and words of Jesus Christ possess a binding and normative authority. The exhortations and commandments of the apostle provide a further obligatory standard for Christian living. And, finally, the orders of creation are essentially normative for Christian conduct.

It is wrong to create a contrast between the *intra nos* and the *extra nos*, i.e. between the inward activity of the Spirit and the external word of God[444]. Even though the Christian existence and the divine norm never become simply identical it is nevertheless true that there is no contradiction between spiritual experience and heteronomy: God's norms and commandments, in the eyes of Paul, always remain an opposite entity ('Gegenüber') for the Christian. Christian behaviour is totally dependent upon the will of God in all its ethical decisions. The Christian is and always remains a

---

443 Cf. W. Schrage, *Einzelgebote*, p.228; T. Herr, *Naturrecht*, pp.131-133.
444 Contra e.g. T.J. Deidun, *Morality*, pp.209-214 who asserts that there exists a dialectical relationship between the two — only to dissolve this 'dialectic' later when he states that the binding external law does not have its *raison d'être* in itself but derives its validity and meaning from its vital connection with the imperative of love (p.224). Deidun seems to have forgotten his earlier, correct statement that God's demand is eternally valid (p.153) and that Paul never condemned the law qua law (p.155). He excludes any *tertius usus legis* but then goes on to assert its possibility using different phraseology (pp.153f.). When he points out that for Paul, the Christian does not "live by" a code of law whatever (!) its nature and origin (!) in the sense of drawing life from its observance, of his love being contained within the limits of prescription, of avoiding evil not because it is evil but merely because it is prohibited by law, and of seeking security in it and boasting of its observance before God (p.155), it is enough to point out that no serious biblical scholar would argue for such a position today. For the following remarks see especially W. Schrage, *Einzelgebote*, pp.71-93 passim.

δουλεύων (cf. 1Thess 1,9; 1Cor 7,22; Rom 7,6; 14,18; 16,18; Col 3,24).

> In the words of Schrage, "niemals kann und soll also der Mensch sein Leben in eigene Regie nehmen, auch nicht das christliche! Auch unter der Gnade stehen heißt unter einer Herrschaft und somit im Gehorsam stehen (Röm 5,21; 6,16.18.22)"[445].

The norm for specific Christian conduct cannot be found or established by consulting one's self or the Spirit in oneself. Paul knows nothing of such an enthusiastic immediateness or of an identity between Christ and the Spirit-filled Christian[446]. Paul never unified or identified the will of the Christian with the will of God, of Christ, or of the Spirit. Christian living is subject to norm and authority *coram Deo*. God's work in us and God's word to us belong together[447].

A final comment is to be made here concerning the relationship between the indicative (§ 16.1.) and the imperative (§ 16.2.). The indicative, with God's justification of the sinner in Christ at its centre, is, as we pointed out already, the *articulus fidei constituens*, with the imperative, or the Christian ethic, as *articulus fidei consequens*[448]. The indicative with its *Heilszusage* is primary but implies and then substantiates the imperative. The latter is grounded on, and appeals to, the indicative and is intended to bring the

---

445 W. Schrage, *Einzelgebote*, p.83 summarizing this concept with the phrase *servitium domini summa libertas*.
446 Cf. E. Reinmut, *Geist und Gesetz*, 1981 who demonstrated that Paul defines the "walk" in the Spirit as factual fulfilment of the commandments: the Spirit comprehends in love the character of the law but does not fulfill the law in the reduction to the commandment of love but fulfills, rather, by love the entire law (Gal 5, 13-6,10; Rom 8,1-11). The presence of the Spirit cannot be reconciled with the transgression of the law (1Cor 6,12-20). Thus, Paul relates the Spirit and the law in a way which links the fulfilment of the law with the presence of the Spirit in the church: the reality of the Spirit is presented as fulfilment of the law by and in love (cf. *ThLZ* 107/1982, cols.633f.).
447 Cf. W. Schrage, *o.c.*, p.85 who asserts that "das *intra nos* schützt den neuen Gehorsam vor einem bloß formalen Legalismus gegenüber dem äußeren Gebot; das *extra nos* aber bewahrt ihn vor einer schwärmerischen Unmittelbarkeit, die sich von allem Hören auf Gottes Gebote entbunden glaubt".
448 On the indicative-imperative relation cf. also supra, § 16.1.3., and generally H.M. Schenke, *Das Verhältnis von Indikativ und Imperativ bei Paulus*, Diss. Berlin, 1956 (not available); V.P. Furnish, *Theology*, pp. 224-227; H. Ridderbos, *Paul*, pp. 253-258; O. Merk, *Handeln*, pp.34-41; W.D. Dennison, "Indicative and Imperative: The Basic Structure of Pauline Ethics", *CThJ* 14 (1979) 55-78; J.F. Collange, *Éthique*, pp.25-27; T.J. Deidun, *Morality*, pp.239-243; H.H. Schade, *Christologie*, pp. 154-156; W. Schrage, *Ethik*, pp.156-161; U. Schnelle, *Gerechtigkeit*, pp.103-106.

indicative to full realization. The relation of indicative and imperative is determined by the present salvation-historical situation as they both represent the 'already' and the 'not yet'. It seems to be clear for Paul, however, that when the imperative is not 'met', the indicative cannot be existent either[449]. Thus, the imperative implies the aspect of human, or rather Christian, responsibility. This leads us to the next and final section.

16.3. Guiding Criteria: The Wisdom Aspect

16.3.1. Introduction. The Christian, according to Paul, is responsible for his specific conduct in everyday life. This responsibility has two aspects: he is responsible to obey the binding norms of the Christian ethos, and he is responsible to realize and implement this obedience specifically and concretely in everyday life. And it is this second aspect which accounts for the freedom in Paul's ethic. Paul did not describe and prescribe the way in which every Christian should behave differently in certain circumstances. There are differences related to creational and earthly conditions (e.g. the difference between male and female, married and single, masters and slaves). There are differences related to the specific existential situations. And there are differences related to the charismatic gifts (e.g. the charisma of celibacy!)[450].

These different situations and conditions are neither all nor totally regulated (cf. 1Cor 7,25!). Different ways of conduct and different decisions concerning the same matter are possible (cf. 1 Cor 6,1-8; 7,1-40). Personal advice ($\gamma\nu\omega\mu\eta$) is valuable (1Cor 1,10; 7,25.40; 2Cor 8,10), but — and this is very clearly implied for Paul here — the personal, responsible decision is necessary. This is especially obvious in Paul's treatment of the relation between the 'strong' and the 'weak' (Rom 14-15; 1Cor 8-10): the personal, responsible decision of the individual is of paramount importance, and the possibility of materially differing decisions is basically acknowledged. This ethical plurality obviously cannot be applied

---

449 Emphasized by W. Schrage, *o.c.*, p.160, following E. Käsemann, "Gottesgerechtigkeit bei Paulus", *Exegetische Versuche und Besinnungen*, 2, p.188.
450 See generally W. Schrage, *Einzelgebote*, pp.141-146; idem, *Ethik*, pp.182-184.

to any- and everything but only to areas of life where the fundamental norms and commandments of the Christian ethos are not affected and where the believer therefore has the *mandatum concretissimum*. The reality of church discipline shows that some limits are not negotiable, i.e. they are absolute.

We suggest that (1) this personal freedom in the realm of the Christian ethic can be understood, partly, on the background of the Jewish wisdom tradition, and (2) the factuality of freedom and simultaneous obedience to binding norms can be explained, partly, on the basis of the correlation of wisdom and law[451].

Some scholars have hinted at the relationship between elements, forms, and parts of Paul's parenesis and the wisdom tradition[452]. Some of the "classified motives" which Grech lists for Paul's ethic[453] — such as the appeal to 'common sense' (1Cor 5,6; 6,12; 9,7; 11,15-16; 2Cor 9,6; Col 3,21; 2Thess 3,10), the appeal to a sense of shame (1Thess 4,4; 1Cor 11,6; 2Cor 9,4; Rom 2,17ff.; 16,17-18), and social reasons (1Thess 4,12; 1Cor 7,4; Rom 13,1-6; Gal 5,15; Col 3,20-25) — are very similar to, if not identical with, motivations in the wisdom literature.

Several important verses have to be pointed out which confirm, on the terminological level, the link between Paul's ethic and the

---

451 We say 'partly' because Paul's understanding of the Christian's position "in Christ" is relevant in these respects as well. M. Black thinks that the attempt to relate Paul's ethic to the correlation of wisdom and law is overstated and seems to claim too much (personal communication). However, we are still convinced that this correlation provides a good basis for understanding the apparent paradoxicality of Paul's ethic which contains both normative-regulative aspects and elements of self-responsibility.

452 As regards the catalogues of virtues and vices (Gal 5,19-23; also Eph 4,32-5,2; cf. also Rom 1,29-31; 13,13; 1Cor 5,10-11; 6,9-10; 2Cor 12,20-21; Col 3,5.8) see A. Vögtle, *Die Tugend- und Lasterkataloge im Neuen Testament*, 1936, pp.92ff.; H. Conzelmann, "Paulus und die Weisheit", p.177 n.5; T. Herr, *Naturrecht*, pp.92f.; H.D. Betz, *Galatians*, p.282 (who, however, sees Hellenistic philosophy as the primary source). As regards the asyndetic sequences of poignant exhortations (1Thess 5,12-22; 2Cor 13,11; Rom 12,9-21) see W. Schrage, *Einzelgebote*, p.125,146; H.H. Schade, *Christologie*, p.143; U. Luz, in R. Smend, U. Luz, *Gesetz*, p.108. See generally also T. Herr, *o.c.*, pp.26f.; F. Festorrazzi, "Originalità", 1979, p.243; W. Schrage, *Ethik*, p.196. Surprisingly R. Hodgson, *Die Quellen der paulinischen Ethik*, Diss.theol. Heidelberg, 1976, does not recognize the Jewish wisdom tradition as important source of Pauline ethic; according to him the OT law tradition and Stoic ethics are the two main "geistesgeschichtliche" sources of Paul's ethic with the former received via "Testimonienbücher" (pp.1-144).

453 Cf. P. Grech, "Motives", 1979, pp.542f.

wisdom tradition. In 1Cor 3 Paul treats the problematic divisions in the Corinthian church and declares as goal of a truly Christian attitude — with the focus on human or, rather, brotherly relations — the γίνομαι σοφός (3,18). In 1Cor 6,5 Paul deplores the fact that nobody in the church is σοφός enough to deal with lawsuits among brothers. In Rom 16,19 Paul commends the believers for being obedient to the Lord and says that he wants them to be wise concerning the good (σοφοὺς εἶναι εἰς τὸ ἀγαθόν) and innocent and pure concerning evil, obviously a reference to the ethical decisions of Christians.

In Col 1,9-10 Paul prays that the believers will be filled with the perception of God's will (ἐπίγνωσις τοῦ θελήματος αὐτοῦ) in all wisdom and spiritual understanding (ἐν πάσῃ σοφίᾳ καὶ συνέσει πνευματικῇ) in order that they may live (περιπατῆσαι) a life worthy of the Lord, bearing fruit in every good work — which is clearly an ethical context. In Col 1,28 Paul asserts that his admonishing (νουθετεῖν) and teaching (διδάσκειν) was done ἐν πάσῃ σοφίᾳ in order that every believer may attain perfection in Christ — thus linking wisdom and the Christian ethic[454]. Similarly, Paul states in Col 3,16 that it is the task of all believers to teach and admonish each other ἐν πάσῃ σοφίᾳ. In Col 4,5 (cf. Eph 5,15) he stresses that the Christian's behaviour should be characterized by wisdom (ἐν σοφίᾳ περιπατεῖτε), also toward non-Christians.

Thus it can be accurately stated with Schrage that "Vernunft und Einsicht, Weisheit und Erkenntnis spielen eine große Rolle in der paulinischen Ethik"[455]. Other conceptions which show that the Pauline ethic is to be linked with the wisdom tradition include the roles of reason and of man's conscience.

16.3.2. Existing orders. The last area of binding norms which we discussed above was the realm of the existing orders of creation. We pointed out that these orders are not seen as absolutely, i.e. for every Christian and in every situation, binding. The believ-

---

454 Cf. J. Gnilka, *Kolosserbrief*, 1980, p.103: "Mahnung und Lehre geschehen in Weisheit. Damit ist im Sinn der alttestamentlichen Sophie die praktisch-ethische Zielsetzung erneut zu verstehen gegeben". Gnilka points out that the comparison with the Stoic ideal of the wise is not helpful here as the wisdom concept in Col is biblically determined (p.200 n.40).

455 W. Schrage, *Ethik*, p.188.

er's position ἐν κυρίῳ implies a potential and effective reservation and even critique of these orders, particularly as regards the respect of conventions. For this reason the submission to existing orders of creation and of the world has to be included among the guiding criteria of Christian behaviour.

Paul's reception of elements of the secular contemporary ethic, especially as regards his attitude to existing orders and conventions, reveals the Christian freedom, rooted in the indicative, which Paul proclaims. But this freedom is also revealed in the way in which Paul presents the specific submission to these received orders and conventions: as they are not *eo ipso* and *semper* identical with that which is appropriate "in the Lord", they are received with potential critique and reservation[456]. As to the received elements of traditional ethics, the process of critical selection and sifting gave a new Christian sense to the various concepts and thoughts – the "in Christ" is not a mere formula! – and often altered even their content.

The existing orders of creation (marriage, family, work, etc.) are essential criteria, or in this case rather binding norms, for Christian conduct. The existing orders of the world, i.e. society (state, social status, property, etc.) are basically to be submitted to by the Christian. The existing conventions regarding τὸ ἀγαθόν (1Thess 5,15; Rom 12,9; 13,3; 14,16; 15,2; 16,19; cf. Gal 6,6; Rom 12,2), τὰ καθήκοντα (Rom 1,28), τὰ διαφέροντα (Rom 2,18; Phil 1,10), ἀνῆκεν (Col 3,18; cf. Phlm 8), εὐάρεστος (Col 3,20; Rom 12,2), and ἀληθῆ, σεμνά, προσφιλῆ, and εὔφημα (Phil 4,8) are to be observed in the Lord. To do that properly "in Christ" is wisdom (Rom 16,19)!

16.3.3. The Spirit. Many scholars seem to have what amounts to an enthusiastic understanding of the Spirit. They regard the Spirit as adequate ethical guide making external norms and controls superfluous[457]. We pointed out above (§16.2.1.) that the Spirit does not invalidate the external norms and commandments but that he is primarily the foundation, locus, and power of the Chri-

---

456 Cf. W. Schrage, *o.c.*, pp.189-192; idem, *Einzelgebote*, pp.201-209; T. Herr, *Naturrecht*, pp.116-133,211-270 for further details.
457 Cf. supra, p.311 with n.395 for references.

stian existence (cf. §16.1.4.). Paul expresses this thought with the phrase ἐν πνεύματι which has a local and an instrumental sense (Rom 1,9; 2,29; 8,9;14,17).

On the other hand, Paul also uses the dat. πνεύματι without preposition (Gal 5,16.18.25; Rom 8,14; 2Cor 12,18), as well as the phrase κατὰ πνεῦμα περιπατεῖν (Rom 8,4.5), which implies that the Spirit is not only the foundation and power of the Christian life but also indicates the 'how' of Christian behaviour[458].

Thus, Paul refers to the Spirit both as foundation or power of the Christian experience and as standard of Christian conduct. Paul relates the latter aspect, i.e. the role of the Spirit as guiding criterion for decisions, to wisdom (σοφία), understanding (σύνεσις), and knowledge (ἐπίγνωσις) of the will of God (Col 1,9-10)[459]. That is, the Spirit helps the Christian, though not automatically (note the scopus of prayer in Col 1,9-12), to discern the will of God in order to know what to do in specific circumstances and how to realize God's claim in everyday life. The Spirit makes the believer wise as to his specific conduct.

16.3.4. Love. The Pauline evidence concerning the role and the significance of ἀγάπη[460] can be stated as follows[461]. First, it is rooted in the love of God and in the life of Christ which was revealed in the salvational mission and action of Christ[462] (cf. Gal 2,20; Rom 5,8; 8,32-37.39). Love is linked with the love of the Spirit (Rom 15,30; 5,5) and is a fruit of the Spirit (Gal 5,22; cf.

---

458 Cf. W. Schrage, *Einzelgebote,* p.74; idem, *Ethik,* pp.167f. See U. Wilckens, *Römer,* 2, 1980, p.129 who asserts regarding Rom 8,5 that κατά, in Paul's usage, designates the fundamental direction of (ethical) action.

459 Thus W. Schrage, *Einzelgebote,* pp.92f.,163. He states that "wo es Paulus um die konkrete sittliche Entscheidung des Christen geht, verweist er nicht auf die Leitung des Geistes" (p.92) but rather to the renewed mind.

460 See generally C. Spicq, *Agapè dans le Nouveau Testament: Analyse des textes,* EB, 3 vols., ³1966 (lit. in 1, pp.317-342), on Paul cf. 1, pp.208-315; 2, pp.9-305. On ἀγάπη in the extra-biblical literature see now O. Wischmeyer, "Agape in der außerchristlichen Antike", *ZNW* 69 (1978) 212-238. For further literature cf. H. Schürmann, *Orientierungen,* p.96 n.29; G. Friedrich, *ThWNT* 10/2 (1979) 948-951; G. Schneider, Art. "ἀγάπη", *EWNT* 1 (1980) 19-21.

461 Following generally W. Schrage, *Ethik,* pp.202-208.

462 See generally K. Romaniuk, *L'amour du Père et du Fils dans la sotériologie de Saint Paul,* AnBibl 15A, 1974; T.J. Deidun, *Morality,* 1981, pp.137-148.

Col 1,8). Thus, love is not a natural human faculty but a salvational-pneumatic reality (1Cor 13,8-13).

Second, love has to do with moral conduct and with specific ways of behaviour (cf. 1Cor 13,4-7; 2Cor 8,7-8.11; Rom 12,9; 13,10). Love is concrete and specific since its sincerity and genuineness can be tested (2Cor 8,8.24). Love is demonstrable[463].

Third, love therefore is oriented towards one's neighbour: the ἕτερος (Rom 13,8; cf. 1Cor 10,24; 13,5), the ἀλλήλους (1Thess 3, 12; 4,9; Gal 5,13; Rom 13,8), the πλησίον (Rom 13,9-10; 15,2).

Fourth, love is self-sacrifice not only for God and Christ (Gal 2, 20; Rom 5,6-11) but also for the Christian (Gal 2,20; Phil 2,4; 1Cor 13,5): it is parallel to δουλεύειν (Gal 5,13; 1Cor 9,19), διακονεῖν (cf. 2Cor 8,8 with 8,19-20), and (παρα-) διδόναι ἑαυτόν (Gal 1,4; 2,20). Love is to give oneself.

Fifth, love is commanded in the context of Paul's parenesis (Gal 5,13-14; 1Cor 14,1; 16,14; 2Cor 8,24; Rom 13,8-10).

Sixth, love is the basic principle, or the summary, of the law (Gal 5,14; Rom 13,8-10): it does not replace the commandments but is rather the criterion for their fulfilment[464]. Love is the *conditio sine qua non* of all Christian behaviour without disclaiming the commandments. When the latter are understood as God's eternally valid and hence normative revelation and as finding their true fulfilment in actual and factual *agape*, there is no dichotomy between law and love. Love according to Paul is therefore not (!) the total formal content of the Christian imperative, totally exhausting God's law[465]. This can be proved by the following observations: (1) the statements in both 1Cor 7,19 and in Gal 5,6 assert

---

463 Cf. W. Schrage, *Einzelgebote*, p.251 arguing against R. Bultmann, "Das christliche Gebot der Nächstenliebe", *Glaube und Verstehen*, 1, pp.239f.; see also T. Holtz, "Frage", *ThLZ* 106 (1981) 393 who emphasizes contra Bultmann that love is not simply or only a state of mind, but is action.
464 Correctly H. Ridderbos, *Paul*, p.282; similarly W. Schrage, o.c., pp.256, 268-271; idem, *Ethik*, pp.198,207f.
465 Thus T.J. Deidun, *Morality*, pp.85-103. It is inconsistent when he insists that love does not replace the law and does not exclude particular ethical claims as the Christian is still liable to the claim of particular ethical demands (pp.150-183). Deidun is ambiguous, also, as regards the character of these ethical demands: he states that they differ formally totally from the precepts of the Mosaic law but are (at the same time?) "substantially identical" with them (p.187). However, he correctly rejects the approach of situation ethics (pp.184f.).

that both circumcision and uncircumcision are irrelevant since (ἀλλά) what matters in the life of the Christian is the keeping of the commandments or, respectively, faith which is operative through love[466]; this means that love is realized specifically by fulfilling the law; (2) even though love occurs often as a subject-matter in Paul's parenesis, it is hardly ever used as substantiation of the exhortations[467]; and (3) Paul does not differentiate or define sins on the basis of their difference to love[468].

Seventh, as love fulfills the law, so love is also expressed in the respecting of institutions and conventions of the world[469].

Eighth, love is of central significance as regards the specific, individual exhortations and their realization in actual life and conduct (cf. 1Cor 13 in the context; cf. the relation of the 'strong' and the 'weak').

Ninth, in certain circumstances love limits and transcends (not breaks!) traditional orders and conventions (cf. 1Cor 7,32-33: celibacy; 1Cor 6,1-8: renunciation of legal rights; Phlm: slavery).

Tenth, love has a critical and creative potency also in those areas in which Paul does not specifically refer to ἀγάπη but where conflicts have to be settled and specific decisions to be made (cf. 1Cor 7,4-5: sexual intercourse in marriage; 1Cor 7,36-38: engagement; cf. the relation between master and slave).

It is especially with regard to the last two points that love is crucially significant for the tackling of new (!) specific situations. True Christian love leads to knowledge (ἐπίγνωσις) and insight (αἴσθησις) in deciding how to behave and conduct oneself in everyday life (Phil 1,9-10), and gives wisdom (σοφία) for settling crucial questions (1Cor 3,18). Love makes the believer act wisely!

16.3.5. Reason and discernment. As regards the perception of

---

466 Cf. W. Schrage, *Einzelgebote*, p.269; T. Holtz, "Frage", *ThLZ* 106 (1981) 393. On 1Cor 7,19 see § 15.2.4.
467 Pointed out by T. Holtz, *a.c.*, p.387. He observes that the commandment of love is therefore not developed as motive but rather as specific commandment (p.396). Cf. T.J. Deidun, *o.c.*, p.220 who asserts that "love, in itself, is not a sufficiently articulated ethical norm for guiding the Christian in the manifold and often complex circumstances of daily life" (ibid.).
468 Cf. W. Schrage, *o.c.*, p.270.
469 As regards the last four points cf. W. Schrage, *o.c.*, pp.256-268; idem, *Ethik*, pp. 204-207.

God's will in the hic et nunc and of the proper ways of realizing God's will as revealed in the commandments, Paul refers the believer also to his cognitive faculties. The evidence is as follows. First, Paul uses the term νουθετεῖν[470] to describe an important aspect of his parenesis: it can be translated as "putting in the right mind" (νοῦν τεθῆναι) and denotes the effort to encourage others to refrain from what is evil and to do what is right[471]. This term indicates that Paul considers the νοῦς to be significant for proper moral behaviour.

Second, this is confirmed by the actual use of the term νοῦς in parenetic contexts[472]. According to Paul man lives under the dominion of the σάρξ which results in a corrupt νοῦς (cf. Rom 1,28; Col 2,28). This is evidenced by corrupt νοήματα (2Cor 3,14; 4,4) and an antagonistic relationship with God's law (Rom 7,23.25). The radical renewal of man by Christ also affects the νοῦς: every νόημα is made obedient to Christ (2Cor 10,5), and the νοῦς is renewed (Rom 12,2; cf. Col 3,10).

> The statement in Rom 12,2 is especially significant[473]. The reference to the crucial function of the renewed mind belongs to the introductory motto of Paul's parenesis in Rom. The application of the human functions of perception, in obedience to Christ, is vital for the discernment of God's will in specific situations and thus for the Christian's conduct in everyday life. Every believer is to be fully convinced in his νοῦς as to the propriety of his actions as a Christian (Rom 14,5).

Third, Paul describes the function of the νοῦς in Rom 12,2 as δοκιμάζειν. This term is often used by Paul[474] and plays an important role in parenetic contexts (1Thess 5,21; Gal 6,2-5; Rom 2, 18; 12,2; 14,22-23; Phil 1,9-11; cf. Eph 5,8-10; Tit 1,15-16). The believers are to be able to recognize, to discern, and to decide in specific situations what the will of God is and how they should therefore behave. The δοκιμάζειν is both "Denk- und Lebensakt ...

---

470 Cf. 1Thess 5,12.14; 2Thess 3,15; 1Cor 4,14; Rom 15,14; Col 1,28; 3,16; (cf. also Acts 20,31!); the noun νουθεσία occurs in 1Cor 10,11; Eph 6,4; Tit 3,10.
471 Cf. C.E.B. Cranfield, *Romans*, 2, p.753 n.3.
472 Cf. W. Schrage, *Einzelgebote*, pp.163-174; R. Jewett, *Paul's Anthropological Terms*, AGAJU 10, 1971, pp.367-390.
473 On Rom 12,1-2 cf. C. Evans, "Romans 12,1-2: The True Worship", *Dimensions de la vie chrétienne*, 1979, pp.7-33 who, however, contributes no insights which might be relevant for our concerns here.
474 Cf. G. Therrien, *Le discernement dans les écrits Pauliniens*, EB, 1973, pp.63-236 (exegetical), 239-301 (thematic).

er äußert sich als kritisches Unterscheiden (Prüfen) wie als praktisches Bewähren eines Erkennens"⁴⁷⁵. It implies norms and standards and is related to experience. It is important to note that Paul himself links δοκιμάζειν both with God's commandments (Rom 2, 18) and with wisdom (Rom 1,18; Phil 1,9-10)⁴⁷⁶.

Fourth, a final term of rational perception used in a parenetic context is λογίζεσθαι (Phil 4,8) which denotes the reflection upon, and evaluation of, what is the appropriate attitude and action in Christian conduct.

Fifth, rational thinking and discernment of God's will do not occur in a vacuum: Paul sees them linked with the context of the church (cf. § 16.1.5.) and as a phenomenon which is controlled by the Spirit (1Cor 12,8; Col 1,9), which is an expression of love (Phil 1,9-10) and faith (Phlm 6), and which is linked with prayer (cf. Phil 1,9-10 and Col 1,9 and the respective contexts). Proper discernment is man's responsibility (note the imperatives in 1Cor 14, 37; 1Thess 5,21; Phil 4,8) but at the same time dependent upon God (note the passive in Col 1,9)⁴⁷⁷. The epistemological potency of man's perception is not absolute⁴⁷⁸.

---

475 G. Schunack, Art. "δοκιμάζω", *EWNT* 1 (1980) 826. J.D.G. Dunn, *Jesus and the Spirit*, pp.233f. is not entirely clear in his definition of δοκιμάζειν in Paul's parenesis: he takes the word to mean "to test, and if the test warrants it, to approve" (p. 233 following C.K. Barrett, *Romans*, p.104), and then goes on to assert that the word does not mean testing by some norm or standard but denotes rather "a spontaneous awareness of what is God's will in the concrete situation... and a recognition and approval of that will as good, acceptable and perfect". If Dunn defines δοκιμάζειν as he does, he should reckon with norms and standards on the basis of which the testing and the approving take place! It is inconsistent to reject such standards without giving any reasons, simply (re-) defining the verb as "spontaneous awareness" and correlating this awareness with the recognition and approval of one's moral decision as the acceptable will of God. Re-cognition as "the mental process of identifying what has been known before"(*Shorter Oxford English Dictionary*, p.1764) and approval also presuppose some sort of standard!

476 The contrast which Dunn sees between Rom 2,18 – the Jew makes moral distinctions and decisions on the basis of the law – and Rom 12,2 – the Christian makes ethical decisions on the basis of the renewal of his mind (*o.c.*, p.223) is certainly not a law/Spirit antithesis: (1) these two passages are not related to each other and belong to different contexts; (2) Rom 12,2 does not refer to the Spirit at all; (3) Rom 2,18 is not a polemical critique of what the Jew is doing 'in theory' but only of what he is doing in practice; (4) Paul accepts the validity and authority of God's revealed law in other passages (cf. § 16.2.2). See further infra.

477 Cf. W. Schrage, *Einzelgebote*, p.168.
478 Cf. T. Herr, *Naturrecht*, pp.170f.

Sixth, the object and content of the believer's rational discernment is the will of God (Rom 12,2; Col 1,9), τὰ διαφέροντα (Rom 2,8; Phil 1,10), the needs of the moment (Phil 4,8-9). The content of discernment is not identical with the σχῆμα of this world (Rom 12,2). The numerous uses of πᾶς in this specific context (Rom 12, 2; Phil 1,9; Col 1,9-10; 4,12; Phlm 6) indicate that the believer's discernment is relevant and crucial for the continuous and progressive concretization of God's will in everyday life and in minor matters. The same thought is expressed by the μᾶλλον καὶ μᾶλλον in Phil 1,9 and by the ἡμέρα καὶ ἡμέρα in 2Cor 4,16 as well as by the imp.praes. in Rom 12,2 (cf. 1Cor 13,9)[479].

Seventh, for Paul there is no conflict or contrast between obedience to the explicitly revealed and stated commandments and norms of God and the always fresh effort to discern God's specific will. This means that the searching reason of the Christian is not (!) particularly relevant for the substantiation of Christian moral behaviour[480], since it never provides the final word in questions of Christian life-style, nor cancels or invalidates God's norms and commandments, nor is it relevant for discerning and deciding basic moral questions, as these have been decided already in God's eternally valid revelation[481]. The believer's reason is revelant for questions of minor importance and for deciding how (not whether!) the binding norms of, and the guiding criteria for, moral behaviour are to be realized *in actu*.

The use of one's cognitive faculties which have been and are still being renewed by God is crucial since the knowledge of God's will is only in part (1Cor 13,9), and since many new situations arise in life in which the application and realization of God's norms is not immediately self-evident[482]. Wisdom is required in order to make appropriate decisions in this context (Phil 1,9-10; Rom 15,

---

479 Cf. W. Schrage, *o.c.*, pp.168-172.
480 Contra e.g. R. Hasenstab, *Modelle*, pp.190-203 for whom the human καρδία and νοῦς are "Organe der Selbstgesetzgebung" (p.192).
481 Cf. W. Schrage, *Einzelgebote*, pp.165,172f.; idem, *Ethik*, pp.188,208.
482 We cannot agree with W. Schrage, *o.c.*, p.208 when he states that new situations are "nur durch die von der Liebe geleitete Vernunft zu bewältigen". According to Paul, the believer has the primary norm of God's revelation in the OT, in Christ, and through the apostle, as well as the secondary guiding criteria of the orders and conventions of creation and the world, and of the Spirit, which will also, apart from love, enable his mind and reason to make the right decisions.

14; cf. 1Cor 6,5). Proper use of the believer's νοῦς enables him to make wise decisions based on knowledge and perception.

16.3.6. The conscience. Paul's use of the term συνείδησις[483] presupposes a meaning of the term which is similar to the Hellenistic (popular) usage: it denotes self-examination, the critical self-reflection of the ego of man, the 'Instanz' and tribunal which occasions the *recognitio sui* "als nachträgliche Selbstprüfung und Reflexion, die auf eine Norm bezogen ist"[484]. The conscience's fundamental reference to a norm — for Paul the revealed will of God in the Scriptures, in Christ, through the apostles, and in the orders of creation — and the sequential subsequence of its operation show that the conscience is not *eo ipso*, materially, the voice of God and therefore does not possess the ultimate or autarchic authority as regards ethical decisions (cf. 1Cor 4,4!)[485].

In Paul's parenesis the conscience is not related primarily to knowing God's will[486] but to man's consciousness of being blameless before God[487]. Paul clearly distinguishes between the require-

---

483 Cf. Rom 2,15; 9,1; 13,5; 1Cor 8,7.10.12; 10,25.27.28.29.29; 2Cor 1,12; 4,2; 5,11; cf. also Acts 23,1; 24,16; 1Tim 1,5.19; 3,9; 4,2; 2Tim 1,3; Tit 1,15; Cf. M.E. Thrall, "The Pauline Use of Συνείδησις", *NTS* 14 (1967/68) 118-125; R. Jewett, *Paul's Anthropological Terms*, pp.402-446; H.J. Eckstein, *Der Begriff Syneidesis bei Paulus*, Diss.theol. Tübingen, 1979, pp.144-341; also J. Stelzenberger, *Syneidesis im Neuen Testament*, 1961; P. Hilsberg, "Das Gewissen im Neuen Testament", *Theologische Versuche* 9 (1977) 145-160; H. Chadwick, Art. "Gewissen", *RAC* 10 (1978) 1025-1107; G. Lüdemann, Art. "συνείδησις", *EWNT* 3 (1983) 721-725.
484 W. Schrage, *Ethik*, p.185 referring to Seneca, De Ira 3,36. Paul probably adopted the term from Hellenistic Judaism: Philo (Decal 87) has a similar understanding of conscience as Seneca and as Paul (cf. Rom 2,15). See further C. Maurer, Art. "σύνοιδα κτλ", *ThWNT* 7 (1964) 897-918; H. Ridderbos, *Paul*, p.288; U. Wilckens, *Römer*, 1, p.139; H.J. Eckstein, *Begriff*, pp.117-121,126-138,338-341. R. Jewett, *Paul's Anthropological Terms*, pp.421-432,436 believes that the term συνείδησις was introduced into Christian theology not by Paul but by the Corinthians. He agrees that the conscience, in parenetic contexts, "plays an active role only after the deed" (p.440).
485 Contra e.g. R. Schnackenburg, *Moral Teaching*, pp.293f.; R. Hasenstab, *Modelle*, pp.195-198 (for whom the conscience is the witness of autonomy which controls the realization of the imperatives established by καρδία and νοῦς); B. Gerhardsson, *Ethos*, p.82. See W. Schrage, *Einzelgebote*, p.153; T. Herr, *Naturrecht*, p.162; H. Ridderbos, *o.c.*, p.292; T.J. Deidun, *Morality*, pp.161f.; W. Schrage, *Ethik*, pp.185f.
486 Cf. W. Schrage, *Einzelgebote*, p.153; H. Ridderbos, *o.c.*, p.292; P. Hilsberg, "Gewissen", 1977, p.155 stating that "bei der Frage: Was sollen wir tun? spielt im NT das Gewissen kaum eine Rolle".
487 Cf. H. Ridderbos, ibid. (cf. pp.289-292 for a careful exegesis of the relevant pas-

ment of God and the verdict of the conscience (1Cor 8,7-8; 10,25-27; cf. Rom 14,14). The conscience is not simply the tribunal which enables the Christian to know the will of God in his ethical decisions[488] but the tribunal "which in these decisions reminds him of the judgment of God and of the necessity in them of preserving inviolate before the judgment of God the liberty wrought by Christ"[489]. One should note in this context that Paul links statements on the conscience occasionally with eschatological issues (Rom 2,12-16; 13,5; 1Cor 4,4-5).

> In the context of the dispute between the 'strong' and the 'weak' over the question of the legitimacy of eating sacrificial meat in 1Cor 8,1-13; 10,23-11,1 Paul is concerned to shift the emphasis from an abstract, impersonal conscience to the respect for and consideration of the brother who possesses a conscience[490]. Paul was convinced that the conscience can and must be educated – contra the 'weak' who regarded the conscience virtually as a superior being which should not be touched – but that this education was possible only indirectly – contra the 'strong' who believed that the conscience could be transformed by the simple infusion of *gnosis*. The necessary change of the conscience can be achieved only through the transformation of the Christian's personality.

Consequently there are two main factors which are of fundamental importance according to Paul. (1) The conscience presupposes and functions in the context of primary norms and standards. The criteria for the moral behaviour of the Christian (and of the non-Christian, cf. Rom 2,15!) is God's claim revealed in the law (Rom 2,15) and in the orders of creation (Rom 13,5) and demanded in the commandment of love (1Cor 8,12). (2) The secondary operation of the conscience has a testing and reviewing function as regards one's ethical decision. The conscience critically controls the behaviour, i.e. the practical realization of the norms, by comparing it with the latter. If this happens *post eventum*, the function of the conscience is one of evaluation and self-judgment. If it happens *ante eventum* (cf. Rom 13,5!), it becomes, still in

---

sages); also T.J. Deidun, *o.c.*, p.162 asserting "a human (hence fallible) power of reflecting upon and assessing the goodness or badness of one's own conduct". It should be noted here that Philo's conception of the conscience belongs to the context of the doctrine of man's struggle against sin; cf. C. Maurer, *a.c.*, pp.910f.

488 Similarly Philo does not really reckon with a (positively) guiding function of the conscience. Cf. C. Maurer, in *ThWNT* 7 (1964) 911.
489 H. Ridderbos, *Paul*, p.292.
490 For these observations cf. particularly J. Murphy-O'Connor, "Freedom of the Ghetto", 1981, pp.30-32.

the context of the primary standards, a criterion for moral action. It is with regard to the second case that one can say that the conscience establishes the responsibility of man as to his actions in everyday life[491].

Although it seems that nobody attempted to link the function of the conscience in Paul to the wisdom tradition, this seems to be nevertheless possible: (1) In 1Cor 4,4; 2Cor 1,12; 4,2; 5,11; Rom 2,15; 9,1 Paul uses συνείδησις in the sense of ἔλεγχος[492]. The Hellenistic-Jewish background of this usage (cf. Philo!) reveals that the LXX uses ἐλέγχειν 38 times in Job, Prov, Sir, and SapSal (from 64 occurrences altogether) with ἐλέγχειν being the task of God or of his wisdom (Sir 8,13; SapSal 1,6-8; 12,2)[493]. (2) When Paul asserts in Rom 2,15 that the Gentiles know the law as to its material content, it is possible to understand this conception not only on the background of the Stoic νόμος ἄγραφος[494] but on the background of universalistic and creational wisdom which had been identified with the Torah and consequently rendered the Torah universal as well[495]. As Paul presents the conscience here as witness of this universal law written in the hearts, it is implicitly also related to (universal) wisdom (cf. in the immediate context Rom 2,17-20 and our discussion above, § 13.2.). (3) In Rom 13,5 Paul exhorts the believers to submit to the state διὰ τὴν συνείδησιν: conscience is here "das verantwortliche Mitwissen um die letzten in Gott bestehenden Grundlagen sowohl des eigenen Seins wie auch des konkreten Staates"[496]. The Christian knows that the state belongs to God's order for this world and is therefore obedi-

---

491 Cf. U. Wilckens, *Römer*, 1, p.138 who defines the conscience as a whole as "die Instanz im Innern des Menschen, die seine Verantwortlichkeit begründet und je und je wahrnimmt". When Wilckens states that the conscience is the representative of God's will in man (ibid.), he implicitly qualifies his definition of conscience: man's responsibility is surely not established by his conscience per se but by God's claim of which the conscience is a witness.
492 Cf. C. Maurer, in *ThWNT* 7 (1964) 915f.
493 Cf. C. Maurer, *a.c.*, p.911.
494 Cf. U. Wilckens, *o.c.*, pp.133-135; disputed by E. Käsemann, *Römer*, p.59. See further supra, p.319.
495 See supra, § 4.2.1., 4.4.1. (Ben Sira), § 10.5.2., 11.3.2., 12.2.1. (Qumran), and p. 164 with nn.376/377 for references and analyses.
496 C. Maurer, in *ThWNT* 7 (1964) 915; also C.E.B. Cranfield, *Romans*, 2, p.668; U. Wilckens, *Römer*, 3, p.36.

ent. As the orders of creation derive essentially and orginally from sapiential theology, conscience is again related with wisdom.

Thus, the basis of the conscience in God's universally revealed law/wisdom, the motivation of the conscience by God's orders of creation, and the function of the conscience as critical self-evaluation and self-judgment as to one's moral conduct establishes an essential link between the conscience and law/wisdom which come from God. To have a clear and good conscience is to act in accordance with God's law and in harmony with God's wise orders.

16.3.7. Admonitory teaching. The very fact that Paul provides motivations in his parenesis shows that he wants understanding and not blind obedience[497]. This coincides with the concern of the Jewish wisdom admonitions. The link between Paul's parenesis as teaching ($διδάσκειν$) and admonishing ($νουθετεῖν$) and wisdom ($σοφία$) is expressly stated in Col 1,28; 3,16.

16.3.8. Summary. We delineated in this section the criteria which guide the believer, according to Paul, in the ongoing process of implementing and realizing *in concreto* and *in actu* the binding norms of the Christian ethos in the context of its broad motivational foundation. We established that the individual's responsibility and freedom in this realm of the practical and specific realization of the Christian ethic in everyday life can be linked with fundamental concepts of wisdom theology.

The Christian is to live in harmony with God's orders of creation and is to follow, basically, the existing conventions. To do so is, in Paul's eyes, fundamentally and essentially wisdom (cf. Rom 16,19). In wisdom theology the orders of creation are the expression of divine wisdom, and human conventions are the manifestation of experiential wisdom. As Christ is the wisdom of God, the Christian is enabled to respect these orders and conventions. Paul does not state this explicitly, but the validity of this conclusion concerning the theological or rather christological basis of the believer's relationship with creation and the world and its orders and conventions is evident.

---

497 Cf. O. Merk, *Handeln*, p.232; W. Schrage, *Ethik*, p.187.

The Christian is not on his own in the effort to make the right decisions in everyday life. The Spirit of God who has been given to him grants the believer wisdom and understanding so that he can know and discern God's will in specific situations and make proper ethical decisions (Col, 1,9-10).

The Christian has been given, by the Spirit, a further criterion which guides him in the realization of the Christian ethos: love. As love can limit and transcend existing orders and conventions, it is particularly important to make the right decision as to one's specific conduct in specific situations. As love is the principle and summary of the law it is obvious that it will not break God's eternally valid norms. As criterion of the latter's fulfilment and realization it will show the Christian how to implement these norms and standards. Christian love provides the believer with knowledge, insight, and wisdom (Phil 1,9-10 ;Col 3,18).

The Christian is further referred to his mind which is constantly being renewed and also to his cognitive faculties which, properly applied in the context of the motivation, the norms, and the guiding criteria, enable him to make decisions which are based on knowledge and perception and characterized by wisdom (Phil 1, 9-10; Rom 15,14; 1Cor 6,5).

The Christian possesses another guideline in this process of making the proper ethical decisions: his conscience. The conscience 'speaks' in harmony with God's norms and standards and prompts the Christian always to stay within the framework of these norms. The conscience evaluates and reviews the Christian's decisions and either leads to self-judgment or provides criteria for proper moral action. The operation of the conscience leads to responsible behaviour which is in accordance with the divine norms, i.e. it leads to wisdom.

Finally, both the form of Paul's parenesis as teaching and admonition and its goal which is behaviour in everyday life characterized by wisdom and knowledge are related to wisdom theology.

Thus, the guiding criteria of Paul's ethic which show the believer how to realize the binding norms and standards of God's eternally valid will in the context of his basic motivation as a Christian are all linked with concepts and elements of wisdom theology. Each individual Christian is personally responsible for the manner in which he behaves in everyday life.

16.4. Conclusion: Normativity and Wisdom in Paul's Ethic

The individual responsibility and freedom of the Christian is carried out, according to Paul, in the framework of God's binding norms and commandments. This relationship of individual responsibility and simultaneous submission to norms and standards is to be explained on the basis of the correlation of law and wisdom. This is evidenced by the fact that all the guiding criteria of the Christian ethic imply and often express both obedience to God's norms and the importance of individual responsibility, knowledge, and perception.

The criterion of the existence of orders of creation and human conventions is in Paul's view both a binding norm, as they manifest God's universal law (§ 16.2.5.), and an expression of wisdom (§ 16.3.2.) as they manifest (this is the Jewish basis of Paul's conception here) God's universal wisdom.

The criterion of the prompting of the Spirit who is God's gift to the believer implies the fundamental and consistent respect of God's norms and standards (§ 16.2.1./4.) and it leads at the same time to wisdom which is knowledge of God's will as regards ethical decisions (§ 16.3.3.).

The criterion of love which is rooted in God's love in and through Christ and which is a gift and a fruit of the Spirit is the summary of the law and realized by the Christian in fulfilling the law and, at the same time, provides the Christian with wisdom and insight regarding his specific conduct in everyday life (§ 16.3.4).

The criterion of reason and discernment functions for Paul in the context of and in harmony with God's eternally valid will and enables the believer to make decisions concerning his behaviour which are based on knowledge and insight and which are characterized by wisdom (§ 16.3.5.).

The criterion of the conscience presupposes the existence and the normative validity of divine norms and standards and – as it is motivated according to Paul by God's orders of creation and as it functions as critical self-judgment and self-evaluation – leads to behaviour marked by wisdom (§ 16.3.6.).

And finally, Paul's preaching as a whole aims, first, as teaching at communicating the fundamental motivations of the indicative of the Gospel. This includes the continued normativity of God's claim as regards the Christian's life revealed in the law, as qualified by Christ, as well as in the words of Jesus Christ, in the exhortations of the apostle, and in the orders of creation. Paul's preaching aims, secondly, as admonition at enabling the Christians to realize and implement these norms and standards in everyday life with wisdom, insight, and understanding.

It is obvious that, in the light of our description of the Christian ethic according to Paul, the concept of an autonomous morality[498] has to be rejected for Paul.

The interpretation of Paul's ethic in the horizon of the autonomy concept, sometimes labelled 'Christian freedom', is clearly related to Kantian philosophy and morality[499]. This is openly acknowledged by scholars who reflect on the 'tradition-historical' origin of their conceptions and viewpoints which they attempt to harmonize with Paul's position[500].

> I. Kant transferred the maxim of the ethos from obedience into man's will, from relevation into reason, from receptivity into creativity and activity. His ethic is the conscious step from heteronomy to the autonomy of the ethic. Morality is to be based upon and derived from practical reason which must determine the will of man and thus his action. These 'imperatives' are relevant for everybody, they are categorical. Morality is based upon the self-legislation of the human will which can be comprehended by reason and which is related to general acceptance. The activity, creativity, and productivity of the *cogito* totally outweigh man's listening to reality[501].

If one attempts to describe the Christian ethic in the context of this modern consciousness of autonomy, it is only consistent that one disregards binding external norms and standards and finally even God himself. And this has actually happened: "Die Moraltheologie hat sich daran gewöhnt, die in den Wissenschaften

---

498 Advocated by many Protestant scholars; cf. recently P. Richardson, *Paul's Ethic of Freedom*, 1979; G. Strecker, "Autonome Sittlichkeit", ThLZ 104 (1979) 865-872, here 871f.; J.F. Collange, *Éthique*, pp.27-29,89,111-127; B. Gerhardsson, *Ethos*, 1981, pp.64-71,81F.; see also J. Ellul, *The Ethics of Freedom*, 1976, and seemingly the majority of the Catholic moral theologians; cf. A. Auer, *Autonome Moral und christlicher Glaube*, 1971; W. Korff, *Theologische Ethik*, 1975; F. Böckle, *Fundamentalmoral*, 1977; R. Hasenstab, *Modelle*, 1977; H. Halter, *Taufe*, 1977 (pp.19-23 on the Catholic majority view).
499 Cf. L. Honnefelder, "Die ethische Rationalität der Neuzeit", *Handbuch der Ethik*, 1, 1978, pp.19-46, here 34-36; and especially G. Huntemann, *Der verlorene Maßstab: Gottes Gebot im Chaos dieser Zeit*, 1983, pp.14-20.
500 Cf. R. Hasenstab, *o.c.*, pp.263f.
501 The last observation was made by R. Hasenstab, *o.c.*, p.264. He continues to discuss the significance of Fichte in this context (pp.264-266).

übliche methodische Ausklammerung der Gottesdimension zu akzeptieren"[502]. It is obviously impossible to 'actualize' Paul's ethic in this context if one is not prepared to manipulate the evidence[503].

The critique of this 'ethic of autonomy' in general has to start with the reference to the sovereignty of God and the factuality of revelation[504]. As regards Paul, it suffices at this point to indicate that (1) Paul indisputably regarded God's revelation in the law (as qualified by Christ) as well as the words of Jesus and the instruction of the apostles as normative for the believer's (faith and) life, and (2) Paul's concept of freedom is irreconcilably different from the modern understanding of autonomy[505].

The evidence for Paul's concept of ἐλευθερία can be very briefly delineated as follows[506].

First, freedom is a gift of Jesus Christ (Gal 2,4; 5,1; Rom 8,21; 2Cor 3,17). Second, Christian freedom as such is freedom from sin (Rom 6, 6-7.18.22;8,2), i.e.

---

[502] R. Hasenstab, o.c., p.281; cf. T. Rendtorff, "Strukturen christlicher Ethik", *Handbuch*, 1, 1978, p.213: "Die Radikalität der modernen Profanität wird als geistiger Ort heutiger moraltheologischer Reflexionen akzeptiert". Cf. also G. Strecker, "Sittlichkeit", *ThLZ* 104 (1979) 872.

[503] Hasenstab's attempt to 'actualize' Paul's ethic in this respect is exegetically extremely weak and totally unconvincing; cf. G. Strecker, "Sittlichkeit", *ThLZ* 104 (1979) 867 (who is himself in favour of Hasenstab's concerns!). Hasenstab asserts, for example, regarding Rom 2,14 (his basic text!) that this verse can be related to the concept of autonomy only (!) by current hermeneutics and not by historical-critical exegesis (*Modelle*, p.22), and admits that in the end he arrives at a "Autonomie-Modell aus paulinischem Geist" rather than at a "Modell paulinischer Ethik im historischen Sinn" (p.25). We ask whether the "umfassende Grundlagenkrise" in moral theology (ibid.) is not related to this very dichotomy!

[504] Cf. K Barth, *Kirchliche Dogmatik*, II/2, pp.572f.; T. Rendtorff, "Strukturen", 1978, p.210-212; G. Huntemann, *Maßstab*, pp.24-34 (with an analysis of K. Barth's contribution in this context on pp.64-68).

[505] It has to be pointed out at this point that the basic structures of Stoic ethics include (1) the fundamental rationalistic structure, (2) man as ultimate measure of morality, (3) the ideal of autonomous (!) and autocratic personality which has arrived at moral perfection in its own strength and on the basis of the inborn (!) standards and norms. Cf. T. Herr, *Naturrecht*, pp.128f. (with lit.).

[506] On the concept of freedom in Paul cf. B. Häring, "Paulinische Freiheitslehre, Gesetzesethik und Situationsethik", *Studiorum Paulinorum Congressus*, AnBibl 17, 1963, pp.165-173; J. Cambier, "La liberté chrétienne selon Saint Paul", *TU* 87 (1964) 315-353; K. Niederwimmer, *Begriff der Freiheit*, 1966, pp.168-220; H. Ridderbos, *Paul*, pp.258-260,288-293; H. Schürmann, *Orientierungen*, pp.13-49; K. Niederwimmer, Art. "ἐλεύθερος", *EWNT* 1 (1980) 1052-1058 (lit.); J. Murphy-O'

from sin as enslaving power. Third, the Christian is consequently freed from performance-oriented piety seeking to attain righteousness and is therefore free from the law as *lex iustificatrix* (and thus *et accusans et condemnatrix*), as the law has now a new locus "in Christ" (Rom 7,5-6; 8,2; also Rom 3,27 ;Gal 6,2; 1Cor 9,21). Fourth, as a result the Christian is able to fulfill the law "in Christ" and "in the Spirit" by love and in faith (Gal 5,14.22-23; Rom 13,8-10), as he is now, as freed man (!), a slave (!) of righteousness (Rom 6,18; also 6,22). True Christian freedom finds its highest expression in service (Gal 5,13; 1Cor 9,19). Fifth, Christian freedom has to be constantly protected against the two dangers of relapse into legalism (Gal 2,4; 5,1) and of antinomism (Gal 5,13). Sixth, Christian freedom is essentially a property of the Christian community whose vitality conditions the reality of freedom[507]. Seventh, Christian freedom is therefore obviously not absolute: it is possible only in servitude to God and in obedience to his will[508]: it implies the Christian's δουλεύειν (1Cor 9,19).

What Murphy-O'Connor said regarding the 'strong' in Corinth applies to many modern exegetes as well: "The fundamental error of the Strong was to transfer the absolute character of 'freedom from sin' to the level of decision and action . . . They confused 'freedom *from* something' with 'freedom *to do* something' without realizing that their exaggeration of the latter would necessarily involve the destruction of the former"[509].

Christian freedom is a characteristic of the believer whose conduct and behaviour in everyday life are marked by obedience to God's revealed will and by wisdom as regards the practical realization of God's will in specific situations. For this reason, true Christian freedom is totally different from autonomy: the autonomous individual establishes, and is interested in, only the experience of the *ego cogitans* and leaves aside the experience of the Creator who reveals himself and who calls man, and of God's orders of creation and the human conventions which enable man

---

Connor, "Freedom", 1981, pp.7-38; G. Galitis, "Das Wesen der Freiheit", *Freedom and Love*, ed. L.de Lorenzi, 1981, pp.127-141.

[507] Cf. J. Murphy-O'Connor, "Freedom", 1981, p.29 referring to the study of F. Mussner, *Theologie der Freiheit*, 1976. Murphy-O'Connor describes here Paul's reaction against the 'strong' in Corinth who understood ἐλευθερία in the framework of a popular cynico-stoic philosophy (cf. 1Cor 10,23!), giving 'freedom' an individualistic interpretation. Cf. R. Schnackenburg, *Moral Teaching*, pp.276f. who asserts that Paul's concept of freedom is fundamentally different from the Stoic ideal of liberty in the sense of αὐτοπραγία and ἀπάθεια.

[508] Emphasized by W. Schrage, *Einzelgebote*, pp.83f.,109; H. Ridderbos, *Paul*, p.259; H. Schürmann, *Orientierungen*, pp.35-37 (for whom, however, God's will ends up being identical with the "Lehrtradition der Kirche", p.37); K. Niederwimmer, in *EWNT* 1 (1980) 1055f.

[509] J. Murphy-O'Connor, *a.c.*, p.29.

to live a life in goodness and harmony. The consciousness of an autonomous morality is automatically "erfahrungs- und geschichts-unfähig"[510], whereas the consciousness of a heteronomous sapiential Christian ethos takes into account both history and experience. It takes into account the history of the world as under the rule of God who created the world and revealed the Word, as well as under the rule of Christ who enables the believer to see and observe the world with its orders as God's creation and to fulfill God's will in Christ and in the power of the Spirit. And it takes into account the experience of man as providing guiding criteria which help the believer to make wise decisions.

Thus, we see that Paul presupposes for his ethic the traditional correlation of law and wisdom. The Christian is called to, and enabled to (!), observe and submit to God's will as revealed in the law, in the words of Jesus Christ, in the pronouncements of the apostles, and in the orders of creation. At the same time the Christian has the free and personal responsibility practically and specifically to realize God's revealed and normative will in the concrete and diverse situations of everyday life which requires wisdom and insight. The Christian ethos according to Paul is neither legalistic nor antinomistic — it is a heteronomous sapiential ethos realizing the correlation of law and wisdom in the horizon of God's salvational action in and through Christ.

---

510 Pointed out by R. Hasenstab, *Modelle*, p.266.

Chapter Five

Conclusions

The universal presence of the correlation of law and wisdom in post-biblical Judaism confirmed the statement which we made in the Preface, that this correlation is of crucial importance for early Jewish and Christian theology and ethics. After our exegetical analysis of all pericopes which express and imply the correlation of law and wisdom in the respective documents or circles of tradition, we are now able to spell out the relevant conclusions concerning the tradition-historical evidence as regards the 'identity' of law and wisdom[1].

(1) The *origin* of the correlation of law and wisdom cannot be entirely illuminated. This is due to the fact that although Sirach is the first document which records the complete identification of law and wisdom, this correlation can be traced back to OT evidence which, however, has not been (and cannot be?) conclusively delineated. The discussion as to the origin of both OT wisdom and OT law, as regards both form and content or intention, is still going on. The OT sapiential tradition sheds no light on our question here. The legal and prophetic traditions of the OT seem to be aware of the correlation. It is especially in the liturgical tradition that the correlation is, in some way, presupposed. Can this be explained simply by reference to a possibly freer usage of terms in hymnody? Or is the cultic and personal (ethical) context of importance at this point? One should note, at any rate, that the relevant psalms betray a profound theological connection between the law as revelation of God's wisdom and the individual's fear of the Lord as personal manifestation of wisdom. Further assump-

---

[1] For references see the relevant summaries and conclusions in the individual chapters and sections.

tions as to the origin of the identification of law and wisdom will be made at the end of the next section on the basis of the identification's basic sociological locus.

(2) The basic *sociological locus* of the correlation of law and wisdom can be established more easily. As Ben Sira was the first author to identify law and wisdom completely and consciously, and as Ben Sira was both a priestly Torah scholar and wisdom teacher, it is natural and logical to relate the established identity of law and wisdom with the circle of scribes who combined the functions of (priestly) Torah scholars and wisdom teachers. We saw that this group was of essential significance in the subsequent promulgation of this identity (see 4Ezr, ApcBar, Qumran).

As the basis sociological locus of a concept is usually not unconnected with its origin, it seems to be possible to assume that the identification of law and wisdom could have arisen in this circle. This would date the origination of the identification to post-exilic but pre-Maccabean times and render the OT evidence to be significant contributing components which were eventually taken up when law and wisdom were fully and consciously identified.

(3) The *historical development* of the identification of law and wisdom cannot be described in precise detail. This is due to the fact that often the exact historical and sociological context of the particular document cannot be established, that in many cases neither the notion of law nor the concept of wisdom is developed to any extent, and that in numerous instances the identification of law and wisdom is simply stated, or implied, without making a careful analysis of the identification possible. The ethical dimension of the identification is always in the centre, with the theological, creational/universalistic, particularistic, eschatological and didactic dimensions being variably present and/or significant. The following observations can be made.

(4) The *ethical dimension* constitutes the main and fundamental focus of the identification of law and wisdom: law and wisdom contain and promulgate the norms and the criteria of moral conduct and lead to a pious, holistic way of life. Already Ben Sira expressed the identification for the most part on the ethical level, and this focus remained the same throughout the intertestamental period as well as in Paul's thinking. It is in this context that both law and wisdom are repeatedly linked with the concept of life as 'walking' in (good) 'ways' which is prominent throughout the

Conclusions 345

early Jewish literature. Similarly, both law and wisdom are often compared with 'light' which gives orientation (to walk aright on the way). Both law and wisdom are intimately linked with righteousness, holiness, and purity as goal of the enlightened walk in the proper way.

Ben Sira emphasized that right ethical behaviour equals wise conduct and results from obedience to God's law. Baruch asserts that law and wisdom both and together lead to an upright walk. The traditions incorporated in Enoch closely relate righteousness, which obviously implies obedience to the law, and wisdom. The circles which are responsible for the Psalms of Solomon were convinced that practical obedience to the law is equivalent with the adoption of divine wise instruction.

In a Hellenistic context the author of the Letter of Aristeas argued that the Jewish law is true wisdom since it enables man to live a morally perfect life. The Jewish Sibylline Oracle teaches that the keeping of the law equals the ability to give sound counsel with both resulting in good deeds. The Wisdom of Solomon yields no clear evidence in this context.

The Qumran Community focused on the ethical dimension of the identification of law and wisdom as well, as the latter is repeatedly linked with the concepts of righteousness of the Community's ethics. Proper conduct and walking in the right way is considered to be possible only in obedience to the law by appropriating God's wisdom in the context of the Community.

The Jewish writings of the first century A.D. equally place the ethical dimension into the centre of their concern. The author of Fourth Maccabees argued that true philo-sophy consists in a pious life obeying the Jewish law. The author of Fourth Ezra was convinced that law and wisdom contain the norms which help man to please God, walking in his ways, and to obtain salvation. The author of the Apocalypse of Baruch believed that obedience to the law equals wisdom amounting to righteousness and guaranteeing salvation.

Regarding Paul the apostle we discovered the identification of law and wisdom as basis of his ethic. He calls the individual to observe God's revealed will and acknowledges at the same time the individual's personal responsibility to realize God's will in everyday life which requires wisdom and insight. The correlation of wisdom and law enables the individual to live in a way which pleases God. The crucial contrast to the Jewish writings consists in the fact that the individual's (or the community's) proper ethical behaviour does not secure, and is not even necessary for, salvation since the latter has been secured already by and in Christ.

(5) The *theological dimension* of the identification of law and wisdom is most explicit in Sirach and is subsequently more implied or presupposed than elaborated on. Ben Sira specified that law and wisdom are one as both law and (!) wisdom are the expression of God's will for life. Both law and wisdom seek to lead the individual and the community into submission to God's will. This objective is summarized in the notion of the fear of the Lord which is obedience to the commandments and practised wisdom. This theological dimension was seen as closely connected with the ethical perspective.

After Ben Sira the theological dimension of the identification was usually simply taken for granted. This coincides with the fact that the notion of fear of the Lord, with the exception of PsSal (and TestXIIPatr), nearly vanishes. However, it is evident in most documents that both law and wisdom are regarded as unique possessions of God, given as gifts to his people.

As regards Paul, the extant evidence does not permit us to draw any definite conclusions regarding the theological dimension of the relatedness of law and wisdom. He did regard the law as gift from God. As for wisdom, i.e. the guiding criteria for decision-making in everyday life, both the Spirit and love, and some of the exisiting orders, are seen as coming from God. But reason and discernment, the function of the conscience, and some existing orders (such as the human conventions), are not *eo ipso* the voice of God. The Christian is given the personal and consistent responsibility to realize God's norms in everyday life and is thus essentially free: free from sin, free from performance-oriented piety, and free to live in harmony with God's will. Thus it seems that the fact that Paul did not link all the components of the wisdom aspect to the divine reality preserved, or rather re-introduced, true and genuine (Christian) freedom.

On the other hand Paul was able to use wisdom language and wisdom theology to describe the person and mission of Jesus Christ. But he was obviously concerned to avoid the correlation of Christ with both wisdom and (!) law. Christ is not described in terms of Torah but, rather, the Torah is described and defined in terms of Christ. Paul dismissed the identity of Torah and wisdom on the christological level for soteriological reasons.

(6) The *universalistic dimension* of law and wisdom was recognized as result, rather than precondition, of the identification of the two notions, with the Torah assuming universalistic aspects. The Torah is henceforth seen as comprehensive order for the communion of God, creation (cosmos), and man or his people. In subsequent early Jewish thought both (Jewish) law and wisdom are related with creation and considered to be universal. Naturally the (Hellenistic) apologetic treatises were more inclined to stress the universal aspect of the law which is wisdom.

The Qumran Community with its monastic exclusivism did not dwell on the universalistic but rather on the *creational dimension* of the identity of law and wisdom. The laws of creation which are seen as embodiment of God's wisdom are considered to be one with the laws of the Community which combined Torah and relevant halakhah.

The Pauline evidence does not allow us to arrive at any conclusions in this area. However, it seems that the creational aspect of the identity of law and wisdom would be implied as well.

(7) The *particularistic dimension* of the identity of law and wisdom which focuses on the Jewish realm is always at least taken for granted. The later writings of the Qumran Community were seen to narrow down this dimension from the wider (and earlier) context of Israel to the desert Community.

Paul makes no relevant statements in the immediate context of the identification of law and wisdom. However, it is possible to say that on the one hand he retains this particularistic dimension — the Christian has to live in submission to the (Jewish) Torah which is the revelation of (Israel's) God and which is qualified by Jesus Christ — and that on the other hand he dismisses it — the Christian life is open to both Jews and Gentiles and the guiding criteria (i.e. wisdom) are not exclusively Jewish but often creational.

(8) The *eschatological dimension* of the identity of law and wisdom was discovered in En(eth), in certain Qumran texts, and in the later Jewish apocalypses 4Ezr and ApcBar. The different messianic figures are related both with law and wisdom. Obedience to the law and faithful wisdom are seen as decisive for obtaining righteousness and for inheriting eschatological salvation (especially

stressed in the apocalypses). The new aeon is characterized both by obedience to the law and by wisdom.

While Paul would agree with the last notion — that the new aeon is characterized by law and wisdom — he rejected the conviction that living in harmony with law/wisdom is the prerequisite for obtaining salvation: salvation is God's free and undeserved gift by and in Christ and is received by faith in Christ. For this reason, as we pointed out, he dismissed the traditional correlation of law and wisdom on the eschatological (christological) level.

(9) As regards a *formal evaluation* of the evidence connected with the identity of law and wisdom in early Judaism it is obvious from our analysis that the tradition of this identification appears in wisdom texts, in parenetic books, in apologetic-philosophical treatises, in apocalypses, and in letters.

(10) The *sociological evidence* of the tradition shows that all circles of early Judaism were aware of, and made use of, the identification of law and wisdom: wisdom teachers, priests, Torah scholars, scribes, hasidic groups, Pharisaic fellowships, the Qumran Community and connected circles, the Jewish Hellenistic diaspora, and the main theologian of early Christianity.

The description and analysis of the identification of law and wisdom which proved to be a fundamental *Interpretament* of early Jewish theology and of Pauline thought has thus been accomplished. The lack of comprehensive studies in several important areas was felt with regret. More work has yet to be done on Ben Sira's understanding of Torah, on his ethical system, on the conceptions of law and covenant and ethics in the Qumran Community, on the history of sapiential literature in Qumran, on the basic theologoumena of Pharisaic apocalyptic, on Paul's knowledge and use of early Jewish literature, and on the relationship between Jewish wisdom concerns and Paul's parenesis. Although a wise man would always like to follow Ben Sira's dictum, "ἐν στόματι μωρῶν ἡ καρδία αὐτῶν, καρδία δὲ σοφῶν στόμα αὐτῶν" (Sir 21,26), occasionally he has to take his heart into his mouth, especially when he is writing a dissertation! For this reason the present study attempted to make some contribution in these areas. The main concern and the main contribution, however, is the presentation of the exegetical and conceptional evidence of the traditional early Jewish identification of law and wisdom.

The Jewish communities in the post-exilic era considered the realms of God's law and of wisdom to be identical on the basis of complex reasons and with complex and varying results. The goal was the same: to ensure the existence of God's people and to attain, on the individual level, a life in harmony and peace under God's approval. The apostle Paul saw the existence of God's people — the Christian community — as being ratified in Christ, of the individual as being realized and realizable (only) in Christ. For the individual Jew obedience to the law and conformity with wisdom remained in some way, but essentially, linked with the attainment of righteousness, holiness, and God's approval. For the individual Christian, according to Paul, righteousness and holiness and God's approval are God's free and unconditional gift which renders obedience to God's revealed will and living in keeping with wise conduct to be the thankful and worshipful response of the believer in Christ *coram Deo*.

Select Bibliography

The following bibliography omits dictionary articles, encyclopedia entries, and works of a complementary and tangential nature. The index of authors serves to facilitate the location of material not listed in the select bibliography.

1. Sources, texts

Albeck, H., ששה סדרי משנה, 6 vols., Jerusalem/Tel Aviv: Bialik Institute, 1954-1959.

Allegro, J.H., ed., *Discoveries in the Judaean Desert of Jordan V — Qumrân Cave 4: I* (4Q158-4Q186) = *DJD* 5, Oxford: Clarendon, 1968.

Andrews, H.T., "The Letter of Aristeas", *APOT* 2 (1913) 83-122.

Baillet, M., ed., *Discoveries in the Judaean Desert VII — Qumrân Grotte 4: III* (4Q482-4Q520) = *DJD* 7, Oxford: Clarendon, 1982.

Baillet, M., Milik, J.T., Vaux, R. de, eds., *Discoveries in the Judaean Desert of Jordan III — Les 'Petites Grottes' de Qumrân. Exploration de la falaise. Les grottes 2Q, 3Q, 5Q, 6Q, 7Q à 10Q. Le rouleau de cuivre. DJD* 3, Oxford: Clarendon, 1962.

Barthélemy, D., Milik, J.T., eds., *Discoveries in the Judaean Desert I — Qumrân Cave 1* = *DJD* 1, Oxford: Clarendon, 1955.

Beer, G., Holtzmann, O., Krauss, S., Rengstorf, H.K., Rost, L., eds., *Die Mischna: Text, Übersetzung, und ausführliche Erklärung.* Mit eingehenden geschichtlichen und sprachlichen Einleitungen und textkritischen Anhängen (= Giessener Mischna), Giessen/Berlin: Töpelmann, 1912ff.

Black, M., *Apocalypsis Henochi Graeci*, PVTG 3, Leiden: Brill, 1970.

Bogaert, P.M., *Apocalypse de Baruch: Traduction du Syriaque*, SC 144, 1, pp.461-528, Paris: Cerf, 1969.

Box, G.H., *The Ezra-Apocalypse (2Esdras 3-14).* Translated from a Critically Revised Text, with Critical Introductions, Notes, and Explanations, London: Pitman, 1912.

— —, Oesterley, W.O.E., "The Book of Sirach", *APOT* 1 (1913) 268-517.

— —, "IV Ezra", *APOT* 2 (1913) 542-624.

Burrows, M., ed., *The Dead Sea Scrolls of St. Mark's Monastery*, 2 vols., New Haven: American Schools of Oriental Research, 1950/1951.

Charles, R.H., ed., *The Apocrypha and Pseudepigrapha of the Old Testament*, (= APOT), 2 vols., Oxford: Clarendon, 1913.

— —, "1Enoch", *APOT* 2 (1913) 163-281.

— —, "2Baruch, or the Syriac Apocalypse of Baruch", *APOT* 2 (1913) 470-526.

Charlesworth, J.H., *The Odes of Solomon: The Syriac Texts.* Edited, with Translation and Notes, Missoula: Scholars Press, 1978.

Danby, H., *The Mishnah.* Translated from the Hebrew with Introduction and Brief Ex-

planatory Notes, Oxford: University Press, 1933 (= 1980).
Denis, A.M., "Fragmenta pseudepigraphorum quae supersunt graeca una cum historicorum et auctorum Judaeorum hellenistarum fragmentis", *PVTG* 3b (1970) 217-228.
Epstein, I., ed., *The Babylonian Talmud*, 35 vols. reprinted in 18 vols., London: Soncino Press, 1935-1952.
Gaster, T.H., *The Dead Sea Scriptures*. In English Translation with Introduction and Notes, New York: Anchor Press, ³1976.
Geffcken, J., *Die Oracula Sibyllina*, GCS 8, Leipzig: Hinrichs, 1902 (= Amsterdam: Hakkert, 1970).
Georgi, D., "Weisheit Salomos", *JSHRZ* III/4 (1980) 389-478.
Gray, G.B., "The Psalms of Solomon", *APOT* 2 (1913) 625-652.
Gunneweg, A.H.J., "Das Buch Baruch", *JSHRZ* III/2 (1975) 165-181.
Habicht, C., "2. Makkabäerbuch", *JSHRZ* I/3 (1976) 165-285.
Hadas, M., *Aristeas to Philocrates (Letter of Aristeas)*, New York: Harper, 1951.
Holmes, S., "The Wisdom of Solomon", *APOT* 1 (1913) 518-568.
Holm-Nielsen, S., *Hodayot: Psalms from Qumran*, AThD 2, Aarhus: Universitetsforlaget, 1960.
——, "Die Psalmen Salomos", *JSHRZ* IV/2 (1977) 49-112.
James, M.R., *The Biblical Antiquities of Philo*. Now First Translated from the Old Latin Version. Translation of Early Documents, Series I: Palestinian Jewish Texts, London: SPCK, 1917 (= New York: Ktav, 1971).
Klijn, A.F.J., "Die syrische Baruch-Apokalypse", *JSHRZ* V/2 (1976) 103-191.
Knibb, M.A., *The Ethiopic Book of Enoch.* A New Edition in the Light of the Aramaic Dead Sea Fragments, 2 vols., Oxford: Clarendon, 1978.
Kurfess, A., *Sibyllinische Weissagungen*, Berlin: Heimeran, 1951.
Lanchester, H.C.O., "The Sibylline Oracles", *APOT* 2 (1913) 368-406.
Lohse, E., ed., *Die Texte aus Qumran: Hebräisch und Deutsch*. Mit masoretischer Punktation, Übersetzung, Einführung und Anmerkungen, Darmstadt: Wissenschaftliche Buchgesellschaft, ²1971.
Maier, J., "Texte der Schriftrollen", *Die Qumran-Essener*, by K. Schubert and J. Maier, UTB 224, München/Basel: Reinhardt, 1973.
——, *Die Tempelrolle vom Toten Meer.* Übersetzt und erläutert, UTB 829, Basel/München: Reinhardt, 1978.
Mansoor, M., *The Thanksgiving Hymns: Translation*, STDJ 3, Leiden: Brill, 1961, pp.98-193.
Martin, J., *Le livre d'Hénoch.* Traduit sur le texte éthiopien, Milano: Archè, 1975.
Meisner, N., "Aristeasbrief", *JSHRZ* II/1 (1973) 35-87.
Milik, J.T., *The Books of Enoch: Aramaic Fragments of Qumrân Cave 4*, Oxford: Clarendon, 1976.
Myers, J.M., *I and II Esdras*. Introduction, Translation and Commentary, Anchor Bible 42, New York: Doubleday, 1974.
Nestle-Aland, *Novum Testamentum Graece*, ediderunt K. Aland, M. Black, C.M. Martini, B.M. Metzger, A. Wikgren, 26. neu bearbeitete Auflage, Stuttgart: Deutsche Bibelstiftung, 1979.
Neugebauer, O., *The 'Astronomical' Chapters of the Ethiopic Book of Enoch (72-82)*. Translation and Commentary, Copenhagen: Munksgaard, 1981.
Nikiprowetzky, V., *La Troisième Sibylle*, Études Juives 9, Paris: Mouton, 1970, pp.291-353.
Oesterley, W.O.E., *II Esdras (The Ezra Apocalypse)*. With Introduction and Notes. Westminster Commentaries, London: Methuen, 1933.
Rahlfs, A., ed., *Septuaginta id est Vetus Testamentum graece iuxta LXX interpretes,*

2 vols., editio nona, Stuttgart: Württembergische Bibelanstalt, 1935.

——, "Machabaeorum IV", *Septuaginta*, 1, pp.1157-1184.

Sanders, J.A., ed., *Discoveries in the Judaean Desert of Jordan IV — The Psalms Scroll of Qumrân Cave 11 (11QPs^a)* = *DJD* 4, Oxford: Clarendon, 1965.

Sauer, G., "Jesus Sirach (Ben Sira)", *JSHRZ* III/5 (1981) 483-644.

Schreiner, J., "Das 4. Buch Esra", *JSHRZ* V/4 (1981) 289-412.

Schunck, K.D., "1. Makkabäerbuch", *JSHRZ* I/4 (1980) 287-373.

Smend, R., *Die Weisheit des Jesus Sirach: Hebräisch und Deutsch*, Berlin, Reimers, 1906.

Tov, E., *The Book of Baruch also called 1 Baruch*, SBLTT 8, Missoula: Scholars Press, 1975.

Townshend, R.B., "The Fourth Book of Maccabees", *APOT* 2 (1913) 653-685.

Vattioni, F., *Ecclesiastico*. Testo ebraico con apparato critico e versioni greca, latina e sirica, Naples: Istituto Orientale, 1968.

Vaux, R. de, Milik, J.T., *Discoveries in the Judaean Desert VI — Qumrân Grotte 4: II Tefillin, Mezuzot et Targums (4Q128-4Q157)* = *DJD* 6, Oxford: Clarendon, 1977.

Vermes, G., *The Dead Sea Scrolls in English*, Harmondsworth: Penguin, ^{2}1975 (= 1982).

Violet, B., *Die Esra-Apokalypse (IV. Esra)*, GCS 18, Leipzig: Hinrichs, 1910.

——, *Die Apokalypsen des Esra und des Baruch in deutscher Gestalt*, GCS 32, Leipzig: Hinrichs, 1924.

Viteau, J., *Les Psaumes de Salomon*. Introduction, texte Grec et traduction, DEB I/4, Paris: Letoazey et Ané, 1911.

Wahl, O., *Apocalypse of Ezra: Greek*, Leiden: Brill, 1977.

Walton, F.R., *Diodorus Siculus*, LCL XII, 1967.

Weber, R., ed., *Biblia Sacra Iuxta Vulgatam Versionem*, 2 vols., editio altera emendata, Stuttgart: Württembergische Bibelanstalt, ^{2}1975.

——, "IV Ezra", *o.c.*, 2, pp.1931-1974.

Wendland, P., *Aristeae ad Philocratem Epistula*. Cum ceteris de origine versionis LXX interpretum testimoniis, Leipzig: Teubner, 1900.

Whitehouse, O.C., "The Book of Baruch", *APOT* 1 (1913) 569-595.

Winston, D., *The Wisdom of Solomon*. A New Translation with Introduction and Commentary, Anchor Bible 43, Garden City, NY: Doubleday, 1979.

Woude, A.S.van der, "Die fünf syrischen Psalmen", *JSHRZ* III/1 (1974) 29-47.

Yadin, Y., *The Scroll of the War of th Sons of Light Against the Sons of Darkness*, Edited with Commentary and Introduction, ET by B. and C. Rabin, Oxford: University Press, 1962.

Ziegler, J., "Baruch", *Septuaginta Vetus Testamentum Graecum*, auctoritate Societatis Litterarum Gottingensis editum, vol. 15, Göttingen: Vandenhoeck & Ruprecht, 1976, pp.450-467.

——, "Sapientia Iesu Filii Sirach", *o.c.*, vol. 12/2, ^{2}1980.

——, "Sapientia Salomonis", *o.c.*, vol. 12/1, ^{2}1980.

2. Subsidia

Aland, K., Werner, H., *Computer-Konkordanz zum Novum Testamentum Graece*, von Nestle-Aland, 26. Auflage und zum Greek New Testament, 3rd edition, ed. Institut für Neutestamentliche Textforschung und vom Rechenzentrum der Universität Münster, unter besonderer Mitwirkung von H. Bachmann, W.A. Slaby, Berlin/New York: de Gruyter, 1980.

Balz, H., Schneider, G., eds., *Exegetisches Wörterbuch zum Neuen Testament*, (= EWNT),

3 vols., Stuttgart: Kohlhammer, 1980/1981/1983.

Barthélemy, D., Rickenbacher, O., *Konkordanz zum Hebräischen Sirach,* mit syrisch-hebräischem Index, Göttingen: Vandenhoek & Ruprecht, 1973.

Bauer, W., *Griechisch-deutsches Wörterbuch zu den Schriften des Neuen Testaments und der übrigen urchristlichen Literatur,* Berlin/New York: de Gruyter, ^{5}1971.

Blass, F., Debrunner, A., Rehkopf, F., *Grammatik des neutestamentlichen Griechisch,* (= BDR), Göttingen: Vandenhoeck & Ruprecht, ^{15}1979.

Botterweck, G.J., Ringgren, H., eds., *Theologisches Wörterbuch zum Alten Testament,* (= ThWAT), Stuttgart: Kohlhammer, 1970ff.

Brockelmann, C., *Syrische Grammatik,* mit Paradigmen, Literatur, Chrestomathie und Glossar, Leipzig: Harrassowitz, ^{5}1938.

Burchard, C., *Bibliographie zu den Handschriften vom Toten Meer,* BZAW 76 (1957), 89 (1965).

Charlesworth, J.H., *The Pseudepigrapha and Modern Research,* SBLSCS 7, Missoula: Scholars Press, 1976.

Dalman, G.H., *Aramäisch-Neuhebräisches Handwörterbuch zu Targum, Talmud und Midrasch,* Göttingen: Vandenhoeck & Ruprecht, 1938 (= Hildesheim: Olms, 1967).

Delling, G., Maser, M., *Bibliographie zur jüdisch-hellenistischen und intertestamentarischen Literatur 1900 – 1970,* TU 106^2, Berlin: Akademie-Verlag, ^{2}1975.

Fitzmyer, J.A., *The Dead Sea Scrolls: Major Publications and Tools for Study,* SBLSBS 8, Missoula: Scholars Press, 1975.

Hatch, E., Redpath, H.A., *A Concordance to the Septuagint and the other Greek Versions to the Old Testament (Including the Apocryphical Books),* 2 vols., Oxford: Clarendon, 1897 (= Graz: Akademische Druck- und Verlagsanstalt, 1975).

Jenni, E., Westermann, C., eds., *Theologisches Handwörterbuch zum Alten Testament,* (= THAT), 2 vols., München: Kaiser, 1971/1976.

Kasowski, H.J., *Thesaurus Mishnae: Concordantiae Verborum quae in Sex Mishnae Ordinibus Reperiuntur,* Jerusalem, 1918.

Kittel, G., Friedrich, G., eds., *Theologisches Wörterbuch zum Neuen Testament,* (= ThWNT), 10 vols., Stuttgart: Kohlhammer, 1933-1979.

Koehler, L., Baumgartner, W., *Hebräisches und Aramäisches Lexikon zum Alten Testament,* Dritte Auflage, 2 vols., Leiden: Brill, 1967/1974.

Kuhn, K.G., et al., *Konkordanz zu den Qumrantexten,* Göttingen: Vandenhoeck & Ruprecht, 1960.

——, "Nachträge zur 'Konkordanz zu den Qumrantexten' ", *RQ* 4 (1963) 163-234.

Liddell, H.G., Scott, R., *A Greek-English Lexicon,* New Edition by H.S. Jones and R. McKenzie, Oxford: Clarendon, ^{9}1940 (= 1966).

Mandelkern, S., *Veteris Testamenti Concordantiae Hebraicae atque Chaldaicae,* editio nona aucta atque emendata, Jerusalem/Tel Aviv: Schocken, 1971.

Metzger, B.M., *A Textual Commentary on the Greek New Testament,* London/New York: United Bible Societies, 1975.

Reicke, B., Rost, L., eds., *Biblisch-historisches Handwörterbuch,* (BHH), 4 vols., Göttingen: Vandenhoeck & Ruprecht, 1962-1979.

Stern, M., ed., *Greek and Latin Authors on Jews and Judaism,* 2 vols., Jerusalem: Israel Academy of Science and Humanities, 1974/1980.

Temporini, H., Haase, W., eds., *Aufstieg und Niedergang der römischen Welt: Geschichte und Kultur Roms im Spiegel der neueren Forschung,* (= ANRW), Berlin/New York: de Gruyter, 1972ff.

3. Commentaries

Barrett, C.K., *A Commentary on the Epistle to the Romans*, Black's New Testament Commentaries, London: Black, (1957) 1971.

——, *A Commentary on the First Epistle to the Corinthians*, Black's New Testament Commentaries, London: Black, 1968.

——, *A Commentary on the Second Epistle to the Corinthians*, Black's New Testament Commentaries, London: Black, (1973) 1982.

Barth, G., *Der Brief an die Philipper*, Züricher Bibelkommentare NT 9, Zürich: Theologischer Verlag, 1979.

Betz, H.D., *Galatians: A Commentary on Paul's Letter to the Churches in Galatia*, Hermenia, Philadelphia: Fortress Press, 1979.

Bogaert, P.M., *Apocalypse de Baruch: Introduction, traduction du Syriaque et commentaire*, 2 vols., SC 144/145, Paris: Cerf, 1969.

Bruce, F.F., *Commentary on the Epistle to the Colossians*, NICNT, Grand Rapids: Eerdmans, (1957) ^{9}1977, pp.159-313.

——, *The Epistle to the Galatians: A Commentary on the Greek Text*, NIGTC, Grand Rapids: Eerdmans, 1982.

Bultmann, R., *Der zweite Brief an die Korinther*, ed. E. Dinkler, KEK Sonderband, Göttingen: Vandenhoeck & Ruprecht, 1976.

Conzelmann, H., *Der erste Brief an die Korinther*, KEK 5, Göttingen: Vandenhoeck & Ruprecht, 1969.

——, *Die Apostelgeschichte*, HNT 7, Tübingen: Mohr, ^{2}1972.

Cranfield, C.E.B., *The Epistle to the Romans*, 2 vols., ICC, Edinburgh: Clark, 1975 (= 1980)/1979.

Ebeling, E., *Die Wahrheit des Evangeliums: Eine Lesehilfe zum Galaterbrief*, Tübingen: Mohr, 1981.

Gnilka, J., *Der Philipperbrief*, HThK X/3, Freiburg: Herder, 1968.

——, *Der Kolosserbrief*, HThK X/1, Freiburg: Herder, 1980.

Haenchen, E., *Die Apostelgeschichte*, KEK 3, Göttingen: Vandenhoeck & Ruprecht, ^{13}1961.

Hughes, P.E., *Paul's Second Epistle to the Corinthians: The English Text with Introduction, Exposition and Notes*, NICNT, Grand Rapids: Eerdmans, (1962) ^{7}1979.

Käsemann, E., *An die Römer*, HNT 8a, Tübingen: Mohr, ^{4}1980.

Lietzmann, H., *An die Korinther*, HNT 9, ergänzt von W.G. Kümmel, Tübingen: Mohr, ^{5}1969.

Lohmeyer, E., *Die Briefe an die Philipper, an die Kolosser und an Philemon*, KEK 9, Göttingen: Vandenhoeck & Ruprecht, ^{13}1964.

Lohse, E., *Die Briefe an die Kolosser und an Philemon*, KEK IX/2, Göttingen: Vandenhoeck & Ruprecht, 1968.

Lührmann, O., *Der Brief an die Galater*, Züricher Bibelkommentare NT 7, Zürich: Theologischer Verlag, 1978.

Marshall, I.H., *The Acts of the Apostles: An Introduction and Commentary*, TNTC, Leicester: Inter-Varsity Press, 1980.

Martin, R.P., *Colossians: The Church's Lord and the Christian's Liberty*, Exeter: Paternoster, 1972.

Michel, O., *Der Brief an die Römer*, KEK 4, Göttingen: Vandenhoeck & Ruprecht, ^{5}1978.

Mussner, F., *Der Galaterbrief*, HThK 9, Freiburg: Herder, ^{3}1977.

Myers, J.M., *I and II Esdras: Introduction, Translation and Commentary*, Anchor Bible 42, New York: Doubleday, 1974.

Neugebauer, O., *The 'Astronomical' Chapters of the Ethiopic Book of Enoch (72 to 82): Translation and Commentary*, with Additional Notes on the Aramaic Fragments by M. Black, The Royal Danish Academy of Science and Letters 40:10, Copenhagen: Munksgaard, 1981.

Noth, M., *Könige I*, BK IX/1, Neukirchen-Vluyn: Neukirchener Verlag, 1968.

Orr, W.F., Walther, J.A., *I Corinthians: A New Translation. Introduction with a Study of the Life of Paul, Notes, and Commentary*, Anchor Bible 32, New York: Doubleday, 1976.

Plummer, A., *A Critical and Exegetical Commentary on the Second Epistle of St. Paul to the Corinthians*, ICC, Edinburgh: Clark, 1915 (= 1956).

Roloff, J., *Die Apostelgeschichte übersetzt und erklärt*, NTD 5, Göttingen: Vandenhoeck & Ruprecht, 1981.

Schlatter, A., *Gottes Gerechtigkeit: Ein Kommentar zum Römerbrief*, Stuttgart: Calwer Verlag, (1935) ^{5}1975.

Schlier, H., *Der Brief an die Galater*, KEK 7, Göttingen: Vandenhoek & Ruprecht, ^{5}1971.

——, *Der Römerbrief*, HThK 6, Freiburg: Herder, 1977.

Schneider, G., *Die Apostelgeschichte*, HThK V/1,2, Freiburg: Herder, 1980/1982.

Schweizer, E., *Der Brief an die Kolosser*, EKK, Zürich/Neukirchen-Vluyn: Benzinger/Neukirchener Verlag, 1976.

Senft, C., *La première Épître de Saint-Paul aux Corinthiens*, Commentaire du Nouveau Testament 2/7, Lausanne: Delachaux & Niestlé, 1979.

Snaith, J.G., *Ecclesiasticus or the Wisdom of Jesus Son of Sirach*, Cambridge Bible Commentary, Cambridge: University Press, 1974.

Strack, H.L., Billerbeck, P., *Kommentar zum Neuen Testament aus Talmud und Midrasch*, 6 vols., München: Beck'sche Verlagsbuchhandlung, (1926) ^{6}1974.

Westermann, C., *Genesis 1-11*, BK I/1, Neukirchen-Vluyn: Neukirchener Verlag, ^{2}1976.

Wilckens, U., *Der Brief an die Römer*, 3 vols., EKK VI/1-3, Einsiedeln/Neukirchen-Vluyn: Benzinger/Neukirchener Verlag, 1978/1980/1982.

Wildberger, H., *Jesaja (1-39)*, BK X/1-3, Neukirchen-Vluyn: Neukirchener Verlag, 1972/1978/1982.

Windisch, H., *Der Zweite Korintherbrief*, KEK 6, Göttingen: Vandenhoeck & Ruprecht, 1924 (= 1970).

Winston D., *The Wisdom of Solomon: A New Translation with Introduction and Commentary*, Anchor Bible 43, New York: Doubleday, 1979.

Wolff, H.W., *Dodekapropheton 4: Micha*, BK XIV/4, Neukirchen-Vluyn: Neukirchener Verlag, 1982.

Zimmerli, W., *Ezechiel*, BK XIII/1,2 Neukirchen-Vluyn: Neukirchener Verlag, 1969.

4. General bibliography

Aalen, S., *Die Begriffe 'Licht' und 'Finsternis' im Alten Testament, im Spätjudentum und im Rabbinismus*, Skrifter Norske Akademi 1, Oslo: Dybward, 1951.

Aletti, J.N., *Colossiens 1,15-20: Genre et exégèse du texte. Fonction de la thématique sapientielle*, AnBibl 91, Rome: Biblical Institute Press, 1981.

Alon, G., *Jews, Judaism and the Classical World: Studies in Jewish History in the Times of the Second Temple and Talmud*, ET by I. Abrahams, Jerusalem: Magnes Press, 1977.

Audet, J.P., "Origines comparées de la double tradition de la loi et de la sagesse dans le

Proche-Orient ancien", *25th International Congress of Orientalists*, Moscow 1960, pp.352-357.
Bacher, W., *Die exegetische Terminologie der jüdischen Traditionsliteratur*, 2 vols., Leipzig, 1899/1905 (= Darmstadt: Wissenschaftliche Buchgesellschaft, 1965).
Balz, H.R., *Methodische Probleme der neutestamentlichen Christologie*, WMANT 25, Neukirchen-Vluyn: Neukirchener Verlag, 1967.
Bammel, E., "Νόμος Χριστοῦ", Studia Evangelica 3, ed. F.L. Cross, *TU* 88 (1964) 120-128.
Banks, R.J., *Jesus and the Law in the Synoptic Tradition*, NTS MS 28, Cambridge: University Press, 1975.
Barbour, R.S., "Creation, Wisdom and Christ", *Creation, Christ and Culture*, FS T.F. Torrance, ed. R.W.A. McKinney, Edinburgh: Clark, 1976, pp.22-42.
——, "Wisdom and the Cross in 1 Corinthians 1 and 2", *Theologia Crucis - Signum Crucis*, FS E. Dinkler, ed. C. Andresen et al., Tübingen: Mohr, 1979, pp.57-71.
Bardtke, H., "Literaturbericht über Qumrân", *ThR* 29-41 (1963-1976).
Barrett, C.K., *Essays on Paul*, London: SPCK, 1981.
Barth, M., "Die Stellung des Paulus zu Gesetz und Ordnung", *EvTh* 33 (1973) 496-526.
Bartsch, H.W., *Die konkrete Wahrheit und die Lüge der Spekulation: Untersuchungen über den vorpaulinischen Hymnus und seine gnostische Mythisierung*, Theologie und Wahrheit No. 1, Bern/Frankfurt: Lang, 1974.
Battistone, J.J., *An Examination of the Literary and Theological Background of the Wisdom Passage in Baruch*, Ph.D. Diss. Duke 1968, University Microfilms No. 69-9061, Ann Arbor, Michigan.
Bauckmann, E.G., "Die Proverbien und die Sprüche des Jesus Sirach: Eine Untersuchung zum Strukturwandel der israelitischen Weisheitslehre", *ZAW* 72 (1960) 33-63.
Baum, H., *Mut zum Schwachsein — in Christi Kraft: Theologische Grundelemente einer missionarischen Spiritualität anhand von 2 Kor*, St. Augustin: Steyler Verlag, 1977.
Baumann, R., *Mitte und Norm des Christlichen: Eine Auslegung von 1 Korinther 1,1-3,4*, NTA NF 5, Münster: Aschendorff, 1968.
Baumgarten, J., *Paulus und die Apokalyptik: Die Auslegung apokalyptischer Überlieferungen in den echten Paulusbriefen*, WMANT 44, Neukirchen-Vluyn: Neukirchener Verlag, 1975.
Baumgarten, J.M., *Studies in Qumran Law*, SJLA 24, Leiden: Brill, 1977.
——, "Form-Criticism and the Oral Law", *JSJ* 5 (1974) 34-40.
——, "The Pharisaic-Sadducean Controversies about Purity and the Qumran Texts", *JJS* 31 (1980) 157-170.
Beasley-Murray, P., "Colossians 1,15-20: An Early Christian Hymn Celebrating the Lordship of Christ", *Pauline Studies*, FS F.F. Bruce, ed. D.A. Hagner et al., Exeter: Paternoster, 1980, pp.169-183.
Becker, J., *Gottesfurcht im Alten Testament*, AnBibl 25, Rome: Biblical Institute Press, 1965.
Becker, J., *Das Heil Gottes: Heils- und Sündenbegriffe in den Qumrantexten und im Neuen Testament*, SUNT 3, Göttingen: Vandenhoeck & Ruprecht, 1964.
——, "Das Problem der Schriftgemäßheit der Ethik", *Handbuch der christlichen Ethik*, ed. A. Hertz et al., 1, Freiburg/Gütersloh: Herder/Mohn, 1978, pp.243-269.
Beckwith, R.T., "The Significance of the Calendar for Interpreting Essene Chronology and Eschatology', *RQ* 9 (1980) 167-202.
——, "The Earliest Enoch Literature and its Calendar: Marks of their Origin, Date and Motivation", *RQ* 10 (1981) 365-403.
——, "The Pre-History and Relationships of the Pharisees, Sadducees and the Essenes: A Tentative Reconstruction", *RQ* 11 (1982) 3-46.

Begrich, J., "Sofer und Mazkir: Ein Beitrag zur inneren Geschichte des davidisch-salomonischen Großreiches und des Königreiches Juda", *ZAW* 35 (1940) 1-29.

Benoit, P., "L'hymne christologique de Col 1,15-20: Jugement critique sur l'état des recherches", *Christianity, Judaism and other Greco-Roman Cults*, FS M. Smith, SJLA, 1, Leiden: Brill, 1975, pp.226-263.

——, "Genèse et évolution de la pensée paulinienne", *Paul de Tarse*, ed. L. de Lorenzi, 1979, pp.75-100.

Berger, K., *Die Gesetzesauslegung Jesu: Ihr historischer Hintergrund im Judentum und im Alten Testament*, Teil 1: Markus und Parallelen, WMANT 40, Neukirchen-Vluyn: Neukirchener Verlag, 1972.

Best, E., "The Power and the Wisdom of God: 1 Corinthians 1,18-25", *Paolo a una chiesa divisa (1Co 1-4)*, ed. L. de Lorenzi, 1980, pp.9-39.

Betz, H.D., "Geist, Freiheit und Gesetz", *ZThK* 71 (1974) 78-93.

Betz, O., *Offenbarung und Schriftforschung in der Qumransekte*, WUNT 6, Tübingen: Mohr, 1960.

Bietenhard, H., "Die Handschriftenfunde vom Toten Meer (Hirbet Qumran) und die Essener-Frage. Die Funde in der Wüse Juda", *ANRW* II/19,1 (1979) 704-778.

Black, M., "The Christological Use of the Old Testament in the New Testament", *NTS* 18 (1971/72) 1-14.

Blank, J., *Paulus und Jesus: Eine theologische Grundlegung*, StANT 18, München: Kösel, 1968.

——, "Erwägungen zum Schriftverständnis des Paulus", *Rechtfertigung*, FS E. Käsemann, ed. J. Friedrich et al., Tübingen: Mohr, 1976, pp.37-56.

——, "Gesetz und Geist", *The Law of the Spirit in Rom 7 and 8*, ed. L. de Lorenzi, 1976, pp.73-100.

Blenkinsopp, J., *Wisdom and Law in the Old Testament: The Ordering of Life in Israel and Early Judaism*, Oxford: University Press, 1983.

Bonnard, P.E., *La Sagesse en personne annoncée et venue: Jésus Christ*, Lectio Divina 44, Paris: Cerf, 1966.

——, "De la Sagesse personnifiée dans l'Ancien Testament à la Sagesse en personne dans le Nouveau", *BETL* 51 (1979) 117-149.

Bornkamm, G., "Das missionarische Verhalten des Paulus nach 1 Kor 9,19-23 und in der Apostelgeschichte" (1966), *Geschichte und Glaube: Zweiter Teil*, Gesammelte Aufsätze, 4, BEvTh 53, München: Kaiser, 1971, pp.149-161.

——, *Das Ende des Gesetzes: Paulusstudien*, Gesammelte Aufsätze, 1, BEvTh 16, München: Kaiser, ^{5}1966.

Brandenburger, E., *Adam und Christus: Exegetisch-religionsgeschichtliche Untersuchung zu Röm. 5,12-21 (1. Kor. 15)*, WMANT 7, Neukirchen-Vluyn: Neukirchener Verlag, 1962.

——, *Fleisch und Geist: Paulus und die dualistische Weisheit*, WMANT 29, Neukirchen-Vluyn: Neukirchener Verlag, 1968.

——, *Die Verborgenheit Gottes im Weltgeschehen: Das literarische und theologische Problem des 4.Esrabuches*, AThANT 68, Zürich: Theologischer Verlag, 1981.

Braun, H., "Vom Erbarmen Gottes über den Gerechten: Zur Theologie der Psalmen Salomos", *ZNW* 43 (1950/51) 1-54.

——, *Spätjüdisch-häretischer und frühchristlicher Radikalismus: Jesus von Nazareth und die essenische Qumransekte*, BHTh 24, 2 vols., Tübingen: Mohr, 1957.

——, *Qumran und das Neue Testament*, 2 vols., Tübingen: Mohr, 1966.

Breitenstein, U., *Beobachtungen zu Sprache, Stil und Gedankengut des Vierten Makkabäerbuches*, Diss. Basel, 1974, Basel: Schwabe, ^{2}1978.

Brekelmans, C., "Wisdom Influence in Deuteronomy", *BETL* 51 (1979) 28-38.

Bring, R., *Christus und das Gesetz: Die Bedeutung des Gesetzes des Alten Testaments*

nach Paulus und sein Glauben an Christus, Leiden: Brill, 1969.
Brinsmead, B.H., *Galatians — Dialogical Response to Opponents*, SBLDS 65, Chico: Scholars Press, 1982.
Brooke, G., "Qumran Pesher: Towards the Redefinition of a Genre", *RQ* 10 (1981) 483-503.
Brownlee, W.H., "The Background of Biblical Interpretation at Qumran", *BETL* 46 (1978) 183-193.
Bruce, F.F., *Biblical Exegesis in the Qumran Texts*, Exegetica III/1, Den Haag: Van Keulen, 1959.
—, "Paul and the Law of Moses", *BJRL* 57 (1974/75) 259-279.
—, *Paul: Apostle of the Free Spirit*, Exeter: Paternoster, 1977.
Bultmann, R., *Glauben und Verstehen*, Gesammelte Aufsätze, 4 vols., Tübingen: Mohr, 1952-1965.
—, *Theology of the New Testament*, 2 vols., London: SCM, 1965.
Burchard, C., *Der dreizehnte Zeuge: Traditions- und kompositionsgeschichtliche Untersuchungen zu Lukas' Darstellung der Frühzeit des Paulus*, FRLANT 103, Göttingen: Vandenhoeck & Ruprecht, 1970.
Burger, C., *Schöpfung und Versöhnung: Studien zum liturgischen Gut im Kolosser- und Epheserbrief*, WMANT 46, Neukirchen-Vluyn: Neukirchener Verlag, 1975.
Cambier, J.M., "La liberté chrétienne est et personnelle et communautaire (Rm 14,1-15, 13)", *Freedom and Love: The Guide for Christian Life*, ed. L. de Lorenzi, 1981, pp.57-84.
Campbell, W.S., "Christ as the End of the Law: Romans 10,4", *Studia Biblica 1978, III: Papers on Paul and other New Testament Authors*, ed. E.A. Livingstone, JSNT Supplement Series 3, Sheffield, 1980, pp.73-81.
Caquot, A., "Le messianisme Qumrânien", *Qumrân: Sa piété, sa théologie et son milieu*, BETL 46, ed. M. Delcor, Leuven: University Press, 1978, pp.231-247.
Carmichael, C.M., "Deuteronomic Laws, Wisdom, and Historical Tradition", *JSS* 12 (1967) 198-206.
—, "Forbidden Mixtures", *VT* 32 (1982) 394-415.
Carmignac, J., "Les rapports entre l'Ecclésiastique et Qumrân", *RQ* 3 (1961) 209-218.
Charlesworth, J.H., "A History of Pseudepigrapha Research: The Reemerging Importance of the Pseudepigrapha", *ANRW* II/19,1 (1979) 54-88.
—, "The Origin and Subsequent History of the Authors of the Dead Sea Scrolls: Four Transitional Phases Among the Qumran Essenes", *RQ* 10 (1980) 213-233.
Christ, F., *Jesus Sophia: Die Sophia-Christologie bei den Synoptikern*, AThANT 57, Zürich: Zwingli-Verlag, 1970.
Collange, J.F., *Enigmes de la deuxième épître de Paul aux Corinthiens: Etude exégétique de 2 Cor 2,14-7,4*, SNTS MS 18, Cambridge: University Press, 1972.
—, *De Jésus à Paul: L'éthique du Nouveau Testament*, Geneva: Labor et Fides, 1980.
Collins, J.J., *The Sibylline Oracles of Egyptian Judaism*, SBLDS 13, Missoula: Scholars Press, 1974.
—, "The Apocalyptic Technique: Setting and Function in the Book of the Watchers", *CBQ* 44 (1982) 91-111.
Collins, J.J., Nickelsburg, G.W.E., eds., *Ideal Figures in Ancient Judaism: Profiles and Paradigms*, SBLSCS 12, Chico: Scholars Press, 1980.
Conzelmann, H., *Theologie als Schriftauslegung: Ausätze zum Neuen Testament*, BEvTh 65, München: Kaiser, 1974.
—, "Die Mutter der Weisheit" (1964), *o.c.*, pp.167-176.
—, "Paulus und die Weisheit" (1965/66), *o.c.*, pp.177-190.
Coughenour, R.A., *Enoch and Wisdom: A Study of the Wisdom Elements in the Book of Enoch*, Ph.D. Diss. Case Western Reserve University, 1972, University Microfilms

72-18,677, Ann Arbor, Michigan.
Cranfield, C.E.B., "St. Paul and the Law", *SJTh* 17 (1964) 43-68.
Crenshaw, J.L., "Method in Determining Wisdom Influence Upon 'Historical' Literature", *JBL* 88 (1969) 129-142.
— —, "Wisdom", *Old Testament Form Criticism*, ed. J.H. Hayes, San Antonio: Trinity University Press, 1974, pp.225-264.
— —, "Prolegomenon", *Studies in Ancient Israelite Wisdom*, Selected by J.L. Crenshaw, New York: Ktav, 1976, pp.1-21.
— —, "Wisdom and Authority: Sapiential Rhetoric and its Warrants", *SVT* 32 (1981) 10-29.
— —, *Old Testament Wisdom: An Introduction*, London: SCM, 1982.
Crouch, J.E., *The Origin and Intention of the Colossian Haustafel*, FRLANT 109, Göttingen: Vandenhoeck & Ruprecht, 1972.
Cullmann, O., *The Christology of the New Testament*, London: SCM, 1959.
— —, "Les conséquences éthiques de la perspective paulinienne du temps de l'Église: Éthique entre le 'déjà' et le 'pas encore'", *Paul de Tarse*, ed. L. de Lorenzi, 1979, pp.559-574.
Dalbert, P., *Die Theologie der hellenistisch-jüdischen Missionsliteratur unter Ausschluß von Philo und Josephus*, Theologische Forschung 4, Hamburg: Reich, 1954.
Dautzenberg, G., *Urchristliche Prophetie: Ihre Erforschung, ihre Voraussetzungen im Judentum und ihre Struktur im ersten Korintherbrief*, BWANT 104, Stuttgart: Kohlhammer, 1975.
— —, "Paulus und das Alte Testament", *BiKi* 37 (1982) 21-27.
Davenport, G.L., "The 'Anointed of the Lord' in Psalms of Solomon 17", *Ideal Figures*, ed. J.J. Collins et al., Chico: Scholars Press, 1980, pp.67-92.
Davies, W.D., *Paul and Rabbinic Judaism: Some Rabbinic Elements in Pauline Theology*, London: SPCK, ²1955 (= 1962).
— —, *Torah in the Messianic Age and/or in the Age to Come*, JBL MS 7, Philadelphia: Society of Biblical Literature, 1952.
— —, "Paul and the Law: Reflections on Pitfalls in Interpretation", *HLJ* 29 (1978) 1459-1504.
— —, "Paul and the Law: Reflections on Pitfalls in Interpretation", *Paul and Paulinism*, FS C.K. Barrett, ed. M.D. Hooker et al., London: SPCK, 1982, pp.4-16.
Davis, J.A., *Wisdom and Spirit: An Investigation of 1 Corinthians 1,18-3,20 Against the Background of Jewish Sapiential Tradition in the Hellenistic-Roman Period*, Ph.D. Diss. Nottingham, 1982.
Deichgräber, R., *Gotteshymnus und Christushymnus in der frühen Christenheit: Untersuchungen zu Form, Sprache und Stil der frühchristlichen Hymnen*, SUNT 5, Göttingen: Vandenhoeck & Ruprecht, 1967.
Deidun, T.J., *New Covenant Morality in Paul*, AnBibl 89, Rome: Biblical Institute Press, 1981.
Delcor, M., ed., *Qumrân: Sa piété, sa théologie et son milieu*, BETL 46, Leuven: University Press, 1978.
Denis, A.M., *Les thèmes de connaissance dans le Document de Damas*, Studia hellenistica 15, Leuven: Publications Universitaires, 1967.
— —, *Introduction aux pseudépigraphes grecs d'Ancien Testament*, SVTP 1, Leiden: Brill, 1970.
Dexinger, F., *Henochs Zehnwochenapokalypse und offene Probleme der Apokalyptikforschung*, SPB 29, Leiden: Brill, 1977.
— —, "Die Sektenproblematik im Judentum", *Kairos* 21 (1979) 273-287.

Dimant, D., "The Biography of Enoch and the Books of Enoch", *VT* 33 (1983) 14-29.
Dodd, C.H., "'Εννομος Χριστοῦ", *Studia Paulina*, FS J.de Zwaan, ed. J.N. Sevenster et al., 1953, pp.96-110 (= *More New Testament Studies*, Manchester: University Press, 1968, pp.134-148).
Domkowski Hopkins, D., "The Qumran Community and 1 Q Hodayot: A Reassessment", *RQ* 10 (1981) 323-364.
Drane, J.W., "Tradition, Law and Ethics in Pauline Theology", *NovTest* 16 (1974) 167-178.
——, *Paul, Libertine or Legalist? A Study in the Theology of the Major Pauline Epistles*, London: SPCK, 1975.
Dubarle, A.M., *Les sages d'Israel*, Lectio Divina 1, Paris: Cerf, 1948.
Dülmen, A. van, *Die Theologie des Gesetzes bei Paulus*, SBM 5, Stuttgart: Katholisches Bibelwerk, 1968.
Duesberg, H., Fransen, I., *Les scribes inspirés: Introduction aux livres sapientiaux de la Bible*, edition remaniée, Paris: Beyaert, [2]1966.
Dunn, J.D.G., *Jesus and the Spirit: A Study of the Religious and Charismatic Experience of Jesus and the First Christians as Reflected in the New Testament*, London: SCM, [2]1978.
——, *Christology in the Making: A New Testament Inquiry into the Origins of the Doctrine of Incarnation*, London: SCM, 1980.
Dupont-Sommer, A., "Trente années de recherches sur les manuscrits de la Mer Morte (1947-1977)", *CRAI* 1978, pp.659-677.
Eberharter, A., *Der Kanon des Alten Testaments zur Zeit des Ben Sira, auf Grund der Beziehungen des Sirachbuches zu den Schriften des Alten Testaments dargestellt*, Münster: Aschendorff, 1911.
Eckstein, H.J., *Der Begriff Syneidesis bei Paulus: Eine neutestamentlich-exegetische Untersuchung*, Diss. Tübingen, 1979.
Eichholz, G., *Die Theologie des Paulus im Umriß*, Neukirchen-Vluyn: Neukirchener Verlag, 1972.
Eissfeldt, O., *Der Maschal im Alten Testament: Eine wortgeschichtliche Untersuchung nebst einer literargeschichtlichen Untersuchung der* משל *genannten Gattungen 'Volkssprichwort' und 'Spottlied'*, Giessen: Töpelmann, 1913.
——, *Einleitung in das Alte Testament unter Einschluß der Apokryphen und Pseudepigraphen*, Tübingen: Mohr, [4]1976.
Ellis, E.E., " 'Wisdom' and 'Knowledge' in 1 Corinthians", *TyndB* 25 (1974) 82-98.
Falk, Z.W., *Introduction to Jewish Law of the Second Commonwealth*, AGSU 11, 2 vols., Leiden: Brill, 1972/1978.
Festorazzi, F., "Coherence and Value of the Old Testament in Paul's Thought", *Paul de Tarse*, ed. L. de Lorenzi, 1979, pp.165-173.
——, "Originalità della morale cristiana secondo San Paolo", *Dimensions de la vie chrétienne*, ed. L. de Lorenzi, 1979, pp.237-256.
Feuillet, A., "La création de l'univers 'dans le Christ' d'après 1 Épître aux Colossiens (1,16a)", *NTS* 12 (1965/66) 1-9.
——, *Le Christ Sagesse de Dieu d'après les Épîtres Pauliniennes*, EB, Paris: Gabalda, 1966.
——, "Loi ancienne et morale chrétienne d'après l'Épître aux Romains", *NRTh* 92 (1970) 785-805.
——, "Loi de Dieu, loi du Christ et loi de l'Ésprit d'après les épîtres pauliniennes: les rapports de ces trois lois avec la Loi Mosaique", *NovTest* 22 (1980) 29-65.
Fichtner, J., *Die altorientalische Weisheit in ihrer israelitisch-jüdischen Ausprägung: Eine Studie zur Nationalisierung der Weisheit in Israel*, BZAW 62, Giessen: Töpelmann, 1933.

Fiddes, P.S., *The Hiddenness of Wisdom in the Old Testament and Later Judaism*, Diss. Oxford, 1976.
Finance, J. de, "La sophia chez St. Paul", *RSR* 25 (1935) 385-417.
Fischer, J.A., "Ethics and Wisdom", *CBQ* 40 (1978) 293-310.
Fitzmyer, J.A., "The Use of Explicit Old Testament Quotations in Qumrân Literature and in the New Testament", *NTS* 7 (1961/62) 297-333.
——, "The Aramaic 'Elect of God' Text from Qumran Cave IV", *CBQ* 27 (1965) 348-372.
——, "Glory Reflected on the Face of Christ (2Cor 3,7-4,6) and a Palestinian Jewish Motif", *ThSt* 42 (1981) 630-644.
Flusser, D., "The Jewish Religion in the Second Temple Period", *WHJP* I/8 (1977) 3-40.
Friedrich, G., "Das Gesetz des Glaubens: Röm 3,27", *ThZ* 10 (1954) 401-417 (= *Auf das Wort kommt es an*, Gesammelte Aufsätze, ed. J.H. Friedrich, Göttingen: Vandenhoeck & Ruprecht, 1978, pp.107-122).
Froitzheim, F., *Christologie und Eschatologie bei Paulus*, Forschung zur Bibel 35, Stuttgart: Katholisches Bibelwerk/Echter, 1979.
Furnish, V.P., *Theology and Ethics in Paul*, Nashville: Abingdon, 1968.
Gabathuler, H.J., *Jesus Christus: Haupt der Kirche — Haupt der Welt. Der Christushymnus Colosser 1,15-20 in der theologischen Forschung der letzten 130 Jahre*, AThANT 45, Zürich: Zwingli Verlag, 1965.
Gabrion, H., "L'interprétation de l'Écriture dans la littérature de Qumran", *ANRW* II/19,1 (1979) 779-848.
Galitis, G., "Das Wesen der Freiheit: Eine Untersuchung zu 1 Kor 9 und seinem Kontext", *Freedom and Love: The Guide for Christian Life*, ed. L. de Lorenzi, 1981, pp. 127-141.
Gammie, J.G., "Spatial and Ethical Dualism in Jewish Wisdom and Apocalyptic Literature", *JBL* 93 (1974) 356-385.
Garnet, P., *Salvation and Atonement in the Qumran Scrolls*, WUNT II/3, Tübingen: Mohr, 1977.
——, "Qumran Light on Pauline Soteriology", *Pauline Studies*, FS F.F. Bruce, ed. D.A. Hagner et al., Exeter: Paternoster, 1980, pp.19-32.
Geffcken, J., *Komposition und Entstehungszeit der Oracula Sibyllina*, TU 23, Leipzig: Hinrichs, 1903.
Georgi, D., "Der vorpaulinische Hymnus Phil. 2,6-11", *Zeit und Geschichte*, FS R. Bultmann, ed. E. Dinkler, Tübingen: Mohr, 1964, pp.263-293.
——, *The Records of Jesus in the Light of Ancient Accounts of Revered Men*, Protocol of the 4th Colloquy of the Center for Hermeneutical Studies in Hellenistic and Modern Culture, Berkeley: University of California, 1975.
Gerhardsson, B., *The Ethos of the Bible*, ET by S. Westerholm, Philadelphia: Fortress, 1981.
Gerstenberger, E., *Wesen und Herkunft des 'Apodiktischen Rechts'*, WMANT 20, Neukirchen-Vluyn: Neukirchener Verlag, 1965.
——, "Zur alttestamentlichen Weisheit", *VuF* 14 (1969) 28-44.
Gese, H., *Lehre und Wirklichkeit in der alten Weisheit: Studien zu den Sprüchen Salomos und zu dem Buche Hiob*, Tübingen: Mohr, 1958.
——, "Das Gesetz", *Zur biblischen Theologie: Alttestamentliche Vorträge*, BEvTh 78, München: Kaiser, 1977, pp.55-84.
——, "Wisdom, Son of Man, and the Origins of Christology: The Consistent Development of Biblical Theology", *HBT* 3 (1981) 23-57.
Gilbert, M., "L'éloge de la Sagesse (Siracide 24)", *RThL* 5 (1974) 326-348.
——, ed., *La Sagesse de L'Ancien Testament*, BETL 51, Leuven: University Press, 1979.
Glasson, T.F., "Colossians 1,18.15 and Sirach 24", *JBL* 86 (1967) 214-216.

Goppelt, L., *Theologie des Neuen Testaments*, ed. J. Roloff, 2 vols., Göttingen: Vandenhoeck & Ruprecht, 1976.

Grabbe, L.L., "Chronography in 4 Ezra and 2 Baruch", *SBL 1981 Seminar Papers*, ed. K.H. Richards, Chico: Scholars Press, 1981, pp.49-63.

Grabner-Haider, A., *Paraklese und Eschatologie bei Paulus: Mensch und Welt im Anspruch der Zukunft Gottes*, NTA NF 4, Münster: Aschendorff, 1968.

Grech, P., "Christological Motives in Pauline Ethics", *Paul de Tarse*, ed. L. de Lorenzi, 1979, pp.541-558.

Green, W.S., ed., *Persons and Institutions in Early Rabbinic Judaism*, BJS 3, Missoula: Scholars Press, 1977.

——, ed., *Approaches to Ancient Judaism: Theory and Practice*, BJS 1, Missoula: Scholars Press, 1978.

——, ed., *Approaches to Ancient Judaism: Volume II*, BJS 9, Chico: Scholars Press, 1980.

Grözinger, K.E., ed., *Qumran*, Wege der Forschung 410, Darmstadt: Harrassowitz, 1981.

Gruenwald, I., "Jewish Apocalyptic Literature", *ANRW* II/19,1 (1979) 89-118.

Guttmann, A., *Rabbinic Judaism in the Making: A Chapter in the History of the Halakhah from Ezra to Judah I*, Detroit: Wayne State University Press, 1970.

Hadas, M., *The Third and Fourth Books of Maccabees*, New York: Harper, 1953.

Hagner, D.A., Harris, M.J., eds., *Pauline Studies*, FS F.F. Bruce, Exeter: Paternoster, 1980.

Hahn, F., "Methodenprobleme einer Christologie des Neuen Testaments", *VuF* 15 (1970) 3-41.

——, *Christologische Hoheitstitel: Ihre Geschichte im frühen Christentum*, FRLANT 83, Göttingen: Vandenhoeck & Ruprecht, ^{4}1974.

——, "Das Gesetzesverständnis im Römer- und Galaterbrief", *ZNW* 67 (1976) 29-63.

——, "Teilhabe am Heil und Gefahr des Abfalls: Eine Auslegung von 1 Kor 10,1-22", *Freedom and Love*, ed. L. de Lorenzi, 1981, pp.149-171.

——, "Die christologische Begründung urchristlicher Paränese", *ZNW* 72 (1981) 88-99.

Halson, B.R., *Hokmah — Sophia: A Study of Wisdom in the Hellenistic Age*, Ph. D. Diss. Liverpool, 1972.

Halter, H., *Taufe und Ethos: Paulinische Kriterien für das Proprium christlicher Moral*, FThS 106, Freiburg: Herder, 1977.

Hamerton-Kelly, R.G., *Pre-existence, Wisdom, and the Son of Man: A Study of the Idea of Pre-existence in the New Testament*, SNTS MS 21, Cambridge: University Press, 1973.

Hanson, A.T., *Studies in Paul's Technique and Theology*, London: SPCK, 1974.

——, "The Midrash in II Corinthians 3", *JSNT* 9 (1980) 2-28.

Harnisch, W., *Verhängnis und Verheissung der Geschichte: Untersuchungen zum Zeit- und Geschichtsverständnis im 4. Buch Esra und in der syr. Baruchapokalypse*, FRLANT 97, Göttingen: Vandenhoeck & Ruprecht, 1969.

——, *Eschatologische Existenz: Ein exegetischer Beitrag zum Sachanliegen von 1 Thessalonicher 4,13-5,11*, FRLANT 110, Göttingen: Vandenhoeck & Ruprecht, 1973.

——, "Die Ironie der Offenbarung: Exegetische Erwägungen zur Zionsvision im 4. Buch Esra", *SBL 1981 Seminar Papers*, ed. K.H. Richards, Chico: Scholars Press, 1981, pp.79-104.

Harrington, D.J., "The Wisdom of the Scribe According to Ben Sira", *Ideal Figures in Ancient Judaism*, ed. J.J. Collins et al., SBLSCS 12, Chico: Scholars Press, 1980, pp.181-188.

Hartman, L., *Asking for a Meaning: A Study of 1 Enoch 1-5*, Lund: CWK Gleerup, 1979.

Hasenstab, R., *Modelle paulinischer Ethik: Beiträge zu einem Autonomie-Modell aus*

paulinischem Geist, Tübinger Theologische Studien 11, Mainz: Matthias-Grünewald -Verlag, 1977.
Haspecker, J., *Gottesfurcht bei Jesus Sirach: Ihre religiöse Struktur und ihre literarische und doktrinäre Bedeutung*, AnBibl 30, Rome: Biblical Institute Press, 1967.
Hegermann, H., *Die Vorstellung vom Schöpfungsmittler im hellenistischen Judentum und Urchristentum*, TU 82, Berlin: Akademie-Verlag, 1961.
Heiligenthal, R., "Strategien konformer Ethik im Neuen Testament am Beispiel von Röm. 13,1-7", *NTS* 29 (1983) 55-61.
Heinisch, P., *Personifikationen und Hypostasen im Alten Testament und im Alten Orient*, Münster: Aschendorff, 1921.
Helfmeyer, F.J., " 'Gott nachfolgen' in den Qumrantexten", *RQ* 7 (1969) 81-104.
Hengel, M., "Die Ursprünge der christlichen Mission", *NTS* 18 (1971/72) 15-38.
——, "Anonymität, Pseudepigraphie und 'Literarische Fälschung' in der jüdisch-hellenistischen Literatur", *Pseudepigrapha*, 1, ed. K. von Fritz, Geneva: Vandoeuvres, 1972, pp.229-308.
——, *Judentum und Hellenismus: Studien zu ihrer Begegnung unter besonderer Berücksichtigung Palästinas bis zur Mitte des 2. Jahrhunderts v. Chr.*, WUNT 10, Tübingen: Mohr, ²1973.
——, "Zwischen Jesus und Paulus: Die 'Hellenisten', die 'Sieben' und Stephanus (Apg 6,1-15; 7,54-8,3)", *ZThK* 72 (1975) 151-206.
——, *The Son of God: The Origin of Christology and the History of Jewish-Hellenistic Religion*, ET by J. Bowden, London: SCM, 1976.
——, "Qumran und der Hellenismus", *Qumran*, BETL 46, ed. M. Delcor, Leuven: University Press, 1978, pp.333-372.
——, "Jesus und die Tora", *ThBeitr* 9 (1978) 152-172.
——, "Jesus als messianischer Lehrer der Weisheit und die Anfänge der Christologie", *Sagesse et religion*, Paris, 1979, pp.148-188.
——, *Zur urchristlichen Geschichtsschreibung*, Stuttgart: Calwer, 1979.
——, *The Atonement: A Study of the Origins of the Doctrine in the New Testament*, ET by J. Bowden, London: SCM, 1981.
Hermisson, H.J., *Studien zur israelitischen Spruchweisheit*, WMANT 28, Neukirchen-Vluyn: Neukirchener Verlag, 1968.
——, "Weisheit und Geschichte", *Probleme biblischer Theologie*, FS G. von Rad, ed. H.W. Wolff, München: Kaiser, 1971, pp.136-154.
——, "Observations on the Creation Theology in Wisdom", *Israelite Wisdom*, FS S. Terrien, Missoula: Scholars Press, 1978, pp.43-57.
Herr, T., *Naturrecht aus der kritischen Sicht des Neuen Testaments*, Abhandlungen zur Sozialethik 11, München: Schöningh, 1976.
Hilsberg, P., "Das Gewissen im Neuen Testament", *Theologische Versuche* 9 (1977) 145-160.
Hodgson, R., *Die Quellen der paulinischen Ethik*, Diss. Heidelberg, 1976.
Höffken, P., "Warum schweigt Jesus Sirach über Esra?", *ZAW* 87 (1975) 184-201.
Hofius, O., *Der Christushymnus Philipper 2,6-11: Untersuchungen zu Gestalt und Aussage eines urchristlichen Hymnus*, WUNT 17, Tübingen: Mohr, 1976.
Holmberg, B., *Paul and Power: The Structure of Authority in the Primitive Church as Reflected in the Pauline Epistles*, CB NT Series 11, Lund: CWK Gleerup, 1978.
Holm-Nielsen, S., *Hodayot: Psalms from Qumran*, AThD 2, Aarhus: Universitetsforlaget, 1960.
——, "Religiöse Poesie des Spätjudentums", *ANRW* II/19,1 (1979) 152-186.
Holtz, T., "Zur Frage der inhaltlichen Weisungen bei Paulus", *ThLZ* 106 (1981) 385-399.
Hooker, M.D., Wilson, S.G., eds., *Paul and Paulinism*, FS C.K. Barrett, London: SPCK, 1982.

Horgan, M.P., *Pesharim: Qumran Interpretations of Biblical Books*, CBQ MS 8, Washington: Catholic Biblical Association, 1979.

Horsley, R.A., "The Background of the Confessional Formula in 1 Kor 8,6", *ZNW* 69 (1978) 130-135.

Hruby, K., "La Torah identifiée à la Sagesse et l'activité du 'Sage' dans la Tradition rabbinique", *Bible et Vie Chrétienne* 76 (1967) 65-78.

Hübner, H., "Pauli theologiae proprium", *NTS* 26 (1980) 445-473.

——, *Das Gesetz bei Paulus: Ein Beitrag zum Werden der paulinischen Theologie*, FRLANT 119, Göttingen: Vandenhoeck & Ruprecht, ³1982.

Huntemann, G., *Der verlorene Maßstab: Gottes Gebot im Chaos dieser Zeit*, Bad Liebenzell: VLM, 1983.

Huntjens, J.A., "Contrasting Notions of Covenant and Law in the Texts from Qumran", *RQ* 8 (1974) 361-380.

Jackson, B.S., *Essays in Jewish and Comparative Legal History*, SJLA 10, Leiden: Brill, 1975.

——, "The Concept of Religious Law in Judaism", *ANRW* II/19,1 (1979) 33-52.

——, ed., *Modern Research in Jewish Law*, Leiden: Brill, 1979.

——, ed., *Jewish Law in Legal History and the Modern World*, Leiden: Brill, 1980.

Jacob, E., "Wisdom and Religion in Sirach", *Israelite Wisdom*, FS S. Terrien, Missoula: Scholars Press, 1978, pp.247-260.

Jansen, H.L., *Die spätjüdische Psalmendichtung: Ihr Entstehungskreis und ihr 'Sitz im Leben'. Eine literaturgeschichtlich-soziologische Untersuchung*, Oslo: Kommisjon H.J. Dybwad, 1937.

Janssen, E., *Das Gottesvolk und seine Geschichte: Geschichtsbild und Selbstverständnis im palästinensischen Schrifttum von Jesus Sirach bis Jehuda ha-Nasi*, Neukirchen-Vluyn: Neukirchener Verlag, 1971.

Jaubert, A., *La notion d'Alliance dans le judaïsme aux abords de l'ère chrétienne*, Patristica Sorbonensia 6, Paris: Seuil, 1963.

Jeremias, G., *Der Lehrer der Gerechtigkeit*, SUNT 2, Göttingen: Vandenhoeck & Ruprecht, 1963.

Jeske, R.L., "The Rock was Christ: The Ecclesiology of 1 Corinthians 10", *Kirche*, FS G. Bornkamm, ed. D. Lührmann et al., Tübingen: Mohr, 1980, pp.245-255.

Jewett, R., *Paul's Anthropological Terms: A Study of their Use in Conflict Settings*, AGAJU 10, Leiden: Brill, 1971.

Joest, W., *Gesetz und Freiheit: Das Problem des Tertius Usus Legis bei Luther und die neutestamentliche Parainese*, Göttingen: Vandenhoeck & Ruprecht, ⁴1968.

Jonge, M. de, Woude, A.S. van der, "11QMelchizedek and the New Testament", *NTS* 12 (1966/67) 301-326.

Jongeling, B., *Le Rouleau de la Guerre des Manuscrits de Qumrân: Commentaire et traduction*, Assen: Van Gorcum, 1962.

Jüngel, E., *Paulus und Jesus: Eine Untersuchung zur Präzisierung der Frage nach dem Ursprung der Christologie*, Hermeneutische Untersuchungen zur Theologie 2, Tübingen: Mohr, ⁵1979.

Käsemann, E., *Exegetische Versuche und Besinnungen*, 2 vols., Göttingen: Vandenhoeck & Ruprecht, ⁶1970/³1970.

Kaiser, O., "Die Begründung der Sittlichkeit im Buche Jesus Sirach", *ZThK* 55 (1958) 51-63.

Kaligula, L., *The Wise King: Studies in Royal Wisdom as Divine Revelation in the Old Testament and its Environment*, CB OT Series 15, Lund: CWK Gleerup, 1980.

Kapelrud, A.S., "Der Bund in den Qumran-Schriften", *Bibel und Qumran*, FS H. Bardtke, ed. S. Wagner, Berlin: Evangelische Haupt-Gesellschaft, 1968, pp.137-149.

Kayatz, C., *Studien zu Proverbien 1-9*, WMANT 22, Neukirchen-Vluyn: Neukirchener Verlag, 1966.
Keck, L.E., "The Law and 'The Law of Sin and Death' (Rom 8,1-4): Reflections on the Spirit and Ethics in Paul", *The Divine Helmsman*, FS L.H. Silberman, ed. J.L. Crenshaw et al., New York: Ktav, 1980, pp.41-57.
Kehl, N., *Der Christushymnus im Kolosserbrief: Eine motivgeschichtliche Untersuchung zu Kol 1,12-20*, SBM 1, Stuttgart: Katholisches Bibelwerk, 1967.
Kim, S., *The Origin of Paul's Gospel*, WUNT II/4, Tübingen: Mohr, 1981.
Kimbrough, S.T., "The Ethic of the Qumran Community", *RQ* 6 (1969) 483-498.
Kittel, B.P., *The Hymns of Qumran: Translation and Commentary*, SBLDS 50, Chico: Scholar Press, 1981.
Klijn, A.F.J., "Textual Criticism of IV Ezra: State of Affairs and Possibilities", *SBL 1981 Seminar Papers*, ed. K.H. Richards, Chico: Scholars Press, 1981, pp.217-227.
Klinzing, G., *Die Umdeutung des Kultus in der Qumrangemeinde und im Neuen Testament*, SUNT 7, Göttingen: Vandenhoeck & Ruprecht, 1971.
Knibb, M.A., "The Date of the Parables of Enoch: A Critical Review", *NTS* 25 (1979) 345-359.
Knox, W.L., *St. Paul and the Church of the Gentiles*, Cambridge: University Press, 1939 (= 1961).
Koch, K. et al., eds., *Apokalyptik*, Wege der Forschung 365, Darmstadt: Wissenschaftliche Buchgesellschaft, 1982.
Koo, T.K., *Wisdom and Torah, with Special Reference to the Wisdom Psalms*, Ph.D. Diss. Edinburgh, 1979.
Koole, J.L., "Die Bibel des Ben Sira", *OTS* 14 (1965) 374-396.
Kramer, W., *Christos Kyrios Gottessohn: Untersuchungen zu Gebrauch und Bedeutung der christologischen Bezeichnungen bei Paulus und in den vorpaulinischen Gemeinden*, AThANT 44, Zürich: Zwingli-Verlag, 1963.
Küchler, M., *Frühjüdische Weisheitstraditionen: Zum Fortgang weisheitlichen Denkens im Bereich des frühjüdischen Jahweglaubens*, OBO 26, Freiburg/Göttingen: Universitätsverlag/Vandenhoeck & Ruprecht, 1979.
Kümmel, W.G., *Einleitung in das Neue Testament*, 18. Auflage, Heidelberg: Quelle & Meyer, 1973.
——, *Die Theologie des Neuen Testaments nach seinen Hauptzeugen: Jesus — Paulus — Johannes*, NTD Ergänzungsreihe 3, Göttingen: Vandenhoeck & Ruprecht, [4]1980.
Kuhn, H.W., *Enderwartung und gegenwärtiges Heil: Untersuchungen zu den Gemeindeliedern von Qumran*, SUNT 4, Göttingen: Vandenhoeck & Ruprecht, 1966.
——, "Der irdische Jesus bei Paulus als traditionsgeschichtliches und theologisches Problem", *ZThK* 67 (1970) 295-320.
Kuss, O., "Nomos bei Paulus", *Münchener Theologische Zeitschrift* 17 (1966) 173-227.
Ladd, G.E., *A Theology of the New Testament*, Grand Rapids: Eerdmans, [2]1975.
Lamarche, P., Le Dû, C., *Epître aux Romains V-VIII: Structure littéraire et sens*, Paris: Centre National de la Recherche Scientifique, 1980.
Lang, B., *Frau Weisheit: Deutung einer biblischen Gestalt*, Düsseldorf: Patmos, 1975.
——, "Schule und Unterricht im alten Israel", *BETL* 51 (1979) 186-201.
Larcher, C., *Études sur le Livre de la Sagesse*, EB, Paris: Gabalda, 1969.
Laub, F., *Eschatologische Verkündigung und Lebensgestaltung nach Paulus: Eine Untersuchung zum Wirken des Apostels beim Aufbau der Gemeinde in Thessalonike*, Biblische Untersuchungen 10, Regensburg: Pustet, 1973.
Lauer, S., "Eusebes Logismos in IV Macc.", *JJS* 6 (1955) 170-171.

Select Bibliography

Lauterbach, J.Z., *Rabbinic Essays*, New York: Ktav, 1973.

Lebram, J.C.H., "Die Theologie der späten Chokma und häretisches Judentum", *ZAW* 77 (1965) 202-211.

——, "Jerusalem, Wohnsitz der Weisheit", *Studies in Hellenistic Religions*, ed. M.J. Vermaseren, Leiden: Brill, 1979, pp.103-128.

Lehmann, M.R., "Ben Sira and the Qumran Literature", *RQ* 3 (1961) 103-116.

——, "The Temple Scroll as a Source of Sectarian Halakhah", *RQ* 9 (1979) 579-587.

Lella, A.A. di, *The Hebrew Text of Sirach: A Text-Critical and Historical Study*, The Hague: Mouton, 1966.

——, "Conservative and Progressive Theology: Sirach & Wisdom", *CBQ* 28 (1966) 139-154 (= *Studies in Ancient Israelite Wisdom*, ed. J.L. Crenshaw, New York: Ktav, 1976, pp.401-416).

Lévêque, J., "Le contrepoint théologique apporté par la réflexion sapientielle", *Questions disputées d'Ancien Testament: Méthode et théologie*, ed. C. Brekelmans, BETL 33, Leuven: University Press, 1974, pp.183-202.

Licht, J., "The Qumran Sect and its Scrolls", *WHJP* I/8 (1977) 125-152.

Lichtenberger, H., "Eine weisheitliche Mahnrede in den Qumranfunden (4Q185)", *Qumrân*, ed., M. Delcor, BETL 46, Leuven: Unviersity Press, 1978, pp.151-162.

——, *Studien zum Menschenbild in den Texten der Qumrangemeinde*, SUNT 15, Göttingen: Vandenhoeck & Ruprecht, 1980.

——, "Atonement and Sacrifice in the Qumran Community", *Approaches to Ancient Judaism*, 2, ed. W.S. Green, BJS 9, Leiden: Brill, 1980, pp.159-171.

Limbeck, M., *Die Ordnung des Heils: Untersuchungen zum Gesetzesverständnis des Frühjudentums*, Düsseldorf: Patmos, 1971.

——, *Von der Ohnmacht des Rechts: Untersuchungen zur Gesetzeskritik des Neuen Testaments*, Düsseldorf: Patmos, 1972.

Lindars, B., "Torah in Deuteronomy", *Words and Meanings*, FS D.W. Thomas, Cambridge: University Press, 1968, pp.117-136.

——, *Jesus Son of Man: A Fresh Examination of the Son of Man Sayings in the Gospels*, London: SPCK, 1983.

Lipscomb, W.L., "Wisdom at Qumran", *Israelite Wisdom*, FS S. Terrien, Missoula: Scholars Press, 1978, pp.277-285.

Löhr, M., *Bildung aus dem Glauben: Beiträge zum Verständnis der Lehrreden des Buches Jesus Sirach*, Diss. Bonn, 1975.

Lohse, E., "ὁ νόμος τοῦ πνεύματος τῆς ζωῆς: Exegetische Anmerkungen zu Röm 8,2", *Neues Testament und christliche Existenz*, FS H. Braun, ed. H.D. Betz et al., Tübingen: Mohr, 1973, pp.279-287.

——, "Zur Analyse und Interpretation von Röm 8,1-17", *The Law of the Spirit in Rom 7 and 8*, ed. L. de Lorenzi, 1976, pp.129-146.

——, "Kirche im Alltag: Erwägungen zur theologischen Begründung der Ethik im Neuen Testament", *Kirche*, FS G. Bornkamm, ed. D. Lührmann et al., Tübingen: Mohr, 1980, pp.401-415.

Lorenzi, L. de, ed., *The Law of the Spirit in Rom 7 and 8*, SMB: Sezione biblico-ecumenica 1, Rome: St. Paul's Abbey, 1976.

——, ed., *Paul de Tarse: Apôtre du notre temps*, SMB: Sezione paolina 1, Rome: St. Paul's Abbey, 1979.

——, ed., *Dimensions de la vie chrétienne (Rm 12-13)*, SBM: Sezione biblico-ecumenica 4, Rome: St. Paul's Abbey, 1979.

——, ed., *Paolo a una chiesa divisa (1Cor 1-4)*, SMB: Sezione biblico-ecumenica 5, Rome: St. Paul's Abbey, 1980.

——, ed., *Freedom and Love: The Guide for Christian Life (1Cor 8-10; Rm 14-15)*, SMB: Sezione biblico-ecumenica 6, Rome: St. Paul's Abbey, 1981.

Luck, U., "Das Weltverständnis in der jüdischen Apokalyptik, dargestellt am äthiopischen Henoch und am 4. Esra", *ZThK* 73 (1976) 283-305.
Lührmann, D., *Das Offenbarungsverständnis bei Paulus und in paulinischen Gemeinden*, WMANT 16, Neukirchen-Vluyn: Neukirchener Verlag, 1965.
——, "Ein Weisheitspsalm aus Qumran (11QPs^{a}XVIII)", *ZAW* 80 (1968) 87-98.
Luz, U., *Das Geschichtsverständnis des Paulus*, BEvTh 49, München: Kaiser, 1968.
Lyonnet, S., "Agapè et charismes selon 1Co 12,31", *Paul de Tarse*, ed. L. de Lorenzi, 1979, pp.509-527.
——, "La charité-plénitude de la loi (Rm 13,8-10)", *Dimensions de la vie chrétienne*, ed. L. de Lorenzi, 1979, pp.150-163.
Mack, B.L., *Logos und Sophia: Untersuchungen zur Weisheitstheologie im hellenistischen Judentum*, SUNT 10, Göttingen: Vandenhoeck & Ruprecht, 1973.
MacKenzie, R.A.F., "Ben Sira as Historian", *Trinification of the World*, FS F.E. Crowe, ed. T.A. Dunne et al., Toronto: Regis College Press, 1978, pp.312-327.
Maier, G., *Mensch und freier Wille: Nach den jüdischen Religionsparteien zwischen Ben Sira und Paulus*, WUNT 12, Tübingen: Mohr, 1971.
Maier, J., *Geschichte der jüdischen Religion: Von der Zeit Alexanders des Grossen bis zur Aufklärung*, Berlin/New York: de Gruyter, 1972.
——, Schreiner, J., eds., *Literatur und Religion des Frühjudentums: Eine Einführung*, Würzburg/Gütersloh: Echter/Mohn, 1973.
——, "Frühjüdische Literatur: Ein Überblick", *o.c.*, pp.117-122.
——, *Die Tempelrolle vom Toten Meer: Übersetzt und erklärt*, UTB 829, Basel/München: Reinhardt, 1978.
——, Schubert, K., *Die Qumran-Essener: Texte der Schriftrollen und Lebensbild der Gemeinde*, UTB 224, München/Basel: Reinhard, 1973.
Maillot, A., "Essai sur les citations vétérotestamentaires contenues dans Romains 9 à 11, ou comment se servir de la Torah pour montrer que le 'Christ est la fin de la Torah' ", *EThR* 57 (1982) 55-73.
Malfroy, J., "Sagesse et loi dans le Deutéronome", *VT* 15 (1965) 49-65.
Mansoor, M., *The Thanksgiving Hymns: Translated and Annotated with an Introduction*, STDJ 3, Leiden: Brill, 1961.
Mantel, H.D., *Studies in the History of the Sanhedrin*, Harvard Semitic Studies 17, Cambridge: Harvard University Press, [2]1965.
——, "The High-Priesthood and the Sanhedrin in the Time of the Second Temple", *WHJP* I/7 (1975) 264-283.
——, "The Development of the Oral Law During the Second Temple Period", *WHJP* I/8 (1977) 41-64.
Marböck, J., *Weisheit im Wandel: Untersuchungen zur Weisheitstheologie bei Ben Sira*, BBB 37, Bonn: Hanstein, 1971.
——, "Sirachliteratur seit 1966: Ein Überblick", *Theologische Revue* 71 (1975) 178-183.
——, "Gesetz und Weisheit: Zum Verständnis des Gesetzes bei Jesus Sirach", *BZ* 20 (1976) 1-21.
——, "Sir. 38,24-39,11: Der schriftgelehrte Weise. Ein Beitrag zu Gestalt und Werk Ben Siras", *BETL* 51 (1979) 293-316.
——, "Henoch – Adam – der Thronwagen: Zu frühjüdischen pseudepigraphischen Traditionen bei Ben Sira", *BZ* 25 (1981) 103-111.
Marcus, R., *Law in the Apocrypha*, Columbia University Oriental Studies 26, New York: AMS Press, 1966.
Marshall, I.H., "Palestinian and Hellenistic Christianity: Some Critical Remarks", *NTS* 19 (1972/73) 271-287.
Martin, R.P., *Carmen Christi: Philippians 2,5-11 in Recent Interpretation and in the Setting of Early Christian Worship*, SNTS MS 4, Cambridge: University Press, 1967.

Mattern, L., *Das Verständnis des Gerichtes bei Paulus*, AThANT 47, Zürich: Zwingli Verlag, 1966.
Mearns, C.L., "Dating the Similitudes of Enoch", *NTS* 25 (1979) 360-369.
Meisner, N., *Untersuchungen zum Aristeasbrief*, 2 vols., Diss. Kirchliche Hochschule Berlin, 1973 (not obtainable).
Mengel, B., *Studien zum Philipperbrief: Untersuchungen zum situativen Kontext unter besonderer Berücksichtigung der Frage nach der Ganzheitlichkeit oder Einheitlichkeit eines paulinischen Briefes*, WUNT II/8, Tübingen: Mohr, 1982.
Merk, O., *Handeln aus Glauben: Die Motivierungen der paulinischen Ethik*, Marburger Theologische Studien 5, Marburg: Elwert, 1968.
Merklein, H., "Zur Entstehung der urchristlichen Aussage vom präexistenten Sohn Gottes", *Zur Geschichte des Urchristentums*, Quaestiones Disputatae 87, ed. G. Dautzenberg et al., Freiburg: Herder, 1979, pp.33-62.
— —, "Die Auferweckung Jesu und die Anfänge der Christologie (Messias bzw. Sohn Gottes und Menschensohn)", *ZNW* 72 (1981) 1-26.
Mettinger, T.N.D., *Solomonic State Officials: A Study of the Civil Government Officials of the Israelite Monarchy*, CB OT Series 5, Lund: CWK Gleerup, 1971.
Meyer, P.W., "Romans 10,4 and the End of the Law", *The Divine Helmsman*, FS L.H. Silberman, ed. J.L. Crenshaw et al., New York: Ktav, 1980, pp.59-78.
Meyer, R., *Tradition und Neuschöpfung im antiken Judentum*, dargestellt an der Geschichte des Pharisäismus, BAL 110/2, Leipzig, 1965, pp.1-88.
Middendorp, T., *Die Stellung Jesu Ben Siras zwischen Judentum und Hellenismus*, Leiden: Brill, 1973.
Milik, J.T., "Milkî-ṣedeq et Milkî-rešaᶜ dans les anciens écrits juifs et chrétiens", *JJS* 23 (1972) 95-144.
— —, *The Books of Enoch: Aramaic Fragments of Qumrân Cave 4*, Oxford: Clarendon, 1976.
Moore, G.F., *Judaism in the First Centuries of the Christian Era: The Age of the Tannaim*, 3 vols., Cambridge: Harvard University Press, 11 1970.
Moore, R.D., "Personification of the Seduction of Evil: 'The Wiles of the Wicked Woman' ", *RQ* 10 (1981) 505-519.
Morgan, D.F., *Wisdom in the Old Testament Traditions*, Oxford: Blackwell, 1981.
Moule, C.F.D., "Obligation in the Ethic of Paul", *Christian History and Interpretation*, FS J. Knox, ed. W.R. Farmer et al., Cambridge: University Press, 1967, pp.389-406.
Mowinckel, S., "Psalms and Wisdom", *SVT* 3 (1955) 204-224.
Mueller, J.R., "A Prolegomenon to the Study of the Social Function of 4 Ezra", *SBL 1981 Seminar Papers*, ed. K.H. Richards, Chico: Scholars Press, 1981, pp.259-268.
Münchow, C., *Ethik und Eschatologie: Ein Beitrag zum Verständnis der frühjüdischen Apokalyptik mit einem Ausblick auf das Neue Testament*, Göttingen: Vandenhoeck & Ruprecht, 1981.
Munck, J., *Christ and Israel: An Interpretation of Romans 9-11*, Philadelphia: Fortress, 1967.
Mundle, W., "Das religiöse Problem des 4. Esrabuches", *ZAW* 6 (1929) 222-249.
Murphy, R.E., "Assumptions and Problems in Old Testament Wisdom Research", *CBQ* 29 (1967) 407-418.
— —, "The Interpretation of Old Testament Wisdom Literature", *Int* 23 (1969) 289-301.
— —, "Wisdom — Theses and Hypotheses", *Israelite Wisdom*, FS S. Terrien, Missoula: Scholars Press, 1978, pp.35-42.
Murphy-O'Connor, J., "A Literary Analysis of Damascus Document VI,2-VIII,3", *RB* 78 (1971) 210-232.
— —, "The Essenes and their History", *RB* 81 (1974) 215-244.
— —, "I Cor.VIII,6: Cosmology or Soteriology?", *RB* 85 (1978) 253-267.

—, "Freedom or the Ghetto (1 Co 8,1-13; 10,23-11,1)", *Freedom and Love*, ed. L. de Lorenzi, 1981, pp.7-38.

Nagata, T., *Philippians 2,5-11: A Case Study in the Contextual Shaping of Early Christology*, Ph.D. Diss. Princeton Theological Seminary, 1981.

Nel, P.J., "A Proposed Method for Determining the Context of the Wisdom Admonitions", *JNSL* 6 (1978) 33-39.

—, *The Structure and Ethos of the Wisdom Admonitions in Proverbs*, BZAW 158, Berlin/New York: de Gruyter, 1982.

Neusner, J., *The Idea of Purity in Ancient Judaism*, SJLA 1, Leiden: Brill, 1973.

—, *Early Rabbinic Judaism: Studies in Religion, Literature and Art*, SJLA 13, Leiden: Brill, 1975.

—, "The Formation of Rabbinic Judaism: Yavneh (Jamnia) from A.D. 70 to 100", *ANRW* II/19,2 (1979) 3-42.

—, *A History of the Mishnaic Law of Holy Things*, SJLA 30, 6 vols., Leiden: Brill, 1979-1980.

—, *Judaism: The Evidence of the Mishnah*, Chicago/London: University of Chicago Press, 1981.

Nickelsburg, G.W.E., "Enoch 97-104: A Study of the Greek and Ethiopic Texts", *Armenian and Biblical Studies*, ed. M.E. Stone, Sion Supplement 1, Jerusalem: St. James, 1976, pp.90-156.

—, "The Apocalyptic Message of 1 Enoch 92-105", *CBQ* 39 (1977) 309-328.

—, *Jewish Literature between the Bible and the Mishnah: A Historical and Literary Introduction*, London: SCM, 1981.

Niederwimmer, K., "Erkennen und Lieben: Gedanken zum Verhältnis von Gnosis und Agape im ersten Korintherbrief", *KuD* 11 (1965) 75-102.

—, *Der Begriff der Freiheit im Neuen Testament*, Theologische Bibliothek 11, Berlin: Töpelmann, 1966.

Nikiprowetzky, V., *La Troisième Sibylle*, Études Juives 9, Paris: Mouton, 1970.

Nissen, A., "Tora und Geschichte im Spätjudentum", *NovTest* 9 (1967) 241-277.

—, *Gott und der Nächste im antiken Judentum: Untersuchungen zum Doppelgebot der Liebe*, WUNT 15, Tübingen: Mohr, 1974.

Nötscher, F., *Zur theologischen Terminologie der Qumransekte*, BBB 10, Bonn, Hanstein, 1956.

Norden, E., *Agnostos Theos: Untersuchungen zur Formengeschichte religiöser Rede*, Leipzig/Berlin: Teubner, 1923.

Östborn G., *Tora in the Old Testament: A Semantic Study*, Lund: Ohlsson, 1945.

Offerhaus, U., *Komposition und Intention der Sapientia Salomonis*, Diss. Bonn 1981 (not available).

Osten-Sacken, P. von der, *Gott und Belial: Traditionsgeschichtliche Untersuchungen zum Dualismus in den Texten aus Qumran*, SUNT 6, Göttingen: Vandenhoek & Ruprecht, 1969.

—, *Die Apokalyptik in ihrem Verhältnis zu Prophetie und Weisheit*, Theologische Existenz heute 157, München: Kaiser, 1969.

—, *Römer 8 als Beispiel paulinischer Soteriologie*, FRLANT 112, Göttingen: Vandenhoeck & Ruprecht, 1975.

—, "Das paulinische Verständnis des Gesetzes im Spannungsfeld von Eschatologie und Geschichte", *EvTh* 37 (1977) 549-587.

—, "Das Evangelium als Einheit von Verheißung und Gesetz: Grundzüge paulinischer Theologie", *ThViat* 14 (1977/78) 87-108.

—, "Paulus und das Gesetz", *VIKJ* 8 (1978) 59-66.

——, "Die paulinische theologia crucis als Form apokalyptischer Theologie", *EvTh* 40 (1979) 477-496.
——, "Geist im Buchstaben: Vom Glanz des Mose und des Paulus", *EvTh* 41 (1981) 230-235.
Otzen, B., "Old Testament Wisdom Literature and Dualistic Thinking in Late Judaism", *SVT* 28 (1975) 146-157.
Patte, D., *Early Jewish Hermeneutic in Palestine*, SBLDS 22, Missoula: Scholars Press, 1975.
Paulsen, H., *Überlieferung und Auslegung in Römer 8*, WMANT 43, Neukirchen-Vluyn: Neukirchener Verlag, 1974.
Pearson, B.A., "Hellenistic-Jewish Wisdom Speculation and Paul", *Aspects of Wisdom in Judaism and Early Christianity*, ed. R.L. Wilken, London, 1975, pp.43-66.
Perdue, L.G., *Wisdom and Cult: A Critical Analysis of the Views of Cult in the Wisdom Literature of Israel and the Ancient Near East*, SBLDS 30, Missoula: Scholars Press, 1977.
Pfeifer, G., *Ursprung und Wesen der Hypostasenvorstellungen im Judentum*, Aufsätze und Vorträge zur Theologie und Religionsgeschichte 37, Stuttgart: Calwer Verlag, 1967.
Pfeiffer, R.H., *History of New Testament Times: With an Introduction to the Apocrypha*, New York: Harper, 1949.
Ploeg, J.P.M. van der, "Le Psaume 119 et la sagesse", *BETL* 51 (1979) 82-87.
Plöger, O., *Theocracy and Eschatology*, Oxford: Blackwell, 1968.
Pöhlmann, W., "Die hymnischen All-Prädikationen in Kol 1,15-20", *ZNW* 64 (1973) 53-74.
Pohlenz, M., *Die Stoa: Geschichte einer geistigen Bewegung*, 2 vols., Göttingen: Vandenhoeck & Ruprecht, 1948/1949.
Provence, T.E., " 'Who is Sufficient for these Things?': An Exegesis of 2 Corinthians 2, 15-3,18", *NovTest* 24 (1982) 54-81.
Pury, A. de, "Sagesse et révélation dans l'Ancien Testament", *RTP* 110 (1977) 1-50.
Rabinowitz, J., "The Qumran Hebrew Original of Ben Sira's Concluding Acrostic on Wisdom", *HUCA* 42 (1971) 173-184.
Rabinowitz, L.I., "The Halakhah as Reflected in Ben Sira" (hebr), *Papers of the 4th World Congress of Jewish Studies*, Jerusalem: World Union of Jewish Studies, 1967, vol. 1, pp.145-148.
Rad, G. von, *Theologie des Alten Testaments*, 2 vols., München: Kaiser, ^{4}1962/^{4}1965.
——, *Wisdom in Israel*, ET by J.D. Martin, London: SCM, 1972.
Räisänen, H., "Paul's Theological Difficulties with the Law", *Studia Biblica 1978, III: Papers on Paul and other New Testament Authors*, ed. E.A. Livingstone, JSNT Supplement Series 3, Sheffield, 1980, pp.301-320.
——, "Das 'Gesetz des Glaubens' (Rom.3,27) und das 'Gesetz des Geistes' (Rom.8,21)", *NTS* 26 (1980) 101-117.
——, *Paul and the Law*, WUNT 29, Tübingen: Mohr, 1983.
Raj, V.A.R., *The Cosmic Christ of Colossians*, Th.D. Diss. Concordia Seminary St. Louis, Mo., 1981.
Rankin, O.S., *Israel's Wisdom Literature: Its Bearing on Theology and the History of Religion*, Kerr Lectures 1933-36, Edinburgh: Clark, 1936.
Rau, E., *Kosmologie, Eschatologie und die Lehrautorität Henoch: Traditions- und formgeschichtliche Untersuchungen zum äthiopischen Henochbuch und zu verwandten Schriften*, Diss. Hamburg, 1970 (not obtainable).
Rayburn, R.S., *The Contrast Between the Old and New Covenants in the New Testament*, Ph.D. Diss. Aberdeen University, 1978.

Reese, J.M., *Hellenistic Influence on the Book of Wisdom and its Consequences*, AnBibl 41, Rome: Biblical Institute Press, 1970.
——, "Paul Proclaims the Wisdom of the Cross: Scandal and Foolishness", *BTB* 9 (1979) 147-153.
——, "Christ as Wisdom Incarnate: Wiser than Solomon, Loftier than Lady Wisdom", *BTB* 11 (1982) 44-47.
Reicke, B., "Da^cat and Gnosis in Intertestamental Literature", *Neotestamentica Semitica*, FS M. Black, ed. E.E. Ellis et al., Edinburgh: Clark, 1969, pp.245-255.
Reindl, J., "Weisheitliche Bearbeitung von Psalmen: Ein Beitrag zum Verständnis des Psalters", *SVT* 32 (1981) 333-356.
Reinmut, E., *Geist und Gesetz: Studien zu Voraussetzungen und Inhalt der paulinischen Paränese*, Diss. Halle, 1981.
Rendtorff, T., "Strukturen christlicher Ethik", *Handbuch der christlichen Ethik*, 1, ed. A. Hertz et al., Freiburg/Gütersloh:Herder/Mohn, 1978, pp.199-216.
Renker, A., *Die Tora bei Maleachi: Ein Beitrag zur Bedeutungsgeschichte von tôra im Alten Testament*, FThS 112, Freiburg: Herder, 1979.
Rhyne, C.T., *Faith Establishes the Law*, SBLDS 55, Chico: Scholars Press, 1981.
Richard, E., "Polemics, Old Testament, and Theology: A Study of 2 Cor 3,1-4,6", *RB* 88 (1981) 340-367.
Richter, W., *Recht und Ethos: Versuch einer Ortung des weisheitlichen Mahnspruchs*, StANT 15, München: Kösel, 1966.
Rickenbacher, O., *Weisheitsperikopen bei Ben Sira*, OBO 1, Freiburg/Göttingen: Universitätsverlag/Vandenhoeck & Ruprecht, 1973.
Ridderbos, H., *Paul: An Outline of his Theology*, ET by J.R. de Witt, Grand Rapids: Eerdmans, ²1977.
Riesner, R., *Jesus als Lehrer: Eine Untersuchung zum Ursprung der Evangelien-Überlieferung*, WUNT II/7, Tübingen: Mohr, 1981.
——, "Präexistenz und Jungfrauengeburt", *ThBeitr* 12 (1981) 177-187.
Ringgren, H., *Word and Wisdom: Studies in Hypostatization of Divine Qualities and Functions in the Ancient Near East*, Lund: Ohlsson, 1947.
Rissi, M., *Studien zum zweiten Korintherbrief: Der alte Bund - Der Prediger - Der Tod*, AThANT 56, Zürich: Zwingli Verlag, 1969.
Rivkin, E., "Ben Sira and the Non-Existence of the Synagogue: A Study in Historical Method", *In the Time of Harvest*, FS S. Silver, ed. D.J. Silver, New York, 1963, pp. 320-354.
——, "Ben Sira – The Bridge between Aaronide and Pharisaic Revolutions", *Eretz Israel* 12 (1975) 95-103.
——, *A Hidden Revolution*, Nashville, Abingdon, 1978.
Rössler, D., *Gesetz und Geschichte: Untersuchungen zur Theologie der jüdischen Apokalyptik und der pharisäischen Orthodoxie*, WMANT 3, Neukirchen-Vluyn: Neukirchener Verlag, 1960 (²1962).
Romaniuk, K., "Le Livre de la Sagesse dans le Nouveau Testament", *NTS* 14 (1967/68) 498-514.
——, "Les motifs parénétiques dans les écrits pauliniens", *NovTest* 10 (1968) 190-207.
——, *L'amour du Père et du Fils dans la sotériologie de Saint Paul*, AnBibl 15A, Rome: Biblical Institute Press, 1974.
——, "Le thème de la sagesse dans les documents de Qumran", *RQ* 9 (1978) 429-435.
Roon, A. van, "The Relation between Christ and the Wisdom of God According to Paul", *NovTest* 16 (1974) 207-239.
Roop, E.F., *A Form Critical Study of the Society Rule (1QS) at Qumran*, Ph.D. Claremont Graduate School 1972 University Microfilms 72-30,564, Ann Arbor, Michigan.

Rosso-Ubigli, L., "Il Documento di Damasco e la Halakah Settaria (Rassegna di Studi)", *RQ* 9 (1978) 357-399.
Rost, L., *Einleitung in die alttestamentlichen Apokryphen und Pseudepigraphen einschließlich der großen Qumran-Handschriften*, Heidelberg: Quelle & Meyer, 1971.
Rowland, C., *The Open Heaven: A Study of Apocalyptic in Judaism and Early Christianity*, London: SPCK, 1982.
Rüger, H.P., *Text und Textform im hebräischen Sirach: Untersuchungen zur Textgeschichte und Textkritik der hebräischen Sirachfragmente aus der Kairoer Geniza*, BZAW 112, Berlin/New York: de Gruyter, 1970.
Rylaarsdam, J.C., *Revelation in Jewish Wisdom Literature*, Chicago: University Press, 1946 (= 1974).

Sandelin, K.G., *Die Auseinandersetzung mit der Weisheit in 1. Korinther 15*, Stiftelsens för Abo Akademi Forskningsinstitut Nr. 12, Abo: Abo Akademi, 1976.
Sanders, E.P., *Paul and Palestinian Judaism: A Comparison of Patterns of Religion*, London: SCM, 1977.
— —, "On the Question of Fulfilling the Law in Paul and Rabbinic Judaism", *Donum Gentilicium*, FS D. Daube, ed. E. Bammel et al., Oxford: Clarendon, 1978, pp. 103-126.
Sanders, J.A., "Two Non-Canonical Psalms in 11QPs^a", *ZAW* 76 (1964) 57-75.
— —, "The Dead Sea Scrolls — A Quarter Century of Study", *BA* 36 (1973) 110-148.
— —, "Torah and Christ", *Int* 29 (1975) 372-390.
— —, *Torah and Canon*, Philadephia: Fortress, ^{3}1976.
— —,"Torah and Paul", *God's Christ and His People*, FS N. Dahl, ed. J. Jervell, Oslo: Universitetsforlaget, 1977, pp.132-140.
Sanders, J.T., *The New Testament Christological Hymns: Their Historical Religious Background*, SNTS MS 15, Cambridge: University Press, 1971.
— —, *Ethics in the New Testament: Change and Development*, London: SCM, 1975.
— —, "Ben Sira's Ethics of Caution", *HUCA* 50 (1979) 73-106.
Schade, H.H., *Apokalyptische Christologie bei Paulus: Studien zum Zusammenhang von Christologie und Eschatologie in den Paulusbriefen*, GThA 18, Göttingen: Vandenhoeck & Ruprecht, 1981.
Schelkle, K.H., *Theologie des Neuen Testaments. III: Ethos*, Düsseldorf: Patmos, 1970.
— —, *Paulus: Leben - Briefe - Theologie*, Erträge der Forschung 152, Darmstadt: Wissenschaftliche Buchgesellschaft, 1981.
Schenk, W., "Christus, das Geheimnis der Welt, als dogmatisches und ethisches Grundprinzip des Kolosserbriefes", *EvTh* 43 (1983) 138-155.
Schiffman, L.H., *The Halakhah at Qumran*, SJLA 16, Leiden: Brill, 1975.
— —, "The Temple Scroll in Literary and Philological Perspective", *Approaches to Ancient Judaism*, 2, BJS 9, ed. W.S. Green, Leiden: Brill, 1980, pp.143-159.
Schlier, H., "Die Erkenntnis Gottes nach den Briefen des Apostels Paulus", *Gott in Welt*, FS K. Rahner, ed. J.B. Metz et al., 1, Freiburg: Herder, 1964, pp.515-535 (= *Besinnung auf das Neue Testament*, Freiburg: Herder, ^{2}1967, pp.319-339).
— —, *Grundzüge einer paulinischen Theologie*, Freiburg: Herder, 1978.
Schmid, H.H., *Wesen und Geschichte der Weisheit: Eine Untersuchung zur altorientalischen Weisheitsliteratur*, BZAW 101, Berlin: Töpelmann, 1966.
Schnackenburg, R., *The Moral Teaching of the New Testament*, London: Burns & Oates, 1965, (= ^{4}1967).
Schnelle, U., *Gerechtigkeit und Christusgegenwart: Vorpaulinische und paulinische Tauftheologie*, GThA 24, Göttingen: Vandenhoeck & Ruprecht, 1983.
Schoeps, H.J., *Paul: The Theology of the Apostle in the Light of Jewish Religious History*, ET by H. Knight, Philadelphia: Westminster, 1961.

Schrage, W., "Zur formalethischen Deutung der paulinischen Paränese", *ZEE* 4 (1960) 207-233.
——, *Die konkreten Einzelgebote in der paulinischen Paränese: Ein Beitrag zur neutestamentlichen Ethik*, Gütersloh: Mohn, 1961.
——, "Zur Ethik der neutestamentlichen Haustafeln", *NTS* 21 (1975) 1-22.
——, "Korreferat zu 'Ethischer Pluralismus im Neuen Testament' ", *EvTh* 35 (1975) 402-407.
——, *Ethik des Neuen Testaments*, NTD Ergänzungsreihe 4, Göttingen: Vandenhoeck & Ruprecht, 1982.
Schubert, K., *Die jüdischen Religionsparteien in der neutestamentlichen Zeit*, SBS 43, Stuttgart: Katholisches Bibelwerk, 1970.
——, "Lebensbild der Gemeinde", *Die Qumran-Essener*, UTB 224, by J. Maier, K. Schubert, München/Basel: Reinhardt, 1973, pp.9-141.
Schüpphaus, J., *Die Psalmen Salomos: Ein Zeugnis Jerusalemer Theologie und Frömmigkeit in der Mitte des vorchristlichen Jahrhunderts*, ALGHJ 7, Leiden: Brill, 1977.
Schürer, E., *The History of the Jewish People in the Age of Christ (175 B.C. – A.D. 135)*, New English Edition by G. Vermes, F. Millar, M. Black, 2 vols., Edinburgh: Clark, 1973/1979.
Schürmann, H., " 'Das Gesetz des Christus' (Gal 6,2): Jesu Verhalten und Wort als letztgültige sittliche Norm nach Paulus", *Neues Testament und Kirche*, FS R. Schnackenburg, ed. J. Gnilka, Freiburg: Herder, 1974, pp.282-300 (= Schürmann, H., *Jesu ureigener Tod: Exegetische Besinnungen*, Freiburg: Herder, [2]1976, pp.97-120).
——, *Orientierungen am Neuen Testament: Exegetische Gesprächsbeiträge*, Düsseldorf: Patmos, 1978.
Schüssler Fiorenza, E., "Wisdom, Mythology and the Christological Hymns of the New Testament", *Aspects of Wisdom in Judaism and Early Christianity*, ed. R.L. Wilken, London, 1975, pp.17-41.
Schütz, J.H., *Paul and the Anatomy of Apostolic Authority*, SNTS MS 26, Cambridge: University Press, 1975.
Schweizer, E., *Erniedrigung und Erhöhung bei Jesus und seinen Nachfolgern*, AThANT 28, Zürich: Zwingli Verlag, (1955) [2]1962.
——, *Neotestamentica: Deutsche und englische Aufsätze 1951-1963*, Zürich: Zwingli Verlag, 1963.
——, "Zur Herkunft der Präexistenzvorstellung bei Paulus" (1959), *o.c.*, pp.105-109.
——, "Die Kirche als Leib Christi in den paulinischen Antilegomena" (1961), *o.c.*, pp.293-316.
——, "Aufnahme und Korrektur jüdischer Sophiatheologie im Neuen Testament" (1962), *o.c.*, pp.110-121.
——, *Beiträge zur Theologie des Neuen Testaments: Neutestamentliche Aufsätze (1955-1970)*, Zürich: Zwingli Verlag, 1970.
——, "Kolosser 1,15-20" (1969), *o.c.*, pp.113-144.
——, "Zum religionsgeschichtlichen Hintergrund der 'Sendungsformel' Gal 4,4f, Röm 8,3f, Joh 3,16f, 1 Joh 4,9" (1966), *o.c.*, pp.83-95.
——, "Ethischer Pluralismus im Neuen Testament", *EvTh* 35 (1975) 397-401.
——, "Zur neueren Forschung am Kolosserbrief", *Theologische Berichte*, ed. J. Pfammatter et al., Zürich: Theologischer Verlag, 1976, pp.163-191.
Scott, R.B.Y., "The Study of the Wisdom Literature", *Int* 24 (1970) 20-45.
——, *The Way of Wisdom in the Old Testament*, New York: Macmillan, 1971.
Sellin, G., "Das 'Geheimnis' der Weisheit und das Rätsel der 'Christuspartei' (zu 1 Kor 1-4)", *ZNW* 73 (1982) 69-96.

Sheppard, G.T., "Wisdom and Torah: The Interpretation of Deuteronomy Underlying Sirach 24,23", *Biblical and Near Eastern Studies*, FS W.S. LaSor, ed. G.A. Tuttle, Grand Rapids: Eerdmans, 1978, pp.166-176.

——, *Wisdom as a Hermeneutical Construct: A Study in the Sapientializing of the Old Testament*, BZAW 151, Berlin/New York, 1980.

Shields, B.E., *Creation in Romans*, Diss. theol. Tübingen, 1981.

Siebeneck, R.T., "May their Bones Return to Life! Sirach's Praise of the Fathers", *CBQ* 21 (1959) 411-428.

Shehan, P.W., "The Acrostic Poem in Sirach 51,13-30", *HThR* 64 (1971) 387-400.

Slomovic, E., "Toward an Understanding of the Exegesis in the Dead Sea Scolls", *RQ* 7 (1969) 3-16.

Smend, R., *Die Weisheit des Jesus Sirach erklärt*, Berlin: Reimers, 1906.

——, Luz, U., *Gesetz*, Biblische Konfrontationen 1015, Stuttgart: Kohlhammer, 1981.

Smitten, W.T. in der, *Esra: Quellen, Überlieferung und Geschichte*, SSN 15, Assen: Van Gorcum, 1973.

Spicq, C., *Agapè dans le Nouveau Testament: Analyse des textes*, EB, 3 vols., Paris: Gabalda, ³1966.

Stadelmann, H., *Ben Sira als Schriftgelehrter: Eine Untersuchung zum Berufsbild des vormakkabäischen Sofer unter Berücksichtigung seines Verhältnisses zu Priester-, Propheten- und Weisheitslehrertum*, WUNT II/6, Tübingen: Mohr, 1980.

Starky, J., "Un texte messianique araméen de la grotte 4 de Qumrân", *Mémorial du cinquantenaire de l'École des langues orientales anciennes de l'Institut Catholique de Paris 1914-1964*, Paris, 1964, pp.51-66.

Steck, O.H., *Israel und das gewaltsame Geschick der Propheten: Untersuchungen zur Überlieferung des deuteronomischen Geschichtsbildes im Alten Testament, Spätjudentum und Urchristentum*, WMANT 23, Neukirchen-Vluyn: Neukirchener Verlag, 1967.

Stoike, D.A., *'The Law of Christ': A Study of Paul's Use of the Expression in Galatians 6,2*, Th.D. Diss. School of Theology at Claremont, 1971, University Microfilms 71-30,520, Ann Arbor, Michigan.

Stone, M.E., "The Book of Enoch and Judaism in the Third Century B.C.E.", *CBQ* 40 (1978) 379-492.

Strecker, G., "Autonome Sittlichkeit und das Proprium der christlichen Ethik bei Paulus", *ThLZ* 104 (1979) 865-872.

Strugnell, J., "The Angelic Liturgy at Qumran, 4Q Serek Sîrôt ᶜOlam Haššabbat", *SVT* 7 (1960) 318-345.

——, "Notes en marge du volume V des 'Discoveries in the Judaean Desert of Jordan", *RQ* 7 (1970) 163-276.

Stuhlmacher, P., *Gerechtigkeit Gottes bei Paulus*, FRLANT 87, Göttingen: Vandenhoeck & Ruprecht, ²1966.

——, *Versöhnung, Gesetz und Gerechtigkeit: Aufsätze zur biblischen Theologie*, Göttingen: Vandenhoeck & Ruprecht, 1981.

——, "Die Gerechtigkeitsanschauung des Apostels Paulus", *o.c.*, pp.87-116.

——, "'Das Ende des Gesetzes': Über Ursprung und Ansatz der paulinischen Theologie" (1970), *o.c.*, pp.166-192.

——, "Achtzehn Thesen zur paulinischen Kreuzestheologie" (1976), *o.c.*, pp.192-208.

——, "Zur paulinischen Christologie" (1977), *o.c.*, pp.209-223.

——, "Das Gesetz als Thema biblischer Theologie" (1978), *o.c.*, pp.136-165.

Suggs, M.J., "'The Word is Near You': Rom 10,6-10 within the Purpose of the Letter", *Christian History and Interpretation*, FS J. Knox, ed. W.R. Farmer et al., Cambridge: University Press, 1967, pp.289-312.

—, *Wisdom, Christology and Law in Matthew's Gospel*, Cambridge, Mass.: Harvard University Press, 1970.
Suter, D.W., *Tradition and Composition in the Parables of Enoch*, SBLDS 47, Missoula: Scholars Press, 1979.
Synofzik, E., *Die Gerichts- und Vergeltungsaussagen bei Paulus: Eine traditionsgeschichtliche Untersuchung*, GThA 8, Göttingen: Vandenhoeck & Ruprecht, 1977.
Theisohn, J., *Der auserwählte Richter: Untersuchungen zum traditionsgeschichtlichen Ort der Menschensohngestalt der Bilderreden des Äthiopischen Henoch*, SUNT 12, Göttingen: Vandenhoeck & Ruprecht, 1975.
Theochares, A., "The Concept of Wisdom in the Ethiopic Book of Enoch" (Greek), *Deltion Biblikon Meleton* 1 (1972) 287-311.
Therrien, G., *Le discernement dans les écrits Pauliniens*, EB, Paris: Gabalda, 1973.
Thomas, C., *A Christian Theology of Judaism*, ET by H. Croner, New York: Paulist, 1980.
Thompson, A.L., *Responsibility for Evil in the Theodicy of IV Ezra*, SBLDS 29, Missoula: Scholars Press, 1977.
Unnik W.C. van, *Sparsa Collecta. The Collected Essays of W.C. van Unnik*, vol. 1: Evangelia, Paulina, Acta, SNT 29, Leiden: Brill, 1973.
—, *La littérature juive entre Tenach et Mischna. Quelques problèmes*, ReBi 9, Leiden: Brill, 1974.
Urbach, E.E., "Halakhah and History", *Jews, Greeks and Christians*, FS W.D. Davies, ed. R. Hamerton-Kelly et al., 1976, pp.112-128.
—, *The Sages: Their Concepts and Beliefs*, ET by I. Abrahams, Jerusalem: Magnes Press, ²1979.
Vanhoye, A., "Un médiateur des anges en Ga 3,19-20", *Bib* 59 (1978) 403-411.
Vawter, B., "Prov 8,22: Wisdom and Creation", *JBL* 99 (1980) 205-216.
Vermes, G., *Scripture and Tradition in Judaism: Haggadic Studies*, SPB 4, Leiden: Brill, ²1973.
—, "Sectarian Matrimonial Halakhah in the Damascus Rule", *JJS* 25 (1974) 197-202.
—, *Post-Biblical Jewish Studies*, SJLA 8, Leiden: Brill, 1975.
—, *The Dead Sea Scrolls: Qumran in Perspective*, London: Collins, 1977.
—, "The Essenes and History", *JJS* 32 (1981) 18-31.
Villiers, P.G.R. de, "Understanding the Way of God: Form, Function, and Message of the Historical Review in 4 Ezra 3,4-27", *SBL 1981 Seminar Papers*, ed. K.H. Richards, Chico: Scholars Press, 1981, pp.357-378. 1936.
Violet, B., *Die Esra-Apokalypse (IV. Esra). Erster Teil: Die Überlieferung*, GCS 18, Leipzig: Hinrichs, 1910.
—, *Die Apokalypsen des Esra und des Baruch in deutscher Gestalt*, GCS 32, Leipzig: Hinrichs, 1924.
Viteau, J., *Les Psaumes de Salomon: Introduction, texte Grec et traduction*, DEB I/4, Paris: Letouzey et Ané, 1911.
Viviano, B.T., *Study as Worship: Aboth and the New Testament*, SJLA 26, Leiden: Brill, 1978.
Vögtle, A., *Die Tugend- und Lasterkataloge im Neuen Testament*, Münster: Aschendorff, 1936.
—, "Paraklese und Eschatologie nach Röm 13,11-14", *Dimensions de la vie chrétienne*, ed. L. de Lorenzi, 1979, pp.179-194.
Vriezen, T.C., *An Outline of Old Testament Theology*, Oxford: Blackwell, 1958 (= 1970).
Weder, H., *Das Kreuz bei Paulus: Ein Versuch, über den Geschichtsbezug des christlichen Glaubens nachzudenken*, FRLANT 125, Göttingen: Vandenhoeck & Ruprecht, 1981.
Weimar, P., "Formen frühjüdischen Literatur: Eine Skizze", *Literatur und Religion des*

Frühjudentums, ed. J. Maier et al., Würzburg/Gütersohl: Echter/Mohn, 1973, pp.123-162.
Weinfeld, M., *Deuteronomy and the Deuteronomistic School,* Oxford: Clarendon, 1972.
Weiss, H.F., *Untersuchungen zur Kosmologie des hellenistischen und palästinensischen Judentums*, TU 97, Berlin: Akademie-Verlag, 1966.
——, "Schöpfung in Christus: Zur Frage der christologischen Begründung der Schöpfungstheologie im Neuen Testament", *Zeichen der Zeit* 31 (1977) 431-437.
Wendland, H.D., *Ethik des Neuen Testaments: Eine Einführung*, Göttingen: Vandenhoeck & Ruprecht, ²1975.
Wengst, K., *Christologische Formeln und Lieder des Urchristentums*, StNT, Göttingen: Vandenhoeck & Ruprecht, 1972.
Whedbee, J.W., *Isaiah and Wisdom*, Nashville: Abingdon, 1971.
Whybray, R.N., *Wisdom in Proverbs: The Concept of Wisdom in Proverbs 1-9*, London: SCM, 1965.
——, *The Intellectual Tradition in the Old Testament*, BZAW 135, Berlin: de Gruyter, 1974.
Wibbing, S., *Die Tugend- und Lasterkataloge im Neuen Testament unter besonderer Berücksichtigung der Qumrantexte*, BZNW 25, Berlin: de Gruyter, 1959.
Wilckens, U., *Weisheit und Torheit: Eine exegetisch-religionsgeschichtliche Untersuchung zu 1. Kor. 1 und 2*, BHTh 26, Tübingen: Mohr, 1959.
——, "Was heißt bei Paulus: 'Aus Werken des Gesetzes wird kein Mensch gerecht'?" (1969), in *Rechtfertigung als Freiheit: Paulusstudien*, Neukirchen-Vluyn: Neukirchener Verlag, 1974, pp.77-109.
——, "Der Gehorsam gegen die Behörden des Staates im Tun des Guten: Zu Römer 13, 1-7", *Dimensions de la vie chrétienne*, ed. L. de Lorenzi, 1979, pp.85-130.
——, "Zu 1 Kor 2,1-16", *Theologia Crucis — Signum Crucis*, FS E. Dinkler, ed. C. Andresen et al., Tübingen: Mohr, 1979, pp.501-537.
——, "Das Kreuz Christi als die Tiefe der Weisheit Gottes: Zu 1. Kor 2,1-16", *Paolo a una chiesa divisa*, ed. L. de Lorenzi, 1980, pp.43-81.
——, "Statements on the Development of Paul's View of the Law", *Paul and Paulinism*, FS C.K. Barrett, ed. M.D. Hooker et al., London: SPCK 1982, pp.17-26.
——, "Zur Entwicklung des paulinischen Gesetzesverständnisses", *NTS* 28 (1982) 154-190.
Wilken, R.L., ed., *Aspects of Wisdom in Judaism and Early Christianity*, London: University of Notre Dame Press, 1975.
Windisch, H., "Die göttliche Weisheit der Juden und die paulinische Christologie", *Neutestamentliche Studien*, FS G. Heinrici, ed. A. Deissmann et al., Leipzig: Hinrichs, 1914, pp.220-234.
Wintle, B.C., *The Law of Moses and the Law of Christ: An Exegetical Study of Pauline Teaching on the Authority of the Law over the Christian Believer*, Ph.D. Diss. Manchester University, 1977.
Wolff, H.W., *Amos' geistige Heimat*, WMANT 18, Neukirchen-Vluyn: Neukirchener Verlag, 1964.
Worrell, J.E., *Concepts of Wisdom in the Dead Sea Scrolls*, Ph.D. Diss. Claremont Graduate School, 1968, University Microfilms 71-21,664, Ann Arbor, Michigan.
——, "עצה: 'Counsel' or 'Council' at Qumrân", *VT* 20 (1970) 65-74.
Young, E.M., " 'Fulfill the Law of Christ': An Examination of Gal 6,2", *SBT* 7 (1977) 31-42.
Zeilinger, F., *Der Erstgeborene der Schöpfung: Untersuchungen zur Formalstruktur und Theologie des Kolosserbriefes*, Wien: Herder, 1974.
Zeitlin, S., *Studies in the Early History of Judaism*, 4 vols., New York: Ktav, 1978.

Zeller, D., *Die weisheitlichen Mahnsprüche bei den Synoptikern*, Forschung zur Bibel 17, Würzburg: Echter, 1977.
Zenger, E., "Die späte Weisheit und das Gesetz", *Literatur und Religion des Frühjudentums*, ed. J. Maier et al., Würzburg/Gütersloh: Echter/Mohn, 1973, pp.43-56.
Ziener, G., *Die theologische Begriffssprache im Buche der Weisheit*, BBB 11, Bonn: Hanstein, 1956.
Ziesler, J.A., *The Meaning of Righteousness in Paul: A Linguistic and Theological Enquiry*, SNTS MS 20, Cambridge: University Press, 1972.
Zimmerli, W., "Zur Struktur der alttestamentlichen Weisheit", *ZAW* 51 (1933) 177-204.
——, "Ort und Grenze der Weisheit im Rahmen der alttestamentlichen Theologie" (1963), = "The Place and Limit of the Wisdom in the Framework of Old Testament Theology", *SJT* 17 (1964) 146-158.
Zink, J.K., *The Use of the Old Testament in the Apocrypha*, Ph.D. Diss. Duke University, 1963, University Microfilms 64-2847, Ann Arbor, Michigan.

Supplement (new publications)

Charlesworth, J.H., ed., *The Old Testament Pseudoepigrapha. Vol. 1: Apocalyptic and Testaments*, New York: Doubleday, 1983.
Dunn, J.D.G., "Mark 2,1-3,6: A Bridge Between Jesus an Paul in the Question of the Law", *NTS* 30 (1984) 395-415.
Hofius, O., "Das Gesetz des Mose und das Gesetz Christi", *ZThK* 80 (1983) 262-286.
Kertelge, K., "Gesetz und Freiheit im Galaterbrief", *NTS* 30 (1984) 382-394.
Martin B.L., "Paul on Christ and the Law", *JETS* 26 (1983) 271-282.
Mohrlang, R., *Matthew and Paul: A Comparison of Ethical Perspectives*, SNTS MS 48 Cambridge: University Press, 1984.
Sanders, E.P., *Paul, the Law and the Jewish People*, Philadelphia: Fortress Press, 1983.
Villiers, P.G.R. de, "Revealing the Secrets: Wisdom and the World in the Similitudes of Enoch", *Neotestamentica* 17 (1983) 50-68.
Westerholm, S., "'Letter' and 'Spirit': The Foundation of Pauline Ethics", *NTS* 30 (1984) 229-248.

Index of Passages

I. Old Testament

Genesis
1,14	43
1,14-16	43
1,26-27	253
1,31	18
2,11-14	72
2,18	314
2,24	313
3,5	254
3,22	254
6,12	3
18,19	3
19,31	3
31,35	3
47,26	36

Exodus
13,21	246
14,21-22	246
16,4	246
16,14-18	246
16,18	313
17,6	246
19-20	44
20,11	312
20,14	47
20,18-19	210
22,6-14	58
23,7	52
23,8	48
23,15	38, 51
29,28	36
30,23-24	61
34,20	38
34,28-35	282

Leviticus
5,1	58
5,14-26	51
5,21	58
6,11	36
18,4ff.	35
19,17-18	47
19,17	46
19,18	275
26,15	35
26,43	35

Numbers
6,24-27	218
14,41	34
18,8-19	51
18,9	51
18,11	51
18,19	51
20,7-14	246
21,18	209
22,18	34
24,13	34
24,17	187
25,13	62

Deuteronomy
1,5	212
1,12	212
1,13	212
1,15	212
4	84
4,1	36
4,5	36
4,6-14	210
4,6-8	12, 13, 84
4,6	5, 11, 13
4,8	36
4,12	210
4,14	36, 210
4,32	84
4,40	25, 82
4,45	36
5,1	36
5,10	56
5,18	47
5,22-23	210
5,31	34, 36
5,33	25, 82
6,1	34,36
6,2	25, 36, 82
6,5	56
6,7	211
6,20	36

6,25	34	*Judges*	
7,8	21	11,39	36
7,9	56		
7,11	34, 36	*1 Samuel*	
7,13	21	12,23	3
8,1	144	15,24	34
8,11	36		
10,12	56	*2 Samuel*	
10,13	21, 36	15,4	52
11,1	36	24,14	61
11,8-9	25		
11,8	34	*1 Kings*	
11,18-21	25	2,3	3
11,22	34	8,32	52
11,26ff.	3		
11,32	36	*2 Kings*	
12,1	36	12,10	64
12,6-7	51	12,11	63
12,9-10	22	17,19	34
15,7-11	38, 48	17,26-27	35
15,18	59	17,37	3, 4
16,16	38, 51, 62	18,37	64
16,19	48, 61	19,2	64
17,7	313	22,3	64
18,3	51	22,8-10	64
23,5	21	22,12	64
25,1	52	25,19	63
25,19	22		
26,1-4	38, 51	*1 Chronicles*	
26,13	34	22,13	36
26,16-17	36		
27,25	48	*2 Chronicles*	
28,1-17	75	7,17	36
28,15	36	19,10	36
28,45	36	24,20	34
30	84, 97, 98	33,8	36
30,11-14	14, 248, 249	34,8	64
30,12-14	247, 292, 298	36,12	21
30,12-13	248, 249		
30,14	249	*Nehemiah*	
31,10	184	1,5	56
32,8-9	61	1,7	36
32,35	313	9,13	36
32,47	25,82	10,30	36
33,2	210	11,7-9	229
33,3	21	11,31-35	229
33,4	61, 72		
33,10	35, 97	*Ezra*	
33,14	14	7,6	84
33,20	26	7,10	32, 84, 210
		7,12	63, 64
Joshua		7,21	63
1,8	34	7,25	5, 71, 84
22,3	34	8,1	64
22,5	34	8,4	64
		8,9	64
		8,13	64

12,6	64	119,56	32
12,36	64	119,63	5
		119,69	32
Job		119,72	21
14,5	36	119,88	21
14,13	36	119,101	234
23,10-11	3	119,105	146
23,12	21	119,110	32
23,14	36	119,115	32
24,13	3	119,129	32
28,26	36	119,130	234
28,28	249	119,145	32
38,10	36	128,1	5
38,33	36	128,4	5
40,2	207	132,13-14	21
40,18	35	147,19	97
		148,2-6	36
Psalms			
1	4, 5, 11, 12, 84	*Proverbs*	
1,2	34	1,1	22
5,13	26	1,7	61
6,6	61	1,8	33
15,5	48	1,31	3
19	4, 5, 12, 14, 84	2,3-6LXX	259
19,6	43	2,6	21
19,8	146	2,8	3
19,9	234	2,12-15	234
19,10	5, 35	3,1	33
30,6	26	3,2	25
30,8	26	3,4	313, 314
33,18	61	3,7	313
36,9	73	3,16	220
46,5	73	3,17	3, 25, 234
56,9	213	4,2	33
69,22	211	4,11-12	234
72,1-2	115	4,11	3
73	5	6,20	33
78,5	97	6,22-23	234
78,7	32	6,23	3, 33, 146
78,68	21	6,35	48
82,3	52	7,2	33
87,2	21	8,12-14	257
89,31	35	8,18	220
105,45	32	8,20	3, 234
111,10	5	8,22-31	13, 250
112,1	5	8,22-25	256
112,9	314	8,22-23	257
119	4, 5, 11, 12, 32, 84	8,22	234
119,2	32	8,27-30	257
119,12	210	8,27	36
119,13	21	8,29	36
119,20	35	8,32	3
119,22	32	8,34	234
119,33	3, 32	8,35	26
119,34	32	9,10	61
119,38	5	11,20	3
119,39	35	12,2	26

12,15	3
12,20	25
14,33	22
15,30	220
17,15	52
17,23	48
18,4	148
18,22	26,61
22,6	3
22,8	314
25,21-22	313
26,27	61
28,7	32
30,1-6	14, 249
30,8	36
31,26	33

Qohelet

1,12	22
1,16-18	250
2,13	234
2,26	250
5,19	220
7,12	250
9,10LXX	250

Isaiah

1,20	21
1,23	48
2	132
2,1-5	288
3,14	35
5,23	52
9,6	117
9,7	115
10,24	3
10,26	3
11,2-3	115
11,2	117
11,3-5	115
12,3	73
16,5	115
22,13	314
24,5	34
25,6-8	288
26,8-9	35
29,13	313
30,18	35
32,1	115
34,16	21
40,5	21
40,12-26	249
41,18	73
42,1-6	132
43,4	21
45,3LXX	259
45,23	21
48,3	21
51,4	35
55,8-11	249
55,10	314
55,11	21
56,6	56
58,2	35
60,10	26
62,2	21
63,9	21

Jeremiah

1,10	61
2,8	32
5,22	36
5,24	36
8,8-9	5
8,8	65, 84
9,11	21
9,19	21
12,16	3
15,19	21
18,18	5
23,5	115, 117
23,16	21
31,12	73
31,31ff.	267
31,33	288
31,36	36
32,11	34
33,15	115
33,25	36
36,10	64
36,12	64
36,20-21	64
38,31-34	282

Ezekiah

3,17	21
5,5-6	36
16,8	21
22,12	48
33,7	21
36-37	282
36,26	284
36,27	288
37,24	288
47	73

Daniel

7,10	213
9	95
9,41	56

Hosea

6,5	21,35
10,3	3

11,4	21		*Habakkuk*	
14,4	21		1,5	217
Joel			*Zechariah*	
4,18	73		8,17	313
			14,8	73
Amos				
4,10	3		*Malachi*	
8,14	3		2,6-7	5, 84
Micah				
4,1-8	288			
4,4	21			

II. Early Jewish Literature

Antiquitates Biblicae			15,3	155
9,8	164, 234		15,5-6	155
10,7	246		15,5	155, 158, 162
11,1-2	164		15,6	155, 159
11,1	164, 234		15,7-8	155
11,5	164, 246		17,1ff.	153
12,2	164		17,1	163
12,4	164		17,4-19,1	154
15,6	164		17,4	154, 156, 159, 234
19,6	164		18,1-2	156, 159, 163
20,2-3	162		18,2	154
21,2	162		19,1ff.	153
21,2	162		19,1	155
21,9	164		19,3	155
23,7	162, 164, 234		21,9-10	158
23,10	164		23,2ff.	153
30,1-2	164		24,1	155
32,7	162		28,1	158
33,3	164		31-34	157
51,4	164, 234		31,5-32,1	157
			32,1	154, 155, 159
Apocalypse of Baruch			38,1-2	154, 156, 159, 162, 163, 234
1,2-4	153			
1,4	153		38,1	158, 159
2,2	155		38,2	150, 158, 159, 164
3,6	154, 157		38,4	159, 162, 164
5,3	153		43-46	157
6,4ff.	153		44,3-7	157
7,1-2	153		44,3	82, 154, 155
8,1-2	153		44,5-6	153
13,2-12	155		44,6	158
14,1-19	155		44,7	154, 155, 157
14,7	155		44,12-13	159
14,8-11	249		44,14	154, 158, 159, 160, 162, 233
14,8	155			
14,9	158		44,15	158
14,12	155		45,1-2	156
15,1ff.	153		45,2	159
15,1-8	154, 155		46,2-3	156, 159, 163

46,3	154, 157	77,13-15	157
46,4	154, 155, 158, 159	77,15-16	154, 155
46,5-6	157, 162	77,15	146, 157, 164
46,5	154, 155, 157, 158, 159, 164	77,16	158, 161, 162
		82,6	154, 155
48,9	158	84,1	154, 155
48,10	155	84,9	154, 157
48,22	154, 160	85,3	154
48,23	160	85,7	154
48,24	158, 160, 162	85,8-9	154
48,26ff.	153		
48,31	160	*Assumptio Mosis*	
48,33-47	160, 162	1,14	272
48,33	160	3,11ff.	107
48,36	148, 158, 160	3,12	272
48,38-41	156		
48,38	160	*Baruch*	
48,40	132, 155, 160	1,5-3,8	97
48,45-47	156	1,15-5,9	96
48,47	160	1,15-3,8	95
49,7	160	1,15-2,19	95
51,3-7	154, 162	1,17-22	98, 99
51,3-4	160	1,18-20	97
51,3	155, 158, 160	1,18	97, 98, 99
51,4	160	2,1-7	98, 99
51,7	155, 158	2,2-28	98
52,7	160, 162	2,2	97
54,3	157	2,10-12	97
54,5	154, 158, 163	2,10	97, 98, 99
54,13	158	2,20-26	98, 99
54,15	154	2,27-35	97
54,16-18	156	2,28-30	98, 99
54,19	154	2,28	97
54,21-22	156	3,2-4	98, 99
54,22	156	3,7	97
55,2	155	3,8-13	98, 99
57,2	155	3,9-5,9	97
59,2	132, 154, 156, 159, 164	3,9-4,4	95, 96, 98
59,4	157, 160, 162	3,9-14	98, 99, 162
59,5	160	3,9	96, 97, 98, 99
59,7	158, 160, 162	3,10-13	98
61, 4-6	160, 162	3,12	96, 98
61,6	160	3,13	97, 98, 99, 164
63,3	155	3,14	96, 97, 98, 99, 164, 220, 234
63,5	160, 162		
66,2	161, 162	3,15	259
66,5	161, 162	3,16-28	96
66,14	154	3,20-21	99
67, 2-4	153	3,20	96
67,6	155	3,23	96, 99
70,5	148	3,24-25	96, 164
75,2	158	3,27	96, 99
76-77	157	3,28	97
76,5	156	3,29-32	249
77,3	155	3,29-31	96, 97, 98
77,5-7	157	3,29-30	248, 249
77,6	157	3,29	96

Index of Passages

3,30	61	20-36	100
3,31	99	21,1-6	107
3,32-36	96	25,13	102
3,32-34	96, 164	32,3	104
3,32	96	33,3-4	106, 164
3,35	96	36,4	107
3,36	96	37-71	100, 101, 103
3,37-4,4	97	37,1-5	102
3,37-4,1	97	37,2	102
3,37-38	96	37,4	105, 111
3,38	96, 97, 200, 257	38-44	100, 102
4,1-4	96, 98, 99, 162	38,2-6	107
4,1	71, 97, 98, 99, 164	38,2	108
4,2	82, 83, 99	39,1-2	100
4,3	99	39,6	108, 165
4,5-5,9	95	39,8	107
4,5-5,4	95	39,9	107
4,12-13	98, 99	41,1	107, 108
4,12	97	41,3-9	104, 105
4,13	82, 97, 98, 99, 164	41,5-6	107
5,4	97	42	103, 148
		42,1-3	110, 111, 162
Enoch (Ethiopic)		42,1-2	103
1-5	100, 101	42,1	103, 164
1,1-9	102	43-44	105
1,9	108	43,1-2	107
1,1-2	102	43,4	104
1,1	102	45-57	100, 102
1,2-3	102	46,2	108
2-5	105	46,3	259
2,1-5,3	104	47,3	213
2,1-2	107, 164	48,1-2	104, 105, 108, 165
5,3-4	109, 111	48,1	104, 105, 110, 111, 162
5,4-9	102, 105	48,7	103
5,4	107, 108, 110	49,1-3	104, 108, 110, 111, 162, 165
5,6-9	111, 164	49,1	106
5,7-9	105, 111	49,2	106, 108, 165
5,8-9	104, 110, 111, 162	49,3	106
5,8	104, 105	51,3	106, 108, 165
5,9	105, 111	52,1-9	104, 105
6-36	100, 101	53,6	108
6-16	100	53,7	108, 165
6-11	101	54,7-55,2	101
10,15	102, 105	58-59	100, 102
12,1-11	102	58,2	102
12,3-4	102	58,3-6	111, 164
13,6	108	58,3	105, 111
13,8	102	58,5	104
14,1-3	111	59	105
14,1	104	59,1-3	104
14,2-4	102	60	101
14,3	104	60,6	110
15,1	102	60,11-23	104, 105, 106, 164
17-26	102	61,1-13	104, 110, 111, 162
17-19	100	61,7	103, 104
18,1-5	106	61,11	103
18,11-16	107		

62,1-63,12	102	91,3-19	108
63,2-3	103	91,3	102
63,3	104, 111	91,10	102, 103, 104, 105, 110, 111, 148, 162, 164
65,1-69,25	101		
66,1-2	106, 164	91,12-17	100, 101
69,15-21	106	92,1	104, 105, 110, 111, 162
69,21-25	106	92,4	108
69,25	106	93,1-14	100, 101
70,1-3	102	93,2	111
71	102	93,5	105
71,1	102	93,6	108, 164
71,3	104	93,8	105, 110
71,5	102	93,10	105, 110, 111, 162
71,14	108, 165	94,1-100,9	102
71,16	108, 165	94,1-5	110, 111, 162, 164
72-82	100, 101, 102, 104	94,1	102
72,3	106	94,5	103, 148, 164
73,1	106, 164	94,6-11	108
75,1	106	94,6	107
75,2	107	95,1-7	108
76,14	106, 164	95,5-6	109
79,1-2	106, 164	96,4-8	108
79,1	102, 105	96,5	109
80,1-6	107	96,7	109
80,1	104, 106	97,8	109
80,2-82,3	104	98,1-102,3	102
80,2-8	105	98,1	102
80,4-6	107	98,3	102
80,4	106	98,6-10	111, 162
80,7	106, 107, 164	98,6	108
81,1-4	110, 111	98,9	109
81,1-2	107, 213	98,11	109
81,1	102, 105	98,13	109
81,2-4	108	98,14-15	109
81,4	102, 105	99,1-16	108
82,1-5	107	99,2	108, 164
82,1-3	104	99,10	102, 104, 110, 111, 162, 164
82,1	102, 105		
82,2-4	104, 105, 111	99,11-12	109
82,2	104	99,14	108, 109, 164
82,3	104	99,15	109
82,4	104, 106	100,6	102
82,7-10	106	100,7-10	108
83-90	100, 101	100,7-8	109
83	102	100,7	108
83,1	102	101,1	111
84,3	103, 104, 164	101,2-8	102
85,1-2	102	102,4-104,13	102
86,1	102	103,3	108
89-90	168	103,5	102
89,16-71	104	103,8	102
89,21-38	107	104,7	108
90,17	213	104,12	102, 104, 110, 111, 162
90,39-42	102	105,1	127, 234
90,41	107	105,2	111
91-105	100, 101, 102, 103, 105	106-108	100
91,1	102	106-107	101

108	101	3,4-27	141, 146, 147
108,1	102, 108	3,5-26	142
108,11-14	111, 164	3,8	82, 142
		3,11	249

Enoch (Slavic)

48,1	148	3,13	148
49,1	148	3,14	143
		3,15-20	145
		3,19	143

Epistula Aristeae

3	120	3,22	160
5	120	3,25	141
10	120	3,28-36	142
15	120, 121	3,29-36	142
30-32	121	3,29-30	145
30	120	3,32-36	144
31	120, 123, 162	3,32-33	145
33-34	121	3,33	144, 145
83-106	121	3,34	141, 145
107	122	3,34-35	145
121	122	3,35-36	145
127	120, 121, 122, 123, 162	3,35	145
128-171	121	3,36	145
130-171	121	4,23	145
130	122	4,24	141
131	120	5,1-12	148
137	122	5,1	148
139	120, 121, 122, 123, 162	5,9-11	149, 151, 162
144	120, 121, 122, 123, 124, 162	5,9-10	148
		5,10	148
		5,20-6,34	140
155	120	5,27	107, 143, 145, 146
158	120	5,28-30	142
161	121, 122, 123, 132, 162	5,29	144, 145
162	122	5,36-40	249
168-169	123, 162	6,1-6	249
168	120, 121, 122	6,5	145, 159
169	121, 122	6,35-9,25	140
171	120	6,53-59	142
172-300	122	7,2-16	144
176-177	121	7,10-16	143
177	120	7,11	145, 146, 164
200	122	7,17-25	143, 144, 145
207	122	17,17-18	144
235	122	7,17	144
240	120	7,20-44	144
260	122	7,20-24	132
271	122	7,20	144
279	121	7,21-25	143, 145
306	121	7,21	144, 145
309	120	7,22-44	145
313	120	7,24	145
		7,35	145

4Ezra

		7,37	144, 145
1-2	139	7,45-46	144
3-14	139	7,45	145
3,1-5,19	140	7,48	144
3,1-3	140	7,60	144
3,1	140	7,62	149

Passage	Page	Passage	Page
7,64	149	12,36-38	140
7,66-67	144	12,36	148
7,70-74	145, 149, 162	12,38	147
7,72	145, 149, 150, 151, 155	12,40-50	141, 151
7,77	159	12,47	148
7,79	82, 143, 145, 146	13,1-56	140
7,81	145	13,23	145
7,82	144	13,42	145
7,83	145	13,53-58	143
7,88-99	146, 149, 151, 162	13,54-55	150, 151
7,88-90	143	13,55	148
7,89	143	13,58	143
7,92	144	14,1-50	140
7,94	143	14,3ff.	107
7,127-131	145	14,3-6	145
7,127-130	143	14,5	143
7,129-131	144	14,6-8	140
7,129	82, 144, 145	14,13	140, 147, 151
7,131	144	14,19-22	151
7,133	82	14,20-21	145, 148, 151, 163, 234
7,137-138	144	14,20	132
8,3	144	14,21-22	143
8,6	144	14,22	144, 145, 148
8,7-13	150, 162	14,23-26	143
8,12-29	146	14,25-26	148
8,12	150, 151, 162	14,25	148, 150, 151, 162
8,16-17	141	14,26	147
8,20-23	249	14,27-35	142
8,27	145	14,28-32	144
8,28-29	151	14,30	141, 144, 145
8,29	151	14,31	146
8,31-36	145	14,34	146
8,39	143, 144	14,35	145
8,41	144	14,37-48	151
8,52-58	150, 162	14,37-44	148
8,52-56	151	14,38-47	140
8,52-54	150	14,40	148, 151
8,52-53	160	14,45-46	147
8,52	148, 150	14,46	147
8,54	144	14,47	148
8,55-58	150	14,48	140
8,56	143, 145, 150	14,50	151
9,7-13	143	15-16	139
9,7	145		
9,13	144	*Jubilees*	
9,15	144	1,4	164
9,26-10,59	139, 140	1,10	164
9,29ff.	107	1,26	164
9,29-37	144	1,27	273
9,29-32	145	1,29	164, 273
9,31	143, 145	1,48-50	107
9,32	145	2,1	273
9,37	143, 146, 164	2,2	162, 164
9,38-10,24	141	2,25-26	273
10,22	145, 163	2,29-30	273
10,29-59	140	2,33	164
11,1-38	140	4,17	162

5,13	82, 164	6,15	135
6,14	164	6,21	135
6,20	273	6,22	137
6,22	273	7,1	138
7,20	164	7,4	138
12,21	82	7,7	135
13,26	164	7,9	135, 136, 137
15,25-28	273	7,16	137
15,25	164	7,21	135, 136, 137
16,3	164	8,1	138
16,30	164	9,1-8	136
20,3	82	9,2	136
21,5	164	9,6-7	137
21,22	82	9,15	136
23,16	164	9,29-30	137
23,21	82	11,20	137
23,26	82	11,27	135
24,11	164	13,6	138
25,15	82	13,12	137
30,21	164	13,24	136
30,22	213	13,26	136
35,13	82	13,27	137
		15,9	136
Judith		15,14	137
13,12	82	16,4	138
		16,14	137
1 Maccabees		16,17-22	136
1,56-57	72	16,17	136, 137
7,12-13	65	16,19	136
7,12	65	17,7	137
		17,16	135, 136
4 Maccabees		17,19	136
1,1	135, 138	18,3	137
1,12	136	19,1	136
1,15-19	136		
1,16-17	132	*Psalms of Solomon*	
1,16	136	1,8	115
1,17	137, 162	2,3	115
1,18	136	2,12	115
1,34	136	2,33	116, 118, 164
2,5	136	3,12	116, 118, 164
2,8	136	4,1	115
2,9-10	138	4,8-13	117, 162
4,23	136	4,9	115, 116, 117
5,2	135	4,11	115, 117
5,6	135	4,12	115, 117
5,7	137	4,19	115
5,9	136	4,21	115
5,11	137	4,23	115, 118, 164
5,16-38	136	4,25	118
5,16	136, 138	5,18	118, 164
5,18	135	6,5	118, 164
5,22	137	6,6	118
5,25	132	7,9	113, 115, 164
5,31	137	8,9	115
5,33	136	8,11	115
5,35	135, 137, 162	8,32	113

9,2	115	1	130
10,2	116, 118	1,5	131
10,3	116, 118	1,6-8	335
10,4	113, 114, 115	1,6	131
11	95	1,15	131
12,1	115	2,11	131
12,3	115	2,12	131, 132, 133, 134, 162
12,4	115, 118, 164	3,1	131
13,10-12	116	3,15	160
13,12	118, 164	5,1	131
14,1-2	117, 162	5,6	82
14,1	116, 117, 118	5,15	131
14,2-3	116	6-10	130, 133
14,2	113, 114, 115, 117, 164	6,4	131, 132
14,3	47	6,12-13	131
14,6	114	6,16	131
15,8	115	6,18	131, 133
15,10	115	6,22	250
15,13	118, 164	7,7	131
16,7-8	118, 162	7,14	259
16,7	116	7,15-21	250
16,8	116	7,15-16	131
16,9	116	7,16	131
16,10	116	7,17-21	131, 132, 164
16,13	116	7,20	234
17,5	115	7,22-30	131
17,11	115	7,22	131
17,18	115	7,23	131
17,20	115	7,24	131, 164
17,21-46	115, 118	7,25-26	131
17,22-31	117	7,25	133
17,22-25	117	7,26-30	250
17,23	115, 116, 117, 118, 165	7,26	133, 134, 164, 256
17,24	114, 115, 118, 165	7,27	131, 133, 134
17,26	118	8,1-4	164
17,29	116, 117, 118, 165	8,1-3	131
17,32-41	117	8,2	131
17,32	115, 118	8,3-4	131
17,34	118	8,3	131
17,35	116, 117, 118, 165	8,4	250
17,36	117	8,7	131, 132
17,37	116, 117, 118, 165	8,8	132
17,39	118	8,9	250
17,40	115, 118	8,13	131
17,41	118	8,18	131
18,7	115, 116, 117, 118, 165	8,21-9,6	131
18,8	118	8,21	131
18,10-14	114	9-18	133
18,10-12	114	9,1-2	131, 164
18,10	114	9,4	131
18,12	114	9,5	131
		9,9-13	250
Psalms (syr)		9,9-10	131
2,1-39	214	9,9	131, 132, 133, 164, 256
		9,10-18	133, 134, 249
Sapientia Salomonis		9,10	131, 241
1-6	129	9,11	234

9,16-17	250	3,686	126, 127, 128
9,17	131, 241	3,687	128
9,29	250	3,702-731	128
10,1-21	134	3,719-720	127
10,10	234	3,719	126, 128
10,17-18	246	3,720	127
10,17	234	3,757	127
11,1-10	134	3,762-763	128
11,15-16	134	3,764-765	128
12,2	335	3,768	126, 127
12,24-27	134	3,776	125
14,2	131	4	125
14,3	131	4,128	126
14,16	131	4,129	126
15,18-19	134	4,143	126
16,6	131, 134	5	125
18,4	131, 132, 133, 134, 146, 163, 234	5,264-265	128
		5,298-305	126
18,9	131	5,360	128
18,15	131	5,384	128
		5,509	128

Sibylline Oracles

2	125	*Sirach*	
3,1-92	125	prol.	
3,46-62	125	1-3	77, 78
3,62-96	125	1-2	37
3,69-70	126, 127	1	38, 40, 42
3,75-92	125	7-11	83
3,194-195	234	8-10	37
3,195	127	8	38, 40, 42
3,219-220	127, 162	12-14	77, 79, 82, 83
3,237-262	126	27-36	79
3,246	126, 127	29	77, 79, 82, 83
3,248-260	126	31-36	83
3,256	126	35-36	77, 79, 82, 83
3,259	126	1	15
3,275-278	127	1,1-10	16, 24
3,275	126	1,1-8	250
3,284	126	1,1	16, 20
3,291	126	1,2-3	18, 19, 73
3,293	126	1,2	78
3,350-380	125	1,4	78, 256, 257
3,372	125	1,5	30, 77, 78, 82, 83, 259
3,496	127	1,6	18, 19, 73, 160
3,558	127	1,8	16
3,569-603	127	1,9-10	21
3,573-600	127, 128, 162	1,9	16, 17, 18, 78
3,573-583	127	1,10	16, 21, 24, 56, 74, 200
3,575-579	127	1,11-20	24, 56
3,580-581	127	1,11-12	25
3,580	128	1,11	25
3,584	128	1,12	25
3,585	128	1,13	25
3,586-596	128	1,14	24, 61, 74, 82
3,600	126, 128	1,16	18, 24, 74, 82
3,669-697	128, 162	1,18	24, 25, 74, 82, 220
3,670	128	1,19	81

1,20	25, 74, 82, 160, 220	8,8-9	58
1,21	25	8,9	18, 58
1,26-27	45	8,13	335
1,26	18, 21, 30, 38, 39, 40, 42, 50, 55, 69, 73, 74, 83	8,15	82
		9,8-9	57
1,27	18, 21, 25, 26	9,9-12	57
1,28	5	9,14-15	58
1,30	58	9,15	45
2,9	78	9,16	5, 45
2,15-16	10, 45, 56, 70, 74	10,1	207
2,15	37, 56, 82	10,2	58
2,16	26, 37, 38, 40, 42, 50, 56, 82	10,4	17
		10,18ff.	30
2,18	61	10,19	34, 35, 38, 40, 42, 51
3,2	87	10,25	207
4,7	57, 59	10,26	18
4,9	35	11,4	18
4,11-19	16, 30	11,7	58, 60
4,12	25, 26, 220	11,17	36, 43, 80
4,13	25, 26, 220	11,18	36
4,16-19	24	12,5	18
4,18	19	12,15	82
4,19	207	13,6	18
4,29	58, 59	14,11	23
5,2	82	14,12	36, 43, 80
5,9	82	14,17	36, 43, 80
6,14-15	181	14,20	26, 34
6,18-37	16, 24, 30	14,21	82
6,18-36	74	14,20-15,10	16, 69
6,19	74	15,1-2	25
6,20-31	181	15,1	10, 11, 15, 31, 32, 33, 40, 42, 45, 50, 55, 69, 70, 82, 83
6,26-27	234		
6,28-31	74		
6,28	22, 25, 26, 220	15,2	18
6,29	25, 26	15,3	73
6,30-31	75	15,7	55
6,31	26, 220	15,9	18
6,32ff.	30	15,13	45
6,33	207	15,14	46, 47, 75
6,35-36	58	15,15-17	75
6,36	25, 29, 34, 35, 38, 40, 42, 50, 55, 70, 74, 82, 83	15,15	26, 32, 34, 38, 40, 42, 50, 56, 75, 82
6,37	5, 15, 29, 45	15,19	61
7,6-7	58, 59	16,20	36
7,6	58	16,24-17,14	14, 17, 44
7,8-10	23	16,24-28	17, 44
7,15	18, 87	16,24	17
7,19	58, 60	16,26	16, 17, 18
7,23	207	16,27	17, 78
7,26	58, 60	16,28	17, 78
7,29-31	23	16,29-17,10	17, 44
7,29	56, 87	17,1-2	43
7,30-33	57	17,2-4	17
7,30	56	17,2	17
7,31	51, 56, 87	17,6-9	21
7,32-35	23	17,7	17, 53
7,33	49	17,8	16, 17, 18

Index of Passages

17,11-14	13, 17, 29, 37, 44, 69	24,1-34	11, 14, 15, 16, 19, 20, 21, 23, 44, 60, 71, 97, 98, 253
17,11-12	11, 42		
17,11	11, 17, 21, 23, 37, 38, 39, 40, 42, 44, 50, 70, 72, 80, 81, 82, 150	24,1-22	9, 22, 71, 75
		24,1-5	250
17,12	17, 37, 39, 40, 42, 44, 72, 81	24,3-29	14
		24,3-6	19
17,13	26, 37, 44	24,3-4	16
17,14	17, 37, 44, 87	24,3	21, 81
17,15	82	24,4-11	257
17,17	44, 61	24,4	61
17,27	61	24,6-12	21
18,1	78	24,6	17
18,4-7	18	24,7-11	23
18,4	18	24,7	22
18,14	39	24,8-12	21, 22, 23, 81
18,20	37	24,8	21, 22, 81
19,4-17	46	24,9	256, 257
19,6	66	24,10-13	22
19,11	38, 42	24,10-11	23
19,14-17	46	24,10	22
19,17	30, 37, 38, 40, 42, 46, 81, 88	24,11	22
		24,12	22
19,18	37, 56	24,13-17	22, 26
19,19	56, 77, 78, 82, 83	24,13-14	61
19,20-30	11	24,15	23, 61
10,20-24	16	24,16-17	25, 26, 61, 220
19,20	10, 11, 30, 37, 38, 40, 42, 50, 55, 70, 74, 75, 82	24,16	25, 26
		24,17	26, 220
		24,18-20	22
19,22-25	75	24,19-22	75
19,24	30, 37, 38, 40, 42, 50, 51, 75, 82	24,20-22	71
		24,22	25, 26, 75, 82, 83
19,25	39	24, 23-29	19
20,27-31	16	24,23-27	72
20,29	61	24,23	9, 10, 11, 12, 13, 14, 23, 30, 33, 38, 40, 42, 43, 44, 61, 69, 71, 72, 73, 80, 81
20,35ff.	30		
21,1-11	30, 46		
21,5	39		
21,9	37	24,25-29	73
21,10	37, 57, 82	24,25-27	72
21,11-28	16, 46	24,26	61
21,11	12, 37, 38, 40, 42, 45, 46, 47, 56, 57, 70, 74, 75, 82	24,28-29	73, 249
		24,30-34	76
		24,30	148
21,12	46	24,31	76
21,13	73, 250	24,32-33	76
23,9-11	58	24,32	76, 83, 234
23,13	62	24,33	76, 83
23,16-27	47	24,34	76
23,22-27	38	25,9-10	26
23,22-25	58	25,21-22	59, 60
23,23	37, 38, 40, 42, 46, 47, 81, 88	25,25-26	59, 60
		26,29	59
23,24	59	26,36	60
23,27	38, 39, 40, 41, 45, 51, 56, 81	27,1-2	59
		27,6	46, 47

Index of Passages

27,26	61	34,8	38, 41, 59, 73, 83
27,30-28,7	47	34,15	88
28,3	25	34,16	61
28,6-7	47, 88	34,30	59
28,6	38, 40, 42, 46, 81	35,1-7	49
28,7	5, 38, 40, 42, 46, 47, 72, 81	35,1	38, 41, 42, 81
		35,2-4	45
28,15	59, 60	35,2	18, 38, 41, 42, 49, 81
28,16	22	35,3-5	52
29,1-3	47	35,3	49
29,1	38, 40, 42, 81, 88	35,4	49
29,9	15, 38, 40, 42, 46, 47, 81, 88	35,5	26
		35,6-7	51
29,11	38, 40, 42, 46, 47, 81, 88	35,6	51, 52, 62
30,4-6	59, 60	35,7	38, 41, 32, 81
30,13	207	35,12	35, 36
30,20	35	35,14	21, 74
31,13	18	35,17	18, 35, 36
31,21-32,20	23	35,23-24	88
31,21-31	23	36,13-17	23
31,27	18	36,19	26
32,1	38	36,22	78
32,1-7	23	36,24	61
32,1	38	36,25	59, 60
32,2	38	37,7-15	49
32,5	35	37,8	18
32,7	38, 88	37,11	49, 59, 60
32,8-13	23	37,12	32, 34, 35, 38, 41, 42, 45, 49, 56
32,14-33,6	48		
32,14-20	23	37,16-26	16
32,14-18	30	37,26	26, 220
32,14-17	48	38,1	18
32,14-16	25, 32, 45	38,2	25
32,14	32, 48	38,6	21
32,15	31, 32, 33, 40, 42	38,9-11	23
32,16	32, 34, 35, 36, 40, 42, 48	38,12	18
32,17	31, 32, 33, 35, 40, 46, 48	38,14	25
32,18-23	48	38,16	35
32,18	31, 32, 33, 34, 35, 40, 42, 48	38,22	36, 43, 80
		38,24-39,14	16
32,22-23	30, 49	38,24-39,11	63, 65
32, 22	32, 34, 35, 40, 42, 48	38,24-34	65
32,23	31, 32, 33, 34, 41, 42, 48, 83	38,24	53, 65, 66
		38,32	59
32,24-33,3	48	38,33	53, 59
32,24-33,1	45	38,34-39,11	38, 52, 65
33,1	32	38,34-39,3	52, 76, 83
33,2-3	50, 55, 76	38, 34	11, 38, 41, 42, 53, 76, 77, 81
33,2	31, 32, 33, 41, 42, 50, 76, 83	39,1-11	11, 52
33,3	31, 32, 33, 37, 41, 42, 50, 76, 83	39,1-5	53
		39,1-4	53
33,4-6	48	39,1-3	53
33,5	76	39,1-2	44
33,7-9	43	39,1	11, 45, 53, 58
33,15	18	39,2-3	53, 59, 66
33,20	72	39,4-5	52

Index of Passages

39,4	53	43,1-2	18
39,5	53	43,1	42
39,6-8	53	43,2-4	43
39,6	25, 53, 54, 74	43,4	60
39,7	54	43,5-10	80
39,8	38, 41, 42, 44, 72, 76, 77, 83	43,5	37, 39, 42, 43
		43,6-8	43
39,9-11	53, 54	43,6	18
39,9	54	43,7	36, 43
39,10	54	43,9-10	43
39,14-35	17	43,10	18, 36, 37, 39, 42, 43
39,16	16, 17, 18, 29	43,12	18, 36
39,18	29	43,13	29, 35
39,20	78	43,26	37, 39, 42, 43
39,21	17, 18	43,28-32	18
39,24	82	43,29	37, 42
39,25	18	43,33	21, 25
39,28	17	44,1-15	23
39,29	35, 36	44,2	18, 26
39,30	17, 18	44,3-4	23
39,31	36, 39	44,4	77, 83
39,33	17, 18	44,5	36
39,34	17	44,15	23
40,1	18	44,20	32, 34, 36, 41, 42, 44, 45, 81, 83
40,17	49		
40,29	207	44,23-45,5	24
41,1-4	43	44,23	22
41,1	33, 43, 88	45,1-5	29, 54
41,2	36, 43, 80	45,3	26, 39
41,3	36, 43, 80	45,5	22, 23, 31, 33, 34, 35, 36, 37, 41, 42, 44, 45, 50, 54, 70, 72, 73, 81, 82
41,4	31, 32, 33, 42, 80		
41,5-13	49		
41,8	31, 32, 33, 41, 42, 46, 49, 56, 81	45,6-22	24, 54
		45,6	35, 54
41,16	35	45,7	36, 42, 45
41,24	60	45,10	35, 36
42,1-8	32	45,11	22
42,2	31, 33, 35, 36, 37, 41, 42, 44, 60, 72, 81	45,14-16	23
		45,17-19	65
42,3	59, 60	45,17	34, 35, 36, 37, 41, 45, 52, 53, 54, 55, 83, 146, 234
42,4	52, 59		
42,7	59		
42,8	60	45,20-21	51
42,11	58, 59	45,22	22
42,15-43,33	17, 18, 43	45,23-26	23
42,15-25	249	45,23-25	24
42,15-16	18	45,23	22, 62
42,15	39	45,24	36, 41, 45
42,16-17	18, 26	45,25	45
42,18-20	18	45,26	21
42,18	16	46,1	22
42,20	16	46,13-20	24
42,21	18	46,16	23
42,23-25	18	47,1-11	24
42,23	78	47,2	22, 23
42,25	18	47,10	35
42,33	18	47,11	22, 36, 41, 45

47,12-23	24	5,1	82
47,12-13	22	5,8	82
47,12	23		
47,14	23	*TJoseph*	
47,17	23	11,1	164
47,18	22		
47,22	37	*TJudah*	
47,23	22	13,2	82
48,1	39	16,2	164
48,3	37, 39, 42	23,5	82
48,5	39	24,1	165
48,7	35, 36	24,3	82, 165
48,17-22	24	24,6	165
49,1-3	24		
49,1	23	*TLevi*	
49,4	31, 33, 41, 42, 81	4,3	164, 234
49,7	61	8,17	65
49,12	26	13	162, 164
49,13	26	13,1	164
50,1-21	23, 24	13,7	164
50,13	22	14,3-4	164, 234
50,17	22	14,4	132, 146
50,19	35, 36	18,2	165
50,20	22	18,3-5	165
50,22	22	18,3	164, 234
50,23	21	18,5	165
50,27-29	24	18,7	165
50,28-29	25	18,9	165
51,8	78	18,11	165
51,12	22	19,1	146, 164, 234
51,13-30	16, 77		
51,13-21	58	*arTLevi*	
51,13-20	58, 81	88-90	162
51,15	77, 82		
51,17	26, 220	*TNaphtali*	
51,23-30	77	2,1-3,3	164
51,23	58	2,8-9	164
51,30	37, 77, 83, 181	2,9	162
		3,2-5	164
Testaments of the Twelve Patriarchs		4,1	82
TAsher		8,7-10	162, 164
2,6	58		
5,4	82	*hebrTNaphtali*	
		1,6	122
TDan			
5,5	82	*TReuben*	
		3,8	164, 234
TGad			
3,2	164	*TZebulun*	
6,4	58	3,4	120
TIssachar		*Tobit*	
3,1-2	82	4,15	122
4,6	82	4,19	82

III. Dead Sea Scrolls

CD			
1,1-12	203	6,19	177
1,3-4	177	6,21	190
1,4-11	175	7,1-3	172
1,4	175	7,2	187
1,6-12	174	7,4-5	187
1,11-12	174, 203	7,5-6	188
1,20-21	187	7,5	207
1,20	177	7,6-8	187
1,21	177	7,8	207
2,3	196, 250	7,14-19	174
2,8	177	7,18-20	187
2,12-13	202	7,18	170, 187, 224
2,14-21	188	8,3	176
2,15-18	188	8,13	176
2,15-16	187	8,16-18	175
2,18	173	8,18-19	175
2,20-3,12	176	8,21	177
2,20	177	9-16	187
2,21	173, 177, 180	9,3	177
3,2-6	188	9,7-8	173
3,2	173	10,6	213
3,5-16	187	12,15	178
3,6	173	12,19-20	172
3,8	177, 180	13-16	198
3,10	175, 177	13,2-3	68
3,11-12	188	13,2	213
3,12-15	176	13,11	204
3,12-13	175	14,7-8	68
3,13-16	175	14,17-19	172
3,14	172	15,5-15	170
3,15-16	188	15,5-11	177
3,15	188	15,9	169
3,16-17	174, 175, 209	15,10-13	172
3,18-20	175	15,12	169
3,20	188	15,13	172
4,1	176	15,15	5
4,9	175	16,1-2	169
5,5	172, 174	16,4-5	169
5,9	172	16,8-9	170
5,16	176	19,1-2	188
5,21	173	19,2	188
6,2-11	174, 209	19,4	207
6,2-5	209, 223, 224	19,32	173
6,2	175	20,3	247
6,3	196	20,4	68, 202
6,4-6	68	20,6-7	187
6,4	212	20,10	169
6,5	176	20,11-12	176
6,7-11	182	20,12	177
6,7	68, 170	20,13	169
6,8-11	209	20,21	189
6,10-11	68	20,27-32	172
6,11	177, 187, 224	20,30-31	207
6,14-21	187		

1QH		7,26	203
1,1-20	210, 222	7,27	203
1,1-19	208	7,34	171, 178
1,5	211	8,6	199
1,7-15	200, 211	8,36	68
1,7	199, 200, 211	9,12	199
1,8	211	9,16	203
1,9-13	179	9,17-30	199
1,9	178, 208, 211	9,17	200
1,10	171, 178, 211	9,31	202
1,12-16	179	10,4	203
1,12	211	10,5	203
1,13	179, 211	10,6-7	203
1,14	200, 211	10,9-12	189
1,16	178, 208, 211	10,13-14	193
1,18-19	250	10,14	203
1,19	211	10,28-29	193
1,21	174, 193, 202	11,3-14	202
1,23	207	11,3-4	193
1,24	178	11,8	177
1,26	199, 207	11,9-10	193, 202
1,27-31	189	11,12	203
1,34-36	217, 223	11,15-17	193
1,35	195	11,22	203
1,36	206	11,27-28	193, 197, 202
2,9-10	203	11,28	203
2,10	206	12,5-11	179, 200, 211, 222
2,17	203	12,5	178
2,18-19	174	12,8-9	178
2,18	199	12,10	199
2,39	68	12,11-13	217
3,14	196	12,29	199
3,22-23	203	12,32	217, 223
4,5-6	174	12,33	203
4,5	174	12,34	174
4,8	201	13,4	201
4,9-11	211, 223	13,7-13	208
4,10	170, 171	13,8-10	200
4,21	187	13,13	200
4,23	174	14,13	193
4,24	187	14,16	172
4,27-30	189	14,17-18	170
4,27-28	203	14,20	178
4,27	174	14,25-26	202
4,31-32	217	14,25	203
5,11	170, 171	14,26	189
5,23	174	15,9-10	189
5,26	199	15,11-12	173
6,4	174	15,12-26	208
6,10	170, 171	15,19	173
6,11	209	16,7	189
6,13	209	16,13	171, 173, 188, 189
6,20	187	16,17	171, 173, 188
7,13	199	17,7	171
7,21-22	174	17,12	175
7,26-33	202	17,22	207
7,26-27	193	18,4	174

18,19	174	3,8-12	187
18,20	174	3,9-11	177
18,22	179	3,9	172
18,24	174	3,13-4,25	189
f2,8	171	3,13-14	204
f2,16	217	3,13	203
f4,15	199	3,15-4,26	194
f5,1	207	3,15-18	200
f17,3	179	3,15-17	179, 208, 222
f20,4	179	3,15-16	179
		3,15	194, 199, 200

1QM

3,6	176, 177	3,16-17	178
3,9	177	3,19-20	174
10,6	175	3,26-4,1	177
10,8-16	210	4,2-12	202
10,8-11	189	4,2-6	216, 223
10,9-11	209, 222	4,2	217
10,10-11	210	4,3-6	217
10,10	68, 171	4,3	172, 188, 196, 250
10,11	172	4,4-5	190
10,12-13	171, 178, 179	4,4	179, 207
10,12	171	4,18	178, 196
11,7-8	189	4,22	187, 196, 203, 206, 250
13,2-4	189	4,24	196, 201
13,12	171	5-9	187
14,7	206	5,2	169
17,8	202	5,3	179
		5,7-11	170
		5,7	179

1QS

1,1-3	169, 204	5,8-9	170, 173, 177
1,2-3	173, 175	5,8	173, 175
1,2	173, 205	5,9	169, 172, 173, 177
1,3	173, 175, 205	5,11-12	205
1,7	173	5,11	172
1,8	176, 177, 209	5,12	172, 176
1,9	172, 173, 190	5,20-21	204
1,10	209	5,20	177
1,11-13	191, 216, 223	5,21-22	182
1,12	172	5,25	190
1,13	187, 209	6,3-4	182
1,14	172	6,4	179
1,16	177	6,6-8	181
1,24	177	6,6-7	68, 187
1,26	187	6,7	182
2,2-3	216, 223	6,8-10	179
2,3	174, 191, 202, 216	6,15	177
2,8-9	68	6,18	204
2,10-13	177	6,19	177
2,15	172, 177	6,22	179
2,18	177	7,21	179
2,24	190	8,1-2	170
2,26-3,1	207	8,1	172, 173
3,1-4	187	8,4	178
3,1	187, 207, 223	8,6	191
3,5	172	8,7	247
3,6	172, 209	8,10	206
		8,11-12	182

8,11	172	1,7	171, 213
8,12-14	181	1,11	171
8,15-21	173	1,17-18	204
8,15	172, 173, 175, 181	1,28	196, 202, 206
8,16	173, 177	2,16	196, 202
8,17-18	172	2,22	171
8,17	171		
8,18	187, 206	*1QSb 9*	
8,19	179	1,1-3	173
8,21	187, 206	1,1-2	187, 188
8,22	175	1,1	171
8,24-25	172	2,26	207
9,2	179, 206	3,22-24	187
9,5	206	3,24	171
9,7	179	5,21	177
9,9	206	5,22	187
9,12-20	204	5,25	203
9,12	178		
9,13-14	203	*1QpHab*	
9,13	172, 173	1,11	173, 176
9,14-15	172	2,1-3	203
9,14	171, 178	2,3-4	177
9,17-18	187	2,7	217
9,17	172, 207, 208, 223, 224	2,8-10	217, 224
9,18	178	2,8-9	187
9,19	172, 187	2,8	182, 217
9,21	179	2,9-10	187, 217, 224
9,23	171, 178	2,15	171, 173
9,24	177	5,5	171, 173
10,1-8	273	5,10-12	170
10,1	171, 178	7,4-5	170
10,5	178	7,4	203
10,6	171, 178	7,13	171, 178
10,7	178	8,1	169, 176
10,8-9	189	8,10	171
10,8	171, 178	8,16-17	173
10,9	178	8,17	171
10,11	171, 178	12,5	169, 176
10,12	199		
10,16	208	*1Q16*	
10,24	196, 197	12,1	171
10,26	171, 178		
11,3-7	202	*1Q22*	
11,3	174, 199	1,1-4	173
11,5	174	1,1	175
11,6	196	1,2-9	187
11,10	178	1,4	171, 173
11,11	179	1,11	175
11,19	172, 179	2,1-5	188
14 f9,6-8	170	2,1-2	173
f55,1	172	2,1	171
		2,7-8	212
1QSa		2,8-9	202, 212, 222, 223, 224
1,1-6	184	2,9-10	188
1,2	177	2,9	171, 187
1,5	171	2,11	171, 173
1,6-18	213	4,3	175

Index of Passages

1Q25			7,9	175
1,4	171		13-14	187
			f3 2,16	175
1Q26	199		f4,8	171, 175
1,4	172		f6,3	171
			f6,12	175
1Q27				
3-8	189		*4QDibHam*	
5,2	171		f121,2	172, 173
f1 f,5-6	172		f122,1	175
1,7	203			
2,1	172		*4QFlor*	
			1,5-6	176
1Q34			1,7	171
f3 2,2	171		1,11	171, 187, 224
2,7	207		f1-3 2,3	175
1Q34^{bis}			*4QM^a*	
2,2-3	179		f1-3,3	171
2,3-4	189		f8-9,5	206
2,6-7	188			
			4QMessAr	
1Q38			1,3-11	212
12,1	171		1,3-10	203
			1,3	213
1Q51			1,5	213, 224
2	171		1,6	213
			1,7-8	213
1Q62				
2	175		*4QOrNab*	199
2Q18	25		*4QOrd^a* (159)	184
18 f1	181		2,17	175
f2	181			
			4QOrd^b (513)	184
4QAhA	203		4,5	175
			f3,5	187
4QBer^a (286)				
10 2,12	170		*4QPrFêtes^b*	
			2,3	171
4QDibHam^a			f2,4	172
f1 2,13	170, 173		f4,2	175
2,13-15	187			
2,13-14	188		*4QPrFêtes^c*	
f1-2 2,9	175		2,4	175
2,12-15	220, 223		f16,7	196
2,13	171, 220		f18,2	175
2,14	220		f55,2	196
3,9	175, 220		f97,98 1,8	175
3,12	175		f188,2	175
3,18	175		f212,1	172
4,3	220			
4,5	220		*4QShir^a* (510)	193, 198, 221
4,6	175		f 1,6	203
5,8-9	175		1,9	206
6,8	175			
f2 5,14	173		*4QShir^b* (511)	193, 198, 221

f1, 7-8	220, 222		4Q158	
f2, 1-6	187		f7-8,3	175
5-7	220, 223			
f10,8	206		4Q159	
f18 2,6	203		f1 2,17	175
f48-51 2,4	171		5,4	175
f63-64 2,3	171		5,7	175
2,5	175			
3,5	175		4Q166	
f63 3,3	206		2,4	173
			2,16	187

4QS1
37-40	203
39 f1	218

4Q175   167

39 f1,17-18	218, 223
1,21-22	217, 223
1,22	206
1,24-25	218

4Q176
16,5   175

4Q177
f5-6,9   172

4QTestim
1	175
12	187
23-24	176

4Q179   167
f1 1,4   175

4Q180   199
1-5   179

4QpHos^a (166)
2,4   171

4QpHos^b (167)
f7-9,2	171
f23,1	171

4Q183
f1 2,3   175

4QpIs^a (161)
D2	171
f8-10,11-24	203

4Q184   167, 198
f1 1,15	171
f1 14-17	187, 218, 223
14-15	218
15	219
16-17	218

4QpIs^b (162)
2,1-10	187
2,7	173

4Q185   167, 193, 198
2,3-4	173
3,3	175

4QpIs^c (163)
12	171
14	171
f4-7 2,5	171

f1-2 1,13-2,1	219, 222, 223
1,14	219
1,15	219
2,1	219
2,2-11	219, 222, 223
2,3-4	220
2,8-13	220
2,11-12	220
2,13-15	220

4QpIs^e (165)
f1-2,3   172

4QpNah (169)
f3 2,5	172
3,4	172

4Q186   167, 199

4Q247   199

4QpPs^a (171)
1,2-5	188
1,3	171
2,3	171
2,15	171
2,23	171
4,8	171

4Q260   199

4Q317   199

4Q485		*11QMelch*	
f3,2	172	12	173
4Q486	193	*11QPs^a*	
		17,2-3	187
4Q487	193, 198	18	200, 214, 215
f2,5	171	18,1-16	214
f2,8	196	18,1	215
f,21,3	171	18,3	196, 215
		18,10-13	214, 223
4Q489	193, 198	18,10	215
		18,11-12	214, 215
4Q491		18,11	215
f8-10 1,7	175	18,12-14	215
		18,12	171, 215
4Q497		18,13	215
1,5	175	18,14	173
		19,1-18	167
4Q501		19,2-3	203
f1,7	172	19,14	203
7	173	21,17	175
1,2	175	21,11-22,1	181
1,7	175	22,1-15	167
		24,8	171, 203, 215
4Q502	186	24,9	173
f1-2	171	26,4-8	200
		26,14	196
4Q503		27,2-11	167, 187, 199, 221, 223, 224
4,3	175		
		27,2	196, 221
4Q512	186	27,3	206, 221
5,15	172	27,4	221
12,12	175	27,11	221
f1 12,4	187		
f82,2	171	*11QT*	
		51,5-9	187
4Q513		54,5-14	173
f4,5	171	54,5	187
		54,14	187
5Q13		56,3-4	187
1,2	172	56,20-21	187
28,3	175	56,21	187
		56,21	187
6Q16		58,18	187
3,1	175	59,3-9	187
3,2	171	59,9-10	188
		59,13-21	187
6QD			
3,4	175		

IV. New Testament

Matthew		*Mark*	
7,12	122	2,16	67
15,24	241	9,37	241
22,36-40	44		

Index of Passages

Luke	
4,18	241
5,30	67
6,31	122

Acts	
4,11	247
5,34	230
6,9	229
7,20-22	228
7,38	120, 210
7,53	210
9,29	229
9,30	230
11,25	230
15,10	113
15,29	122
20,31	330
20,35	315
21,39	227
22,3	227, 230
22,27-28	229
23,1	333
23,6	229, 230
23,9	67
23,16	229
24,16	333
26,5	230
26,10	229, 230
26,14	229

Romans	
1-2	319
1,2	295
1,5	303
1,8	303
1,9	327
1,18-3,20	285, 293
1,18ff.	251
1,18	331
1,26	320
1,28	326, 330
1,29-31	324
2,5-11	308
2,7	308
2,8	332
2,12-16	334
2,12	280
2,13	280, 286, 290
2,14-15	319
2,14	280, 340
2,15	333, 334, 335
2,16	308
2,17ff.	324
2,17-29	285
2,17-24	232
2,17-20	232, 233, 234, 235
2,17-18	232
2,17	233
2,18	233, 326, 330, 331
2,19-20	232, 233
2,19	234
2,20	233, 234
2,29	327
3,1-8	285
3,2	120
3,20	286
3,21-31	285
3,21-26	285, 293
3,21	287
3,22	287
3,27-31	285
3,27	266, 268, 285, 286, 287, 293, 294, 314, 341
3,28-30	293
3,28	285, 286, 287, 293
3,29-30	285
3,31	269, 270, 281, 288, 294, 297
4,15	314
5,5	305, 327
5,6-11	328
5,8	327
5,12ff.	251
5,13-14	314
5,20-21	290
5,21	322
6,6-7	340
6,12-23	303
6,13	303
6,14	293
6,15	293
6,16	322
6,18	322, 340, 341
6,19	303
6,22	322, 340, 341
7	289, 319
7,1-6	293
7,5-6	341
7,6	288, 322
7,7	288
7,12	294, 295
7,13-23	288, 293
7,13	288
7,14	289
7,22	295
7,23	330
7,24	288
7,25	288, 295, 330
8,1ff.	305
8,1-11	322
8,1-4	288
8,1	288, 290
8,2-4	281

Index of Passages

8,2	266, 268, 270, 278, 286, 288, 289, 290, 293, 294, 314, 340, 341	13,8-10	274, 275, 280, 294, 328, 341
8,3-4	289	13,8	290, 328
8,3	291, 293	13,9-10	328
8,4	280, 290, 294, 305, 327	13,9	275
8,5	327	13,10	276, 290, 328
8,7	295	13,11-14	309
8,9-11	294	13,13	320, 324
8,9	305, 327	14-15	323
8,14	305, 327	14,5	330
8,15	305	14,7-9	303
8,16-17	305	14,9-10	303
8,18	306	14,9	302
8,19ff.	251	14,11	314
8,21	340	14,14	317, 334
8,26-27	305	14,16	326
8,29-30	253	14,17	327
8,29	250	14,18	322
8,32-37	327	14,20	319
8,39	327	14,22-23	330
9,1	333, 335	15,1	312
9,23	249	15,2	326, 328
9,31	291, 293	15,3	314, 316
10,1-21	290	15,5	306, 307
10,2	290	15,7	301, 316
10,3-4	291	15,13	305
10,4	284, 290, 293, 297	15,14	330, 332, 337
10,6-8	298	15,16	305
10,6-7	247, 248, 261, 263, 292	15,18	303
11,1	229	15,27	312
11,2	250	15,30	305, 327
11,32	250	16,17-18	324
11,33-36	249, 263	16,17	318
11,33-35	261	16,18	322
11,33	249	16,19	303, 317, 325, 326, 336
11,34-35	249	16,20	304
11,34	250		
11,36	250, 260, 261, 262	*1 Corinthians*	
12-13	301, 310	1-4	242
12,1-2	303, 330	1-3	243
12,1	295, 305, 306	1,8	309
12,2	304, 306, 326, 330, 331, 332	1,10	317, 323
		1,13	303
12,4ff.	305	1,18-25	263
12,4-8	305	1,19	249
12,9-21	324	1,20	244
12,9	326, 328	1,21	250
12,16	306, 313	1,24	242, 243, 244, 250, 261
12,17	313	1,30	242, 243, 244, 250, 258, 261
12,19	313, 314	2,6-17	244
12,20	313	2,6-16	244
13,1-7	320	2,9	250
13,1-6	324	2,10-16	305
13,3	319, 326	2,12	250
13,5	312, 333, 334, 335	2,16	250
13,7-8	312	3	325

Index of Passages

3,8	308	8,7-8	334
3,13	308	8,7	333
3,14	308	8,10	333
3,18	325, 329	8,11-13	303
3,23	303	8,12	333, 334
4,4-5	334	9,1	280
4,4	333, 335	9,7ff.	280
4,5	308	9,7	324
4,14	330	9,14	315
4,16-17	318	9,19-23	231, 280
4,17	318	9,19	280, 328, 341
5,6	324	9,20-22	281
5,7	303	9,20-21	280, 285
5,10-11	324	9,20	280, 281, 292, 293
5,13	313, 314	9,21	280, 281, 294, 295, 296, 341
6,1-20	301		
6,1-8	323, 329	9,22	280
6,5	325, 333, 337	9,24-25	308
6,6	314	9,25	306
6,9-11	280	10	246, 247
6,9-10	324	10,1-4	247
6,12-20	303, 322	10,3-4	247
6,12	324	10,4	246, 247, 261, 262
6,13	306	10,11	330
6,16	313	10,13	305
6,17	294	10,14-22	303
7,1-40	320, 323	10,20	317
7,3	312	10,23-11,1	334
7,4-5	329	10,23	304, 341
7,4	324	10,24	328
7,5	304	10,25-27	334
7,7	317	10,25	333
7,9	306, 313	10,26	319
7,10	314, 315, 317	10,27	333
7,11	314	10,28	333
7,15	314	10,29	333
7,17-24	279	10,32	319
7,17	279, 317	11,1	316, 318
7,19	279, 292, 294, 295, 328, 329	11,3-5	303
		11,6	324
7,20	279	11,10	312
7,21-24	303	11,11	303
7,22	322	11,14	320
7,25	323	11,15-16	324
7,26	314	11,16	306
7,32-35	303	11,17	317
7,32-33	329	11,23-26	316
7,32	317	11,23	315
7,35	320	11,34	317
7,36-38	329	12-14	305
7,39	303	12-13	301
7,40	305, 323	12,3-11	305
8,1-11,1	301	12,4-6	294
8-10	244	12,8	306, 331
8,1-13	334	12,11	305
8,3	250	13	329
8,6	242, 244, 245, 260, 261, 262, 319	13,4-7	328
		13,5	313, 320, 328

13,8-13	328	8,21	313
13,9	332	8,24	328
14	305	9,4	324
14,1	328	9,6	324
14,37	331	9,7	314
14,40	320	9,9-10	314
15,22-28	261	9,9	314
15,24-26	261	10,5-6	303
15,32	313	10,5	330
15,44-49	261	11,22	229
15,45	294	12,14	312
15,57	261	12,18	327
15,58	308	12,20-21	324
16,1	317	12,20	317
16,14	328	13,11	306, 324

2 Corinthians

		Galatians	
1,12	333, 335	1,22	228
2,9	317	2,4	340, 341
2,11	305	2,6	307
2,17	317	2,14	277, 307
3	284, 285	2,19	274
3,3	283, 284	2,20	278, 327, 328
3,4-18	265, 282, 285, 293, 294, 296	3	268
		3,3	305
3,4-6	282	3,13	294
3,6	293	3,15-18	271
3,7-11	283, 284, 293, 294	3,17	271
3,7	283	3,19-25	271, 274, 293
3,11	283	3,19-20	269, 272
3,12-18	284, 293	3,19	210, 271, 272, 273, 296
3,13	283, 283	3,20-25	271
3,14	283, 330	3,20	271, 272
3,17-18	284	3,21-25	271
3,17	340	3,21	271, 273, 292, 296
3,18-4,6	253	3,22-25	271
4,2	333, 335	3,23-24	273, 292
4,4	256, 330	3,23	273
4,13	305	3,24	273
4,16	332	3,25	273, 292
4,17	306	4,4	240, 241, 242, 261, 262
5,9-10	308	4,5	293
5,11	333, 335	4,6	241, 305
5,13-15	303	4,9	250
5,14-15	302	4,10	273, 277
5,17	290	4,21	293
6,2	304	5-6	310
8-10	323	5,1	113, 340, 341
8-9	301	5,3	274
8,7-8	328	5,5-6	275
8,8-9	303	5,5	278
8,8	328	5,6	278, 279, 328
8,9	316	5,13-6,10	301, 322
8,10	323	5,13ff.	278, 279, 305
8,11	328	5,13-14	305, 328
8,15	313, 314	5,13	328, 341
8,19-20	328	5,14	274, 275, 276, 277, 278,

	281, 294, 328, 341	4,8	306, 326, 331
5,15	324	4,9	318
5,16	278, 305, 327	4,19	249
5,17	280		
5,18	293, 327	*Colossians*	
5,19-23	324	1,8	328
5,19-21	304	1,9-12	327
5,22-25	305	1,9-10	305, 306, 325, 327, 332,
5,22ff.	278		337
5,22	305, 327	1,9	331, 332
5,23	306	1,15-20	253, 255, 258
5,25	305, 327	1,15-18	225, 262
6,1	305	1,15-17	242
6,2-5	330	1,15	256, 258, 260, 261, 262,
6,2	266, 268, 269, 277, 278,		263
	279, 281, 294, 296, 314,	1,16-18	256
	341	1,16	257, 258, 260
6,6	326	1,17-18	256
6,7-10	308	1,17	257, 258, 260
6,8	308	1,18-20	255
6,14	274	1,18	257, 261
6,15	279, 290	1,19	257
6,16	312	1,27	249
		1,28	325, 330, 336
Ephesians		2,2	259, 260, 313
4,32-5,2	324	2,3	259, 261, 263
5,8-10	330	2,28	330
5,15	325	3,1-4	301
6,4	330	3,5	324
		3,8	324
Philippians		3,10	330
1,6	309	3,16	305, 325, 330, 336
1,9-11	330	3,17-18	303
1,9-10	306, 329, 331, 332, 337	3,18	312, 326, 337
1,9	332	3,20-25	324
1,10	308, 326, 332	3,20	326
2,2	306	3,21	324
2,4	328	3,24	322
2,6-18	301	3,25	208
2,6-11	248, 251, 252, 254, 261,	4,5	319, 325
	262, 303, 316	4,12	332
2,6	241, 253, 254		
2,8	252	*1 Thessalonians*	
2,12-13	304	1,6-7	305
2,12	303	1,6	316
2,15	313	1,9	322
2,16	309	2,13	317
2,17	303	3,5	305
3	269	3,12-13	308
3,5	229, 230	3,12	328
3,6	229	4	310
3,14	308	4,1-8	305
3,17	318	4,1-2	312, 328
3,20	309	4,1	327
4,2	306	4,3-6	308
4,4	403	4,4	324
4,8-9	332	4,6-8	301

4,6	308	1,19	333
4,9	328	3,9	333
4,12	319, 320	4,2	333
4,15	315		
5,1-11	309	2 Timothy	
5,1-10	301	1,3	333
5,9-10	308		
5,10	303	Titus	
5,12-22	324	1,15-16	330
5,12	330	1,15	333
5,14	320, 330	3,10	330
5,15	326		
5,21	304, 330, 331	Philemon	329
5,23	308	6	331, 332
		8	326
2 Thessalonians			
3,4	317	Hebrews	
3,6-7	320	5,12	120
3,7	312	8,6	272
3,10	324	9,15	272
3,11	320	12,19	210
3,15	330	12,24	272
		22,2	210
1 Timothy			
1,5	333		

V. Jewish-Hellenistic Literature

Aristobulos		2,163	166
PrEv		2,292	233
7,14,1	257	6,291	69
8,10,4	162		
13,12,1-2	162	Vita	
13,12,4	162	10-11	166
13,12,8-13	162		
		Contra Apionem	
Josephus		2,41	234
Antiquitates			
12,142	63, 65	Philo	
12,256	233	De Abrahamo	
13,171	166	16,60	132
15,136	210	19	234
16,203	63		
17,149-150	69	De Decalogo	
17,152	69	1	92
18,13-21	166	84-86	58
18,16	67	87	333
		Quod Det. Pot. insidiari soleat	
De Bello Judaico		115-118	246
1,24	63		
1,87ff.	191	Quis Rer. Div. Heres sit	
1,648	69	98	249
2,121-123	166	189	257
2,128-142	166	199	257
2,139-142	170		
2,147-149	166	De Migratione Abrahami	
2,159	191	130	92

De Ebrietate
30-31	256

De Fuga et Inventione
97	92
108-109	92
112	257

De Mutatione Nominum
236-239	249

De Opificio Mundi
3,143	132

De Posteritate Caini
18	92
84-88	249

De Praemiis et Poenis
80-81	249

Quod Omnis Probus liber sit
68	249
72-91	191
75-76	166

Quaestiones in Genesin
2,118	257
4,97	256

De Somniis
2,180	249
2,252	92
2,242	92
2,245	92

De Specialibus Legibus
1,301	249
2,2-5	58
3,6	92

De Virtutibus
8	249
62-65	92
62	256
183-184	249

De Vita Mosis
2,52	44, 132
3,19	272
76	249

VI. Rabbinic Literature

Mishnah
Abot
1,4	212
1,9	58
3,3-4	214
3,5	113
4,1	47

Kelim
13,7	68

Keraioth
1,1	58
1,7	59

Baba Mesia
5,11	68

Gittin
3,1	68
7,2	68
8,8	68
9,8	68

Orla
3,9	68

Para
11,4-6	68

Pesahim
3,1	68

Sanhedrin
7,2	67
11,1	58
11,3	68
4,3	68
5,5	68

Shebiit
10,1	59

Shebuot
5,1	58

Shabbat
12,5	68

Sota
9,15	69

Index of Passages

Tohorot	
4,7	68
4,11	68
Yebamot	
2,4	68
4,13	58
9,3	68
Yadayim	
3,2	68
Tosefta	
Baba Mesia	
11,23	59
Pea	
4,5	59
4,19	49
Ketubot	
4,13	59
Megilla	
3,19	68
4,38	68
Sota	
6,2	68
Sukkah	
3,11ff.	246
Babylonian Talmud	
Baba Bathra	
21b	68
Ketubot	
105a	68
Qiddushin	
30a	63
30b	47

Shabbat	
31a	122
Sanhedrin	
23a	58
52b	67
Baba Qamma	
62a	212
Sota	
49b	230
Palestinian Talmud	
Pea	
21a	68
Megilla	
74a	68
Taanit	
69a	68
Yebamot	
13a	68
Berachot	
7,2	214
Pesiqta Rabbati	
21(103b-104a)	210
Exodus Rabbah	
29(88d)	210
Numeri Rabbah	
11(164b)	210
14,11	212
Pesiqta	
108a	210
Targum Onkelos	
Num 21,19-20	246

VII. Greek and Roman Literature

Cicero	
De natura deorum	
2,14	84
2,37	84
De re publica	
3,33	85

De legibus	
1,6	85
1,18	85
2,8	85
Tusculanae Disputationes	
4,57	136

Diogenes Laertius
7,88   85

Plinius Maior
Naturalis Historia
5,73   166

Ps.-Menander
39-40   122

Seneca
Epistulae morales
89,4   136

De ira
3,36   333

VIII. Early Christian and Gnostic Literature

Barnabas
5,4   155

Didache
1,2   122

Odes of Solomon
6,8ff.   148

Nag Hammadi
Codex VII Silvanus
111,13-111,20   252
112,8-113,23   252

Index of Authors

Aalen, S. 36, 83, 99, 106, 111, 131, 133, 145, 155, 156, 157, 158, 236
Ackroyd, P. R. 26, 61
Adam, A. 166
Agnew, F. 317
Aland, B. 252
Aland, K. 93, 231
Aletti, J. N. 240, 255, 256, 257, 258
Allegro, J. M. 167, 179, 184, 186, 218, 219, 220
Allo, E. B. 239
Alon, G. 58, 59
Alonso-Schökel, L. 25, 70, 75
Alt, A. 1
Anderson, G. W. 1
Andresen, C. 238, 239
Andrews, H. T. 120, 122, 123
Audet, J. P. 2
Auer, A. 339
Avi-Yonah, M. 6

Baillet, M. 167, 181, 184, 186, 193, 220, 221
Balz, H. 281
Balz, H. R. 242
Bammel, E. 230, 255, 266, 277
Banks, R. J. 37, 79, 86, 94, 97, 105, 107, 108, 109, 115, 121, 126, 132, 136, 143, 145, 149, 154, 157, 158, 161, 175, 178, 189, 190
Baras, Z. 6
Barbour, R. S. 240, 243, 244, 245, 246, 252, 256
Bardtke, H. 195, 214
Barr, J. 94
Barrett, C. 247, 248, 250, 269, 274, 276, 279, 280, 281, 283, 286, 289, 331
Barth, G. 251, 252
Barth, K. 259, 340
Barth, M. 235, 265
Barthelemy, D. 16, 31, 167
Bartsch, H. W. 251, 252, 253, 255, 305
Battistone, J. J. 95, 96, 97, 98, 99
Bauckmann, E. G. 9, 10, 11, 39, 42
Bauer, W. 233
Baum, H. 282
Baumann, R. 239, 242, 250
Baumgarten, J. 231

Baumgarten, J. M. 169, 172, 173, 184, 185, 186, 187
Baumgartner, W. 1, 34, 207
Beardslee, W. A. 236
Beasley-Murray, P. 257
Becker, Jo. 5
Becker, Jü. 168, 174, 175, 178, 189, 211, 216, 217, 310, 311
Beckwith, R. T. 64, 101, 102, 168, 185, 186
Begrich, J. 1, 64
Behm, J. 233
Beker, J. C. 240
Belkin, S. 230
Benoit, P. 255, 270
Berger, K. 30, 31, 131, 275
Best, E. 243
Betz, H. D. 240, 241, 246, 265, 271, 272, 273, 274, 275, 276, 278, 286, 324
Betz, O. 68, 166, 167, 169, 170, 172, 174, 181, 183, 187, 197, 209
Bieder, W. 270
Bietenhard, H. 166
Billerbeck, P., see Strack, H. L.
Black, M. 89, 100, 230, 248, 324
Blank, J. 235, 265, 266, 286, 289, 290
Blenkinsopp, J. 1, 4, 15, 19, 72
Böckle, F. 339
Bogaert, P. M. 152, 153, 154, 155, 156, 159
Bonnard, P. E. 16, 96, 130, 237, 240, 243, 250, 259
Bornkamm, G. 232, 246, 249, 280, 311
Botte, B. 237
Bourke, M. M. 240
Bouttier, M. 244
Box, G. H. 8, 26, 32, 34, 43, 46, 47, 48, 56, 58, 59, 70, 73, 139, 148
Brandenburger, E. 139, 140, 141, 142, 143, 144, 145, 146, 147, 148, 149, 150, 153, 154, 156, 232, 240
Braun, H. 113, 169, 170, 173, 176, 177, 181, 188, 197, 205, 206, 265, 286
Breitenstein, U. 134, 135, 136, 137, 138
Bright, J. 4
Bring, R. 272, 291
Brinsmead, B. H. 270, 271, 272, 274, 277, 278

Index of Authors

Brock, S. P. 100
Brooke, G. 183
Brownlee, W. H. 180, 181
Bruce, F. F. 170, 181, 183, 229, 230, 231, 235, 240, 241, 257, 259, 266, 272, 273, 274, 275, 277, 278, 286, 296
Brunt, J. C. 311
Bühner, J. A. 317
Bultmann, R. 233, 236, 283, 284, 286, 295, 313, 328
Burchard, C. 166, 228, 229 230
Burger, C. 255, 256, 257
Burgmann, H. 186
Burnett, F. W. 237

Cahill, H. 261
Callan, T. 272
Calvin, J. 272
Cambier, J. M. 340
Campbell, W. S. 269, 291
Carmichel, C. M. 2
Carmignac, J. 94, 166, 181, 212, 213
Cazelles, H. 178
Ceriani, A. M. 152
Chadwick, H. 249, 333
Charles, R. H. 100, 108, 152, 153, 154, 159
Charlesworth, J. H. 93, 100, 112, 113, 118, 120, 125, 134, 139, 140, 152, 153, 167, 168, 185
Christ, F. 236
Collange, J. F. 261, 277, 282, 283, 284, 285, 302, 306, 308, 311, 316, 322, 339
Collins, J. J. 14, 52, 100, 105, 108, 112, 116, 125
Colpe, C. 194, 239
Conzelmann, H. 19, 228, 229, 231, 232, 234, 238, 243, 244, 246, 247, 255, 281, 324
Coughenour, R. A. 100, 101, 102, 103, 104, 105, 109, 110
Cranfield, C. E. B. 234, 248, 266, 268, 270, 272, 273, 274, 283, 284, 285, 286, 287, 289, 290, 291, 295, 296, 303, 305, 330, 335
Cremer, H. 286
Crenshaw, J. L. 1, 2, 8, 9, 16, 20, 21, 87, 98, 269, 291
Crowe, F. E. 27
Cullmann, O. 240, 247, 252, 304, 313

Dahl, N. A. 266
Dalbert, P. 120, 121, 125, 126, 127, 130, 135
Daube, D. 230, 266

Dautzenberg, G. 183, 238, 269
Davenport, G. L. 116, 117
Davies, P. R. 176, 210
Davies, W. D. 9, 105, 108, 110, 112, 115, 118, 237, 243, 247, 248, 256, 259, 264, 265, 269, 270, 278, 291, 296
Davis, J. A. 15, 207, 209, 223, 242, 243, 244
Dednering, S. 152
Deichgräber, R. 249, 251, 255, 256
Deidun, T. J. 276, 279, 281, 283, 289, 291, 304, 306, 307, 311, 315, 316, 321, 322, 327, 328, 329, 333, 334
Deissmann, A. 237
Delcor, M. 170, 181, 214
Delekat, L. 77
Delling, G. 134, 135, 136
Denis, A. M. 93, 100, 101, 112, 113, 118, 119, 125, 152, 168, 190, 199
Dennison, W. D. 322
Dexinger, F. 93, 94, 100, 105, 193
Dimant, D. 102
Dinkler, E. 238, 239
Dodd, C. H. 280, 281
Domkowsi Hopkins, D. 211
Drane, J. W. 265, 270
Du, C. le 289
Dülmen, A. van 264, 265, 272, 276, 277, 278, 281, 286, 289, 291, 295
Duesberg, H. 18, 77
Dunn, J. D. G. 20, 131, 235, 238, 239, 241, 242, 243, 244, 245, 247, 248, 249, 250, 251, 252, 253, 254, 255, 256, 257, 258, 259, 260, 261, 262, 263, 282, 283, 294, 311, 331
Dupont-Sommer, A. 166

Ebeling, G. 271, 274
Eberharter, A. 60, 61
Eckart, K. G. 255
Eckstein, H. J. 333
Edwards, R. A. 236
Eichholz, G. 302, 303, 305
Eissfeldt, O. 8, 93, 95, 100, 101, 112, 113, 118, 119, 123, 125, 129, 134, 135, 136, 139, 140, 152, 153, 154
Ellis, E. E. 230, 231, 253, 261
Ellul, J. 304, 339
Emerton, J. A. 1
Evans, C. 330

Falk, Z. W. 57, 58, 59, 60
Farmer, W. R. 233, 291
Festorazzi, F. 266, 302, 306, 307, 324
Feuillet, A. 236, 239, 245, 247, 248, 251, 252, 255, 256, 257, 259, 265, 269, 277, 280, 281, 283, 284, 289, 296, 316

Index of Authors

Fichtner, J. 12, 47, 122
Fiddes, P. S. 9, 13, 14, 15, 20, 39, 42, 79, 81, 84, 133
Finkelstein, L. 66
Fischer, J. A. 231
Fitzmyer, J. A. 212, 213, 214, 282, 285
Flusser, D. 184
Fohrer, G. 5
Friedrich, G. 264, 266, 286, 287, 289, 327
Friedrich, J. 266
Fritz, K. von 93
Froitzheim, F. 241, 243, 246, 247, 251, 258, 262
Furnish, V. P. 300, 301, 302, 311, 316, 322

Gabathuler, H. J. 255, 256
Gabrion, H. 170, 172, 176, 181, 182, 183, 184, 207, 226
Galitis, G. 280, 341
Galling, K. 5, 64
Gammie, J. G. 192, 195
Garnet, P. 168, 170, 189, 190
Gasque, W. W. 296
Gaster, T. H. 209, 212, 213, 214, 215, 218, 219, 220
Geffcken, J. 124, 125
Georgi, D. 129, 130, 132, 133, 232, 251, 252, 255
Gerhardsson, B. 230, 301, 311, 313, 333, 339
Germann, H. 181
Gerstenberger, E. 2, 5
Gese, H. 5, 20, 21, 22, 23, 84, 87, 193, 237, 240, 246, 256, 257, 261, 288
Giblin, C. H. 245, 272
Gilbert, M. 9, 13, 79, 84
Ginzberg, L. 185
Gnilka, J. 235, 251, 252, 255, 256, 257, 258, 259, 266, 325
Gooding, D. W., 120
Goppelt, L. 240, 241, 251, 258
Grabbe, L. L. 140, 143, 153
Grabner-Haider, A. 300, 302
Gray, G. B. 112, 113, 114
Grech, P. 301, 303, 306, 307, 308, 313, 316, 324
Green, W. S. 167, 178
Grözinger, K. E. 167
Gruenwald, I. 93, 94, 193
Grundmann, W. 236
Gunkel, H. 141
Gunneweg, A. H. J. 95
Gutbrod, W. 9, 123, 127, 133, 229
Guttmann, A. 64, 69

Hadas, M. 118, 119, 120, 123, 134, 135
Haenchen, E. 228, 230
Häring, B. 340
Hagner, D. A. 257
Hahn, F. 240, 245, 247, 266, 267, 270, 272, 274, 278, 286, 289, 290, 291, 311, 317
Hainz, J. 306
Halter, H., 276, 301, 302, 303, 304, 305, 306, 307, 311, 316, 339
Hamerton-Kelly, R. G. 236, 238, 241, 243, 245, 246, 247, 248, 251
Hanson, A. T. 247, 282
Hanson, P. D. 94
Harnisch, W. 94, 139, 140, 141, 142, 143, 144, 145, 146, 147, 148, 149, 150, 151, 152, 153, 154, 155, 156, 157, 309
Harrington, D. J. 14, 52, 67
Hasenstab, R. 236, 300, 302, 311, 332, 333, 339, 340, 342
Haspecker, J. 16, 18, 24, 25, 29, 32, 33, 37, 44, 45, 46, 47, 50, 51, 56, 62, 67, 69, 70, 73, 73, 75
Hatch, E. 31, 39
Haufe, C. 265
Hayman, A. P. 141
Hegermann, H. 130, 131, 135, 225, 256
Heiligenthal, R. 320
Heinemann, I. 135
Heinrici, G. 237
Helfmeyer, F. J. 176
Hengel, M. 8, 9, 11, 12, 19, 20, 27, 39, 52, 53, 62, 63, 65, 71, 84, 85, 86, 87, 88, 93, 98, 101, 119, 121, 123, 125, 126, 167, 168, 169, 173, 174, 185, 188, 191, 194, 195, 196, 197, 199, 201, 202, 207, 212, 214, 215, 226, 228, 229, 230, 236, 237, 238, 240, 241, 242, 243, 244, 246, 247, 251, 253, 256, 259, 261, 263, 279, 291, 294, 296, 297
Herford, R. T. 82
Herr, T. 309, 313, 314, 318, 320, 321, 324, 326, 331, 333, 340
Hertz, A. 310
Hickling, C. J. A. 282
Hilsberg, P. 333
Hock, R. F. 229
Hodgson, R. 309, 324
Höffken, P. 27
Hofius, O. 251, 252
Holmberg, B. 317
Holmes, S. 129, 132
Holm-Nielsen, S. 112, 113, 117, 171, 174, 211, 217

Holtz, T.   254, 295, 313, 314, 315, 317, 319, 328, 329
Honnefelder, L.   339
Hooker, M. D.   254, 269
Horgan, M. P.   182, 183, 217
Horsley, R. A.   243, 244
Howard, G.   251
Hübner, H.   230, 235, 264, 268, 270, 272, 273, 274, 275, 278, 283, 286, 287, 289, 290, 291
Hughes, P. E.   284, 285
Huntemann, G.   339, 340
Huntjens, J. A.   169, 175, 177, 178, 184, 188, 189

Ilg, N.   175

Jackson, B. S.   57, 58, 59, 185
Jacob, E.   5, 9, 84, 87
James, M. R.   139
Jansen, H. L.   116
Janssen, E.   9, 22, 26, 27, 28, 94, 151, 157
Jastrow, M.   217
Jaubert, A.   107, 114, 121, 132, 135, 157, 175, 177, 186
Jellicoe, S.   119, 120
Jeremias, G.   180, 187, 202
Jeremias, J.   67, 68, 69, 229, 230, 265
Jervell, J.   155, 255, 266
Jeske, R. L.   246, 247
Jewett, R.   330, 333
Joest, W.   300
Johnson, M. D.   236
Jonas, H.   252
Jonge, H. J. de   237
Jongeling, B.   166, 210
Joüon, P.   69
Jüngel, E.   274, 278, 288, 289, 295

Käsemann, E.   232, 233, 234, 247, 248, 249, 250, 255, 266, 270, 285, 289, 296, 303, 323, 335
Kaiser, O.   9, 10, 19, 44, 82, 86
Kant, I.   339
Kapelrud, A. S.   175
Kautzsch, E.   141
Kayatz, C.   64
Keck, L. E.   269, 289
Kehl, N.   255, 256, 257
Kellermann, U.   27
Kerst, R.   244
Kertelge, K.   285, 317
Kim, S.   228, 229, 230, 231, 235, 237, 238, 239, 240, 241, 243, 246, 247, 248, 251, 252, 253, 255, 256, 257, 258, 259, 260, 261, 263, 292

Kimbrough, S. T.   184, 205, 206, 223
Kirk, J. A.   317
Kittel, B. D.   211
Klijn, A. F. J.   139, 152, 153, 154, 155, 157, 158, 161
Klinzing, G.   176, 189, 206
Knibb, M. A.   100, 101
Knox, J.   233, 291
Knox, W. L.   9, 19, 71, 72
Koch, K.   94, 192, 193
Koehler, L.   34, 207
Koester, K.   239
Koo, T. K.   5
Koole, J. L.   79, 84
Korff, W.   339
Küchler, M.   6, 66, 87, 88, 94, 95, 96, 97, 98, 103, 105, 109, 130, 136, 148, 149, 158, 163, 190, 191, 196, 197, 199, 200, 201, 202, 219, 220
Kümmel, W. G.   228, 235, 240, 241, 251, 252, 254, 255, 258, 265, 276, 290, 291, 296
Kuhn, G.   25
Kuhn, H. W.   174, 177, 193, 194, 195, 197, 202, 203, 211, 217, 235
Kuhn, K. G.   171, 174, 186, 194, 220
Kuss, O.   264
Kutsch, E.   71

Lacey, D. R. de   272
Lacocque, A.   140
Ladd, G. E.   286, 291
Lähnemann, J.   255
Lamarche, P.   289
Lanchester, H. C. O.   126
Lang, B.   19
Langkammer, H.   245, 257
Larcher, C.   129, 130, 131, 132
LaSor, W. S.   14
Laub, F.   300, 309
Lauer, S.   137, 138
Lauterbach, J. Z.   64
Lebram, J. C. H.   19, 21, 22, 23, 27, 44, 71, 73, 135, 200
Lehmann, M. R.   181, 186, 212
Lella, A. A. Di   8, 86
Levine, B. A.   167
Lewis, J. J.   122
Licht, J.   166, 167
Lichtenberger, H.   166, 167, 168, 169, 170, 171, 175, 176, 177, 178, 180, 183, 189, 191, 192, 193, 195, 198, 205, 206, 208, 210, 215, 216, 219, 220, 226
Liddell, H. G.   48
Liedke, G.   32, 34, 35, 36
Lietzmann, H.   243, 245, 246, 280, 281, 286

Index of Authors

Limbeck, M. 43, 94, 106, 107, 108, 113, 114, 127, 143, 146, 147, 154, 155, 156, 157, 158, 169, 170, 171, 172, 175, 176, 177, 178, 179, 180, 186, 189, 273, 280, 295
Lindars, B. 101
Link, C. 312
Lipscomb, W. L. 190, 191, 192, 195, 201, 203, 204, 214
Livingstone, E. A. 269
Löhr, M. 15, 16, 18, 21, 24, 30, 37, 39, 43, 50, 54, 62, 70, 72, 73, 74, 75, 76, 84
Lohmeyer, E. 251
Lohse, E. 167, 207, 209, 217, 235, 250, 256, 257, 259, 265, 266, 286, 287, 289, 290, 311
Lorenzi, L. De 239, 243, 244, 265, 266, 275, 341
Luck, U. 94, 109, 149, 236, 240
Lüdemann, G. 333
Lührmann, D. 181, 200, 201, 214, 215, 246, 272, 277, 311
Luyten, J. 5
Luz, U. 246, 248, 269, 270, 272, 275, 287, 288, 291, 324
Lyonnet, S. 275, 276

McDermott, J. M. 306
Mack, B. L. 9, 19, 62, 130
MacKenzie, R. A. F. 27, 29, 39
MacKinney, R. W. A. 240
McL.Wilson, R. 242
Maier, G. 8, 47, 53, 75, 113, 114
Maier, J. 9, 20, 88, 93, 135, 185
Maillot, A. 269
Malfroy, J. 2
Mansoor, M. 211, 212
Mantel, H. D. 64, 67, 186
Marböck, H. 9, 11, 12, 13, 15, 16, 17, 18, 19, 20, 21, 22, 24, 26, 27, 28, 29, 30, 32, 33, 37, 42, 43, 44, 46, 48, 52, 53, 60, 62, 64, 66, 69, 70, 71, 72, 73, 74, 77, 79, 80, 81, 84, 85, 86, 87
Marshall, I. H. 228, 229, 230, 258
Martin, R. P. 251, 252, 259
Mattern, L. 308
Maurer, C. 333, 334, 335
Mayer, G. 94, 139, 141
Mearns, C. L. 101
Meisner, N. 118, 119, 120, 122
Mengel, B. 251, 252
Merk, O. 276, 278, 279, 287, 290, 291, 300, 301, 302, 303, 304, 305, 306, 307, 309, 310, 313, 316, 322, 336
Merklein, H. 238, 241, 251, 258, 275, 296

Mettinger, T. N. D. 64
Metz, J. B. 250
Metzger, B. M. 93, 278
Meyer, P. W. 268, 291
Meyer R. 52, 63, 64, 65, 66, 67
Michaelis, W. 119
Michel, O. 234, 247, 249, 286, 289, 301, 306
Middendorp, T. 27, 32, 33, 35, 48, 52, 58, 60, 61, 62, 86
Milgrom, J. 182, 185
Milik, J. T. 100, 101, 102, 167, 170, 185, 212
Momigliano, A. 86
Moore, C. A. 95
Moore, G. F. 87
Moore, R. D. 198, 218
Morgan, D. F. 4, 5
Moule, C. F. D. 259, 291
Mowinckel, S. 64
Moyne, J. Le 67
Mueller, J. R. 143
Müller, H. P. 4, 5
Müller, K. 88, 145, 147, 149, 150
Münchow, C. 93, 94, 102, 105, 106, 109, 110, 139, 141, 143, 145, 149, 152, 153, 154, 155, 156, 157, 158, 193, 302, 308, 309, 311, 320
Mullins, T. Y. 236
Munck, J. 291
Mundle, W. 140, 143, 145
Murphy, R. E. 1, 6, 24
Murphy-O'Connor, J. 178, 185, 209, 244, 245, 251, 252, 255, 306, 334, 340, 341
Mussner, F. 240, 241, 265, 272, 273, 274, 277, 278, 341
Myers, J. M. 139, 140, 146, 148, 149, 150

Nagata, T. 251, 252, 316
Nel, P. J. 1, 4, 9, 14, 15, 70, 74, 84, 85, 301
Neugebauer, O. 103, 104
Neusner, J. 59, 64, 65, 67, 68, 167, 185
Nickelsburg, G. W. E. 8, 14, 44, 93, 94, 95, 97, 98, 100, 101, 109, 112, 113, 118, 119, 121, 125, 129, 130, 134, 135, 137, 139, 140, 141, 152, 153, 166, 167
Nieder, L. 300
Niederwimmer, K. 239, 294, 311, 340, 341
Nikiprowetzky, V. 125, 126, 127
Nissen, A. 55, 56, 88, 94, 102, 107, 108, 109, 110, 122, 140, 145, 149, 151, 152, 153, 154, 155, 156, 157, 275

Nötscher, E. 169, 172, 190, 195, 197, 199, 201, 202, 207, 212, 216
Norden, E. 244, 255
Nyberg, H. S. 3

Oepke, A 229
Östborn, G. 3
Oesterley, W. O. E. 8, 26, 32, 34, 43, 46, 47, 48, 56, 58, 59, 70, 73, 139
Ogg, G. 228
Ollrog, W. H. 235
O'Neill, J. C. 255
Orr, W. F. 246, 279
Osten-Sacken, P. von der 168, 177, 192, 193, 208, 210, 217, 240, 265, 266, 267, 270, 282, 283, 286, 287, 289, 290
Otzen, B. 195, 205

Panikulam, G. 306
Patte, D. 181, 183
Paulsen, H. 231
Pearsen, B. A. 238, 240, 248
Perdue, L. G. 23, 24, 54
Perrin, N. 236
Pesch, R. 245
Peters, N. 20, 26, 77
Pfammatter, J. 255, 306
Pfeifer, G. 20
Pfeiffer, R. H. 52, 66
Philonenko, M. 214
Places, E. des 130
Plevnik, J. 275
Ploeg, J. P. M van der 5
Plöger, O. 178
Pöhlmann, W. 254
Pohlenz, M. 85, 136
Pohlmann, K. F. 26
Provence, T. E. 282, 283, 284
Prümm, K. 239
Pury, A. de 3

Rabin, C. 185
Rabinowitz, I. 183, 217
Rabinowitz, J. 181
Rabinowitz, L. I. 57, 58, 66
Rad, G. von 2, 5, 9, 12, 16, 22, 24, 25, 29, 46, 87, 147, 192, 193
Räisänen, H. 269, 270, 272, 273, 275, 277, 279, 281, 285, 286, 288, 289, 290, 291, 295
Rahlfs, A. 113, 134
Rahner, K. 250
Raj, V. A. R. 256, 263
Rankin, O. S. 122
Rau, E. 100, 103
Rayburn, R. S. 282, 283, 284, 295, 313

Redpath, H. A. 31, 39
Reese, G. 147
Reese, J. M. 130, 243, 246, 256, 263
Reicke, B. 195, 197
Reinmut, E. 313, 322
Rendtorff, T. 340
Rengstorf, K. H. 229, 317
Renker, A. 1
Rhyne, C. T. 268, 269
Richard, E. 282, 283, 284
Richards, K. H. 140, 311
Richardson, P. 339
Richter, W. 2, 3
Ricken, F. 130
Rickenbacher, O. 15, 16, 17, 18, 21, 22, 24, 25, 26, 31, 33, 34, 35, 44, 46, 47, 51, 52, 54, 66, 69, 70, 71, 72, 73, 74, 75, 76, 77, 78
Ridderbos, H. 276, 281, 301, 302, 304, 305, 308, 309, 310, 311, 313, 322, 328, 333, 334, 340, 341
Riesenfeld, H. 279
Riesner, R. 64, 65, 67, 68, 69, 187, 203, 237, 238, 241, 251
Ringgren, H. 19, 20, 201
Rissi, M. 282, 283, 284
Rist, J. M. 85
Rivkin, E. 26, 39, 57, 60, 63, 65, 66, 67
Robinson, J. A. T. 235
Robinson, J. M. 236
Rössler, D. 94, 107, 157
Roloff, J. 228, 229, 230
Romaniuk, K. 190, 195, 196, 197, 207, 232, 247, 301, 307, 327
Roon, A. van 235, 239, 259
Roop, E. F. 167, 198, 203
Rosenthal, F. 153
Rosso-Ubigli, L. 186
Rost, L. 8, 93, 95, 100, 101, 102, 112, 113, 118, 119, 125, 129, 134, 135, 139, 140, 152, 153
Rowland, C. 93, 94, 101, 140, 153, 193, 194, 201
Rudolf, W. 64
Rüger, H. P. 8

Sabatier, A. 102
Samburski, S. 85
Sandbach, F. H. 85
Sandelin, K. G. 240, 242, 261
Sanders, E. P. 169, 175, 177, 185, 189, 202, 205, 207, 266, 270
Sanders, J. A. 166, 167, 181, 200, 201, 214, 215, 221, 266
Sanders, J. T. 252, 255, 256, 311
Sauer, G. 8, 17, 24, 32, 33, 37, 43, 48, 50, 54, 58, 59, 71, 73, 75, 77, 79, 86

Index of Authors

Schade, H. H. 235, 251, 252, 253, 308, 309, 322, 324
Schaeder, H. H. 64, 65
Scharlemann, M. H. 239
Schelkle, K. H. 230, 311, 313, 315, 316
Schencke, W. 20
Schenk, W. 256, 258
Schenke, H. M. 252, 255, 322
Schiffman, L. H. 167, 169, 172, 182, 183, 184, 185, 186, 187
Schilling, O. 9
Schischkoff, G. 90
Schlier, H. 233, 234, 241, 249, 250, 264, 266, 272, 274, 275, 278, 281, 286, 289, 290, 291, 295, 296, 312
Schlink, E. 300
Schmid, H. H. 20, 88
Schnackenburg, R. 236, 237, 266, 311, 333, 341
Schneider, G. 229, 327
Schnelle, U. 242, 277, 278, 281, 282, 307, 322
Schniewind, J. 300
Schoeps, H. J. 275, 278
Schrage, W. 229, 275, 276, 277, 279, 290, 300, 302, 303, 304, 305, 306, 307, 308, 309, 310, 311, 312, 313, 314, 315, 316, 317, 318, 319, 320, 321, 322, 323, 324, 325, 326, 327, 328, 329, 330, 331, 332, 333, 336, 341
Schreiner, J. 139, 140, 141, 149, 152
Schrenk, G. 25, 279
Schubert, K. 12, 84, 107, 167, 176
Schüpphaus, J. 113, 114, 115, 116, 117, 118
Schürer, E. 52, 63, 64, 67, 68, 69, 166
Schürmann, H. 236, 265, 266, 277, 306, 307, 310, 311, 327, 340, 341
Schüssler-Fiorenza, E. 19, 240, 252
Schütz, J. H. 317, 318
Schulz, S. 236
Schunack, G. 331
Schweizer, E. 235, 238, 239, 240, 241, 245, 246, 247, 248, 252, 255, 256, 257, 259, 309
Schweitzer, A. 304
Scott, R. B. Y. 1
Scroggs, R. 237, 239
Segal, M. S. 18, 47, 77
Sellin, G. 242, 243, 244, 246
Senft, C. 245, 247, 279, 281
Sharvit, B. 202, 207
Sheppard, G. T. 1, 9, 14, 60, 61, 71, 72, 84, 95, 96, 97, 98, 248
Sigal, P. 9, 23, 27, 57, 63, 65, 66, 67, 69, 88, 186

Silbermann, L. H. 269, 291
Silver, A. H. 26
Sint, J. A. 93
Skehan, P. W. 58
Slomovic, E. 181
Smend, R. 8, 24, 25, 26, 27, 32, 33, 34, 43, 47, 73, 77, 83, 269, 270, 287, 288, 291, 324
Smith, M. 93, 255
Smitten, W. T. in der 27, 64
Snaith, G. 8, 18, 27, 32, 33, 34, 43, 44, 46, 48, 53, 56, 58, 59, 69, 70, 71, 72, 73, 75, 76
Speyer, W. 93
Spicq, C. 254, 327
Stadelmann, H. 8, 23, 24, 28, 29, 35, 37, 47, 48, 50, 51, 52, 53, 54, 55, 58, 62, 65, 66, 67, 69, 70, 71, 72, 73, 75, 77, 80, 88
Stähli, H. P. 32, 34
Stählin, G. 312
Stanley, D. M. 235
Starky, J. 203, 212, 213
Steck, O. H. 94, 95, 147, 149, 150, 153, 157
Stelzenberger, J. 333
Stendahl, K. 119, 120
Störig, H. J. 85
Stoike, D. A. 277
Stone, M. E. 100, 101
Strack, H. L. 210
Strecker, G. 277, 302, 311, 318, 339, 340
Strobel, A. 186
Strolz, W. 236
Strugnell, J. 218, 219, 220
Stuhlmacher, P. 241, 243, 246, 251, 256, 260, 262, 266, 267, 268, 270, 285, 288, 291, 292, 294, 313
Suggs, J. M. 233, 236, 248
Suter, D. W. 100, 101, 102
Synofzik, E. 308

Talbert, C. H. 251
Taylor, A. E. 90
Tcherikover, V. 53, 120, 121
Theisohn, J. 105
Theochares, A. 103, 105
Therrien, G. 311, 330
Thompson, A. L. 141, 149
Thrall, M. W. 296, 333
Thüsing, W. 245
Todd, R. B. 85
Tödt, H. E. 312
Torrance, T. F. 240
Tov, E. 95
Townshend, R. B. 134
Trilling, W. 254

Turbessi, G. 231
Tuttle, G. A. 14

Unnik, W. C. van 228, 229, 231, 284
Urbach, E. E. 59, 63, 65

Vanhoye, A. 272
Vattioni, F. 8, 25, 32, 75
Vaux, R. de 167
Vawter, B. 19
Vermaseren, M. J. 19, 21
Vermes, G. 22, 166, 167, 175, 180, 181, 185, 186, 187, 191, 198, 204, 207, 209, 212, 213, 217, 218, 219, 220, 221
Villiers, P. G. R. de 117, 141, 143, 147, 148, 203
Violet, B. 138, 139, 140, 147, 148, 149, 152, 153, 154, 155
Viteau, J. 112, 113, 114, 115, 116, 117
Viviano, B. T. 9, 133
Vögtle, A. 308, 309, 324
Vriezen, T. C. 3, 4, 15

Wacker, M. T. 103
Wagner, S. 175, 195, 288
Wallace, D. H. 254
Walther, J. A., see Orr, W. F.
Weder, H. 243, 244, 251, 252, 260, 294
Weimar, P. 20, 93
Weiss, H. F. 9, 16, 72, 86, 88, 90, 130, 131, 246
Weiss, K. 21
Wendland, H. D. 302, 304, 305, 306, 311, 315
Wendland, P. 119, 120
Wengst, K. 244, 252, 255
Westermann, C. 254

Wever, R. 139
Whedbee, J. W. 1
Whitehouse, O. C. 95
Wilckens, U. 9, 19, 71, 73, 103, 130, 190, 232, 233, 234, 239, 242, 243, 244, 247, 248, 249, 250, 269, 270, 271, 272, 273, 274, 275, 276, 277, 278, 279, 280, 281, 282, 283, 284, 285, 286, 287, 289, 290, 291, 292, 294, 295, 296, 303, 305, 307, 308, 319, 320, 327, 333, 335
Wildberger, H. 288
Wilken, R. L. 19, 236, 238, 240
Windisch, H. 237, 248, 259
Winston, D. 129, 130, 131, 132, 133
Wintle, B. 265, 267, 272, 273, 277, 281, 282, 289, 291, 311, 316, 318
Wischmeyer, O. 327
Wolff, H. W. 2, 94, 288
Worrell, J. 6, 181, 190, 192, 193, 194, 195, 196, 197, 199, 201, 202, 203, 204, 205, 207, 214
Woude, A. S. van der 93, 214
Wuellner, W. W. 266

Yadin, Y. 77, 210
Young, E. M. 266, 277

Zahavy, T. 186
Zeilinger, F. 255, 256, 257, 259
Zeller, D. 4, 30, 87, 236
Zenger, E. 9, 12, 16, 79, 88
Ziegler, J. 8, 59, 77, 78, 95, 129
Ziener, G. 129, 130, 131, 132, 133
Ziesler, J. A. 285
Zimmermann, F. 129
Zink, J. K. 60, 61, 95

Index of Subjects

Aaron 23, 35, 36, 52, 54f., 65, 83, 187, 209
Abiram 65
Abraham 34, 44, 272f.
Adam 142, 145f., 154, 156, 252, 254f.
Adam christology 252f.
Adultery 38, 47, 58, 116
Aggadah 11, 88
Alcimus 65
Alexandria 8, 11, 123, 129f., 134, 162
Allegorical exegesis 92, 121, 124, 247
Angels 210, 272f.
Anthropos myth 252
Antinomism 341
Antioch 134f., 230
Antiochos III 63
Apocalyptic
 — literature 138f., 140, 152
 — Paul 231
 — Pharisaism 140
 — prophecy 193
 — tradition 94, 125, 129, 139, 163
 — wisdom 147, 192f., 197
Apollos 243
R. Aqiba 153
Aretalogy 19f.
Aristeas, Letter of 119f.
 — Hellenism 120f.
 — law 120f.
 — table-talk 121f.
 — wisdom 121-123
Ark of the covenant 21, 23
Astarte 19
Athene 19

Baruch, Apocalypse of 152f.
 — apocalyptic 152, 157
 — and 4Ezra 152-154
 — law 154-158
 — rabbinic circles 153, 161
 — scribes 157, 161
 — wisdom 158
Baptism 307
Baptismal terminology 242
Baruch, Book of 11, 95
 — covenant 97
 — creation 96
 — faith 97
 — law 95, 97f.

 — salvation history 97
 — wisdom 96f.
 — wisdom figure 96f.
Ben Sira 8f.
 — covenant 42, 44f., 54, 72, 81
 — creation 11-13, 16-20, 32, 42-44, 79f.
 — cult 21, 23f., 51f., 81
 — death 32, 43
 — didactic thrust 12
 — eternal life 56f.
 — eternity 78
 — fear of the Lord 12, 14, 24f., 29, 33-39, 42, 45f., 54, 56, 81f.
 — grandson 8, 78f.
 — halakhah 57-60
 — Hellenism 12, 19f., 27, 31, 86
 — inspiration 53, 66f.
 — Israel 12f., 21-23, 25
 — jurisdiction 52
 — *laus patrum* 22, 26-28, 44, 54, 81
 — and OT 60-63, 84
 — revelation 15, 19, 81
 — salvation history 20-28, 44f., 81
 — sin 46, 49, 56
 — as scribe 28, 30, 51, 67, 76, 80, 181
 — on scribes 44
 — Stoicism 84-86
 — teaching 52-55, 83
 — text 61
Ben Sira, Law
 — commandments 17
 — correlation with wisdom 9-15, 69-91
 — background 10-14, 84-87
 — characteristics 79-83
 — consequences 11f., 87f.
 — cosmic 72, 79f., 85
 — covenant 42, 44ff.
 — and creation 12f., 32, 42f.
 — cult 42, 51f.
 — fear of the Lord 29, 32-39, 42, 45f., 50, 53, 56, 74
 — function of 46-55
 — God 42
 — inscrutability 73
 — and Israel 12f.
 — jurisdiction 52
 — obedience to 55-57
 — and revelation 12, 73
 — and salvation history 44f.

- study of 14, 53
- and teaching 52-55

Ben Sira, Wisdom 10-14, 16-28
- acquisition of 55
- activity 11, 17
- cosmological 16, 79f.
- and creation 11-13, 16-20
- and cult 21-24, 80
- fear of the Lord 24f., 70, 81
- fruit of 25f., 74
- God 16-18, 21, 53, 74, 81
- and history 12, 17f., 22
- human 16
- hymn 11
- hypostasis 14, 20
- inscrutability 73
- and Israel 16, 21-23, 25, 81
- primeval 16
- rule of 16
- and salvation history 16, 20-28, 81
- search for 15
- source of 50
- universalistic 11, 13, 15-17, 87
- wisdom figure 19f.

Bribery 48

Caligula 129
Cardinal virtues 136
Celibacy 307, 314, 323, 329
Charismata 305f., 323
Charity 49
Cheti, Instruction of 66
Christological formulae 238, 240
Christology
- development 11, 88
- and Jewish wisdom 236

Christology, Pauline
- Adam christology 252f.
- Christ and the Torah 264-297
    abrogatio legis 267-269, 273-277, 283, 283, 287, 290-292, 294f., 297, 299
    Christ as end of the Torah 265, 268, 271, 291-293
    Christ as 'new Torah' 237, 264f., 267, 273, 281, 296
    Christ replacing the Torah 243f.
    law of love 266, 268, 274-277, 279, 294f., 334
    'law of Christ' 266-269, 271, 277-279, 280
    messianic Torah 278
    nuda lex 272, 274, 293
    Zion Torah 268, 287f.
- divinity of Jesus 241
- and ethics 302f.
- finality of Christ 239
- 'firstborn of creation' 256
- 'firtborn from the dead' 257
- humiliation/exaltation 248, 253f.
- 'image of God' 238, 256
- mediator of creation 238f., 245, 247, 256-258, 261, 319
- mediator of salvation 243-245, 247, 250f., 258, 261, 293f.
- pre-existence christology 237f., 241f., 246f., 251, 253f., 257f., 260, 262f.
- resurrection 248, 260, 267
- sending of the Son 238, 241f., 261
- Son of God 238, 261
- wisdom christology 236-264

Circumcision 34, 36, 45, 273, 279, 292, 329
Clan ethos 1
Common sense 324
Conscience 333-336
Convention 320, 329
Corinth, Church in
- opponents 239, 242
- division 325

Cosmology
- cosmic order 3, 36
- law 106f.
- material in En(eth) 102
- Stoic 84-86, 245
- Torah as cosmol. principle 88
- universal cosmic law 79f.
- universal cosmic wisdom 79f.
- wisdom 96, 103f., 147
- Yahwistic 14f.

Covenant 145, 282-285
- Abrahamic 34, 36
- Ben Sira 10, 39, 42-45, 54, 72
- companions of 47
- Enoch 107
- Israelitic 10, 39, 42, 44f., 54, 72, 81, 97, 145
- Mosaic 10, 39, 42, 44f., 54, 175
- new covenant 282-285
- old covenant 282, 284
- Qumran Community 175-178, 202f., 222f.

Creation
- Christ as mediator of 238f., 245, 247, 256f., 258, 261, 319
- hymns 17f., 210f.
- order(s) of
    and law (Torah) 13, 42-44, 79f., 106-108, 178-180, 208
    in Pauline ehtics 318-321, 325., 334, 336, 338
    and wisdom 11, 17f., 87, 158
- Qumran Community 179f.
- and wisdom 13, 16-20, 87, 96, 103f., 130f., 200, 211, 222, 256f.

Index of Subjects

Cult 21-24, 38, 42, 51f., 81

Damascus 292
Dathan 65
David 24, 36, 49, 72, 160, 221, 224
Davidic King
— Psalms of Solomon 115-118, 165
Death 32, 43
Decalogue 2, 108, 312
Deuteronomistic tradition 4, 14, 34, 44, 72, 84, 90, 142
Dialogue 140f., 147, 149
Diatribe 130, 135
Divorce 58f., 314
Doxology 18
Dreams 102, 126
Dualism 177, 192, 194f., 205, 232

Egypt 64, 79, 119, 129, 219
Eleazar 121, 137
R. Eliezer b. Zadok 67
Endtime 153
Engedi 26
Enoch 102
Enoch, Book of
— aim 107
— apocalypse 100
— Aramaic 100
— cosmology 102, 104-107
— covenant 107
— creation 103, 106
— date 100f.
— eschatology 105f.
— ethic 102
— Exodus 107
— Hasidim 102, 107
— inspiration 102
— judgment 108
— law 106-109
    eschatological 108
    ethos 108f.
    correlation with wisdom 109-112
    cosmic 106
    Torah 107f., 110
    universalistic 106
— parables 100, 102, 109
— Pharisees 107
— predestination 107
— Qumran theology 101f.
— righteousness 105f., 111
— Son of Man 105f., 108, 110, 112
— wisdom 103-106
    eschatological 105f.
    figure of 103
    particularistic 104f.
    personification 103
    universalistic 103f.

Yahweh 104
— wisdom genres 102
— wisdom traditions 102f.
Essenes, see Qumran Community
Eternal life
— Ben Sira 56f.
— Enoch 105
— Psalms of Solomon 115f.
— 4Ezra 143
— Qumran 188
Ethics, Christian
— development 88, 300
Ethics, Pauline
— 'already'/'not yet' 304, 308, 323
— apostolic dicta 305, 316-318
— autonomy 312, 339-342
— catalogues of virtues/vices 324
— charismata 305f.
— christology 302f.
— common sense 324
— conscience 333-336, 337f.
— conventions 320, 329, 336, 338
— dominical sayings 315f.
— ecclesiology 306f., 311, 331, 341
— eschatology 307-309, 334
— *ethica viatorum* 304
— freedom 324, 336, 340f., 346
— heteronomy 312, 321, 342
— interim ethics 303-305
— indicative/imperative 304, 312, 322f.
— judgment 308, 334
— law, see norms
— love 305, 311, 327-329, 334, 337f.
— *mimesis* 316, 318
— motivation 301-310
— norms 310-323
— obedience 303f., 310, 317, 324, 332, 336, 341
— orders of creation 318-321, 325f., 334, 336, 338
— perception 305f.
— prayer 305
— reasons 311, 329-333, 337f.
— reward 308
— and the Spirit 304f., 326f., 331, 337f.
— temptation 305
— *tertius usus legis* 321
— theocentricity 301
— Torah (Old Testament) 313-315
— wisdom 300, 312f., 323-337
Eudaemonism 10
Euphrates 72
Exile 27, 95f., 176, 260
Exodus 10, 104, 107, 126, 132f., 219f., 246f., 261
Ezra 26-28, 64, 66, 87, 140, 147, 174
Ezra, Fourth Book of 138-143

– apocalyptic 139f., 147
– cosmology 147
– covenant 145
– eternal life 143
– 'Ezra' 140f., 151
– inspiration 148
– law 143-147
– Pharisees 140
– rabbinic circles 152
– revelation 143
– secret revelations 143
– wisdom 147-149

Fear of the Lord 164
– correlation law/wisdom 14, 81f., 346
– law 5, 12, 29, 33f., 36-39, 42, 45f., 50, 146, 264, 187
– righteousness 115, 118
– will of God 56, 346
– wisdom 24f.

Galilee 101
Gamaliel 230
Gihon 72
Gnosticism 194, 239, 242, 252
God (Yahweh)
– cosmic significance of 3f., 17f.
– inscrutability 249
– love for 50, 56
– omniscience 18, 199, 211
– providence 131
– punishment of 47
– righteousness of 113
– will of 3, 46, 53, 55f., 81f., 188, 305, 306, 317f., 327, 329f., 331-333, 346
– wisdom of 17f.
Golden Rule 122
Gossip 46

Hades 57, 248
Hakhamim, see Wise men
Halakhah 82
– Ben Sira 57-60
– development 52, 65-67
– Qumran 183-186
– rabbinic 88
Hasidim 6, 27, 65, 86, 102, 162, 185, 215, 220, 232
Hasmoneans 67
Hellenism
– Ben Sira 12, 19f., 27, 65, 86
– correlation wisdom/law 12, 84
– ethics 319
– literature 19f., 120, 125, 129
– opposition to 12, 27, 65, 67
– Paul 228, 319

– philosophy 135, 228, 324
Heracles myth 252
Hermon 26
Hezekiah 24, 49, 161
Hilkiah 174
Hillel 58, 122
Horoscope 212
huq 21, 36f., 171, 178
Hymnody 343
Hymns 343
Hypostasis 14, 20, 242

Identity, law of 90f.
Immortality 56, 130f., 135
Inspiration 53, 66f., 148, 173, 182, 221
Isis 19f.
Israel 10, 12f., 21-23, 25, 33, 37, 44, 72, 144, 155, 176f., 220, 247

Jacob 22f., 33
Jericho 26
Jerusalem
– Ben Sira 8
– destruction of 104
– Enoch 101
– Ezra 64
– fall of 141, 153
– messiah 117
– Paul 228f.
– priests 64
– Psalms of Solomon 113
– restoration of 28
– Teacher of Righteousness 180f., 203
– Temple 120, 127
– wisdom 21-23
Jesus
– and wisdom 236, 263
– words of 315f.
Jordan 72
Josephus 67, 69
Josiah 24, 49, 161
Judea 64
Judgment
– conscience 334
– doxology 142
– eschatological 108
– fall of Jerusalem 153
– natural disasters as 126
– Torah 145
– according to works 308
– of Yahweh 35f., 38, 334

Kantian philosophy 339
Kings 23, 33, 64
Kelal 275
Kenosis 277
Korah 65

Law
- apodictic 1 – and Christ 264-297
- content 2f.
- correlation with wisdom
  history 4, 87, 163, 343f.
  Old Testament 1-6, 10-14, 84
  Ben Sira 9-15, 69-91
  Baruch 95, 98f.
  Enoch 109-112
  Psalms of Solomon 117-119
  Letter of Aristeas 123f.
  Sibylline Oracles 127f.
  Sapientia Salomonis 132-134
  4 Maccabees 136-139
  4 Ezra 149-151
  Apocalypse of Baruch 158-161
  Qumran 207-226
  Paul 232-234, 298f., 338-342
- creation 178-181
- eschatological 108, 115f., 143-145, 187
- eternal 108, 115, 146
- ethos 46-49, 88, 98, 108f.
- fear of the Lord 5, 12, 29, 33f., 36-39, 42, 45f., 50, 146, 164, 187
- history 1
- inspiration 148
- intention 4
- *ius talionis* 144, 146, 151, 154-156
- origin 4
- revelation 5, 12, 73, 120, 156
- *Sitz im Leben* 2
- society 4, 46-49
- theology 1
- universalistic 79f., 85, 88, 121, 127, 132, 136
Lasterkataloge 31, 324
Lebanon 22, 26
Legalism 109, 188-190, 282, 291-293, 341
Lehreröffnungsformel 102
Leontopolis 120
Levi 36
Levites 27
Life
- as walk/path 82, 198, 234, 344
- eschatological 144
Light 111, 132f., 145f., 156f., 158f., 174, 198, 234, 344
Literary genres 93
Logos 92

Maat 19
Macarisms 220
Maccabees, Fourth Book of 134f.
- hellenistic philosophy 135
- law 135f.

- SapSal 135
Marriage 314, 320, 326, 329
Martyrdom 136f.
Messiah 115-119, 165
- expectations 101
- fear of the Lord 115, 118
- law 118
- messianic woes 147
- priestly 187, 217, 224
- righteousness 115, 118
- royal 187, 212f., 224
- saviour priest 165
- wisdom 116-118
- see also Son of Man, Davidic King
Methuselah 104
Miracles 20, 134
Mishnah 7, 68
mishpat 21, 35f., 171f., 178
Monism 85f.
Monotheism 30, 131, 245
Moses 24, 33, 147, 212
- contrasted with righteousness 247
- covenant 175
- glory 284
- lawgiver 97f., 123, 136, 154, 156, 160
- mediator of God's will 173
- mediator of the Torah 10, 23, 33, 42, 44, 50, 72, 136, 173, 175, 272f., 281
- ministry 282f.
- oral law 183
- teacher of the law 54
- wisdom 50, 123, 158, 160
Music 36
Mythology 19f.

Naherwartung 308
Nehemiah 27, 64
New covenant 267
Nile 72
Nomism 23, 51
Nomos agraphos 319, 335

Oath 58
Obedience
- Ben Sira 55-57, 69
- Paul's ethic 303f., 310, 317, 324, 332, 336, 341
Onomastica 105
Oracle literature 125
Oral law, see Halakhah

Pantheism 85
Parable 53, 100, 102, 109
Paradise 72f., 150
Parenesis, see Ethics
Parousia 304, 308

Patriarchs 72
Paul
– apocalyptic 231, 253
– baptism 307
– Christology, see ibid.
– Christophany 238, 292
– covenant 282-285, 293
– creation 238, 245, 256f., 318-321, 325f.
– dualism 232
– education 228-230
– ethics, see Ethics, Pauline
– Hellenism 229, 231f., 319, 324f.
– justification 280, 285, 287, 290, 292f., 303, 307, 322
– legalism 282, 291f., 292f., 341
– Pharisaism 229-232
– Pneumatology 241, 284, 290, 305, 321f., 326f.
  fruit of the Spirit 284, 327
  gift of the Spirit 278, 305
  life in the Spirit 276, 284, 290, 294, 297, 305, 311, 322
– revelation 263f., 295, 340
– righteousness 285, 287, 290
– sacraments 307
– sanctification 303, 307
– soteriology 260f., 292f., 297, 348
– teaching 318, 325, 336, 338
– theology, development of 268, 269, 270
– theology of the law
  cultic-ritual 277, 295, 313
  development 268, 269, 270
  divine origin 271f., 274, 295f., 340
  freedom from the law 276, 279, 289
– wisdom school 232, 237
Pentateuch 13, 26, 32, 39, 42, 61, 65, 171, 173, 184, 222
Persia 64f.
Pharisees 162
– Enoch 107
– 4Ezra 140
– halakhah 67, 185
– and Paul 229f.
– Psalms of Solomon 113
– and Qumran 168, 185
– scribes 66-68
– Temple Scroll 167
– Torah 67
– wisdom 6
Philo 92, 130f.
Philosophiy of religion 11
– Alexandrian 88
– Stoic 12f.
Phinehas 24, 36, 45
Phylacteries 185

Physicist 86
Piety 50f., 65, 69, 82f., 98, 137
Pishon 72
Pneumatics 243
Polygamy 314
Prayer 53, 305
Pre-existence christology 237f., 241f., 246f., 251-254, 257f., 260, 262f.
Predestination 107, 147, 211
Priests 3, 5, 35, 50, 64
– as scribes 65, 67
– Zadokite 86
Prophecy 126, 131
Prophets 23, 39, 50, 66f., 173
Protreptic 130
Psalter 221
Psalms of Solomon 112f.
– eternal life 115f.
– Davidic King 115-118
– fear of the Lord 115f., 118
– law 113-116
– messiah 115-119, 165
– Pharisees 113f.
– righteousness of God 113
– wisdom 116f.
Pseudonymity 93
Ptolemaios II 119, 122
Purity, ritual 186f.
Qumran Community
– apocalyptic 192f., 197, 204
– and Ben Sira 181, 209
– calendar 177, 186, 188
– covenant 175-178, 202f., 222f.
– creation 178-181, 200, 208, 210f., 222
– dualism 177, 192, 194f., 205
– election 210, 220
– entrance into 169f., 177f., 180, 191, 193, 202, 204, 216
– eschatology 187f., 203, 224f.
– Essenes 6, 66, 166, 168
– ethics 204-206, 223f.
– fear of the Lord 187, 225
– halakhah 182-186, 188, 205f., 216
– hasidim 168, 185, 209
– history 167f., 209, 217
– inspiration 173, 182f., 221
– interpretation 172, 182-184, 209
– Israel 176f., 222
– messiah 187, 212f., 217, 224
– pesharim 167, 171, 182f.
– Pharisees 168, 185, 209
– priesthood 67, 186
– priests 182
– proto-Essenes 168, 214f.
– revelation 172-174, 184f., 194, 199, 200-203

- sabbath 186, 188
- Sadducees 168, 186
- salvation 189, 206
- scribes 66f., 209, 212, 224
- Spirit 174, 180, 203, 217
- study of the law 181-183
- Teacher of Righteousness 68, 170, 174, 178, 180-182, 202-204, 224
- teaching 202-204
- Temple 176
- Temple Scroll 167, 182, 184-186
- temple symbolism 177
- Torah 67
- wisdom 66, 190, 206, 215, 220
  background 194f.
  genres 191, 198f.
  personification 195, 200f., 222
  terminology 195-198
- worldview 194

Rabbinic theology 5, 9, 11, 14, 49, 66f., 72, 88, 155, 183
Rabbis 6, 67, 152f., 161
- proto-rabbis 63, 65f., 68
Reasons 4, 135-138, 311, 329-333
Resurrection 248, 260, 267
Retribution 118, 135, 144, 146, 151, 154-156
Revelation 4f., 10, 12, 15, 19, 67, 81, 143
- ecstatic 125, 199-201
Righteousness
- Enoch 105f., 111
- Paul 285, 287, 290
- Psalms of Solomon 114f.
Riddle 53, 132

Sabbath 186, 188
Sacrifice 23, 36, 51
Sadducees
- and Qumran 168, 186
- scribes 67f.
- Torah 67
Sage, see Wise men
Sirach, see Ben Sira
Salvation
- Christ as mediator 243-245, 247, 250f., 258, 261, 293f.
- Qumran 189, 206
Salvation history 20-28, 44f., 81, 97
Samuel 24
Sanhedrin 229
Satan 304
Scribes (*sopherim*)
- activities 44, 50, 52-54
- Ben Sira 44, 52-54
- Ezra 26, 87, 151

- history 63-69
- identity 59, 157
- importance 87, 344
- and inspiration 53, 66f.
- Pharisees 66-68, 157, 209
- Qumran 67, 180f., 209
- Sadducees 67f.
- term 63f.
- wisdom 6, 75, 157
Septuagint 120
Shame 324
Shammai 58
Shekhina 22f., 246
Sibylline Oracle 124f.
- apocalyptic 125
- Hellenism 125
- law 126f.
- revelation 125
Simon II 24
Simon b. Gamaliel I 230
Sin 46, 49, 56, 98
Sinai 17, 29, 31, 33, 36f., 39, 42, 44, 50, 81, 107f., 126, 173, 175, 183, 210
Situation ethics 328
Solomon 23f., 132, 160
Son of Man 105f., 108, 110, 112, 165, 259
Sopherim, see Scribes
State 320, 326, 335
Stephen 279, 296f.
Stoicism
- Ben Sira 12f., 84-86
- cosmology 85f., 245
- ethics 136, 309, 324, 340
- *nomos agraphos* 335
- origin 86
- philosophy 12
- popular philosophy 12f., 84, 135
- wise 325
Synagogue 282
Syncretism 125
Syria 129, 134

Talmud 66
Tannaim 68
Tannaitic literature 64
Tarsus 227-230
Temple 28, 65, 68, 120, 127, 176
Tertius usus legis 321
Tetragrammaton 184
Theodicy 141f.
Tigris 72
Torah, see Law
torah 3, 21, 31-34, 72, 171
Translation, ecstatic 102
Transmission, written 184
Trinitarian question 263

Typological exegesis 247
Tugendkataloge 31, 324

Uriel 104
Urim and thummim 50

Visions 102, 126, 140f.

Water 72, 174, 198
Wisdom
— apocalyptic 192f.
— christology 236-264
— content 2f.
— correlation with Torah, see Law
— court 2, 21-24, 80
— creation 11-13, 16-20, 42f., 96, 130f.
— cult 3
— eschatological 105f., 116f., 147-149, 158
— ethics 1f.
— fear of the Lord, see ibid.
— figure 19f., 96f.
— fruit of 25f., 104f.
— gift of God 11, 21, 74, 81, 104
— and God 16-18, 21
— hiddenness 133
— history 1-6
— hypostasis 14, 20, 242
— inscrutability 73
— logos 131
— obedience 5
— origin 2, 4
— personification 19f., 96f., 103, 130, 148, 195
— profane 11, 87
— prophecy 131

— research 1
— *Sitz im Leben* 2
— Spirit 131, 133
— teacher of 33
— theology 1
— universalistic 11, 13, 15-17, 87, 96, 103fd., 122f., 158
— wisdom psalms 4f.
Wisdom of Solomon, Book of 129f.
— apocalyptic 129
— covenant 132f.
— Hellenism 129
— immortality 130f.
— law 131f.
— Philo 130
— wisdom 130f.
  creation 130f.
  figure 130
  logos 131
  Spirit 131, 133
Wise men (*hakhamim*) 2f., 13, 23, 33, 52-54, 65-67, 87, 147, 151, 158, 224
Woe formula 102
Work 320, 326
Worship service 305

Yahweh, see God
Yahwistic tradition 3, 14
Yabneh 68, 153
R. Yohanan b. Zakkai 68
R. Yose b. Joezer 212

Zealots 66
Zeus 85f., 289
Zion 21-23, 142

www.ingramcontent.com/pod-product-compliance
Lightning Source LLC
Chambersburg PA
CBHW070651300426
44111CB00013B/2372